Supervision

Concepts and Skill Building

Supervision
Concepts and Skill Building

FOURTH EDITION

Samuel C. Certo
Steinmetz Professor of Management
Roy E. Crummer Graduate School of Business
Rollins College

Boston   Burr Ridge, IL   Dubuque, IA   Madison, WI   New York   San Francisco   St. Louis
Bangkok   Bogotá   Caracas   Kuala Lumpur   Lisbon   London   Madrid   Mexico City
Milan   Montreal   New Delhi   Santiago   Seoul   Singapore   Sydney   Taipei   Toronto

McGraw-Hill Higher Education

*A Division of The **McGraw-Hill** Companies*

SUPERVISION: CONCEPTS AND SKILL-BUILDING
Published by McGraw-Hill/Irwin, a business unit of The McGraw-Hill Companies, Inc.,
1221 Avenue of the Americas, New York, NY, 10020. Copyright © 2003, 2000, 1997,
1994 by The McGraw-Hill Companies, Inc. All rights reserved. No part of this
publication may be reproduced or distributed in any form or by any means, or stored in a
database or retrieval system, without the prior written consent of The McGraw-Hill
Companies, Inc., including, but not limited to, in any network or other electronic storage
or transmission, or broadcast for distance learning.
Some ancillaries, including electronic and print components, may not be available to
customers outside the United States.

This book is printed on acid-free paper.

2 3 4 5 6 7 8 9 0 QPD/QPD 0 9 8 7 6 5 4 3 2

ISBN 0-07-248839-5

Publisher: *John E. Biernat*
Senior sponsoring editor: *Andy Winston*
Editorial coordinator: *Sara E. Ramos*
Marketing manager: *Lisa Nicks*
Producer, Media technology: *Jennifer Becka*
Project manager: *Natalie J. Ruffatto*
Production supervisor: *Gina Hangos*
Senior designer: *Jennifer McQueen*
Supplement producer: *Matthew Perry*
Cover Designer: *Ellen Pettengell*
Cover Images: © *Digital Vision*
Typeface: *10/12 Jansen*
Compositor: *Shepherd Incorporated*
Printer: *Quebecor World Dubuque Inc.*

Library of Congress Cataloging-in-Publication Data

Certo, Samuel C.
   Supervision : concepts and skill building / Samuel C. Certo.—4th ed.
      p.   cm.
   Includes bibliographical references and index.
   ISBN 0-07-248839-5 (alk. paper)
   1. Supervision of employees. I. title.
   HF5549.12 .C42 2003
   658.3'02—dc21   2002067154

www.mhhe.com

To Samuel Skylar Certo . . .
Not yet a year old, you're already impacting lives in profound ways
As you grow and develop, your impact on others can be immeasurable
Look to spiritual roots for best guidance

Preface

Supervision in modern organizations is both challenging and exciting. Never in the past have supervisors had the wealth of reported research and experiences of practicing supervisors to provide insights for building their success. Your career as a supervisor can be extremely interesting and dynamic. Your rewards for competence will inevitably be significant both personally and monetarily.

Like the third edition, this book prepares students to be supervisors and is based on the premise that the modern supervisor's job is extremely intricate. Modern organizations need professional supervisors due to such constantly changing variables as diversity in the workforce, the Internet and computer technology, and organizational structure and goals. With such constantly changing circumstances in mind, *Supervision: Concepts and Skill Building* helps students learn how to be successful supervisors. This title reflects the author's commitment to discuss important supervision concepts *and* to provide to students foundational skills to help apply these concepts.

The continuing success of previous editions of this book reinforces my personal philosophy about what constitutes a high-quality supervision text: *A worthwhile supervision text must contain important theoretical material but must also facilitate student learning and the instructional process.* The following sections explain the many new and updated elements of this edition that reflect this philosophy even more so than in previous editions.

Overview of Text Development

The Foundation

This fourth edition, like all previous editions, is built on a solid foundation. To generate this foundation, a survey was mailed to instructors of supervision courses as well as supervisors nationwide to gather information about what would be needed to develop the highest-quality supervision learning package available in the marketplace. The main themes generated from the results of this survey were summarized and presented to a focus group around the country for refinement and expansion. Supervision professors and practicing supervisors then acted as individual reviewers to help fine-tune the book plan, and they were the final advisers before writing began. A web services company was involved in the process early, to plan how to best design and integrate Internet ancillaries. An illustration

■ FIGURE A

Supervision: **The Professional Team**

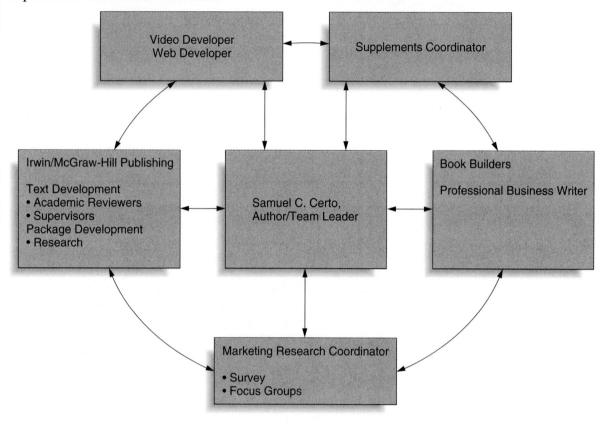

depicting the focus of various professionals during the development of this text is presented in Figure A.

The Fourth Edition

Supervision: Concepts and Skill Building is divided into five main parts: "What Is a Supervisor?" "Modern Supervision Challenges," "Functions of the Supervisor," "Skills of the Supervisor," and "Supervision and Human Resources." The following sections describe the parts and chapters of the fourth edition.

Part One, "What Is a Supervisor?" consists of the first chapter, "Modern Supervision: New Era Management." Chapter 1 is aimed at providing the student with a thorough introduction to supervision before embarking on a more detailed study of the supervision process.

Part Two, "Modern Supervision Challenges," covers areas in which supervisors will have to meet important contemporary organizational challenges. Chapter 2, "Ensuring High Quality," Chapter 3, "Teamwork: Emphasizing Powerful Meetings," and Chapter 4, "Meeting High Ethical Standards," discuss the supervisor's critical role in the organizational quest for building quality into all phases of operations, the characteristics and types of groups and teams and their importance in supervision, and the relationship between ethics and supervision. Chapter 5, "Managing Diversity," is an important chapter that focuses on how diversity can affect the supervision process. Major topics include defining diversity, prejudice, stereotypes, sexism, and ageism. A boxed feature in chapters throughout the text called "Supervision and Diversity" (explained more fully on page xi) ensures that this diversity theme is carried throughout the book. Major supervisory challenges are presented early in the text so that students can focus on them at the beginning of the course and reflect on them as they read the rest of the book.

Part Three, "Functions of the Supervisor," comprises four chapters. Chapter 6, "Reaching Goals and Objectives," is a combination of the planning and control functions of a supervisor. Chapter 7, "Organizing and Authority," focuses on organizing and delegating. Chapter 8, "The Supervisor as Leader," and Chapter 9, "Problem Solving and Decision Making," give students insights about how supervisors relate to people as leaders, the kinds of problems and decisions that supervisors face, and possible steps for solving the problems and making the decisions.

Part Four, "Skills of the Supervisor," discusses important abilities that supervisors must have to be successful. These abilities include communication (Chapter 10), motivating employees (Chapter 11), improving productivity (Chapter 12), supervising "problem" employees (Chapter 13), managing time and stress (Chapter 14), and managing conflict and change (Chapter 15). These chapters focus on how supervisors can share information in organizations, motivate workers, attend to special-needs workers and how to deal with various problems this might present, understand what stress is and how it relates to supervision, and become familiar with conflict and change and use them to enhance supervisory success. The material in this part stresses the practical aspects of the skills presented in the chapters and emphasizes helping students to actually build these skills.

New to this edition and appearing at the end of Part Four is "Appendix: Organizational Politics." This appendix provides students with a special and unique vehicle for learning about the impact of politics on supervision in modern organizations. The material provides a clear definition of organizational politics and discusses various levels of political action as well as political tactics. Also emphasized is a related topic called impression management, along with special coverage of how to manage organizational politics.

The text concludes with Part Five, "Supervision and Human Resources." Chapter 16, "Selecting Employees," focuses on the process of choosing the right person to fill an open position and the sources, methods, and legal issues that must be considered. Chapter 17, "Providing Orientation and Training," discusses the process of orienting new employees, developing skills in employees, and evaluating training methods. Chapter 18, "Appraising Performance," discusses the importance of a systematic performance appraisal and provides several appraisal methods, while Chapter 19, "The Impact of the Law," emphasizes supervision and health and safety in the workplace along with a discussion of the role of unions.

Overview of Text Learning System

The pedagogy for each chapter of this text has been designed to make the study of supervision interesting, enjoyable, effective, and efficient. Special pedagogical improvements in this edition described in the following sections are particularly exciting.

New to This Edition

Supervision Across Industries   New to this edition are "Supervision Across Industries" boxed features that illustrate how text content relates to various industries. "Supervision Across Industries" boxes, which are spread throughout the text, have the purpose of ensuring that students get a full, rich understanding of how supervision concepts can be applied to many different situations. Situations presented in "Supervision Across Industries" boxes emphasize real companies and industries such as Citibank in the banking industry, Kennedy Wieden in the advertising industry, and Murray's Print Shop in the printing industry.

Key Features

Several important components of this text are discussed below. All components reflect new and revised content in this new edition.

Chapter Quotations   The quotes that begin each chapter are drawn from business experts, historical figures, and company policies. They are specifically chosen to help frame the topics presented in the chapters, and the identities and affiliations of those quoted are provided. Each chapter has a new quote in this edition. The quote that opens Chapter 3 (on teamwork) reads as follows:

> Teamwork means focusing on the team's success, realizing that ultimately the team's success is your success. It also means that you succeed by helping other members of the team to succeed.—from Intuit's list of 10 core values

Chapter Outlines   The Chapter Outlines provided at the beginning of each chapter are tools that students can use to preview the chapter and review the material prior to testing. These outlines can also be used to help students understand the relationship of certain topics to other chapter topics.

Learning Objectives   The key points of the chapter's content form the basis for the Learning Objectives. The Learning Objectives serve as a guide for studying the material and also as a means of organizing the material both in the Summary at the end of the chapter and in the *Instructor's Manual.*

Opening Vignettes   The chapter opening vignettes are episodes primarily about actual supervisors on the job, and all are new to this edition. For example, Chapter 9 opens with a story about the supervisors at Hallmark Cards who have tried to find ways to encourage creative thinking among their staff by changing the office environment.

Margin Definitions   Key terms are defined in the margins. Students can use these definitions to test their understanding of the terms and to find the places where important concepts are discussed.

Tips from the Firing Line   In each chapter, this boxed feature highlights practical guidelines that can help students be successful supervisors. New tips in this current edition include how to avoid frustration with quality improvement efforts, how to build an effective team, how to best set organizational goals, and how to delegate successfully.

Meeting the Challenge   This boxed feature addresses current challenges faced by supervisors as they conduct their work each day and sets forth an example of someone who has managed challenge well. These boxes are designed to give students the most current information available. For instance, in Chapter 5, we learn about the physically disabled guest relations team at Red Lobster restaurants and the steps this department has taken to allow these workers to perform to full capacity by using special software and the ability to telecommute for their jobs.

Supervision and Diversity   Each of these boxed features illustrates an important diversity issue related to chapter content and emphasizes how modern supervisors can deal with the issue. The "Supervision and Diversity" features, which are spread throughout the text, have been extensively revised and updated for this edition. For example, new features include bringing diversity to problem solving at Ford Motor Company and advice from the Proskauer Rose law office in New York on how to fairly judge the performance of minorities in organizations.

Summary   Learning Objectives are recapped at the end of each chapter in brief summaries of the chapter concepts for each Learning Objective. This unique format allows students to review what they've learned from each learning objective.

Figures and Tables   Illustrations and tables are used extensively to clarify and reinforce text concepts.

Key Terms   Each chapter includes a list of Key Terms at the end of the chapter. Reading this list can help students review by testing their comprehension of the terms. The page number where a term is first defined is also included in the Glossary at the end of the book. These terms also are highlighted throughout the book as margin definitions.

Review and Discussion Questions   These questions test understanding of the chapter concepts. These questions can be used independently by students or by instructors as a method of reviewing the chapters.

A Second Look   This is a special feature of the Review and Discussion Questions that returns to the scenario presented in the chapter opening vignette. A Second Look asks students to respond to questions by applying the chapter's concepts to that opening scenario. For instance, Does the creativity described at Hallmark Cards and Joe Designer mean letting employees do whatever they want? How can you apply some of the techniques described in the opening story?

Skills Module   As discussed earlier, a renewed commitment of this edition is to emphasize student skills in applying supervision concepts. Consistent with this skills focus is the Skills Module at the end of each chapter. Each Skills Module contains a number of elements that instructors can use as a formal part of a course to develop students' application abilities. Students can also use the elements independently. The elements are:

> *Cases.* The concluding pages of each chapter contain a short case that further applies the chapter's concepts to various supervision situations. Questions following each case provoke students' thinking and help them to synthesize ideas. This feature also can be used independently by students or instructors

for course assignments or classroom discussion. For instance, in Chapter 11, the case describes how the introduction of a new incentive plan for the employees helped to improve the sales of Billy Ross's RV dealership, Super 1, near Atlanta.

Exercises. There are two types of exercises at the end of chapters. Class Exercise sections suggest activities to be done during class sessions. Team-Building Exercises provide recommendations for group activities.

Self-Quizzes. Each chapter contains a short, engaging, self-assessment quiz, which helps students to see the kinds of supervisors they can be. For instance, Chapter 4 includes a test to determine how ethical a student might be.

Glossary   Terms and definitions are gathered from each chapter and provided at the end of the book in the Glossary, which provides ready reference for students and instructors. To encourage student review, the text pages where the terms are first defined and discussed are included.

Ancillaries

One of my objectives is to provide the best teaching package available. I hope you have seen evidence of this in the description of the text and *video series*. But there is more—additional instructional materials are available to further enrich the supervision learning experience. A description of each ancillary and its highlights follows.

New to This Edition

Manager's Hot Seat Videos. This series of provocative programs has particular relevance to the supervision course. In each show you will see a real manager handle difficult, unscripted situations in the workplace. These improvised tapes show you how issues like diversity, discrimination, telecommuting, and teams really shape the way business is done. Teaching notes provide background information and extensive teaching ideas. These videos are the perfect way to expose students to the interpersonal side of supervisory work in organizations.

TechBox: Leading a high-profile project can bring a supervisor under tough scrutiny. Through this scenario you can explore issues such as group dynamics, conflict management, negotiation, and project management. This video supports Part 2 particularly well.

Beck N Call: Selecting between equally qualified candidates of different races can be tricky, especially when one manager behaves in a questionable manner. Through this scenario you can explore issues such as hiring practices, employment law, workplace diversity. This video supports Part 3 particularly well.

Saber Union Insurance: Telecommuting and other "virtual" workplace arrangements have raised the bar for managers' ability to communicate effectively. Through this scenario you can explore issues such as communication, conflict management, and contemporary supervisory challenges. This video supports Parts 1 and 4 particularly well.

EarthFirst Pharmaceuticals: Diverse workplaces mean that teams often contain people who have conflicting beliefs. Supervisors have to be ready to respond to solutions that are legally correct and supportive of a productive work environment. Through this scenario you can explore issues such as conflict management, diversity, and discrimination. This video supports Parts 4 and 5 particularly well.

Online Learning Center

We now provide an Online Learning Center (OLC) for *Supervision*. Visit this website at *http://www.mhhe.com/certo4e* to access a wealth of materials for both instructors and students. Make use of our links to professional resources, Internet exercises and assignments, skills modules, career corner, and flash cards to help review key terms. The material from the OLC can also be exported for use in WebCT, Blackboard, or PageOut.

Test Bank and Computerized Test Bank   We all know the importance of a high-quality *Test Bank* in teaching. The development of such a *Test Bank* to accompany the fourth edition of *Supervision* was of the utmost importance. The *Test Bank* includes more than 2,000 questions and is available both in printed form and in computerized format. Each chapter includes multiple-choice questions with miniature cases to allow application of the principles, true/false questions, short essay questions, and matching questions. Additionally, a prepared quiz is provided for each chapter and can be duplicated or used as a transparency. Each question in *Test Bank* includes the answer, the corresponding text page where the answer can be found, and the rationale for the answer. All questions are graded by level of difficulty and are organized according to the text learning objectives for consistency with the entire teaching package.

Sylvia Ong of Scottsdale Community College is the author of the *Test Bank*.

Instructor's Manual   Each chapter of the *Instructor's Manual is* organized according to the text learning objectives. Part I provides a quick summary for each chapter. Part II, "Teaching the Concepts by Learning Objectives," includes the following for each learning objective:

1. Key terms and their definitions from the text.
2. Teaching notes. These notes describe the focus of the text section where the learning objective is discussed and point out areas where the student might become confused. Suggestions for clarifying the material are provided.
3. Fresh examples not used in the text are provided and are frequently supported by supplementary transparencies or handouts.
4. A new exercise also is provided, and details on using the exercise and the anticipated results are included.

Part III, "Notes on the Boxed Features," provides a synopsis of the "Meeting the Challenge," "Tips from the Firing Line," "Supervision and Diversity," and "The Supervisor and the Internet" boxes. Some teaching tips are also included on how to utilize these materials in your lectures.

Part IV, "Answers to Review and Discussion Questions," provides the answers or suggested answers for each question.

Part V provides answers and solutions to the end-of-chapter exercises and cases, including the Self-Quizzes, Team-Building Exercises, and Skills Modules.

Throughout the *Instructor's Manual*, each transparency is referenced in the chapter next to the area of possible use and highlighted in the margin.

Dr. Amit Shah of Frostburg State University is the author of the *Instructor's Manual*.

Experience indicates that the highest-quality supervision courses expose students to appropriate concepts, give students an opportunity to apply these concepts to solve problems, and provide an opportunity for students to learn from their experiences.

The teaching package for the fourth edition of *Supervision* has been designed to allow flexibility in emphasizing any or all of these components in your supervision course. I sincerely wish you well in building your course around *Supervision: Concepts and Skill Building*. Have a great class!

Acknowledgments

For the author, the many years of success of *Supervision: Concepts and Skill Building* have been very gratifying. As with any book, however, the success of this book has been due, in very large part, to the hard work and commitment of many respected colleagues. I am pleased to be able to acknowledge the input of these professionals.

A special thanks to Supervision experts who have provided feedback over the years:

Reviewers

Win Chesney
St. Louis Community College at Meramac
James Day
Grambling State University
Medhat Farooque
Central Arizona College
Carson Gancer
Kalamazoo Valley Community College
Brad Gilbreath
New Mexico State University
Debbie Jansky
Milwaukee Area Technical College
Bonnie Johnson
Fashion Institute of New York
Vincent Kafkaa
Effective Learning Systems
Corinne Livesay
Mississippi College
Lynda Massa
Santa Barbara Business College
Noel Matthews
Front Range Community College
James Mulvihill
Mankato Technical Institute
Sylvia Ong
Scottsdale Community College
Smita Jain Oxford
Commonwealth College

Robert Payne
Baker College
Carl Sonntag
Pikes Peak Community College
Barbara Whitney
St. Petersburg Junior College

Focus Group Participants

Dick Brigham
Brookhaven College
Arnold Brown
Purdue University North Central
Randy Busch
Lee College
Gloria Couch
Texas State Technical Institute
Richard Gordon
Detroit College of Business
Ruby Ivens
Lansing Community College
James Kennedy
Angelina College
Russell Kunz
Collin County Community College, Spring Creek
Sue Kyriazopoulous
DeVry Institute of Technology
Allen Levy
Macomb Community College Center
John Maloney
College of DuPage

Kim McDonald
IPFW
L. E. Banderet
Quinsigamond Community College
E. Ronald Cornelius
University of Rio Grande
Mike Dougherty
Milwaukee Area Technical College
Patrick G. Ellsberg
Lower Columbia College
Janice M. Feldbauer
Austin Community College
William G. Graham
Palm Beach Community College
Carnella Hardin
Glendale College
J. Donald Herring
State University of New York–Oswego
Joshua Holt
Ricks College
Sue Jones
Odessa College
Iris Jorstad
Waubonsee Community College
Jack E. Kant
San Juan College
Dominic A. Montileone
Delaware Valley College
David A. Phillips
Purdue University

George Stooks
*State University of New York–
Oswego*
Michael R. White
University of Northern Iowa
Steven Pliseth
University of Wisconsin, Platteville
Charles Riley
Tarrant County Community College
Ralph Schmitt
Macomb Community College South
David Way
Galveston College
Dan Yovich
Purdue University North Central

Survey Respondents
Raymond Ackerman
Amber University
Rex Adams
*Southside Virginia Community
College, Daniels*
Musa Agil
Cape Fear Community College
Linda Alexander
*Southeast Community College,
Lincoln*
Gemmy Allen
Mountain View College
Scott Ames
North Lake College
E. Walter Amundsen
Indiana University Southeast
Paul Andrews
Southern Illinois University
Solimon Appel
College for Human Services
Bob Ash
Rancho Santiago College
Glenda Aslin
Weatherford College
Bob Baker
Caldwell Community College
James Bakersfield
*North Hennepin Community
College*
Robert Barefield
Drury College, Springfield
Laurence Barry
Cuyamaca College

Perry Barton
Guinnett Area Technical
Becky Bechtel
Cincinnati Technical College
Kenneth Beckerink
Agricultural and Technical College
Gina Beckles
Bethune-Cookman College
Jim Beeler
*Indiana Vocational and Technical
College, Indianapolis*
Robert Bendotti
Paradise Valley Community College
Jim Blackwell
Park College
David Bodkin
Cumberland University
Arthur Boisselle
Pikes Peak Community College
Robert Braaten
Tidewater Community College
James Brademas
University of Illinois, Urbana
Suzanne Bradford
Angelina College
Richard Braley
Eastern Oklahoma State College
Janis Brandt
Southern Illinois University
Stanley Braverman
Chestnut Hill College
Duane Brickner
*South Mountain Community
College*
Eugene Buccini
West Connecticut State University
Gary Bumbarner
Mountain Hope Community College
Kick Bundons
Johnson County Community College
Bill Burmeister
New Mexico State University
Randy Busch
Lee College
Oscar S. Campbell
Athens State College
Marjorie Carte
D. S. Lancaster Community College
Joseph Castelli
College of San Mateo

James Chester
Cameron University
William Chester
University of the Virgin Islands
Jack Clarcq
Rochester Institute of Technology
Charles Clark
Oklahoma City Community College
Sharon Clark
Lebanon Valley College
Virgil Clark
Sierra College
Jerry Coddington
*Indiana Vocational and Technical
College, Indianapolis*
Bruce Conners
Kaskaskia College
Ronald Cornelius
University of Rio Grande
Gloria Couch
Texas State College Institute
Darrell Croft
Imperial Valley College
Joe Czajka
University of South Carolina
Beatrice Davis
Santa Fe Community College
Irmagard Davis
*University of Hawaii, Kapiolani
Community College*
Richard De Luca
Bloomfield College
Edwin Deshautelle, Jr.
*Louisiana State University
at Eunice*
Richard Deus
Sacramento City College
Ruth Dixon
Diablo Valley College
Leroy Drew
Central Maine Technical College
Janet Duncan
City College of San Francisco
Ron Eads
Labette Community College
Patrick Ellsberg
Lower Columbia College
Earl Emery
Baker College, Flint
Roland Eyears
Central Ohio Technical College

Tom Falcone
Indiana University
Jim Fatina
Triton College
Jack Fleming
Moorpark College
Lee Fleming
El Centro College
Charles Flint
San Jacinto College Central
Toni Forcioni
Montgomery College, Germantown
Laurie Francis
Mid State Technical College
Cheryl Frank
Inver Hills Community College
Connie French
Los Angeles City College
Larry Fudella
Erie Community College South
William Fulmer
Clarion University of Pennsylvania
Autrey Gardner
*Industrial Technology Department,
Warren Air Force Base*
David Gennrich
Waukesha County Technical College
Sally Gillespie
Broome Community College
Catherine Glod
Mohawk Valley Community College
Tim Gocke
Terra Technical College
Richard Gordon
*Detroit College of Business,
Dearborn*
Greg Gorniak
*Pennsylvania State University,
Behrend*
Valerie Greer
University of Maryland
James Grunzweig
Lakeland Community College
James Gulli
Citrus College
Bill Hamlin
Pellissippi State Technical College
Willard Hanson
Southwestern College
James Harbin
East Texas State University

Carnella Hardin
Glendale Community College
Scott Harding
Normandale Community College
Louis Harmin
Sullivan County Community College
Lartee Harris
West Los Angeles College
Edward L. Harrison
University of South Alabama
Paul Hedlund
Barton County Community College
Kathryn Hegar
Mountain View College
Gene Hilton
Brookhaven College
Jean Hiten
Owensboro Community College
Roger Holland
Cerritos College
Larry Hollar
Catawba Valley Community College
Russ Holloman
Augusta College
Tonya Hynds
Indiana University at Kokomo
Robert Ironside
North Lake College
Ellen Jacobs
College of St. Mary
Bonnie Jayne
Bryant & Stratton
Sarkis Kavooyian
*Delaware Technical and Community
College*
Bernard Keller
Pikes Peak Community College
Robert Kemp
Peralta Laney College
Howard Keratin
Fashion Institute of Technology
James Kerrigan
Stonehill College
Scott King
Sinclair Community College
Jay Kingpin
University of South Florida
Edward Kingston
*Piedmont Virginia Community
College*

Ronald Kiziah
Caldwell Community College
Mary Lou Kline
Reading Area Community College
Sue Kyriazopoulous
DeVry Institute of Technology
Thomas Lloyd
*Westmoreland County Community
College*
Barbara Logan
*Albuquerque Technical-Vocational
Institute*
Rosendo Lomas
Lawrence Technical University
Frances Lowery
Brewer State Junior College
Henie Lustgarten
University of Maryland
Alvin Mack
Everett Community College
Jon Magoon
Santa Rosa Junior College
Marvin Mai
Empire College
Joseph Manno
Montgomery College
Edward Mautz
El Camino College
Ron Maxwell
*Indiana Vocational and Technical,
Terre Haute*
Robert McDonald
Central Wesleyan College
William McKinney
University of Illinois, Urbana
Joseph McShane
*Gateway Technical Institute,
Kenosha*
Raymond Medeiros
Southern Illinois University
Unny Menon
*California State Polytechnic
University*
Dorothy Metcalfe
*Fashion Institute of Design and
Merchandising, Los Angeles*
Eugene Meyers
Western Kentucky University
Charles Miller
Los Angeles Southwest College

Dominick Montileone
Delaware Valley College
Wayne Moorhead
Brown Mackie College
Peter Moran
Wisconsin Indianhead Technical College
Ed Mosher
Laramie County Community College
Donald Mossman
Concordia College
John Mudge
Community College of Vermont, Rutland
James Mulvihill
South Central Technical College
Hershel Nelson
Polk Community College
John Nugent
Montana Technical College
Randy Nutter
Geneva College
Cruz Ortolaza
Catholic University of Puerto Rico
Joseph Papenfuss
Westminster College, Salt Lake City
Mary Papenthien
Milwaukee Area Technical College
John Parker
Manchester Community College
James Peele
Carl Sandburg College, Galesburg
Joe Petta
Regis College
Bonnie Phillips
Casper College
Martha Pickett
University of Arkansas at Little Rock
Barbara Pratt
Community College of Vermont
Robert Priester
Madison Area Technical College
Barbara Prince
Cambridge Community College Center
John Pryor
Northern Nevada Community College

Marcia Ann Pulich
University of Wisconsin–Whitewater
Margaret Rdzak
Cardinal Stritch College
William Redmon
Western Michigan University
Arnon Reichers
Ohio State University
Charles Reott
Western Wisconsin Technical Institute
Peter Repcogle
Orange County Community College
Richard Rettig
University of Central Oklahoma
Harriett Rice
Los Angeles City College
Robert Richardson
Iona College
Charles Riley
Tarrant County Junior College
Richard Riley
National College
Michael Rogers
Albany State College
Robert Roth
City University, Bellvue
Larry Runions
North Carolina Vocational Textile
Henry Ryder
Gloucester County College
Larry Ryland
Lurleen B. Wallace Junior College
Duane Schecter
Muskegon Community College
S. Schmidt
Diablo Valley College
Irving Schnayer
Peralta Laney College
Greg Schneider
Waukesha County Technical College
Arthur Shanley
Milwaukee School of Engineering
Margie Shaw
Lake City Community College
Allen Shub
Northwestern Illinois University
Pravin Shukla
Nash Community College

Clay Sink
University of Rhode Island
Ron Smith
DeKalb Institute of Technology
Steve Smith
Mid State Technical College
Wanda Smith
Ferris State University
Carl Sonntag
Pikes Peak Community College
Marti Sopher
Cardinal Stritch College
Jerry Sparks
Cannon International Business College
David Spitler
Central Michigan University
Richard Squire
Northwest Technical College
Dick Stanish
Tulsa Junior College
Gene Stewart
Brookhaven College
John Stout
University of Scranton
Art Sweeney
Troy State University
Sally Terman
Scottsdale Community College
Sherman Timmons
University of Toledo
Don Tomal
Purdue University
Donna Treadwell
Johnson County Community College
Ron Tremmel
Rend Lake College
Guy Trepanier
Iona College
John Tucker
Purdue University
Bill Tyer
Tarrant County Junior College
Robert Ulbrich
Parkland College
Diann Valentini
Fashion Institute of Technology
Steven Vekich
Washington State Community College

Michael Vijuk
William Rainey Harper College
Charles Wall
Bakersfield College
Kathy Walton
Salt Lake City Community College
Robert Way
Milwaukee Area Technical College
Rick Webb
Johnson County Community College
Ronald Webb
Messiah College Grantham
Alan Weinstein
Canisius College
Bill Weisgerber
Saddleback College
Julia Welch
*University of Arkansas Medical
School*
Floyd Wente
*St. Louis Community College
at Florissant Valley*
Ron Weston
Contra Costa College
Charles Wetmore
California State University, Fresno
Jerry Wheaton
North Arkansas Community College
Luther White
*Central Carolina Community
College*
Michael White
University of Northern Iowa
Sara White
University of Kansas Medical Center

Barbara Whitney
St. Petersburg Junior College
Tim Wiedman
Thomas Nelson Community College
Stephen Winter
Orange County Community College
Arthur Wolf
Chestnut Hill College
Barry Woodcock
Tennessee Technological University
Michael Wukitsch
American Marketing Association
Catalina Yang
Normandale Community College
Charles Yauger
Arkansas State University
Morrie Yohai
New York Institute of Technology
Teresa Yohon
Hutchinson Community College
James Yoshida
*University of Hawaii, Hawaii
Community College*
Allan Young
Bessemer State Technical College
Marilyn Young
Waukesha County Technical College
Richard Young
Pennsylvania State University
Fred Ziolhowski
Purdue University
Karen Zwissler
Milwaukee Area Technical College

**Application Exercises
Contributors**
E. Walter Amundsen
Indiana University Southeast
Stanley A. Braverman
Chestnut Hill College
Bruce L. Conners
Kaskaskia College
James E. Fatina
Triton Allege
Peter J. Gummere
Community College of Vermont
Bernard Keller
Pikes Peak Community College
Edward A. Kingston
*Piedmont Virginia Community
College*
Joseph R. Manno
Montgomery College
Arnon E. Reichers
Ohio State University
John P. Wanous
Ohio State University
Charles Wetmore
California State University
Michael R. White
University of Northern Iowa
Timothy G. Wiedman
Thomas Nelson Community College
Stephen I. Winter
Orange County Community College
Fred Ziolkowski
Purdue University

New to this edition is the appendix to Chapter 15—"Appendix: Organizational Politics." This important appendix was added to provide students with special insights regarding organizational politics and how supervisors might deal with politics in organizations. This appendix is based upon the work of Robert Kreitner and Angelo Kinicki. I am grateful to these respected colleagues for allowing their work to be a part of this project.

Members of my McGraw-Hill family deserve personal and sincere recognition. Andy Winston, my editor, has been professional, patient, supportive, and unquestionably dedicated to this project. He has been a true partner and I would like to thank him and the rest of the McGraw-Hill staff for their expertise and advice. Other people who deserve special recognition are Sara Ramos, Lisa Nicks, Jennifer Becka, Natalie Ruffatto, Gina Hangos, Jennifer McQueen, and Matthew Perry.

Orlando businessman Charles Steinmetz, a longtime leader in the pest control industry, and his wife, Lynn, recently established the Steinmetz Chair in Management to recruit or retain a nationally recognized scholar for the management program in the Roy E. Crummer Graduate School of Business at Rollins College. I am extremely honored and personally excited to be the first recipient of the Steinmetz Chair of Management. I feel very fortunate to have been selected for this honor and can only hope to relate to students the keen business acumen and high moral and ethical standards that have made Charles Steinmetz a world-class entrepreneur and manager. I would like to thank Dr. Rita Bornstein, Rollins College President, and Dr. Craig McAllaster, Crummer Dean, for creating an educational climate in which professionalism can grow and flourish and for supporting me as the first recipient of the Steinmetz Chair in Management.

On a personal note, my family has been a source of energy and dedication throughout this project. A very special thank you goes to my wife, Mimi, for her love and support throughout all aspects of my life. She helps me to maintain my spiritual, family, and professional balance. Our children Brian, Sarah, Matthew, and Trevis continually support me unconditionally. In giving us Samuel Skylar Certo, the beginning of our family's next generation, our son, Trevis, and his wife, Melissa, help me to keep the true meaning of life in perspective. Last, my parents, Sam and Annette, instilled within me a discipline and work ethic. I am truly grateful for their support and love.

About the Author

Dr. Samuel C. Certo is professor of management and former dean at the Roy E. Crummer Graduate School of Business at Rollins College. He has been a professor of management for over 20 years and has received prestigious awards, including the Award for Innovative Teaching from the Southern Business Association, the Instructional Innovation Award granted by the Decision Sciences Institute, and the Charles A. Welsh Memorial Award for outstanding teaching at the Crummer School. Dr. Certo's numerous publications include articles in journals such as *Academy of Management Review*, *Journal of Experiential Learning and Simulation*, and *Training*. He also has written several successful textbooks, including *Modern Management* and *Supervision: Concepts and Skill Building*. Most recent books include *the Strategic Management Process* (available at studystrategy.com) and *Digital Dimensioning: Finding the E-Business in Your Business*. A past chairman of the Management Education and Development Division of the Academy of Management, he has been honored by that group's Excellence of Leadership Award. Dr. Certo also has served as president of the Association for Business Simulation and Experiential Learning, as associate editor for *Simulation & Games*, and as a review board member of the *Academy of Management Review*. His consulting experience has been extensive, with notable experience on boards of directors.

Contents in Brief

Contents

PART ONE

What Is a Supervisor?

1

Working in the knowledge economy requires the ability to recognize patterns, to share ideas with people inside and outside your organization, to maintain relationships with people who have common interests, and to pull value out of those relationships.

—Chris Meyer, director of Ernst & Young's Center for Business Innovation

Modern Supervision: New-Era Challenge

■ CHAPTER OUTLINE

Types of Supervisory Skills

Categorizing the Skills
Supervising a Diverse Workforce

General Functions of the Supervisor

Planning
Organizing
Staffing
Leading
Controlling
Relationships among the Functions

Responsibilities of the Supervisor

Types of Responsibilities
Responsibilities after Restructuring or Reengineering
Responsibilities and Accountability

Becoming a Supervisor

Preparing for the Job
Obtaining and Using Power and Authority
Characteristics of a Successful Supervisor

About This Book

■ LEARNING OBJECTIVES

After you have studied this chapter, you should be able to:

1.1 Define what a supervisor is.

1.2 Describe the basic types of supervisory skills.

1.3 Describe how the growing diversity of the workforce affects the supervisor's role.

1.4 Identify the general functions of a supervisor.

1.5 Explain how supervisors are responsible to higher management, employees, and co-workers.

1.6 Describe the typical background of someone who is promoted to supervisor.

1.7 Identify characteristics of a successful supervisor.

■ SUPERVISION BY REMOTE CONTROL

Tracey Curvey had just taken on a new assignment as a marketing executive for Fidelity Investments. She now had 40 people reporting to her, five of them working under an arrangement known as telecommuting. Telecommuters are full-time employees of a firm who work at home instead of in the office. They keep in touch by telephone, conference calls, and e-mail. "Was I willing to continue that situation?" Tracey asked herself. "Was I willing to take that risk?" In the fast-paced department she now headed, she was doubtful the telecommuters could keep up with customers' demands.

One of Tracey's first steps was to assess the value of each individual to the firm. She then sat down with each telecommuter and put in writing when each would be in the office for occasional face-to-face meetings, when each would be at home and available to work with office colleagues, and when each would be traveling on Fidelity business. She also conferred with each telecommuter to reach agreement on how deadlines for assignments would be met.

Once those plans were written, Tracey monitored progress to be sure that work was getting done. She checked that the five remained in regular contact with their colleagues in the office, looking at measurable factors like their participation in conference calls and phone and e-mail contacts. She compensated her telecommuters fairly for their work, once it was established that "business was happening as usual." She gave them their share of top assignments and made sure that, even though it raised a few eyebrows, they were given appropriate office space for the time they spent "in house."

The group met all her expectations, and Tracey was recently promoted to a senior vice presidency with Fidelity.

Source: Robert Barker, "So Your Workers Want to Telecommute," *Business Week*, October 12, 1998, p. 154E8.

Tracey's successful experience with telecommuting employees demonstrates several of the key functions that today's managers and supervisors perform. Planning, organizing, staffing (which includes appraising worker performance), leading, controlling or monitoring performance are all basic aspects of the supervisor's In today's increasingly technological world, the supervisor is also becoming sponsible for supporting the transfer of information between groups and networks of knowledge within the organization.[1]

supervisor
A manager at the first level of management.

To define the term, a **supervisor** is a manager at the first level of which means that the employees reporting to the supervisor are From this definition, you can see that many different kinds of orsupervisors. Figure 1.1 reprints actual want ads for a variety of sup

The basic job of a manager is to see that an organization yet there are distinctions. For the top executives of an organi tails making sure that the organization's vision and busine

■ FIGURE 1.1

A Sampling of Supervisory Positions to Be Filled

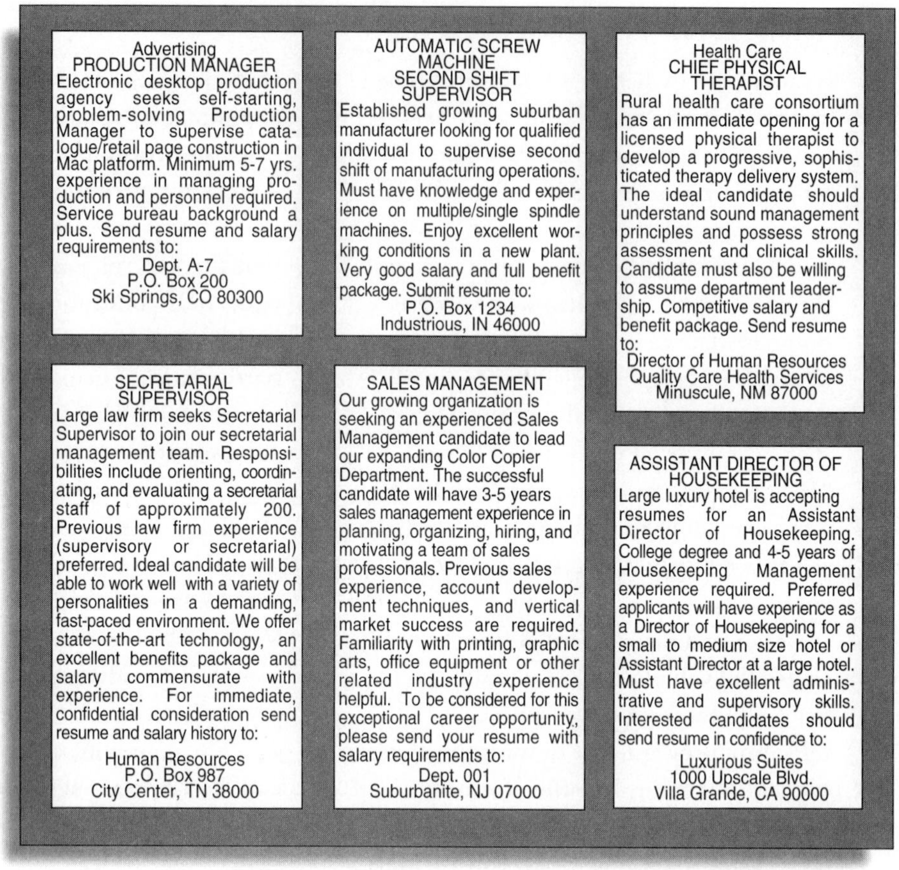

Advertising
PRODUCTION MANAGER
Electronic desktop production agency seeks self-starting, problem-solving Production Manager to supervise catalogue/retail page construction in Mac platform. Minimum 5-7 yrs. experience in managing production and personnel required. Service bureau background a plus. Send resume and salary requirements to:
Dept. A-7
P.O. Box 200
Ski Springs, CO 80300

AUTOMATIC SCREW MACHINE SECOND SHIFT SUPERVISOR
Established growing suburban manufacturer looking for qualified individual to supervise second shift of manufacturing operations. Must have knowledge and experience on multiple/single spindle machines. Enjoy excellent working conditions in a new plant. Very good salary and full benefit package. Submit resume to:
P.O. Box 1234
Industrious, IN 46000

Health Care
CHIEF PHYSICAL THERAPIST
Rural health care consortium has an immediate opening for a licensed physical therapist to develop a progressive, sophisticated therapy delivery system. The ideal candidate should understand sound management principles and possess strong assessment and clinical skills. Candidate must also be willing to assume department leadership. Competitive salary and benefit package. Send resume to:
Director of Human Resources
Quality Care Health Services
Minuscule, NM 87000

SECRETARIAL SUPERVISOR
Large law firm seeks Secretarial Supervisor to join our secretarial management team. Responsibilities include orienting, coordinating, and evaluating a secretarial staff of approximately 200. Previous law firm experience (supervisory or secretarial) preferred. Ideal candidate will be able to work well with a variety of personalities in a demanding, fast-paced environment. We offer state-of-the-art technology, an excellent benefits package and salary commensurate with experience. For immediate, confidential consideration send resume and salary history to:
Human Resources
P.O. Box 987
City Center, TN 38000

SALES MANAGEMENT
Our growing organization is seeking an experienced Sales Management candidate to lead our expanding Color Copier Department. The successful candidate will have 3-5 years sales management experience in planning, organizing, hiring, and motivating a team of sales professionals. Previous sales experience, account development techniques, and vertical market success are required. Familiarity with printing, graphic arts, office equipment or other related industry experience helpful. To be considered for this exceptional career opportunity, please send your resume with salary requirements to:
Dept. 001
Suburbanite, NJ 07000

ASSISTANT DIRECTOR OF HOUSEKEEPING
Large luxury hotel is accepting resumes for an Assistant Director of Housekeeping. College degree and 4-5 years of Housekeeping Management experience required. Preferred applicants will have experience as a Director of Housekeeping for a small to medium size hotel or Assistant Director at a large hotel. Must have excellent administrative and supervisory skills. Interested candidates should send resume in confidence to:
Luxurious Suites
1000 Upscale Blvd.
Villa Grande, CA 90000

to meet its goals through the years ahead. Managing at the supervisory level means ensuring that the employees in a particular department are performing their jobs such that the department will make its contribution to the organization's goals. Usually, supervisors focus on day-to-day problems and on goals to be achieved in one year or less. This chapter introduces what supervisors do and what skills and characteristics they need to be effective.

Types of Supervisory Skills

Although a supervisor in a Pizza Hut restaurant and a supervisor in a Bethlehem Steel factory work in very different environments, the skills they need to be successful fall into the same basic categories. The categories of skills are used by all levels of managers in all kinds of organizations. If these skills are developed during a beginning supervisory job, they will prove useful in every job held throughout a management career. The basic categories of skills are technical, human relations, conceptual, and decision-making skills.

Categorizing the Skills

technical skills
The specialized knowledge and expertise used to carry out particular techniques or procedures.

Technical skills are the specialized knowledge and expertise used to carry out particular techniques or procedures. A United Way fund-raiser's ability to persuade executives to write big checks is a technical skill. A Goodyear mechanic's ability to bring an automobile engine back to life relies on technical skills. And selling ability is the technical skill of an insurance salesperson who earns big commissions. As you can see from these examples, skills do not have to be mechanical or scientific in order to be "technical"; they can involve any work-related technique or procedure.

human relations skills
The ability to work effectively with other people.

Supervisors also have to be able to work effectively with other people, or possess **human relations skills.** Human relations skills include the ability to communicate with, motivate, and understand other people. Supervisors use their human relations skills to impress their superiors, to inspire employees to work efficiently, to defuse conflicts, to get along with co-workers in other departments, and in many other ways.

conceptual skills
The ability to see the relation of the parts to the whole and to one another.

In addition, supervisors need **conceptual skills,** or the ability to see the relationship of the parts to the whole and to one another. For a supervisor, conceptual skills include recognizing how the department's work helps the entire organization achieve its goals and how the work of the various employees affects the performance of the department as a whole. For example, the supervisor of a manufacturing department at General Motors should be able to see that the company's reputation depends on the department's making high-quality products. The supervisor also should realize that for the company's salespeople to be able to keep their promises, the manufacturing department must meet its production quotas.

decision-making skills
The ability to analyze information and reach good decisions.

Supervisors must have **decision-making skills,** or the ability to analyze information and reach good decisions. For example, a supervisor might have to decide which of three candidates for a job will work out best or which of two conflicting deadlines has a higher priority. Someone who has strong decision-making skills can think objectively and creatively. (Chapter 9 provides a more detailed look at how to make decisions effectively.)

knowledge skills
The ability to utilize e-mail, voice mail, fax, intranet, and Internet to manage and distribute continuous streams of data.

Finally, supervisors must have **knowledge skills,** or the ability to deal competently with the rewards and challenges of communication technology such as e-mail, voice mail, fax, intranets, and the Internet, all of which contribute to a continuous stream of data that must be managed and distributed.[2]

The relative importance of each type of skill depends on the level of management. As shown in Figure 1.2, human relations skills are important at every level of management. However, supervisors rely more on technical skills than do higher-level managers because employees who have a problem doing their jobs go to the supervisor and expect help. Also, top managers tend to rely more on decision-making and knowledge skills simply because they tend to make more complex decisions and provide broader and more complex streams of data to nizational stakeholders.

What is the purpose of learning why management skills can be categorized this way? Supervisors can use this information to recognize the different skills needed. For example, a salesperson can see that being able to sell fully does not in itself make him or her a good sales manager. They also have to develop skills in working with others and making decisions.

To develop the variety of skills needed to be a good supervisor, practice the concepts discussed in this book. Get to know good managers and observe how they handle situations. Supervisors

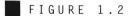

■ FIGURE 1.2

Relative Importance of Types of Skills for Different Levels of Managers

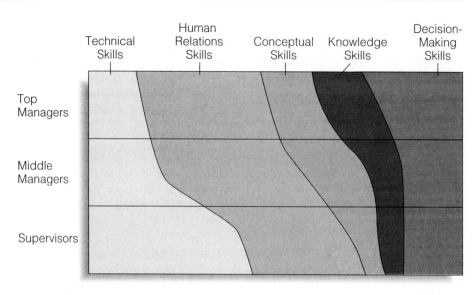

develop their skills in each area are the ones most likely to be promoted to higher levels of management.

Supervising a Diverse Workforce

Good human relations skills are especially important in today's environment because of the increasing diversity of the U.S. workforce. Whereas almost half (45 percent) of the workforce in 1986 consisted of white males, this group's share of the workforce is expected to fall to 38 percent by the year 2006.[3] While the share of white males in the workforce declines, the share of black, Hispanic, and Asian workers is expected to rise, although the greatest diversity continues to be concentrated in a few urban areas.[4] Women are entering the workforce at about the same rate as men, and now make up over 46 percent of the adult labor pool, holding a majority of the jobs in 151 occupations.[5] In addition, the over-65 segment is expected to be 17 percent of the U.S. population by 2020.[6]

Opportunities and Challenges   Together, these changes mean that supervisors can expect to have more employees who are female, nonwhite, and experienced—perhaps senior citizens holding a retirement job. As described in later chapters, these trends enable supervisors to draw on a greater variety of talent and gain insights into a greater variety of perspectives than ever before.

Diversity is not an entirely new issue. Management professor William P. Anthony describes how his grandfather, Alberto Spina, addressed similar needs during his career with American Manganese Steel Company in Chicago Heights, Illinois, from 1907 to 1944.[7] Most of the immigrant workers Spina supervised were white males, but they came from different cultural and linguistic backgrounds that reflected their countries of origin: England, Germany, Italy, Ireland, and the Slavic-speaking nations. Sometimes Spina had to use a translator to communicate with his employees. Today the immigrants are just as likely to be from Bosnia, Somalia, Congo, or Ethiopia, like the employees of Robinwood Inc., a Boston maker of candles and giftware. Company co-founder Philip Celeste works with the International Rescue Committee to hire and train refugees.[8]

Although diversity is not a new issue, the even greater diversity expected in the U.S. workforce of the future—coupled with laws and policies intended to ensure fair treatment of the various groups—requires supervisors to work successfully with a much wider variety of people.

Subtle Discrimination   Today hardly anyone would say that it is all right to discriminate or that a manager should be allowed to give preference to employees of the manager's race or sex. However, subtle forms of discrimination persist in every workplace, and everybody holds some stereotypes that consciously or unconsciously influence their behavior. The subtle discrimination that results may include ignoring the input from the only woman at a meeting or mistaking an African-American professional for someone with a less prestigious job such as receptionist or janitor.

Supervisors and other managers can use several tactics to improve attitudes:

- Have employees work with someone who is different. This gives the employees a chance to educate themselves about the customs and values others hold.
- Use the kind of behavior they expect their employees to exhibit, including demonstrations of respect for others.
- Question negative stereotypes. When an employee makes an offensive comment, point out the damage it does and ask the employee to avoid such remarks in the future.

Unfortunately, many supervisors still work for organizations that fail to see the advantages of hiring and developing a diverse workforce. Even in an organization where management is not committed to these goals, supervisors can provide advice and coaching to female and nonwhite employees, helping them get along in the organization. Supervisors also can make a point of learning about the various employees in the department, such as what motivates them and what their career goals are. Throughout this book, you will find more specific ideas for meeting the diversity challenge as it relates to the chapter topics. See "Supervision and Diversity" for an assessment of affirmative action.

General Functions of the Supervisor

Jennifer Plotnick is a supervisor at her city's board of education. Her responsibilities include ensuring that the employees in her department are doing a good job, preparing a budget for her department, making sure not to spend more than the budgeted amounts, explaining to employees what they are expected to do, and justifying to her manager why she needs to add people to her department next year. In contrast, supervisors in other settings may spend most of their time enabling employees to do their jobs and may handle fewer responsibilities than Jennifer.

Although the settings and degrees of responsibility may differ, supervisors and other managers carry out the same types of functions. To describe these common activities, management experts categorize them as planning, organizing, staffing, leading, and controlling. The management functions are illustrated in Figure 1.3. The figure shows that all of the activities should be directed toward enabling employees to deliver high-quality goods and services, whether to customers of the organization or to colleagues in another department.

Affirmative Action or Reverse Discrimination?

Some observers detect a change in public attitudes about affirmative action, a backlash against policies put into effect to right the wrongs of discrimination against minorities. Critics of affirmative action suggest that it has resulted, perhaps unintentionally, in "reverse discrimination," which puts white males at a disadvantage.

Recent legislation in California has limited bilingual education in that state, and voters in Washington state have accepted a ban on state-sponsored affirmative action programs despite the opposition of their governor and well-known Washington employers like Boeing, Eddie Bauer, Microsoft, and Starbucks. Lobbyists hope to put similar legislation to the vote in Nebraska, Michigan, Florida, and Texas.

What exactly is affirmative action, and what is its intent? One authority defines affirmative action as any combination of these four basic forms:

1. *Recruiting underrepresented groups.*
2. *Changing management attitudes*, attempting to eliminate conscious or unconscious prejudices.
3. *Removing discriminatory obstacles*, identifying employment policies and practices that place women and minorities at a disadvantage in the employer's workforce.

4. *Giving preferential treatment* to women and minorities in staffing decisions.

Preferential treatment is the issue at the heart of the most vocal public debates. It seems to many that preferential treatment goes well beyond the meaning and intention of "equal opportunity," which means that all individuals must be treated equally regardless of race, color, religion, sex, or national origin.

Few recent debates have stirred as much feeling as the contrast between the intent of affirmative action and the possibly undesirable results of preferential treatment. Federal courts seem to agree that the government should remove the effects of discrimination against its citizens, as long as it does not commit another wrong in the process. Recent decisions indicate that the courts are less in favor of giving preferential treatment to members of groups that have suffered discrimination in the past but who, as individuals, have been slighted. Where do you stand?

Sources: Robert K. Robinson, Joseph G. P. Paolillo, and Brian J. Reithel, "Race-Based Preferential Treatment Programs," *Public Personnel Management*, Fall 1998, pp. 349 ff.; Steven A. Holmes, "Victorious Preference Foes Look for New Battlefields," *New York Times*, November 10, 1998.

FIGURE 1.3

Functions of Supervisors and Other Managers

Planning

planning
Setting goals and determining how to meet them.

Common sense tells us that we do our best work when we know what we are trying to accomplish. Thus, the supervisor's job includes determining the department's goals and the ways to meet them. This is the function of **planning.** Sometimes a supervisor has a substantial say in determining the goals themselves, while another supervisor must focus his or her efforts on how to achieve goals set by higher-level managers.

As mentioned earlier, the supervisor's job is to help the organization meet its goals. Organizational goals are the result of planning by top managers. The purpose of planning by supervisors, then, is to determine how the department can contribute to achieving the organization's goals. This includes planning how much money to spend—and, for a retailer or sales department, how much money to bring in—what level of output to achieve, and how many employees will be needed. Computer technology has made new planning tools possible as well. (Chapter 6 discusses planning in greater detail.)

Organizing

organizing
Setting up the group, allocating resources, and assigning work to achieve goals.

Once the supervisor figures out what needs to get done, the next step is to determine how to set up the group, allocate resources, and assign work to achieve the goals efficiently. This is the function of **organizing.**

Somebody has to decide how to set up the overall organization, creating departments and levels of management. Of course, few supervisors have much of a say in those kinds of decisions. At the supervisory level, organizing usually involves activities such as scheduling projects and assigning duties to employees (or, as will be discussed later, enabling employees to carry out these organizing tasks). In addition, modern supervisors are increasingly responsible for setting up and leading teams of workers to handle special projects or day-to-day operations. Virtual teams rely on electronic communication to function effectively even when team members and supervisors are widely separated. (Chapter 7 discusses organizing in greater detail, and Chapter 3 addresses leading a team.)

Staffing

staffing
Identifying, hiring, and developing the necessary number and quality of employees.

The supervisor needs qualified employees to carry out the tasks that he or she has planned and organized. The activities involved in identifying, hiring, and developing the necessary number and quality of employees are known as the function of **staffing.** While an operative (nonmanagement) employee's performance is usually judged on the basis of the results that the employee has achieved as an individual, a supervisor's performance depends on the quality of results that the supervisor achieves through his or her employees. Therefore, staffing is crucial to the supervisor's success. (The various activities of the staffing function are addressed in Chapters 16 through 18.)

Leading

Even if the supervisor has the clearest and most inspired vision of how the department and its employees should work, this vision will not become a reality unless employees know and want to do their part. The supervisor is responsible for letting employees know what is expected of them and for inspiring and motivating

leading
Influencing people to act (or not act) in a certain way.

employees to do good work. Influencing employees to act (or not act) in a certain way is the function of **leading.** Good leadership is even more important for supervisors in a time of rapid change, fueled by the widespread use of the Internet.

Whereas organizing draws heavily on the supervisor's conceptual skills, leading requires good human relations skills. The supervisor needs to be aware of and use behaviors that employees respond to as he or she desires. [Chapter 8 includes a more detailed discussion of leading. Other chapters discuss the ways in which supervisors influence employees to act, such as by communicating (Chapter 10), motivating (Chapter 11), and disciplining (Chapter 13).]

Controlling

controlling
Monitoring performance and making needed corrections.

The supervisor needs to know what is happening in the department. When something goes wrong, the supervisor must find a way to fix the problem or enable employees to do so. Monitoring performance and making needed corrections is the management function of **controlling.**

In an increasing number of organizations, the supervisor is not supposed to control by dictating solutions. Rather, the supervisor is expected to provide employees with the resources and motivation to identify and correct problems themselves. In these organizations, the supervisor is still responsible for controlling, but he or she works with others to carry out this function. (Chapter 6 discusses these and more traditional principles of controlling in more detail.) Now the control function can also include the use of e-mail controls that monitor employees' use of the computer, and "e-supervision technology," which uses both the Internet and audiovideo technology to monitor store operations for safety, customer service, stock level, and other supervisory issues.[9]

Relationships among the Functions

Notice that Figure 1.3 shows the management functions as a process in which planning comes first, followed by organizing, then staffing, then leading, and, finally, controlling. This order occurs because each function depends on the preceding function or functions. Once the supervisor has planned what the department will do, he or she can figure out the best way to organize work and people to accomplish those objectives. Then the supervisor needs to get the people in place and doing their jobs. At that point, the supervisor can direct their work and inspire their efforts. The results are then evaluated by the supervisor to ensure that the work is getting done properly. During the controlling function, the supervisor may wish to revise some goals, at which point the whole process begins again.

Of course, real-life supervisors do not spend one week planning, then one week organizing, and so on. Instead, they often carry out all the management functions during the course of a day. For example, a patient care coordinator in a hospital might start the day by checking the nurses' performance (controlling), then attend a meeting to discuss the needs of the patients (planning), then help resolve a dispute between a nurse and a physical therapist (leading). Thus, Figure 1.3 is a very general model of managing that shows how the functions depend on each other, not how the supervisor structures his or her work.

Typically, supervisors spend most of their time leading and controlling. That is so because supervisors work directly with the employees who are producing or selling a product or providing support services. Planning, staffing, and organizing take up less of a supervisor's time. In contrast, higher-level managers are responsible for setting the overall direction for the organization; thus, they spend more time on planning and organizing.

Responsibilities of the Supervisor

"I wish I were the manager," grumbled Hal O'Donnell, a cook at a pizza restaurant. "Then I'd be in charge and wouldn't get bossed around all the time." Perhaps Hal has not considered that a promotion to supervisor (or any level of management) would not lessen a person's burdens. Indeed, an employee who becomes a supervisor assumes all the responsibilities listed in Table 1.1. In other words, supervisors have more power than nonmanagers but also many responsibilities—to higher management, to employees, and to co-workers.

Types of Responsibilities

Supervisors are responsible for carrying out the duties assigned to them by higher-level managers. This includes giving managers timely and accurate information for planning. They also must keep their managers informed about the department's performance. Supervisors are expected to serve as a kind of "linking pin" between employees and management. Thus, their responsibilities include building employee morale and carrying employee concerns to the relevant managers.

Some supervisors may question the notion that they have a responsibility to their employees. After all, the employees are responsible for doing what the supervisors say. Nevertheless, because supervisors link management to the employees, the way they treat employees is crucial. Supervisors are responsible for giving their employees clear instructions and making sure they understand their jobs.

TABLE 1.1 **Responsibilities of the Supervisor**	<ul><li>Recognize the talents of each subordinate.</li><li>Share your vision of where the organization wants to go.</li><li>Treat employees with dignity and respect.</li><li>Conduct necessary meetings efficiently and ensure they accomplish their intended tasks.</li><li>Keep your staff informed and up to date.</li><li>Be accessible to those under your supervision.</li><li>Conduct periodic evaluations of your group's progress.</li><li>Provide an opportunity for employees to evaluate you.</li><li>Praise your staff for their accomplishments.</li><li>Keep in touch with your industry.</li><li>Be able to perform the duties of those you supervise.</li><li>Keep a sense of humor.</li><li>Be fair.</li><li>Follow proper hiring practices.</li><li>Know the law as it applies to your company and your job.</li><li>Adhere to workplace safety rules and regulations.</li><li>Keep accurate employee records.</li><li>Avoid sexual harassment and discrimination based on gender, age, race, pregnancy, sexual orientation, and national origin.</li><li>Know how to fire an employee without violating his or her rights.</li></ul>

Sources: Nolo.com, "When You're the Boss," reprinted at http://www.workingwoman.com/wwn/article.jsp?contentId=513&ChannelID=210; Rona Leach, "Supervision: From Me to We," *Supervision*, February 2000, p. 8.

They must look for problems and correct them before employees' performance deteriorates further. They also need to treat their employees fairly and to speak up for their interests to top management.

Finally, supervisors are responsible for cooperating with their co-workers in other departments. They should respond promptly when a co-worker in another department requests information. They should share ideas that will help the organization's departments work together to accomplish common goals. And supervisors should listen with an open mind when co-workers in other departments make suggestions about improving the way things are done. When supervisors learn from each other's ideas, the whole organization benefits and the supervisors have the satisfaction of working together as members of a team.

Responsibilities after Restructuring or Reengineering

In recent years, many organizations have attempted to cut costs by reducing the number of levels of management. In this process, many middle managers, who rank between supervisors and the top executives, usually are eliminated. (By one account, middle-management positions accounted for about one-fifth of jobs eliminated in the United States since 1988.)[10] The Diner's Club unit of Citicorp was reduced from eight layers of management between the president and first-line supervisors to four layers. Other companies that have cut out layers of management include Monsanto, Digital Equipment, McDonnell Douglas, and General Electric.[11]

When organizations eliminate layers of management—whether they call this process restructuring, reengineering, or something else—they generally push responsibility lower in the organization's hierarchy. Today's supervisors often have responsibilities that only a decade ago would have been the province of middle management. Supervisors not only must continue to work closely with employees but also must handle much of the planning and organizing once done by middle managers.

Furthermore, the organization may expect that operative employees will play an active role in traditional management tasks such as setting goals, allocating work, and monitoring and improving quality. An old-fashioned "command-and-control" approach to supervision in this setting would not be effective. It stifles the very creativity and empowerment that this kind of reorganization seeks to foster. (See "Meeting the Challenge.")

Rather, the supervisor's role in such situations is to make it easier for employees to carry out their broad responsibilities. This role assumes that employees are able and willing to contribute if only they have the information and other resources they need. Lawrence A. Bossidy, Allied Signal's CEO, refers to this new role of enabler and empowerer when he says, "We need people who are better at persuading than at barking orders, who know how to coach and build consensus."[12]

Consultant Frank Quisenberry has summarized three basic ways in which a supervisor can carry out this redefined role:[13]

1. The supervisor *empowers* employees, making sure they understand the organization's goals and have enough freedom to make decisions in support of those goals.
2. The supervisor *communicates* with employees and higher-level managers, sharing information extensively. He or she communicates the needs and concerns of management to employees and the needs and concerns of employees to management. (This can require skill in negotiating.)

Supervising in the New Millennium

With the shape of organizations changing faster than ever before, the job of the supervisor is changing and expanding as well.

Today's organizations are open systems—that is, they obtain inputs from their environment, put them through a transformation process, and deliver output back to the organization's external environment. Firms focus on serving the customer's needs, on continuously improving essential functions, and on forming strategic alliances and networks with other firms.

Supervisors in these organizations find themselves in flatter, more horizontal hierarchies. They are expected to adapt and update their skills to the changing needs of the organization, to work well with teams that may be cross-functional or virtual, and to communicate and cooperate with those above, below, and on their own level in the firm. Supervisors are the ones who instill trust in their employees through delegating, team problem solving, and sharing of information. Simply encouraging people to do their jobs is no longer enough.

Some believe that supervisors can contribute to the firm's "organizational health," which has eleven related components:

1. Good internal communication.
2. Participation and involvement in decision making by workers at all levels.
3. Loyalty and commitment to the organization.
4. High morale and motivation.
5. A strongly positive reputation.
6. A positive ethical climate.
7. Recognition for outstanding performance and achievement.
8. Goal alignment.
9. Leadership.
10. Employee development.
11. Appropriate use of resources.

Supervisors can recognize the links between each of these components of health and their own departmental responsibilities in such measures as absenteeism, turnover, and productivity. By using benchmarks to assess their contributions to organizational health, supervisors can ensure that they are managing for the new millennium.

Sources: Julie A. Lyden and William E. Lingele, "Supervising Organizational Health," *Supervision*, December 1, 2000, p. 3; Patricia M. Buhler, "Managing in the New Millennium," *Supervision*, October 1, 2000, p. 15.

3.   The supervisor *develops* the skills of his or her team or of individual team members by recognizing the importance of developing problem-solving and teamwork skills in addition to technical skills.

All these activities rely heavily on interpersonal skills. Thus, the changes occurring in the modern workplace require managers to rely much less than before on their technical expertise and more on their ability to understand, inspire, and enhance cooperation among people.

For some supervisors who view their job as telling others what to do and then checking that the work gets done, this new style of supervision can feel awkward. However, many supervisors discover that their employees can, and do, contribute ideas and commitment that improve performance and the satisfaction of customers and employees alike.

Supervisors may find their jobs changing in other ways as well. As new technology makes telecommuting—working on a computer from a remote location such as one's home—more appealing to workers and employees alike, the supervisor's job becomes both more important and more challenging. George Piskurich, a consultant and writer, says, "If you have a lot of telecommuters, you need even better supervisory skills."[14]

Responsibilities and Accountability

accountability
The practice of imposing penalties for failing to adequately carry out responsibilities and of providing rewards for meeting responsibilities.

Whatever the responsibilities of a particular supervisor, the organization holds the supervisor accountable for carrying them out. **Accountability** refers to the practice of imposing penalties for failing to adequately carry out responsibilities, and it usually includes giving rewards for meeting responsibilities. Thus, if customer service supervisor Lydia Papadopoulos effectively teaches the telephone representatives on her staff to listen carefully to customers, the company might reward her with a raise. In contrast, a higher-level manager who gets frustrated with a supervisor who fails to provide information about what is happening in the department might eventually fire the supervisor for not carrying out this responsibility.

Becoming a Supervisor

Most supervisors started out working in the department they now supervise. Because technical skills are relatively important for first-level managers, the person selected to be supervisor is often an employee with a superior grasp of the technical skills needed to perform well in the department. The person also might have more seniority than many of the other employees in the department. Good work habits and leadership skills are also reasons for selecting an employee to be a supervisor. Sometimes a company will hire a recent college graduate to be a supervisor, perhaps because the person has demonstrated leadership potential or a specialized skill that will help in the position.

Unfortunately, none of these bases for promotion or hiring guarantees that a person knows how to supervise. A hotel employee promoted to a supervisory position, for instance, might be at a loss for ways to motivate those who now report to her. Gene Ference, president of HVS/The Ference Group of Weston, Conn., suggests that coaching is a more effective means of encouraging performance and development than simply saying, "Do your best." According to Ference, coaching means asking questions like, "How do you think we can apply these culinary principles to our new spa menu?" and "The guest corridors in the west wing were exceptionally clean today. How can we ensure that happens all of the time?"[15]

Becoming a supervisor marks a big change in a person's work life. The new supervisor suddenly must use more human relations and conceptual skills and devote more time to planning ahead and keeping an eye on the department's activities. Also, a change takes place in the supervisor's relationships with the employees in the department. Instead of being one of the crowd, the supervisor becomes a part of management—even the target of blame or anger when employees resent company policies. All these changes are bound to lead to some anxiety. It is natural to wonder whether you are qualified or how you will handle the problems that surely will arise. See "Tips from the Firing Line" for ways to ease the transition into management.

Preparing for the Job

One way to combat the anxiety is to prepare for the job. A new supervisor can learn about management and supervision through books and observation. He or she can think about ways to carry out the role of supervisor. More important than friendliness are traits such as fairness and a focus on achieving goals. A supervisor can also strive to learn as much as possible about the organization, the department, and the job.

How to Survive the Rise into Supervisory Ranks

Many talented workers look forward to that first big promotion and the rewards that come with it. For those who make the move up into the supervisory ranks, the change is both exhilarating and stressful. One of the most challenging aspects of the new supervisor's job is learning how to make the transition from peer to supervisor. What will happen to friendships with co-workers? How should the new boss build his or her new authority?

Here are some suggestions on avoiding five common mistakes new managers make.

1. *Change your work habits.* As an employee you were responsible for motivating yourself. Now your job includes motivating others to produce the best products or services they are capable of, as efficiently as possible. Doing so requires a brand new set of skills (many of which are covered in this book). Measuring performance quality, setting schedules and standards, and training others are among the new habits supervisors must actively work to acquire.

2. *Don't let down your guard.* While friendships with former co-workers can be enhanced by your new job, remember that business is business. You will need to deal with employee relations issues, use discipline, and sometimes terminate another person's employment. True friends will respect your new responsibilities. Those who try to use personal friendship as leverage on the job don't have your best interest at heart.

3. *Don't try to be a hands-on boss.* It's your turn to pass along to others the knowledge and experience that have brought you to the supervisor's job. As frustrating as it may be, resist the temptation to do tasks yourself. Educating your workers will enhance their productivity and their confidence and job satisfaction as well. That's better for both of you in the long run.

4. *Plan for tomorrow.* Don't get stuck in the here and now. Failure to attend to long-term planning as part of your daily routine can leave you offering your manager excuses instead of results. Take into account training, production schedules, absenteeism, and other factors and develop an effective plan to deal with them.

5. *Accept the responsibility of representing your firm.* While there is no need to change your circle of friends or activities, consider that as a member of the management team you now represent the company to outsiders. Act in a way that will not compromise or embarrass the firm, and others will follow your example.

Source: Ed Lisoski, "Rising from the Ranks to Management: How to Thrive versus Survive," *Supervision*, July 1998, p. 6.

Once on the job, a supervisor needs to continue the learning process. More important than understanding the layout of the workplace is knowing about the employees in the department or work group. Who are the quiet but productive workers, for example, and who are the unofficial leaders? To get to know employees, a supervisor can talk to his or her own manager and read performance appraisals, but the most reliable sources of information are the employees themselves. Particularly in the early days on the job, a supervisor should take time to discuss goals with employees and observe their work habits.

A supervisor may learn that one or more employees had been candidates for the supervisor's job and therefore may be jealous. One constructive approach that a supervisor might take to this problem is to acknowledge the other person's feelings, to ask for the employee's support, and to discuss his or her long-term goals. An important aspect of this approach is that the supervisor is helping employees to meet or exceed their own goals. For example, a sales supervisor can help a potentially jealous salesperson increase sales. Most employees will regard someone as a better manager who helps them make more money.

Obtaining and Using Power and Authority

To carry out his or her job, a supervisor needs not only knowledge but also power (the ability to do certain things) and authority (the right to do certain things). To acquire power upon assuming the job of supervisor, it may help to have the new supervisor's boss make an official announcement of the promotion. When accepting the job, a supervisor can ask his or her boss to announce the promotion at a meeting of the employees. There the supervisor can take the opportunity to state his or her expectations, desire to work as a team, and interest in hearing about work-related problems.

A new supervisor should not rush to make changes in the department, but should first understand how the department works and what employees expect. Making changes quickly and without seeking their input can alienate employees and put them on the defensive. The supervisor can build support for change by introducing it gradually after inviting suggestions where appropriate.

Using new supervisory authority can take some getting used to. Marsha Wells was promoted to deputy project manager at CACI International, Inc., when she was just 26. The promotion is a big opportunity for Marsha, but she is still learning to be comfortable in her new position. "Sometimes," she says, "I have the realization [that] people are coming in and expecting me to give them guidance. That can be humbling."[16]

(Chapter 7 discusses the delegation of authority. Chapter 15 covers sources and types of power along with more information about managing change.)

Characteristics of a Successful Supervisor

Unfortunately, many of us have worked for someone who seemed to stifle our best efforts or to anger us with unfair decisions. Many of us also have worked for a supervisor who taught us new skills, inspired us to do better than we thought possible, or made us look forward to going to work each day. What is behind the success of this second category of supervisors? Figure 1.4 illustrates some characteristics of successful supervisors. Take the Self-Quiz on page 22 to see whether supervising is a good fit with your current traits and interests.

A successful supervisor has a *positive attitude*. Employees tend to reflect the attitudes of the people in charge. When the supervisor's attitude toward work and the organization is positive, employees are more likely to be satisfied with and interested in their work. Furthermore, managers and co-workers alike prefer working with someone who has a positive attitude.

Successful supervisors are *loyal*. As a part of the management team, they must take actions that are best for the organization. This may include making decisions that are unpopular with employees. In such situations, supervisors must recognize that taking on a supervisory job means they cannot always be "one of the gang."

Successful supervisors are *fair*. Supervisors who play favorites or behave inconsistently will lose the support and respect of their employees, and thus not be able to lead effectively. Furthermore, when supervisors make assignments and decisions based on those they like best, they will not necessarily make the assignments and decisions best suited to the organization. Another aspect of being fair is to follow the rules yourself. The supervisor can set a good example, for example, by being on time and refraining from doing personal work on the job or taking supplies home.

Supervisors also need to be *good communicators*. Employees and bosses alike depend on the supervisor to keep them informed of what is going on. Employees

■ FIGURE 1.4

Characteristics of a Successful Supervisor

who receive clear guidance about what is expected of them will not only perform better but also will be more satisfied with their jobs. Good communication also includes making contact with employees each day and listening to what they have to say. (Chapter 10 takes an in-depth look at the communications skills that supervisors need to develop.)

To be successful, supervisors must be *able to delegate;* that is, to give their employees authority and responsibility to carry out activities. As supervisors tend to have excellent technical skills, delegating may be a challenge. They may resist giving an assignment to an employee who may not carry it out as easily or as well as they, the supervisors, could do. Nevertheless, supervisors cannot do the work of the whole department. Therefore, they must assign work to employees. Equally important, a supervisor should give employees credit for their accomplishments. This, in turn, makes the supervisor look good; the employees' successes show that the supervisor is able to select and motivate employees as well as delegate effectively. (Chapter 7 discusses delegation in greater detail.)

Finally, a successful supervisor must *want the job.* Some people are happier carrying out the technical skills of their field, whether it is carpentry, respiratory therapy, or financial management. People who prefer this type of work to the functions of managing will probably be happier if they turn down an opportunity to become a supervisor. In contrast, people who enjoy the challenge of making plans and inspiring others to achieve goals are more likely to be effective supervisors.

About This Book

This book introduces the many kinds of activities supervisors must carry out to accomplish their overall objective of seeing that employees contribute toward achieving the organization's goals. Part One is devoted to a broad view of the supervisor's role. Chapter 1 serves as an introduction to the general activities and responsibilities of supervisors.

Part Two describes the challenges modern supervisors face in meeting their responsibilities. Ever-higher expectations of customers, business owners, and the general public have made high quality a necessary concern of employees at all levels, including the supervisory level. Therefore, Chapter 2 addresses how supervisors can understand and carry out their role in maintaining and constantly improving quality. Chapter 3 covers groups and teamwork, reflecting the increasingly common role of the supervisor as a team leader. Supervisors (and others in the organization) also must consider the ethical implications of their decisions, the topic of Chapter 4. The value of diversity is the topic of Chapter 5.

Part Three takes a deeper look at the supervisory functions introduced earlier in this chapter. Chapter 6 discusses how supervisors use planning and controlling to enable their work groups to reach goals and objectives. Chapter 7 covers the function of organizing, including supervisors' use of delegation to share authority and responsibility. Chapter 8 examines the supervisor's role in carrying out the management function of leading. Chapter 9 explains how supervisors can be effective at solving problems and making decisions.

Part Four describes skills needed by supervisors in all kinds of organizations. Individual chapters cover ways supervisors can communicate, motivate their employees, improve productivity, supervise "problem" employees, manage time and stress, and manage conflict and change. These skills are important at all levels of management and in all types of organizations. A special appendix new to this edition follows this section and emphasizes how supervisors negotiate and handle organizational politics.

The last part of this book addresses activities related to managing the organization's human resources: its employees. Chapter 16 covers the supervisor's role in selecting new employees. Chapter 17 discusses the process of training new and current employees. Chapter 18 describes how supervisors appraise employees' performance. Finally, Chapter 19 introduces some of the many government laws and regulations that guide supervisors' roles and decisions with regard to human resources.

Throughout the book, the chapters include special features designed to help you apply the principles of supervision to the practice of supervising real people in a real organization. These features include "Tips from the Firing Line" and "Meeting the Challenge," which discuss actual examples of modern supervisory challenges—quality, teamwork, ethics, and technology—as well as provide practical tips on effective supervision. "Supervision and Diversity" boxes demonstrate how the diverse workforce of the future is already affecting the lives of supervisors. "Across Industries" boxes demonstrate the applicability of supervision practices in a wide variety of business areas. Chapter-opening cases and end-of-chapter cases show how real supervisors and organizations have approached the issues covered in the chapter.

An end-of-book notes section, divided by chapter, provides source and additional reading material for various topics covered within the chapters. The glossary at the end of this text provides a quick reference for all key terms. For review, each definition is followed by the number of the page where the boldfaced key term is defined.

The Skills Modules at the end of each chapter contain self-assessments, skill-building exercises, role-playing exercises, information applications, and miniature case studies. These allow you to use text concepts and develop leadership abilities.

Summary

1.1   Define what a supervisor is.
A supervisor is a manager at the first level of management. That is, the employees reporting to the supervisor are not themselves managers.

1.2   Describe the basic types of supervisory skills.
The basic supervisory skills are technical, human relations, conceptual, and decision-making skills. Technical skills are the specialized knowledge and experience used to carry out particular techniques or procedures. Human relations skills enable the supervisor to work effectively with other people. Conceptual skills enable the supervisor to see the relation of the parts to the whole and to one another. Decision-making skills are needed to analyze information and reach good decisions. Knowledge skills include the ability to utilize e-mail, voice mail, fax, the intranet, and the Internet to manage a stream of information and data.

1.3   Describe how the growing diversity of the workforce affects the supervisor's role.
Compared with the current makeup of the U.S. workforce, an increasingly large share of employees will be female, nonwhite, and older. As a result, supervisors in the future will typically manage a more diverse group of employees. This means that supervisors can benefit from a greater variety of talents and viewpoints, but it also requires them to draw on more sophisticated human relations skills than in the past.

1.4   Identify the general functions of a supervisor.
The general functions of a supervisor are planning, organizing, staffing, leading, and controlling. Planning involves setting goals and determining how to meet them. Organizing is determining how to set up the group, allocate resources, and assign work to achieve goals. Staffing consists of identifying, hiring, and developing the necessary number and quality of employees. Leading is the function of getting employees to do what is expected of them. Controlling consists of monitoring performance and making needed corrections.

1.5   Explain how supervisors are responsible to higher management, employees, and co-workers.
Supervisors are responsible for doing the work assigned to them by higher management and for keeping management informed of the department's progress. They link higher management to the employees. Supervisors are responsible for treating employees fairly, making instructions clear, and bringing employee concerns to higher management. Organizations that have undergone restructuring or reengineering often make supervisors responsible for empowering and enabling employees instead of focusing on command and control. Supervisors are responsible for cooperating with co-workers in other departments. Organizations hold supervisors accountable for meeting these various responsibilities.

1.6   Describe the typical background of someone who is promoted to supervisor.
Most supervisors begin as employees in the department they now supervise. They usually have superior technical skills and may have seniority or demonstrate leadership potential.

1.7   Identify characteristics of a successful supervisor.
A successful supervisor is usually someone who has a positive attitude, is loyal, is fair, communicates well, can delegate, and wants the job.

Key Terms

Review and Discussion Questions

1. What are some ways that a supervisor's job is similar to that of managers at other levels? How does a supervisor's job differ from that of other managers?

2. Identify whether each of the following skills is a technical skill, a human relations skill, a conceptual skill, a decision-making skill, or a knowledge skill.

   a. The ability to communicate well with one's manager.

   b. The ability to create advertisements that grab people's attention.

   c. The ability to select the most appropriate safety training program for the housekeeping staff.

   d. The ability to create and distribute a spreadsheet of employees' vacation preferences.

   e. The ability to see the big picture in order to understand a situation fully.

   f. Knowledge of how to machine a part without unnecessary changes in the setup of equipment.

3. Imagine that you have just been promoted to supervisor of the cashiers in a supermarket. List specific technical, human relations, conceptual, and decision-making skills you think you might need to succeed at this job. How might you develop them continually to achieve the job of store manager?

4. Population trends suggest that the workforce will become increasingly diverse. What are some advantages of greater diversity? What challenges does it pose to the supervisor?

5. What are the basic functions of a supervisor? On which functions do supervisors spend most of their time?

6. As the controlling function changes in many organizations, supervisors should no longer control by dictating solutions. How do they carry out the controlling function?

7. What responsibilities do supervisors have to each of these groups?

   a. Higher management.

   b. The employees they supervise.

   c. Co-workers in other departments.

8. Emma has just been promoted to office manager in a small real estate office. Some of the people she will supervise are her former peers; she is aware that one of them also applied for the office manager's job. How can Emma prepare for her new position? What might be the best way to approach the co-worker who did not get the manager's job?

9. What are some ways a new supervisor can use power and authority effectively?

10. List the characteristics of a good supervisor. Besides the characteristics mentioned in the chapter, add any others you believe are important. Draw on your own experiences as an employee and/or supervisor.

A SECOND LOOK

How might Tracey Curvey ensure that her in-house employees felt everyone in the department received fair treatment?

SKILLS MODULE

CASE

Two Supervisors' Tales

Joyce Gurtatowski and John David are both supervisors, but their jobs look quite different on the surface. Gurtatowski is an assistant vice president with La Salle Bank Matteson in Calumet City, Illinois. She supervises six personal bankers. David is a senior property manager for Standard Parking. He supervises 30 employees in several parking garages in Chicago.

On a typical day, Gurtatowski arrives at the bank at about 7:30 A.M. She begins her day with paperwork such as auditing department accounts. When the bank is open for business, she spends much of her time answering questions from personal bankers and tellers about nonroutine customer problems and questions. According to Gurtatowski, "Every customer is a new situation," and that variety is what poses challenges to her employees—and what makes her own job interesting. From the time the bank lobby closes (at 3:00 P.M. on most days) until she leaves at about 5:30 P.M., Gurtatowski returns phone calls from customers and prepares her department schedule for the next day. In addition, she trains staff members at weekly meetings and conducts performance appraisals.

David spends about 60 percent of his day with people, both customers and employees. He devotes most of his time with employees to follow-up: to see that they are carrying out instructions. Most of the remainder of David's day is taken up with paperwork, including monthly parking accounts, market analyses, and efforts related to marketing the garages. David finds working with employees particularly interesting and challenging because they come from many countries, including Ethiopia, Kuwait, Ghana, Pakistan, and Nigeria, as well as the United States. Sometimes, the cultural differences of the employees mandate special training for serving American customers. For example, an employee from Ethiopia would speak in a monotone, a tone of voice that shows respect in his culture. David had to train this employee to speak more enthusiastically to American customers.

1. Which supervisory skills seem to be most important to Gurtatowski's and David's jobs? Why?
2. What types of responsibilities does each undertake?
3. Do you think Gurtatowski and David are examples of successful supervisors? Why or why not?

■ SELF-QUIZ

Is Supervising Right for You?

Answer each of the following questions Yes or No.	Yes	No
1. Do you consider yourself a highly ambitious person?	_____	_____
2. Do you sincerely like people and have patience with them?	_____	_____
3. Could you assume the responsibility of decision making?	_____	_____
4. Is making more money very important to you?	_____	_____
5. Would recognition from others be more important to you than taking pride in doing a detailed job well?	_____	_____
6. Would you enjoy learning about psychology and human behavior?	_____	_____
7. Would you be happier with more responsibility?	_____	_____
8. Would you rather work with problems involving human relationships than with mechanical, computational, creative, clerical, or similar problems?	_____	_____
9. Do you desire an opportunity to demonstrate your leadership ability?	_____	_____
10. Do you desire the freedom to do your own planning rather than being told what to do?	_____	_____
Total	_____	_____

Give yourself 1 point for each Yes answer. If your score is 6 or more, you might be happy as a supervisor. If your score was 5 or less, you should think hard about your preferences and strengths before jumping into a supervisory job.

Source: From *Supervisor's Survival Kit: Your First Step*, by Elwood N. Chapman. Copyright © 1993 Pearson Education, Inc. Reprinted by permission of Pearson Education, Inc., Upper Saddle River, NJ.

Class Exercise

Which of the five management functions would you rely on in each of the following situations? Discuss your choices in class.

1. One of your employees is chronically late for work.
2. Your department has switched to a new word-processing program and some people are having difficulty making the change.
3. Your manager has asked you to have your staff complete a special project without incurring any overtime.
4. It's time to prepare your department's budget for the coming year.
5. Your team's productivity is not meeting the standards the team set.

Team-Building Exercise

Performing Supervisory Functions

Instructions

1. Imagine you are the supervisor in each scenario described below, and you have to decide which supervisory function(s) you would use in each.

2. Many of the scenarios require more than one function. The "Answers" column lists the number of functions your answer should include. Mark your answers using the following codes:

Code	Supervisory Function	Brief Description
P	Planning	Setting goals and determining how to meet them
O	Organizing	Determining how to set up the group, allocate resources, and assign work to achieve goals
S	Staffing	Identifying, hiring, and developing the necessary number and quality of employees
L	Leading	Getting employees to do what is expected of them
C	Controlling	Monitoring performance and making needed corrections

3. As a class, compare and discuss your answers and the reasoning you used in determining them.

Scenarios

Your group's work is centered on a project that is due in two months. Although everyone is working on the project, you believe that your subordinates are involved in excessive socializing and other time-consuming behaviors. You decide to meet with the group to have the members help you break down the project into smaller subprojects with minideadlines. You believe that this will help keep the group members focused on the project and that the quality of the finished project will then reflect the true capabilities of your group.

Your first impression of the new group you will be supervising is not too great. You tell your friend at dinner after your first day on the job: "Looks like I got a babysitting job instead of a supervisory job."

Your boss asks your opinion about promoting Andy to a supervisory position. Andy is one of your most competent and efficient workers. Knowing that Andy lacks leadership skills in many key areas, you decide not to recommend him at this time. Instead you tell your boss you will work with Andy to help him develop his leadership skills so that the next time an opportunity for promotion occurs, Andy will be prepared to consider it.

You begin a meeting of your work group by letting the members know that a major procedure the group has been using for the past two years is being significantly revamped. Your department will have to phase in the change during the next six weeks. You proceed by explaining the reasoning management gave you for this change. You then say, "Take the next five to ten minutes to voice your reactions to this change." The majority of comments are critical of the change. You say, "I appreciate each of you sharing your reactions; I, too, recognize that *all*

Answers

(four functions)
1. _____

(three functions)
2. _____

(one function)
3. _____

(three functions)
4. _____

Source: This team-building exercise was prepared by Corinne Livesay, Belhaven College, Jackson, Mississippi.

change creates problems. However, either we can spend the remaining 45 minutes of our meeting focusing on why we don't want the change and why we don't think it's necessary, or we can work together to come up with viable solutions to solve the problems that implementing this change will most likely create." After five more minutes of an exchange of comments, the consensus of the group is that they should spend the remainder of the meeting focusing on how to deal with the potential problems that may arise from implementing the new procedure.

You are preparing the annual budget allocation meetings to be held in the plant manager's office next week. You decide to present a strong case to support your department's getting money for some high-tech equipment that will help your employees do their jobs better. You will stand firm against any suggestions of budget cuts in your area.

(one function)

5. _____

Early in your career you learned an important lesson about employee selection. One of the nurses on your floor unexpectedly quit. The other nurses pressured you to fill the position quickly because they were overworked even before the nurse left. After a hasty recruitment effort, you made a decision based on insufficient information. You regretted your quick decision during the three months of problems that followed, until you finally had to discharge the new hire. Since that time, you have never let anybody pressure you into making a quick hiring decision.

(two functions)

6. _____

Team-Building Exercise

Building Teams with Supervisory Skills

In Chapter 1 ("Modern Supervision: New-Era Challenge"), you learned to categorize the different skills that supervisors use in order to decide which skills apply to any given situation. Here you will apply your knowledge of these skill categories to several team-building situations.

Instructions

Imagine that you are the supervisor in each of the following situations. On the line provided at the end of each situation, write which of the following skills will best help you to build a team: technical, human relations, conceptual, decision making. Each situation requires more than one skill.

1. As the supervisor of a group of production workers in a plant that manufactures parts for telephones, you have been asked by upper management to join a team of supervisors from different departments. Your objective will be to investigate ways to improve the time required to fill large orders from major customers. Which two skills do you think will be most important to you on this team?

2. You supervise 20 telephone operators on the night shift at a mail-order catalog company. You used to be an operator yourself, so you know a great deal about the job. Management has been pressing you and other supervisors to reduce the amount of time operators spend on the telephone with each order. You believe that a potentially negative situation for your employees can be solved in a friendly competition between two teams of operators. There are no punishments for the team that comes in second, but there is a reward for the team that wins. Team members are encouraged to find new ways to reduce telephone time without reducing customer satisfaction. Which two skills do you think would be most important as you get your teams up and running?

3. You are a supervisor in the engineering department and a member of a team that includes people from production, finance, marketing, and engineering. After conducting marketing research, your team must determine whether to recommend that your company expand its operations overseas. Which three skills do you think would be most important in your contribution to the team?

PART TWO

Modern Supervision Challenges

2

Quality has become bigger than life.
—Si Sloman, vice president of operations, Best Western International

Ensuring High Quality

■ LEARNING OBJECTIVES

After you have studied this chapter, you should be able to:

2.1 Describe consequences suffered by organizations as a result of poor-quality work.

2.2 Compare product quality control and process control.

2.3 Identify techniques for quality control.

2.4 Explain how employee involvement teams work and what makes them successful.

2.5 Describe principles for successfully using total quality management.

2.6 Identify ways organizations measure their success in continuous quality improvement.

2.7 Describe guidelines for quality control.

■ WHEN QUALITY IS MEASURED IN MPH

How do you measure quality if you are the manager of a fleet of bicycle messengers? For Chris Neal, founder of the Bay Area messenger firm called Zap Courier, the answer was speed. That's why he recently put in place a state-of-the-art, computer-aided dispatching system called "free call."

In the past, harried dispatchers in the office handled calls from the firm's 200 clients, did the troubleshooting when problems arose, and assigned each delivery call, or "tag," to one of 15 messengers on a bike. Through two-way radios, the new system puts the information about tags where it belongs—with the messengers, who evaluate each job and pick the best rider

to make the delivery. "Instead of dispatchers telling you what to do, you tell them what you *can* do," says Justin De Jesus, one of the firm's expert riders.

Now Zap is one of the fastest-growing bike messenger services in the area, making more than 300 deliveries a day to clients like Levi Strauss and Miller-Freeman. That's about 20 deliveries per messenger per day. Chris Neal is not surprised. "When a messenger is allowed to follow his or her own initiative and intimate knowledge of the street, the job just gets done faster."

Source: Alex Frankel, "The Need for Speed," *Fast Company*, September 1998, p. 68.

For Zap Courier, high-quality service is defined in terms of getting packages into clients' hands as fast as possible. There are many other ways to define quality, depending on the business a firm is in. A logical way to understand the meaning of *high quality* is to think of it as work that meets or exceeds customers' expectations. Table 2.1 describes eight dimensions that can be used to measure the quality of goods or services.

Many of the supervisor's activities, including planning, leading, and controlling, are directed toward improving the quality of the organization's goods and services. This chapter considers the supervisor's role in maintaining and improving quality. The chapter begins with a description of the consequences of poor quality. Then the types of quality-control efforts and several techniques for quality control are introduced, followed by an explanation of how managers at all levels can measure whether they are improving quality and meeting high-quality standards. Finally, some general guidelines for maintaining and improving quality are discussed.

Consequences of Poor Quality

Like employees at all levels, supervisors must care about quality. They must care because poor quality limits the organization's access to resources and raises its costs.

TABLE 2.1	Dimension	Explanation
Dimensions of Quality	Performance	The product's primary operating characteristic, such as an automobile's acceleration or the picture clarity of a television set
	Features	Supplements to the product's basic operating characteristics—for example, power windows on a car or the ceremony with which a bottle of wine is opened in a restaurant
	Reliability	The probability that the product will function properly and not break down during a specified period—a manufacturer's warranty is often seen as an indicator of this
	Conformance	The degree to which the product's design and operating characteristics meet established standards, such as safety standards for a baby's crib
	Durability	The length of the product's life—for example, whether a stereo lasts for 5 years or 25 years
	Serviceability	The speed and ease of repairing the product—for example, whether a computer store will send out a repairperson, service the computer in the store, or provide no maintenance service at all
	Aesthetics	The way the product looks, feels, tastes, and smells, such as the styling and smell of a new car
	Perceived quality	The customer's impression of the product's quality, such as a buyer's belief that an Audi is a safe and reliable car

Source: Adapted from David A. Garvin, "Competing on the Eight Dimensions of Quality," Nov.–Dec. 1987 *Harvard Business Review.*

Limited Resources

When the quality of an organization's goods or services is poor, the whole organization suffers. As word spreads about problems with the product, customers look for alternatives. The organization develops a negative image, which drives away customers and clients. The organization loses business and therefore revenues, and it also has more difficulty attracting other important resources. An organization with a poor reputation has a harder time recruiting superior employees and borrowing money at favorable terms.

Many firms know that the potential for lost business is a major reason to invest in quality. "The Achilles' heel of our industry has been poor reliability, and we've solved that," says Gary Van Spronsen, a vice president of Herman Miller, Inc., the nation's second-largest manufacturer of office furniture. In the mid-1990s the company built a new plant in Michigan based around a quality initiative called SQA, for "simple, quick, affordable." By linking sales and purchasing operations via the Internet, the new system, which has now been folded back into the operations of the main company, has reduced order entry errors to almost nothing, from the more than 20 percent it suffered before implementation. Market research also indicates the firm's original SQA unit now has the highest customer-satisfaction rating in the industry.[1]

Technology and Quality Control

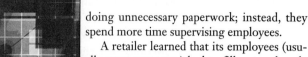

How can a computer decide whether a chocolate chip cookie tastes as good as it should? Debbi Fields, founder of Mrs. Fields Cookies, found a way to use a computer to ensure product quality even in the Mrs. Fields Cookies stores in locations farther away than she could visit regularly. In 1980, Fields visited the Hawaii store and found that the cookies tasted nothing like her original recipe. "They looked like little cakes," she recalls. The store's baker had allowed the recipe to shift slightly each day until the cookies had become an entirely different product that did not conform to the company's quality standards. Customers who develop loyalty to foods such as Mrs. Fields Cookies, McDonald's cheeseburgers, and Ben & Jerry's ice cream expect consistency in the products wherever they shop; Debbi Fields had to find a way to give her customers the value they wanted in the form of product quality. She ultimately discovered computer software that tells managers everything they need to know about their products' quality—at a low cost.

Other businesses have used this type of software to maintain both product and process quality. At a national chain of pizza restaurants, employees clock in and out of work on a computer instead of a manual punch clock. The computer compiles and transmits this data daily to the company's headquarters, relieving individual restaurant managers from having to tabulate the data themselves. How does this improve quality? The managers no longer waste valuable time

doing unnecessary paperwork; instead, they spend more time supervising employees.

A retailer learned that its employees (usually store managers) had to fill out and wade through 260 forms companywide to keep the business running. The same information might appear on several forms, sometimes sent to the same people, sometimes not. Thus, there was not only overlap in information received, but also a gap in information received—and plenty of wasted time filling out forms. When the information concerned sales, the confusion and time lag could prove disastrous for a company trying to create value for its customers. So the company automated its reporting process, cutting the number of forms to 50. Reports were distributed electronically, and information was accessible to everyone. After automation, store managers were able to increase the time they spent on activities that directly affected customers.

Technology can help supervisors do the job they were hired to do: supervise employees and processes in a way that boosts quality and creates greater value for customers. It can even tell if a cookie contains enough chocolate chips.

Source: From *Management Review* by Randall Fields and Nicholas Imparato. Copyright 1995 by American Management Association. Reproduced with permission of American Management Association via Copyright Clearance Center.

Higher Costs

Poor-quality work can also lead to high costs. Some managers might think it expensive to ensure that things are done right the first time. But the reality is that businesses spend billions of dollars each year on inspections, errors, rework, repairs, customer refunds, and other costs to find and correct mistakes. Attracting new customers costs several times more per customer than keeping customers satisfied, so marketing costs are higher, too. Thus, poor quality often results in much wasted time and materials, besides requiring that unacceptable items be fixed or discarded. If the problems remain undetected until after the goods have been sold, the manufacturer may have to recall its products for repair or replacement. In addition, poor goods and services may result in lawsuits by disgruntled or injured customers.

Quality programs may carry some start-up costs, but the cost of poor quality is higher. When General Electric set out to improve quality in 1995 with its now-famous Six Sigma initiative, the firm's investment of $300 million in the program reaped savings between $400 and $500 million, with an additional $100 to $200 million in incremental savings that would have been lost without the program.[2]

Even more costly, in terms of money, reputation, injury, and death, was the recall of millions of Firestone tires in 2000 and 2001. Ford Motor Company, which had used the tires in its Ford Explorer sport utility vehicles, blamed failure rates of up to 450 per million tires on Firestone, while the tire company in turn insisted that the design of the vehicle was partly to blame for more than 100 deaths in which Explorers were involved. Both companies were required to testify before congressional committees on energy and commerce in the summer of 2001.[3] In the meantime, however, Ford's quality problems were not over. Its new Focus and Escape models were each recalled several times in 1999 and 2000 for safety problems and emissions failures. Quality efforts at the company are being stepped up and include joint quality programs with its many suppliers.[4]

Types of Quality Control

quality control
An organization's efforts to prevent or correct defects in its goods or services or to improve them in some way.

Because of the negative consequences of poor quality, organizations try to prevent and correct such problems through various approaches to quality control. (See "Meeting the Challenge.") Broadly speaking, **quality control** refers to an organization's efforts to prevent or correct defects in its goods or services or to improve them in some way. Some organizations use the term *quality control* to refer only to error detection, while *quality assurance* refers to both the prevention and the detection of quality problems. However, *quality control* in the broader sense will be used in this chapter because it is the more common term.

Whichever term is used, many organizations—especially large ones—have a department or employee devoted to identifying defects and promoting high quality. In these cases, the supervisor can benefit from the expertise of quality-control personnel. Ultimately, however, the organization expects its supervisors to take responsibility for the quality of work in their departments.

In general, when supervisors look for high-quality performance to reinforce or improvements to make, they can focus on two areas: the product itself or the process of making and delivering the product. These two orientations are illustrated in Figure 2.1.

■ F I G U R E 2 . 1

Types of Quality Control

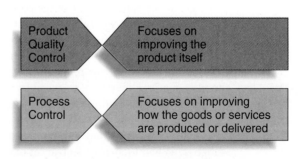

Product Quality Control

product quality control
Quality control that focuses on ways to improve the product itself.

An organization that focuses on ways to improve the product itself is using **product quality control.** For example, employees in a print shop might examine a sample of newsletters or envelopes to look for smudges and other defects. A city's park district might consider ways to upgrade its playground equipment or to improve the programs it offers senior citizens.

New software tools can greatly improve product quality control. At Morton Metalcraft Co., of Morton, Ill., sheetmetal components are made for farm and industrial vehicles like John Deere backhoes. Morton employees now work with a software system that uses digital photos, drawings, and key dimensions of products to create software routines for quality-checking both the entire product and subsections of it. To cope with last-minute design changes by its customers, Morton has undertaken the task of programming the system with customized routines. Programmer Jason Granneman notes, "If the change is something like the relocation of a headliner mount, we can do that here in about five minutes." The system has cut inspection time for the cab of the John Deere backhoe, for example, from 4½ hours for two operators to less than 45 minutes and one operator.[5]

Process Control

process control
Quality control that emphasizes how to do things in a way that leads to better quality.

An organization might also consider how to do things in a way that leads to better quality. This focus is called **process control.** The print shop, for example, might conduct periodic checks to make sure its employees understand good techniques for setting up the presses. The park district might ask the maintenance crew to suggest ways to keep the parks cleaner and more attractive. In this way, the park district can improve the process by which the crew members do their job.

A broad approach to process control involves creating an organizational climate that encourages quality. From the day they are hired, employees at all levels should understand that quality is important and that they have a role in delivering high quality. In our city park district example, managers and employees might consider ways to be more responsive to citizens' input. The greater responsiveness, in turn, could enable park district employees to recognize ways to better serve the community.

Process control techniques can be very effective for product manufacturers. The Boeing Company, a giant maker of aircraft, has reduced scrap rates, inventory turns, and other indicators of poor quality, with the help of a multimillion dollar investment in new plants and equipment dedicated to lean production. Employee teams now analyze ways to make production processes more efficient, and at the Wichita, Kansas, plant, where orders for the company's new 737 are pouring in, a philosophy of inspecting the process, not just the product, prevails. The company regularly inspects tools and machinery to ensure that its processes run as planned. "Inspecting the product after it is made does not add value," according to Danny High, a company metrologist. "It just tells us if we did a good job. Inspecting the process before we manufacture the part helps minimize errors in the final product."[6]

Techniques for Quality Control

Within this broad framework, managers, researchers, and consultants have identified several quality-control techniques, including statistical quality control, the zero-defects approach, employee involvement teams, and total quality management. Figure 2.2 summarizes these techniques.

■ F I G U R E 2 . 2

Quality-Control Techniques

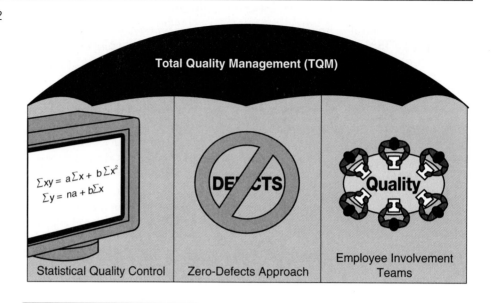

In choosing a technique—or, more commonly, applying the techniques selected by higher-level management—supervisors need to remember that a technique alone does not guarantee high quality. Rather, these techniques work when the people who use them are well motivated, understand how to use them, and exercise creativity in solving problems. In the words of Veronica T. Hychalk, R.N. and vice president of professional services for Northeastern Vermont Regional Hospital, "Do extensive quantitative data measurements reflect the quality that patients expect? They want compassion caring, time, skill, communication, education, listening, and good results from their caregivers. It's apparent that the patient-defined characteristics of quality serve as the foundation of our profession."[7]

Statistical Quality Control

It rarely makes economic sense to examine every part, finished good, or service to make sure it meets quality standards. For one thing, that approach to quality control is expensive. Furthermore, examining some products, such as packages of cheese or boxes of tissues, can destroy them. Therefore, unless the costs of poor quality are so great that every product must be examined, most organizations inspect only a sample. Looking for defects in parts, finished goods, or other outcomes selected through a sampling technique is known as **statistical quality control.**

statistical quality control
Looking for defects in parts or finished products selected through a sampling technique.

The most accurate way to apply statistical quality control is to use a random sample. This means selecting outcomes (such as parts or customer contacts) in a way that each has an equal chance of being selected. The assumption is that the quality of the sample describes the quality of the entire lot. Thus, if 2 percent of the salad dressing bottles in a sample have leaks, presumably 2 percent of all the bottles coming off the assembly line have leaks. Or if 65 percent of customers surveyed report they were treated courteously, presumably about 65 percent of all customers feel that way.

■ FIGURE 2.3

Chart Used for Statistical Process Control

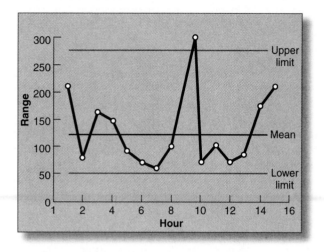

Source: From John A. Lawrence, Jr., and Barry A. Pasternack, *Applied Management Science: A Computer-Integrated Approach for Decision Making*. Copyright © 1998 John Wiley & Sons, Inc. This material is used by permission of John Wiley & Sons, Inc.

statistical process control (SPC)
A statistical quality-control technique using statistics to monitor production quality on an ongoing basis and making corrections whenever the results show the process is out of control.

Rather than wait until a process is complete to take a random sample, the operators of a process can use statistics to monitor production quality on an ongoing basis. This quality-control technique is known as **statistical process control (SPC).** The operator periodically measures some aspect of what he or she is producing—say, the diameter of a hole drilled or the correctness of an account number entered into a computer—then plots the results on a control chart such as the simplified one shown in Figure 2.3. The middle line in the chart shows the value that represents the standard—in this case, the mean (average). Above and below the mean value are lines representing the acceptable upper and lower limits. When a measured value falls between these limits, the operator may assume the process is working normally. When a value falls outside these limits, the operator is supposed to correct the process.

Thus, if a machine operator is supposed to make a part 0.0375 inch in diameter (the mean value in this case), the lower and upper limits might be 0.0370 inch and 0.0380 inch, respectively. If the operator measures a part and finds that its diameter is 0.0383 inch, the operator would adjust the machine or modify his or her actions to keep such errors from recurring. The measurements in Figure 2.3 indicate that the operator made some needed adjustments after one measurement exceeded the upper limit. After that point, the measurements are clustered much closer to the mean; the process is again under control. Clearly, SPC gives the operator a great deal of control in maintaining quality, so the task does not need to be assigned to specialized personnel. That is one reason SPC is increasingly popular today, especially in manufacturing firms.

The idea of using SPC or other statistical methods makes some supervisors nervous. They worry that they or their employees will be unable to handle the statistics. However, the process requires only a basic knowledge of statistics, coupled with an understanding of what level of quality is desirable and achievable. The supervisor should see that employees get the training they need in using the

SPC technique and in adjusting the processes for which they are responsible. (Chapter 17 describes the supervisor's role in employee training.)

Zero-Defects Approach

zero-defects approach
A quality-control technique based on the view that everyone in the organization should work toward the goal of delivering such high quality that all aspects of the organization's goods and services are free of problems.

A broad view of process quality control is that everyone in the organization should work toward the goal of delivering such a high degree of quality that all aspects of the organization's goods and services are free of problems. The quality-control technique based on this view is known as the **zero-defects approach.** An organization that uses the zero-defects approach would have products of excellent quality not only because the people who produce them are seeking ways to avoid defects, but also because the purchasing department is ensuring a timely supply of well-crafted parts or supplies, the accounting department is seeing that bills get paid on time, the human resources department is helping to find and train highly qualified personnel, and so on.

Thus, in implementing a zero-defects approach, managers and employees at all levels seek to build quality into every aspect of their work. To do so, employees work with supervisors and other managers in setting goals for quality and in identifying areas where improvement is needed. Management is responsible for communicating the importance of quality to the whole organization and for rewarding high-quality performance.

Employee Involvement Teams

employee involvement teams
Teams of employees who plan ways to improve quality in their areas of the organization.

Teams of employees who plan ways to improve quality in their segments of the organization became popular in the United States during the 1970s. These **employee involvement teams** may take slightly different forms, depending on their specific functions: quality circles, problem-solving teams, process improvement teams, or self-managed work groups. The concept of employee involvement teams was created in the 1920s by Walter Shewhart of Bell Laboratories and later expanded by American statistician W. Edwards Deming, whose ideas are described later in this chapter.

The typical employee involvement team consists of up to 10 employees and their supervisor, who serves as the team leader. In this role, the supervisor schedules meetings, prepares agendas, and promotes the participation and cooperation of team members. (The next chapter describes general principles of teams, including the role of the team leader.)

How Employee Involvement Teams Work   Each employee involvement team in an organization holds periodic meetings, which usually take place at least once or twice a month for an hour or two during the workday. At these meetings, participants examine areas where quality needs improvement, and they develop solutions. The problems discussed may be identified by management or by operative employees. In either case, the problems should be related to the employees' everyday work because this is where they have the greatest expertise.

In a typical process, the members of the team might take the following steps (see Figure 2.4):

1. Identify quality problems related to the employees' areas of responsibility.
2. Select the problems to focus on first. A newly formed group may find it helpful to focus on simple problems, so that the group can build on its successes.

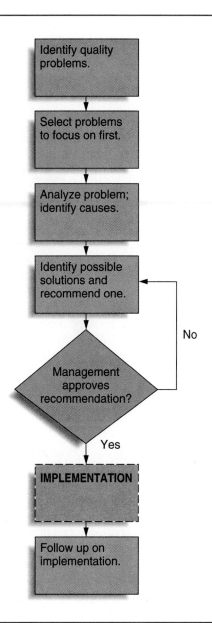

■ FIGURE 2.4

Typical Procedure for an Employee Involvement Team

3. Analyze the problem to identify its causes.
4. Identify possible solutions and select one to recommend to management.

Depending on the organization's policies, one or more managers usually must approve the recommendations of the employee involvement team. Once a recommendation is approved, the appropriate people in the organization must implement it. The team should follow up on the implementation to ensure that the problem actually was solved.

Employee involvement has been a theme for several years at several plants run by the Elkay Manufacturing Company's Elkay Division, which makes stainless steel sinks. Quality and productivity have steadily improved at the Broadview,

FIGURE 2.5

Characteristics of Successful Employee Involvement Teams

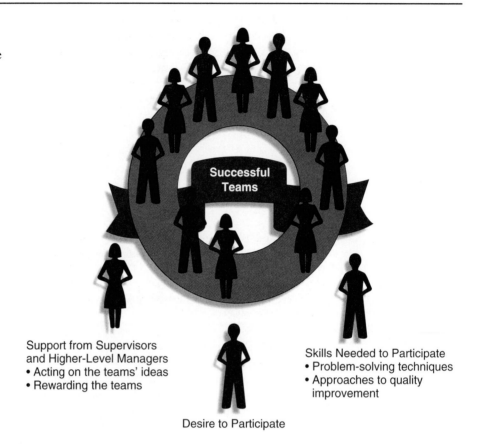

Support from Supervisors
and Higher-Level Managers
• Acting on the teams' ideas
• Rewarding the teams

Skills Needed to Participate
• Problem-solving techniques
• Approaches to quality
  improvement

Desire to Participate

Illinois, plant, for example, as employee teams have become increasingly instrumental in selecting and installing machinery, relocating and designing the layout of departments, introducing demand-flow technology, improving the setup process of hydraulic presses, and even developing a training program for press setup. Line employees work with engineers and other technical specialists to create and monitor new programs, and supervisors at one plant received 36 hours of training in teamwork skills such as feedback and conflict resolution.[8]

Characteristics of Successful Employee Involvement Teams   A number of things help a supervisor to make employee involvement teams a success. These include the principles of problem solving (described in Chapter 9) and the guidelines for supervising groups (discussed in Chapter 3). In addition, teams are most likely to achieve improvements in quality when they have certain characteristics (see Figure 2.5).

First, employee involvement teams must have support from supervisors and higher-level managers. The teams are most likely to succeed when the organization's top management supports them. (Of course, supervisors have little control over top managers' attitudes, but they must be enthusiastic themselves.) Managers can demonstrate support for employee involvement teams by acting on and rewarding the ideas that these groups produce.

In addition, employee involvement teams work best when participants have the skills necessary to contribute. To get the group off to a good start, the organization should provide training at the first meeting or meetings. Participants may need training in problem-solving techniques and approaches to quality improvement. The group's leader may need assistance in learning to lead a group discussion and to encourage participation.

Employee involvement teams will be more successful when all group members are eager to participate. For that reason, it is a good idea to make membership in the team voluntary. Employees who are interested in problem solving will make the most valuable contributions.

Total Quality Management

**total quality management (TQM)
An organizationwide focus on satisfying customers by continuously improving every business process for delivering goods or services.**

Bringing together aspects of other quality-control techniques, many organizations have embraced the practice of **total quality management (TQM),** an organizationwide focus on satisfying customers by continuously improving every business process for delivering goods or services. Some of the leading users of TQM are Federal Express, Hewlett-Packard, Motorola, 3M, Westinghouse, and Xerox Business Products and Systems.

The objective of TQM is to meet or exceed customer expectations. Thus, it is not a final outcome but, in the words of quality consultant Roy Duff, "a philosophical approach to running a business."[9] As such, it requires commitment at all levels and time for results to become evident. (See "Tips from the Firing Line.")

One example of how that kind of commitment can achieve results occurred at Weyerhaeuser Co., the forest products company, where the insurance department, which serves other departments within the firm, adopted total quality management principles. The 12 members of the department took weekly classes in TQM over the course of a year and learned how to work in small teams to evaluate risk management software, improve departmental recordkeeping, and accomplish other departmental goals. The teams plan and evaluate their quality efforts and, thanks to special leadership training, also run brainstorming sessions with outside vendors and internal customers to find ways to improve their services. With TQM, "you don't end up doing things three or four times," says the company's insurance manager and office administration manager John Lambdin. "You get the team together, you decide what the problem is and the best way to attack it. Then you are done with it. You don't have to go back to the same problem over and over." And best of all for the insurance department, a recent outsourcing and layoff initiative at Weyerhaeuser left the group intact.[10]

Advocates for Quality The popularity of TQM has been due largely to the compelling case that management experts have made for an organizationwide focus on quality. The three experts most frequently associated with TQM are Philip B. Crosby, W. Edwards Deming, and Joseph M. Juran.

Crosby, known worldwide as a quality expert, pioneered the quality movement in the United States. To achieve product quality, Crosby maintains, the organization must be "injected" with certain ingredients, much as a vaccination serum is intended to keep a person healthy. An organization needs to add five types of ingredients:

1. *Integrity*—Managers and employees at all levels must be dedicated to their role in providing quality to customers.

Avoiding Frustration with Quality Improvement Efforts

No matter which quality initiative is in place at a firm, the pressure to get the job done better, more quickly, and with fewer errors ultimately rests with the front-line supervisor. Though they may have little freedom to "change the system," whether it is management by objectives, total quality management, continuous improvement, or reengineering, supervisors must find a way to instill in their subordinates a sense of responsibility for quality and a desire to constantly reach for improvement.

It is easy to become discouraged. Change often meets resistance, and it comes about only slowly. Those supervisors who are aware of the causes of frustration, however, can guard against them and ensure that quality efforts accomplish their goals. Here are a few reasons supervisors can find the task a challenging one.

- Communications sometimes break down and messages are misunderstood.
- Subordinates fail to understand the concept of quality.
- Training for quality is poor or nonexistent.
- Objectives are not clearly defined and/or understood.
- Expectations are vague, confusing, or unrealistic.

How can supervisors best counter these negatives? They should:

- Insist on good communications, ensuring clarity and understanding by all parties above and below them in the organization.
- Maintain their own technological competence.
- Be ready to learn new skills and competencies to apply to the quality effort.
- Hone their interpersonal and problem-solving skills in order to guide, coach, and motivate their subordinates through the change period.
- Accept that quality is an ongoing goal.
- Most important, demonstrate, through their own words and behavior, that they care about quality and expect it of their team.

Source: From Donald S. Miller, "Q-u-a-l-i-t-y: Realities for Supervisors," *Supervision*, May 2000. Reprinted by permission of © National Research Bureau, 320 Valley Street, Burlington, Iowa 52601.

2. *Systems*—The organization needs various kinds of systems to indicate whether quality is acceptable and customers are satisfied.
3. *Communications*—Employees must be aware of their progress, and the organization must recognize employee achievements.
4. *Operations*—The organization must educate suppliers, train employees, and examine and improve its procedures, all in support of high quality.
5. *Policies*—The organization needs clear policies on quality.

Deming taught statistical quality control in Japan shortly after World War II and became an important contributor to quality improvement efforts in that country. Deming so impressed the Japanese with his lectures on quality that they named a prize after him. The Deming Prize is Japan's prestigious international quality award. Not until decades later was Deming's emphasis on total quality widely discussed in the United States. Deming's approach is this: To achieve product quality, the organization must continually improve not only the product's design but also the process of producing it.

Juran also taught quality concepts to the Japanese. He emphasizes the view that management should seek to maintain and improve quality through efforts on two levels: (1) the mission of the organization as a whole to achieve and maintain high quality and (2) the mission of individual departments in the organization to achieve and maintain high quality. In pursuing these missions, Juran says that managers must be involved in studying the symptoms of quality problems, identifying the underlying problems, and carrying out solutions.

Successfully Using TQM   An organization that wants to use total quality management begins by deciding what strategies to use, who will do what to carry out the strategies, and when these steps will take place. A basic strategy for implementing TQM is to use groups, such as employee involvement teams, to identify and solve problems. Another is to review criteria for improving quality (such as the categories for the Baldrige Award, to be described later), then seek to meet those criteria. The organization also may focus on improving the processes used for delivering goods and services, rather than on the products themselves. Finally, it may form self-managing work teams (see Chapter 3), groups of employees with broad responsibility for producing particular goods, services, or parts.

Because these strategies call for the involvement of employees at all levels, the organization needs to educate employees about why quality improvement is needed and how the TQM process will work. The Self-Quiz on page 53 consists of questions that identify whether a person has the kind of quality awareness that can make TQM work. Try taking it yourself to see where you stand.

According to a study by the General Accounting Office, the organizations that have used TQM most successfully have six characteristics in common:[11]

1. The company's attention is focused on meeting customers' requirements for quality.
2. Management leads in spreading TQM values throughout the organization.
3. Management asks and empowers employees to continuously improve all key business processes.
4. Management fosters a corporate culture that is flexible and responsive.
5. The organization's management systems support decision making based on facts.
6. The organization uses partnerships with suppliers to improve the delivery of the goods or services it buys.

An important way supervisors and other managers can build an organization with these characteristics is to behave as if quality is important. Among TQM users, this commonly is called "walking the talk." For example, if everyone is to receive training in quality improvement, supervisors who walk the talk will not look for ways to get out of the training sessions, even if they do have a lot of urgent matters to attend to.

Customer Satisfaction   One of the key values of total quality management is the focus by employees at all levels on meeting or exceeding the expectations of their customers. This principle assumes that everyone has a customer to serve. It is clear whom a salesclerk or a nurse serves, but even the back-office personnel at a manufacturer are delivering services to someone. Thus, part of satisfying customers is knowing who they are. They may be the people who buy the company's products, the taxpayers who support the government agency, or the other employees in the organization who use the reports, advice, or other support prepared in a given department.

Dell Computer has become a premier supplier of personal computers by knowing its customers firsthand. It sells directly to them via the Internet, where it is perhaps the leading merchant in any category, and it has seen its profitability and revenues shoot straight up since its founding. Although it also competes on price, Dell seems to be able to keep its edge through a track record of quality in customer service. John Delta, director of NASDAQ's interactive services, commented on an order Dell filled within 36 hours: "Originally, Dell got in with us on price, but that's not the issue now. Their customer support and service is what's driving our relationship."[12]

Knowing the customer is key to achieving quality in the hospitality industry. Ritz-Carlton Hotel Co., a leader in the search for quality and a 1999 winner of the Malcolm Baldrige National Quality Award (see below), starts its quality efforts with the customer. Pat Mene, vice president of quality for the giant chain, explains the company's philosophy about customer satisfaction in this way: "Standards are set by the customers, and then we organize a plan." This puts knowledge of what the customer wants, and the process of delivering it, squarely at the center of the firm's winning quality efforts. And because customers' expectations are always changing, Ritz-Carlton's quality process includes always performing better just to maintain the status quo. "People are constantly coached, every day," says Mene. "Most of the coaching is done at the front-line management level."[13]

A supervisor can help employees focus on customers by having employees ask themselves whether they would buy the goods or services. Would they be satisfied with the work? If they can put themselves in their customers' shoes and honestly say they would be satisfied, it is a good indicator that their work is up to quality standards.

Six Sigma

Six Sigma
A process-oriented quality control method designed to reduce errors to 3.4 defects per 1 million operations, or 99.9997 percent perfect.

Six Sigma is a process-oriented quality control method designed to reduce errors to 3.4 defects per 1 million operations, or 99.9997 percent perfect. (Sigma is a statistical expression defining how much variation there is in a product. Operations can be defined as any unit of work, such as an hour of labor, completion of a circuit board, a sales transaction, or a keystroke.) So the goal of Six Sigma is to reduce variation from the standard to almost nothing. Over time, however, its meaning has broadened to include a rigorous analytical process for anticipating and solving problems, improving profits through defect reduction, yielding improvements in products and processes, increasing customer satisfaction, and delivering best-in-class organizational performance.[14]

To get an idea of how much it can cost to fall below Six Sigma standards of quality, consider a couple of examples from the health care field: If quality standards were met 99.73 percent of the time in the United States, there would be 54,000 incorrectly filled drug prescriptions each year, more than 40,500 newborns accidentally dropped in the hospital, and unsafe drinking water almost two hours each month. At Six Sigma standards, there would be one wrong prescription every 25 years, three babies dropped in 100 years, and unsafe drinking water for one second every 16 years.[15]

In the mid-1980s Motorola became the first U.S. company to institute a large-scale Six Sigma program, and the firm now teaches Six Sigma concepts and courses to other organizations through its education and training arm, Motorola University. General Electric also offers its own customers high-level instruction in Six Sigma methods. Its first effort, undertaken by GE Medical Systems, brought the quality program to a handful of health care customers and resulted in over $94 million in benefits. The program included two weeks of intensive training in statistical process control and required completion of two projects that directly improve either company or customer performance.[16]

Many firms adopt more than one kind of quality program. Firms using Six Sigma now include General Electric, IBM, Asea Brown Boveri, Allied Signal/Kodak, and Whirlpool, all of whom find it an effective, though challenging,

The Banking Industry

Six Sigma Boosts Citibank

Quality programs like Six Sigma have become more and more popular in the manufacturing industries. But can they work for employees and supervisors in a service business like banking?

Citibank's goal is to be the premier international finance company in the world. To reach that ambitious aim, the company needed to begin by implementing quality initiatives that would satisfy customers quickly and reliably in every interaction around the world.

Citibank responded to the challenge by adopting a number of well-known manufacturing methodologies, of which Six Sigma was one. With the help of trainers from Motorola, the company that pioneered the Six Sigma program with great success, the bank devised a cross-functional program to identify areas for improvements, empower employees to make the needed changes, and eliminate wasteful steps in its operations.

Shortly after the program had begun, one manager for Citibank's Asset-Based Finance (ABF) division faced serious challenges when his back-office operation relocated from New York to Delaware. Some employees chose not to make the move, and John Podkowsky, managing director of the group,

soon realized that the new employees brought in to replace them—and sometimes their supervisors too—were inexperienced and needed training fast if the day-to-day operations of the business were to keep running smoothly.

A critical component of the training process was empowering employees *and* supervisors to sign off on more loans, which reduced the number of steps in the approval process and cut the time required by about 75 percent. The result? "It's been very successful with reduced cycle time," says Podkowsky. "Instead of getting complaints from customers, we are now getting compliments."

When it comes to quality and customer satisfaction, supervisors should expect to be in the forefront of the company's efforts, whether that means taking more training in state-of-the-art procedures, supporting employees' quality-improvement efforts, or serving as a role model in a period of rapid change. In the case of Citibank's ABF, supervisors did all three.

Source: Rochelle Rucker, "Citibank Increases Customer Loyalty with Defect-Free Processes," *Journal for Quality & Participation*, October 1, 2000, pp. 32–36.

quality initiative. Du Pont, Dow Chemical, Microsoft, Ford Motor Company, and American Express have also recently begun instituting Six Sigma methods.

Executives at the Defense Systems Electronics Group (DSEG), a unit of Texas Instruments at the time and now part of Raytheon, adopted it in the 1990s after comparing its results to those of Motorola and realizing that "we were less than four sigma and Motorola was close to six. We couldn't believe someone was 2,000 times better than us. It really got our attention."[17] Within a couple of years, DSEG had won the Malcolm Baldrige National Quality Award, which Motorola had won in 1988. Says the unit's Ron Randall, manager of quality improvement, "Winning gave a lot of validity to the Six Sigma approach. I'm confident Six Sigma helped."[18]

Both TQM and Six Sigma are customer-focused analytical methods. Unlike TQM, which is philosophical and avoids explicit goals, Six Sigma is highly structured and bottom-line oriented. Its leadership structure relies on the formation of process improvement teams and change agents called Black Belts. Black Belts also act as liaisons with upper management and are usually well-regarded and technically competent product or line personnel. At Ford Motor Company, for instance, a typical Black Belt is middle manager Chris Davis, an engineer who successfully traced the source of vibrations in some of the company's trucks and sport utility vehicles. Ford's Black Belts commit to working on quality improvement projects for two years.[19]

The heart of the Six Sigma approach consists of five steps[20]:

1. Define the problem.
2. Measure defects inherent in the existing process, using customer expectations to define "out of specification" conditions.
3. Analyze the reasons for defects, using statistical analysis to examine variables, identify root causes, and prioritize a list of the factors that influence the desired outcome.
4. Develop and test a plan of action for implementing and confirming the solution, ensuring that the revised method yields results within customer expectations.
5. Institute ongoing control measures to keep the problem from coming back.

Implementation of the training program usually occupies 10 days that are spread over a three-month period.

Measurement of Quality

Quality-control techniques such as statistical process control provide information about when defects occur in processes and products. But when an organization is engaged in a long-term process such as TQM, how can supervisors and others in the organization know whether they are satisfying their internal or external customers? How can they tell whether they are using practices likely to foster high quality? Guidelines for answering such questions come from the Baldrige Award, the standards known as ISO 9000, a practice called benchmarking, and a focus on customer value.

The Baldrige Award

Malcolm Baldrige
National Quality
Award
**An annual award
administered by the
U.S. Department of
Commerce and given
to the company that
shows the highest-
quality performance in
seven categories.**

Organizations using a TQM approach often measure their progress in terms of the criteria used to judge applicants for the **Malcolm Baldrige National Quality Award.** This is an annual award administered by the U.S. Commerce Department's National Institute of Standards and Technology and given to the organization that shows the highest-quality performance as measured by seven categories[21]:

1. Leadership.
2. Information and analysis.
3. Strategic planning.
4. Human resource focus.
5. Process management.
6. Business results.
7. Customer and market focus.

Many organizations, whether or not they apply for the award, use the Baldrige evaluation categories as a basis for assessing their own performance. Pat Mene of the Ritz-Carlton Hotel Co. says, "The Malcolm Baldrige Award is the road map for business excellence."[22] And while there has yet to be a national winner from the health care industry, the average score achieved on each Baldrige criterion has been steadily rising among the many firms that have requested the standards from the National Institute of Standards and Technology (NIST) since education and health care was added as an award category in 1999.[23] (The other categories are manufacturing, service, and small business.)

The Baldrige Award has had far-reaching effects on quality awareness and recognition. There are nearly 60 international awards, including the Deming

Prize (Japan), and over 40 states have or are establishing award programs, most of which are modeled after the Baldrige programs. Participation in these awards is increasing; in 1998 there were 830 applications for various state and local quality award programs, and no wonder. From 1994 to 2001, the NIST has compared stock performance of the winners of the Baldrige Award and the Standard & Poor's 500. The Baldrige winners have consistently outperformed the S&P 500, most recently (in April 2001) by 4.4 to 1.[24]

The risk of focusing on award criteria is that an organization or department can get caught up in winning an award or meeting certain criteria instead of focusing on the intended goal of delivering quality to the customer. Competing for a challenging award such as the Baldrige can be costly in terms of dollars and managers' time. Many organizations find that the key is to proceed with moderation.

ISO 9000

ISO 9000
A series of standards adopted by the International Organization of Standardization to spell out acceptable criteria for quality systems.

Another measure of success in quality management is ISO 9000 certification.[25] **ISO 9000** is a series of standards adopted in 1987 by the International Organization of Standardization to spell out acceptable criteria for quality systems. To be certified, an organization is visited by independent audit teams; if the auditors determine that the key elements of the standard are in place, they issue certification of compliance. (Note that they are evaluating quality processes, not product quality.) Organizations seek ISO 9000 certification for a number of reasons. For example, a customer may require it as a condition of doing business, or a nation's government may require it of organizations selling in that nation. As more businesses become certified, those that want to remain competitive will have to be certified as well.

Certification has become a little easier to achieve with the appearance of ISO 9000 compliance software programs, which automate many tasks such as document management, supplier management, and internal audits and training. These programs provide a wide range of information and simplify ISO 9000 compliance procedures.[26]

Like the Baldrige Award, ISO 9000 has also had ripple effects. The FS 9000 Association is a group of financial services firms that aims to speed the process of standardization in its industry. This group has recently proposed new standards for privacy, security, and risk that are based on the latest version of the ISO standards.[27]

Benchmarking

benchmarking
Identifying the top performer of a process, then learning and carrying out the top performer's practices.

Managers at all levels can evaluate their success in improving quality by comparing their processes and results with those at other departments and organizations. This practice is known popularly as **benchmarking:** identifying, learning, and carrying out the practices of top performers. In this sense, the term first referred to the practice of comparing the products and processes at one's own company with those that are the best in the world. For example, Xerox has benchmarked the highly successful distribution system of L. L. Bean. While this might seem to be an activity for higher-level managers, supervisors can certainly apply the technique to their own department's operations or even to their own career and management style. For those who want to use benchmarking, one source of information is the business-supported International Benchmarking Clearinghouse, http://www.em.doe.gov/bch/ibc.html.

Customer Value

While quality improvement practices can make the organization very efficient at whatever it does, they carry the risk of never ensuring that it is doing what customers *want*. For example, an accounting department might use the zero-defects approach so well that it produces a year's worth of reports without a single error. But if the reports do not contain information useful to the recipients, has the department done high-quality work? Or suppose a maintenance group reduces its response time to requests for repair of an office's photocopiers. The office staff might benefit more from training in the prevention and correction of the most common causes of malfunctions.

Recognizing this principle, an increasing number of organizations have concluded that they need to provide a context for their efforts at quality improvement.[28] In other words, quality improvement should be directed at a larger goal, and that goal should be to deliver greater customer value. In this sense, **value** refers to the worth the customer places on what he or she gets (the total package of goods and services) relative to the cost of acquiring it.

Quality improvement directed toward value begins when the organization's employees communicate with customers to determine their needs and wants. This step defines what the organization should focus on doing. The organization is then prepared to consider ways to make those processes more efficient.

A study by the Boston Consulting Group found that insurance companies take, on average, 22 days to process a customer's application, yet the work done to carry out that task takes only 17 minutes.[29] Value-directed quality improvement would question whether these organizations are delivering value to their customers during the remainder of that time. This approach would seek process improvements that lower customers' costs and frustrations by reducing cycle time without reducing the worth of what customers get from insurers. A value orientation thus does not replace the tactics described in this chapter, but directs them and detects whether they are delivering useful results. See "Supervision and Diversity" for a look at how customer value can be defined by management philosophy.

value
The worth a customer places on a total package of goods and services relative to its cost.

Guidelines for Quality Control

As with the other responsibilities of supervisors, success in quality control requires more than just picking the right technique. The supervisor needs a general approach that leads everyone involved to support the effort at improving quality. To develop such an approach, the supervisor can start by following the guidelines illustrated in Figure 2.6.

Prevention versus Detection   It is almost always cheaper to prevent problems from occurring than it is to solve them after they happen; designing and building quality into a product is more efficient than trying to improve the product later. Therefore, quality-control programs should not be limited to the detection of defects. Quality control also should include a prevention program to keep defects from occurring.

One way to prevent problems is to pay special attention to the production of new goods and services. In a manufacturing setting, the supervisor should see that the first piece of a new product is tested with special care, rather than wait for problems to occur down the line. In the delivery of services, the supervisor should spend extra time evaluating the work carried out by new employees or employees

SUPERVISION AND DIVERSITY

It Isn't a Man's World Anymore

Some people still think the Silicon Valley is a man's world, but they may change their minds after Ann Livermore has spent some time in her new job as head of Hewlett-Packard's Enterprise Computing Solutions Organization. Her division markets all of Hewlett-Packard's computers (except for desktops) and has annual sales of $15 billion. It employs 44,000 people. As one of the most powerful women in the male-dominated world of corporate computing, Ann brings to the job a remarkable intensity of purpose and dedication to quality.

As an eight- or nine-year-old, she volunteered to be a keypunch operator in her father's insurance company office. In her first year at Stanford University's business school, Ann won the right to manage the student snack bar and made enough money to completely pay for her MBA. In her first 16 years at Hewlett-Packard, including her most recent post as vice president and general manager of the software and services group, she established herself as a quick learner and a manager with both an iron will and a gracious manner. Her performance benchmarks are high; in each one of the last four years she set growth goals for her areas that were twice the industry average—and she met them.

What is the key to that impressive growth? For Ann it comes down to quality, which she defines in terms of customer satisfaction. The three components of customer satisfaction that get equal weight in her management philosophy are (1) pure satisfaction with the product, (2) the likelihood that the customer will buy it again, and (3) the likelihood that the customer will recommend the product to someone else. Judging by her track records, it seems to be working.

Source: John Markoff, "Trailblazer in the Silicon Jungle," *New York Times*, November 1, 1998, section 3, p. 2.

FIGURE 2.6

Guidelines for Quality Control

---

performing a new procedure. In these situations, particularly, the supervisor might seek out feedback on customer satisfaction, rather than wait for complaints to come in. Furthermore, when prevention efforts show that employees are doing good work, the supervisor should praise their performance. Employees who are confident and satisfied are less likely to allow defects in goods or services.

Standard Setting and Enforcement   If employees and others are to support the quality-control effort, they must know exactly what is expected of them. This calls for quality standards. In many cases, the supervisor is responsible for setting quality standards as well as for communicating and enforcing them. These standards should have the characteristics of effective objectives: They should be written, measurable, clear, specific, and challenging but achievable. (For more on setting objectives, see Chapter 6.) Furthermore, those standards should reflect what is important to the client. Employees or the supervisor may benefit from asking customers how they measure the quality of the goods or services. TeleTech, a firm that handles customer service phone calls for a variety of clients, customizes its quality measurements by asking each client what measures, such as the number of calls answered or the cost per call, it considers most important.[30]

In communicating standards, a supervisor should make sure that employees know why quality is important. Specific information about the costs of poor quality and the benefits of excellent quality needs to be provided. For example, if employees know how much it costs to make a component, they can understand the costs of remaking one that is defective. Similarly, a Taco Bell manager could tell employees that a typical repeat customer accounts for several thousand dollars' worth of life time total sales. Therefore, providing the quality of food and service that makes a customer want to come back is more valuable than the price of a single meal might suggest.

In addition, employees must understand the difference between poor quality and excellent quality. One way to do this is through the use of examples. In teaching a new employee how to manufacture a part, a supervisor could show a sample of a part that meets specifications and one that does not. Katherine Nicastro, customer service manager for Whittaker, Clark and Daniels (a distributor of minerals, colors, and chemicals to manufacturers), provides her staff with detailed instructions and feedback. Nicastro and her employees developed a sourcebook that explains how to deliver high-quality service. Furthermore, she not only provides feedback herself but has established a practice of sending customer service reps on occasional sales calls so they can talk with customers and learn about their needs.[31]

To enforce the standards, a supervisor must participate in inspecting the quality of goods and services that employees produce. This may entail examining a random sample of parts, accompanying a salesperson on sales calls, or visiting the workplace where employees interact with customers. The timing of these inspections should be unpredictable enough that employees cannot adjust their performance with the knowledge that the supervisor will be checking up on them that day.

When an inspection uncovers a quality problem, the supervisor should inform the responsible employees immediately. Then they should get to work on solving the problem. The appropriate response may include apologizing to customers as well as fixing a problem within the organization. Requiring a quick response demonstrates the importance of quality to the organization.

For enforcement of standards to be effective, the employees must know that management is serious about quality. A catchy slogan posted on bulletin boards, inscribed on buttons, or taped to cash registers is meaningless unless supervisors and higher-level managers pay attention to these principles, reward employees for following them, and live up to them themselves.

The Impact of Diversity

Organizations that effectively draw on the variety of talents available from a diverse workforce are in the best position to deliver high-quality goods and services.

Likewise, a supervisor who values diversity is in a position to help all his or her employees develop their full potentials. This supervisor appreciates the various strengths of different kinds of people, which boosts employees' morale. In such a climate, working relationships among people are positive.

The supervisor who values diversity also helps to make the organization a desirable place to work, which gives the organization the largest possible pool of available talent from which to recruit. In addition, employee turnover in such an organization is likely to be low.

An organization that recruits employees who represent the various kinds of people in its markets will be most attractive to customers. A business that sells to people of various races will appeal to more customers if its sales force consists of people of those races. Customers and clients of various national and ethnic backgrounds appreciate a company where employees speak their languages and know their customs. Not only is this kind of diverse organization more attractive to current and prospective customers, it is in a better position to understand and identify needs, giving the organization an edge in developing new goods and services.

Finally, many of the quality-control techniques described in this chapter rely on the creativity of managers and employees. An organization that attracts and draws on the talents of a diverse group of employees will have the widest pool of creative thinking that it can hire. In such an organization, thinking and problem solving tend to be more flexible.

The Role of Suppliers

Organizations depend on suppliers in a variety of ways. An automaker relies on manufacturers of many types of components, and a law office relies on a printer to provide elegant stationery. Many businesses depend on outside suppliers of advice in areas such as accounting, investments, and the law.

An organization's performance is only as good as its suppliers' inputs. To avoid or correct problems, the quality-control effort should include setting and enforcing standards for acceptable work from suppliers. For example, the supervisor should make sure that employees have tools, materials, and supplies of acceptable quality. When choosing suppliers, the organization needs to stick to those that will be able to live up to the standards.

Rewards for Quality

As with any area of performance that the supervisor wants to encourage, employees need valued rewards. Thus, a supervisor's job includes making sure that employees receive rewards for high-quality work. Performance measures must include an evaluation of the quality of the goods or services produced by the employees. Teams that meet or exceed the quality standards would then receive appropriate rewards (see Chapter 11). If the organization's strategy for maintaining and improving quality is TQM or some other approach that emphasizes process control, then the rewards should reflect that emphasis. In other words, supervisors should look at improvements in the process as well as the final results achieved.

Summary

2.1 Describe consequences suffered by organizations as a result of poor-quality work.

Poor-quality work gives an organization a negative image, which drives away customers and makes it harder to recruit superior employees and borrow money. Poor-quality work can also lead to higher costs to attract customers, inspect for and correct defects, replace defective products, and defend against lawsuits.

2.2 Compare product quality control and process control.

Both types of quality control involve preventing and detecting quality-related problems. Product quality control focuses on ways to improve the product. Process control focuses on how to do things in a way that results in higher quality.

2.3 Identify techniques for quality control.

Statistical quality control involves looking for defects in parts or finished products selected through a sampling technique. In statistical process control, the operator takes samples during the process, plots the results on a chart, and makes corrections when the chart indicates the process is out of control. The zero-defects approach holds that everyone in the organization should work toward the goal of delivering such high quality that all aspects of the organization's goods and services are free of problems. Employee involvement teams plan ways to improve quality in their areas of the organization. Total quality management is an organization-wide focus on satisfying customers by continuously improving every business process involved in delivering goods or services.

2.4 Explain how employee involvement teams work and what makes them successful.

Each employee involvement team holds periodic meetings during which participants examine needs for improvement and develop solutions. When management has approved suggested solutions, the team follows up to make sure that the problem is solved. These teams are most likely to achieve improvements in quality when they have management support, when participants have the skills necessary to contribute, and when all group members want to participate.

2.5 Describe principles for successfully using total quality management.

TQM must be seen as a continuous process that unfolds gradually as employees find more and more ways to improve quality. The organization should start by deciding what strategies to use and how to carry them out. Employees must play an active role in carrying out TQM, so they must be educated about the need for quality improvement and the way the TQM process will work. The organization must focus on satisfying customers and operate in a flexible, responsive manner.

2.6 Identify ways organizations measure their success in continuous quality improvement.

Organizations compare their practices and performance with various sets of guidelines. They may compete for the Malcolm Baldrige National Quality Award or assess their performance using its evaluation categories. They may seek certification for meeting the standards of ISO 9000. Also, they may compare their performance with that of organizations that excel in particular areas—a practice known as benchmarking.

2.7 Describe guidelines for quality control.

The organization should focus on preventing quality problems, which is cheaper than detecting them. Supervisors and other managers should set, communicate, and enforce standards for quality control. The organization should insist upon high quality from its suppliers inside and outside the organization. Supervisors and higher-level managers should provide valued rewards for high-quality work.

Key Terms

quality control, p. 33

product quality control, p. 33

process control, p. 33

statistical quality control, p. 34

statistical process control (SPC), p. 35

zero-defects approach, p. 36

employee involvement teams, p. 36

total quality management (TQM), p. 39

Six Sigma, p. 42

Malcolm Baldrige National Quality Award, p. 44

ISO 9000, p. 45

benchmarking, p. 45

value, p. 46

Review and Discussion Questions

1. Brand X Corporation seeks to be the lowest-cost maker of lawn chairs and toboggans. To keep costs down, management tells the production department, "Keep that assembly line moving. We have an inspector on staff to catch the mistakes later." What are the consequences Brand X Corporation is likely to experience as a result of this approach to manufacturing?

2. What is the difference between product quality control and process control? Is balancing a checkbook a type of product quality control or process control? Explain.

3. The manager of a restaurant wants to make sure that her staff is delivering good customer service, but she does not have time to investigate the service given to every customer. So every evening at 5:30, the manager stops at customers' tables to ask if they are satisfied with their service. In effect, this is a form of statistical quality control because she is talking to a sample of the customers. How can the manager improve the accuracy of the information she gets from this quality-control technique?

4. Define the zero-defects approach to quality control. Do you think zero defects is attainable? Why or why not?

5. Michelle LeVerrier supervises a group of tellers at a bank located in a city. The bank manager has asked her to lead an employee involvement team designed to improve the processes of serving individual customers at the teller windows. The four steps the team must take are (1) to identify quality problems in the specific area of responsibility, (2) to select one problem to focus on, (3) to analyze the problem, and (4) to identify solutions and select one to present to management. How might Michelle use this four-step procedure to conduct her first team meeting?

6. What is total quality management (TQM)?

7. Louise Ho supervises a group of editorial assistants who read book manuscripts and write reports evaluating the manuscripts for editors at a book publishing company. How might Louise determine whether her group is providing the best value to her customers—the editors?

8. Describe how organizations can use the Malcolm Baldrige National Quality Award as a tool for measuring their success at continuous quality improvement.

9. Imagine that you are the supervisor responsible for a pharmacy. You have received a few complaints about mistakes in customers' prescriptions. To improve the quality of service delivered by the pharmacists, you can concentrate on (*a*) doing a better job of catching errors in the future or (*b*) doing a better job of avoiding errors. Which approach would you choose? Explain.

10. Sean Riley supervises the produce department at a supermarket. How can he set and enforce standards from his suppliers? What impact will his decisions have on the sales of products in his department?

11. Why is it important for employees to receive rewards for high-quality work?

A SECOND LOOK

What kind of benchmark might Chris Neal set for Zap Courier's bicycle fleet?

SKILLS MODULE

CASE

Embracing TQM, but Not Overnight

After 36 years of autocratic management, Fielding Manufacturing of Cranston, Rhode Island, was ready for a change. It took four years to transform the custom injection-molding company into a firm based on the principles of total quality management (TQM), and vice president of operations Stan Valencia feels it was worth it. With the company's operations under the leadership of the employees, many of the old top-to-bottom flows of communication and authority have been swept away.

In the old way, "the people at the middle management [level] did not understand what upper management wanted," Stan says. "They were holding on to their autocratic practices. People in the rank and file did not understand what all the fuss was about." To smooth the introduction of TQM, a continuous process of employee education was put in place and still operates; its goal is to have everyone in the firm participating in the TQM way of management.

Yet, throughout the struggle to reshape the company, productivity and quality remained high, because Fielding set up a team to oversee those very issues. A Productivity Improvement Team consisting of middle managers, front-line supervisors, and line workers scrutinized jobs in progress, looking for ways to improve them and setting up benchmarks for safety, quality, and customer service. At weekly meetings, the team identified projects that were running late, failed performance standards, or had quality problems. A champion for each problem project was appointed to ensure that corrective actions were put in place, but since every member on the team contributed to the solutions, all were given credit. Results were evident within the first six months, and productivity went up between 15 and 20 percent. Late shipments are down to almost zero, whole processes have been streamlined, and employees have a greater sense of responsibility and importance.

Other aspects of the TQM process that were put in place at Fielding include a Customer Service Team, an ISO Fast-Track Team that monitors the company's progress toward ISO 9000 certification, and a Continuous Improvement Council that oversees all the company's new quality teams and appoints the members.

Despite the successes, temporary complications in work processes and communications sometimes arise as new ways replace the old, and Stan still senses some resistance among employees who have not totally embraced the TQM concept. He estimates it will take another year for the teams and the new TQM processes to be fully integrated and predicts that those who don't adapt will be "sticking out like sore thumbs."

1. What steps taken by Fielding Manufacturing do you think contributed to the success it has had in implementing TQM?
2. Can you think of anything the firm could have done that it hasn't to encourage employees reluctant to adapt to the new methods? What should Stan do if there are still "sore thumbs" at the end of the next year?
3. Team members who have an idea for improvements in a manufacturing process at Fielding are expected to fill out a form with details about the idea and give it to a member of the Continuous Improvement Council, who presents the idea to the council. Comment on the pros and cons of this system.

Source: Samantha Hoover, "Productivity-Improvement Team Does Its Job," *Quality*, September 1, 1998, p. 50.

SELF-QUIZ

Your Level of Quality Awareness

Answer each question by checking Yes or No.	**Yes**	**No**
1. Do you trust your co-workers? Is there a feeling of cooperation rather than competition?	_____	_____
2. Are you truly interested in the welfare of those with whom you work?	_____	_____
3. Can you communicate openly and honestly with the people in your department?	_____	_____
4. Do you understand your department's quality performance goals?	_____	_____
5. Are you committed to the attainment of those goals?	_____	_____
6. When you need special help, do you try to tap the resources of others?	_____	_____
7. Can you resolve conflict successfully?	_____	_____
8. When your department has a meeting, do you participate by preparing and providing your own input?	_____	_____
9. Whether you agree or not, do you respect individual differences?	_____	_____
10. Do you really like your job and your fellow workers?	_____	_____
Total	_____	_____

Score yourself: If you had 8 to 10 Yes answers, you're a quality-oriented person and well suited for being part of a work effort aimed at quality awareness. A lower score, however, indicates that you may have good reason for self-doubt. But don't give up. We are not born with an appreciation for quality performance or even with a grasp of what constitutes a quality lifestyle. Rather, we learn these. Seek help from the members of your department. If a commitment to quality is your mutual goal, they will support you—and everyone will benefit.

Source: Reprinted with the permission from Dartnell, 360 Hiatt Drive, Palm Beach Gardens, FL 33418. Copyright © 2002. All rights reserved. For more information on this or other products published by Dartnell, please call (800) 621-5463, ext. 567.

Class Exercise

Divide the class into groups of four to six people. Each group receives the following materials: 20 index cards, a roll of tape, a pair of scissors, and a felt-tipped pen. To complete the exercise, the groups may use these supplies and no others.

The instructor specifies how much time the groups will have to complete the project (10 or 15 minutes). When the instructor gives the signal to begin, each group is to use the materials provided to construct a house. The teams may use the materials in any way they see fit, but they may not use additional materials of their own.

When time is up, someone from each group brings the group's house to a table or other designated location in the classroom. The instructor appoints five class members to serve on a panel of judges. They rate each house on a scale of 1 to 5 (with 5 representing the highest quality). The judges' scores are totaled, and the house with the highest score is deemed the winner of this quality contest.

Finally, the class discusses the following questions:

• On what basis did the judges rate the quality of the houses? How many of the criteria in Table 2.1 did they use?

• How did your group decide on a way to make its house? How well did your group work together to produce the house?

• Given your group's experience and the information about how the judges arrived at their scores, how would you want to improve the quality of your house if you could repeat the exercise? Are your changes process improvements or product improvements?

Team-Building Exercise

Applying Control and Quality Principles to Customer Service

Because nearly 8 out of every 10 jobs in this country are in the service sector, it is important to understand the significance of providing quality customer service. This exercise is designed to help you apply what you learned in this chapter to a service-sector job.

Instructions

1. Form groups of two or three people. Identify a work setting where customer service is critical.

The place should be one that all of you are familiar with. It might be a workplace where one of you has worked or at least has been a customer (some examples: retail store, post office, bank, hospital, university, resort, restaurant).

2. Identify a specific job title for the work setting (e.g., waiter/waitress, nurse, clerk at the university bookstore, shoe salesperson at a store).

3. Review some of the principles covered in this chapter (see Figure A). Select those that are appropriate to the job you have identified, and develop specific customer service guidelines for the employees.

 **F I G U R E   A**

Quality Principles from Chapter 2

• Process control

• Zero-defects approach

• Employee involvement teams

• Philip Crosby's five ingredients for quality (integrity, systems, communications, operations, and policies)

• Benchmarking

• Prevention versus detection

• Standard setting and enforcement

• The role of suppliers

• Rewards for quality

• Dimensions of quality (performance, features, reliability, conformance, durability, serviceability, aesthetics, and perceived quality from Table 2.1)

4. Now select principles appropriate for a supervisor of employees in the job you have identified, and develop some supervisory guidelines that focus on customer service. For example, how should the supervisor monitor performance to determine that employees are practicing the quality service standards you have established?

5. Share your group's efforts with the class by presenting a written statement that includes work setting, job title, principles from Figure A and how your group applied them to the job, and principles from Figure A on the next page and how your group applied them to the supervisor.

Source: This team-building exercise was prepared by Corinne Livesay, Belhaven College, Jackson, Mississippi.

3

Teamwork means focusing on the team's success, realizing that ultimately the team's success is your success. It also means that you succeed by helping other members of the team to succeed.

—Intuit's list of 10 core values

Teamwork: Emphasizing Powerful Meetings

■ CHAPTER OUTLINE

Reasons for Joining Groups

Groups in the Workplace

Functional and Task Groups
Formal and Informal Groups
Getting the Group to Work with You

Characteristics of Groups

Roles
Norms
Status
Cohesiveness
Size
Homogeneity
Effectiveness

The Development of Groups

Teamwork

Benefits of Teamwork
Leading the Team
Labor Law and Teamwork

Meetings

Reasons for Meetings
Preparing for a Meeting
Conducting a Meeting
Overcoming Problems with Meetings

■ LEARNING OBJECTIVES

After you have studied this chapter, you should be able to:

3.1 Explain why people join groups.

3.2 Distinguish types of groups that exist in the workplace.

3.3 Discuss how supervisors can get groups to cooperate with them.

3.4 Describe characteristics of groups in the workplace.

3.5 Identify the stages in the development of groups.

3.6 Explain why teamwork is important.

3.7 Describe how the supervisor can lead a team so that it is productive.

3.8 Discuss how to plan for effective meetings.

3.9 Provide guidelines for conducting effective meetings.

VIRTUAL OFFICE MAKES LONG-DISTANCE TEAMWORK SUCCEED

When some work teams go out to a restaurant together, it's a routine occasion in which the most discussion might center around whether to try the special of the day. For Judy Duplisea and her team from CheckFree, however, lunch or dinner together is a real, and rare, event that calls for a reservation in the back room so the loud talk and laughter doesn't disturb other diners.

Duplisea, a regional vice president for the Atlanta firm, lives in Canton, Ohio, while the rest of her sales and client relationship staff live in Connecticut, Maryland, Michigan, New Hampshire, and New York. Their meetings are more like reunions.

CheckFree is a provider of electronic financial services that let consumers receive and pay their bills online or electronically. Duplisea's team members, like some 23 million other employees in the United States today, work out of their homes and use computers, fax machines, and conference calls to create their "virtual" office.

When Duplisea started at CheckFree in 1997, she had some doubts about whether working virtually was effective. "I didn't know if I could deal with the lack of socialization and control over my sales people," she says. But her experiences with her team, which began with good foundation of personal relationships built on regular conference calls and face-to-face meetings as frequent as possible, has changed her mind. "My group is probably tighter now than any of the groups that I was working with in regular offices," says Duplisea. "We go out of our way to stay in contact with each other," using instant messaging throughout the day, to ask quick questions or just have a little fun.

What makes a virtual team really work? Duplisea advises hiring "good people who you are certain you don't have to see every day. You must be able to trust them."

Source: Michael Rosenwald, "Long-Distance Teamwork as 'Virtual Offices' Spread, Managers and Their Staffs Are Learning to Adapt to New Realities," *Boston Globe*, April 29, 2001, p. J1.

Teams or groups like those at CheckFree are among the newest ways to boost productivity at many of today's firms. Much of the work that involves supervisors takes place in such groups, whether "virtual" or real world.

group
Two or more people who interact with one another, are aware of one another, and think of themselves as a group.

To define that term formally, a **group** is two or more people who interact with one another, are aware of one another, and think of themselves as a group. The supervisor must see that groups of employees work together to accomplish objectives. An increasing number of organizations are expanding group efforts by forming teams. As leaders or members of a team, supervisors help plan and carry out a variety of activities. Many group and team efforts take place in meetings.

How the supervisor can work effectively as a leader and member of a team or other group is covered in this chapter. Some general characteristics of groups— why people join them, what kinds of groups operate in the workplace, how groups can be described, and how they develop—are described. Then efforts to build employee participation through the use of teamwork are discussed, and basic benefits of teamwork and ways supervisors can lead teams effectively are outlined. Finally, the chapter provides guidelines for holding meetings.

Reasons for Joining Groups

When Felicia Watt accepted a position as math teacher at West Junior High School, she became a member of two groups: the teaching staff at the school and the teachers' union representing her district. She also joined a citywide organization of black education professionals to receive moral support and to participate in service projects sponsored by the organization. In addition, the principal of West Junior High asked Felicia to serve on a committee to plan an innovative math and science curriculum. Upon learning that Felicia liked to eat sushi, one teacher invited her to join a group of four teachers who visited a local Japanese restaurant about once a month.

This example shows that people belong to groups for many reasons. Sometimes group membership simply goes along with being an employee. In particular, all employees are members of the organization that employs them, most are part of a division or department, and some also join a union when they go to work for a particular company. At other times, employees join a group because their supervisor or some other manager asks them to. In such cases, an employee may join the group to advance his or her career or simply to avoid going against the manager's wishes. Finally, an employee may join a group because being a member satisfies personal needs. The most common personal reasons for joining a group include the following:

- *Closeness*—Being members of the same group builds ties among people. Friendships generally result from the shared experiences that come from membership in some kind of group—for example, a class at school or a bowling team.
- *Strength in numbers*—Having ties to others gives people confidence they may lack when they act alone. Their sense of confidence is well founded. In an organization, a group of people tends to be more influential than one person acting alone.
- *Common goals*—When people have a goal to meet, they can get moral and practical support by working with or alongside others who have similar goals.
- *Achievement of personal objectives*—Membership in a group can help people achieve personal objectives in a variety of ways. The time spent with group members can be enjoyable. Membership in certain groups can enhance a person's prestige. In a related vein, group membership can satisfy people's desire to feel important.

Groups in the Workplace

As mentioned earlier, all the employees of an organization form a group. On a practical level, however, most organizations are too large for all their members to interact with one another. Therefore, except at very small organizations, most employees cluster into smaller groups. Some examples are departments, task forces, and groups that meet for lunch to play cards, do needlework, or talk about baseball. References to groups in this chapter generally mean these small groups; that is, groups small enough that all members interact with one another.

To fully benefit from the various groups in an organization, the supervisor needs to be able to identify them. The first step is to recognize the various categories of an organization's groups. Then the supervisor can apply several principles for building cooperation on the part of the groups.

Functional and Task Groups

functional groups
Groups that fulfill ongoing needs in the organization by carrying out a particular function.

Some groups fulfill ongoing needs in the organization by carrying out a particular function, such as producing goods, selling products, or investing funds. These are called **functional groups.** For example, a hospital's accounting department has the ongoing responsibility for keeping accurate records of the flow of money into and out of the organization. In most cases, a functional group is one that appears on a company's organization chart.

task groups
Groups that are set up to carry out a specific activity and then disband when the activity is completed.

Other groups, called **task groups,** are set up to carry out a specific activity, and they disband when that activity has been completed. Another kind of group is formed for an ongoing purpose. For example, at Royal Dutch/Shell Group, several six-member teams meet every week in the company's Exploration & Production Divisions in Houston and Rijswijk (Netherlands), to evaluate cost-saving and new-product suggestions that employees send in via e-mail. Four of Shell's five top business projects in early 1999 were developed in one of these GameChanger teams.[1] This kind of group could operate for years with no definite end date, since the need to create new business opportunities is never likely to be finished.

Formal and Informal Groups

formal groups
Groups set up by management to meet organizational objectives.

The examples of functional and task groups are also types of **formal groups.** These are groups set up by management to meet organizational objectives. Thus, these groups result from the management function of organizing (introduced in Chapter 1). A customer service department and a committee charged with planning the company picnic are formal groups.

informal groups
Groups that form when individuals in the organization develop relationships to meet personal needs.

Other groups result when individuals in the organization develop relationships to meet personal needs. These are **informal groups.** Figure 3.1 shows two informal groups in a small store. Perhaps the china department manager and three clerks like to jog after work; they might find themselves jogging together. Eventually they could build friendships around this shared activity. Most employees welcome the opportunity to be part of informal groups because these groups help satisfy social needs. The friendships established within the group can make work more enjoyable.

Informal subgroups can develop among members of a formal group when the formal group fails to meet some personal needs. For example, when some group members feel angry at the group's leader or uncertain about whether they really belong, they may form a subgroup. Subgroups may also form when some group members feel uncomfortable with the way they are expected to behave; for example, they might be expected not to express their feelings. In such a situation, the people who form a subgroup may feel more comfortable with the other members of the subgroup.

Getting the Group to Work with You

Groups have a lot to offer with regard to decision making and problem solving. A group can generate a creative solution that a single person might not think of, and the group process can build support by letting people make decisions about what

FIGURE 3.1

Informal Group Structures

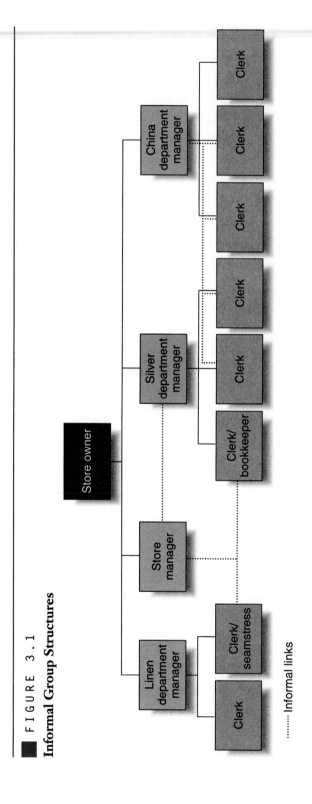

······ Informal links

Source: From Samuel C. Certo, *Human Relations Today: Concepts and Skills*, 1995. Copyright © 1995 by The McGraw-Hill Companies. Reproduced with permission of The McGraw-Hill Companies.

Merging 20 Little Businesses at Once

When Carl Friedrich took on the job of managing 20 independent-minded doctors at New York's Hospital for Special Surgery, at first "it was like trying to merge 20 little businesses at once." To meet his goal of getting the physicians to work as a team and combine the business side of their practices, he faced several challenges. The doctors resisted change; they were reluctant to share financial information with one another; they regarded Carl as an outsider and were displeased that he was not a doctor himself; and they were full of complaints that at first struck him as petty. It seemed that leading this team was going to be an uphill battle.

By training himself to listen carefully, however, Carl discovered that some of the complaints were symptoms of other problems. Sometimes, he learned, "they just want to tell [their problem] to someone; they want someone to be an advocate." He began to win them over by doing what he could to resolve small things and gain the doctors' trust. He accepted responsibility when his ideas didn't work, which won their respect. He persisted, too, spending a year lobbying one member of the group to join the billing consortium he had set up. Once she did so, he was able to show her results: a 40 percent increase in her revenue and a $30,000 drop in costs.

Carl offered choices. Rather than forcing two groups to use the same software, he set software performance standards and let each group choose its own program. Soon 90 percent of the doctors were using the same product anyway, because it was the only one that met the mark. "I told them I won't force anything on them that compromises them as a physician," Carl said. "You give them options, but you try to limit the options."

Finally, Carl learned to work toward a series of small victories rather than trying to generate a "master plan" that would have to be constantly changed. "When you go for home runs," he said, "you strike out a lot." Meanwhile, the group has grown to 30 doctors.

Source: Hal Lancaster, "A Lesson in Whipping an Unruly Bunch into a Working Unit," *Wall Street Journal*, November 10, 1998, p. B1.

---

affects them. To make the most of the potential benefits of working with groups, supervisors can use several tactics.

An important step is for the supervisor to make sure all members of a formal group know what they can and should be doing. This includes setting effective group objectives (described in Chapter 6) and clearly communicating those objectives. Group members also need to understand their authority, including the limits on what they can do. For example, a group assembled to solve a problem should know whether it is to implement the solution or simply to suggest solutions, leaving to the supervisor the task of choosing an alternative and implementing it.

Besides communicating expectations, the supervisor should keep groups informed about what is happening in the organization and what changes are planned for the future. Making the effort to communicate with groups is a way of demonstrating that they are important to the organization. It also tends to create a climate in which group members will readily let the supervisor know what is happening in the group.

The supervisor should support the group when it wants to bring legitimate concerns to higher management. For example, if some problem is keeping employees from getting their work done on time or up to standards, the supervisor should do what is possible to get the problem corrected. However, this does not mean adopting an "us versus them" attitude toward management. The supervisor is a part of management and must act accordingly. See "Meeting the Challenge" for more information on getting the group to work with you.

A supervisor who is responsible for setting up a group can help it function well by making good choices about whom to assign to the group. In many cases, the group can benefit from a combination of people with a variety of strengths or backgrounds. At the same time, the supervisor needs to be careful about splitting up informal groups when creating a formal one; doing so could hurt morale within the formal group. In addition, the number of group members can be important. Although including all employees is sometimes important, for many tasks a group will work best with only 5 to 10 members.

Some of the guidelines for supervision discussed in other chapters also will help get the group's cooperation. Supervisors should treat all employees fairly and impartially, respect the position of the group's informal leader, and find ways to give rewards to the group as a whole, rather than to individual employees only. Finally, supervisors should encourage the group to participate in solving problems. As a result of following these practices, the supervisor can benefit by receiving the group's support.

Characteristics of Groups

You can readily conclude from this discussion and from personal experience that working with a group is not like working alone. Social scientists have summarized a number of group characteristics, including ways to describe them, how effective they are, and what pressures they place on individuals. Supervisors who are aware of this theoretical information can use it to understand what is happening in a group situation. They can decide whether the group is effectively supporting the achievement of organizational objectives or whether they need to step in and make changes.

When looking at how groups are the same or different, it helps to consider some basic ways of describing them. Some of the most useful characteristics include roles, norms, status, cohesiveness, size, homogeneity, and effectiveness (see Figure 3.2).

Roles

roles
Patterns of behavior related to employees' positions in a group.

The character taken on by each actor in a play is the actor's role. In an organization's groups, the various group members also take on **roles,** or patterns of behavior related to their position in the group. Some common roles that you may have encountered or even held include the (formal or informal) leader of a group, the scapegoat, the class clown, and the person to whom others take their problems.

What leads a person to take on a role? Sometimes a person's formal position in an organization dictates a certain role. For example, as described in Chapter 1, certain kinds of behavior are expected of a supervisor. Another source of a person's role is a combination of the person's beliefs about how he or she ought to behave and other people's expectations about how that person will act. For example, if Anne displays empathy toward a colleague who is going through a divorce, Anne may eventually find that everyone in the department wants to cry on her shoulder when a problem arises. If she continues to respond with sympathy and concern, she may take on a role in which she hears other people's troubles but is expected not to complain herself. Similarly, if Stuart makes wisecracks during a couple of meetings, group members may start expecting to hear jokes and funny remarks from him on a regular basis.

The kinds of roles people select serve different purposes. People may take on a role, such as leader or organizer, that helps the group get its work done. Or they may take on a role that holds the group together—the person who can be counted on to

FIGURE 3.2

Ways to Describe Groups

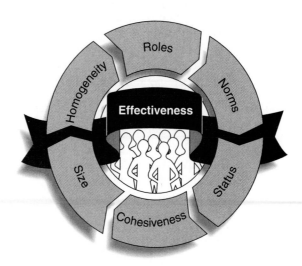

smooth ruffled feathers whenever conflicts arise among group members. Finally, group members may take on roles that help them meet personal needs. Thus, Stuart may be making jokes to cover up his own discomfort with being a group participant.

Awareness of roles is important because recognizing them can help the supervisor encourage desirable behavior or bring about a change in undesirable behavior. The supervisor would probably want to include an informal group's leader in planning how to carry out a change in policy. Or a supervisor who finds an employee's wisecracks to be a distraction during meetings needs to understand that other people may be encouraging this employee's behavior. Thus, to get the employee to stop, the supervisor will have to end the encouragement of the wisecracks as well as the wisecracks themselves.

Sometimes supervisors also have to resolve problems involving **role conflicts,** situations in which a person has two different roles that call for conflicting types of behavior. Suppose, for example, that several employees have been members of a volleyball team for a number of years. At work, one of them is promoted to be supervisor of the others, with the expectation that he will end the goofing off that has been common in the department. The supervisor's role as teammate conflicts with his role as strict supervisor. The way the supervisor resolves this conflict—which role he chooses—will influence his performance as a supervisor as well as his relationship with the employees.

role conflicts
Situations in which a person has two different roles that call for conflicting types of behavior.

Norms

Groups typically have standards for appropriate or acceptable behavior. These are called the group's **norms.** For instance, in some work settings the employees have a norm of doing only what is expected of them and no more. They may fear that if they do an exceptional amount of work, management will expect that much from them every day. A new employee eager to develop a strong work record could anger the others if he or she violates the norm by doing "too much." Other norms may be stated rather than implied; for example, an organization has an expectation that everyone will arrive at work on time.

norms
Group standards for appropriate or acceptable behavior.

When a member of the group violates a norm, the group responds by pressuring the person to conform. Formal groups have procedures for handling violations of norms that are group policies, such as arriving at work on time. With unofficial norms, a typical first step would be for someone to point out to the violator how he or she is expected to behave. If that does not work, the group may resort to shutting the person out, ridiculing the person, or even threatening him or her with physical harm.

Employees whose norm is doing no more than is required have a norm that hurts the organization. When a supervisor finds that a group of employees seems to be behaving in a way that works against the achievement of organizational objectives, the supervisor could investigate whether these employees are following some norm of an informal group. This might be the case if half a dozen employees in the department regularly leave work 15 minutes early. One way to change this kind of norm is to look at the way the organization treats the behavior. Perhaps the organization or supervisor does not properly reward those who do follow the rules. In trying to persuade employees to change or ignore an informal group's norm, the supervisor must remember that violating norms carries negative consequences for group members.

Status

status
A group member's position in relation to others in the group.

A group member's **status** is his or her position relative to others in the group. Status depends on a variety of factors, including the person's role in the group, title, pay, education level, age, race, and sex. Thus, in one group, the person with the highest status might be a male who is the tallest and owns a cottage by a lake. The others find this person's presence impressive and hope for invitations to the cottage, so his status is high.

Status is important to supervisors because group members with the highest status have the most effect on the development of group norms. Group members with lower status tend to pattern their behavior after that of high-status members. A supervisor who wants to reinforce or change group norms will have the greatest success by focusing on the high-status members of the group.

Cohesiveness

cohesiveness
The degree to which group members stick together.

The degree to which group members stick together is known as **cohesiveness.** In other words, cohesiveness refers to the "glue" that holds the group together. A cohesive group has members who want to stay with the group even during periods of stress on the group. They abide by group norms even when under pressure to follow other norms.

Groups that are cohesive work harder than others and are more likely to accomplish their objectives. Thus, when a group's objectives support those of the organization, the supervisor will want the group to be cohesive. The supervisor can foster cohesiveness in several ways:

- By emphasizing to group members their common characteristics and goals. A supervisor of a research department might point out proudly that this is a select group of talented individuals working on an important project.
- By emphasizing areas in which the group has succeeded in achieving its goals. A history of successes, such as accomplishing a task or increasing the status of members, tends to improve cohesiveness.

- By keeping the group sufficiently small—ideally no more than eight members—so that everyone feels comfortable participating. When a larger number of employees report to a single supervisor, he or she might want to support the formation of more than one group.
- By encouraging competition with other groups. In contrast, cohesiveness diminishes when group members are competing with one another.
- By encouraging less active members to participate in group activities. Groups tend to be more cohesive when everyone participates equally.

Size

An organization's groups may vary widely in size. As few as two people can form a group. Up to 15 or 16 group members can get to know and communicate well with one another. Beyond 20 members, however, informal subgroups tend to form.

Big groups typically operate differently than small ones. Small groups tend to reach decisions faster and to rely less on formal rules and procedures. Also, quiet group members are more likely to participate in a small group. If group processes seem overly cumbersome—for example, if the group tends to take too long in reaching decisions—the supervisor might consider dividing the group into subgroups of about 8 to 12 members. A bigger group might make sense when a lot of work needs to get done and the individual group members can work independently most of the time.

Homogeneity

homogeneity
The degree to which the members of a group are the same.

The degree to which the members of a group are the same is known as **homogeneity.** Thus, a *homogeneous* group is one in which group members have a lot in common. When group members have many differences, the group is said to be *heterogeneous.* Group members can be alike or different according to age, sex, race, work experience, education level, social class, personality, interests, and other characteristics.

The members of a homogeneous group enjoy a number of benefits. Perhaps most significant is that people feel most comfortable being around others who are like themselves. This may be the reason that homogeneous groups offer better cooperation among members, greater satisfaction, and higher productivity, at least for simple tasks.

At the same time, the U.S. workforce is becoming more diverse. But for complex, creative tasks, a heterogeneous group can perform better than a homogeneous one because group members offer a variety of skills, experience, and viewpoints. The heterogeneous group as a whole has broader skills and knowledge, and it can examine problems from different points of view. Studies show that groups with diverse membership perform complex tasks better than homogeneous groups.

Effectiveness

The preceding characteristics of groups can affect whether a particular group is effective—that is, whether it achieves what it set out to do. To the supervisor, a group's effectiveness is one of its most important characteristics. In general, the organization's formal groups should be as effective as possible. The supervisor

FIGURE 3.3

Stages of Group Development

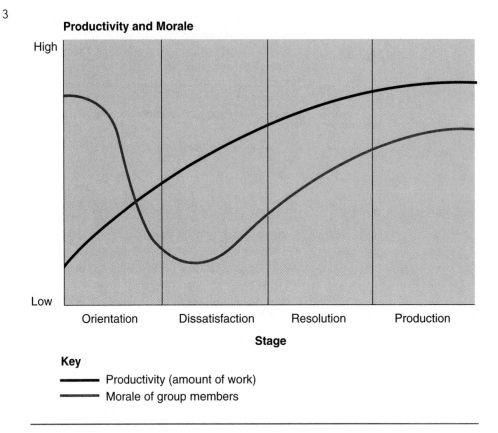

wants informal groups to be effective only to the extent that this supports organizational goals. For example, a company softball team that builds morale and improves working relations is properly effective. A clique that hurts morale among the employees who feel left out is not supporting organizational objectives.

The Development of Groups

In a sense, groups are living organisms with life stages. They grow, are subjected to stresses, and either mature or die as a result. Figure 3.3 shows one view of group development, that of groups passing through the following stages:[2]

- *Orientation*—When a group first forms, its members tend to be highly committed to the group, but they do not yet have the experience and skills to work together efficiently. Group members tend to be concerned about what the group is supposed to do and how they will fit in. The supervisor's role is primarily to clarify objectives and provide direction.
- *Dissatisfaction*—If group members are able to learn their roles and the group's objectives, the group moves to the dissatisfaction stage. Although group members are more competent at working together, their initial enthusiasm has given way to disappointment with the day-to-day reality of being part of the group. While continuing to help group members develop competence, the supervisor must focus more on encouraging and motivating them.

- *Resolution*—If group members are able to reconcile the differences between their initial expectations and the realities they experience, the group moves to the resolution stage. During this stage, group members continue to be more productive and their morale also improves. The supervisor should focus on helping with conflict resolution and encourage group members to participate in planning and decision making.
- *Production*—If group members continue to resolve conflicts and develop a workable structure for the group, their output and morale will continue to increase. The group is effectively working as a team. When group structure must change or other issues arise, the group resolves them quickly. The supervisor should give group members as much autonomy as possible.
- *Termination*—At some point, many groups must come to an end. If the group had reached the production stage, group members may be sad. If the group ends before that stage, members are more likely to be relieved.

Getting a group to the resolution and production stages is challenging for supervisors who are most comfortable telling employees what to do. Instead, this process requires skill in resolving conflicts and fostering employee development (topics of Chapters 15 and 17).

Teamwork

team
A small number of people with complementary skills who are committed to a common purpose, goal, and an approach to work for which they hold themselves mutually accountable.

Organizations today are increasingly looking for ways to involve employees in decision making and problem solving. For a growing number of organizations, teamwork is the means to employee involvement. A **team** is a small number of people with complementary skills who are equally committed to a common purpose, goals, and a working approach for which they hold themselves mutually accountable.[3] When most organizations form a team, someone is appointed to be team leader. Often the team leader is a supervisor, and the team consists of operative employees.

Being an effective team leader draws on many of the same skills required of an effective supervisor. The team leader needs excellent communication skills, patience, fairness, and good rapport with team members. In addition, because the purpose of the team is to draw on the expertise of all team members, the team leader will need to rely most on a leadership style that encourages involvement. (For more on this type of leadership, see Chapter 8.)

self-managing work teams
Groups of 5 to 15 members who work together to produce an entire product.

In the 1970s, it became popular to form teams in which employees suggest ways to improve the quality of their work. More recently, organizations have expanded their use of teams by creating **self-managing work teams.** These are groups of 5 to 15 members who work together to produce an entire product. The team members rotate jobs, schedule work and vacations, and make other decisions affecting their area of responsibility. Companies using self-managing work teams include Toyota, General Electric, and Xerox.[4] At GM's Saturn plant in Spring Hill, Tennessee, over 150 work teams interview and approve new team members, decide how to run their own area, and accept budget responsibility.

Benefits of Teamwork

A basic benefit of using work teams is that they enable the organization to increase its usage of the insights and expertise of all its employees. In the marketing area, some companies are setting up sales teams that combine technical and sales experts to better address the needs of their major customers. For example, many high-tech and Internet firms combine experts in hardware, software, and technical support to help customers fully use the hardware and software they buy. Nike is seeking ways to increase the company's share of the market for athletic footwear and apparel among 15- to 35-year-old women, and its marketing managers meet regularly, sometimes with Cynthia Cooper, coach of the Phoenix Mercury of the Women's National Basketball Association (WNBA), as a guest and participant.[5]

Teams can also serve as motivators. Employees who participate in planning and decision making are more likely to take responsibility for the quality of what they do. They also tend to be more enthusiastic about their work. Responsible, enthusiastic employees are more likely to work hard and deliver high quality.

When New York City's public television station, WNET, moved into its new headquarters, among the benefits president William F. Baker anticipated were greater efficiency, more spontaneous interaction, and even greater comfort for all its employees. The reason? The spacious new offices bring most of the station's approximately 600 employees and volunteers together in open work areas that occupy one and a half floors. "The old building was not conducive to a television station," said Baker. "We had people in rabbit warrens [on many different floors], while television is a team effort."[6]

Ultimately, motivating employees and drawing on their strengths should enhance the performance of the organizations that use self-managing work teams. For instance, at General Electric's Durham, North Carolina, plant, jet engines are produced by nine self-managing teams of technicians, each of which "owns" an engine from the moment its part are uncrated to the moment the finished engine is placed on a truck for shipment. Perfection in an 8.5-ton object with 10,000 parts is hard to achieve, but the teams come very close. After each step in the process, the technician responsible initials the work via computer. "It matters," says technician Bill Lane about the drive for perfection at the plant. "I've got a 3-year-old daughter, and I figure that every plane we build engines for has someone with a 3-year-old daughter riding on it."[7]

The story at many small businesses also is positive. Growing Green, a St. Louis–based company that supplies and maintains plants for corporate clients, adopted the use of teamwork, charging its teams of employees with making decisions in their areas of responsibility. Co-owners Joel and Teri Pesapane credit employee empowerment for the company's steady revenue growth. Furthermore, notes Teri Pesapane, "We have a reputation in St. Louis for finishing a job on time and on budget, and that's because of team management."[8]

Leading the Team

Many teams fall short of their potential.[9] Whether an organization's teams achieve the benefits of teamwork depends in part on the teams' leaders. Broadly speaking, the goal of a team leader is to develop a productive team. Experts in teamwork have linked team productivity to the team characteristics described in Table 3.1. In general, these characteristics describe a team whose members want to participate, to share ideas freely, and to know what they are supposed to accomplish. (See "Tips from the Firing Line" for more on building and leading a team.)

When Tony Tallarita tried to encourage his team of 14 fellow hourly workers to improve the fit and finish of trunk hinges and lids at Ford's Chicago plant, where the Taurus and Sable lines are made, he met resistance. Trunk-fitting problems have long been a source of quality failures at the plant, but Tallarita

	Characteristic	Significance
TABLE 3.1 **Management Activities Related to Quality Improvement**	Openness and honesty	These are signs that group members trust one another. Tact and timing also are important.
	Leadership that does not dominate	The leader is flexible, changing with conditions and circumstances.
	Decisions made by consensus	The leader will sometimes have to make a decision alone or reject suggestions, but all team members should have a voice in making many decisions, not simply a vote without a full opportunity to be heard.
	Acceptance of assignments	Team members should willingly take on the tasks that must be done, then do them correctly and on time. Team members should view work as a cooperative effort, helping each other out as needed.
	Goals that are understood and accepted	Goals give the team purpose and direction. Team members should view accomplishing them as the team's primary purpose.
	Assessment of progress and results	Team members should focus on results.
	Comfortable atmosphere	Some conflict can stimulate desirable action and change, but there should be a basic level of cooperation.
	Involvement and participation	Team members should be involved in the work of the group. When a team member is reluctant to speak up at meetings, the leader should seek his or her input during or outside the meeting.
	Debate and discussion	If everyone agrees all the time, it may signify that team members are unable or unwilling to contribute.
	Atmosphere of listening	Team members should listen to each other, even when they disagree.
	Access to information	All team members need to know what is happening.
	Win-win approach to conflict	Team members should work to resolve conflicts in ways that let everyone be a winner.
	Relatively low turnover	Members of a team must have a close relationship, which is impossible when the team's membership keeps changing.

Sources: Adapted from Edward Glassman, "Self-Directed Team Building without a Consultant," *Supervisory Management*, March 1992, p. 6; Louis V. Imundo, "Blueprint for a Successful Team," *Supervisory Management*, May 1992, pp. 2–3.

thought his proposed new layout of the team's work area would save each employee walking some 2,000 steps per shift and eliminate wasted effort. Co-workers' fear that his effort was a prelude to downsizing at the plant earned him scorn, and one fellow employee swore at him. Tallarita is persisting in his efforts, gradually persuading his team that the step-saving measures and other improvements are cutting waste only, and not jobs.[10]

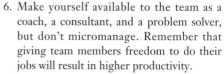

How to Build an Effective Team

One of the most exciting opportunities you will face as a supervisor is the chance to lead a team. With some thought and preparation, as well as a few management skills, you can build a successful group. Here are some useful tips for doing just that.

1. Set goals. The better you define your primary goal, the greater your chance of success. Prioritize your remaining goals below the top one or two.

2. Build the team well. Keep the team as small as you can while still including all the skills needed to meet your goal. In selecting team members, consider technical qualifications, past experience with similar tasks, availability, level of interest in the team's project or goals, and good chemistry with other members of the team. Balance the team so that it includes members with different backgrounds who are more likely to offer a wide variety of ideas.

3. Hold an initial meeting or two. The first meeting can serve to introduce members of the team and give them a chance to get to know one another. The second meeting's purposes are to review the budget, the deadline or timeline for the project, and the available resources, and to identify members' responsibilities.

4. Hold frequent or regular status meetings. Keep these brief and use them to get the whole team updated on members' progress. Review goals and renew commitment.

5. Monitor the progress of individuals and of the team as a whole. Maintain and distribute a written report that measures progress against deadline and budget.

6. Make yourself available to the team as a coach, a consultant, and a problem solver, but don't micromanage. Remember that giving team members freedom to do their jobs will result in higher productivity.

7. Remember that communication is two-way. Talk over problems with the team, but also listen carefully and watch body language, facial expression, and tone of voice.

8. Step in when you sense a conflict. Ask questions until you understand the problem; then ask for suggested solutions.

9. Update your manager. Provide regular updates to your own boss as well as to the managers of any team members who are from other departments.

10. Be a good team player yourself. Participate in meetings by listening actively, speaking plainly, and demonstrating your investment in the goals and tasks of the group. Be open to other points of view and learn to compromise, but beware the words "can't" and "won't."

11. Give credit where it is due. Make sure that all members of the team are rewarded for their contributions to the successful accomplishment of the goal.

Sources: "Helpline," *RN Magazine*, April 2001, p. 23; Renee Evenson, "Team Effort: Beyond Employees to Team, Beyond Manager to Coach," *Supervision*, February 2000, p. 11; David King, "Team Management," *CMA Management*, May 2001, pp. 101ff.; Michael Thomas, "Building and Managing a Winning Project Team," *Manage*, August 1, 2000, pp. 4–5.

Coaching the Team   The team leader who can stimulate this high-quality performance is one who focuses on enabling team members to do their best. *Enabling* in this context means providing employees with the resources they need to do their job and removing obstacles that interfere with their work (such as procedures that slow employees down without adding value from the customer's perspective). Providing resources includes making sure employees have the training they need to be effective team members. Typically, employees are not used to working on a team and can benefit from training in decision making, conflict resolution, meeting management, interpersonal skills, problem solving, negotiation, and dealing with customers.[11] When a new member joins a team, the team leader can enable that person's full participation by making an experienced team member responsible for showing him or her the ropes and by ensuring that the team gives the new member an assignment as soon as possible.[12]

This kind of leader coaches employees—asking them questions that help them decide how to handle a situation instead of simply telling them what to do. The team leader encourages team members by expressing understanding and appreciation of their ideas and feelings, and limits his or her advice and criticism because these can interfere with members' creativity and stifle their motivation to find solutions.[13] The team leader knows when it is time to help the group stay on track and when to promote balanced participation from team members.

This style of leading may seem to leave a supervisor with less power than one who gives directions and checks up on performance. However, coaching enables the supervisor to build on the strengths and expertise of the whole group. The likely result is a stronger position for everyone, including the supervisor.

Selection of Team Members   A team leader may be charged either with selecting candidates for jobs that involve teamwork or with selecting existing employees to participate in a team devoted to a particular task. In either case, the supervisor should look for people who work well with others. If the team is to include people from several departments, the team leader should talk to other supervisors and employees to learn which employees would do best on the team.

team building
Developing the ability of team members to work together to achieve common objectives.

Team Building   Once the team leader knows who will be on the team, he or she must develop the group's ability to work together to achieve common objectives. This process is known as **team building.** Team building includes several activities: setting goals, analyzing what needs to be done and allocating work, examining how well the group is working, and examining the relationships among the team members.

At some organizations, a consultant with expertise in team building carries out this process. However, hiring someone often can be too expensive, especially at small organizations. Consultant Edward Glassman describes a three-step approach by which a supervisor can conduct team building:[14]

1. Set aside time at the end of team meetings to discuss the quality of the interactions during the meeting as well as the creativity of the results. Ask what went well and what needs to be improved.
2. Ask each team member to rate, on a scale of 1 to 10, how well the meeting went in terms of (*a*) whether everyone participated equally, (*b*) whether the team member influenced the outcome, and (*c*) whether the outcome was creative. Prepare a written summary of the ratings and discuss them at the next team meeting.
3. Use a questionnaire to ask team members how effective the team and team leader were in accomplishing goals. Such questionnaires are readily available from consultants in training, management, and human resources development.

Supervisors and other team leaders can embellish on this approach by drawing on the resources and talents they have available. However, supervisors need not go to the extreme that Harvey Kinzelberg did—the CEO of the Meridian Group, a computer leasing firm, took his management team on scuba-diving expeditions to stretch their creative thinking and make them aware of how much they depended on one another.[15]

Ray Evernham, crew chief extraordinary for champion race car driver Jeff Gordon, relies on some basic team-building skills to achieve success with his team, called the Rainbow Warriors. Evernham's philosophy readily applies to business situations. "Racing is a team sport," he says. "Everyone who races has pretty much the same car and the same equipment. What sets us apart is our people. . . . I think a lot about people, management, and psychology: Specifically, how can I motivate my guys and make them gel as a team? I surround them with ideas about teamwork. I read every leadership book I can get my hands on. . . . When the Rainbow Warriors meet, we always put our chairs in a circle. That's a way of saying that we're stronger as a team than we are on our own."[16]

Communication in Teams   The way the team leader communicates with the other team members will influence the success of the team. In general, the team leader should create a climate of trust and openness, and encourage team members to collaborate. The team leader also should acknowledge disagreement, not squelch it. To see whether you already have a communication style that would make you an effective team leader, or whether you need to make some changes to fill that role, take the Self-Quiz at the end of this chapter, on page 83.

Team leaders need this kind of communication style because successful teamwork requires open and positive communication among team members. Feeling able to express one's viewpoint and knowing how to do so constructively are essential for reaping the benefits of diverse viewpoints. Otherwise, peer pressure can lead to a uniformity that stifles creative thinking.[17]

Building effective communication was among the key challenges faced by Brian Wilson, charged with leading three of the production teams at GE Fanuc Automation North America. Before the company instituted teamwork, explains Wilson, "We had a situation where some people had been working together side by side for 10 or 15 years and hadn't had to speak to each other." Furthermore, the employees were used to taking orders instead of planning and making decisions. GE Fanuc helped with the change to teamwork by providing training in these skills, along with feedback on the organization's performance. Wilson (whose job under the old structure was that of a supervisor) and his team learned together that they were responsible for implementing decisions and for discussing and solving any problems that resulted. The change to teamwork has been good for GE Fanuc's business performance, but, Wilson admits, "I'm still learning to let go of the reins."[18]

Rewards   For teams to remain productive, members must be rewarded appropriately. The organization should reward the entire team for its accomplishments instead of emphasizing individual rewards. The 1,100 employees of Behlen Manufacturing in Columbus, Nebraska, are organized into 32 teams. Employees are paid an hourly wage in addition to rewards based on group performance. Bonuses based on the amount a team produces free of defects can boost the pay of the team's employees by up to $1 an hour. In addition, Behlen divides 20 percent of its profits among its employees. Since Behlen has been using this compensation plan, employees have made thousands of suggestions for improvement that have saved the company almost $5 million and helped it exceed its profit goals.[19] (For more on group incentives, see Chapter 11.)

Team members also are likely to value different rewards; therefore, the rewards should be varied enough so that everyone will feel motivated. For example, the typical salesperson is motivated by money, whereas technical people might be more interested in recognition and promotion. Thus, one approach might be to use the company's basic incentive plan and also to ask the team members to reach a consensus on what additional reward they would enjoy receiving for a specific accomplishment.

Tape Resources, Inc., one of *Inc.* magazine's 500 top companies for 1998, rewards team members with a new incentive system that specifically recognizes teamwork. It has helped sales grow to $4.7 million, about a 70 percent increase over 1996. Because the company, which sells blank video- and audiocassettes to television stations and production companies, competes on service and not on price, this system makes sense for its 12 employees, who work more effectively as a team now than when the firm used a commission system in 1997.[20]

Labor Law and Teamwork

An important issue concerning teamwork is whether employee teams violate federal labor law. Specifically, the National Labor Relations Act of 1935 forbids employers to dominate or interfere with the formation of any "labor organization," defined as "any organization of any kind, or any employee representation committee which exists for the purpose of dealing with employers concerning grievances, wages, hours of employment, or conditions of work." This provision—designed to prevent employers from interfering with organizing efforts by setting up "fake unions"—seems to prohibit teams that address the issues identified.[21]

The labor Policy Association, an antiunion group, recently pressed the North American Free Trade Association (NAFTA) to push for employers' rights to create labor-management teams at nonunion firms, saying that NAFTA encourages what the Act forbids.[22]

In practical terms, teamwork probably need not lead to government sanctions. First, a ruling by the National Labor Relations Board suggests that while this government agency will set limits, it will not seek to prohibit most teams.[23] Furthermore, unions are unlikely to challenge unionized companies in this area, because most have approved of teams. However, during an organizing drive at a nonunionized company, the union could challenge the use of teams.

Supervisors and other managers should take some precautions to avoid violating the law. Managers who participate in team meetings should make sure they do not criticize the union at those meetings. Some legal experts recommend that supervisors avoid any discussion of topics that could become a matter for union bargaining, such as working conditions or pay, and focus instead on specific work-related projects or problems.[24] Teams also should *not* be set up to represent the company's employees. Teams should have power to solve problems, not to deal with management to seek a resolution.[25] Perhaps most important, a supervisor or other manager who wants to form a team should get legal advice on how to form and operate it without violating the law.[26]

Meetings

Much of the work of teams and other groups takes place in meetings. When groups plan, solve problems, and reward successes, they usually do so in a meeting. Although the supervisor's role may be either that of participant or that of leader of the meeting, this chapter emphasizes the latter. The principles described here apply to other situations as well, but supervisors will have less ability to make improvements when someone else is conducting the meeting.

Reasons for Meetings

Meetings should take place when they serve a purpose. As obvious as this sounds, many supervisors and other managers hold meetings at a regularly scheduled time, whether or not they have something particular to accomplish. Thus, when the supervisor is thinking of calling a meeting, he or she should consider specifically what the meeting is intended to accomplish. It should be possible for the group to achieve its stated purpose by the end of the meeting.[27] If the supervisor wants to call a meeting as a way to make small matters seem important, to prove he or she is being democratic, or to rescue a lost cause (such as building a groundswell of support for an idea the boss has vetoed), the supervisor should not call the meeting.

Another way of easing communication among team members is to make communication visual, even touchable. At E-Lab LLC, a team-based firm, cofounder Rick Robinson set aside a special room "with a floor-to-ceiling tackable surface on one side and whiteboards on the other. Project teams put up an emerging story in the form of documents, slide shows, flow charts, and maps. The walls accumulate layers of information as people wander through and paste comments on giant Post-it-notes, and as teams attach new versions on top of old ones."[28]

There are several valid reasons for holding a meeting. One is to convey news to a group of people. Doing this in a meeting gives the supervisor a chance to see and respond to people's reactions to the news. A meeting is also appropriate when the supervisor wants the group to participate in decision making. (Chapter 9 describes the pros and cons of decision making in a group.) Finally, the supervisor may use meetings to prepare group members for a change and to build support for the change. (Chapter 15 describes this process.)

As much as possible, a meeting should be scheduled at a time that is convenient for all participants. Times that tend to cause problems are peak working hours and the last few hours before a weekend or holiday. However, if a meeting is supposed to be brief, it makes sense to schedule the meeting for a half-hour before lunch or quitting time.

Preparing for a Meeting

To prepare for a meeting, the supervisor should decide who is to attend and where to meet. When the purpose of a meeting is to convey information to the whole department, naturally the whole department should be invited. In many cases, however, the participants are to provide or evaluate information. In these cases, the supervisor should invite only those who have the needed information or expertise.

The location of the meeting usually depends on the available facilities. For a very small meeting, the participants might be able to meet in the supervisor's office. Larger meetings can take place in a conference room. When the whole department is called, finding a big enough space can be a challenge. In general, it is more comfortable to meet casually in the work area than to squeeze a big group into a stuffy conference room.

agenda
A list of the topics to be covered at a meeting.

One of the most basic preparation tasks is to draw up an **agenda.** This is a list of the topics to be covered at the meeting. A practical approach is to put the most important topics first, to be sure they will be covered before time runs out. To keep the focus on important topics, it is helpful to recall the purpose of the meeting. Figure 3.4 is an agenda that was used at a meeting called by an editor to discuss progress on a book. Notice that in addition to the topics to be covered, the agenda states the name of the group that is meeting, the location, the date, and the starting and ending times of the meeting.

The agenda should be distributed to all participants before the meeting is to take place. Participants should receive the agenda in time to review it before the meeting and make any necessary preparations. In addition, the person calling the meeting should make sure that participants have received any other documents they might need, so that they are prepared to contribute.

■ FIGURE 3.4

Sample Agenda

Team for *Supervision* Text

Sheraton O'Hare

June 24, 2002

8:30 A.M.–3:00 P.M.

1. Workbook (8:30–10:00)

    a.   Components and process

    b.   Possible sources of material

    c.   Tentative schedule

2. Remaining manuscript work (10:00–12:00)

    a.   Examples in text

    b.   Opening vignettes

    c.   End-of-chapter material

    d.   Changes based upon reviewer feedback

3. Working lunch (12:00–1:00)

4. Videos (1:00–2:00)

5. Ancillaries (2:00–3:00)

    a.   Components

    b.   Process

Conducting a Meeting

Meetings should begin promptly at the scheduled starting time. This demonstrates respect for all participants' schedules and it encourages people to be on time. It helps to announce an ending time and to end the meeting promptly at that time. When critical issues come up near the end of a meeting, the group can reach an agreement to extend the meeting or continue the discussion at another time.

It can be difficult to ensure that meetings run as efficiently as possible and do not extend beyond the planned time. At OpenAir.com Inc., a software provider based in Boston, about 25 engineers gather every morning to share information gathered in their customer phone calls from the day before. No chairs are allowed at the meeting. As chief of operating officer Morris Panner says, "The stand-up meeting is both a discipline—nobody can talk too long because people get antsy— and a way to get a jump on the morning. We huddle, then someone says, 'Break,' and off we go to do our stuff for the day."[29]

To make sure that meetings are as fruitful as possible, the supervisor can facilitate the discussion in several ways. One is to rephrase ideas that participants express. For example, if an employee on a printing company's health and safety committee says, "We've got to do something about the fumes in the shop," the supervisor might comment, "You're recommending that we improve ventilation." This type of response helps to ensure that the supervisor and other participants understand what has been said. Of course, the supervisor has to use this technique with care; participants might become annoyed if the supervisor sounds like their echo. Also, the supervisor should summarize key points often enough to make sure everyone is following the discussion. Times to summarize include at the conclusion of each agenda item, at the end of the meeting, and at times when people have trouble following the discussion.

The supervisor should be careful not to dominate the discussion; instead, he or she should make sure that everyone has a chance to participate. Having everyone sit around a table or in a circle makes people feel more involved as Ray Evernham recognizes in promoting teamwork with his Rainbow Warriors.[30] Some people find it easier than others to speak up during a meeting. The person leading the meeting is responsible for encouraging everyone to contribute, a task that can be as simple as saying, "Mary, what do you think about the suggestions that have been proposed so far?"

Quieting participants who are monopolizing a discussion can be a more delicate matter. One approach is to begin with someone other than the talkative person, then go around the table and hear each person's views on some topic. Also, the supervisor could have a one-on-one talk with the person monopolizing discussions, letting the person know his or her contributions are important but that the lengthy discourse is unnecessary. For more on dealing with problems among meeting participants, see "Supervision and Diversity."

Throughout the meeting, the supervisor should take notes on what is being decided. This helps the supervisor summarize key points for participants. In addition, it helps the supervisor recall what actions are to be taken later and by whom.

When it is time for the meeting to end, the supervisor should help bring it to a close. A direct way to do this is to summarize what has been covered, state what needs to happen next, and thank everyone for coming. For example, at the end of a meeting called to decide how to make the company's purchasing decisions more efficient, the supervisor might say, "We've selected three interesting possibilities to explore. Max will research the costs of each, then we'll meet back here in two weeks to select one." Then the supervisor's job becomes one of following up to make sure that plans are carried out. As in the example, following up may include planning another meeting.

Figure 3.5 summarizes these guidelines for conducting a meeting.

Overcoming Problems with Meetings

A frequent complaint about meetings is that they waste time because participants stray from the main topic and go off on tangents. Thus, an important job for the supervisor is to keep the discussion linked to the agenda items. When a participant

SUPERVISION AND DIVERSITY

Participants' Styles Can Make or Break Your Meeting

People differ widely in their work habits and in their ways of dealing with others, and these two traits are perhaps nowhere more evident at work than in meetings. Some members will be prompt, attentive, communicative, and constructive. Others are more problematic. The way you deal with problem participants can help determine whether your meetings are successful. Here are some suggestions.

The Nonparticipant. It may not be necessary to have everyone participate at every meeting. If some people never participate at all, however, and if apprehension or shyness is the cause, you can ease members' concerns and help them contribute to the group by providing chances for them to get involved in discussions. Make eye contact more often with these members to show your interest, and avoid putting them on the spot with direct questions. Respond positively when they do contribute and let them know you value their input.

The Loudmouth. The person who talks so much that no one else has a chance to speak is a common problem in meetings. You may need to interrupt the loudmouth to say that you acknowledge and understand his or her point. Then take the opportunity to ask other group members for their views. If the loudmouth remains a problem, remind him or her that it's important to get input from everyone. At the next meeting, try asking the problem participant to take the minutes, to shift his or her focus from talking to listening.

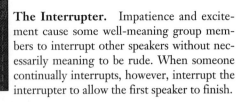

The Interrupter. Impatience and excitement cause some well-meaning group members to interrupt other speakers without necessarily meaning to be rude. When someone continually interrupts, however, interrupt the interrupter to allow the first speaker to finish.

The Whisperer. Group members who must whisper to one another during the meeting distract everyone and deter the group from its agenda and goals. Staring at whisperers may make them more conscious that you are aware of their behavior, as will making a deliberate pause in your presentation until you regain their attention. As a last resort, you can ask them to share their conversation with the group. You never know what you may find out.

The Latecomer and the Early Leaver. Train those who come late to mend their ways by starting your meetings on time and not backtracking to tell tardy arrivals what they missed. After the meeting, you can talk to them about the importance to the group of their arriving on time. If you have group members who come and go to attend to other business, or who work on other business during the conference, politely ask them to give their full attention to the entire meeting or to take care of other work in advance.

Source: Isa N. Engelberg and Dianna R. Wynn, *Working in Groups: Communication Principles and Strategies* (Boston, Houghton Mifflin, 1997), chap. 9.

---

begins discussing an unrelated topic, the supervisor can restate the purpose of the meeting and suggest that if the topic seems important, it could be covered in another meeting.

In steering the discussion back on course, it is important to avoid ridiculing the participants and to respect their efforts to contribute. The supervisor can do this by focusing on the effects of particular kinds of behavior instead of on the personalities of the participants. For example, if a participant tends to interrupt when others are speaking, the supervisor should not say, "Don't be so inconsiderate." A more helpful comment might be, "It's important that everyone in our group have a chance to state his or her ideas completely. Interruptions discourage people from participating."

Other problems arise because the meeting leader and participants have failed to prepare for the meeting. If there is no agenda, the discussion may ramble

FIGURE 3.5

Guidelines for Conducting a Meeting

Begin and end on time.
Restate key points.
Encourage participation by all.
Take notes.
Bring the meeting to a close.

aimlessly. If someone failed to bring necessary background information, the participants may be unable to make plans or reach decisions, and the meeting will be unproductive. These kinds of problems lead to frustration and anger among participants who feel they are wasting precious time. The solution is to follow the guidelines described earlier, including creation and distribution of an agenda well before the meeting. When the supervisor is prepared to lead the meeting but others are unprepared to participate, the supervisor should probably consider rescheduling the meeting.

Summary

3.1   Explain why people join groups.
People may join a group because membership in that group goes along with being an employee. (All employees are members of the organization that employs them.) Employers may ask employees to join particular groups such as committees or task forces. An employee also may join a group because doing so satisfies personal needs such as closeness, common goals, and achievement of personal objectives.

3.2   Distinguish types of groups that exist in the workplace.
Functional groups fulfill ongoing needs in the organization by carrying out a particular function. Task groups are set up to carry out a specific activity, disbanding when the activity is completed. Formal groups are set up by management to meet organizational objectives. Informal groups result when individuals in the organization develop relationships to meet personal needs.

3.3   Discuss how supervisors can get groups to cooperate with them.
The supervisor should make sure all members of a formal group know what they can and should be doing. The supervisor also should keep groups informed about what is happening in the organization and what changes are planned. The supervisor should support the group when members want to bring legitimate concerns to higher management.

When the supervisor is responsible for setting up a group, he or she should combine people with a variety of strengths and backgrounds while avoiding separation of members of informal groups. Finally, general principles of effective supervision apply to supervising groups as well as individuals.

3.4 Describe characteristics of groups in the workplace.

Group members have various roles, or patterns of behavior related to their position in the group. Group members are expected to follow norms, or the group's standards, for appropriate or acceptable behavior. The status of each group member depends on a variety of factors, which may include his or her role in the group, title, pay, education level, age, race, and sex. Some groups are more cohesive than others; that is, the members of some groups are more likely to stick together in the face of problems. Groups may vary widely in terms of size, with subgroups likely to form in groups of more than 20 members. Homogeneity refers to the extent to which group members are the same. All these characteristics can influence the effectiveness of a group. In general, a supervisor wants a group to be effective when its goals support the achievement of organizational goals.

3.5 Identify the stages in the development of groups.

In the orientation stage, the group forms, and its members are highly committed to the group but lack the experience and skills to work together efficiently. In the dissatisfaction stage, group members are more competent at working together but their initial enthusiasm has given way to disappointment with the day-to-day reality of being in the group. During the resolution phase, group members become more productive and their morale improves as group members begin to resolve their conflicts. By the production phase, the group is working effectively as a team with still higher morale and productivity. At some point, many groups pass through a termination phase, during which group activity ends.

3.6 Explain why teamwork is important.

Teams bring employees together to collaborate on solving problems and making decisions. By using teams, the organization can more fully draw upon the insights and expertise of all its employees. Teams also can motivate employees by giving them a say in how things are done. As a result, organizations that use teams can benefit from improved performance, which is measured by higher quality and greater productivity and profits.

3.7 Describe how the supervisor can lead a team so that it is productive.

If building the team includes selecting team members, the supervisor should include people who work well with others. The supervisor should adopt a coaching role, enabling employees by providing them with the resources they need and removing any obstacles in their way. Then the supervisor builds the team by helping it set goals, analyzing what needs to be done and allocating the work, examining how well the group is working, and examining the relationships among team members. The supervisor can increase the success of the team through effective communication that creates a climate of trust and encourages collaboration. The supervisor should see that teams receive group rewards valued by team members.

3.8 Discuss how to plan for effective meetings.

The supervisor should hold a meeting only when there is a valid reason for doing so. He or she should schedule the meeting at a convenient time and should plan who is to attend and where the meeting will take place. The supervisor should create an agenda, which lists the topics to be covered at the meeting. The agenda should be distributed to all participants far enough in advance so that they can be prepared to contribute at the meeting.

3.9 Provide guidelines for conducting effective meetings.

Meetings should start and end promptly. The supervisor should facilitate the discussion through such means as rephrasing what participants say and summarizing key points, without dominating the discussion. The supervisor should make sure that everyone participates in the discussion, take notes of what is being decided, and keep the discussion on track by reminding participants of the topic under consideration. After the meeting, the supervisor should follow up to make sure plans are carried out.

Key Terms

group, p. 57	roles, p. 62	homogeneity, p. 65
functional groups, p. 59	role conflicts, p. 63	team, p. 67
task groups, p. 59	norms, p. 63	self-managing work teams, p. 67
formal groups, p. 59	status, p. 64	team building, p. 71
informal groups, p. 59	cohesiveness, p. 64	agenda, p. 74

Review and Discussion Questions

1. Think of your current job or the most recent job you have held. (If you have never been employed, consider your role as a student.)
   a. What groups are you a member of? For example, what organization employs you? In which division or department do you work? Are you a member of any informal groups?
   b. Why did you join each of these groups?
2. State whether each of the following groups is formal or informal. Then state whether it is a functional group or a task group.
   a. Six employees who have decided on their own to research the possibility of establishing an on-site day care facility.
   b. The board of directors of a major corporation.
   c. Three employees who decide to plan a birthday celebration for a co-worker.
   d. Software developers at an educational publisher.
3. Joseph Dittrick is a supervisor in the marketing department of a toy manufacturer. He is responsible for leading a group of employees in finding ways to improve a problematic product. In what ways can Joseph encourage the group to be as effective as possible?
4. Why do supervisors need to know about each of the following characteristics of groups?
   a. Roles of group members.
   b. Status of group members.
5. Yolanda Gibbs supervises employees in the reference department of a public library. Her team meets once a month to discuss ways to improve the quality of services delivered at the library. Yolanda wants the team to be cohesive, so that its members will work hard. How can she encourage the cohesiveness of this group?

6. A supervisor observes that the members of a committee are not as enthusiastic about their work as they initially were. How can the supervisor help the committee move into the resolution stage of group development?
7. Describe briefly Edward Glassman's three-step approach to team building.
8. Peter Wilson is a supervisor who also leads a team that has been working on revamping an old product—snow saucers—to make them seem new and more attractive to a new generation of customers. The team includes both design people and salespeople. What type or types of rewards might Peter consider for his team members if the project is successful?
9. How can a supervisor at an organization with self-managing work teams help the organization avoid violations of federal labor law?
10. Bonnie First supervises respiratory therapists at a large community hospital. One day her manager said, "Your department used too much overtime again last week. I want you to propose a solution to this problem, and I think you need to involve the employees in finding the solution. Get back to me in a week with your ideas." To prepare for the next meeting with her manager, Bonnie decided she needed to hold a department meeting at 1:00 the next afternoon. She asked two therapists to spread the word about this meeting.

    At the meeting, Bonnie described the problem. To her disappointment, no one seemed to have any suggestions. She said, "Unless someone has a better idea, you're just going to have to help each other out more when someone is having trouble keeping up. And don't hesitate to ask me to pitch in, too."

    How could the supervisor have better planned this meeting?

11. As a supervisor, you have done everything you can to prepare for a meeting, including writing up and distributing an agenda. At the meeting, you have problems with two of the participants. Ken dominates the conversation, drifting off to subjects that are not on the agenda. Sheryl refuses to talk at all, even though you know she has read the agenda and probably has something insightful to contribute. What steps might you take to elicit more positive participation from Ken and Sheryl?

A SECOND LOOK

How cohesive do you think the team at CheckFree is? Why?

SKILLS MODULE

CASE

Behlen Manufacturing

One of the ways a supervisor can help ensure continued success of a team is to figure out what type of reward team members value, and provide it if possible. For organizations that use financial rewards, the issue can be particularly complex: Does everyone on the team deserve the same monetary reward? If not, how should the amount of reward be determined? Who decides which team members get what? Behlen Manufacturing in Columbus, Nebraska, has found a way to solve this problem.

Rewards for team achievement at Behlen are folded into each team member's total compensation package: A combination of base pay, bonuses, profit sharing, and employee stock ownership reflect company goals and individual as well as team performance. One reason for establishing such a plan is that Behlen's teams are permanent. Rather than forming task groups to solve a particular problem and then disband, Behlen uses teamwork to manufacture and sell its products. Behlen's teams vary in size: One team might have up to 60 people, another only 6.

"We are getting an increasing amount of cross-training all the time," notes CEO Tony Raimondo, "and productivity is rising." Increased productivity has solidified Behlen's commitment to teamwork. That is how the organization can work certain reward programs into its pay system. For instance, workers can receive bonuses of up to $1 per hour when their groups meet productivity goals. This amount may not sound like much at the outset, but the time can add up if the team has been working on a project for more than a month. (These bonuses also are tied to quality: Defects are subtracted from the total produced by the group.) One of the best parts of the bonus system is that it is simple: Both workers and supervisors understand it, and anyone can calculate it.

Actual profit sharing is another part of the Behlen reward system: Employees receive 20 percent of profits. As teams improve their performance and increase productivity, profits rise and so do members' paychecks.

What about team members who slack off, do less work than their co-workers, or pay less attention to quality? That doesn't seem to be a problem at Behlen. According to Raimondo, "Performance has exceeded plan and expectations." Since the beginning of the team compensation program, workers have submitted 5,000 ideas for improving safety, quality, and efficiency; those ideas have saved the company $5 million. Indirectly, those savings drop right into employees' pockets.

1. Team members at Behlen seem to value the reward system that is in place. What steps might the company take to add less tangible rewards for employees who value them?
2. Do you think that rewarding an entire team for its overall performance is fair? Why or why not?
3. The Behlen teams are considered permanent. How might this affect their development?

Source: Reprinted from *HR Focus*, September 1994. © 1994 American Management Association International. Reprinted by permission of American Management Association International, New York, NY. All rights reserved. http://www.amanet.org.

How Do You Communicate as a Team Leader?

In response to each item, circle the answer that reflects what you think you always do (SA), often do (A), rarely do (D), and never do (SD). Your answer should reflect your own perceptions of the way you communicate. Be honest with yourself; you are the only one who will see the results.

1. When people talk, I listen attentively; that is, I do not think of other things, such as my response or a deadline, or read while someone is talking to me.	SA	A	D	SD
2. I provide the information the group needs, even if someone else is its source.	SA	A	D	SD
3. I get impatient when people disagree with me.	SA	A	D	SD
4. I ask for and carefully consider advice from other people.	SA	A	D	SD
5. I cut off other people when they are talking.	SA	A	D	SD
6. I tell people what I want, speaking rapidly in short, clipped sentences.	SA	A	D	SD
7. When people disagree with me, I listen to what they have to say and do not respond immediately.	SA	A	D	SD
8. I speak candidly and openly, identifying when I am expressing opinions or feelings rather than reporting facts.	SA	A	D	SD
9. I finish other people's sentences.	SA	A	D	SD
10. I find it difficult to express my feelings, except when stresses build up and I become angry.	SA	A	D	SD
11. I am conscious of how I express myself: facial expressions, body language, tone of voice, and gestures.	SA	A	D	SD
12. When people disagree with me, I avoid arguments by not responding.	SA	A	D	SD
13. During meetings, I prefer to listen rather than to talk.	SA	A	D	SD
14. When I talk, I am concise and to the point.	SA	A	D	SD
15. I prevent arguments during team meetings.	SA	A	D	SD

Agreeing (SA or A) with items 1, 4, 8, 11, and 14 and disagreeing (D or SD) with the rest suggests that you encourage openness and candor; you create a climate of trust by involving the team in important decisions that affect their lives. You communicate clearly and concisely and balance task and process dynamics.

Agreeing with items 2, 3, 5, 6, and 9 suggests you tend to be task oriented and dominate the team. You are frequently intolerant of disagreement and may squelch involvement and discussion. Disagreeing with these items does not necessarily indicate that you encourage collaboration; it could be blocked by passive communication.

Agreeing with items 7, 10, 12, 13, and 15 suggests you squelch disagreement by avoiding it and therefore undermine the team's task and process dynamics. A lack of leadership will more likely destroy a team than tyrannical leadership. At least people know what to expect from a tyrant.

Source: From *Supervisory Management* by AMA. Copyright 1992 by American Management Association. Reproduced with permission of American Management Association via Copyright Clearance Center.

Class Exercise

A key characteristic of any effective meeting is participants who know how to listen. Write a list of dos and don'ts for being a good listener in a meeting, and share your ideas with the class. Here are a few to get you started: *Do:* Be alert, concentrate on the speaker, and avoid making hasty judgments about what is said. *Don't:* Interrupt, talk to others in the room, or let your feelings about the speaker get in the way.

Team-Building Exercise

Understanding the Benefits of Working in Teams

In working with teams, most managers believe in the following axiom: "None of us is as smart as all of us." Let's see if this axiom holds true for this exercise.

Instructions

1. Perform this part of the exercise on your own. When your instructor starts the clock, you will have two minutes to fill in the U.S. state names on Chart 1. The first letter of each of the 50 states is provided. Write the state name out in full; do not use abbreviations. Do not talk among yourselves during this step.
2. Form teams of three to five students to work on Chart 2. Your team should select someone to record your group's list. Without looking back at the first chart you completed, your group will have two minutes to fill in the second chart. Speak quietly among yourselves so that other teams will not overhear your answers.
3. Your instructor will read the 50 state names so that you may check your answers. Then fill in the information about your team's performance.

Chart 1: Working alone

Number of correct answers for each team member:

_____ _____ _____ _____

What is the average of these scores? _____

Chart 2: Working in teams

Number of correct answers your team completed: _____

How many in your team got the same or a better score on Chart 1 than the group got on Chart 2? _____

Questions for Discussion

1. How many individual students, working alone, did as well or better than students working in one of the teams?
2. Benefiting from the collective knowledge of a group to help solve a problem is but one advantage to working in groups. Name some other advantages of working in an effective group or team that normally cannot be realized when individuals work alone.

Source: The Team-Building Exercise was prepared by Corinne Livesay, Belhaven College, Jackson, Mississippi.

■ CHART 1 **Working Alone**

1. A	26. M
2. A	27. N
3. A	28. N
4. A	29. N
5. C	30. N
6. C	31. N
7. C	32. N
8. D	33. N
9. F	34. N
10. G	35. O
11. H	36. O
12. I	37. O
13. I	38. P
14. I	39. R
15. I	40. S
16. K	41. S
17. K	42. T
18. L	43. T
19. M	44. U
20. M	45. V
21. M	46. V
22. M	47. W
23. M	48. W
24. M	49. W
25. M	50. W

■ CHART 2 **Working in Teams**

1. A	26. M
2. A	27. N
3. A	28. N
4. A	29. N
5. C	30. N
6. C	31. N
7. C	32. N
8. D	33. N
9. F	34. N
10. G	35. O
11. H	36. O
12. I	37. O
13. I	38. P
14. I	39. R
15. I	40. S
16. K	41. S
17. K	42. T
18. L	43. T
19. M	44. U
20. M	45. V
21. M	46. V
22. M	47. W
23. M	48. W
24. M	49. W
25. M	50. W

4

Having integrity means more to us than simply the absence of deception. It means we are completely forthright in all our dealings. We say what needs to be said, not simply what people want to hear.

—**Scott Cook, founder of Intuit**

Meeting High Ethical Standards

■ LEARNING OBJECTIVES

After you have studied this chapter, you should be able to:

4.1 Define ethics, and explain how organizations specify standards for ethical behavior.

4.2 Identify benefits of ethical behavior and challenges that make ethical behavior more difficult in the modern workplace.

4.3 Discuss the impact of cultural differences on ethical issues.

4.4 Describe major types of ethical behavior that supervisors should practice.

4.5 Outline ways to make ethical decisions.

4.6 Provide guidelines for supervising unethical employees.

4.7 Define whistleblowers, and describe how the supervisor should treat such employees.

■ MAINTAINING SOCIAL RESPONSIBILITY IN GOOD TIMES AND BAD

How does a company grow to be noteworthy not only for its high-quality products but also for its high ethical standards? In the case of children's clothier Hanna Andersson Corporation, the impetus for the company's caring culture came from the original motives of founder Gun Denhart. She says, "When we started Hanna, we just wanted to create a place where we wanted to be. It was important to me to spend time with my family as well. So I just assumed that was what other people preferred, too."

From that beginning came generous employee benefits like 50 percent reimbursement for child care expenses, family-friendly work schedules, and an unwritten understanding that no one with five years' seniority would be laid off or fired. The firm, which operates mainly through its mail-order catalog, also began a charitable endeavor called Hannadowns. Customers could return outgrown clothing and Hanna Andersson would distribute it to needy children, acknowledging the donation with a credit toward the next order worth 20 percent of the value of the used clothes.

The company flourished, but rising costs and stiff competition began to cut into profits. Better management practices and improved marketing strategies are in place for a brighter long-term outlook, but in the short term, faced with a conflict between social responsibility and fiscal soundness, Gun had to find a way to retrench while holding onto her ideals. Among other cost-cutting measures, she reluctantly eliminated the 20 percent credit for Hannadowns, a program that had grown so successful that it also became costly to administer. Over one million garments have been collected and given away over the years as the program has continued, with customers now donating outgrown clothing in their own communities. New charitable programs include giving assistance to a school for homeless children and to a support group for teenage parents. The firm also donates 5 percent of pretax profits to a wide range of charities that help meet children's needs.

One constant theme is Hanna Andersson's commitment to balancing social and fiscal responsibility. The basis for that, as Gun says, is "a socially responsible product. It's a quality product that lasts a long time, and that's something we won't change."

Source: Diane Cyr, "Gun Denhart," *Working Woman*, June 1998, pp. 28–29; and www.hannaandersson.com, accessed June 27, 2001.

This chapter covers the role of ethics in the workplace. Ethical behavior is distinguished from unethical behavior and supervisors are told how they can behave ethically. Suggestions are provided for handling the challenge of supervising unethical employees and employees who report unethical or illegal behavior in the organization.

Ethics in the Workplace

ethics
The principles by which people distinguish what is morally right.

In general, **ethics** refers to the principles by which people distinguish what is morally right. For example, most people would agree that cheating is wrong, or at least they would agree that it is unethical to cheat an elderly widow out of her life savings. Many decisions about ethics are more difficult. For example, is it cheating or just clever to pad an expense report or to take advantage of a supplier's mistake in totaling a bill? The Self-Quiz on page 103 is a chance for you to examine your own standards of ethical behavior. To get an accurate score, be honest with yourself!

Some people say that "business ethics" is an oxymoron—that is, a contradiction in terms. Can businesspeople behave ethically, and if so, should they? One view is that profitability should be the overriding concern of business. This view makes it easy to behave ethically unless an ethical choice is also costly to the organization. Another view is that organizations and their employees have an obligation to behave ethically, even if doing so cuts into short-term economic advantages. The implication is that we are all better off if organizations and individuals consider the common good.

Michael Deck, of KPMG Ethics and Integrity Services in Toronto, sees ethics as beginning and ending with individuals. "Decisions are made by individuals. Actions are taken by individuals. Companies are nothing without individual human beings, and that's where the problems start or end."[1] As a supervisor, you will be looking for ethical behavior in your employees and also making sure you contribute to an environment that encourages such actions. Deck adds, "The desired behavior must start from the top and work its way through the entire organization."

code of ethics
An organization's written statement of its values and its rules for ethical behavior.

Ethical issues are of particular concern in today's workplace and many organizations have adopted a **code of ethics.** This is an organization's written statement of its values and its rules for ethical behavior. According to a recent survey, 73 percent of U.S. companies have codes of ethics, and 40 percent have ethics training programs for their employees.[2] (Furthermore, to help people resolve ethical dilemmas, one-third of the companies surveyed have an office or ombudsman charged with ethics.) To help U.S. organizations address ethical issues, the Clinton administration drafted a voluntary code of ethics for conducting international business in a way that is fair and respects workers' rights. Figure 4.1 shows the code of ethics for Johnson & Johnson Corporation, and the Carnegie Council of the United States and Uehiro Foundation of Japan have established a code of ethics based on the common world heritage of Plato, Aristotle, and Confucius.[3]

Codes of ethics provide guidelines for behavior and, perhaps more importantly, support top management's assertion that they care about ethical behavior. However, a code of ethics cannot ensure ethical behavior.

Benefits of Ethical Behavior

Besides being morally right, ethical behavior offers some potential advantages to the organization. To be known as an ethical individual or organization is a satisfying way of maintaining a reputation for high standards. St. Louis–based Bi-State Development Agency sent the following letter to its suppliers to help them handle the ethics of giving holiday gifts to the organization's employees:

We have chosen to buy your product or service over the year solely because of its quality, price, and service, and we confidently hope to do so in the future. Product excellence is the best gift we can receive at any time. Hence, at this time of the year, we

FIGURE 4.1

The Johnson & Johnson Code of Ethics

We believe our first responsibility is to the doctors, nurses, and patients, to mothers and all others who use our products and services.

In meeting their needs everything we do must be of high quality.

We must constantly strive to reduce our costs in order to maintain reasonable prices.

Customers' orders must be serviced promptly and accurately.

Our suppliers and distributors must have an opportunity to make a fair profit.

We are responsible to our employees, the men and women who work with us throughout the world.

Everyone must be considered as an individual.

We must respect their dignity and recognize their merit.

They must have a sense of security in their jobs.

Compensation must be fair and adequate, and working conditions clean, orderly and safe.

Employees must feel free to make suggestions and complaints.

There must be equal opportunity for employment, development, and advancement for those qualified.

We must provide competent management, and their actions must be just and ethical.

We are responsible to the communities in which we live and work and to the world community as well.

We must be good citizens—support good works and charities and bear our fair share of taxes.

We must encourage civic improvements and better health and education.

We must maintain in good order the property we are privileged to use, protecting the environment and natural resources.

Our final responsibility is to our stockholders.

Business must make a sound profit.

We must experiment with new ideas.

Research must be carried on, innovative programs developed and mistakes paid for.

New equipment must be purchased, new facilities provided, and new products launched.

Reserves must be created to provide for adverse times.

When we operate according to these principles, the stockholder should realize a fair return.

know you will refrain from presenting seasonal gifts of a more personal nature to those of our organization you meet and work with. Actually, it's a policy based on our own feeling—which we know you share—that the best thing an organization like ours can do for the public is to deliver high quality service with the utmost efficiency and courtesy.[4]

Not only does this letter set high ethical standards, it spotlights the agency's commitment to quality.

Ethical behavior can also improve the organization's relations with the community, which tends to attract customers and top-notch employees. In addition,

SUPERVISION AND DIVERSITY

Denny's Is Still Trying

Denny's, the restaurant chain, has been in the process of remaking itself. In the early 1990s it was the defendant in several costly civil rights suits brought by African-American customers who charged it with blatant racial discrimination. As late as 1994, managers at some Denny's locations routinely barred black customers or required them to prepay their dinner checks. Only one of Denny's 512 franchise operations was owned by a member of a minority group. Minority suppliers got little if any of Denny's business.

Now, under a new management philosophy imposed by James Adamson, CEO of Denny's parent company, Advanttica, the company hopes that things are changing. Diversity training is mandatory, managers who show racism are fired, civil rights charges are monitored, and the number of complaints received is tracked and posted in the restaurants. Women and minorities represent nearly 25 percent of Denny's franchise owners, and 5 percent of Denny's corporate managers are black. Minority contracts soared, reaching nearly $80 million in 1996, up from almost nothing two years before. Managers' bonuses are tied to their record of diversity in hiring and promoting employees, and the company was ranked among the top 10 companies for minorities by *Fortune* magazine.

Nonetheless, there have been some lingering complaints, including a suit filed in early 1999 alleging discrimination at a Denny's restaurant in San Jose, California. Adamson remains confident that the corporate culture will change, however, because of "all the initiatives that have taken place, including training people in racial sensitivity [and] to understand how their actions are received by others."

But with $46 million already paid to customers who claimed racial discrimination in class-action suits and more suits pending, Denny's may still have a distance to go. The company was exonerated in a discrimination suit brought by Asian-American customers in New York, but it was recently forced to settle a case brought by the Justice Department in response to charges that the company requested excessive documentation from aliens applying for work in its stores. The managers of all 835 company-owned Denny's restaurants must be trained to work with the Immigration and Reform and Control Act of 1986, and almost $90,000 in civil penalties must be paid.

Sources: Jane Bokun, "Denny's Tries to Repair Image with TV Ads," *St. Petersburg Times*, March 8, 1998; David M. Herszenhorn, "Punitive Actions Are Advised in Discrimination at Denny's," *New York Times*, August 15, 1997, p. B4; "Denny's Serving All of America," special advertising section in *Fortune*, June 23, 1997; Nicole Harris, "A New Denny's—Diner by Diner," *Business Week*, March 25, 1996, pp. 166, 168; Reuter's News Service, January 12, 1999; Theodore Kinni, "The Denny's Story: How a Company in Crisis Resurrected Its Good Name," *Training*, Aug. 2000, pp. 74–76; "Denny's To Retrain Managers," *Times Union* (Albany), April 12, 2000, p. E1.

---

ethical behavior tends to reduce public pressure for government regulation—a situation that most managers would view as beneficial.

In contrast, the costs of unethical behavior can be high. Organizations whose employees are unethical may lose respect, customers, and qualified employees who are uncomfortable working in an environment that compromises their moral standards. Following the disclosure of a fraud and embezzlement scheme at Phar-Mor, a discount drugstore chain, top management was fired and the company entered bankruptcy. Rebuilding Phar-Mor involved slashing the number of employees by two-thirds and closing one-third of the stores.[5] See "Supervision and Diversity" for the effect of charges of racial discrimination against customers.

Unethical behavior has personal consequences as well. Federal employees who accept gifts that fall outside federal government regulations can be suspended, demoted, or even fired. The restrictions require that the gifts not be given as a result of the recipient's position or office and not come from a "prohibited source," such as a person or organization that does business with the employee's agency.[6] And MBA students at the University of Maryland know that even jail sentences can result from unethical acts. Before they graduate, the students travel to the Federal Correction Institute in Cumberland, Maryland, to meet white-collar executives and professionals like Gerard Evans, Monte Greenbaum, and Greg Gamble, all serving time for fraud or embezzlement. The careers and families of all three have suffered for their actions.[7]

On a more mundane level, a supervisor may simply find that tolerating lapses of ethics leads employees to behave in increasingly unacceptable ways. For example, if the supervisor looks the other way when employees take home small items like pencils or screws, employees may eventually start "borrowing" bigger items.

Challenges to Ethical Behavior

In spite of these implications, the restructurings, cutbacks, and layoffs of recent years have made ethical behavior harder to encourage. With greater responsibilities, supervisors and other managers in restructured or downsized organizations cannot monitor employees' day-to-day behavior.[8] At the same time, the uncertainty of the work environment has made many employees afraid of being ethical when doing so conflicts with other goals. Fudging numbers on performance records or producing shoddy merchandise to keep costs down is tempting, if the alternative is to be laid off for failing to meet cost or performance goals.

Other challenges arise from the supervisor's environment. In a recent national study of organizational integrity that polled nearly 2,400 workers, 76 percent said they had observed violations of the law or of company standards in the past 12 months, 61 percent thought their companies would not discipline workers guilty of an ethical breach, 57 percent believed management was unaware of the type of behavior that occurred within the company, and 38 percent actually thought management would authorize illegal or unethical conduct to meet business goals.[9]

Differing Measures of Ethical Behavior

Meeting high ethical standards is especially challenging for those who work with people from more than one culture because ethical standards and behavior can vary from one culture to another. A survey of expatriate managers (managers from other countries) ranked the levels of corruption in business in several Asian countries (see Figure 4.2). According to the survey, the biggest risk of operating in the most corrupt countries is shifts in the political winds. An organization that has dealt with a bureaucrat or government-controlled enterprise in an Asian country may become the object of suspicion if that person or organization falls out of favor. The risks are greatest if the organization is relatively small or the matters handled are routine and require contact with lower-level officials.[10]

One reason for perceived differences in corruption levels is that gift giving in the workplace can have different meanings from one culture to another. In the United States, the giving of gifts often is interpreted as bribery, an attempt to buy influence. However, in many parts of the world, giving a gift is the proper way to indicate one's gratitude toward and respect for the receiver. Furthermore, although bribery is a violation of U.S. law, it may not be in other countries, which have different legal standards. For example, bribes paid by Danish companies to foreign companies are tax-deductible business expenses.[11]

Cross-cultural gift giving and receiving can present sensitive issues, and it can be difficult for the supervisor to apply accepted U.S. standards to situations in international business or with employees and managers from different cultures. In

MEETING THE CHALLENGE

Is It Too Hard to Be Good?

American businesses struggle with ethics at home and abroad. Two researchers, Joseph Badaracco of the Harvard Business School and Allen Webb of the McKinsey consulting agency, conducted interviews with young businesspeople to learn about their attitudes toward ethics in business. The results were published in the *California Management Review*.

Many of the people interviewed believed that the companies they worked for interpreted "ethics" as turning in a good performance and remaining loyal to the company. Unethical behavior by managers was often overlooked in these companies, as long as the managers were successful. Two-thirds of the interviewees believed their organizations would not respect an employee who disclosed unethical behavior. "The ethical climate of an organization is extremely fragile," note Badaracco and Webb.

Does a clear code of ethics help? Not necessarily. Even some of the best-known and most respected organizations have fought some battles over ethics. Johnson & Johnson, whose code of ethics pledges that managers' actions "must be just and ethical," was lauded for its level-headed, responsible behavior during the crises caused when criminals laced bottles of the company's Tylenol pills with cyanide. But recently, Johnson & Johnson admitted that the company had shredded documents related to a federal probe of its marketing strategy for the drug Retin-A. The company will pay $7.5 million in fines and other costs. Prudential, which has a strict code of ethics directing employees "to strive to be the best at helping each of our customers achieve financial security and peace of mind," must now settle claims for its subsidiary, Prudential Securities, because of the subsidiary's improper sale of $8 billion of limited partnerships.

Another difficulty is the reality that supervisors are often caught in the middle. Young, idealistic employees may be able to afford blowing the whistle or quitting a job. Top managers may insulate themselves from these problems. But supervisors, who are partway up the career ladder and often have mortgages to pay and families to support, are more apt to remain loyal to the company's business purposes.

Finally, doing business abroad has its own set of challenges. Cheap labor in developing countries, along with differing sets of ethical standards in different countries, tend to cloud the issue.

But some American companies have begun to turn the trend around, even capitalizing on their reputations for ethical practices. Levi Strauss, Nike, and Cannondale are well known for their business ethics. In addition to adopting formal codes of ethics, some companies have ethics offices or ombudsmen that operate like watchdogs over procedures. Many business schools now require M.B.A. candidates to take courses in business ethics, and the federal government recently announced the establishment of a voluntary code of business ethics and workers' rights for U.S. companies that conduct business overseas. The code is supposed to designate "a worldwide standard for the conduct of American business."

Wrestling the ethics beast to the ground is not an easy task, but American businesses should try on a continual basis. Eventually, maybe they can tame it.

Source: "Good Grief," *The Economist*, April 8, 1995. Copyright © 1995 The Economist Newspaper Group, Inc. Reprinted with permission. Further reproduction prohibited. *www.economist.com*

Japan politeness requires a gift to be declined up to three times before it may be accepted, and it is never opened in front of the giver, to avoid showing any embarrassing disappointment. In Switzerland gifts should be small; craft gifts are preferred and are opened immediately. Among black and mixed-race communities in South Africa it is improper to present a gift with the left hand, and to avoid misinterpretation in Brazil, a man who gives a female subordinate a gift of a scarf or perfume should always say, "This is from my wife."[12]

Here are a few guidelines for successful gift giving in a multinational environment:

1. Avoid gifts and cards of a religious nature.
2. Make it clear that you intend the gift as a gift and not a bribe. Sometimes this will mean giving a group gift rather than an individual one.
3. Be aware of food preferences. Ham and pork are forbidden to Jews and Muslims, Hindus do not eat beef, and many Asians are lactose intolerant and do

■ FIGURE 4.2

**Ratings of
Corruption Levels in
11 Asian Countries**

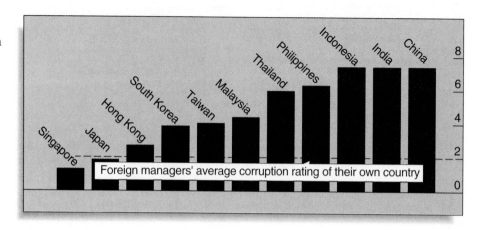

Source: From "Hard Graft in Asia," *The Economist*, May 27, 1995. Copyright © 1995 The Economist Newspaper Group, Inc. Reprinted with permission. Further reproduction prohibited. www.economist.com

    not eat cheese. In some countries gourmet popcorn would be insulting because corn is considered animal feed.

4. If you give liquor, consider the source. Many of the world's finest grapes are grown in France, Italy, and Argentina; it is hard to make a good impression there with a bottle of wine. And, of course, some cultures such as Muslim countries forbid the consumption of alcohol.

5. Consider the implications of luck in numbers. In Asian cultures some numbers are considered good luck and others bad. The numbers 4 and 9 are unlucky in Japan, while gifts in sets of 8 are welcomed. The number 4 is unlucky in China, while 1 is considered an ill omen in Taiwan.

6. Know the meanings of everyday objects. Leather goods are not acceptable among Hindus; the Chinese consider watches and clocks to be reminders of death. In Latin America and Asia, sharp objects such as knives and scissors symbolize the end of a relationship; handkerchiefs signal grief. Flowers have special meanings in many cultures as well.

7. Know how to give and receive. The U.S. custom of gleefully tearing the package open is not universal.[13]

    What can a supervisor do if refusing a gift might insult the giver? Most important, the supervisor must follow company policy, and in many cases that means turning down the gift. At the same time, however, the supervisor should explain carefully and politely the reason for not accepting the gift. If a supervisor has immigrant employees who might not understand U.S. views about gift giving, this might be an area about which to educate all employees before such a problem arises.

Ethical Behavior of Supervisors

If supervisors wish to see a high standard of ethical behavior in the workplace, they must behave ethically themselves. Supervisors in particular must exhibit important dimensions of ethical behavior including loyalty, fairness, and honesty (see Figure 4.3).

**Important
Dimensions of
Ethical Behavior
by Supervisors**

As a leader, a supervisor is expected to be loyal to the organization, to his or
her manager, and to his or her subordinates (see Chapter 8). When these loyalties
conflict, ethical dilemmas result. These loyalties also may at times come into conflict with the supervisor's self-interests. If supervisors are seen by others in the organization to put their own interests first, they will have difficulty earning the loyalty, trust, and respect of others.

Fairness is another important trait of a supervisor. Employees expect to be
treated evenhandedly. They resent it if the supervisor plays favorites or passes the
blame for mistakes on to them. Supervisors may find it harder to be fair—or to
convince others that they are fair—when they supervise their own relatives.
Therefore, supervisors may find it wise to avoid **nepotism,** the hiring of one's
own relatives. A related problem can arise when supervisors accept a gift from a
supplier or someone else who may wish to influence their judgment. Even if a supervisor is sure about remaining objective in the acceptance of cash, lavish entertainment, or other gifts, other people may question whether the supervisor can be
fair. When supervisors place themselves in such a position, management tends to
doubt their ability to exercise good judgment. See "Tips from the Firing Line" for
ways to deal with an unethical boss.

A recent survey of 30 graduates of Harvard Business School found that
most of them said they had been pressured by their bosses to do things they felt
were unethical or even illegal. One reported being told to exaggerate return-on-
investment figures, and another was told to make up data about a new product introduction. Such examples are especially disturbing because subordinates tend to
follow the instructions as well as the example of their supervisor. As Martha Clark
Gross, vice president of the consulting firm Booz Allen & Hamilton, Inc., reports,
"People almost always follow the example of the senior partners." At Booz Allen, a

**nepotism
The hiring of one's
relatives.**

What to Do When Your Boss Is Unethical

Management books and articles are full of advice to supervisors about how to deal with dishonest subordinates. But what do you do when your *boss* is a crook? The International Association of Administrative Professionals reports that most secretaries say they have witnessed lying, expense report fakery, and other forms of manipulation. But most people do nothing about such incidents, figuring that their job security is tied to their boss's fate.

There are some steps you should take, however, before your loyalty is put to a severe test.

1. Check on your boss's ethics before you sign on if possible. Tell the headhunter or each agency that you want to work for someone whose values meet the test of your behavioral standards.

2. Discuss ethical behavior early in your employment. Ask how to avoid inadvertently violating ethical standards or what to do if anything suspicious happens. Questions can get a conversation going in which you can feel out your employer's expectations.

3. Assume your boss is unaware that his or her actions are wrong. Express your concern that he or she may be exposed to the censure of others if matters go unchecked. This lets a crooked boss know you're aware of the dishonest behavior and gives an honest one a chance to correct the mistake.

4. Protect yourself with a paper trail. Politely ask in writing for an explanation of any unusual procedures or requests. Even if answers don't materialize, your concerns are on record.

5. Cut through vague language and euphemisms. Say, "Am I right that you want me to lie to this client?" Most employers will be forced to backpedal when faced with such directness.

6. If nothing else works, know where to go next. Your firm may have internal auditors, an ombudsman, or a legal department. If not, find your own attorney. Remember, you can be held personally responsible for undertaking actions you know to be wrong.

Source: "Coping with a Crooked Boss," *U.S. News & World Report,* September 28, 1998, p. 76.

rule called the "sunshine rule" discourages dishonesty by requiring employees to consider standing in front of the firm's partners to explain a business expense.[14]

Honesty includes several types of behavior by the supervisor. First, when employees make a suggestion or accomplish impressive results, the supervisor should be sure that the employees get the credit. Pretending that other people's accomplishments are your own is a type of dishonesty. So is using the company's resources for personal matters. For example, a supervisor who spends work time chatting with friends on the phone or who takes supplies home for personal use in effect is stealing what belongs to the organization. Furthermore, the supervisor is demonstrating that such behavior will be overlooked, thus encouraging employees to be equally dishonest. Finally, supervisors should be honest about what the organization can offer employees.

Making Ethical Decisions

Assuming that it is desirable to choose ethical behavior and to help employees do so, the challenge is to decide what action is ethical in a particular situation and then determine how to carry it out. There are no hard-and-fast rules for making ethical decisions. In some cases, two possibilities might seem equally ethical or unethical. Perhaps someone will get hurt no matter what the supervisor decides. Furthermore, as discussed earlier, people from different cultures may have different measures of ethical or unethical behavior.

■ FIGURE 4.4

Steps to Take When an Employee Is Suspected of Unethical Behavior

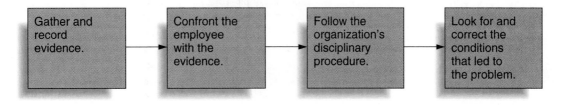

Sometimes, the supervisor can promote ethical decision making by involving others in the process. When the group discusses the issue, group members can discuss their perspective of the situation and the underlying values. Discussing the ethical implications of the decision can help the supervisor see consequences and options that he or she might not have thought of alone. (Chapter 9 provides further guidelines for group decision making.)

Deciding what behavior is ethical does not always end an ethical dilemma. Employees are sometimes afraid that doing what is morally right will cause their performance to suffer and may even cost them a job. While such decisions are never easy, sometimes good triumphs, as it did when Douglas D. Keeth reported fraudulent billing practices at the defense contracting firm where he worked, United Technologies Corporation. Keeth was given the option of keeping his job as division vice president of finance and was awarded $22.5 million by the U.S. government.[15]

Supervising Unethical Employees

It is tempting to ignore the unethical behavior of others, hoping they will change on their own. However, the problem usually gets worse as the unethical employee sees that he or she can get away with the behavior. Consequently, when the supervisor suspects that an employee is behaving unethically, the supervisor needs to take prompt action. The steps to take are summarized in Figure 4.4.

The first step is to gather and record evidence. The supervisor needs to be sure that unethical behavior is actually occurring. For example, if the supervisor suspects that one or more employees are padding their expense accounts, the supervisor regularly should review expense reports. As soon as the supervisor sees something that looks odd, he or she should ask the employee about it. After confronting the employee with the evidence, the supervisor should follow the organization's disciplinary procedure. (Discipline is discussed in Chapter 13.)

After dealing with the specific problem, the supervisor should try to understand what conditions contributed to this problem. That can help the supervisor avoid similar ethical lapses in the future. In analyzing why an employee has behaved unethically, consider whether you have created a climate for ethical behavior in the department. Have you set a good example through your own ethical behavior? Are the rewards for productivity so great that they tempt employees to cut ethical corners? Do the employees hear messages that say the organization cares only about achievements, such as, "I don't care how you get it done, just do it"? Martin Marietta's A. Thomas Young says, "If you expect honesty, you get honesty. If you don't, you get what you probably deserve."[16]

SUPERVISION ACROSS INDUSTRIES

The Printing Industry

Their Ink Is Green

In the St. Louis printing business his grandfather founded, Tim Alton is seeing his efforts to run a "green" shop pay off. Thanks to his many years of recycling paper and chemicals and using environmentally friendly inks, solvents, and paper, Alton's Murray Print Shop has won a top regional award from Choose Environmental Excellence. It counts the Missouri Botanical Garden and St. Louis University among its many steady customers.

In fact, word-of-mouth and repeat business is so high, the print shop needed no sales person to generate sales of $1.5 million in 2000. Being "green" has been good business for Murray Print Shop.

Alton, who owns the firm with his sister and brother, stands by his commitment to such "green" resources as soy-based (instead of oil-based) inks and recycled paper stock. Among his plans for further improvements to the shop's environmentally conscious

operations are large hoods over the presses and plate-cleaning areas to capture solvent fumes. "It's a matter of $50,000 to do it," says Alton, but the cost is justified when he thinks about his 18 employees. "People's health is more important than money," he feels. "A lot of our employees have been with us for a long time."

For Alton's nephew Jeremy, who works on one of the presses, upholding the family tradition of environmental responsibility will be a matter of following a well-established path. Managers and supervisors may find themselves in a similar position, or they may have opportunities to raise environmental standards through patience and a little cost-benefit analysis. For Murray Print Shop, it's profitable to be green.

Source: Repps Hudson, "Printing Business Learns that Being Green Can Pay Off," *St. Louis Post-Dispatch*, April 29, 2001, p. B1.

Treatment of Whistleblowers

whistleblower
Someone who exposes a violation of ethics or law.

Someone who exposes a violation of ethics or law is known as a **whistleblower.** Typically, a whistleblower brings the problem first to a manager in the organization. If management seems unresponsive, he or she then contacts a government agency, the media, or a private organization. In England, employees of any British firm can contact senior management anonymously through a free service at www.forensicaccounting.co.uk.

A whistleblower's report may be embarrassing as well as costly to the organization. Nevertheless, whistleblowers are protected by federal laws, the laws of several states, and some recent court decisions. For example, federal laws protect employees who make complaints pertaining to violations of antidiscrimination laws, environmental laws, and occupational health and safety standards. Thus, in general, employers may not retaliate against someone for reporting a violation. Suppose an employee files a complaint of sexual harassment; the organization may not react by firing the employee who complained.

In addition, under a Civil War–era law that was little used until the late 1980s, whistleblowers who report on companies that are cheating the government stand to receive up to 30 percent of whatever money the company ultimately pays as a penalty for the fraud. The number of cases filed under the False Claims Act jumped from 33 a year in 1987 to 533 in 1997, and the average award to the whistleblower has been around $1.2 million.[17]

In spite of these protections, whistleblowers often do suffer for going public with their complaints. Typically, the whistleblower is resented and rejected by co-workers, and the whistleblower may be demoted or terminated. Even when the courts agree that the whistleblower was treated unlawfully, it can take years for that person to be compensated by the organization or even appreciated by the public. Engineer Thomas D. Talcott quit Dow Corning in 1976 to protest what he saw as safety problems with the company's silicone breast implants.[18] Not until 15 years later did that issue receive widespread publicity. Talcott at least had the credentials to start a successful consulting business when he left his job, whereas many people would have a much harder time finding work. Because of these consequences—and out of fairness to one's employer—a would-be whistleblower should try to resolve problems within the organization before blowing the whistle.

One case of whistle blowing, which revealed the presence of devastating toxins in the groundwater of Hinkley, California and resulted in a $333 million lawsuit against Pacific Gas & Electric Company, was made famous in the 2000 Hollywood film named for the whistleblower, Erin Brockovich. The payment was the largest legal settlement in U.S. history and was made to more than 600 residents of the town of Hinkley.[19]

The supervisor's general attitude toward whistleblowing should be to discourage reports of wrongdoing when these are motivated simply by pettiness or a desire to get back at someone. Nevertheless, when someone does complain, the supervisor should investigate the complaint quickly and report what will be done. This lets employees know that their complaints are taken seriously and that the supervisor wants to handle them fairly and appropriately. The supervisor should bear in mind that the typical whistleblower is not simply a troublemaker but a person with high ideals and competence. Keeping communication flowing and responding to problems will allow the organization to find solutions without the costs and embarrassment of public disclosure. Finally, engaging in ethical behavior can eliminate the need for whistleblowing—and the other negative fallout of misconduct—in the first place.

Summary

4.1 Define ethics, and explain how organizations specify standards for ethical behavior.

Ethics refers to the principles by which people distinguish what is morally right. Organizations are particularly concerned about ethical behavior because modern technology has made the potential consequences of unethical behavior enormous. Recognizing the importance of preventing ethical lapses, many organizations have adopted a code of ethics. Codes of ethics provide guidelines for behavior and support top management's assertion that they care about ethical behavior.

4.2 Identify benefits of ethical behavior and challenges that make ethical behavior more difficult in the modern workplace.

To be known as an ethical organization is a satisfying way of maintaining a reputation for high standards. When customers, clients, and suppliers see that they are treated ethically, they are more likely to want to work cooperatively with the organization and to do their best for it. Ethical behavior can also improve community relations, attracting customers and qualified employees. Unethical behavior, on the other hand, can cause an organization to lose both respect and the best employees (who may be uncomfortable working for an unethical organization). Unethical behavior may even land employees and managers in jail, if they break the law.

An uncertain work environment can make ethical behavior harder to encourage. Fear of losing one's job can lead employees to cooperate with unethical activities sponsored by others, so it is important for supervisors to foster a climate that encourages ethical behavior.

4.3 Discuss the impact of cultural differences on ethical issues.

In some cases, ethical standards and behavior vary among cultures. The biggest risk of operating in the most corrupt countries is shifts in the political winds. One reason for perceived differences in levels of corruption is that gift giving in the workplace is interpreted differently from country to country. The supervisor should always follow company policy, but should do so carefully and politely in order not to offend members of another culture.

4.4 Describe major types of ethical behavior that supervisors should practice.

Supervisors should be loyal to the organization, their manager, and their subordinates. Supervisors should treat others, especially employees, fairly. Ways to dispel any doubts about one's fairness are to avoid nepotism and to decline gifts from suppliers and others seeking influence. Finally, supervisors should be honest, which includes giving subordinates credit for their accomplishments and avoiding personal use of the company's resources.

4.5 Outline ways to make ethical decisions.

There are no hard-and-fast rules for making ethical decisions, but asking some essential questions can help. The supervisor can promote ethical decision making by involving others in the thought process. Discussing the ethical implications of the decision can help the supervisor see consequences and options that he or she might not have thought of alone.

4.6 Provide guidelines for supervising unethical employees.

When the supervisor believes an employee is doing something unethical, the supervisor should take immediate action. First, the supervisor should gather and record evidence. Then the supervisor confronts the employee with the evidence and follows the organization's disciplinary procedure. After dealing with a specific problem, the supervisor should try to understand what conditions contributed to the problem and then seek to correct those conditions.

4.7 Define whistleblowers, and describe how the supervisor should treat such employees.

Whistleblowers are people who expose a violation of ethics or law. They are protected from retaliation by federal and state laws as well as recent court decisions. The supervisor should discourage reports of wrongdoing when they are motivated simply by pettiness or a desire for revenge. However, when someone does complain, the supervisor should quickly investigate the complaint and report what will be done. This lets employees know that their complaints are taken seriously. Keeping communication flowing and responding to problems ultimately allows the organization to find its own solutions.

Key Terms

ethics, p. 89	nepotism, p. 95	whistleblower, p. 98
code of ethics, p. 89		

Review and Discussion Questions

1. What are some of the benefits of ethical behavior? What are some of the challenges to ethical behavior?
2. Gift giving in the workplace is interpreted differently from culture to culture. What can a supervisor do if his or her company prohibits accepting gifts but a customer from another culture insists on offering one?
3. In what ways can loyalty create conflict for a supervisor?
4. In what ways should a supervisor practice honesty in the workplace?

5. In each of the following situations, what would have been the ethical thing for the employee or supervisor to do? What criteria did you use to decide? What would you have done in that situation? Why?
   a. Upon being hired, a new employee offers his supervisor confidential information about his former employer's marketing plan for a new product. The two companies have competing product lines.
   b. The associate editor of a magazine learns that a particularly newsworthy individual

wants to be paid to grant an interview with the magazine. The magazine's policy is never to pay for interviews, but the editor knows she could "bury" the expense elsewhere in her budget. She desperately wants the story; she knows it will be good for both the magazine and her career.

6. Devon Price supervises a crew of maintenance workers. One day a secretary at the company took him aside and asked, "Do you know that Pete [a member of the crew] has been taking home supplies like nails and tape to work on personal projects?" What should Devon do?

7. Assume that Pete, the maintenance worker in question 6, was discovered pilfering supplies and was disciplined. Upset, he decides to act

on some safety problems he has observed and complained about, and he reports them to the local office of the Occupational Safety and Health Administration (OSHA). When Devon, Pete's supervisor, finds out that the department will be investigated by OSHA, he is furious. It seems as though Pete is nothing but a troublemaker. What should Devon do?

A SECOND LOOK

Do you feel Hanna Andersson's internal policies are as ethical as its socially responsible attitudes toward those outside the firm? Why or why not?

SKILLS MODULE

CASE

Lawyers, Ford, and Firestone: Who's To Blame?

One of the country's top traffic-safety consulting firms, Strategic Safety, identified 30 cases of Firestone tire failure on Ford Explorers in 1996, after Texas lawyers bringing suits against Bridgestone and Firestone retained the company's services. Although a few of these cases had resulted in deaths, Strategic Safety and the lawyers passed on several opportunities to tell the National Highway Traffic Safety Administration (NHTSA) about them. Sean Kane, a partner in Strategic Safety, says lawyers were "very leery" of letting the government know, lest an investigation find nothing wrong and the firm's pending individual lawsuits be compromised. "You don't want to be tipping your hand to the defendants," Kane said, who later also claimed that he had tried to alert the media with information he had gotten from NHTSA's own database.

After 1996, however, more problems with Firestone tires surfaced, particularly in Texas where prolonged high-speed driving in hot weather contributes to deadly tread separation in the tires. Kane disclosed in July 2000 that Ford was recalling Firestone tires in Venezuela, and the resulting pressure forced a similar recall in the United States. Firestone recalled 6.5 million tires in the fall of 2000, all of which had been sold to Ford Motor Company for its Ford Explorer sport utility vehicle, and it was revealed that accidents related to the Explorer were responsible for 203 deaths in the United States, all but 13 of them occurring after 1996.

Ford claims the tires were flawed and voluntarily recalled 13 million more of them, giving drivers free replacements. Firestone countered with data that it claims show the design of the Explorer to be fatally flawed. It says, for instance, that tread separations occur 10 times as often on the Explorer as they do on the Ford Ranger pickup, which uses the same tires and the same chassis. The National Highway Traffic Safety Administration has fallen behind in its investigation for lack of funding and has yet to investigate Firestone's claims about the Explorer's design. Meanwhile, victims' lawyers say that Ford and Firestone knew more than anyone else about the reasons for the accidents but kept everyone in the dark.

While it does seem clear that, as former NHTSA administrator Joan Claybrook says, "For some reason, a Firestone tire on a Ford Explorer is a deadly combination," it appears it will be a long time before the truth is finally known.

1. Do you think anyone involved in the Ford-Firestone case acted unethically? Why or why not?
2. If there had been a whistleblower early on in the situation, do you think the problem would have grown as large as it did? Why or why not?
3. What do you think will be the ultimate costs to Ford, Firestone, Strategic Safety, and the NHTSA?

Sources: Joann Muller and Nicole St. Pierre, "Ford vs. Firestone: A Corporate Whodunit," *Business Week*, June 11, 2001, pp. 46–47; Keith Bradsher, "Lawyers Hid Tire Failures from Agency Attorneys," *Denver Post*, June 24, 2001, p. A1; James Cox and Jayne O'Donnell, "Consultant Denies Withholding Ford/Firestone Accident Data," *USA Today*, June 25, 2001, p. B2.

How Ethical Is Your Behavior?

Below are the actual questions posed in a recent survey of 1,300 workers who said they had engaged in unethical activities. Check those you would do or consider doing, and rate yourself using your own values (there is no score!). If you wish, you can compare your standards to those of the respondents at the end.

1. _____ Cut corners on quality control.
2. _____ Covered up incidents.
3. _____ Abused or lied about sick days.
4. _____ Lied to or deceived customers.
5. _____ Put inappropriate pressure on others.
6. _____ Falsified numbers or reports.
7. _____ Dismissed or promoted an employee unfairly.
8. _____ Lied to or deceived superiors on serious matters.
9. _____ Withheld important information.
10. _____ Misused or stole company property.
11. _____ Engaged in or overlooked environmental infractions.
12. _____ Took credit for someone's work or idea.
13. _____ Discriminated against a co-worker.
14. _____ Abused drugs or alcohol.
15. _____ Engaged in copyright or software infringement.
16. _____ Lied to or deceived subordinates on serious matters.
17. _____ Overlooked or paid or accepted bribes.
18. _____ Had extramarital affair with business associate.
19. _____ Abused an expense account.
20. _____ Abused or leaked proprietary information.
21. _____ Forged name without person's knowledge.
22. _____ Accepted inappropriate gifts or services.
23. _____ Filed false regulatory or government reports.
24. _____ Engaged in insider trading.

Percent of original respondents who admitted to each infraction: (1) 16%, (2) 13%, (3) 11%, (4) 9%, (5) 7%, (6) 6%, (7) 6%, (8) 5%, (9) 5%, (10) 4%, (11) 4%, (12) 4%, (13) 4%, (14) 4%, (15) 3%, (16) 3%, (17) 3%, (18) 3%, (19) 2%, (20) 2%, (21) 2%, (22) 1%, (23) 1%, (24) 1%.

Source: From Henry Fountain, "Of White Lies and Yellow Pads," *New York Times*, July 6, 1997. Copyright © 1997 The New York Times. Reprinted with permission.

Class Exercise

Each student completes the survey in Figure 4.5 anonymously, circling all the answers that apply. The instructor tabulates the results and distributes them for discussion at the next class session.

For each item in the survey, the class discusses the following questions:

- Which answer or answers were selected by most students?
- What is the justification for the answers selected?

- If you were the supervisor of an employee who acted in this way, how would you respond (assuming that you observed the behavior)?
- If your supervisor learned that you had acted in the way indicated by the survey response, how do you think your career would be affected?

Source: This exercise is based on a suggestion submitted by James Mulvihill, Mankato, MN.

Team-Building Exercise

Making Ethical Choices

Ethical issues are seldom clear-cut. Form small groups and consider the following scenarios. Although there will be disagreement, choose the action your group most strongly supports, and compare your decisions with those of the other groups. Be prepared to defend your choices.

1. You believe your company is overcharging a client. Do you:
   a. Report the fraud to the Justice Department, which will keep your complaint confidential and award you a percentage of any money recovered.
   b. Keep the matter within the company, going up the chain of command until you find someone who's not involved and is willing to take action.
   c. Discuss the matter with your company's corporate ethics or human resources staff.
2. You become aware of a case of sexual harassment. Do you:
   a. Report your concerns to the Equal Employment Opportunity Commission and get their advice.

   b. Intervene carefully and go to the suspected victim first and ask whether you can help. If so, go to officials within the company.
   c. Assume that with today's heightened awareness of sexual harassment the victim will know what to do without your help.
3. An employee is taking home inventory or equipment, or padding his or her time sheet. Do you:
   a. Report the matter to a company official.
   b. Report the matter to your local law enforcement agency.
   c. Ignore the matter, since the monetary value of the items is small and you fear creating an unpleasant atmosphere of suspicion if you overreact.

Source: Adapted from Geanne Rosenberg, "Truth and Consequences," *Working Woman*, July–August 1998, pp. 79–80.

■ FIGURE 4.5

Survey for Class

Exercise

Which of the following actions would you take?

Circle the letters of as many choices as apply to you.

1. Put false information in your résumé:
   a. If necessary to get a job.
   b. Only about minor details.
   c. If most people are doing it.
   d. Never.

2. Tell a competing company secrets about your employer's product or procedures:
   a. To land a job with the competitor.
   b. In exchange for $100.
   c. In exchange for $1 million.
   d. Never.

3. Cheat on a test used as the basis for promotion:
   a. If you have a family to support.
   b. If you think the test is unfair.
   c. If your co-workers are doing it.
   d. Never.

4. Use the office copier:
   a. To make a copy of your dentist's bill.
   b. To make six copies of a report that is related to charitable work you do.
   c. To make 50 copies of your résumé.
   d. Never.

5. Pad your expense account for a business trip:
   a. If you believe you are underpaid.
   b. Only for small amounts that the employer won't miss.
   c. Only when you are experiencing financial problems.
   d. Never.

6. Call in sick when you aren't sick:
   a. If you're worn out from working on a big project.
   b. If your child is sick.
   c. If you need to recover from the weekend.
   d. Never.

7. Lie about your supervisor's whereabouts when he or she takes a long, liquid lunch:
   a. Only if specifically instructed to do so.
   b. If the supervisor gives you a generous raise in return.
   c. Only when the person asking is your supervisor's superior.
   d. Never.

5

Being black is never incidental. It's central to who I am.
—Dr. Joyce F. Brown, president, Fashion Institute of Technology

Managing Diversity

■ CHAPTER OUTLINE

What Is Diversity?

A Look at Our Diversity

Challenges to Working in a Diverse Society
Prejudice and Discrimination
Stereotypes
Sexism
Ageism

Implications for the Supervisor
Advantages of Diversity
Communication
Diversity Training
Legal Issues

■ LEARNING OBJECTIVES

After you have studied this chapter, you should be able to:

5.1 Define diversity.

5.2 Discuss how the U.S. workforce is changing and its impact on the supervisor.

5.3 Differentiate between prejudice, discrimination, and stereotypes in the workplace.

5.4 Explain how sexism and ageism are barriers to diversity, and how supervisors can be more aware of them.

5.5 Describe some ways to communicate more effectively in the diverse workplace.

5.6 Describe the goals of diversity training.

5.7 List the most important recent legislation affecting diversity and its provisions.

■ DIVERSIFICATION UNDER FIRE

New York City's Fire Department (FDNY) has a force 11,334 members strong that is nearly 94 percent white and almost entirely male. So it would seem that a new program designed to attract minority and female recruits to its ranks would be an unqualified good thing. But the story of the FDNY's new Cadet Program shows just how difficult it is to devise a diversity program that everyone will welcome.

The department's December 2000 graduating class was the first to include participants in the program, which allowed candidates who underwent long and intensive instruction and training as emergency medical technicians to enter the fire academy with lower written and physical scores than the firefighter's job usually requires. The class was 2.9 percent Asian, 10.7 percent black, 14.3 percent Hispanic, and 1.4 percent female.

But because the Cadet Program is actually open to anyone, only 60 percent of entrants have been women or minority group members, and some critics contend that the remaining 40 percent of white males is a high enough proportion to prevent the program from realizing its goals. Another possible flaw in the program, detractors say, is that those whites who have benefited from its admissions policy are sons and close relatives of high-ranking supervisors in the department and the firefighters' union.

The union, for its part, opposes the Cadet Program on the grounds that it relaxes standards and increases the dangers of the job. Says Uniformed Firefighters Association president Kevin Gallagher, "We have a hundred-year history of the merit system. This job is too dangerous a job to be lowering standards in order to address the diversity issue."

But the Fire Department remains proud of the program. Says Commission Thomas Von Essen, "This is a terrific program which has helped provide us with the largest percentage of minorities we've ever had. If we could duplicate this once a year, we would go a long way towards bringing greater diversification to the ranks."

Source: Elissa Gootman, "Effort to Diversify Fire Department Bears Fruit, While Drawing Criticism," *New York Times*, November 16, 2000, pp. B1, B6.

What Is Diversity?

The New York City Fire Department's diversity efforts may be controversial, but they reflect a growing awareness of diversity in the workplace. Dealing successfully with cultural, ethnic, age, gender, and racial diversity is a lifelong process for most of us. However, being ready to work successfully in a multicultural environment is a goal supervisors can set immediately and work toward in every business encounter.

Our understanding of cultural diversity has matured in recent decades. The old "melting-pot" model, in which immigrants were expected to assimilate their

diversity
Characteristics of individuals that shape their identities and the experiences they have in society.

language and culture into the mainstream, has long since been left behind. The view today is that our diversity is our strength. We define **diversity** as the characteristics of individuals that shape their identities and the experiences they have in society.[1] Visible reminders and celebrations of our diverse heritage, such as Martin Luther King, Jr., Day and Gay Pride celebrations, enrich and renew our society and our culture. Ensuring diversity within an organization offers supervisors the opportunity to make the best fit between the employee and the job, allowing varied points of view to be aired and improving decision making. Many forms of discrimination, in hiring and elsewhere in business practice, are illegal in the United States. Yet even if they were not, ethical considerations would encourage the supervisor to seek many kinds of diversity within his or her department or team.

Businesses and governments too are striving to acknowledge diversity in their communications and interactions with citizens, employees, and customers. In Oregon, for example, an appeals court recently ruled that the state constitution gives homosexual government employees the right to health and life insurance benefits for their life partners, making Oregon the first state to issue such a decision.[2] Vermont recently became the first state to recognize civil unions for gay partners, but businesses such as Boeing, Citigroup, Cummins Engine, Deloitte Touche, General Mills, Goldman Sachs, Motorola, Nationwide Insurance, Prudential, SAIC, Texas Instruments, and U.S. Bancorp have led the way in offering benefits to unmarried domestic partners of either gender.[3]

A Look at Our Diversity

The face of the United States is changing. This process is not new; the country was built on the concept of diversity as waves of immigrants and homesteaders arrived on its shores. Today, however, we recognize both subtle and obvious differences among employees at every organizational level. These differences call upon all the supervisor's management skills.

As recently as 1980 white men accounted for half of U.S. workers. Today, the number of white women in the workforce has risen to nearly 40 percent, women-owned businesses are growing, and, the proportion of women and minorities in the workforce is expected to rise to over 80 percent soon. Mothers of young children in particular have entered the workforce as a permanent contingent, at a rate that shows no sign of slowing down. The workforce is expected to continue to age as well, as some older workers postpone retirement to continue working and as the first wave of the large generation commonly called "baby boomers" (those born between 1946 and 1964) reaches their 50s and 60s. The proportions of African Americans, Asian Americans, and Hispanics in the U.S. population and workforce are rising gradually and are expected to continue to do so.[4] This is confirmed in recent Bureau of Labor *Statistics.*[5] These changes at work reflect overall trends in the U.S. population and were reflected in a report prepared for the U.S. Department of Labor called *Workforce 2020: Work and Workers for the Twenty-First Century* (see Figure 5.1). Supervisors will deal with older workers, telecommuters, flextime scheduling, ethnic holidays, and many other reflections of diversity that affect day-to-day operations in the workplace.

Other kinds of changes are occurring, although on a smaller scale. Advances in technology, such as voice synthesis and Braille software for visually impaired computer users, can bring more disabled into the workforce, with their valuable skills and insights, though the employment rate of disabled men and women fell

■ FIGURE 5.1

Composition of the American Workforce, by Ethnic Group, Percent, 1995–2020 (Projected)

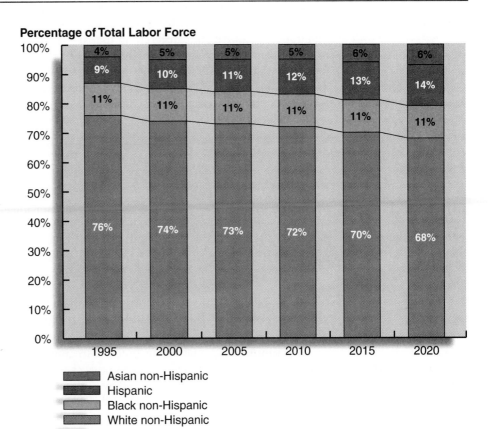

Percentage of Total Labor Force

	1995	2000	2005	2010	2015	2020
Asian non-Hispanic	4%	5%	5%	5%	6%	6%
Hispanic	9%	10%	11%	12%	13%	14%
Black non-Hispanic	11%	11%	11%	11%	11%	11%
White non-Hispanic	76%	74%	73%	72%	70%	68%

Asian non-Hispanic
Hispanic
Black non-Hispanic
White non-Hispanic

Sources: Bureau of Labor Statistics projections to 2005, Hudson Institute projections 2010–2020; Richard W. Judy and Carol D'Amico, *Workforce 2020: Work and Workers in the 21st Century* (Indianapolis, IN: Hudson Institute, 1997).

steadily from 1989 to 1999.[6] The shifting fortunes of various regions in the United States, such as the so-called Rust Belt and California's famed Silicon Valley, draw workers to and from those areas in steady internal migrations. Events around the world, such as the breakup of the Soviet Union and the political and economic struggles of emerging nations, lead highly trained and sophisticated technical workers in many fields to the United States in search of employment. All these factors combine to raise the level of diversity that supervisors find in the workplace, and to increase opportunities to build a strong and flexible team.

Challenges to Working in a Diverse Society

corporate culture
Beliefs and norms that govern organizational behavior in a firm.

These trends are changing the way business firms operate. Supervisors today need new skills to communicate and collaborate effectively with a broader range of people. More generally, however, awareness of differences of all kinds is creating changes in the way firms go about selecting, training, and motivating employees. It can also have a profound impact on the **corporate culture,** or those beliefs and norms that govern organizational behavior in a firm.

Even within the company, differences can flourish between one location and another. At US Interactive, for instance, work hours, office decor, and even communication styles are quite different in the New York City office from what workers experience in the suburban environment of the firm's Malvern, Pennsylvania, location only about 100 miles away. With the support of its supervisors, this firm has had to make special efforts, including an interactive website and quarterly sales meetings, to improve communication between its offices and help employees work successfully around their differences. This is just one way in which firms can benefit from its diversity.[7]

Prejudice and Discrimination

prejudice
A preconceived judgment about an individual or group of people.

Prejudice, or a preconceived judgment about an individual or group of people, is a sometimes subtle force. Obviously, we don't always recognize our own prejudices for what they are, even when they are affecting our behavior. For instance, a supervisor with a position to fill, who assumes that a female job applicant could not make sales calls at night, that an older worker is not as physically strong as a younger one, or that a working parent will abuse sick day privileges, is making judgments on the basis of prejudice. When those judgments motivate business decisions relating to hiring, appraisal, and promotion, they can be construed as discrimination.

discrimination
Unfair or inequitable treatment based on prejudice.

Discrimination, unfair or inequitable treatment based on prejudice, is prohibited by law, as we will discuss later in this chapter. The United States has been a nation of immigrants from its founding, although it has also borne a history of slavery. But the principles of religious and civic freedom extend deep into the U.S. legal system, beginning with the Constitution (1787), the Emancipation Proclamation (1862–1863), and continuing to the influential Civil Rights Act of 1964 and its later updates, and the Americans with Disabilities Act (1990). Specifically, Title VII of the Civil Rights Act of 1964 makes it illegal for an employer to discriminate on the basis of race, color, gender, religion, or national origin in making decisions regarding hiring, firing, training, discipline, compensation, benefits, classifications, or other terms or conditions of employment.

The effects of discrimination are divisive to a firm as well as illegal. If a supervisor treats employees unfairly for any reason, the outcome is never a positive one. Such treatment becomes widely known among employees, lowers morale and trust, and can eventually affect productivity. It often becomes the responsibility of the supervisor to guard against such disparate treatment. Some types of discrimination are more obvious than others, and some are more easily countered than others. An important first step for any supervisor is to know and acknowledge his or her own prejudices. Once recognized, prejudices can be countered or even eliminated.

While it is all too easy to think that our past experiences with members of different ethnic, racial, or religious groups can be applied to those subordinates and co-workers we may meet in the future, generally they cannot. Believing they can is the source of prejudice. If, for instance, you assign workloads or responsibilities differently because you feel that "blacks have trouble keeping jobs" or "teenagers are unreliable," you are letting your prejudices control your business decisions. Aside from the ethical and legal problems of such beliefs, they can lead supervisors to make less than optimal use of a firm's resources and to abuse the trust the firm has placed in them.

Stereotypes

Supervisors need to be aware of the many distinctions between U.S. culture and behavior and the norms of other countries. For example, the thumbs-up gesture in the United States is understood to mean OK or "all clear." In Iran, however, it is considered obscene. Bowing indicates respect in Japan, where smiling and nodding, important cultural expressions of politeness, do not necessarily signify agreement. In the United States, bowing is unknown, and when someone smiles and nods we generally assume they concur with our statements.

Even time has a different value in certain cultures. In some cultures, it is considered rude or careless to act quickly in a business situation. The speed at which people speak, and the number of times they consider it proper to repeat themselves, can also vary from culture to culture. In the United States, businesses that operate 24 hours a day are common. In France, it took an act of legislation to allow such businesses as Swatch and the Gap to keep their doors open 24 hours a day, 7 days a week.[8]

stereotypes
Generalized, fixed
images of others.

What matters in dealing with racial and cultural differences is avoiding **stereotypes,** or generalized, fixed images of others. In other words, supervisors must always guard against generalizing what they believe or observe about a culture and using that to unfairly classify its members. Imagine, for instance, how you would respond to an employee or supervisor who said, "All Americans are aggressive and loud." Yet without much effort you can probably think of similar negative statements you have heard about blacks, gays, elderly people, or the physically handicapped. Such stereotypes, usually based on false or incomplete information, prevent us from seeing people as individuals and treating them accordingly. Knowing that the Japanese revere their elders, for instance, or that Hispanic cultures are centered around the family, may enable a supervisor to understand why special tact is needed when delegating work to an older Japanese employee or why a Dominican worker might require time off during a parent's illness. It does not justify drawing erroneous conclusions based on stereotypes. While avoiding stereotypes may take some effort, it is well repaid in improved interpersonal relationships and successful supervision of a diverse team.

One communication expert offers two reasons why stereotypes may persist despite our realization that they are inaccurate.[9] First, we tend to think they are helpful shortcuts to forming opinions; second, we sometimes find it comforting to think we know what people are like without taking the time to get to know them in their real complexity. Supervisors should be aware of the pitfalls of relying on stereotypes, particularly commonly held assumptions about racial and cultural differences, and work to overcome them. Remaining aware that such stereotypes are outdated, and that they can lead us into offensive behavior patterns, is an important first step toward removing them.

Sexism

To take over the management of its Saturn division, General Motors was looking for someone with a particular kind of experience that few of its managers have. One candidate had spent most of the last 20 years working in transmission and engine factories and a foundry—the grittiest and most dangerous workplaces in the macho auto industry. GM made her an offer, and on January 1, 1999, Cynthia Mary Trudell became the first woman to head a car division for any U.S. or foreign automaker.[10]

This story may surprise you, but it shouldn't. Women have long been a growing factor in the labor force, and their participation has changed the workplace in

The Airline Industry

Diversity Makes a Mark at Continental Airlines

The financial turnaround of Continental Airlines in the late 1990s was due in large part, observers say, to its strong commitment to diversity at every level of the firm.

An aggressive program of hiring, training, and retaining minorities has brought the firm not only 23 percent of its managers and 37 percent of its employees, but also several years of profits and double-digit growth. A leader in recruiting and retaining Hispanics, who make up a large proportion of the population around the company's Houston, Texas, hub, Continental has also hired record numbers of crew members who speak French or Japanese and is increasing its efforts to attract African-American pilots and attendants.

Once a diverse employee pool is on board, however, the manager or supervisor's job is not over. "Many groups are uncomfortable and insecure with diversity initiatives," says Stephen Klineberg, a professor at Rice University who conducts a yearly demographic study of the Houston area. "But companies must recognize the points of view of people from all ethnic groups in order to find balance and succeed."

Some of the ways in which Continental has sought that balance is through programs designed to encourage teamwork among employees from many cultures. Supervisors play a major role in making diversity successful at the work-team level by supporting the company's goals and modeling acceptance of differences. One program that has been a big success rewards team efforts at Continental by giving each employee $65 every month the carrier ranks among the top three airlines nationwide for on-time arrivals. Says Pat Bissonnet, the airline's director of diversity and fair employment practices, "Employees tell us these programs have driven home the importance of looking at the person next to you as a team member, regardless of their ethnicity or lifestyle." With new diversity programs always in the works at Continental, management counts on its supervisors to help make each a success.

Continental's commitment to diversity extends from CEO Gordon Bethune through all the ranks and areas of the company. And word is getting around. The airline ranks 18th on *Fortune's* list of the "100 Best Companies to Work For," has repeatedly appeared on *Hispanic Business's* list of best places to work for Latinos, and was *Air Transport World's* Airline of the Year for 2001.

Source: Kate Fitzgerald, "Diversity Turns Airline Around," *Advertising Age*, February 19, 2001, pp. S6–S7.

sexism
Discrimination based on gender stereotypes.

many ways. **Sexism,** or discrimination based on gender stereotypes, is a barrier to diversity that many employers have taken steps to combat and prevent. Whether sexist language, sexual harassment, or discrimination against gays or lesbians, sexism challenges the supervisor's efforts to ensure a fair and harmonious work environment.

More women head companies and divisions than ever before, and female entrepreneurs are making a strong mark on U.S. business (see Figure 5.2). Cross-Worlds Software, Pearson PLC, the AFL-CIO, Digital City, Coopers & Lybrand, NFL Properties, Motorola, Hewlett-Packard, Netscape, Pitney Bowes, Lucent Technologies, and Mattel, among many others, join GM in having female CEOs or heads of divisions. Many firms are developing flextime and work-at-home policies that make it easier for all workers—but particularly women, still the traditional care givers for children and elderly relatives—to blend work and family responsibilities. Yet the number of single fathers with primary custody of their children has risen 50 percent from 1990 to 2000, making up at least one-sixth of the nation's single parents, or about two million people whose special needs society, and employers, may be slow to recognize.[11] Sometimes benefits can backfire. See "Tips from the Firing line" for ways to ease conflicts over family-friendly policies.

Subtle use of language, such as the word "chairman" applied to a woman or "stewardess" instead of the gender-neutral "flight attendant," is a form of sexism

■ FIGURE 5.2

Growth among Women-Owned Firms in the United States, 1987–1999

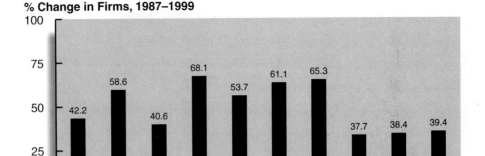

% Change in Firms, 1987–1999

TCPU = transportation/communications/public utilities.
FIRE = finance insurance/real estate.
W/R Trade = wholesale/retail.

Source: Data from Center for Women's Business Research, Washington, DC.

that conscientious supervisors can most readily overcome. More obvious sexism, such as passing over a woman for a physically demanding job, asking a pregnant job applicant about child care arrangements, or denying a promotion to a qualified woman, raises legal and ethical questions that a supervisor would have difficulty answering. Such actions are rarely, if ever, justified, although the difficulty women and minorities have experienced in rising through the corporate ranks is well-enough documented to be given a name. The "glass ceiling" refers to a certain level of responsibility to which many qualified applicants find themselves rising, and then no higher, despite their ability and willingness to contribute further to the goals of the firm. Changes for the better are taking place every day, but much progress remains to be made.

sexual harassment
Unwanted sexual attentions, including language, behavior, or the display of images.

The most blatant form of sexism is **sexual harassment,** defined as unwanted sexual attentions, including language, behavior, or the display of images. Offenses have ranged from sexual jokes and displays of explicit pictures in the workplace to touching, sexual advances, and requests for sexual favors. While women have been the victims and men the aggressors in most cases of sexual harassment, that need not be the case. In any event, sexual harassment is illegal, and experts advise supervisors to adopt a policy of "zero tolerance," to take any complaints seriously, and to investigate them at once.

Ageism

Your chances of someday supervising older workers are fairly high. The newest report from the Hudson Institute, *Workforce 2020*, projects that by 2020 almost 20 percent of the U.S. population will be age 65 or older.[12] And while *Business*

Balancing Needs of Parents and Nonparents in the Workplace

Many employers are creating new options at work to allow parents to better balance the needs of their families and their jobs. Flex-time, job sharing, on-site day care, sick days that apply to the worker's children or aging parents, and telecommuting are just some of the many ways in which firms try to help employees manage the stress of working and being a parent. Single parents especially benefit from, and welcome, such flexibility.

But these options have had an unintended effect in some workplaces. They have created tension among nonparents who feel that their needs are unmet or their value to the company is underestimated. Those who must pitch in to cover for absent colleagues attending a school play or taking long vacations during school holidays can become impatient and create as many problems for the supervisor as parents who must come in late, leave early, or miss work more frequently than others.

Here are some ways to ensure that your parent and nonparent employees can work together in harmony.

1. Avoid taking sides if a dispute arises. Be fair and emphasize the positive contributions of all your staff.
2. Don't let anyone fume or shout; insist on keeping discussions calm and cordial.
3. Suggest that parents take home paperwork, for example, to make up for the workload their colleagues shoulder during weekends and school holidays.

4. Remind everyone that performance is judged on results, not on the number of hours worked or missed.
5. Make sure you have looked into all possibilities for flexible work arrangements, and if possible extend them equitably to all members of your department, parents and nonparents alike. (Remember that nonparents may have family members other than children to care for, and consider substituting a "personal leave" policy for "maternity" or "paternity" leave.)
6. Lobby for on-site day care if it will ease the burden on members of your team.
7. Defend your company's family-friendly policies as essential to the organization's commitment to the community at large, and not as special treatment for parents.
8. Plan work-related social events that include the families of employees. Giving people a chance to know one another's children, parents, and other relatives can go a long way toward increasing acceptance of worker's special needs.
9. Remember that conflicts about benefits like these should not have winners and losers. Work to minimize conflict and maximize cooperation; then everyone wins.

Source: From Robert D. Ramsey, "Easing Tensions Between Parent and Non-Parent Employees," *Supervision*, November 2001. Reprinted by permission of © National Research Bureau, 320 Valley Street, Burlington, Iowa 52601.

Week recently reported that some older men are leaving the workforce earlier than ever, most of them still want to work part time or handle special projects.[13] But a recent survey of 35- to 60-year-old men and women job seekers found that the older they were, the fewer interviews they got and the longer it took them to find a job.[14] "It's a young person's industry," said Margit Gerow of the software business in Seattle, where she is trying to find a new job since being laid off. "I stick out like a sore thumb because I'm over 60. But I'm a national resource, like iron. And I think I'm worth mining for a bit."[15] Does **ageism,** discrimination based on age, prevent workers from finding opportunities?

ageism
Discrimination based on age.

As the baby-boomer generation begins to age, and as improvements in health care and nutrition allow for longer and healthier lives, older workers (both men and women) are sure to become a more common sight. The Age Discrimination in Employment Act (1967) makes it illegal to fail to hire, or to fire, based on age. When inexperienced younger workers are given preference over equally or better-

■ FIGURE 5.3

**Percentage of
People over Age 65
in the United States,
1946–2030**

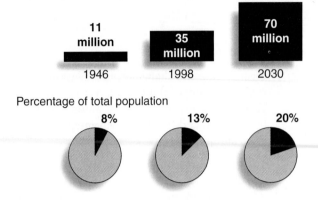

The number of Americans over 65, actual and projected, from the
beginning of the baby boom through the boomers' retirement.

11 million	35 million	70 million
1946	1998	2030

Percentage of total population

8%   13%   20%

Source: From *New York Times*, November 29, 1998. Copyright © 1998 The New York Times.
Reprinted with permission.

**bona fide occupational
qualification (BFOQ)
An objective
characteristic required
for an individual to
perform a job properly.**

qualified elders, or when downsizing lets disproportionately more older (and often better-paid) workers go, ageism costs the organization the benefit of experience, perspective, and judgment that senior workers can bring. John Renner, a psychologist with Hagberg Consulting Group, says the firm's collected data on 4,000 executives shows that while willingness to take risks declines after about 40, patience, a key management trait, doesn't blossom until after the age of 45, while open-mindedness and teamwork are abilities that actually increase with age.[16]

In a few rare cases, such as the Federal Aviation Agency's limit of 64 years of age for airline pilots or acting roles that call for persons of very young or very advanced age, age can be shown to be what is called a **bona fide occupational qualification (BFOQ),** an objective characteristic required for individual to perform a job properly. In all other cases, experts suggest that supervisors beware of making decisions based on assumptions about age, such as that older employees are less physically capable or have failing eyesight that prevents them from performing well on the job. Tests that measure proven job qualifications, such as a vision test, can ensure that age is not being used as a discriminator and that valuable workers are not being overlooked or lost.

There is no longer a mandatory age for retirement, and many workers find it economically necessary to continue their careers. It is estimated that 20 percent of the population will be over 65 by 2030: (see Figure 5.3), and it's likely that many of those citizens will remain on the job. They will be a potent force, and while many firms are prepared to train retirees who decide to return to work, one area where they apparently already excel is computer use. Seniors are said to make up the fastest-growing segment of Internet users, and they demonstrate longer attention spans than the young, in addition to a higher-than-average interest in government, politics, investing, news, travel, spirituality and religion, medicine, and culture.[17]

One firm that's already taken the lead in tapping the experience of older workers is Queens Surface Corporation, the largest privately owned bus company in New York City. With age-neutral hiring, promotion, and training practices, along with plentiful job opportunities for workers over 50, the firm recently earned the first Age Diversity in the Workplace Award granted by the American Association of Retired Persons (AARP).[18]

Implications for the Supervisor

Advantages of Diversity

Overcoming the challenges to supervising a diverse workforce can require consistent effort and a willingness to learn from mistakes, particularly for the new supervisor. But there are rewards, among them the confidence that such behavior is both ethical and fair. Other advantages for the individual supervisor are more concrete and include:

1. The opportunity to learn from the varied perspectives of those unlike ourselves.
2. A better motivated and more loyal team of employees.
3. Enhanced communication skills.
4. Improved management ability.
5. Enhanced opportunities for career advancement.

The firm as a whole can also benefit from a supervisor's successful efforts. Some of the advantages of diversity for the business organization are:

1. Greater ability to attract and retain the best employees for the job.
2. Increased productivity.
3. Higher morale and motivation throughout the company.
4. More resilient workforce.
5. Greater innovation.
6. Reduced turnover.
7. Enhanced performance leading to greater market share.

See "Meeting the Challenge" for an example of the advantages of diversity.

It is important to remember that even the best and most necessary efforts to manage diversity will need to be handled with care. Among the many challenges supervisors face in the newly diverse workplace is the task of adjusting job schedules and workloads to religious and ethnic holidays, to family needs such as a sick child or an elderly parent needing temporary or ongoing care, and to unique arrangements such as job sharing and telecommuting. Special equipment and training are sometimes needed to ease the stress of a disability in a capable employee or to tailor a workstation to an employee's physical needs. Bilingual employee manuals and the creation of benefit programs that offer medical coverage to life partners of either sex are other examples. Adjustments like these, while beneficial to the firm, can occasionally create dissatisfaction among other employees. Supervisors need to be aware that these problems also can occur and be prepared to deal with them.

Communication

Our attitudes toward others are perhaps nowhere as evident as in our communication with them. Communication in the workplace, therefore, is one area where supervisors can serve as particularly good role models of managing diversity constructively.

Nonverbal communication is just as powerful in many contexts as the actual words we say, and body language differs from one culture to another (and even

Red Lobster Hires Stars

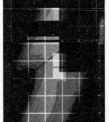

The 22-member guest relations department of the Red Lobster restaurant chain responds to an average of 2,000 customer contacts a week. All phone contacts are answered the same day, and letters are answered within 24 hours. Arlene Marcus, supervisor of guest relations, has this to say about her staff: "I'm not sitting here holding their hands. . . . These people are stars."

Arlene's people are also severely physically disabled. Nineteen of the 22 employees have handicaps ranging from missing limbs to quadriplegia, and a few of them are unable to commute. Those workers telecommute, and all the guest relations workers use Star 2000, a Windows-based software program modified to capture information from customer calls and personalize form letters to each situation with a reduced number of keystrokes and mouse movements. An autocapitalization feature was added to the software package for name and address entry, another custom feature inserts a city name in response to the entry of a zip code, and special "jump keys" are designed to make it easier to navigate around the computer screen. Callers are generally unaware that the Red Lobster representative they've reached is typing with one hand or entering data by means of a mouth wand.

What Arlene characterizes as a "win-win situation" is for Betty Salem, one of the disabled workers, "the best job I've ever had." Betty is confined to a wheelchair by cerebral palsy and is saving more than 10 hours a week by telecommuting to her Red Lobster job. She logs onto the data processing network and remains connected for the length of her eight-hour shift. Dick Monroe, the restaurant chain's vice president of public relations, says the opportunity to hire disabled workers through a local vocational-rehabilitation agency fits well with Red Lobster's policy of matching abilities to the job. The department is cost effective and generates more valuable information about the chain's customers than the outside firm that handled guest relations in the past.

To Arlene Marcus, however, the workers are simply "stars."

Source: "Guests Benefit as Hardware, Software Unite Red Lobster, Physically Challenged Workers," *Nation's Restaurant News*, August 5, 1996, p. 22.

---

between genders) as much as spoken language does. It's important to try not to rely too much on generalizations about culture, because even within cultures that differ from our own, there are variations in behavior among individuals. But to draw some basic conclusions about how supervisors might best shape their communications with others, both managers and subordinates, we will need to rely on a few simple statements. Keep in mind that they do not reflect the real complexity of any foreign culture or of any individual.[19]

Here are a few examples[20]:

- The Japanese value the ability to be physically still.
- The French see the way Americans walk as "uncivilized."
- Whites in North America interpret eye contact as a sign of honesty, while in many other cultures eyes are dropped as a sign of respect to one's superiors.
- Americans tend to smile at everyone, while in Germany smiles are reserved for friends. The Japanese smile not just to express gladness but also to cover embarrassment and even anger.
- In Bulgaria, people nod their heads to signal no and shake their heads to mean yes.
- Latin Americans stand closer to people of the same sex than North Americans do, but North Americans stand closer to those of the opposite sex.
- In Asia, the Middle East, and South America, friends of the same sex can hold hands or walk arm-in-arm in public, while opposite-sex couples who touch in public are seen as slightly shocking.

- In North America, the person sitting at the head of a table is generally assumed to be the leader of the group unless it is a woman, in which case observers tend to assume the leader is one of the men.
- In Japan, it is considered good manners to accept another's business card with both hands and to store it carefully in a distinctive case made for this purpose.[21]

Nonverbal communication or body language seldom occurs without some accompanying words. Verbal communication, both written and spoken, offers many opportunities for bridging the gaps between cultures, and just as many chances for us to fail to convey our intended meaning. Just one of the many ways in which supervisors can improve their communication with others in the diverse workplace of the future is to choose words with extra care, particularly when giving directions.

Many English words have more than one meaning, and the English language is full of slang, idioms, and borrowed expressions such as "on the ropes" or "from left field."[22] These have the potential to mislead, confuse, and frustrate nonnative speakers of English and should be used with care, if at all. Here are a few examples of expressions we may take for granted but others would find puzzling at best[23]:

- Head for home.
- Grasp at straws.
- Out to pasture.
- A sitting duck.
- Up the creek without a paddle.
- A fish out of water.
- Tearjerker.
- Circle the wagons.
- Shoot from the hip.

Supervisors should also be aware that every industry has its own particular jargon, and that specialized terms can pose particular problems. Publishing, for example, has its own specific meanings for such terms as *widow, orphan, register*, and *river*. Since even native speakers of English will find jargon unfamiliar at first, explanations of terms should be a standard part of orientation and training.

The point of all these examples is not that the supervisor must become an expert in other cultures. That would be an impossible and probably pointless goal. What these differences do suggest, however, is that it is most important not to make assumptions in one's communications with others, particularly regarding the way one's own words and actions are interpreted. Thinking before communicating, in order to understand the potential reaction to our words and gestures, is a good habit to foster. Checking for understanding is a simple but very effective way to ensure that we are conveying the meaning we intend.

Diversity Training

To fully reap the benefits of having a diverse workforce, supervisors first need to ensure that cultural differences are perceived by everyone as a positive force within the firm. Sometimes formal diversity training such as a two- or three-day workshop is needed to raise employee awareness of multiculturalism and to help reduce such barriers to success as prejudice and stereotypes. It's interesting to note that three out of four Fortune 500 firms have implemented diversity training programs.[24] These programs are often credited with attracting minority recruits and raising sensitivity to differences among people. Improved communications skills are also a common goal of diversity training, along with improving interpersonal and technical skills, improving English proficiency, and facilitating mentoring. Some firms, however, have experienced a backlash against diversity training; problems include the reinforcement of group stereotypes and even lawsuits based on offensive statements made during "awareness raising" sessions.[25] Appropriate controls and guidelines should accompany the training, which should be administered by professional trainers.

When diversity is embraced by top management and is built into policies and procedures that are fairly enforced, and when the goals of diversity training are continually reinforced within the corporate culture, it has the greatest chance of contributing to the company's goals. If such ideal support is lacking, supervisors can still support diversity by consistently setting a good example in their dealings with others. Such seemingly innocent practices as hiring only people who appear to fit into the "corporate culture" can lead supervisors to staff a firm with workers from similar backgrounds; with identical religious, ethnic, or racial characteristics; or all within the same age bracket. Even if no legal actions are brought against such firms, they still are losing one of their best potential resources—the creativity and vitality that come from bringing people into contact with others from whom they can learn.

Legal Issues

A review of all the relevant employment law is beyond the scope of this text. Table 5.1 summarizes some of the major legislation that governs the areas of workplace diversity and that supervisors should be aware of. These rules govern

■ TABLE 5.1 **Some Important Equal Employment Opportunity Legislation**	**Legislation**	**Result**
	Title VII of 1964 Civil Rights Act, as amended	Created the Equal Employment Opportunity Commission; bars discrimination based on race, color, religion, sex, or national origin.
	Equal Pay Act of 1963	Requires equal pay for men and women performing similar work.
	Age Discrimination in Employment Act of 1967	Bars discrimination against those 40 years old and over because of age.
	Vocational Rehabilitation Act of 1973	For jobs connected with the federal government, requires affirmative action to employ qualified handicapped persons and prohibits discrimination against them.
	Pregnancy Discrimination Act of 1978	Bars discrimination in employment against women based on pregnancy, childbirth, or related conditions.
	Vietnam Era Veterans' Readjustment Assistance Act of 1974	Mandates affirmative action in employment for veterans of the Vietnam War era.
	Americans with Disabilities Act of 1990	Prohibits discrimination against disabled employees in the private sector and encourages reasonable accommodations for them.
	Civil Rights Act of 1991	Places the burden of proof on the employer and allows for compensatory and punitive damages in discrimination cases.

hiring, pay, promotion, and evaluation, all within the scope of the supervisor's responsibilities.

Note that the Equal Employment Opportunity Commission (EEOC) was instituted by Title VII of the 1964 Civil Rights Act as amended in 1972. The EEOC consists of five members appointed by the president to serve a five-year term. This agency acts as the federal government's major means of enforcing equal employment opportunity laws and has the power to investigate complaints, use conciliation to eliminate discrimination when found, and file discrimination charges on behalf of an individual if needed. Individual states have also passed their own laws to fill perceived gaps in federal law.[26]

Summary

5.1   Define diversity.

Diversity refers to the characteristics of individuals that shape their identities and the experiences they have in society. Racial, cultural, ethnic, age, gender, and other kinds of diversity are welcomed and considered a strength in business organizations today.

5.2   Discuss how the U.S. workforce is changing and its impact on the supervisor.

The number of women and minorities in the workforce is increasing. The workforce is aging as well, and new technologies are bringing the disabled into the workforce with valuable skills and insights. Technical workers from abroad are bringing their expertise to many U.S. firms. All these changes offer supervisors both a challenge to their management skills and an opportunity to build a strong and flexible team of workers.

5.3   Differentiate between prejudice, discrimination, and stereotypes in the workplace.

Prejudice is a preconceived judgment about an individual or group of people. Discrimination is unfair or inequitable treatment based on prejudice. Stereotypes are generalized, fixed images we hold of others.

5.4   Explain how sexism and ageism are barriers to diversity, and how supervisors can be more aware of them.

Sexism and ageism discriminate against others on the basis of sex or age. Supervisors should be aware that sexism can be either subtle, as in sexist language, or blatant, as in sexual harassment, defined as unwanted sexual attentions including language, behavior, or the display of images. Sexual harassment is illegal. Ageism can cost the organization the benefit of experience, perspective, and judgment that older workers bring. Discrimination based on age is illegal except in the (rare) case of a bona fide occupational qualification (BFOQ).

5.5   Describe some ways to communicate more effectively in the diverse workplace.

Supervisors can communicate more effectively by being aware that verbal and nonverbal communication varies in meaning across cultures. Avoiding slang and idioms, explaining technical jargon, and checking for meaning will help improve communication.

5.6   Describe the goals of diversity training.

Diversity training is intended to raise employee awareness of multiculturalism and help reduce such barriers to success as prejudice and stereotypes. Other goals include improved communications, and interpersonal and technical skills.

5.7   List the most important recent legislation affecting diversity and its provisions.

Title VII of the 1964 Civil Rights Act, amended in 1972, created the Equal Employment Opportunity Commission, which investigates and acts on complaints of discrimination. See Table 5.1 for a full summary of legislation.

Key Words

diversity, p. 108

corporate culture, p. 109

prejudice, p. 110

discrimination, p. 110

stereotypes, p. 111

sexism, p. 112

sexual harassment, p. 113

ageism, p. 114

bona fide occupational
qualification (BFOQ), p. 115

Review and Discussion Questions

1. What is diversity? How has its meaning changed?

2. Rasheen supervises the mailroom for a large financial services firm. He has been told he will be attending a diversity training program next week. Rasheen believes that since he has recently hired three women from his native country he does not need to know any more about diversity. As his supervisor, what would you say to Rasheen to prepare him for the training program?

3. Some research suggests that the increasing racial and cultural diversity in the United States is limited to the larger cities. How would you account for this trend? Does it suggest that only supervisors in these cities need be concerned about diversity?

4. Distinguish between prejudice and discrimination. How do stereotypes contribute to each?

5. Aaron, clerical supervisor for a health maintenance organization, wants to hire the best person for the receptionist job. Ramona, his manager, is doubtful that the candidate Aaron has selected will be capable because she uses a wheelchair. Ramona is concerned that other workers will have to spend a lot of time helping the receptionist get in and out of the office for lunch, breaks, and so on. How can Aaron ensure that his candidate will be an asset to the firm?

6. List as many English expressions as you can think of that might be confusing to a nonnative speaker of the language. Next to each, write a brief expression that conveys the same meaning with greater clarity.

7. Mariah's boss calls her "honey" although he refers to her co-workers as Jason, Rick, and Harrison. How can Mariah ask her boss to correct this situation?

8. Several members of your team are out ill and you are falling behind your production schedule for the week. A new employee comes to you and asks for a half day off for a religious holiday you have never heard of. What should you do?

9. What is the EEOC, and what are its responsibilities and powers?

A SECOND LOOK

What would you recommend to the New York City Fire Department to ensure that its recruitment policies balance the goal of diversity and the goal of getting the best people for the job?

SKILLS MODULE

CASE

Coming Out in Corporate America

The last several years have seen what some writers call "a quiet revolution" in corporate America. Hundreds of companies of all sizes have barred discrimination based on sexual orientation, and dozens of these have gone further, offering "domestic partner" benefits to their gay and lesbian staff. While some older companies such as Disney, Colgate Palmolive, Coors, United Way, Chevron, and General Mills are among these, observers note the trend toward greater openness and acceptance of gay and lesbian workers who are "out" (that is, open about their sexual orientation) is strongest among firms in high-tech industries, entertainment, and health care, where the best creative minds are actively sought regardless of their sexuality, and where managers and supervisors tend to be younger and more progressive.

Hilary Rosen is president of the Recording Industry Association of America. When she began her career (as a lobbyist), she told no one that she is gay. But she grew tired of pretense and finally let her orientation be known. In what she terms a "macho industry," she feels her male colleagues are more comfortable with her because she is gay. Now, she says, "You just can't do as good a job if you are afraid. You are as free as you choose to be, which is not to say you don't pay a price for being out. I just never understood why the price was worth it." As for employees she supervises who may be gay, "I want them to give 150 percent and they will not if they are preoccupied with stuff like [pretense]."

Jane (a pseudonym) is a 38-year-old vice president for a telecommunications firm who manages 1,200 employees and is considered to be on the fast track for further promotion. She always planned on coming out at work, "until I found out firsthand what my superiors really thought. It was just awful. Much worse than I ever thought. . . . My mentor, the man who had helped me rise, got up [at a meeting] and said he did not know anyone who was gay and didn't want to know them." Jane's hope of declaring herself and giving up her pretense of having a boyfriend has been abandoned, and she is quietly looking for another job. "I always said to myself that if I got one more promotion, I would come out. . . . I thought I could be so good at my job that it would be impossible for my colleagues to hurt me if they found out I was gay. Now I know that could never be true."

1. Do you think Hilary's or Jane's experience is more typical for gay employees in industries you are familiar with?
2. Hilary feels her subordinates cannot turn in a top performance if they are concerned about reactions to their sexual orientation. How far would you go to bring your own subordinates to the level of comfort at work that Hilary feels is optimal?
3. Jane's firm runs a diversity training program. What flaws do you see in its results? Should improvements in the program depend on someone like Jane coming out and filing a complaint against a colleague?
4. If you heard a colleague expressing the opinion of Jane's mentor, how would you react? What, if anything, would you do?

Source: Kara Swisher, "Coming Out in Corporate America," *Working Woman*, July–August 1996, pp. 50 ff.

■ SELF-QUIZ

Avoiding Age Bias

Place a 0 next to any statements you believe are true; write 10 for those you think are false.

_____ 1. Worker productivity declines with age.

_____ 2. Older employees are more expensive.

_____ 3. Older employees are more difficult to get along with.

_____ 4. Older employees are coasting until they can retire.

_____ 5. Older employees are prone to accidents and absenteeism.

_____ 6. Older employees can retire because they are financially secure.

_____ 7. Retraining older employees is more expensive because their future with the company is shorter than average.

Scoring: The higher your score, the less likely you are to be biased [about] an employee's age. All the statements are false.

Source: Adapted from Margaret J. Cofer, "How to Avoid Age Bias," *Nursing Management*, November 1, 1998, p. 11.

Class Exercise

Cultural Analysis Inventory

For each topic, there are two questions. Write brief responses to each. After you are finished, your instructor may wish to discuss your responses in class; or you may share them in small groups; or you may conduct a "culture hunt" by trying to find people in your class who answered the questions as you did.

1. Weddings
   a. What is the most important part of the wedding ceremony?
   b. What is the most important part of the reception?
2. Dinners
   a. Who carves the meat at large family dinners?
   b. Who clears the kitchen at large family dinners?
3. Funerals
   a. What is the correct decision regarding "viewing" the remains?
   b. Where should a funeral be held?

4. Family
   a. What is the most important activity that your family does together?
   b. How far down the family tree does the obligation go to be responsible for a family member (for example, lend money, take care of children, pay for food, or let the person live with you temporarily)?
5. Ethnicity
   a. How does your family identify itself ethnically?
   b. What represents your family's cultural and ethnic identity? (For example, if you put "Hungarian" you might refer to a Hungarian lullaby or food that your family eats.)

Source: From Dan O'Haire and Gustav Friedrich, *Strategic Communication in Business and the Professions*, Second Edition. Copyright © 1995 by Houghton Mifflin Company. Used with permission.

Team-Building Exercise

Your work team is responsible for interviewing candidates for openings in the group and making hiring recommendations. For a current opening you have interviewed several qualified people and decided which is the best. However, the candidate is quite young, and most of the members of your work group are in their fifties. Although they are impressed with the candidate's skills, you sense that they are reluctant to change the composition of the team so drastically. You are concerned that the workflow should continue without disruption, and that the team spirit you have developed should remain high.

Assume the candidate is hired. Break into groups and brainstorm strategies for bringing the new person onto the team in such a way that the existing team members are accepting and welcoming.

PART THREE

Functions of the Supervisor

6

Whenever an individual or a business decides that success has been attained, progress stops.
—Thomas Watson

Reaching Goals and Objectives

■ LEARNING OBJECTIVES

After you have studied this chapter, you should be able to:

6.1 Describe types of planning that take place in organizations.

6.2 Identify characteristics of effective objectives.

6.3 Define *management by objectives (MBO)* and discuss its use.

6.4 Discuss the supervisor's role in the planning process.

6.5 Explain the purpose of using controls.

6.6 Identify the steps in the control process.

6.7 Describe types of control and tools for controlling.

6.8 List characteristics of effective controls.

■ "IF YOU HAVE A PLAN, YOU KNOW WHAT TO DO"

Every supervisor's job is part preparation and part execution. But for Bruce Lemmerman, director of college scouting for the New Orleans Saints, the preparation takes up 363 days of the year, while the execution takes exactly two.

During those two days each year in April, the National Football League holds its annual college draft, and Bruce must ensure that he is prepared to help his team choose the best new players for the coming season. He travels throughout the year, interviewing dozens of college football coaches and trainers and observing their most talented players in action. He watches hundreds of football games, both live and on video. He collects and organizes huge amounts of facts, some of them hard statistics and some of them his own personal impressions of the players he's seen. At the end of each day on the road, he transmits all his data to the network in the Saints' New Orleans office.

A sophisticated planning process precedes Bruce's 363 days of efficient data collection. Right after each year's draft, he meets with his scouts to draw up a new plan of action for the following year, with detailed travel schedules and scouting assignments for each member of the team. "We plan a whole year to make about 20 primary decisions," says Bruce. "And some of those are million-dollar decisions."

Creating the plan and sticking to it are critical for success. Without such complete scheduling and attention to logistics and detail, it would be impossible to cover all the necessary groundwork to prepare for the draft. Bruce's plans are so successful that the group usually needs to meet only six or seven times during the year, and unexpected developments are easily accommodated. "If you have a clear game plan," he says, "you know what to do."

Source: Emily Esterson, "Game Plan," *Inc.* no. 4 (1998), pp. 43–44.

Through careful planning, Bruce Lemmerman ensures that his group reaches its goals and objectives. Doing this requires knowledge of what the group is supposed to accomplish and whether the group is actually accomplishing it. Supervisors acquire that important knowledge by carrying out the functions of planning and controlling.

This chapter describes how supervisors can and should carry out those functions. The chapter begins with a description of how planning takes place in organizations, including the types of objectives and planning that are common. Next, the chapter discusses the supervisor's role as planner: setting and updating objectives and including employees in these processes. The second half of the chapter addresses the management function of controlling. It describes the process supervisors follow and some of the tools they use in controlling, as well as the characteristics of effective controls.

Planning in Organizations

planning
Setting goals and determining how to meet them.

As you learned in Chapter 1, **planning** is the management function of setting goals and determining how to meet them. For supervisors, this includes figuring out what tasks the department needs to carry out to achieve its goals, as well as how and when to perform those tasks. For action-oriented people, planning can seem time-consuming and tedious. But the need for planning is obvious, especially if you consider what would happen in an organization where no one plans. For example, if a store did not implement planning, customers would not know when the store would be open, and employees would not know what inventory to order or when to order it. The location of the store might be an accident, with no marketing research to determine where business would be sufficiently good to generate a profit. The managers would not know how many employees to hire, because they would have no idea how many customers they would be serving. Clearly, this business would fail in the mission of providing its customers with high-quality service and merchandise.

Supervisors and other managers plan for several reasons. Knowing what the organization is trying to accomplish helps them set priorities and make decisions aimed at accomplishing their goals. Planning forces managers to spend time focusing on the future and establishes a fair way for evaluating performance. It helps managers use resources efficiently, thus minimizing wasted time and money. Time spent in planning a project can reduce the time required to carry it out. The total time for planning and execution can actually be shorter for a thoroughly planned project than for one started in haste.

Many inexpensive software packages are now available to help supervisors plan projects efficiently. Templates that supervisors can customize for their own purposes lead the way through the various planning steps and help establish project phases and the order in which they need to be accomplished, project goals and deadlines, people and departments involved in the project, anticiapted obstacles and action plans for overcoming them, and budgets and other resources.[1]

Finally, the other functions that managers perform—organizing, staffing, leading, and controlling—all depend on good planning. Before supervisors and other managers can allocate resources and inspire employees to achieve their objectives, or before they can determine whether employees are meeting those objectives, they need to know what they are trying to accomplish.

Supervisors rarely have much input into the way an organization does its planning. Rather, they participate in whatever process already exists. To participate constructively, supervisors should understand the process.

Objectives

objectives
The desired accomplishments of the organization as a whole or of part of the organization.

Planning centers on the setting of goals and objectives. **Objectives** specify the desired accomplishments of the organization as a whole or of a part of it. According to one school of thought, **goals** are objectives with a broad focus. For example, an organization seeks to be the number one supplier of nursing home care by the end of next year. That would be considered a goal. In contrast, the accounting department seeks to have all invoices mailed within two weeks of a patient's departure; this is more specific and is therefore an objective. One steering committee, made up of Roadway Express Inc. employees from all levels and departments, created a set of goals for transforming the company that

goals
Objectives, often those with a broad focus.

they dubbed an "opportunity map" of needs and priorities.[2] This text uses the term *objectives* in most cases and treats the terms *objectives* and *goals* synonymously.

Strategic Objectives   Planning should begin at the top, with a plan for the organization as a whole. **Strategic planning** is the creation of long-term goals for the organization. These typically include the type and quality of goods or services the organization is to provide and, for a business, the level of profits it is to earn. When Wal-Mart readied itself to move into the urban markets once dominated by Kmart, it concentrated on its skill in discount retailing and adopted a strategy of building superior operations: its order and distribution systems. Kmart, in contrast, emphasized marketing to boost its image, and the company diversified by acquiring specialty retailers, including the Sports Authority.[3]

Similarly, when Procter & Gamble announced its goal to double net sales by 2006, it had to build a risky strategic plan based on structural change unlike anything the company had attempted before. In the first two years of the plan, the giant consumer products firm missed its goals and refined its plans. As Watts Wacker, chairman of consulting firm FirstMatter, notes, "This is a very big deal, for Procter and for all the companies that watch Procter's moves. But great plans often come with great obstacles."[4]

Usually it is the top managers who engage in strategic planning; in other cases, a planning department prepares objectives for approval by top management. Either way, the managers at the top decide where the organization should be going.

Operational Objectives   The objectives for divisions, departments, and work groups support the goals developed in strategic planning. These objectives, developed through **operational planning,** specify how the group will help the organization achieve its goals. Operational planning is performed by middle managers and supervisors. Table 6.1 summarizes the characteristics of strategic and operational planning.

Middle managers set objectives that will enable their division or department to contribute to the goals set for the organization. Supervisors set objectives that will enable their department or work group to contribute to divisional or departmental goals. For example, if the organizational objective for a bank is to increase profits by 8 percent next year, the goal of a branch located in a high-growth area might be to increase its own profits by 9 percent. At this branch, the vice president (supervisor) in charge of lending operations might have the objective of increasing loans to businesses by 15 percent. The head teller might have the objective of keeping customer waits to five minutes or less. (The good service is designed to support organizational objectives by attracting new customers to the bank.)

strategic planning
The creation of long-term goals for the organization as a whole.

operational planning
The development of objectives that specify how divisions, departments, and work groups will support organizational goals.

■ TABLE 6.1

Characteristics of Strategic and Operational Planning

	Strategic Planning	Operational Planning
Planners	Top managers, possibly with a planning department	Middle managers and supervisors
Scope	Objectives for the organization as a whole	Objectives for a division, department, or work group
Time Frame	Long range (more than one year)	Short range (one year or less)

■ FIGURE 6.1

Characteristics of Effective Objectives

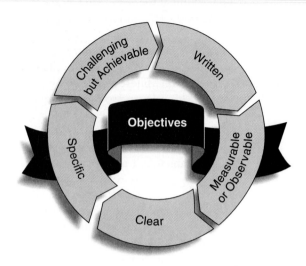

Notice in the example that the objectives become more specific at lower levels of the organization, and planning tends to focus on shorter time spans. This is the usual pattern for planning in an organization. Thus, top managers spend a lot of their time thinking broadly over several years, whereas much of the supervisor's planning may involve what actions to take in the current week or month.

Personal Objectives Besides planning for the department as a whole, each supervisor should apply good planning practices to his or her individual efforts. This includes determining how to help the department meet its objectives, as well as how to meet the supervisor's own career objectives. Another important application of planning is effectively managing one's use of time. (Chapter 14 discusses time management.

Characteristics of Effective Objectives For objectives to be effective—that is, clearly understood and practical—they should have certain characteristics. They should be written, measurable or observable, clear, specific, and challenging but achievable (see Figure 6.1).

Putting objectives *in writing* might seem like a nuisance, but doing so gives them importance; employees can see they are something to which managers have devoted time and thought. The people required to carry out the objectives can then look them up as a reminder of what they are supposed to be accomplishing, and they can take time to make sure they understand them. Finally, writing down objectives forces the supervisor to think through what the objectives say.

Making objectives *measurable* or at least observable provides the supervisor with a way to tell whether people are actually accomplishing them. Measurable objectives might specify a dollar amount, a time frame, or a quantity to be produced. Examples are number of sales calls made, parts manufactured, and customers served. The words *maximize* and *minimize* are tip-offs that the objectives are not measurable. If the objective is to "maximize quality," how will anyone be

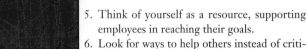

Hints for Setting Goals

If you can think of goals as agreements between you and your employees, you will see that goal setting is as much an art as a science. Goals that are too high are discouraging to your employees; goals that are too low fail to motivate them. Many supervisors find that the best strategy for goal setting is to include employees in the process as much as possible.

Here are a few tips for goal setting.

1. Try to set individual goals for each employee, particularly if you can allow each to create his or her own goals.
2. Help people enhance their sense of their own worth by getting to know their individual strengths and abilities.
3. Use your employees' perspective to determine what is realistic and what isn't.
4. Make goals concise and measurable, with target completion dates.
5. Think of yourself as a resource, supporting employees in reaching their goals.
6. Look for ways to help others instead of criticizing them or giving them ultimatums.
7. Remain flexible and open-minded to new ideas and suggestions as your team works toward its goals.
8. Allow employees to take risks and make mistakes, recognizing that mistakes and minor setbacks are part of the growing process.
9. Celebrate progress. Celebrate mistakes and learn from them.
10. Make sure that everyone keeps the company's mission or vision firmly in mind.

Sources: Jody Urquhart, "Manage by Mobilizing," *Journal of Property Management*, May–June 2001, p. 6; Ken Fracaro, "Optimism on a Rainy Day," *Supervision*, May 1, 2001, p. 5.

---

able to know whether maximum quality has been obtained? Rather, the objective might call for a defect rate of no more than 2 percent or for no customer complaints during the month. Other objectives that are difficult to measure are those that simply call for something to "improve" or get "better." The person writing the objective should specify a way to measure or observe the improvement.

Making objectives *specific* means spelling out who is to do what and by what time to accomplish the objective. Specific objectives describe the actions people are to take and what is supposed to result from those actions. For example, instead of saying, "Computer files will be backed up regularly," a specific objective might say, "Each word-processing operator will back up his or her files at the end of each workday." Being specific simplifies the job of ensuring that the objectives are accomplished; the supervisor knows just what to look for. Also, specific objectives help the employees understand what they are supposed to be doing.

When the supervisor needs other people to play a part in accomplishing objectives, those people must understand the objectives. Thus, it is easy to see why objectives should be clear. The supervisor makes sure the objectives are clear by spelling them out in simple language and asking employees whether they understand them.

Objectives that are challenging are more likely to stimulate employees to do their best than those that are not. However, the employees have to believe they are capable of achieving the objectives. Otherwise, they will become frustrated or angry at what seem to be unreasonable expectations. Most of us have had the experience of tackling a challenging job and enjoying the sense of pride and accomplishment that comes with finishing it. In setting goals, the supervisor should remember how stimulating and confidence building such experiences can be. See "Tips from the Firing Line" for ideas on goal setting.

Policies, Procedures, and Rules

To meet his objective of staffing his information systems department with top-quality employees, Bruce Frazzoli hired some people he used to work with at his former job. He was later embarrassed to be called on the carpet for violating his employer's policy that managers must work with the personnel department in making all hiring decisions. Bruce learned that supervisors and other managers must consider the organization's policies, procedures, and rules when setting objectives. The content of the objectives and the way they are carried out must be consistent with all three.

policies
Broad guidelines for how to act.

Policies are broad guidelines for how to act; they do not spell out the details of how to handle a specific situation. For example, a firm might have a policy of increasing the number of women and minorities in its workforce. Such a policy does not dictate whom to hire or when; it merely states a general expectation.

procedures
The steps that must be completed to achieve a specific purpose.

Procedures are the steps that must be completed to achieve a specific purpose. An organization might specify procedures for hiring employees, purchasing equipment, filing paperwork, and many other activities. Publishing company McGraw-Hill's management guidelines include suggested procedures for how to conduct performance appraisals and employment interviews. A supervisor may be responsible for developing the procedures for activities carried out in his or her own department. For example, a restaurant manager might spell out a cleanup procedure or a maintenance supervisor might detail the shutdown procedure for a piece of machinery. Procedures free managers and employees from making decisions about activities they carry out repeatedly.

rules
Specific statements of what to do or not do in a given situation.

Rules are specific statements of what to do or not do in a given situation. Unlike policies, they are neither flexible nor open to interpretation. For example, one rule at G & W Electric Company states that safety glasses and safety shoes (shoes with steel toes or leather uppers) must be worn in the factory. Restaurants have rules stating that employees must wash their hands before working. Rules of this kind are often imposed by law.

Action Plans

action plan
The plan for how to achieve an objective.

Objectives serve as the basis for action plans and contingency plans (see Figure 6.2). An **action plan** is a plan for how to achieve an objective. If you think of objectives as statements of where you want to go, then an action plan is a map that tells you how to get there. For a successful trip, you need to have both kinds of information.

■ FIGURE 6.2

Areas of Planning

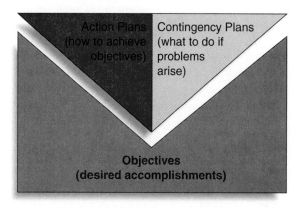

The supervisor creates an action plan by answering the questions *what, who, when, where,* and *how:*

- *What* actions need to be taken? Do sales calls need to be made, customers served in a certain way, goods produced? The supervisor should outline the specific steps involved.
- *Who* will take the necessary steps? The supervisor may perform some tasks, but many activities will be assigned to specific employees or groups of employees.
- *When* must each step be completed? With many types of processes, certain steps will determine when the whole project is completed. The supervisor should be particularly careful in scheduling those activities.
- *Where* will the work take place? Sometimes this question is easy to answer, but a growing operation may require that the supervisor plan for additional space. Some activities may require that the supervisor consider the arrangement of work on the shop floor or the arrangement of items in a warehouse or supply room.
- *How* will the work be done? Are the usual procedures and equipment adequate, or does the supervisor need to innovate? Thinking about how the work will be done may alert the supervisor to a need for more training.

Contingency Planning

contingency planning
Planning what to do if the original plans don't work out.

A lot of people believe in Murphy's law: "If anything can go wrong, it will." Even those who are less pessimistic recognize that things don't always go as planned. A delivery may be delayed by a strike or a blizzard, a key employee may take another job, a "foolproof" computer system may crash. The sign of a good supervisor is not so much never having these nasty surprises, but being prepared with ideas about how to respond.

Planning what to do if the original plans don't work out is known as **contingency planning.** The wise supervisor has contingency plans to go with every original plan. One useful technique for contingency planning is to review all objectives, looking for areas where something might go wrong. Then the supervisor determines how to respond if those problems do arise.

Peter White travels 100,000 miles a year in his capacity as president of Wave Phore Newscast. He learned the hard way to make contingency plans for his frequent trips around the country. On a recent trip to Boston he found himself walking for an hour through the December night to reach his hotel after taking a bus and a subway from the airport. "I've never been so cold," he recalls. "Now, before I leave, I always research what I'm going to face at my destination airport. I ask the hotel to describe the fastest, easiest, most direct way to get there. I look at maps."[5]

Contingency planning is not always formal. It would be too time-consuming to create a written contingency plan for every detail of operations. Instead, the supervisor simply has to keep in mind how to respond if some details of the operation do not go as planned.

Management by Objectives

management by objectives (MBO)
A formal system for planning in which managers and employees at all levels set objectives for what they are to accomplish; their performance is then measured against those objectives.

Many organizations use a formal system for planning known as **management by objectives (MBO).** This is a process in which managers and employees at all

■ FIGURE 6.3

Sample Objectives in an Organization Using MBO

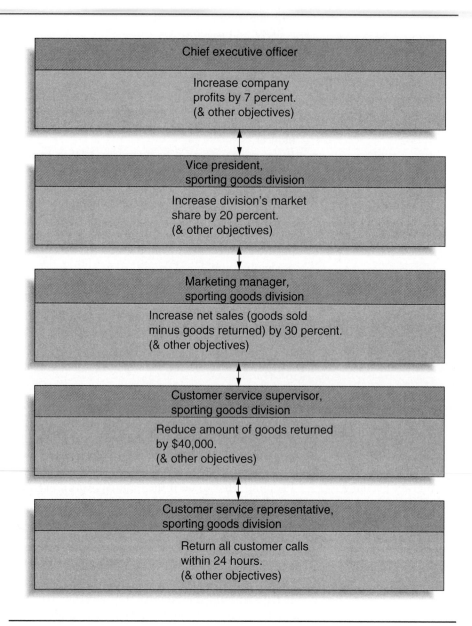

levels set objectives for what they are to accomplish. Their performances are then measured against those objectives. Basically, MBO involves three steps:

1. All individuals in the organization work with their managers to set objectives, specifying what they are to do in the next operating period (such as a year).

2. Each individual's manager periodically reviews the individual's performance to see whether he or she is meeting the objectives. Typically, these reviews take place two to four times a year. The reviews help the individual and the manager decide what corrective actions are needed, and they provide information for setting future objectives.

3. The organization rewards the individuals based on how close they come to fulfilling the objectives.

Figure 6.3 shows examples of objectives for employees at several levels of an organization using MBO. Notice that the sample objective for the nonmanagement employee supports the achievement of the supervisor's objective, which in turn supports the achievement of his or her manager's objective, and so on up the hierarchy. (In practice, of course, each person in the organization would have several objectives to meet.)

For effective use of MBO, the managers at all levels (especially top management) must be committed to the system. Also, the objectives they set must meet the criteria for effective objectives described earlier. For example, a salesperson would not be expected merely to "sell more," but to help develop specific objectives, such as "make 40 sales calls a month" and "sell 50 copiers by December 31." Finally, managers and employees must be able to cooperate in the objective-setting process.

Some people dislike MBO because setting and monitoring the achievement of objectives can be time-consuming and requires a lot of paperwork. However, the organization can benefit from involving employees in setting goals, which may lead to greater commitment in achieving them. Furthermore, the employees can benefit from a system of rewards that is rational and based on performance rather than personality. In light of these advantages, a supervisor may want to use the principles of management by objectives with the employees in his or her own department even if the organization as a whole has not adopted a formal MBO system.

The Supervisor as Planner

In most organizations, supervisors are responsible for the creation of plans that specify goals, tasks, resources, and responsibilities for the supervisor's own department. Thus, at the supervisor's level, objectives can range from the tasks he or she intends to accomplish on a certain day to the level of production the department is to achieve for the year. To be an effective planner, the supervisor should be familiar with how to set good objectives in these and other areas.

Although supervisors might resist doing the necessary paperwork, thoughtful planning is certainly worth the investment of time and effort. In carrying out their planning responsibilities, supervisors may engage in a variety of activities, from providing information to allocating resources, involving employees, coaching a team's planning effort, and updating objectives. (Take the "Self-Quiz" on page 155 to see whether you are a planner.)

Providing Information and Estimates

As the manager closest to day-to-day operations, the supervisor is in the best position to keep higher-level managers informed about the needs, abilities, and progress of his or her department or work group. For that reason, higher management relies on supervisors to provide estimates of the personnel and other resources they will need to accomplish their work.

Allocating Resources

The department for which the supervisor is responsible has a limited number of resources—people, equipment, and money. The supervisor's job includes deciding how to allocate resources to the jobs that will need to be done.

TABLE 6.2

Sample Budget for a Machine Shop Project

BUDGET MONITORING REPORT

Organizational unit <u>Machine shop</u> Job number <u>1763</u> Period <u>January–June</u> Total parts needed <u>6,000</u> Parts produced to date <u>2,700</u> Remaining work <u>3,300</u> Parts per month projection <u>1,000</u> Current production per month <u>900</u> Difference <u>(–100)</u>

ACTUAL EXPENDITURES

Line Item	Budgeted Amount	January	February	March	April	May	June
Direct labor	$60,000	10,000	$10,000	$10,000			
Indirect labor	5,400	900	900	900			
Material	13,200	2,195	3,156	1,032			
Operating supplies	3,000	1,200	0	296			
Equipment repair	5,400	0	0	3,600			
Total	**$87,000**	**$14,295**	**$14,056**	**$15,828**			

Source: From *Industrial Supervision: In The Age of High Technology*, by David L. Goetsch. Copyright © 1992 Pearson Education, Inc. Reprinted by permission of Pearson Education, Inc., Upper Saddle River, NJ.

The process of allocating human resources includes determining how many and what kind of employees the department will need to meet its objectives. If the department's workload is expanding, the supervisor may need to plan for hiring new employees. He or she also must plan for employee vacations and other time off, as well as for employee turnover.

The process of allocating equipment resources includes determining how much equipment is needed to get the job done. For example, does every book-keeper need a personal computer, or will adding machines be enough? The supervisor may find that the department needs to acquire more equipment. In that case, the supervisor must justify the request to buy or rent it by showing how it will benefit the organization.

Developing a Budget The process of allocating money resources is called budgeting. A **budget** is a plan for spending money. Many households use budgets for deciding how much of each paycheck should go for housing, car payments, food, savings, and so on. Businesses use budgets to break down how much to spend on items such as wages and salaries, rent, supplies, insurance, and so on. These items would be part of an *operating budget*; big-ticket items such as machinery or a new building would more likely be accounted for separately as part of a *capital budget*.

budget
A plan for spending money.

Some organizations expect their supervisors to prepare a budget showing what they think they will need to spend in the next year to meet departmental goals or carry out a specific project. Table 6.2 illustrates a sample budget for a machine shop project. The line items show different categories of expenses. The first column of figures contains the amounts budgeted for expenses in each category. The right-hand columns have the actual amounts spent each month in each category. The supervisor uses the actual amounts in controlling, which is described later in this chapter.

In preparing a budget, the supervisor typically has rules and guidelines to follow. For example, one company may say that pay increases for the department as a

FIGURE 6.4

Sample Gantt Chart for Building a Church

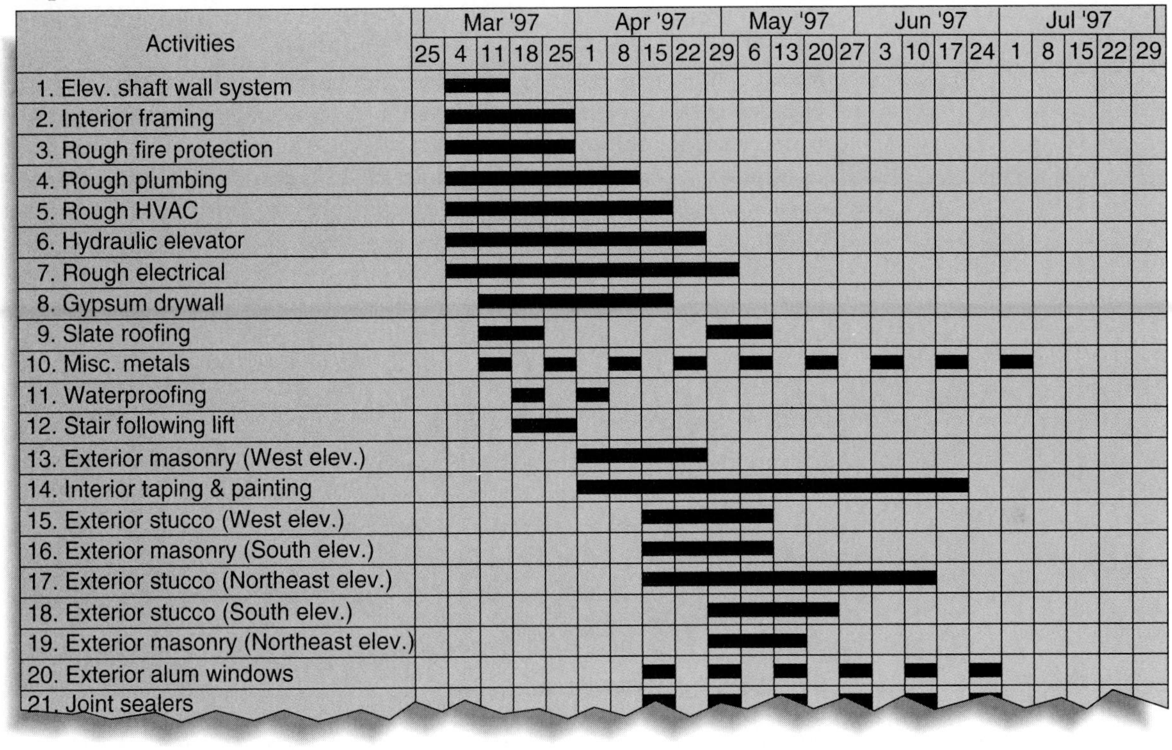

Activities	Mar '97 25	4	11	18	25	Apr '97 1	8	15	22	29	May '97 6	13	20	27	Jun '97 3	10	17	24	Jul '97 1	8	15	22	29
1. Elev. shaft wall system		█																					
2. Interior framing		█	█	█																			
3. Rough fire protection		█	█	█																			
4. Rough plumbing		█	█	█	█	█	█																
5. Rough HVAC		█	█	█	█	█																	
6. Hydraulic elevator		█	█	█	█	█	█	█	█	█	█												
7. Rough electrical		█	█	█	█	█	█	█	█	█	█												
8. Gypsum drywall			█	█	█	█	█																
9. Slate roofing			█	█							█	█											
10. Misc. metals			▬	▬	▬	▬	▬	▬	▬	▬	▬	▬	▬	▬	▬	▬	▬						
11. Waterproofing				█	█																		
12. Stair following lift																							
13. Exterior masonry (West elev.)							█	█															
14. Interior taping & painting							█	█	█	█	█	█	█	█	█	█							
15. Exterior stucco (West elev.)									█	█	█	█											
16. Exterior masonry (South elev.)									█	█	█	█											
17. Exterior stucco (Northeast elev.)									█	█	█	█	█	█									
18. Exterior stucco (South elev.)											█	█	█	█									
19. Exterior masonry (Northeast elev.)											█	█	█										
20. Exterior alum windows									█		█		█		█		█						
21. Joint sealers																							

Source: From "How to Plan Any Project: A Self-Teaching Guide." by Thomas C. Belanger. Reproduced with permission of Sterling Planning Group, Sterling, MA, 1991.

whole must be no more than 5 percent of the previous year's budget for salaries. Another organization may specify a total amount that the department may spend, or it may give the supervisor a formula for computing the department's overhead expenses. Based on these guidelines, the supervisor then recommends how much to spend in each area. In most cases, the supervisor and his or her manager review the budget. The supervisor must be willing to modify it when higher-level managers require a change.

scheduling
Setting a precise timetable for the work to be completed.

Scheduling   The supervisor continually needs to think about how much work the department needs to accomplish in a given time period and how it can meet its deadlines. Setting a precise timetable for the work to be done is known as **scheduling.** This includes deciding which activities will take priority over others and deciding who will do what tasks and when.

Gantt chart
Scheduling tool that lists the activities to be completed and uses horizontal bars to graph how long each activity will take, including its starting and ending dates.

Many organizations expect supervisors to use one or more of the techniques and tools that have been developed to help with scheduling. Two of the most widely used techniques are Gantt charts and PERT networks. A **Gantt chart** is a scheduling tool that lists the activities to be completed and uses horizontal bars to graph how long each activity will take, including its starting and ending dates (see Figure 6.4).

program evaluation and review technique (PERT)
Scheduling tool that identifies the relationships among tasks as well as the amount of time each task will take.

The **program evaluation and review technique (PERT)** is a scheduling tool that identifies the relationships among tasks and the amount of time each task will take. To use this tool, the planner creates a PERT network. For example, in Figure 6.5, the circles represent the tasks that must be completed in order to change a tire. The lines with arrows between the circles represent the sequence of activities needed to carry out each task. The numbers in the circles represent the order of tasks, in this case, counting by fives. The numbers in parentheses next to the arrows represent the time (number of minutes) required to complete each task. An important piece of information in a PERT network is the *critical path*— the sequence of tasks that will require the greatest amount of time. A delay that occurs in the critical path will cause the entire project to fall behind.

Besides these tools, supervisors may use a computer to help with scheduling. Many project management software packages have been developed for this application.

Involving Employees

To make sure that employees understand objectives and consider them achievable, supervisors may involve them in the goal-setting process. Employees who are involved in the process tend to feel more committed to the objectives, and they may be able to introduce ideas that the supervisor has not considered. In many cases, employees who help set objectives agree to take on greater challenges than the supervisor might have guessed.

One way to get employees involved in setting objectives is to have them write down what they think they can accomplish in the coming year (or month or appropriate time period). Then the supervisor discusses the ideas with each employee, modifying the objectives to meet the department's overall needs. Another approach is to hold a meeting of the entire work group at which the employees and supervisor develop objectives as a group. (Chapter 3 provides ideas for holding successful meetings.)

To set objectives for salespeople at Davis & Geck (a medical supply company), sales manager Dave Jacobs asks the salespeople and their regional supervisors to come up with sales levels they can guarantee. The supervisors are expected to discuss each salesperson's figures with him or her to assess how realistic they are. Jacobs then may modify those numbers in light of broad industry trends. The first year Jacobs used this bottom-up approach, some projections were overly optimistic. Since then, supervisors have begun asking salespeople to prepare action plans detailing how they expect to achieve their numbers. The result: more accurate numbers.[6]

Planning with a Team

In many applications of teamwork, teams, not individual managers, are charged with planning. In these cases, supervisors are expected not only to seek employee involvement in planning, but also to coach their team in carrying out the planning function. This requires knowing and communicating a clear sense of what the plan should encompass and encouraging team members to cooperate and share ideas freely.

When teams draw on the many viewpoints and diverse experience of team members, they can come up with creative plans that dramatically exceed past performance. At one time, Toshiba had the objective of producing a VCR with half

PERT Network for Changing a Flat Tire

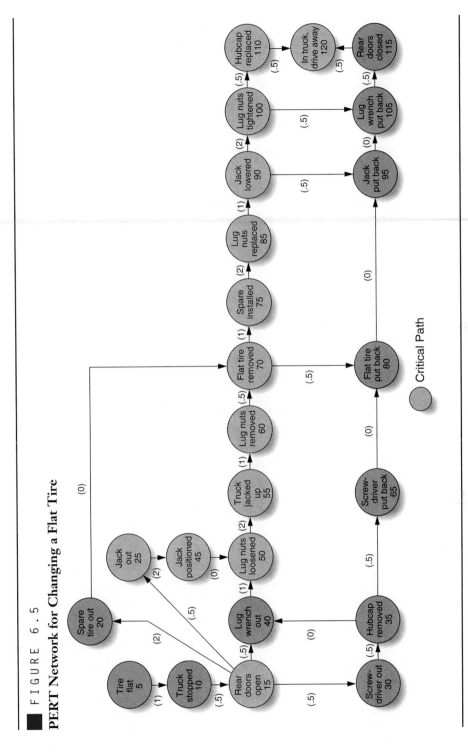

Critical Path

Source: From *Experiencing Modern Management*, by Samuel C. Certo and Lee A. Graf. Copyright © 1992 Pearson Education, Inc. Reprinted by permission of Pearson Education, Inc., Upper Saddle River, NJ.

the parts of the previous model, in half the time, and at half the cost. It assigned a team to develop an action plan for accomplishing that objective. The team cut the number of necessary parts by more than half and had the VCR in production in one year (compared with two years for previous models).[7] (Chapter 3 provides a more detailed discussion of managing teamwork.)

Updating Objectives

Once the supervisor has set objectives, he or she should monitor performance and compare it with the objectives. The control process will be described later in this chapter. Sometimes the supervisor determines that objectives need to be modified.

When should supervisors update the objectives for their department or work group? They will need to do so whenever top management updates organizational objectives. Also, organizations with a regular procedure for planning will specify when supervisors must review and update their objectives.

The Supervisor as Controller

controlling
The management function of ensuring that work goes according to plan.

As you learned in Chapter 1, **controlling** is the management function of making sure that work goes according to plan. Supervisors carry out this process in many ways. Consider the following fictional examples:

- Bud Cavanaugh told his crew, "I expect the work area to be clean when you leave each day. That means the floors are swept and all the tools are put away."
- Once or twice each day, Maria Lopez took time to check the documents produced by the word-processing operators she supervised. Maria would look over a few pages each employee had produced that day. If one of the employees seemed to be having trouble with some task—for example, deciphering handwriting or preparing neat tables—Maria would discuss the problem with that employee.
- Sonja Friedman learned that citizens calling her housing department complained of spending an excessive amount of time on hold. She scheduled a meeting at which the employees discussed ways they could handle calls faster.

As shown in these examples, supervisors need to know what is going on in the area they supervise. Do employees understand what they are supposed to do and can they do it? Is all machinery and equipment (whether a computer-operated milling machine or a touch-tone telephone) operating properly? Is work getting out correctly and on time?

To answer such questions, a supervisor could theoretically sit back and wait for disaster to strike. No disaster, no need for correction. More realistically, the supervisor has a responsibility to correct problems as soon as possible, which means that some way to *detect* problems quickly must be found. Detection of problems is at the heart of the control function.

By controlling, the supervisor can take steps to ensure quality and manage costs. Visiting the work area and checking up on performance, as Maria Lopez did, allows the supervisor to make sure that employees are producing satisfactory work. By setting standards for a clean workplace, Bud Cavanaugh reduced costs related to spending time looking for tools or to slipping on a messy floor. Sonja Friedman engaged her employees in improving work processes. In many such ways, supervisors can benefit the organization through the process of control.

■ FIGURE 6.6

The Control Process

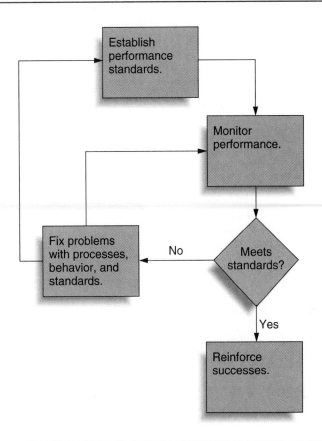

The Process of Controlling

While the specific ways in which supervisors control vary according to the type of organization and the employees being supervised, the basic process involves three steps. First, the supervisor establishes performance **standards,** which are measures of what is expected. Then the supervisor monitors actual performance and compares it with the standards. Finally, the supervisor responds, either by reinforcing success or by making some adjustment to bring performance and the standards into line. Figure 6.6 illustrates this process.

If the control system is working properly, the supervisor should be uncovering problems before customers and management discover them. This gives the supervisor the best opportunity to fix a problem in time to minimize damage.

Establish Performance Standards   Performance standards are a natural outgrowth of the planning process. Once the supervisor knows the objectives employees are to achieve, he or she can determine what employees must do to meet those objectives. Assume that the objective of an eight-person telephone sales (telemarketing) office is to make 320 calls an evening, resulting in 64 sales. To achieve this objective, each salesperson should average 10 calls an hour, with 2 in 10 calls resulting in a sale. Those numbers could be two of the office's performance standards.

standards
Measures of what is expected.

Standards define the acceptable quantity and quality of work. (The measure of quantity in the example is the number of telephone calls made; the number of sales measures the quality of selling; that is, turning a telephone call into a sale.) Other standards can spell out expectations for level of service, amount of money spent, amount of inventory on hand, level of pollution in the workplace, and other concerns. Ultimately, all these standards measure how well the department contributes to meeting the organization's objectives for serving its customers and—for a business—earning a profit.

The way supervisors set standards depends on their experience, their employer's expectations, and the nature of the work being monitored. Often, supervisors use their technical expertise to estimate reasonable standards. Past performance also is a useful guide for what can be expected. However, the supervisor must avoid being a slave to the past. In creating a budget, some supervisors assume that because they have spent a given sum in a given category in the past, that expense will be appropriate in the future. Sometimes there are better alternatives. Supervisors may have additional sources of information in setting performance standards. Equipment manufacturers and systems designers can provide information about how fast a machine or computer system will perform. Some companies arrange for time-and-motion studies to analyze how quickly and efficiently employees can reasonably work.

To be effective, performance standards should meet the criteria of effective objectives; that is, they should be written, measurable, clear, specific, and challenging but achievable. Standards also should measure dimensions of the goods or services that customers care about. Finally, because standards serve as the basis for deciding whether to make changes, they should measure things the group, supervisor, or organization has the ability to act on.[8]

Not only should the supervisor have standards in mind, but the employees should be aware of and understand those standards. In communicating performance standards, the supervisor should put them in writing so that employees can remember and refer to them as necessary. (Chapter 10 provides more detailed suggestions for communicating effectively.)

The supervisor should also be sure that the employees understand the rationale for the standards. It is human nature to resist when someone lays down restrictive rules, but the rules seem less of a burden when they serve a purpose we can understand. Thus, if a law office's word-processing department is to produce error-free documents, the department's supervisor can explain that it is part of the firm's plan to build a prestigious clientele by delivering an excellent product. With such an explanation, the word processors are less likely to feel overwhelmed by the stringent quality standard and more likely to feel proud that they are part of an excellent law firm.

Monitor Performance and Compare with Standards   Once performance standards are in place, the supervisor can begin the core of the control process: monitoring performance. In the example of the telephone sales force, the supervisor would want to keep track of how many calls each salesperson made and how many of those calls resulted in sales.

One way to monitor performance is simply to record information on paper or enter it into a computer, a task that can be done by the supervisor, the employees, or both. The telephone salespeople in the example might provide the supervisor with information to enter into a log such as the one shown in Table 6.3. Some types of machinery and equipment have electronic or mechanical counting sys-

TABLE 6.3 **Sample Performance Record**	Week of <u>November 22, 2002</u>			
	Performance Standard: <u>40</u> calls, <u>8</u> sales			
	Name	**Number of Calls Completed**	**Number of Sales Made**	**Action**
	Forrest	32	6	Discuss slow pace of work.
	French	41	8	Praise performance.
	Johnson	39	7	None.
	Munoz	47	9	Praise performance.
	Peterson	38	8	Praise performance.
	Spagnoli	50	7	Praise hard work; discuss how to turn more calls into sales.
	Steinmetz	29	5	Discuss poor performance; discipline if necessary.
	Wang	<u>43</u>	<u>9</u>	Praise performance.
	Total	**319**	**59**	

tems that provide an unbiased way to measure performance. For instance, the electronic scanners at store checkout stations can keep track of how fast cashiers are ringing up merchandise.

One new means of monitoring performance in a growing number of firms is software that allows supervisors to track employees' use of the Internet. Management Recruiters International recently reported that 64 percent of nearly 3,500 companies surveyed had a policy prohibiting using the Internet for personal reasons at work, 40 percent had monitoring software in place to track such usage, and nearly 35 percent restricted employee's access to Internet websites.[9]

Of course, the monitoring must be efficient and accurate. After investigating a series of fatal bus crashes in U.S. cities in 1997, the National Transportation Safety Board announced that the reason the federal government cannot identify hazardous public transit conditions before accidents occur is that the data collection and oversight methods are poor. "Somebody needs to be there in an oversight role, overseeing safety," said James E. Hall, the board's chairman, emphasizing the need not only to have controls in place but for those controls to be effective.[10]

From a quality perspective, monitoring performance should include assessing whether customers are satisfied. Supervisors of groups that provide services to other employees in the organization should ask those internal customers whether they are getting what they need, when they need it. They may find it helpful to conduct a survey assessing whether the customers are happy with the group's reports, response times, ideas, repairs, or other services.[11]

When monitoring performance, the supervisor should focus on how actual performance compares with the standards he or she has set. Are employees meeting standards, exceeding them, or falling short? Two concepts useful for maintaining this focus are variance and the exception principle.

In a control system, **variance** refers to the size of the difference between actual performance and the standard to be met. When setting standards, the

variance
The size of the difference between actual performance and a performance standard.

SUPERVISION AND DIVERSITY

Controlling with Rules, Communication, and Faith

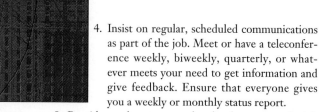

A reporter recently uncovered the ways three successful firms help their supervisors control the efforts of the workforce. While the tips they offered were focused on controlling telecommuters, they apply generally to subordinates both in and out of the office. Here's what American Management Systems (a computer consulting firm), AT&T, and PeopleSoft (a software firm) had to say:

1. Set rules for workers with unorthodox locations and schedules that require them to do the work they are supposed to do and not abuse the privilege of working at home or during flextime.
2. Trust your people to follow tip 1.
3. Don't be compulsive about checking up on them, such as calling them at home to be sure they really are working.

4. Insist on regular, scheduled communications as part of the job. Meet or have a teleconference weekly, biweekly, quarterly, or whatever meets your need to get information and give feedback. Ensure that everyone gives you a weekly or monthly status report.
5. Provide ample support and technology to get the job done, on- or off-site.
6. Make sure there's a well-equipped "home" for telecommuters when they do come into the office.
7. In return for real-time updates from your staff, provide them with relevant and timely information, online if that's convenient.

Source: Carol A.L. Dannhauser, "The Invisible Worker," *Working Woman*, November 1998, p. 38.

---

supervisor should decide how much variance is meaningful for control purposes. It can be helpful to think in terms of percentages. For example, if a hospital's performance standard is to register outpatients for lab tests in 10 minutes or less, the supervisor might decide to allow for a variance of 50 percent (5 minutes). (In a manufacturing setting, a variance of 5 to 10 percent might be more appropriate for most standards.) As described in Chapter 2, some organizations strive for a standard of accepting zero defects.

exception principle
The control principle stating that a supervisor should take action only when a variance is meaningful.

According to the **exception principle,** the supervisor should take action only when a variance is meaningful. Thus, when monitoring performance in the previous example, the supervisor would need to take action only if outpatients spent more than 15 or fewer than 5 minutes registering for lab tests.

The exception principle is beneficial when it helps the supervisor to manage his or her time wisely and to motivate employees. A supervisor who did not tolerate reasonable variances might try to solve the "problem" every time an employee made one component too few or went over the budget for office supplies by the cost of a box of paper clips. In such a case, employees might become frustrated by the control system, and morale would deteriorate. At the same time, the supervisor would be too busy with trifles to focus on more significant issues. See "Supervision and Diversity."

Reinforce Successes and Fix Problems   The information gained from the control process is beneficial only if the supervisor uses it as the basis for reinforcing or changing behavior. If performance is satisfactory or better, the supervisor needs to encourage this. If performance is unacceptable, the supervisor needs to make changes that either improve performance or adjust the standard. The right-hand column in Table 6.3 lists some ways the telemarketing supervisor plans to respond to performance data.

reinforcement
Encouragement of a behavior by associating it with a reward.

When employees are doing excellent work, customers are happy, and costs are within budget, the supervisor needs to reinforce these successes. **Reinforcement** means encouraging the behavior by associating it with a reward. Praise from the supervisor for performance that meets standards not only gives the employee a good feeling, but also clarifies what is expected. For exceptionally high performance, the supervisor also may reward the employee with a monetary bonus. The supervisor's actions will depend on company and union rules regarding superior performance.

problem
A factor in the organization that is a barrier to improvement.

When performance significantly falls short of standards, the supervisor should investigate. Below-standard performance is the sign of a **problem**—some factor in the organization that is a barrier to improvement. The supervisor's task is to identify the underlying problem. For example, if the supervisor in the telephone sales company learns that the group is not meeting its sales objectives, the supervisor could find out who is falling short of the sales goals: everyone or only one or two employees. If everyone is performing below standard, the problem may be that the sales force needs better training or motivation. Or the problem may lie outside the supervisor's direct control; the product may be defective or customers may lack interest for some other reason, such as poor economic conditions. If only one employee is failing to make sales, the supervisor needs to search for the problem underlying that employee's poor performance. Does the employee understand how to close a sale? Does the employee have personal problems that affect performance?

symptom
An indication of an underlying problem.

Poor performance itself is rarely a problem, but a **symptom**—an indication of an underlying problem. To make effective use of information gained through controlling, the supervisor needs to distinguish problems from symptoms. For instance, some health care experts estimate that 42 percent of life-threatening medication errors that occur in U.S. hospitals could be prevented. Seeing the number of unnecessary emergencies as a symptom rather than a problem, one team of writers suggests that the real remedy has little to do with drugs themselves but instead includes developing hospital systems that do not depend on human memory, simplifying and standardizing drug administration processes and dosages, using protocols wisely, avoiding reliance on handwritten or verbal orders, and eliminating long hours, particularly overtime, for physicians and nurses.[12]

Sometimes a problem underlying a significant variance is that the standard is too low or too high. For example, if no employees on the telephone sales force are achieving the desired number of sales, the standards may be too high, given current economic or market conditions. In other cases, what the manager learns about performance may indicate that a standard is not measuring the right thing.

Fixing the problem may entail adjusting a process, the behavior of an individual employee, or the standard itself. For process and behavioral problems, supervisors can choose from among a number of possible actions:

- Develop new rewards for good performance.
- Train employees.
- Improve communications with employees.
- Counsel and/or discipline poor performers.
- Ask employees what barriers are interfering with their performance, then remove those barriers. (Common barriers include insufficient supplies or information, poorly maintained equipment, and inefficient work procedures.)

The best response to problems related to standards is to make the performance standard more appropriate. The supervisor may need to make the standard less stringent or more challenging.

Whatever actions the supervisor selects, it is important to give employees feedback soon after observing a deviation from the standard. This enables the employees to make changes before performance deteriorates further. A problem that has been allowed to continue is often harder to correct. For example, an employee may get into the habit of doing a task the wrong way or may fall so far behind that it is impossible to catch up.

Modifying standards brings the control process full circle. With new standards in place, the supervisor is again ready to monitor performance.

Types of Control

From the description of the control process, it might sound as though controlling begins when employees' work is complete. The employees finish their jobs, then the supervisor checks whether a job was done well. However, this is only one type of controlling. There are three types of control in terms of when it takes place: feedback control, concurrent control, and precontrol.

feedback control
Control that focuses on past performance.

Feedback control is the type just described; that is, control that focuses on past performance. A supervisor reviewing customer comments about service is practicing feedback control. The customers provide information about the quality of service; the supervisor reacts by reinforcing or trying to change employee behavior.

concurrent control
Control that occurs while the work takes place.

The word *concurrent* describes things that are happening at the same time. Thus, **concurrent control** refers to controlling work while that work is taking place. A restaurant manager who greets customers at their tables and visits the kitchen to see how work is progressing is practicing concurrent control. This supervisor is gathering information about what is going smoothly and what problems may be developing. The supervisor can act on any problems before customers or employees become upset. Another technique for concurrent control is statistical process control, described in Chapter 2.

precontrol
Efforts aimed at preventing behavior that may lead to undesirable results.

Precontrol refers to efforts aimed at preventing behavior that may lead to undesirable results. Such efforts may include setting rules, policies, and procedures. A production supervisor might provide employees with guidelines about the detection of improperly functioning machinery. The employees can then request repairs before they waste time and materials on the machinery. Precontrol is one of the functions of the management philosophy known as total quality management (see Chapter 2).

Tools for Control

When considering how to monitor performance, the supervisor can start with some of the basic tools used by most managers. Budgets and reports are common in most organizations. In addition, supervisors can benefit from personally observing the work taking place.

Budgets   Creating a budget—a plan for spending money—is part of the planning process. In controlling, a budget is useful as a kind of performance standard. The supervisor compares actual expenses with the amounts in the budget.

Table 6.4 is a sample budget report based on the example in Table 6.2. The left-hand column shows each category of expenses for the machine shop project, which was scheduled to last for six months, from January through June. Thus, the six-month budget represents the total the supervisor expected to spend in each category for the project. This report was prepared on March 31 (halfway through the project), so the next column shows what would be budgeted for half of the project. The next column shows the amounts that actually were spent during the

TABLE 6.4
Budget Report for a Manufacturing Project

Line Item	Organizational Unit Machine Shop Job Number 1763 Date March 31, 20xx			
	Six-Month Budget	Budgeted Year to Date (Jan.–Mar.)	Actual Year to Date (Jan.–Mar.)	Variance
Direct labor	$60,000	$30,000	$30,000	$ 0
Indirect labor	5,400	2,700	2,700	0
Material	13,200	6,600	6,383	217
Operating supplies	3,000	1,500	1,496	4
Equipment repair	5,400	2,700	3,600	–900
Total	**$87,000**	**$43,500**	**$44,179**	**–$679**

Source: From *Industrial Supervision: In The Age of Technology*, by David L. Goetsch. Copyright © 1992 Pearson Education, Inc. Reprinted by permission of Pearson Education, Inc., Upper Saddle River, NJ.

first three months. In the right-hand column appears the variance between the actual and budgeted amounts. In this case, the machine shop has a negative total variance because the project is $679 over budget for the first three months.

When using such a budget report for controlling purposes, the supervisor focuses on the variance column, looking for meaningful variances. In Table 6.4, the supervisor would note that the total unfavorable variance is due entirely to a large expense for equipment repair. The machine shop is otherwise under budget or exactly meeting the budget standards. Following the exception principle, the supervisor takes action when a meaningful variance occurs. Typically, this involves looking for ways to cut costs when the department goes over budget. The supervisor in the example will want to focus on avoiding further equipment breakdowns. Sometimes the supervisor can change the budget when a variance indicates that the budgeted figures were unrealistic. See "Meeting the Challenge" for a look at budgeting in art museums.

Performance Reports   A well-structured report can be an important source of information. **Performance reports** summarize performance and compare it with performance standards. They can simply summarize facts, such as the number of calls made by sales representatives or the number of deliveries completed by delivery personnel, or they can be analytical; that is, they may interpret the facts.

Most supervisors both prepare and request performance reports. Typically, the organization requires that the supervisor do a particular type of reporting of the department's performance. The supervisor's role is to prepare this report. Supervisors also may request that employees prepare reports for them. In that case, the supervisor can influence the type of reporting.

As much as possible, supervisors should see that reports are simple and to the point. A table or log may be more useful than an essay-style report. Graphs can sometimes uncover a trend better than numbers in columns. Figure 6.7 shows how the data from Table 6.3 can be converted into a graph. In this case, variances were first computed of the difference between each employee's performance and the performance standards. Notice how easy it is to tell from the graph the wide variation in the number of calls made by each employee. Does this mean some

performance report
A summary of performance and comparison with performance standards.

FIGURE 6.7

Graph of Variances Determined from Table 6.3

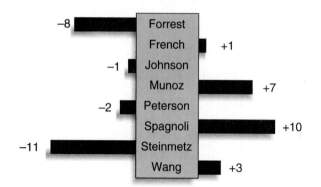

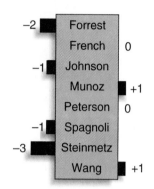

employees are working harder than others? Maybe, but remember the process of searching for a problem. It is also possible that some employees are better at keeping calls short and to the point.

Perhaps even more important is the supervisor's role in creating a climate that fosters full and accurate reporting. The example of Wal-Mart and Kmart early in this chapter described two very different strategies for the retailers. After several years of pursuing those strategies, Wal-Mart surged past Kmart in several measures, including sales, income, and stock price. However, the strategy difference may have been less important than the behavior of managers. At Wal-Mart, executives routinely visited stores and sought suggestions for improvement. In contrast, Kmart CEO Joseph Antonini reportedly discouraged criticism.[13] Although this example describes the behavior of top management, supervisors also can shape a favorable climate by actively seeking ideas from employees and being willing to listen to reports that something may be wrong.

The supervisor also should determine whether every report he or she is receiving is still useful. Many reports continue to be generated long after they have lost their usefulness. In deciding whether to continue using a report, the supervisor can consider whether it has the characteristics of effective controls, described at the end of this chapter.

Personal Observation A supervisor who spends the entire day behind a desk reading budgets and reports is out of touch. An important part of controlling involves spending time with employees and observing what is going on. Management consultant Tom Peters has popularized this approach, which he calls "management by walking around." While engaged in this approach, the supervisor can listen to employees, help them discover better ways of doing their jobs, and make the changes necessary to help employees carry them out. For example, a nursing supervisor might observe that the nurses frequently spend time debating which demands to respond to first. The supervisor could discuss this with the nurses and help them develop criteria for setting priorities.

Museums Look for Ways to Control Costs

Most art museums have had to come face-to-face with a new business reality: To pay their bills, they need to market themselves. "Blockbuster" shows and exhibits, extended hours, and expanded gift shop and catalog offerings all demonstrate how hard museum directors are working to balance their budgets.

Art prices have risen steeply, along with the costs of security, insurance, shipping, printing catalogs, marketing, and sharing and borrowing works of art for shows. In the past most institutions tried to keep admission fees low, and some even experimented with "pay what you wish" policies. They made little or no attempt to link what an exhibition cost with what it earned for the institution. Now, however, it is becoming a struggle to keep ticket prices in line with the price of a movie, which was the pricing benchmark for many years. Fortunately, tracking costs is becoming easier, and most museum directors are becoming more financially sophisticated. They perform careful profit-and-loss analyses on individual events and sell special tickets for popular shows, priced accordingly.

All this budgetary caution is, of course, in the service of art. Not every show will feature such popular painters as Monet, nor do museums want to. "I want to balance the museum's finances, I don't want to be a blockbuster junkie," says Malcolm Rogers, director of the Museum of Fine Arts in Boston.

Source: Judith H. Dobrzynski, "Blockbuster Shows and Prices to Match," *New York Times*, November 10, 1998, pp. E1, E13.

Personal observation can help the supervisor understand the activities behind the numbers in reports. However, the supervisor must be careful in interpreting what he or she sees. Often the presence of a supervisor causes workers to alter their behavior. Also, the supervisor must visit work areas often enough to be sure of witnessing routine situations, not just an unusual crisis or break in the action. At the same time, the supervisor must not spend so much time among employees that they feel the visits interfere with their work. How much time is the right amount to spend in management by walking around? The supervisor probably will have to rely on trial and error, weighing employee reactions and the amount of information obtained.

The inability to control through personal observation is a challenge of supervising employees who work at home. This issue is growing in importance as communications technology makes telecommuting possible for people with disabilities, working parents, and others who simply prefer not to dress up. How can a supervisor make sure employees are not devoting their time to raiding the refrigerator and catching up on the latest soap operas?

Evidence suggests that employees who choose to work at home tend to be self-motivated. If anything, they have trouble taking a break. One telecommuter reportedly became so wrapped up in his computer programming that he gave himself headaches by working for hours without interruption. He eventually had to set a clock radio to go off every two hours, reminding him to take a break. Dramatic examples aside, supervisors and employees alike can benefit from training in handling the long-distance relationship.

"The telecommuter has to understand what the supervisor's problems are going to be and vice versa," says George Piskurich, a management consultant. Roger Herman, CEO of the Herman Group, points out, "One of the things the supervisor has to be sensitive to, of course, is maintaining that high level of communication, keeping [telecommuters] involved and realizing that managing someone you can't see is considerably different than walking around the cubicle wall to see that they're there at eight in the morning."[14]

Characteristics of Effective Controls

No supervisor can keep track of every detail of every employee's work. An effective control system is one that helps the supervisor direct his or her efforts toward spotting significant problems. Normally, a supervisor has to use whatever control system higher-level managers have established. However, when making recommendations about controls or setting up controls to use within the department, the supervisor can strive for the following characteristics of effective controls.

Timeliness

The controls should be *timely*, enabling the supervisor to correct problems in time to improve results. For example, an annual budget report does not let the supervisor adjust spending in time to meet the budget's goals. In contrast, monthly budget reports give the supervisor time to identify spending patterns that will pose a problem. If the supervisor's annual budget includes $500 to spend on overnight couriers but the department has already spent $200 by the end of February, the supervisor knows that work must be planned far enough ahead that materials can be sent by other, less expensive means.

Cost-Effectiveness

The controls should be *economical*. In general, this means that the cost of using the controls should be less than the benefit derived from using them. In a supermarket, for example, an elaborate system designed to ensure that not a single item of inventory gets lost or stolen may not save the store enough money to justify the cost of the system.

Acceptability

The controls should be *acceptable to supervisors and employees*. Supervisors want controls that give them enough information about performance so that they can understand what is going on in the workplace. Employees want controls that do not unduly infringe on their privacy. One area of controversy has been electronic monitoring of employee performance. For example, computers can keep track of how many telephone calls operators handle and how much time they spend on each call. Electronic monitoring gives the supervisor a lot of information, including how much time operators spend going to the bathroom. Does this close scrutiny enhance performance by encouraging employees to work hard, or does it merely lower morale and remove the incentive to take time to greet customers in a friendly way? The answer lies partly in the way supervisors use this information.

Employees also appreciate controls that focus on areas over which they themselves have some control. For example, a control that measures the number of units produced by an employee would be acceptable only if the employee always has the parts needed to produce those units. An employee whose performance looks poor because of an inventory shortage would feel frustrated by the control.

Flexibility

Finally, the controls should be *flexible*. This means that the supervisor should be able to ignore a variance if doing so is in the best interests of the organization. For example, in comparing expenditures to a budget, a supervisor should be aware of occasions when spending a little more than was budgeted actually will benefit the company. That might be the case when employees have to put in overtime to fill an order for an important customer. In the future, better planning might make it possible to avoid the overtime, but the immediate goal is to satisfy the customer.

One reason flexibility is important is that performance measures might be incompatible. For instance, employees may find it impossible to cut costs and improve quality at the same time. In that case, the supervisor may have to set priorities or adjust the control measures. Such actions are in effect a type of planning, an example of how controlling and planning work together to help the organization reach its goals.

Summary

6.1 Describe types of planning that take place in organizations.

At the top level of an organization, managers engage in strategic planning, which is the creation of long-term goals for the organization. The plans for divisions, departments, and work groups are known as operational plans and are set by middle managers and supervisors. Operational plans support the strategic plan; they are more specific and focus on a shorter time frame. Supervisors also must apply good planning practices to their individual efforts.

6.2 Identify characteristics of effective objectives.

Effective objectives are written, measurable or observable, clear, specific, and challenging but achievable.

6.3 Define *management by objectives (MBO)* and discuss its use.

Management by objectives is a process in which managers and employees at all levels set objectives for what they are to accomplish, after which their performance is measured against those objectives. In MBO, all individuals in the organization work to set objectives; each employee's manager periodically reviews the employee's performance against the objectives, and the organization rewards individuals based on how close they come to fulfilling the objectives. To use MBO effectively, managers at all levels of an organization must be committed to the system.

6.4 Discuss the supervisor's role in the planning process.

Supervisors are responsible for the creation of plans that specify goals, tasks, resources, and responsibilities for their own departments. Supervisors keep higher-level managers informed about the needs, abilities, and progress of their groups. They decide how to allocate resources to the jobs that need to be done, including creating budgets. Supervisors also engage in scheduling. Where possible, they should involve employees in the planning process.

6.5 Explain the purpose of using controls.

By identifying problems in time for them to be corrected, controlling enables supervisors to ensure high-quality work and to keep costs under control.

6.6 Identify the steps in the control process.

First, the supervisor sets and communicates performance standards in writing. The supervisor then monitors performance and compares it with the standards. Depending on whether performance is above, at, or below the standards, the supervisor reinforces successes or fixes problems. Fixing a problem may entail adjusting a process, the behavior of an employee, or the standard itself.

6.7 Identify types of control and tools for controlling.

Feedback control focuses on past performance. Concurrent control occurs while the work is taking place. Precontrol is aimed at preventing behavior that may lead to undesirable results. Budgets, performance reports, and personal observation are all tools for controlling.

6.8   List characteristics of effective controls.
Effective controls are timely, economical, acceptable to both supervisor and employee, and flexible.

Key Terms

planning, p. 128

objectives, p. 128

goals, p. 128

strategic planning, p. 129

operational planning, p. 129

policies, p. 132

procedures, p. 132

rules, p. 132

action plan, p. 132

contingency planning, p. 133

management by objectives (MBO), p. 133

budget, p. 136

scheduling, p. 137

Gantt chart, p. 137

program evaluation and review technique (PERT), p. 138

controlling, p. 140

standards, p. 141

variance, p. 143

exception principle, p. 144

reinforcement, p. 144

problem, p. 145

symptom, p. 145

feedback control, p. 146

concurrent control, p. 146

precontrol, p. 146

performance report, p. 147

Review and Discussion Questions

1. Why is it important for supervisors and other managers to spend time planning?
2. Define policies, procedures, and goals. How does each relate to an organization's objective?
3. Jill Donahue is the supervisor of the telephone operators who handle emergency calls from citizens and dispatch police, firefighters, and ambulances. One of her objectives for the coming year is to reduce the average time it takes for calls to be answered from 1 minute to 30 seconds. How can Jill go about creating an action plan to achieve this objective? What questions must she answer? Suggest a possible answer for each question.
4. Assume you are the supervisor of the machine shop whose budget appears in Table 6.2.
   a. Modify the budgeted amounts to create a budget for a new project of the same size and type. Use the following assumptions and guidelines:
      • The organization says that direct labor costs may increase by no more than 6 percent.
      • You have been instructed to cut expenses for equipment repair by 10 percent.

   • You expect that materials costs will increase about 5 percent.
   b. What additional assumptions did you make to create the budget?
5. What is wrong with each of the following objectives? Rewrite each so that it has the characteristics of an effective objective.
   a. Improve the procedure for responding to customer complaints.
   b. Meet or exceed last year's sales quotas.
   c. Minimize the number of parts that are defective.
   d. Communicate clearly with patients.
6. What are some advantages of involving employees in the process of developing objectives? How can supervisors do this?
7. Your best friend just got promoted to a position as a supervisor and feels uncomfortable about "checking up on people." How can you explain to your friend why controlling plays an important role in helping the organization meet its goals?
8. What are the steps in the process of controlling?
9. How is the control process related to the management function of planning?

10. Bonnie Goode supervises telephone operators in the customer service department of a software company. The operators are expected to handle 50 phone calls per day (250 in a five-day workweek). Every Monday, Bonnie receives a report of each operator's weekly performance relative to this standard. Her most recent report contained the following information:

Operator	Mon.	Tues.	Wed.	Thurs.	Fri.	Total	Variance
Brown	10	28	39	42	16	135	–115
Lee	48	51	58	43	49	249	–1
Mendoza	65	72	56	83	61	337	87
Smith	53	48	47	40	45	233	–17

    a. As supervisor, how should Bonnie respond to each operator's performance?

    b. Is this control system an effective one for ensuring quality performance? Explain.

11. If failure to meet a performance standard indicates some type of underlying problem, how might the supervisor attempt to solve the problem?

12. Mildred Pirelli supervises salespeople in a department store. One day she walked around her department to observe the salespeople in action. She saw a salesperson approve a charge card purchase without following the company's policy of verifying the signature on the card.

    a. How should Mildred respond to this variance from company policy?

    b. Should the way Mildred obtained the information (personal observation) influence her choice of how to act? Explain.

13. Why do controls need to be timely and economical?

A SECOND LOOK

What tools for control does Bruce Lemmerman appear to use? How might he improve his use of control mechanisms?

SKILLS MODULE

CASE

Management by Dropping In

One way to set performance standards for your department is to keep checking on the competition. That's exactly what Staples CEO Tom Stemberg does on a regular basis. Every week he visits at least one of his competitors' retail outlets and one of his own, and sometimes he even drops in on stores with whom Staples doesn't compete, like Toys "R" Us and Price Club. "I've never visited a store where I didn't learn something," he says.

A key to Stemberg's standard setting is his attitude. He looks for things the competition does better than Staples, no matter how many things he may find to criticize. He takes note of the quality of the service, how well stocked the store is, how neatly items are displayed and how accurately priced. He asks salesclerks where items are located and notices whether they show him or merely tell him. He once sent his mother-in-law to an Office Depot store in Florida to test that competitor's delivery and return policies and asked some simple questions of the truck driver to estimate the strength of Office Depot's delivery business.

One drawback to using the competition as a control-setting mechanism, says Stemberg, is that it takes the focus away from the customer. As examples he cites Barnes and Noble and Borders, whom he suspects spend most of their time looking at each other "when both of them should be paying attention to Amazon.com."

1. Rate Stemberg's use of personal observation as a control device against this chapter's set of characteristics of effective controls (timeliness, cost-effectiveness, acceptability, and flexibility).
2. Stemberg says he has visited about 690 of the 740 Staples stores. What are some things he probably looks for when he visits them?
3. What lessons might a supervisor learn from Stemberg's example? Other than the drawback cited above, are there any other pitfalls to his approach?

Source: Stephanie Gruner, "Spies Like Us," *Inc.*, August 1998, p. 45.

■ SELF-QUIZ

Are You a Planner?

Answer each of the following questions with a yes or no.

1. Do you decide the night before what to wear each day? _____
2. Do you buy birthday gifts at the last minute? _____
3. Do you divide up household chores with your roommates or family members? _____
4. When you receive a paycheck, do you designate certain portions of it for specific expenses? _____
5. At the beginning of the workday or school day, do you make a list of what you must accomplish? _____
6. Do you buy a big-ticket item because a friend has the same item and raves about it? _____
7. Do you start studying for final exams before the last week of classes? _____
8. When you purchase a new piece of electronic equipment, such as a computer or CD player, do you read the instructions about how to use it? _____
9. Before taking a trip, do you study a map? _____
10. When you have several projects to handle at once, do you first tackle the one that appeals to you most? _____

Scoring: Answering Yes to questions 1, 3, 4, 5, 7, 8, and 9 and No to questions 2, 6, and 10 indicates that you are a planner.

Class Exercise

This exercise provides you with an opportunity to practice what you learned in this chapter. You will practice setting personal goals (objectives) that are written, measurable, specific, clear, and challenging.

Instructions

1. In the space provided on the next page, write four goals that are important for you to achieve during the remainder of this semester.
2. Some of the goals should be short term (maybe something you need to finish by the end of this week); others should have a longer time frame (maybe by the end of the semester).
3. Write your goal statement so you can check all four boxes (measurable, specific, clear, and challenging) as being represented. Provided here is a brief summary of each term:

- *Measurable*—Provide a tangible way (dollar amount, time frame, or quantity) to determine whether you have reached your goal—avoid *maximize, improve*, and other terms that cannot be measured.
- *Specific*—Describe the actions you will need to take to achieve your goal.
- *Clear*—Use simple language.
- *Challenging* (yet realistic and obtainable)—Choose motivating and stimulating goals that when achieved will give you a sense of pride and build your confidence.

4. Your four goals should represent several different areas; for example, academic, job, career, spiritual, family, financial, social, or physical goals. An example of a financial goal that meets all four criteria is "I will save

20 percent of every paycheck starting this Friday so I'll have enough to pay for my auto insurance when it comes due the last week of the semester." If you are having trouble meeting any of the four criteria in your personal goals, discuss your goal with a classmate or your professor to see if one of them can help you define your goal more clearly.

5. After successfully achieving each goal, write the date in the "Follow-Up" column next to the goal.

Source: This class exercise was written by Corinne Livesay, Belhaven College, Jackson, Mississippi.

Goal:	Follow-up (When you've achieved this goal, write the date here.)
✓ if statement is: Measurable ☐ Specific ☐ Clear ☐ Challenging ☐	

Goal:	Follow-up (When you've achieved this goal, write the date here.)
✓ if statement is: Measurable ☐ Specific ☐ Clear ☐ Challenging ☐	

Goal:	Follow-up (When you've achieved this goal, write the date here.)
✓ if statement is: Measurable ☐ Specific ☐ Clear ☐ Challenging ☐	

Goal:	Follow-up (When you've achieved this goal, write the date here.)
✓ if statement is: Measurable ☐ Specific ☐ Clear ☐ Challenging ☐	

■ FIGURE 6.8

Instructions for Origami Yachts

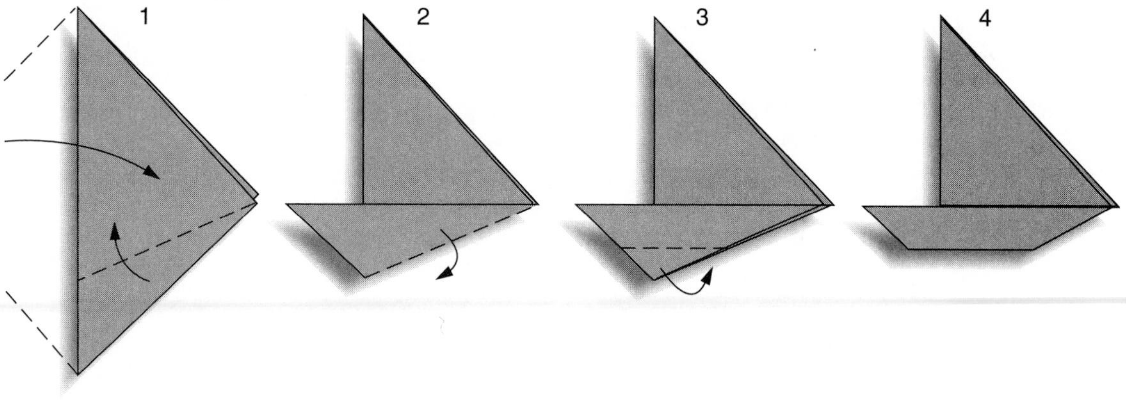

Source: Corinne Livesay of Belhaven College, Jackson, Mississippi, supplied the origami instructions.

Team-Building Exercise

Controlling a Yacht-Making Operation

Divide the class into groups of five or six members. One member of each group will act as the supervisor; the rest are employees. Since few real-life work groups get to choose their supervisor, the instructor might arbitrarily designate the supervisor in each group. The instructor provides each group with square sheets of paper; 5⅞ in. × 5⅞ in. is a good size.

1. Each person reviews instructions for making origami yachts (see Figure 6.8).
2. The supervisor in each group sets performance standards for making the yachts in 10 minutes. These should include quality as well as quantity standards. In setting the standards, the supervisor may use whatever information he or she can obtain; it is up to the supervisor whether to seek input from the group.

   At the same time, each employee estimates how many yachts he or she can make correctly in 10 minutes. The employee writes down this estimate but does not reveal it to the supervisor at this time.
3. For 10 minutes, the employees make as many yachts as they can according to the instruc-

tions. During that time, the supervisor tries to monitor their performance in whatever way seems helpful. If employees seem to be falling short of the performance standard, the supervisor should try to find ways to improve performance. (This may include simply waiting patiently for skills to improve, if that seems most beneficial.)

4. After the 10 minutes have ended, determine how many yachts each group made and assess the quality of the work. As a class, discuss the groups' performance. Did each group meet its supervisor's performance standards? If not, was any variance significant? Based on their own estimates of how much they could do, do employees think their supervisor's standards were reasonable?
5. The class should also consider supervisors' efforts to take corrective action. Did supervisors intervene too much, or not enough? How did supervisors' attempts help or hurt employees' efforts? What does this experience reveal about the way supervisors should behave in the workplace?

7

The best executive is the one who has sense enough to pick good men to do what he wants done, and self-restraint enough to keep from meddling with them while they do it.

—Theodore Roosevelt, 26th president of the United States

Organizing and Authority

■ LEARNING OBJECTIVES

After you have studied this chapter, you should be able to:

7.1 Describe organization charts.

7.2 Identify basic ways in which organizations are structured.

7.3 Distinguish between line and staff authority and between centralized and decentralized authority.

7.4 Compare and contrast *authority*, *power*, *responsibility*, and *accountability*.

7.5 Identify the steps in the process of organizing.

7.6 Describe four principles of organizing.

7.7 Discuss why and how supervisors delegate.

7.8 Identify causes of reluctance to delegate.

■ THE BEST OF BOTH WORLDS

It doesn't seem likely that a company of only 83 people would need to locate itself in two different offices. Yet for John and Debbi Milner, who run a computer reselling operation called Jade Systems Corporation, the two-office organization is perfect.

One location is a former ice-cream machine factory in Long Island City, New York, across the East River from Manhattan. There, previously owned computers are received, configured to customer specifications, tested, and shipped. The neighborhood is heavily industrial, gritty, and uninviting.

The second location houses the company's sales, customer service, and management information services offices. These are found in a suburban home converted to office space, 65 miles away in the village of Cold Spring on the Hudson River. The Milners live next door, where they started the business; they bought and converted the second house, says Debbi, when "one day we realized there were eight people in our bedroom."

Cold Spring wasn't central enough, commercial enough, or close enough to Jade Systems' major customers, 90 percent of whom are big New York City firms, so part of the operation was moved to Long Island City. John and Debbi have organized their own responsibilities to reflect the geographic split. In spite of a long and sometimes difficult commute, Debbi spends two days a week there and finds it both convenient to New York City and very affordable for the business. Cold Spring, where John tends to take charge, draws plenty of attention from suppliers who just want to make a sales call in a beautiful neighborhood, and it's an ideal place to raise a family. So it isn't likely the two locations will be consolidating any time soon. The Milners like their offices and their business organized just the way they are.

Source: Eric Hubler, "Making the Best of Both Worlds," *Inc. 500*, 1998, p. 45.

---

organizing
Setting up the group, allocating resources, and assigning work to achieve goals.

In the opening story, the physical organization of a firm has evolved to meet the owners' needs. As you read in Chapter 1, **organizing** is the management function of setting up the group, allocating resources, and assigning work to achieve goals. By organizing, supervisors and other managers put their plans into action. When done well, organizing helps to ensure that the organization is using its resources—especially human resources—efficiently. For this reason, a business that is well organized is in a better position to be profitable.

Managers in even the simplest organizations need to organize. If you were to set up a softball team, you would have to collect equipment, arrange for a place to play, find players, decide what position each is to play, and create a batting lineup. If you were operating a one-person business, you would have to decide where you would work, what activities you would need to accomplish, and whether you should contract with vendors to provide some services.

Define "Minority Firm"

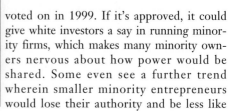

To call itself a minority firm and be eligible for corporate development programs that award millions of dollars in business, a company must have a simple 51 percent minority equity ownership. But this definition may soon be history. A growing number of minority firms are finding that to acquire the funding they need to grow, they may have to sell ownership stakes of up to 75 percent to nonminority investment firms, in effect taking on a nonminority partner and a new organizational form.

"This is no small issue," say Harriet R. Michel, president of the National Minority Supplier Development Council. A plan before the council to allow a redefinition of "minority firm" to take place will be voted on in 1999. If it's approved, it could give white investors a say in running minority firms, which makes many minority owners nervous about how power would be shared. Some even see a further trend wherein smaller minority entrepreneurs would lose their authority and be less like business owners and more like employees of white investors. "It's business ownership and economic empowerment that bring freedom," says one minority business consultant who is also a member of the council's board.

Source: Leon E. Wynter, "Minority Firms May Redefine Themselves." *Wall Street Journal*, November 4, 1998, p. B1.

This chapter describes the ways organizations are structured and the way supervisors organize. The process of organizing includes sharing authority and responsibility. The chapter explains how supervisors share both of these with the people who report to them.

The Structure of the Organization

Some of the most fundamental and far-reaching organizational decisions involve the structure of the organization as a whole. For example, top management could assign a manager authority for a particular product, a particular geographic region served by the organization, or a particular specialty such as sales or finance. Supervisors have little, if any, input into this type of decision. However, supervisors need to understand how they and their departments fit into the big picture, and that includes understanding the structure of the organization. "Supervision and Diversity" illustrates one of the factors that can cause organizational change.

Organization Charts

Businesspeople have come up with a standard way to draw the structure of an organization: the organization chart. These charts use boxes to represent the various positions or departments in an organization (usually just at management levels). Lines connecting the boxes indicate who reports to whom. Figure 7.1 is an organization chart showing the structure of an international company. Note, for example, that someone is in charge of all North American operations, and someone is in charge of all international operations. These two managers report to the person who serves as president and chief operating officer of the entire company.

The positions at the top of an organization chart are those with the most authority and responsibility. Logically, the people in these positions are referred to as the top managers. By following the lines from the top managers down the chart to the lower levels, you can see which middle managers report to these top managers. In other words, the top managers are authorized to direct the work of the

■ FIGURE 7.1

Organization Chart: An International Company

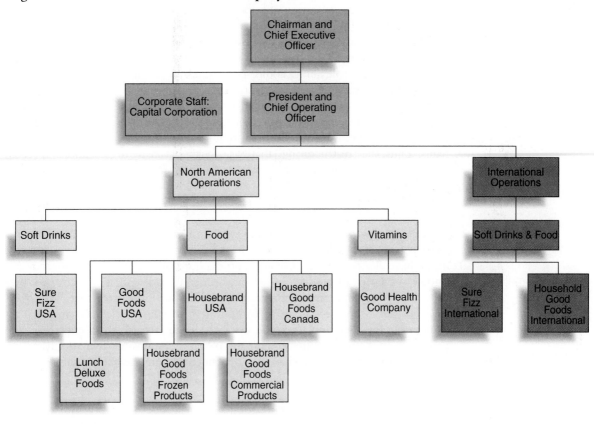

middle managers who report to them and are responsible for the performance of those middle managers. The bottom of the chart may show the first-level managers (or sometimes the operative employees). Supervisors are not shown on the chart in Figure 7.1.

Organization charts sometimes show only a portion of an organization. Like Figure 7.1, a chart may show only the top levels of management or it may show a single division in a large company. Reading the titles of the people associated with each box gives an indication of the scope of a particular organization chart.

Being able to understand organization charts enables supervisors to figure out where they fit in the organization and where opportunities might lie for future promotions. Supervisors can see the variety of responsibilities held by others at their level in the organization. Knowing where they fit in helps supervisors see how their department or group contributes to achieving the goals of the organization.

Types of Structures

department
A unique group of resources that management has assigned to carry out a particular task.

An organization with more than a handful of people works most efficiently when it is grouped into departments. A **department** is a unique group of resources that management has assigned to carry out a particular task, such as selling the company's products to customers in the Midwest, treating patients with cancer, or teaching mathematics. The way management sets up the departments—an activity called **departmentalization**—determines the type of structure the organization has.

departmentalization
Setting up departments in an organization.

Over the years, organizations have been structured in a limited number of ways. Traditionally, organization charts have indicated structures that fall into four categories: functional structure, product structure, geographic structure, and customer structure. More recently, organizations have sought other structures that achieve greater flexibility and responsiveness to customer needs.

In deciding which types of structure to use and how to combine them, managers look for the organizational arrangement that will best achieve the company's goals. As top managers learn from their experiences or as the company and its environment change, the structure may require minor adjustments or major overhauls. Thus, the "restructuring" that has occurred at many organizations in recent years consists of changes in the structure designed to respond to stiffer competition, tougher economic conditions, or the desire to benefit from new practices such as decision making by teams of employees.

Functional Structure   A functional structure groups personnel and other resources according to the types of work they carry out. For example, a business might have vice presidents of finance, production, sales, and human resources. Assigned to each vice president is the staff needed to carry out these activities. Figure 7.2 provides an example of a company with a functional structure. Wiss, Janney, Elstner Associates is an architectural firm where one vice president is responsible for operations (i.e., the work of all the architects and engineers who provide services to customers), and the other is responsible for administration (i.e., support services). Under the vice president of administration, the organization is divided into such functions as marketing and personnel.

Product Structure   In an organization with a product structure, work and resources are assigned to departments responsible for all the activities related to producing and delivering a particular product (good or service). In an automobile business, there might be one department for each make of automobile. Colleges and universities are often departmentalized according to the subject matter taught. At the company shown in Figure 7.1, North American operations are departmentalized according to three product categories: soft drinks, food, and vitamins. Figure 7.3 illustrates a product structure at a division of the Evangelical Lutheran Church in America (ELCA). One director is concerned with disaster relief, another is responsible for health care programs, and so on.

Geographic Structure   A geographic structure results when an organization is departmentalized according to the location of the customers served or the goods or services produced. A manufacturing company might have a department for each of its factories scattered around the world. An insurance company might have a department for each of its 12 sales territories. The manager of each department would be responsible for producing and/or selling all the company's goods or services in that geographic region. At the architectural firm in Figure 7.2, operations are departmentalized on the basis of the cities where the offices are located: Dallas, Denver, Seattle, Washington, D.C., and other cities not shown.

Customer Structure   A customer structure departmentalizes the organization according to the type of customer served. For example, an aerospace company might

■ FIGURE 7.2

Functional Structure

Partial organization chart for Wiss, Janney, Elstner Associates

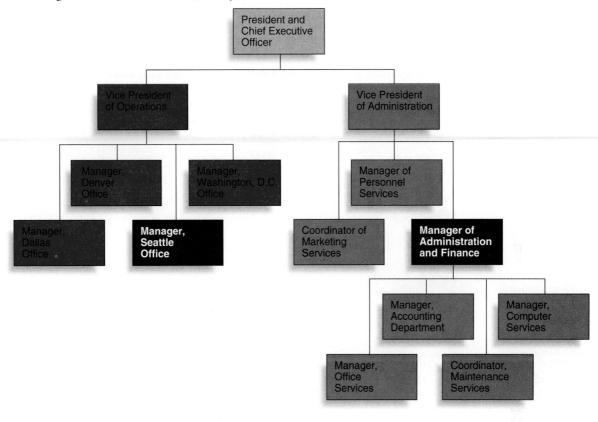

have different departments serving business, the military, and the space program. Digital Equipment Corporation recently reorganized its sales force so that each account manager is responsible for all locations of each of his or her accounts (e.g., all factories or branch offices of a single business client) rather than a single geographic location.[1]

Combinations As you can see from the figures, organizations often combine the basic types of structures. Thus, Figure 7.1 combines geographic and product structures, while Figure 7.2 combines functional and geographic structures. A typical arrangement would be a large corporation with divisions for each of its product lines. Within each division, managers are assigned responsibility for carrying out a particular function, including sales and operations (i.e., making goods or delivering services). Each sales department in turn is structured geographically.

Various combinations of structures occur when the organization forms teams of employees to meet objectives such as improving quality, developing products, or applying new technology. These teams may require diverse kinds of expertise, so the organization brings together people who perform different functions or

■ FIGURE 7.3

Product Structure

Partial organization chart for ELCA Division for Social Ministry

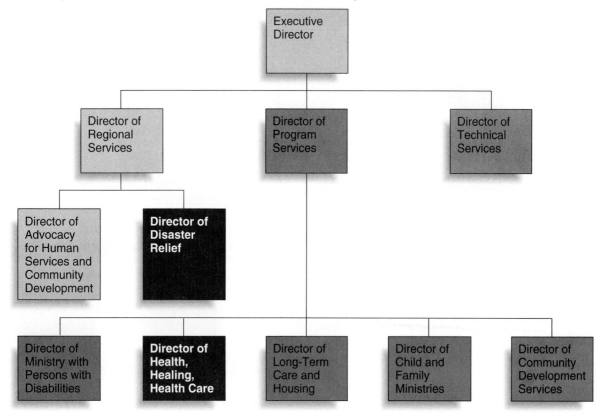

work in different geographic areas. Often these teams of employees are grouped according to product or customer. For example, a team formed to develop a new kind of stereo speaker might combine people from sales, engineering, and production functions under the umbrella of that new product. For a more in-depth discussion of forming and leading teams, see Chapter 3.

New Organizational Structures   The managers of many organizations consider the basic forms of departmentalization too rigid for a turbulent, highly competitive environment. Grouping people according to function or geographic area can create barriers that interfere with coordinating activities and sharing ideas. A rigid structure is rarely suitable for a very small organization. Such organizations typically have a highly **organic structure,** one in which the boundaries between jobs continually shift and people pitch in wherever their contributions are needed.

Larger organizations, too, are seeking the flexibility of organic structures. They may do so by organizing around teams and *processes* (series of activities that deliver value to customers) or *projects* (groups of tasks with defined scope and ending). The customer service division of Sun Life of Canada (U.S.), based in Wellesley, Massa-

organic structure
Organizational structure in which the boundaries between jobs continually shift and people pitch in wherever their contributions are needed.

chusetts, reorganized from functional groups, such as sales and product development, to process-related teams. The former functional managers became coaches for those teams. The teams are responsible for meeting performance standards, and the coaches are accountable to the teams for guiding them to high performance.[2]

Ford Motor Company has reorganized from geographic departmentalization to a structure in which product development takes place in teams called vehicle-platform centers (VPCs). Each VPC brings together stylists, design engineers, and production experts—but not necessarily at a single site. Thanks to modern communications technology, including videoconferencing and groupware such as Lotus Notes, team members can collaborate, even if some are in Michigan and others in Germany.[3]

network organizations
Organizations that maintain flexibility by staying small and contracting with other individuals and organizations as needed to complete projects.

A growing number of organizations are trying to stay flexible by staying small. Rather than adding employees to meet customer demands, these organizations, called **network organizations,** contract with other individuals and organizations as needed to complete specific projects.[4] In practice, this structure may involve *outsourcing,* or paying another organization to carry out a function. Woodspirits Limited, based in St. Paris, Ohio, has only three employees but makes arrangements with three contractors to produce the company's old-fashioned soaps.[5] Other organizations arrange *alliances,* or relationships based on partnership, including joint ventures, minority investments linked to contractual agreements, agreements to jointly fund research, and other, less formal arrangements. At the extreme is a *virtual organization,* in which a small core organization (maybe a single person) arranges alliances as needed to carry out particular projects. In Hollywood, Free Willy Two Inc.—a temporary corporation responsible for making the film *Free Willy II*—was at the hub of a virtual organization. Its scores of contractors, handling everything from payroll to special effects, included Cinnabar, the group that made the miniature seascapes and robotic whale props used in the sequence where an oil tanker is wrecked during a storm.[6]

A growing number of firms are creating "intrapreneurships," in which a small team or group within the company is given the resources to develop new ideas and new ventures without leaving the parent organization. One such intrapreneurship was formed at Elite Information Systems in Los Angeles when Mark Goldin, who had been the company's chief technical officer, launched an Internet venture called Elite.com with funding, office space, and resources from within Elite. One of the best things about the decision, according to CEO Chris Poole, was that Goldin can work without the "That's how we've always done it" constraints.[7]

Like the organizations themselves, supervisors in these new structures must be flexible. They have to contribute wherever the organization currently needs their talents—a requirement that calls for continually knowing, updating, and communicating one's skills. They may have to identify how they can contribute to a particular project, then be ready to move to a new assignment when they no longer add value to the current one. In addition, supervisors in the new structures must rely more on human relations skills than on technical skills. Coaching a team or project group requires the ability to motivate, lead, and communicate as the team handles many project- or process-related decisions. This is especially true for coaching teams that bring together people from a variety of functions.

Authority

authority
The right to perform a task or give orders to someone else.

When a supervisor assigns duties, he or she gives employees the authority to carry them out. **Authority** is the right to perform a task or give orders to someone else (see Table 7.1). The supervisor in turn has authority in certain areas, and his or her manager has even broader authority.

■ TABLE 7.1

Everyday Meaning of Terms Related to Organizing

Term	Everyday Meaning
Departmentalization	"Let's divide up the work."
Authority	"I (or you) get to decide how this is going to get done."
Responsibility	"I (or you) own this job; you can hold me accountable for it."
Accountability	"The buck stops here."
Unity of command	"No matter who else you work with, you are accountable to only one person."
Span of control	"There are limits to how many people a manager can effectively manage."
Delegation	"You have the responsibility and authority to accomplish this assignment."
Empowerment	"I trust you to perform these functions and accomplish these results; this means much more than just delegating a task to you."

Source: Adapted from Brad Lee Thompson, *The New Manager's Handbook* (Burr Ridge, IL. Richard D. Irwin, Inc., 1995), p. 49.

Line, Staff, and Functional Authority

line authority
The right to carry out tasks and give orders related to the organization's primary purpose.

The basic type of authority in organizations is **line authority,** or the right to carry out tasks and give orders related to the organization's primary purpose. Line authority gives a production supervisor at Deere & Company the right to direct a worker to operate a machine; it gives the head chef in a restaurant the right to direct the salad chef to prepare a spinach salad using certain ingredients. At the architectural firm represented in Figure 7.2, the manager of the Seattle office has line authority.

staff authority
The right to advise or assist those with line authority.

In contrast, **staff authority** is the right to advise or assist those with line authority. For example, the employees in the human resource department help the other departments by ensuring that they have qualified workers. The quality-control manager at a manufacturing company helps the production manager see that the goods produced are of acceptable quality. In Figure 7.2, the manager of administration and finance has staff authority.

One way to appreciate the difference between line authority and staff authority is to think of a lawyer's job. In a law firm, the lawyer has line authority (he or she delivers the services the firm is selling). But in the legal department of a manufacturing company, the lawyer has staff authority (supporting the firm by offering legal advice in matters related to producing and selling goods).

Conflicts often arise between line and staff personnel. Line personnel may feel that staff workers are meddling and don't understand their work or how important it is. Staff personnel may conclude that line personnel are resisting new ideas and don't appreciate the valuable assistance they are getting. Whether the supervisor has line or staff authority, he or she can benefit from being aware that these kinds of conflicts are common and trying to appreciate the other person's point of view.

functional authority
The right given by higher management to specific staff personnel to give orders concerning an area in which the staff personnel have expertise.

Supervisors and other personnel with staff authority may also have **functional authority.** This is the right given by higher management to specific staff personnel to give orders concerning an area in which the staff personnel have expertise. For example, members of the accounting department might have authority to request the information they need to prepare reports. Or the human resource manager might have authority to ensure that all departments are complying with the laws pertaining to fair employment practices.

Centralized and Decentralized Authority

In some organizations, the managers at the top retain a great deal of authority; in others, management grants much authority to middle managers, supervisors, and operative employees. Organizations that share relatively little authority are said to be centralized; organizations that share a lot of authority are said to be decentralized.

These terms are relative. In other words, no organization is completely centralized or decentralized, but organizations fall along a range of possibilities from one extreme to another. An organization can even make changes in the degree to which it centralizes authority, depending on its strategic plan and goals. For instance, in an effort to combat depressed oil prices around the world, Texaco announced that it would revamp its oil exploration and development business. One element of the plan is to take some decision-making authority away from Texaco's units around the world and centralize it at company headquarters, to take better advantage of opportunities such as the chance to invest in foreign oil producers. Now, decisions about where to look for new oil will be made at headquarters instead of at the outlying offices.[8]

Supervisors who know whether their employer has a centralized or decentralized structure understand how much authority they can expect to have. Suppose that a supervisor wants to expand the authority of her position so she can make improvements in the department. This ambition probably will be viewed less favorably in a centralized organization than in a decentralized one.

Power, Responsibility, and Accountability

power
The ability to get others to act in a certain way.

It is easy to confuse authority with power, accountability, or responsibility. However, when used precisely, these terms do not mean the same thing. **Power** is the ability (as opposed to the right) to get others to act in a certain way. The supervisor's authority usually confers a degree of power; employees usually do what their supervisor asks them to do. However, some people have power that comes from sources other than their positions in the organization. Also, some people with authority have trouble getting others to act in the desired way. (Chapter 15 discusses power in greater detail.)

responsibility
The obligation to perform assigned activities.

Responsibility is the obligation to perform assigned activities. People who accept responsibility commit themselves to completing an assignment to the best of their ability. Of course, doing a good job is easier when you have authority to control the necessary resources, including personnel. An important aspect of the supervisor's job, therefore, is to ensure that people have accepted responsibility for each of the tasks that the work group must complete—and that they clearly understand what those responsibilities are. The supervisor also must ensure that people have enough authority to carry out their responsibilities.

Employees who accept responsibility may be rewarded for doing a good job, and those who do not may be punished. This practice is called *accountability* (see Chapter 1). Assume an organization makes a supervisor responsible for communicating policies to his or her employees. Accountability means the supervisor can expect consequences related to whether that responsibility is met. Thus, account-ability is a way of encouraging people to fulfill their responsibilities.

The authority to transfer (delegate) responsibility to employees and hold them accountable adds to a supervisor's power. At the same time, even when a supervisor delegates, the supervisor remains accountable for employees' performance.

As Malcolm VandenBerg, management trainer for a firm called Positive Under Pressure, says, "Delegate, don't abdicate. You may be able to pass over most of your job to another person but you can't pass over the responsibility for checking it. You cannot delegate accountability."[9]

The Process of Organizing

For a supervisor, organizing efforts are generally focused on allocating responsi-bilities and resources in a way that makes the department or work group operate effectively and efficiently. In addition, supervisors may want or need to set up teams (see Chapter 3). Whether the organizing job involves setting up a whole new company, restructuring an existing one, or deciding how to organize a de-partment or team, the process should be basically the same. The supervisor or other manager should define the objective, determine what resources are needed, and then group activities and assign duties. This three-step approach leads to a structure that supports the goals of the organization (see Figure 7.4).

Define the Objective

Management activities should support the objectives developed during the plan-ning process. In the case of organizing, the supervisor or other manager should begin by defining what objective the department or work group is supposed to be achieving. If the supervisor does not know, then he or she has not finished plan-ning and should complete that job before trying to organize work. Long-range objectives at the Ritz-Carlton Hotel Company are 100 percent guest satisfaction, 100 percent customer retention, and zero defects in customer transactions.[10] Or-ganizing decisions support these companywide objectives.

Determine the Needed Resources

The planning process also should give the supervisor an idea of what resources—including personnel, equipment, and money—are needed to achieve goals. The supervisor should review the plans and identify which resources are needed for the particular areas being organized.

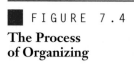

FIGURE 7.4

The Process of Organizing

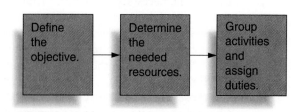

Define the objective. → Determine the needed resources. → Group activities and assign duties.

To achieve Ritz-Carlton's lofty quality goals, its managers have determined that they need employees committed to ensuring high quality. They also realize that every employee must be empowered to contribute to customer satisfaction. This in turn requires that employees have access to information about what customers want and how well the company's processes are working. Modern information systems help fulfill that need.

Group Activities and Assign Duties

The final step in the process is what most people think about when they consider organizing. The supervisor groups the necessary activities and assigns work to the appropriate employees. To ensure that all the necessary responsibilities are assigned, the supervisor also can foster a climate that encourages all the employees working on a project to raise the question, "Who is taking care of this?"[11]

At the Ritz-Carlton in New York, this step has included creating the position of director of quality. Paul Roa, who holds that job, says technology and training help keep the hotel's staff knowledgeable about what customers want. The hotel's employees receive training in how to notice guest preferences (e.g., feather rather than polyester pillows or more oranges than apples in fruit baskets). Employee observations are entered into the company's national database. Each day, the hotel prints a report highlighting the preferences of the guests scheduled to arrive the next day. A full-time guest history coordinator analyzes the report so that the hotel can cater to those preferences. Furthermore, all employees are empowered to resolve guest complaints and rebate up to $2,000 a day per guest without management approval. They also are expected to analyze the problem and prepare an action plan for solving it. If defects recur, the company forms a team to engage in a formal problem-solving process to eliminate future occurrences.[12] In sum, staffing decisions and highly decentralized authority contribute to achieving the Ritz-Carlton's quality objectives. "Meeting the Challenge" illustrates some unique job responsibilities.

The remainder of this chapter discusses how to carry out the third step of the organizing process.

Principles of Organizing

Supervisors, especially those who are new to the job, may be unsure how to group activities and assign duties. The task seems so abstract. Fortunately, management experts have developed some principles that can guide the supervisor: the parity principle, unity of command, chain of command, and span of control.

Parity Principle

parity principle
The principle that personnel who are given responsibility must also be given enough authority to carry out that responsibility.

Parity is the quality of being equal or equivalent. Thus, according to the **parity principle,** personnel must have equal amounts of authority and responsibility. In other words, when someone accepts a responsibility, he or she also needs enough authority to be able to carry out that responsibility. If a head teller at a Citicorp branch is responsible for providing high-quality customer service but does not have the authority to fire a surly teller, the head teller will find it difficult or impossible to carry out this responsibility.

MEETING THE CHALLENGE

What Title Would You Like on Your Business Cards?

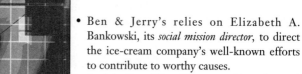

This is the age of the creative entrepreneur. If you had any doubt, take a look at the novel ways that some innovative firms are naming new supervisory positions and assigning responsibilities.

- DoubleClick, a New York–based firm that places ads on the Internet, employs Lee Nadler as its *marketing Sherpa*. Lee chose the title himself after a vacation spent hiking in Nepal, where he gained a new respect for his Himalayan guides and their strength, calm, and focus.
- Yahoo! Inc., the Internet search engine, calls its co-founders Jerry Yang and David Filo—what else?—the *chief yahoos*.
- Sun Microsystems employs *corporate evangelists* who promote the firm to developers.
- Lexica Holdings LLC is a technology consulting firm in San Francisco that specializes in virtual reality projects. Jan Darwin, a kind of chief administrative assistant, is called the company's *reality facilitator*.

- Ben & Jerry's relies on Elizabeth A. Bankowski, its *social mission director*, to direct the ice-cream company's well-known efforts to contribute to worthy causes.
- And the Republic of Tea, a small producer of specialty teas in Novato, California, is searching for someone to fill the newly created post of *minister of propaganda*, otherwise known as public relations director.

Can you see yourself as a future supervisor with a similarly imaginative title?

Sources: Heather Green, "The Organization Sherpa," *Business Week*, May 11, 1998, p. 6; "Job Titles of the Future," *Fast Company*, November 1998, p. 86; Constance L. Hays, "Getting Serious at Ben & Jerry's," *New York Times*, May 22, 1998, pp. D1, D3; "Help Wanted: The Republic of Tea . . . ," *Wall Street Journal*, November 17, 1998, p. B18.

Unity of Command

Meredith Buckle handled the maintenance jobs for a small office building. When building occupants experienced a problem, such as a leaky faucet or a cold office, they would call Meredith. Often, to get a faster response, they would call her repeatedly, complaining about how the problem was interfering with work. As a result, Meredith felt she could never keep everyone satisfied, and she had trouble deciding which jobs to do first.

unity of command
The principle that each employee should have only one supervisor.

According to the principle of **unity of command,** each employee should have only one supervisor. Employees who receive orders from several people tend to get confused and aggravated. As a result, they tend to do poor work. The example of Meredith is a case in point. It would have helped her if the building manager had collected messages from the occupants and assigned the jobs to Meredith along with a schedule for completing them.

Sometimes a supervisor's manager violates this principle by directing the employees who report to the supervisor. This puts the employees in the awkward position of receiving directions from two people, and it puts the supervisor in the awkward position of needing to correct his or her manager's behavior. In this kind of situation, the supervisor might want to approach his or her boss with a tactful way of restoring unity of command. The supervisor might say, for instance, "I've noticed that my team gets confused when you and I both give directions. I'd like to suggest that you let me know what you want, and I'll relay it to the team." Of course, the supervisor also should refrain from directing employees who report to someone else.

Chain of Command

chain of command
The flow of authority in an organization from one level of management to the next.

In a chain, each link is connected to no more than two links, one on either side. In an organization, authority progresses like the links on a chain. Along this **chain of command,** authority flows from one level of management to the next, from the top of the organization to the bottom.

When someone skips a level, the principle of chain of command is violated. For example, suppose that Fred Paretsky wants to take Friday off, but he suspects that the division manager will be more sympathetic to his request than his supervisor. So Fred goes directly to the division manager, who grants permission. Unfortunately, the division manager does not know it, but Fred's group now will be understaffed on Friday because two other workers also will be absent. By violating the chain of command, Fred and the division manager have created a staffing problem that the supervisor could have avoided with a little planning. Similarly, in the earlier example of a supervisor's manager directing the supervisor's employees, the boss is violating both the principles of chain of command and unity of command.

Of course, taking every decision through every level of the organization can be time-consuming and difficult, especially in an organization with many layers of management. The solution is to use common sense. For example, a request for information probably does not have to travel through every layer of management. In contrast, a decision that will affect the group's operations should probably pass through the chain of command.

Span of Control

span of control
The number of people a manager supervises.

Clearly, keeping track of and developing the talents of one employee is easier than supervising 100 employees, but hiring a supervisor for every employee would be tremendously expensive. The number of people a manager supervises is known as the manager's **span of control.** The more people the manager supervises, the greater the span of control.

In organizing, managers must be aware of how many people they can supervise effectively. Ideally, managers supervise as many people as they can effectively guide toward meeting their goals. That number depends in part on several factors that describe the work situation:[13]

- *Similarity of functions*—The more similar the functions performed by employees, the greater the span of control can be.
- *Geographic closeness*—The closer subordinates are physically, the greater the span of control can be.
- *Complexity of functions*—The simpler the functions performed by subordinates, the greater the span of control can be.
- *Coordination*—This refers to how much time managers must spend coordinating the work of their subordinates with that of other employees. The less time they need to spend on coordination, the greater the span of control can be.
- *Planning*—The less time a manager needs to spend on planning, the greater the span of control can be.
- *Availability of staff support*—The more staff specialists available to provide support in a variety of areas, the larger the span of control can be.
- *Performance standards*—If there are clear, objective standards for performance, and employees are familiar with them, the span of control can be larger than in a situation where the supervisor continually must clarify what is expected of employees.

Characteristics of the managers and employees also are important. Managers may find that, as their experience grows, so does the number of people they can supervise effectively. Managers with strong skills in time management and decision making also are likely to be able to supervise more employees. As to employees, the better able they are to work independently, the greater their span of control can be.

Delegating Authority and Responsibility

A recent nationwide survey of U.S. employees found that over half felt they were overworked, were overwhelmed by their workload, and lacked the time needed to complete their tasks.[14] The concept of organizing implies that one person cannot do all the work of an organization. Even a one-person business usually contracts with outside people to provide some services. For example, Lars Hundley runs a one-person business from a corner of his living room. His firm, CleanAirGardening.com, is the largest on-line dealer in the United States of Brill push-reel lawn mowers, a top German brand, and made $300,000 in 2000. Hundley now outsources his incoming telephone orders to a professional call service so he can spend more time on testing and selecting new products and fielding customer-service calls.[15] Giving someone else the authority and responsibility to carry out a task is known as **delegating.** You can explore your delegation effectiveness by taking the Self-Quiz on page 181.

delegating
Giving another person the authority and responsibility to carry out a task.

Benefits of Delegating

Whereas the performance of most nonmanagement employees is evaluated in terms of their individual accomplishments, a supervisor's performance is evaluated according to the achievements of the whole department. Thus, the department's output will be of the highest quality and the supervisor looks best when he or she draws on the expertise of employees. W. H. Weiss, a writer and consultant in industrial management, says that a supervisor's effectiveness and success "depend greatly on your ability to delegate responsibility and authority to others and to hold those so delegated accountable for results. . . . The best way to expand your personal authority is to delegate as much responsibility as you can. Hoarding authority serves to diminish your own status and importance."[16]

For example, a production supervisor might establish a team of employees to devise ways to make the workplace safer. Those employees are likely to come up with more ideas than the supervisor could identify alone. Some employees might have backgrounds or areas of expertise that lead them to notice where improvements are needed—improvements that the supervisor might never have considered.

A supervisor who delegates also has more time for the jobs only a supervisor can do, such as planning and counseling. Kelly Hancock, who supervises the order takers for classified ads at the *Toronto Sun*, says, "Delegating gives me more opportunity to do tasks of a more pressing, creative nature. I can work on special projects . . . such as sales contests for the staff." One way to think of this benefit of delegating is that it is an important tool for time management (discussed in Chapter 14). If the production supervisor in the example handled all aspects of safety, it could take weeks simply to identify and describe safety problems and solutions. That time might be better spent in scheduling and arranging for employees to receive various types of training.

Roxanne Donovan recalls starting her real estate public relations firm, Great Ink Communications, and struggling with the task of delegating. "My first employee sat around a lot because I was used to doing things myself." With a greater effort, she was able to delegate more and focused on making her business grow. Now, while she still signs every check, she always takes a junior staff member with her on sales calls. That is the person who is going to do the actual work on the account.[17]

Delegating also has a beneficial effect on employees. Delegation of work gives employees a chance to develop their skills and their value to the organization. Depending on the kinds of tasks delegated, this can enhance their careers and their earning potentials. It also can make employees' work more interesting. It is reasonable to expect that employees who are more interested in their work and more involved in meeting the organization's objectives are likely to do higher-quality work and remain with the organization longer. (This topic will be discussed in Chapter 9.) Thus, the production employees who serve on the safety team might find that this added responsibility leads them to care more about the quality of their day-to-day work.

Executive Petty Officer Rodney Randall heads the Coast Guard rescue mission at Eaton's Neck, on Long Island Sound (New York). He sees delegating as a major way for the crew members under his supervision to gain the experience they need, and he frequently avoids going out on calls with them. "If you've got somebody there who you think has the answers," he says, "it's easier [for them] to ask the question than to think it out. They ask me, 'What do you think? What do you think?' " Instead of giving answers, Chief Randall trains the men and women he supervises to think on their feet by giving them the authority to make decisions, right or wrong.[18]

"More and more people are seeking meaning in their work," says Raymond Smilor, vice president of Ernst & Young's Kauffman Center for Entrepreneurial Leadership. "They look for a place where they can pursue their own dreams while following the organization."[19]

Empowerment

empowerment
Delegation of broad decision-making authority and responsibility.

These benefits of delegating explain why many organizations use employee involvement to improve the quality of their goods and services (see Chapter 2). In other words, they delegate decision-making authority and responsibility in a variety of areas to employees. This practice—called **empowerment**—is based on the expectation that employees will provide more insight and expertise than managers can provide alone, and that this participation will make employees more committed to doing their best.

BriskHeat Corporation, a manufacturer of electric heating elements based in Columbus, Ohio, uses empowerment extensively. BriskHeat charges employees at all levels to make whatever decisions are necessary to further the organization's best interests. Operative employees organize their work—setting work hours, scheduling shifts, and even deciding how tools should be laid out. They also recommend and vote on capital expenses and order their own materials. The company enables skilled decision making by providing training and feedback about organizational performance. CEO Richard E. Jacob reported that after the employees learned the company's needs and priorities from experience, they began making decisions that helped to fuel substantial sales growth in a mature industry.[20]

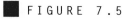

FIGURE 7.5

The Process of Delegating

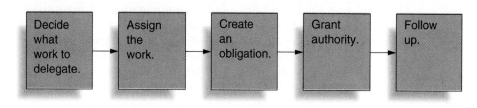

| Decide what work to delegate. | Assign the work. | Create an obligation. | Grant authority. | Follow up. |

The Process of Delegating

When delegating effectively, the supervisor is not merely handing out jobs at random but should be following a logical process: deciding what work to delegate, assigning the work, creating an obligation, granting authority, and following up (see Figure 7.5).

Decide What Work to Delegate There are several ways to select which tasks to delegate. When an employee knows how to do a particular task better than the supervisor, delegation certainly makes sense. Another approach is to delegate simple tasks that employees clearly can handle. For example, Kelly Hancock of the *Toronto Sun* has her employees handle administrative duties such as counting the lines for birth and death notices. The supervisor also can delegate the tasks that he or she finds most boring. This approach can backfire, however, if employees perceive they always are chosen to do the dirty work. Tasks performed regularly are good candidates for delegation because it may be worth the effort to train employees to do them.

Of course, there are some tasks a supervisor should *not* delegate, including personnel matters and activities assigned specifically to the supervisor. Thus, the supervisor should not assign duties such as appraising performance and resolving conflicts. Likewise, if a sales supervisor's boss has asked her to fly to Vancouver to resolve a customer complaint, it would be inappropriate for the supervisor to delegate this assignment to someone else.

Assign the Work The supervisor continues the delegation process by selecting employees to carry out the work. In delegating a particular task, the supervisor considers who is available and asks questions such as the following[21]:

- Who can do the job best?
- Who can do it least expensively?
- Who can save the most time?
- Who would gain the most growth from the assignment?

The supervisor also weighs the personalities involved, safety considerations, and any company policies or union rules that may apply. Supervisors can be most effective in carrying out this step when they know their employees well.

A manager who makes a point of knowing his employees is Rick Hess, a general manager at Massachusetts-based M/A Com, a microwave electronics firm. Hess goes out of his way to learn about employees in an effort to support their development. For instance, one of the engineers reporting to Hess told him she felt pigeonholed and frustrated. He responded by giving the engineer new assign-

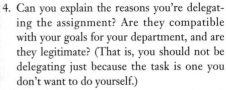

How Well Are You Delegating?

You've looked at your workload, checked your calendar, and assessed your employees. It's time to delegate some of the tasks in your department. How can you be sure you are handling this task well?

Here are some things to consider *before* you assign your employees a task.

1. Is delegating the right way to accomplish the goal? Make sure the task is not one that you should do yourself or work on cooperatively with another supervisor or department. Some jobs should even be outsourced to others outside the company.

2. Does the employee you've selected have the required background, training, and skills? Be sure you know your team's abilities well. There is nothing wrong with assigning a task to someone who will need to learn a new procedure or skill in order to accomplish the goal, and in fact additional responsibility can help motivate employees. But the person should have the basic skills needed to begin the job, and any additional training should be readily available.

3. Is the task one that you can assign to a small subgroup or team within your department, or should just one person shoulder it?

4. Can you explain the reasons you're delegating the assignment? Are they compatible with your goals for your department, and are they legitimate? (That is, you should not be delegating just because the task is one you don't want to do yourself.)

5. Do you understand all the details of the task so you can tell the employee what he or she needs to know in order to do it? If not, assemble all the needed information before you begin.

6. Have you thought about what you will say to the employee so that your delegating this task will prove to be motivating and not burdensome?

7. Is this the best time to delegate the task? If you are going on vacation and will be unavailable to answer questions or offer help, for instance, or if training is needed that cannot be completed before the task deadline, then the timing is probably not right for this task to be delegated.

Source: Based on ideas in Ted Pollock, "A Personal File of Stimulating Ideas, Little-Known Facts and Daily Problem Solvers," *Supervision*, September 1, 2000, p. 16.

ments where her accomplishments would be noticed, a move that increased her motivation.[22] As in this example, matching assignments to employee desires as well as their skills can help the organization reap the full potential of its human resources.

When two jobs must be done at the same time and the same person is best qualified to do both, the process of selecting an employee to do the work becomes complex. In such cases, the supervisor must set priorities. The supervisor must consider how important the particular task is to achieving the department's goals and serving customers. If priorities among jobs are unclear, the supervisor should check with his or her manager.

To finish the step of assigning work, the supervisor tells the designated employees what they are supposed to do. (See "Tips from the Firing Line" for an overview of good delegation skills.) The supervisor must be sure that the employees understand what they are supposed to be doing and have the necessary knowledge and skills. (Employees should be able to exercise some freedom in deciding exactly how to carry out the assignment, however.) Employees also need to know which jobs have the greatest priority. To communicate this information clearly, it helps to be specific and to ask employees to restate the assignment in their own words. (Chapter 10 provides more information about how to communicate clearly.)

Create an Obligation When the supervisor makes an assignment, he or she needs to be sure that the employee accepts responsibility for carrying it out. A supervisor can encourage employees to accept responsibility by involving them in making decisions and by listening to their ideas. Workers who feel involved are more apt to feel responsible. Supervisors cannot force employees to feel responsible, but fortunately many employees willingly take on responsibility as a matter of course. In addition, by making employees accountable for their actions, supervisors lead them to accept responsibility.

Although the employee should accept responsibility for carrying out a task, this does not mean that the supervisor gives up the responsibility for its proper completion. The organization still holds the supervisor accountable. Therefore, following delegation, both parties have responsibility for the work. The supervisor's job becomes one of ensuring that the employee has the necessary resources and that the task is completed and meets quality standards. The supervisor does so through the management function of controlling, described in the previous chapter.

Grant Authority Along with responsibility, supervisors must give employees the authority they need to carry out their jobs. This is how supervisors follow the parity principle, discussed earlier in this chapter. Thus, if a supervisor at Abbott Laboratories gives a researcher responsibility to carry out a particular procedure, the researcher must also be given the authority to obtain the materials and equipment needed to do the job.

Follow Up After assigning duties and the authority to carry them out, the supervisor needs to give the employees some freedom to act independently and creatively. This does not mean that the supervisor should abandon employees to succeed or fail on their own; after all, the supervisor is equally responsible for the success of the work. Therefore, it should be made clear to employees that the supervisor is available for guidance. The supervisor also should set forth a plan for periodically checking on the progress of the work. The supervisor may find that employees need additional information or help in removing obstacles to success, or perhaps they simply need praise for the work they have done so far.

If an employee's performance of an unfamiliar task is less than perfect, the supervisor should not be discouraged from delegating in the future. Everyone needs time to learn, and disappointing performances may offer a chance for the supervisor to learn what is needed to strengthen an employee's skills. In addition, poor performance may have resulted from the way the work was delegated, not from a problem with the employee. The supervisor can check whether the guidelines for delegation mentioned in "Tips from the Firing Line" on page 175 have been observed.

Reluctance to Delegate

Ruby Singh works late every night, reviewing all her employees' work and preparing detailed instructions for them to carry out the next day. Her own manager has suggested that she give the workers more freedom, which would save her a lot of time and probably increase their job satisfaction. However, Ruby is afraid that if she does not keep close tabs on her employees, the department's performance will suffer.

Many supervisors are convinced that they are able to do a better job than their employees. They might even say, "If you want something done right, you have to do it yourself." Often they may be correct, particularly if their own promotion to a supervisory post resulted from high performance. Observing an employee making mistakes can be difficult, especially if the supervisor will look bad for allowing the mistake to occur.

AES Corporation experiences its share of mistakes by operative employees. AES, a power producer that sells electricity to public utilities and steam to industrial customers, uses delegation extensively throughout the organization. As its employees shoulder responsibilities more typical of managers, they are bound to make mistakes until they learn the ropes. For instance, when chemical engineer Ann Murtlow took on the task of buying air pollution credits (which industrial companies trade to gain flexibility in meeting emissions regulations), she first spent $10,000 for an option on a type of credit that turned out to be worthless for the AES plant.[23]

Overall, however, a department's long-term performance requires that its supervisor let employees work up to their potential. This means the supervisor must overcome reluctance, delegate work, and let employees learn from their experiences. Ann Murtlow's mistake inspired her to educate herself, and she became the company's expert on air pollution permits. AES's top management credits such fruits of delegation for its low employee turnover and growing profits.

In some cases, employees may really be unable to carry out jobs that they have been delegated. If so, the supervisor must consider ways to bring the workforce's talents into line with the department's needs. Perhaps employees need training or the department's hiring practices need improvement. (For more on selecting and training employees, see Chapters 16 and 17.)

As mentioned earlier, delegating frees supervisors to concentrate on the tasks that they do best or that only they can do. Sometimes a supervisor is more comfortable being an expert at employees' work than struggling with supervisory responsibilities such as motivating employees and resolving conflicts. However, the supervisor must overcome discomfort or fear, because the organization needs supervisors who supervise.

Summary

8.1 Describe organization charts.

Organization charts are a standard way to draw the structure of an organization. Boxes represent the departments or positions, and connecting lines indicate reporting relationships. The positions at the top of the organization chart have the most authority and responsibility.

8.2 Identify basic ways in which organizations are structured.

Unless they are very small, organizations are grouped into departments. An organization with a functional structure groups personnel and other resources according to the types of work they carry out. A product structure groups work and resources according to the product produced and delivered. In a geographic structure, the departments are set up according to the location of the customers served or the goods or services produced. A customer structure departmentalizes the organization according to the category of customer served.

Organizations now often combine the basic types of structures, particularly where teams of employees are formed to meet objectives such as improving quality or applying new technology. Those seeking flexibility often favor an organic structure—one in which boundaries between jobs continually shift and people pitch in wherever their contributions are needed. They may form network organizations, which contract with other individuals and organizations to complete specific projects (instead of adding permanent employees).

8.3 Distinguish between line and staff authority and between centralized and decentralized authority.

Authority is the right to perform a task or give orders to someone else. Line authority is the right to

PART THREE FUNCTIONS OF THE SUPERVISOR

carry out tasks and give orders related to the organization's primary purpose. Staff authority is the right to advise or assist those with line authority. When authority is centralized, it is shared by a few top managers; when authority is decentralized, it is spread among a greater number of people.

8.4 Compare and contrast *authority, power, responsibility,* and *accountability.*

Authority is the right to perform a task or give orders. Power is the ability (as opposed to the right) to get others to act in a certain way. Responsibility is the obligation to perform certain tasks. Accountability is the practice of imposing penalties for failure to adequately carry out responsibilities and giving rewards for success in meeting responsibilities. The authority to transfer responsibility to employees and hold them accountable adds to a supervisor's power. (However, a supervisor always is held accountable for his or her employees' performance.)

8.5 Identify the steps in the process of organizing.

To organize a department or work group, the supervisor should first define the objective of the department or work group, then determine what resources are needed. Finally, the supervisor groups activities and assigns duties to appropriate employees.

8.6 Describe four principles of organizing.

According to the parity principle, personnel with responsibility must also be given enough authority to carry out that responsibility. The principle of

unity of command states that each employee should have only one supervisor. A chain of command is the flow of authority from one level of the organization to the next; most decisions and information should flow along the chain of command. Finally, supervisors and other managers should have an appropriate span of control; the best number of employees for a specific situation depends on a variety of factors.

8.7 Discuss why and how supervisors delegate.

Supervisors delegate to enhance the quality of the department's and supervisor's performance by drawing on the expertise of employees. Delegation also frees time for supervisory tasks. It may improve employee morale and performance by empowering them to make decisions in a variety of areas. To delegate, supervisors follow a five-step process: Decide what work to delegate, assign the work, create an obligation, grant authority, and follow up. When delegating, supervisors must make sure employees understand and are able to do the work, and they retain the responsibility to see that the work is done properly.

8.8 Identify causes of reluctance to delegate.

Many supervisors are reluctant to delegate because they believe no one else can do the job as well. They may not want to give up activities they enjoy. Some supervisors are more comfortable doing what their employees should be doing than in carrying out supervisory responsibilities.

Key Terms

organizing, p. 159

department, p. 161

departmentalization, p. 162

organic structure, p. 164

network organizations, p. 165

authority, p. 165

line authority, p. 166

staff authority, p. 166

functional authority, p. 166

power, p. 167

responsibility, p. 167

parity principle, p. 169

unity of command, p. 170

chain of command, p. 171

span of control, p. 171

delegating, p. 172

empowerment, p. 173

Review and Discussion Questions

1. Emily Sanford has just been promoted to supervisor of the salespeople in the gift department at a department store. Which of the following organizing activities is she likely to carry out?
   a. Scheduling her employees' work hours.
   b. Forming a team of her employees to work on a promotional event within the department.
   c. Helping decide the best location for a new branch of the department store.
   d. Assigning an employee to sit at the bridal registry desk.
   e. Determining whether the department store should launch its own line of products.

2. What might be the best structure for each of the following organizations?
   a. A three-person company that sells complete, prepackaged gourmet dinners to specialty grocery stores.
   b. A small organization that supplies antique cars to movie studios.
   c. A manufacturer of windows, with offices in Toronto, Seattle, Miami, and Chicago.

3. What special attributes must supervisors have to be successful in some of the new types of organizational structures?

4. Which of the following supervisors have primarily line authority? Which have staff authority?
   a. The production supervisor at a publishing company, who is responsible for getting books typeset and printed.
   b. The housekeeping supervisor at a hospital.
   c. The word-processing supervisor at a law firm.
   d. The payroll department supervisor for a fire department.

5. In recent years, many organizations have become more decentralized. Typically this change involves eliminating middle-management jobs and sharing more control with those at lower levels of the organization. How do you think this affects the role of supervisors in those organizations?

6. Does someone with authority always have power? Does a person who accepts responsibility necessarily have authority? Explain.

7. What are the steps in the process of organizing? How would they apply to the manager of an Olive Garden restaurant who needs to schedule employees? Explain in general how this supervisor could follow each step.

8. Describe each of the following principles of organizing.
   a. Parity principle.
   b. Unity of command.
   c. Chain of command.
   d. Span of control.

9. A production supervisor at a company that makes furniture learns about the factors that should influence the span of control. The supervisor believes that his own span of control is too large for him to supervise effectively. Is there anything a person in his position can do? If not, explain why. If so, suggest what he can try.

10. Harry Jamison, CPA, is planning to set up a business to prepare tax returns. Harry is the only person in the business, at least for now. Can he delegate any work? Should he? Explain.

11. What steps do you think a supervisor who is reluctant to delegate could take to overcome this discomfort?

A SECOND LOOK

The story at the beginning of this chapter describes an interesting form of geographic organization. How do you think the Milners decided on their respective responsibilities?

SKILLS MODULE

CASE

To Reorganize or Not to Reorganize

Sometimes a family-owned business is handed down from generation to generation with few if any changes. Yet the distribution of power and authority in one family firm almost became a major stumbling block in the transition from father to children.

Emerald Packaging sells plastic packaging to the produce industry in California. Just about the time that founder Jim Kelly, Sr., was considering stepping down in favor of his three children, the packaging industry was undergoing an unusual amount of change. Emerald's customers were looking for new ways to package fruits and vegetables to meet consumers' growing desire for pre-sliced and ready-to-eat produce. To keep up with its competitors, Emerald was going to have to invest millions of dollars in new machinery.

The question of how much to spend and what kind of equipment to buy put extra pressure on the next generation of Kellys as they considered their reorganizing options. Jim Jr. was handling sales, Maura managed customer service, and Kevin was in charge of operations. While this had worked well during Jim Sr.'s tenure, everyone wanted a change. Kevin wanted a corporate structure in which the siblings shared power as equal partners and advocated going after new markets. Jim, who had seniority, wanted to make the decisions and favored serving Emerald's established market. Maura wanted a bigger role in sales no matter which market was chosen and worried about being overshadowed by her brothers.

With the help of a consultant, the Kellys put together a five-year plan to start focusing on new markets while they ran the business as partners, collaborating on making all the business's major decisions. As Jim Sr. gradually reduces his role, the children will assume his tasks and remain equal shareholders. It looks like Jim Sr. won't have to make good on his joking threats to leave the business to the cat after all.

1. What special issues of authority and delegation would face the Kelly siblings if any one of them had become the head of their family firm?
2. What on-the-job advantages might the firm's three directors gain from being members of the same family?
3. Would you have trouble delegating work to a family member? What about relinquishing authority on the job? Why or why not?

Source: Kevin Kelly, "Surviving Succession," *Business Week Enterprise*, June 22, 1998, p. Ent24.

Do You Delegate?

To test your delegating skills, answer the following questions with Yes or No.

1. Do you regularly work a lot of overtime? _____
2. Are you usually busier than the people you work with? _____
3. Must you often rush to meet deadlines? _____
4. Are you ever unable to complete important projects? _____
5. Are you too busy to plan or prioritize your work? _____
6. Do you return from vacation to find piles of unfinished business waiting for you? _____
7. Have you neglected training someone to take over your job on short notice? _____
8. Do you feel other people are taking breaks or leaving on time while you do their work for them? _____
9. Do you feel you are the only one who can do the job right? _____
10. Do you have difficulty expressing yourself? _____

The more Yes answers you give, the more likely it is that you are having trouble delegating.

Source: Janet Mahoney, "Delegating Effectively," *Nursing Management*, June 1997, p. 62. Reprinted with permission of Lippincott Williams & Wilkins.

Class Exercise

Six Degrees of Separation

Some experts feel that no matter how an organization is designed, the key to efficiency is the creation of shortcuts between different levels of the firm. Studies have shown that it takes only a few such connections between well-connected individuals to make a very small world out of a large one. This is the idea that underlies the concept of "six degrees of separation," which originated in the work of Harvard social psychologist Stanley Milgram in the 1960s.

Milgram gave randomly selected people in Kansas and Nebraska each a letter addressed to someone they did not know in Massachusetts. He asked them to mail the letter to an acquaintance who would bring it closer to the target addressee. Each participant needed an average of only five intermediaries to make the connection.

Break into small groups and recreate Milgram's experiment as a thought exercise. Let one person in the group name a friend at a different school or university than the one you attend. Go around your group to see whether each person can mention someone who can lead you closer to your target friend. See whether you can at least reach the right campus, if not the person named, and compare notes with the other groups in your class to see how many "degrees of separation" were needed in the smallest and the largest chain.

Team-Building Exercise

Organizing a Fund-Raising Team

Divide the class into teams of four to six members. Appoint a leader to act as supervisor for each team. Each team will hold the initial meeting to organize a fund-raising event for a cause of their choice. The teams should define their objectives, determine the needed resources, group activities, and assign duties. The supervisor should delegate whatever responsibilities he or she can, including asking for a volunteer to take notes at the meeting itself.

Before the end of class, a spokesperson for each team may report to the class on the effectiveness of the meeting: How quickly were objectives defined? How evenly were duties assigned? What was each member's responsibility? How efficient was the supervisor at delegating? Did some members seem to have more power than others?

8

A leader's job is to make people's strengths effective and their weaknesses irrelevant.
—**Peter Drucker**

The Supervisor as Leader

■ LEARNING OBJECTIVES

After you have studied this chapter, you should be able to:

8.1 Discuss the possible link between personal traits and leadership ability.

8.2 Compare leadership styles that a supervisor might adopt.

8.3 Explain contingency theories of leadership.

8.4 Identify criteria for choosing a leadership style.

8.5 Describe guidelines for giving directions to employees.

8.6 Tell why supervisors need to understand and improve their views of themselves.

8.7 Explain how supervisors can develop and maintain good relations with their employees, managers, and peers.

EMPATHIC STYLE IN A TOUGH ENVIRONMENT

Peter Callais is certainly an empathic manager. He has been known to advance money to his workers to pay their debts, alimony, or cost of a new pair of shoes. He's even bailed one of them out of jail.

As CEO of Abdon Callais Boat Rentals (Louisiana), which serves the oil-drilling industry, Peter knows he must win the loyalty of the workers on whom he relies. Most of them are young, low skilled, and restless, and competition for their services is high. Louisiana's unemployment rate is low and falling, and rival firms often try to lure deckhands away from Peter's boats with offers of a few extra dollars a day. But in the five years since he took over the firm from his brother, Peter has expanded the fleet from 1 to 22 boats and now employs 120 people, with a turnover rate only one-third its previous level.

Peter's supervision combines a personal touch with good benefits to meet the diverse and individual needs of his crews, who usually spend months at a time on the firm's four-man, high-speed boats. He offers health insurance, life insurance, and a 401(k) plan to steady his workers and to meet what he looks upon as a corporate commitment to "treat them like individuals." While it may be unusual in his industry, Peter's people-oriented style of leadership is paying off for his firm in terms of growth and stability.

Source: Robert Keough, "Personal Touch Keeps Bayou Services Afloat," *Inc. 500*, 1998, p. 39.

When the supervisor knows what employees should be doing and who should be doing it, the job becomes one of creating the circumstances in which employees will do what is required of them. In other words, supervisors must be leaders. As you learned in Chapter 1, **leading** is the management function of influencing people to act or not act in a certain way.

leading
Influencing people to act or not act in a certain way.

What makes leadership work is examined in this chapter. A variety of leadership styles are described and criteria for matching a style to a situation are provided. In the opening story, Peter Callais chose an empathic style to help retain workers in a grueling and competitive environment. Next, the chapter discusses how to carry out an important activity related to leadership: giving directions. Because leading mainly requires human relations skills, a discussion of how supervisors can relate effectively to the various people in an organization concludes the chapter.

Characteristics of a Successful Leader

What is the difference between a manager and a leader? According to Patty Miller, senior vice president of franchise services for Sylvan Learning Center, leaders "think about things entirely differently. They are usually about 10 steps ahead of the group. They bring a different perspective. And it is not unusual for the rest of the group to be thinking, 'Where is this person coming from?'" Miller

FIGURE 8.1

What Managers Admire and Look For in a Leader

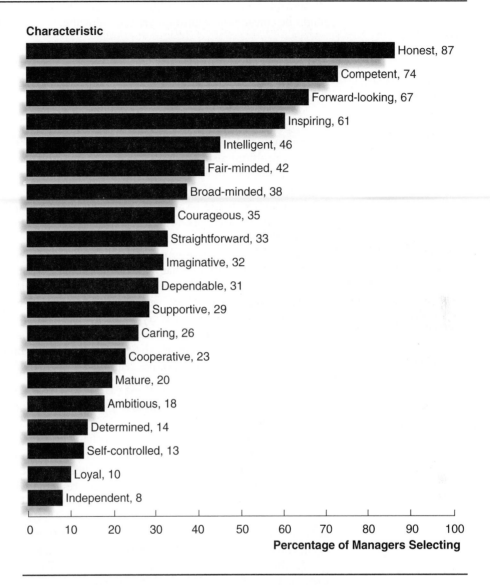

Characteristic

Honest, 87
Competent, 74
Forward-looking, 67
Inspiring, 61
Intelligent, 46
Fair-minded, 42
Broad-minded, 38
Courageous, 35
Straightforward, 33
Imaginative, 32
Dependable, 31
Supportive, 29
Caring, 26
Cooperative, 23
Mature, 20
Ambitious, 18
Determined, 14
Self-controlled, 13
Loyal, 10
Independent, 8

0 10 20 30 40 50 60 70 80 90 100

Percentage of Managers Selecting

Source: Data from James M. Kouzes and Barry Z. Posner, "The Credibility Factor: What Followers Expect from Their Leaders," *Management Review*, January 1990, p. 33.

quotes one of her clients who says, "Managers are followed because they are bosses. Leaders are followed because we believe in them."[1] A leader gives employees such feelings by instilling in them a sense of common purpose, a belief that together they can achieve something worthwhile. Are some people better equipped to do this than others? Figure 8.1 shows the results of a survey that asked more than 5,200 top-level managers to identify the traits they most admire and look for in a leader. Most managers reported that they seek leaders who are honest, competent, forward-looking, and inspiring.

To find out whether people are natural leaders, social scientists have studied the personalities of effective leaders, looking for traits they hold in common.

Presumably, such traits would be predictors of good leadership. Some traits that might be considered significant are the following:

- *Sense of responsibility*—A person who is promoted to a supervisory position is given responsibility for the work of others as well as for his or her own performance. Supervisors must be willing to take this responsibility seriously.
- *Self-confidence*—A supervisor who believes in his or her ability to get the job done will convey confidence to employees.
- *High energy level*—Many organizations expect supervisors to put in long hours willingly to handle the variety of duties that come with the job. Some supervisory positions also are physically challenging, requiring that the supervisor actively observe and participate in what is happening in the workplace.
- *Empathy*—In settling disputes, answering questions, and understanding needs, supervisors should be sensitive to the feelings of employees and higher management. Supervisors who have difficulty understanding what makes people tick will be at a disadvantage.
- *Internal locus of control*—An **internal locus of control** is the belief that you are the primary cause of what happens to yourself. People with an external locus of control tend to blame others or events beyond their control when something goes wrong. Those with an internal locus of control are thought to be better leaders because they try harder to take charge of events.
- *Sense of humor*—People with a good sense of humor are more fun to work with and to work for (assuming they use appropriate humor—not racist or sexist anecdotes—and do not overuse rehearsed jokes that are unrelated to work).

internal locus of control
The belief that you are the primary cause of what happens to yourself.

Focusing on traits such as these, ask yourself whether you have leadership qualities. Further, determine whether you are CEO material by taking the Self-Quiz on page 207.

While these traits sound plausible as characteristics of a successful leader, results of the various studies of leadership traits have been inconsistent. Some studies have found one set of traits to be significant, while others have identified a completely different set of traits. As a result, research has not established a clear link between personality traits and leadership success. Thus, if you have most of the traits described here, you may be a successful leader, but your success is not guaranteed. Also, if you have only a few of these traits, you need not be discouraged; you can still develop the skills that effective leaders use.

Kevin Kelly, officer of family-owned Emerald Packaging that was discussed in the case for Chapter 7, recalls that the reason Evelyn Martin, then 53, made such a successful transition from packer to production supervisor is that "she has a vision of how she wants her department to run. She's committed to increasing productivity and quality, she expects her people to work together, and she lets them know it . . . she holds them accountable . . . [and] rewards her crew for success." With no formal management training, Evelyn turned her unit around and brought production up and absenteeism down.[2]

Leadership Styles

Anita O'Donnell runs a tight ship; she lays down the rules and tolerates no deviation from them. Greg Petersen focuses on what he perceives to be the needs of his employees; they in turn do good work out of loyalty to him. George Liang is an easygoing supervisor when the work is routine, but when a big order comes in, he turns tough.

The Arts

Keeping Everyone on the Same Page

Roger Nierenberg is the conductor of Connecticut's Stamford Symphony Orchestra. His experience leading a group of highly skilled but vastly different individuals in a collaboration that yields beautiful music has given him many insights into the art of leadership. In fact, Nierenberg teaches managers at companies like Georgia-Pacific and Lucent Technologies what he has learned in his career as a leader, and the lessons are useful for supervisors in all fields.

Here are some of Nierenberg's observations about leadership.

Your job as a leader is to communicate a sense of how things could be—and to show people how to achieve that vision.

How do you do all that? By giving direction, not criticism. Direction points to the way things could be. Criticism, on the other hand, points to the way things were. It doesn't enlighten people. Direction tells people what to do, whereas criticism tells people what not to do. Here's a criticism: "The percussion section is playing too loudly." A direction is, "Make sure the audience can hear the woodwinds."

It's much harder to process a "do not" instruction, because the "do not" means you have to locate a behavior, inhibit it, figure out what to replace it with, and then replace it. The "do" instruction means something more direct: "Do this." You're offering a new vision, a different tool. Leadership is about preparation. It means actually inventing a whole new experience and then communicating it to the people you work with. If your team executes your direction and the results improve, then people begin to put their trust in you. That's how you gain credibility as a leader.

Source: Jill Rosenfeld, "Lead Softly, But Carry a Big Baton," *Fast Company,* July 2001, pp. 46–48.

If you have worked for more than one boss, chances are you have experienced more than one leadership style. Anita, Greg, and George illustrate only some of the possibilities. Some supervisors instinctively lead in a way they are comfortable with; others adopt their style of leadership consciously. However, a supervisor who is aware of basic types of leadership styles is probably in the best position to use the style (or styles) that will get the desired results.

Degree of Authority Retained

One way to describe leadership styles is in terms of how much authority the leader retains. Do employees get to make choices and control their own work? Or does the supervisor make all the decisions? To describe the possibilities, management theorists refer to authoritarian, democratic, and laissez-faire leadership.

In **authoritarian leadership,** the leader retains a great deal of authority, making decisions and dictating instructions to employees. An example would be a military commander who expects unquestioning obedience.

Some supervisors share more authority than authoritarian supervisors. With **democratic leadership,** the supervisor allows employees to participate in decision making and problem solving. A supervisor with a democratic style of leadership might have the staff meet weekly to discuss how to improve client relations. When a conflict arises, this supervisor asks the group to discuss possible solutions and to select one.

At the opposite extreme from authoritarian leadership is **laissez-faire leadership.** A laissez-faire manager is uninvolved and lets employees do what they want. Supervisors are rarely, if ever, able to practice this style of leadership because the nature of the supervisor's job requires close involvement with employees.

authoritarian leadership
A leadership style in which the leader retains a great deal of authority.

democratic leadership
A leadership style in which the leader allows subordinates to participate in decision making and problem solving.

laissez-faire leadership
A leadership style in which the leader is uninvolved and lets subordinates direct themselves.

◼ FIGURE 8.2

Possibilities for Retaining Authority

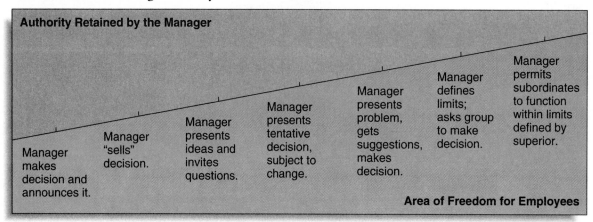

Source: Adapted from Robert Tannebaum and Warren Schmidt, "How to Choose a Leadership Pattern," May-June 1973 *Harvard Business Review*.

Nor are many supervisors totally authoritarian or totally democratic. Most supervisors give employees some degree of freedom to do their jobs but they still make some of the decisions for the department. Years ago, Robert Tannenbaum and Warren H. Schmidt drew a graph showing the continuum, or range of possibilities, for the degree of authority a manager can retain. This continuum is still popular today as a way to picture the possibilities (see Figure 8.2).

Task Oriented versus People Oriented

Another way to look at differences in leadership styles is to consider what supervisors focus on in making decisions and evaluating accomplishments. In general terms, leaders may be task oriented or people oriented. A task-oriented leader is one who focuses on the jobs to be done and the goals to be accomplished. When the work gets done correctly and on time, a task-oriented leader is satisfied. On the other hand, a people-oriented leader is concerned primarily with the well-being of the people he or she manages. This type of leader emphasizes issues such as morale, job satisfaction, and relationships among employees.

Of course, the organization expects that its supervisors and other managers will care about meeting organizational objectives. However, it seems reasonable to assume (other things being equal) that satisfied, healthy, cooperative workers will perform best. In that regard, consultant Peter L. Thigpen has concluded that one source of the high level of commitment in the Marine Corps lies with some unwritten rules of behavior for the officers. The four rules that Thigpen recalls reflect deep concern for the troops[3]:

1. Never eat before your troops eat.
2. Never bed down until your guards are posted and your troops are bedded down.

3. Your job, up to and including the commandant of the Marine Corps, is to support the private rifleman on the front line.
4. Never ask your troops to do something you wouldn't do.

These rules incorporate a people-oriented view of leadership in an organization where leaders are committed to getting the job done.

Most organizations expect that their supervisors can combine some degree of task orientation with some degree of people orientation. A supervisor who tends to focus on getting out the work should remember to check sometimes how employees are feeling and getting along. A supervisor who regularly sticks up for employees' welfare should make sure that he or she also remembers to promote the organization's goals.

Researchers Robert R. Blake and Jane S. Mouton recommend that supervisors and other managers be strong in both leadership orientations. They developed a Managerial Grid® (see Figure 8.3) that identifies seven styles of leadership by managers. Along one axis is the manager's concern for people and along the other is the manager's concern for production. Blake and Mouton's research led them to conclude that productivity, job satisfaction, and creativity are highest with a (9,9), or team management, style of leadership. To apply this model of leadership, supervisors identify where their current style of leadership falls on the managerial grid, then determine the kinds of changes they must make to adopt the (9,9) style, which is high in concern for both people and production.

Leader Attitudes

Theory X
A set of management attitudes based on the view that people dislike work and must be coerced to perform.

In observing the behavior of managers, Douglas McGregor noted that many tended to have a group of attitudes that reflected their beliefs about workers and the workplace. He termed this set of attitudes **Theory X.** To summarize, a Theory X manager assumes that people dislike work and try to avoid it, that they therefore must be coerced to perform, that they wish to avoid responsibility and would prefer to be directed, and that their primary need is for security. Not surprisingly, these beliefs influence how supervisors and other managers behave. A Theory X supervisor would adopt an autocratic role, keeping a close eye on employees and looking for occasions when they need to be disciplined to keep them performing adequately.[4]

Theory Y
A set of management attitudes based on the view that work is a natural activity and that people will work hard and creatively to achieve objectives they are committed to.

McGregor advises that managers can benefit from adopting a much different set of attitudes, which he terms **Theory Y.** According to Theory Y, working is as natural an activity as resting or playing, and people will work hard to achieve objectives they are committed to. They can learn to seek responsibility and to be creative in solving organizational problems. Supervisors and other managers who adhere to Theory Y focus on developing the potential of their employees. Their style of leadership tends to be democratic. Table 8.1 summarizes these two sets of assumptions.

Today a common view among people studying management is that Theory Y is appropriate for many situations. To see what a Theory Y manager looks like, consider Louis Lenzi, general manager of design for Thomson Consumer Electronics. Lenzi coaches cross-functional teams charged with ensuring that the Indianapolis-based company's products are user-friendly. He provides each team with a goal; in one case, the team was to develop a remote-control device for helping consumers navigate the channels of a satellite system. Then he lets each team determine how it wants to accomplish its goal while Lenzi concentrates on

■ FIGURE 8.3

The Managerial Grid

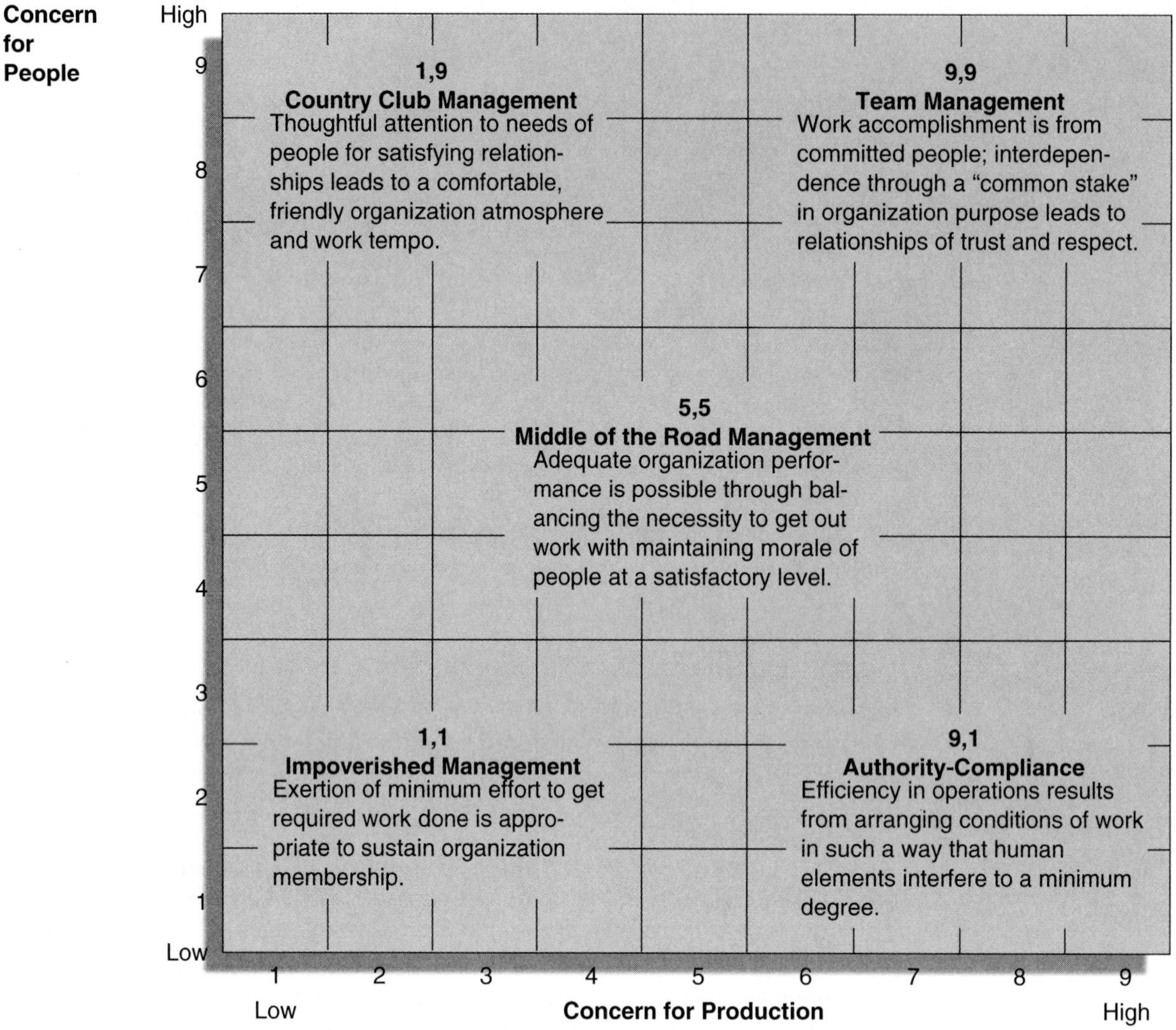

Concern for People

High

9

1,9
Country Club Management
Thoughtful attention to needs of people for satisfying relation-ships leads to a comfortable, friendly organization atmosphere and work tempo.

9,9
Team Management
Work accomplishment is from committed people; interdepen-dence through a "common stake" in organization purpose leads to relationships of trust and respect.

8

7

6

5,5
Middle of the Road Management
Adequate organization perfor-mance is possible through bal-ancing the necessity to get out work with maintaining morale of people at a satisfactory level.

5

4

3

1,1
Impoverished Management
Exertion of minimum effort to get required work done is appro-priate to sustain organization membership.

9,1
Authority-Compliance
Efficiency in operations results from arranging conditions of work in such a way that human elements interfere to a minimum degree.

2

1

Low

1   2   3   4   5   6   7   8   9

Low — **Concern for Production** — **High**

Source: The Leadership Grid® figure for *Leadership Dilemmas—Grid Solutions*, by Robert R. Blake and Ann Adams McCanse (formerly the Managerial Grid® figure by Robert R. Blake and Jane S. Mouton), (Houston: Gulf Publishing Company), p. 29. Copyright 1991 by Scientific Methods, Inc. Reproduced by permission of the owners.

Theory Z
A set of management attitudes that emphasizes employee participation in all aspects of decision making.

removing any corporate obstacles and making sure that the team has whatever re-sources it needs. At the same time, Lenzi requires frequent updates on team progress, and he is firm in insisting on change from those teams that don't keep up or that lapse into complacency or bickering.[5]

In the last decade, management experts extended their view of managing and leading to include **Theory Z.** Theory Z supervisors seek to involve employees in making decisions, to consider long-term goals when making plans, and to give employees relatively great freedom in carrying out their duties. This theory is

	Theory X	Theory Y
TABLE 8.1 **Contrasting Leader Attitudes**	People dislike work and try to avoid it.	Working is as natural an activity as resting or playing.
	People must be coerced to perform.	People will work hard to achieve objectives they are committed to.
	People wish to avoid responsibility.	People can learn to seek responsibility and prefer to be directed.
	People's primary need is for security.	Many people are able to be creative in solving organizational problems.

Source: Based on Douglas McGregor, *The Human Side of Enterprise* (New York: McGraw-Hill, 1960).

based on comparisons of management styles in the United States and Japan; it assumes that where Japanese workers are more productive than their U.S. counterparts, the difference stems in part from different management styles. Thus, Theory Z was developed in an attempt to adapt some Japanese management practices to the U.S. workplace. The Japanese practices include employee involvement and lifetime employment.

Contingency Theories of Leadership

With all these possibilities, is there one best approach to leading employees? Should the supervisor consciously cultivate one leadership style? A common view is that the best style of leadership depends on the circumstances.

Fiedler's Contingency Model   One of the first researchers to develop such a theory—called a contingency theory—was Fred Fiedler. According to Fiedler, each leader has a preferred leadership style, which may be relationship oriented (i.e., people oriented) or task oriented. Whether relationship-oriented or task-oriented leaders perform better depends on three characteristics of the situation: leader-member relations, task structure, and the position power of the leader (see Figure 8.4). Leader-member relations refers to the extent to which the leader has the support and loyalty of group members. Task structure describes any specified procedures that employees should follow in carrying out the task. Position power refers to the formal authority granted to the leader by the organization.

Fiedler recommends that a leader determine whether his or her preferred leadership style fits the situation. For instance, if a situation involves good leader-member relations, a structured task, and strong position power, the situation calls for a leader who is task oriented. If the leader's preferred style does not fit, Fiedler says, the leader should try to change the characteristics of the situation. In the preceding example, a relationship-oriented leader might try to make the task less structured; the result would be a situation in which the leader is likely to be more effective.

Hersey-Blanchard Theory   Fiedler's work led others to develop their own contingency theories of leadership. For example, Paul Hersey and Ken Blanchard developed a model called the life cycle theory. This model, like Fiedler's, considers

■ FIGURE 8.4

Fiedler's Contingency Model of Leadership

Leader–Member Relations	Good	Good	Good	Good	Poor	Poor	Poor	Poor
Task Structure	Structured	Structured	Unstructured	Unstructured	Structured	Structured	Unstructured	Unstructured
Leader Position Power	Strong	Weak	Strong	Weak	Strong	Weak	Strong	Weak
Which Leader Performs Better?	Task-Oriented Leader	Task-Oriented Leader	Task-Oriented Leader	Relationship-Oriented Leader	Relationship-Oriented Leader	Relationship-Oriented Leader	Task- or Relationship-Oriented Leader	Task-Oriented Leader

■ Characteristics of the situation   ■ Optimal leadership style for situation

Source: Adapted from Fred E. Fiedler, "Engineer the Job to Fit the Manager," September–October 1965 *Harvard Business Review.*

degrees to which managers focus on relationships and tasks. Unlike Fiedler's model, however, the Hersey-Blanchard theory assumes that the leader's behavior should adapt to the situation. Specifically, the leadership style should reflect the maturity of the followers as measured by traits such as ability to work independently.

According to the Hersey-Blanchard life cycle theory, leaders should adjust the degree of task and relationship behavior in response to the growing maturity of their followers. As followers mature, leaders should move through the following combinations of task and relationship behavior:

1. High task and low relationship behavior.
2. High task and high relationship behavior.
3. Low task and high relationship behavior.
4. Low task and low relationship behavior.

Under special conditions, such as short-term deadlines, the leader may have to adjust the leadership style temporarily. However, Hersey and Blanchard maintain that this pattern of choosing a leadership style will bring about the most effective long-term working relationship between leader and followers.

FIGURE 8.5

FIGURE 8.5

Characteristics Affecting Choice of Leadership Style

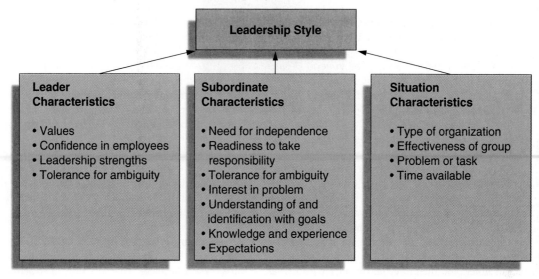

Leadership Style

Leader Characteristics

- Values
- Confidence in employees
- Leadership strengths
- Tolerance for ambiguity

Subordinate Characteristics

- Need for independence
- Readiness to take responsibility
- Tolerance for ambiguity
- Interest in problem
- Understanding of and identification with goals
- Knowledge and experience
- Expectations

Situation Characteristics

- Type of organization
- Effectiveness of group
- Problem or task
- Time available

Choosing a Leadership Style

Viewing contingency theories as a whole provides some general guidelines for choosing a leadership style. To identify the most effective style, the supervisor should consider the characteristics of the leader, of the subordinates, and of the situation itself. Figure 8.5 shows some key characteristics to weigh. (For more ideas on leading, even in difficult times, see "Meeting the Challenge.")

Characteristics of the Leader   Thanks to sources of variation such as personality type and cultural values, different leaders prefer different styles of leading. Whereas one supervisor might feel more comfortable backed up by a clear system of rules, regulations, and schedules, another might prefer to come up with creative approaches on the spur of the moment. One supervisor may like the results of involving employees in decision making, whereas another cannot get used to the time and effort this requires.

One common characteristic of good leaders is the ability to act as a good role model. One writer asks, "Are you always on time? Do you provide a fair day's work for the compensation you receive? Are you eager for information and knowledge? Are you receptive to change? It may not always seem obvious to you, but your people are watching you like a hawk. They observe every move you make—and every move you fail to make."[6]

To some extent at least, a supervisor gets the best results using a leadership style with which he or she feels comfortable. That comfort level depends on characteristics such as the following:

- *The manager's values*—What is most important to the supervisor in carrying out his or her job? Is it the department's contribution to company profits?

MEETING THE CHALLENGE

Leadership in Tough Times

To their subordinates, supervisors represent the company. They are role models, coaches, facilitators, counselors, and communicators. As challenging as these roles may be in good times, when the company's performance is strong, they become even more demanding when cutbacks, layoffs, and poor economic performance beset the firm.

How does a supervisor maintain a leadership role in such times?

Maintaining a positive attitude is important, experts say. Subordinates react more positively to motivated and enthusiastic supervisors than to those who act depressed, confused, or demotivated.

Relaying high-quality information quickly and honestly, without seeking to blame anyone, is another fail-proof leadership strategy. Rumors fly during uncertain times, and therefore the supervisor who seeks good information, thinks before speaking, and gets the news out to his or her employees is seen as a leader.

Sometimes a leader must deal with tough questions by saying, "I don't know, but I'll find out."

Leaders understand that people worry when things are tough, and they earn trust by remaining visible, listening to concerns, answering questions, dealing with difficult situations, and not hiding in their office hoping no one will come in.

Finally, strong leaders know how to create a problem-solving climate that encourages everyone to continue putting forth their best efforts. They define the problem, gather input about solutions, and free up the resources to help others reach the goal.

Sources: Bob Lewis, "In Rough Seas, Does Your Leadership Style Inspire Buoyancy—or Mutiny?" *InfoWorld*, April 16, 2001, p. 49; Victor Buzzotta, "Trust as a Style," *Executive Excellence*, May 2001, p. 19; Donald S. Miller, "Q-u-a-l-i-t-y: Realities for Supervisors," *Supervision*, May 2000, p. 3.

The employees' or the manager's own growth and development? A manager concerned about developing employees is most likely to involve them in making decisions.

- *Level of confidence in employees*—The more confidence the supervisor has in employees, the more he or she will involve them in planning and decision making. Jim Schaefer of British Petroleum's Ohio plants has such faith in his employees that he spent three years commuting between BPs Lima and Toledo operations in order to eat lunch with all 900 workers. He believed the productivity gains he needed to save the plants would only come from the rank-and-file workers and their supervisors, so he actively sought—and acted on—their advice and suggestions. Bringing fast-food lunches to tank fields and control rooms, he asked about strategies, obstacles, and process improvements. When someone suggested that maintenance inspectors should carry tool boxes in their trucks, Schaefer purchased the tools that day.[7]
- *Personal leadership strengths*—Some supervisors have a talent for leading group discussions; others are better at quietly analyzing information and reaching a decision. Some are good at detecting employee wants and needs; others excel at keeping their focus on the numbers. Effective leaders capitalize on their strengths.
- *Tolerance for ambiguity*—When the supervisor involves employees in solving problems or making decisions, he or she cannot always be sure of the outcomes. Supervisors differ in their level of comfort with this uncertainty, which is called ambiguity.

Logically, greater diversity in the workplace would generate greater diversity in some of these characteristics, such as values and leadership strengths. Particularly noteworthy is the possibility that women bring a different set of values and experiences to the workplace than men do, a theory that has received wide attention in the business press. UCLA professor Helen Astin, who conducted a study of well-known women leaders, believes that there is a "feminine way of leadership." She claims that women tend to focus on interpersonal issues and to emphasize collective leadership, which involves empowering one's followers. The women leaders Astin studied tended to describe accomplishments as being accomplishments of the whole group, not just the leader.

Similarly, Alice H. Eagly, a social psychology professor at Purdue University, reviewed more than 360 studies on gender and leadership. She found that the only significant difference between men and women in these studies was that women tend to be more democratic in their leadership style. In many cases, this leadership style is supported by a view that the people in an organization are interdependent. A leader with this belief is more likely to respond to a problem by saying to employees, "Let's work out a solution together."

Characteristics of the Subordinates   In selecting a leadership style, smart supervisors consider their employees as well as themselves. Employees who are at their most creative and productive when they have a lot of freedom will dig in their heels if their supervisor is autocratic with them, even if that is the supervisor's natural leadership style. At the other extreme, employees who expect and rely on structure and direction will tend to drift and even become paralyzed if their leader has a laissez-faire or even democratic style.

What should the supervisor look for in deciding on the kind of supervision employees want? Here are some characteristics that should influence the choice:

- *Need for independence*—People who want a lot of direction will welcome autocratic leadership.
- *Readiness to assume responsibility*—Employees who are eager to assume responsibility will appreciate a democratic or laissez-faire style of leadership.
- *Tolerance for ambiguity*—Employees who are tolerant of ambiguity will accept a leadership style that gives them more say in solving problems.
- *Interest in the problem to be solved*—Employees who are interested in a problem and think it is important will want to help solve it.
- *Understanding of and identification with goals*—Employees who understand and identify with organizational or departmental goals will want to play an active role in deciding how to meet those goals. Furthermore, the supervisor will find that such employees are reliable in carrying out their responsibilities. Employees who don't identify with goals may need more active direction and control from the supervisor.
- *Knowledge and experience*—Employees with the knowledge necessary to solve a problem are more apt to want to help find a solution. Furthermore, their input will be more valuable to the supervisor. Thus, someone who is new on the job will probably need a supervisor who engages in both task-oriented and relationship-oriented behavior, but the supervisor can become less involved as the employee gains experience.
- *Expectations*—Some employees expect to participate in making decisions and solving problems. Others think that a supervisor who does not tell them what to do is not doing a good job.

Organizations that use self-managing work teams (see Chapter 3) generally encourage a variety of employee characteristics that are associated with successful use of democratic leadership and a low degree of task-oriented behavior. They tend to train employees to assume extensive responsibility (or to select such employees). They generally provide the team with information about issues to be handled and about the performances of the organization and the team. This information should produce knowledgeable employees with an understanding of the problems faced by the team. Finally, the members of a self-managing work team expect to be involved in making a wide variety of decisions. What is left for a leader to do? Much of importance: communicating a vision of the team's mission and fostering a climate in which team members contribute to and care about the success of the team and the organization.

Characteristics of the Situation   Besides the personalities and preferences of supervisor and subordinates, the situation itself helps to determine what leadership style will be most effective. Several characteristics are important:

- *Type of organization*—Organizations often lend themselves to one leadership style or another. If the organization expects supervisors to manage large numbers of employees, a democratic leadership style may be time-consuming and relatively challenging to use. If higher-level managers clearly value one style of leadership, the supervisor may find it difficult to use a different style and still be considered effective. At Federal Express, a high degree of empowerment in addition to annual surveys asking employees about management (including whether their supervisor is open to their ideas) requires a relatively democratic leadership style.[8]
- *Effectiveness of the group*—Regardless of the characteristics of individual employees, some groups are more successful in handling decisions than others. If a department, team, or other work group has little experience in making its own decisions, the supervisor may find that an authoritarian approach is easier to use. Supervisors should delegate decisions to groups that can handle the responsibility.
- *The problem or task*—The work group or individual employees can easily reach a solution to relatively simple problems, but the supervisor should retain greater control of complex or difficult problems. Besides difficulty, the supervisor should consider how structured a task is. A structured task—that is, one with a set procedure to follow—is best managed by an autocratic leader. However, some tasks, such as generating ideas to improve customer service or planning the department picnic, are relatively unstructured. These tasks benefit from the employee involvement sought by a democratic, people-oriented leader.
- *Time available*—An autocratic leader is in a position to make decisions quickly. Group decision making usually requires more time for discussion and the sharing of ideas. Thus, the manager should use a relatively democratic leadership style only when time allows for it.

One study reported in the Harvard Business Review found that the most effective leaders choose from six distinctive styles, depending on their goals and on the situation in which they acted. The style can be briefly summarized as:

1. Coercive, which demands compliance. (the leader says, "Do what I tell you!")
2. Pace-setting, which sets extremely high performance standards. ("Do as I do, now!")
3. Coaching, which focuses on developing people. ("Try this.")
4. Democratic, which seeks consensus through participation. ("What do you think?")

5. Affiliative, which creates harmony and emotional bonds. ("People come first.")
6. Authoritative, which mobilizes employees with enthusiasm and vision. ("Come with me.")[9]

When employees and managers work in teams, a democratic leadership style based on Theory Y, which emphasizes people, is appropriate. Some management experts think that a coach is a good analogy for this leadership style. Coaches delegate responsibility to carry out operations, and they are willing to share authority. They focus on picking qualified people, helping them learn to do their jobs well, and inspiring peak performance. Joseph Lipsey, who manages training and development for a major insurance company, credits this leadership style with transforming his department from one with little impact to one that works effectively:

> By driving out fear, hiring top-notch people . . . implementing a team structure, making decisions by consensus, and unleashing the tremendous creativity and desire to contribute and to find meaning in work that is innate to everyone, we have created a real "force" within this organization.[10]

Giving Directions

Supervisors can practice leadership by giving directions. In the workplace, giving directions can range from issuing detailed formal procedures for a particular task to inspiring the work group with a mission that unites them in a common cause. The supervisor can give directions simply by stating what an employee is to do in a particular situation. Or, if the supervisor leads a group that is expected to make many of its own decisions, the supervisor's directions may emphasize broad principles: "In our group, we don't waste time blaming; we figure out how to convert this angry customer into a happy one." In all cases, the way the supervisor gives directions can influence how willingly and how well employees respond.

The supervisor should make sure that the employee understands the directions. If the supervisor says, "I need those figures today," can the employee leave a note on the supervisor's desk at 6:00 P.M., half an hour after the supervisor has left? Or does the supervisor need time to review the numbers, so that he actually needs them by a specific time, say, 3:00 P.M.? Thus, the supervisor should state directions in specific, clear terms. Another way to make sure employees understand is to ask them to restate what they are supposed to do and to check on their progress before they are finished. (Chapter 10 provides further guidelines for effective communication.)

Supervisors may benefit from regularly asking their employees for feedback about their ability to give directions. The most useful feedback comes from specific questions: "Are my directions usually clear, or do you depend on co-workers to help you figure out what I want?" and "Do I often change my mind about what you should do after you've already started an assignment?" When the supervisor emphasizes conveying broad goals and letting employees work out the details, the supervisor will need to seek evidence that employees know what those broad goals are.

The supervisor should make sure that employees also see the reason for the directions. In a crisis, people are willing to pitch in; they easily can see a need. Thus, if a hospital patient has a cardiac arrest, the staff members do not object to someone barking orders in an effort to revive the patient. But sometimes the supervisor has to identify the crisis or explain the need. The supervisor on a loading dock could say, "This order is for our biggest customer, who's getting fed up with late shipments. If we don't get the order on the truck today, we'll be in deep trouble." That approach is more likely to get results than giving no reason and shouting, "Get moving!"

The most effective way to give instructions is to do so confidently and politely, but without apologies. If a supervisor says, "I'm sorry—I know you're busy, but I'd appreciate seeing those lab results by noon," the employee may think that he or she has been given an option, not instructions. The employee also may be unclear about who is in charge of the department. Instead, the supervisor can say, "Please have those lab results ready by noon." Of course, it is never appropriate to be rude.

If employees are not complying with a supervisor's directions, the supervisor can examine whether the directions follow these guidelines. Perhaps employees do not understand what is expected of them, or perhaps they do not realize that the supervisor is giving them directions, not a suggestion.

Human Relations

Leading is clearly an application of human relations skills and is perhaps the most important measure of whether the supervisor excels at relations with his or her employees. Of course, supervisors need good human relations skills for other relationships as well. They need to work effectively with their manager and peers, and to be positive about themselves.

Most books about business focus on the technical skills of managing. How can a supervisor develop human relations skills? Ways to get along with almost anyone include projecting a positive attitude, taking an interest in other people, and helping out. In addition, the supervisor can take some steps to work on each of the categories of relationships that are important to his or her success.

Supervisors' Self-Images

Order-processing supervisor Eleanor Chakonas thinks of herself as a risk taker and a person who makes things happen. When she was asked to plan the expansion of her department, she attacked the job with a gusto that inspired her employees to contribute to the effort. The result was a plan that called for extra efforts by employees but would result in the department performing beyond management expectations. A supervisor who considers him- or herself more cautious or prone to error than Eleanor would have approached the planning job differently.

self-concept
A person's self-image.

The self-image a supervisor has—that is, the supervisor's **self-concept**—influences the supervisor's behavior. Someone who believes that he or she has power will act powerfully; someone who thinks of him- or herself as intelligent is apt to make careful decisions. It is worthwhile for supervisors to be aware of the thoughts they have of themselves.

Doing this can also help supervisors cultivate positive thoughts, which will help them act in positive ways. When you find yourself thinking "I'm so stupid" or "I wouldn't lose my cool the way he did," notice what you are thinking, and consider what it says about your self-concept. Take time to consider what your strengths and goals are. When you do something well, give yourself credit. When someone compliments you, smile and say thank you. Making the effort to behave this way will not only allow you to understand yourself better, but also to discover that your beliefs about yourself are more positive.

Could You Be a Good Mentor?

Many outstanding employees are eager to learn from their supervisors and advance. While it is never a good idea to develop personal relationships with subordinates that extend outside the business, there is, nevertheless, room in the supervisory role for a relationship that allows you to pass along important insights and experience. That is the function of *mentoring*, which is sometimes described as being a "servant leader."

Being a mentor to an up-and-coming subordinate requires time, effort, patience, and readiness. It also requires the consent of both parties. How do you know you are ready to be a mentor? Ask yourself:

- Am I prepared to give the role the time it needs?
- Can I control the amount of time the mentor relationship requires of me and still do it well?
- Am I willing to share my experience and knowledge freely?
- Am I eager for the personal growth in leadership and people skills that mentoring brings?
- Have I examined my own motives in undertaking the role?

- Can I take care of my protégé's needs as well as my own?
- Can I value my protégé's unique path and not force him or her to do what I think is best?
- Can I persevere if my protégé does not always recognize the value of my help?
- Am I prepared for us to occasionally disagree?
- Can I accept the fact that others may hold me responsible for my protégé, for good or for ill?
- Do I understand fully that this relationship will end, and that if my mentoring is successful, my protégé will eventually move on?
- Am I ready to accept my protégé as a future peer and colleague?

If you answered Yes to all the questions, you are ready to be an effective mentor.

Source: Taunee Besson, "Caveat Mentor," "Dos and Don'ts for Mentors," and "Are You Ready for a Mentor?" Working Woman.com accessed at http://www.workingwoman.com/wwn/article.jsp?contentId=4465&ChannelId=211 on June 14, 2001.

Supervisors' Relationships with Their Employees

A supervisor who is liked and respected by employees will inspire them to work harder and better. This does not mean that the supervisor should be friends with employees. Rather, the supervisor should consistently treat them in a way that reflects his or her role as a part of management. Today's supervisor empowers rather than commands employees, seeking consensus and spending time with employees to learn what they need for job success and career development. See "Supervision and Diversity" for ways to ease supervisor-employee relations when age difference is a factor.

Jack Welch, former CEO of General Electric, built a masterful leadership style in his 17 years as head of the giant firm. One of the ways in which he kept in touch with his many employees at all levels of the company was to fax them countless handwritten notes that guided and counseled them. "We're pebbles in an ocean," said GE marketing manager Brian Nailor, "But he knows about us."[11]

See "Tips from the Firing Line" for some ideas about being a mentor.

Supervisors as Role Models   For employees, the supervisor is the person who most directly represents management and the organization. Thus, when employees evaluate the organization, they look at the supervisor's behavior. They also use the supervisor's behavior as a guide for how they should act. If a supervisor takes long lunch breaks, employees either will think that the use of their time is unimportant or will believe that the company unfairly lets managers get away with violating rules.

Smoothing the Way Between Older Workers and Younger Managers

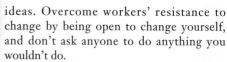

A tight labor market and a booming economy are combining to draw many older people in the United States back into the workforce, where they often find themselves reporting to younger bosses who may or may not respect their skills and experience. Without the seniority they may feel they deserve, many of these older workers can become frustrated and quit.

How can a young manager make a comfortable environment for workers of all ages? First, avoid being critical or negative about employees. Be positive and reinforcing, and suggest, don't order. Next, it's important to demonstrate respect by listening to older workers' opinions. Acknowledging their experience and wisdom can go a long way toward defusing any resentment they may feel toward a "young upstart." Words like "You can really help me with this assignment" can mean a lot. In addition, rely on your supervisory skills of delegating and leading to make your older workers feel they are part of the team. Delegate authority as well as tasks; for instance, ask an older employee to train new hires, make decisions when appropriate, and regularly contribute new ideas. Overcome workers' resistance to change by being open to change yourself, and don't ask anyone to do anything you wouldn't do.

What can older workers do to improve their relationships with younger bosses? Older workers in turn can help bridge the age gap by supporting their boss instead of competing, and by being tactful about suggesting better ways to do things. It's not a good idea to tell your boss how to do his or her job even if you are older and more experienced. Phrases like "You're too young to know" and references to how long you've been in the business will damage the relationship, not strengthen it. Listening to what your supervisor says about his or her needs is important, as is being an energetic and willing team player who is prompt, reliable, and quietly confident about your special skills or expertise.

Good advice for both parties: Focus on the mission, not on your age.

Source: Steve Atlas, "Mature Ways to Bridge Boss-Worker Age Gaps," *Washington Times*, October 21, 1998.

To set a good example for employees, the supervisor should follow all the rules and regulations that cover employees. The supervisor should be impartial in the treatment of employees—for example, assigning unpopular tasks to everyone, not just to certain employees. Supervisors also should be ethical, that is, honest and fair. (Chapter 4 discusses ethics in greater detail.)

Developing Trust   Here is management consultant and author Tom Peters on the subjects of trust: "In a world gone nuts, we cry out for something or someone to rely on. To *trust*. The fearless leader may . . . change his or her mind with the times. But as a subordinate, I trust a leader who shows up, makes the tough calls, takes the heat, sleeps well amidst the furor, and then aggressively chomps into the next task in the morning with visible vitality."[12]

Building trust takes time and effort, yet the supervisor can lose it with a single unreasonable act. The most important way to build trust is to engage in fair, predictable behavior. The supervisor should fulfill promises and give employees credit when they do something well. Keeping the lines of communication open also builds trust. When the supervisor listens carefully and shares information, employees will not think that he or she is hiding something from them. Training and education consultant Jim Kouzes keeps his firm's computer printer next to his desk. He considers the resulting interruptions worthwhile because of what he learns from his employees when they stop by to pick up their documents.

FIGURE 8.6

What Managers Expect of Supervisors

Supervisors' Relationships with Their Managers

No matter how good you are at planning, organizing, and leading, your ability to get along with your manager can determine the course of your career at a particular organization. That may not always seem fair, but your manager is the person who usually decides whether you will be promoted, get a juicy assignment or a raise, or even have a job next week. A manager who likes to work with you is more likely to take a favorable (or at least tolerant) view of your performance.

Expectations   While every manager is different, most expect certain kinds of behavior from the people they manage. As summarized in Figure 8.6, a supervisor can reasonably assume that the manager expects loyalty, cooperation, communication, and results.

- *Loyalty* means that the supervisor says only positive things about company policies and about his or her manager. If the supervisor cannot think of anything positive to say, silence is better than criticism.
- *Cooperation* means that the supervisor works with others in the organization to achieve organizational goals. If the manager offers criticism, the supervisor should listen and try to make improvements. If the criticism seems unreasonable, the supervisor should first make sure that there was no misunderstanding and then try to find constructive aspects of the criticism.
- *Communication* means that the manager expects the supervisor to keep him or her informed about the department's performance.
- *Results* means that the supervisor should see that the department meets or exceeds its objectives. The best way to look good to the manager is to have a high-performing department.

Learning about Your Manager   You can better meet your manager's expectations if you understand him or her as an individual. Observe how your manager handles various situations, try to determine his or her leadership style, and notice what issues are of most importance to your manager. As much as possible, adapt your own style to match your manager's when you are with this person. Also, ask what your manager's expectations are for you and how your performance will be measured.

If You Are Dissatisfied   Despite your best efforts, you may find that you are dissatisfied with your manager. It happens to many people at some point in their career. If you are unhappy, begin by considering the source of the problem. Most interpersonal problems arise from the behavior and attitudes of two people, so determine what changes you can make to improve the situation.

If you cannot improve the situation enough by changing your own behavior, talk to your manager, stating the types of actions you are dissatisfied with and how those actions are affecting you. If you cannot resolve the problem, your best bet is probably to hunt for another job. But try to keep your present job while you look for a new one. Prospective employers look more favorably on job candidates who are already employed.

Supervisors' Relationships with Their Peers

If you get along well with your peers in the same and other departments, they will help you look good and get your job done. Their resentment or dislike for you can cause an endless stream of problems. Therefore, supervisors need to cultivate good relations with their peers.

Competition   Sometimes your peers will be competing with you for raises, bonuses, or promotions. Remember that the more you can cooperate, the better you will all look. This means that your competition should be fair and as friendly as possible. If you try to sabotage a co-worker, you probably will be the one who ultimately ends up looking bad.

Criticism   Because you are trying to maintain a positive attitude, you should not go looking for things to criticize about your peers or anyone else. However, if you know that a co-worker has done something that works against the organization's best interests, you should go directly to that person and point out the problem. It usually helps to be polite and diplomatic and to assume that the problem was unintended—an error or an oversight.

If the co-worker resists listening to your criticism and the problem will harm the company, its employees, or its customers, then you should go to your manager to discuss the problem. Focus on the problem and its consequences to the organization, not on the personalities involved. Gossip is not the behavior of a leader; overcoming problems is.

Summary

9.1   Discuss the possible link between personal traits and leadership ability.

To find which people will succeed as leaders, researchers have looked for traits that successful leaders hold in common. Traits that may be significant include a sense of responsibility, self-confidence, high energy level, empathy, an internal locus of control, and a sense of humor. However, research results have been inconsistent, leading to the conclusion that traits alone do not predict success as a leader.

9.2   Compare leadership styles that a supervisor might adopt.

Depending on how much authority they retain, supervisors can be authoritarian (retaining much authority), democratic (sharing authority), or laissez faire (giving up most authority). Supervisors may also be task oriented, people oriented, or both. They may build their leadership style on Theory X assumptions that employees must be coerced to work, on Theory Y assumptions that employees can be motivated to seek responsibility and achieve objectives creatively, or on Theory Z values such as employee involvement and focus on long-term goals.

9.3   Explain contingency theories of leadership.

These theories hold that leaders can be most effective by matching different leadership styles to varying circumstances. For example, Fiedler's contingency model says that whether people- or task-oriented leaders perform better depends on leader-member relations, task structure, and the leader's position power. Fiedler recommends that, if the leader's preferred leadership style does not fit the situation, the characteristics of the situation should be changed. In contrast, Hersey and Blanchard's life cycle theory maintains that the leader should modify his or her behavior to fit the situation. As followers mature, leaders should use varying levels of task and relationship behavior.

9.4   Identify criteria for choosing a leadership style.

The supervisor should select a leadership style that suits his or her own characteristics, as well as those of the employees and the situation. Criteria for evaluating the characteristics of the leader are his or her values, level of confidence in employees, leadership strengths, and tolerance for ambiguity. Criteria for evaluating the characteristics of employees include their need for independence, readiness to assume responsibility, tolerance for ambiguity, interest in the problem, expectations, understanding of and identification with goals, and knowledge and experience. Criteria for evaluating the characteristics of the situation include the type of organization, effectiveness of the group, the nature of the problem or task, and the time available.

9.5   Describe guidelines for giving directions to employees.

The supervisor should make sure that employees understand the directions and the reasons behind them. The supervisor should give the instructions confidently and politely, but without being apologetic.

9.6   Tell why supervisors need to understand and improve their views of themselves.

The supervisor's self-concept influences how he or she behaves. People who believe they are capable tend to act capably. The supervisor needs to cultivate the self-concept of an effective leader.

9.7   Explain how supervisors can develop and maintain good relations with their employees, managers, and peers.

The supervisor should project a positive attitude, take an interest in others, and help out as needed. With employees, the supervisor should set a good example, be ethical, and develop trust. The supervisor should give his or her manager loyalty, cooperation, communication, results, and adapt to the manager's style. The supervisor should keep competition with peers as fair and friendly as possible and should offer any necessary criticism in a constructive way.

Key Terms

leading, p. 184

internal locus of control, p. 186

authoritarian leadership, p. 187

democratic leadership, p. 187

laissez-faire leadership, p. 187

Theory X, p. 189

Theory Y, p. 189

Theory Z, p. 190

self-concept, p. 198

Review and Discussion Questions

1. Describe the six traits that researchers believe may indicate a good leader. However, research has *not* established a clear link between personality traits and leadership success. What other factors do you think might contribute to success or failure?

2. Claire Callahan supervises the camping department of a large outdoor-equipment store. The store manager (Claire's boss) has given her the objective of increasing sales by 10 percent during the next quarter. Choose one of the three leadership styles for Claire (authoritarian, democratic, or laissez-faire). Then state three or more steps that she might take to influence her employees to meet the new sales objective.

3. Ann Wong is the accounts payable supervisor at an insurance company. During a time of layoffs, she decides to adopt a more people-oriented leadership style than the style she normally uses. What does this change mean?

4. Pete Polito supervises a cross-functional team whose task is to evaluate whether the in-line skates his company manufactures are safe and up-to-date in design and style. Using Theory Y, what steps might Pete take to lead his team to its goal?

5. Do you think it is more realistic to expect supervisors to adjust the situation to meet their preferred leadership style, as suggested by Fiedler's contingency model of leadership, or to adjust their leadership style to fit the situation, as suggested by Hersey and Blanchard? Explain your reasoning.

6. In which of the following situations would you recommend that the supervisor use an authoritarian style of leadership? In which situation would you recommend a democratic style? Explain your choices.

   a. The supervisor's manager says, "Top management wants us to start getting employees to suggest ways to improve quality in all areas of operations." Each department is given wide latitude in how to accomplish this.

   b. A supervisor is uncomfortable in meetings and likes to be left alone to figure out solutions to problems. The supervisor's employees believe that a good supervisor is able to tell them exactly what to do.

   c. A shipment of hazardous materials is on its way to a warehouse. The supervisor is responsible for instructing employees how to handle the materials when they arrive later that day.

7. Prakash Singh prefers a very democratic style of leadership and is uncomfortable telling someone what to do. His solution is to make his instructions as general as possible, so that employees will feel they have more control. He also tends to apologize for being authoritarian. Do you think this method of giving directions is effective? Why or why not?

8. Why should supervisors have a positive view of themselves? What are some ways a supervisor can be aware of and improve his or her self-concept?

9. Identify the human relations error in each of the following situations. Suggest a better way to handle each.

   a. Carole Fields's boss compliments her on the report she submitted yesterday. She says, "It was no big deal."

   b. When Rich Peaslee was promoted to supervisor, he told the other employees, "Now, remember, I was one of the gang before this promotion, and I'll still be one of the gang."

c. The second-shift supervisor observes that the first-shift employees have not left their work areas clean for the last three days. He complains to his manager about the lax supervision on the first shift.

10. Carla Santos doesn't get along with her new manager; the two have disliked each other since the first day they met. Carla was transferred to a new department when the previous supervisor left the company, so neither Carla nor her manager actually chose to work together. Carla doesn't want her job as a supervisor to be jeopardized by an unpleasant relationship. What steps might she take to improve the situation?

A SECOND LOOK

Which characteristics of a successful leader does Peter Callais of Abdon Callais Boat Rentals exhibit? Does he exhibit any other qualities that you think contribute to his success but that are not discussed in the chapter or listed in Figure 8.1?

SKILLS MODULE

CASE

Top-Down and Bottom-Up Style

Rakesh Gangwal is the new chief executive of US Airways Group (formerly USAir). He plans to expand US Airways' route network, increase its fleet, improve profitability, and enhance several key aspects of service such as on-time performance. His management style is an active one that matches his ambitious goals, but what many observers have noticed about Rakesh is that he manages in two ways—from the top down and from the bottom up.

The top-down part of his method is apparent in the way he reviews decisions made deep within the organization. At the same time, the dozens of task forces he has established ask employees to look into and report on everything from in-flight safety to corporate competitive advantages, and that is where the bottom-up style comes in. As he says, "I love it when front-line employees come up with ideas, because I know they are the things that generally work."

While Rakesh is happiest working in two different directions at once, some of his division heads must adjust to the flow of information and input from below. Far from allowing them to relinquish their authority, however, Rakesh still demands that his managers also develop and implement their own ideas. Known for his candor, he has admitted that his expectations are high—about three-quarters of the firm's vice presidents have been replaced since he came on board. "I do impose my views in setting direction and in what we are trying to attain, but then I let the process take over. It's a very fine line," he says.

Another characteristic of Rakesh's style is that he pays attention to details, such as personally reviewing training videos for the airline's flight attendants and worrying about awkward body language in the films. He also reviews menu changes, edits the script that flight attendants use for their preflight and in-flight announcements, and makes adjustments in the duties of maintenance supervisors. He hopes at some point in the future to step back from the details, but he admits he first wants to put his "imprint" on US Airways. So, for the moment he puts in 12-hour days at the office and works several more hours at home each night. Time will tell whether he can repeat the success he had at his previous employers, Air France and United.

1. Would you characterize Rakesh Gangwal as an authoritarian, a democratic, or a laissez-faire leader? Why?
2. Do you think Rakesh has a Theory X, Theory Y, or Theory Z attitude? Explain your answer.
3. What do you think his self-concept is? Why?

Source: Adam Bryant, "Like His Mentor at US Airways, the Chief Has an Eye for Details," *New York Times*, November 29, 1998, sec. 3, p. 2.

SELF-QUIZ

Could You Be a CEO?

Every year *Inc.* magazine surveys the 500 fastest-growing firms in the country and reports on their success. In 1998 *Inc.*'s editors also examined the personal and professional characteristics of the 500 company CEOs. The quiz below will tell you how you stack up, with scoring based on the game of baseball.

1. *Marriage*—More than 80 percent of the CEOs in *Inc.*'s survey were married with a stable home life. You get two hits for being married and staying that way. Anything else is a strikeout.

2. *Education*—Education matters more than family income among this elite group; nearly half the CEOs are graduates of four-year colleges. Give yourself two hits if you plan a graduate degree, one for a college degree, and a strikeout for anything less.

3. *Age*—More than three-quarters of the CEOs were 40 or younger. Two hits are awarded for being under 41, and one hit for being between 41 and 50. Outside that range, you've struck out.

4. *Business sector*—The service sector has grown at the expense of manufacturing and selling and distribution. You get one hit if you run a service company; otherwise, you strike out.

5. *Industry*—The percentages of computer-related and telecommunications businesses among the top 500 have grown dramatically and almost all other kinds of firms have lost ground. Add two hits if you're in computers or telecommunications and one if you're in business services. Everything else earns a strikeout.

6. *Capital*—One of five of the top firms started with less than $5,000 in capital, and most of the company founders on the list never borrowed their start-up costs. If you have enough cash right now to get under way, you score one hit. Otherwise, you strike out.

7. *Advantage*—Technology skills or the rights to some intellectual property drove the success of most of the top firms. If you control valuable intellectual property you get two hits, one if you know more about your field than anyone else, and a strikeout if neither of the above.

8. *Revenues*—"Meat and potatoes" selling by an in-house sales staff compensated under traditional salary-plus-bonus structures has produced an average growth rate of about 75 percent a year for the Inc. 500. You get one hit for doing things the old-fashioned way and keeping your firm growing 25 percent a year. Otherwise, you strike out.

Here's how to score. You've had 34 turns at bat, so divide your total number of hits by 34. If your "batting average" is above .300, you're doing well. Above .350 and you're doing extraordinarily well. Keep up the good work.

Source: *Inc. 500* by Eric Kriss. Copyright © 1998 by Business Innovator Group Resources/Inc. Reproduced with permission of Business Innovator Group Resources/Inc. via Copyright Clearance Center.

Class Exercise

Divide the class into groups of four or five students. Each group is assigned one of the four sections in Figure A, which is a checklist of ways that employees, including supervisors, can demonstrate competence in human relations.

Each group discusses the principles in its section of the checklist. Based on jobs they have held or situations they have observed, group members describe good or bad human relations practices. In particular, consider how you have seen supervisors practice or fail to practice these principles.

After the groups have discussed these principles among themselves, they take turns making presentations. Each group selects one principle to present to the class. One representative (or more) from the group gives a brief illustration of that principle.

Source: This exercise was suggested by Corinne R. Livesay, Belhaven College, Jackson, Mississippi.

Team-Building Exercise

Trying On a Team Leadership Style

Divide the class into teams of four to six. Either appoint a supervisor for each team, or ask for volunteers. The teams have the following objective: to determine whether the campus library is as user-friendly as it could be, and to come up with suggestions for improvement if necessary.

Each supervisor should privately choose a leadership style (task oriented or people oriented) and an attitude (following Theory X or Theory Y)

and practice these during the exercise. Team members should decide on their own characteristics, such as a need for independence, readiness to assume responsibility, and so forth.

At the end of the exercise, each team should discuss with the rest of the class how effective its leader and team members were. Also, they should present their results: Did they come up with some good suggestions for the library?

■ FIGURE A

Human Relations Competencies Checklist

1. Consistently communicate the following attitudes to co-workers, superiors, customers, or patients:

☐ Send out positive verbal and nonverbal signals in all contacts, including telephone.
☐ Remain positive while working with those who are negative.
☐ Be positive and sensitive when those you are dealing with are not.
☐ Deal with all people in an honest, ethical, and moral way.
☐ Avoid ethnic or sexual remarks that could be misinterpreted.
☐ Maintain a sense of humor.
☐ Recognize when you begin to become negative, and start an attitude renewal project.
☐ Develop and maintain a good service attitude.

2. Demonstrate the following human relations skills in dealing with co-workers:

☐ Build and maintain equally effective horizontal working relationships with everyone in your department. Refuse to play favorites.
☐ Build a productive, no-conflict relationship with those who may have a different set of personal values.
☐ Build relationships based on mutual rewards.
☐ Develop productive, healthy relationships with those who may be substantially older or younger.
☐ Maintain a productive relationship even with individuals who irritate you at times.
☐ Treat everyone, regardless of ethnic or socioeconomic differences, with respect.
☐ Work effectively with others regardless of their sexual orientation.
☐ Do not take human relations slights or mistakes from others personally; do not become defensive or attempt to retaliate in kind.
☐ Repair an injured relationship as soon as possible.
☐ Even if you are not responsible for the damage to a working relationship, protect your career by taking the initiative to restore it.
☐ Permit others to restore a relationship with you.
☐ Release your frustrations harmlessly without damaging relationships.
☐ Handle teasing and testing without becoming upset.

3. Demonstrate the following human relations skills in dealing with your superiors:

☐ Build a strong vertical relationship with your supervisor without alienating co-workers.
☐ Be a high producer yourself and contribute to the productivity of co-workers.
☐ Survive, with a positive attitude, under a difficult supervisor until changes occur.
☐ Establish relationships that are mutually rewarding.
☐ Show you can live up to your productivity potential without alienating co-workers who do not live up to theirs.
☐ Live close to your productivity potential without extreme highs or lows regardless of difficult changes in the work environment.
☐ Do not underestimate or overestimate a superior.
☐ Report mistakes or misjudgments rather than trying to hide them.
☐ Show that you can turn any change into an opportunity, including accepting a new supervisor with a different style.
☐ Refuse to nurse small gripes into major upsets.

4. Demonstrate the following professional attitudes and human relations skills:

☐ Be an excellent listener.
☐ Establish a good attendance record.
☐ Keep a good balance between home and career so neither suffers.
☐ Demonstrate that you are self-motivated.
☐ Communicate freely and thoroughly.
☐ Prepare yourself for a promotion in such a manner that others will be happy when you succeed.
☐ Share only positive, nonconfidential data about your organization with outsiders.
☐ Pass only reliable data on to others.
☐ Keep your business and personal relationships sufficiently separated.
☐ Concentrate on the positive aspects of your job while trying to improve the negative.
☐ Make only positive comments about a third party not present.
☐ Leave a job or company in a positive manner; train your replacement so that productivity is not disturbed.
☐ If you prefer to be a stabilizer, develop patience; if you prefer to be a zigzagger, don't stomp on other people's feet, hands, or heads while climbing the success ladder.
☐ Always have a Plan B (a contingency plan for your career).
☐ Avoid self-victimization.

Source: From *Your Attitude Is Showing*, by Elwood N. Chapman. Copyright © 1995 Pearson Education, Inc.. Reprinted by permission of Pearson Education, Inc. Upper Saddle River, NJ.

9

We're in the age of the idea. The organizations that can develop a culture of creativity and idea generation will be the winners.

—Kevin Roberts, CEO, Saatchi & Saatchi

Problem Solving and Decision Making

■ CHAPTER OUTLINE

■ LEARNING OBJECTIVES

After you have studied this chapter, you should be able to:

9.1 Identify the steps in the rational model of decision making.

9.2 Discuss ways people make compromises in following the decision-making model.

9.3 Describe guidelines for making decisions.

9.4 Explain how probability theory, decision trees, and computer software can help in making decisions.

9.5 Discuss advantages and disadvantages of making decisions in groups.

9.6 Describe guidelines for group decision making.

9.7 Describe guidelines for thinking creatively.

9.8 Discuss how supervisors can establish and maintain a creative work climate.

9.9 Identify ways to overcome barriers to creativity.

BRINGING CREATIVITY TO PROBLEM SOLVING

Creativity is a gift, we're told, the ability to see solutions that no one else can find. Either you have it or you don't, right?

Not exactly. Some firms have found ways to encourage creative thinking and bring all the resources they can to bear on stubborn problems. At Hallmark Cards, for example, supervisors recognize that coming up with just the right wording for a new card is a difficult task made even harder by the restrictions of an office environment. So periodically, the company's 600 writers and artists are encouraged to head off-campus for poetry workshops, storytelling festivals, or plays. At the company's Victorian house about 50 miles from the office they can toil in a metalworking studio, fire a pottery kiln, or just walk in the woods. Eileen Drummond, creative director of writing at the company's headquarters in Kansas City, says the result is "appreciable improvements and new things happening."

At Joe Designer in New York, the two heads are Joe Moya and Joe Raia. The first thing they did to the new offices of their product design and development firm was knock the walls down to make room for a Nurf basketball court and two Harley-Davidsons to tinker with while thinking. They put one wall back up, however, and now they hang everyone's ideas on it, often leaving them there for weeks. Sometimes the solution to a design problem comes when somebody walks by the wall and turns something upside down, saying, "Wow, look at that!"

Source: Carol A.L. Dannhauser, "Harnessing Your Muse," *Working Woman*, September 1998, p. 46.

Creativity is an important skill to cultivate. No matter how carefully a supervisor plans or how effectively a supervisor leads, he or she is bound to encounter problems. Human imperfections, new challenges from the environment in which the department operates, and the desire to achieve higher quality are only three sources of problems for a supervisor to solve creatively. Being successful does not mean not having any problems. In fact, it has been said that success simply means solving the right problems, or, as Winston Churchill once remarked, "Success is the ability to go from failure to failure without losing your enthusiasm."[1] The best managers, including supervisors, are those who know what issues to focus on and who respond to problems in a positive way. By solving the right problems—the ones that can improve the quality of work—effective supervisors, like those at Hallmark and Joe Designer in our opening story, improve their department's activities and the service they deliver to their customers.

decision
A choice from among available alternatives.

A **decision** is a choice from among available alternatives. Solving problems involves making a series of decisions: deciding that something is wrong, deciding what the problem is, deciding how to solve it. Successful problem solving depends on good decisions. This chapter describes how supervisors make decisions and offers some guidelines for doing so effectively. The chapter includes a discussion of decision making in groups and suggestions for thinking creatively.

The Process of Decision Making

Much of a supervisor's job is making decisions that cover all the functions of management. What should the supervisor or the department accomplish today or this week? Who should handle a particular project or machine? What should a supervisor tell his or her manager about the customer who complained yesterday? Do employees need better training or just more inspiration? How can a supervisor end the ongoing dispute between two staff members? These are only a few of the issues a typical supervisor has to act on.

In many cases, supervisors make decisions like these without giving any thought to the process of deciding. A supervisor automatically does something because it feels right or because he or she always has handled that problem that way. When a decision seems more complex, a supervisor is more likely to give thought to the decision-making process. For example, in deciding whether to purchase an expensive piece of machinery or to fire an employee, a supervisor might make a careful list of pluses and minuses, trying to include all the relevant economic, practical, or ethical concerns. (Making ethical decisions is discussed in Chapter 4.) Even though making many decisions seems to be automatic, supervisors can improve the way they make them by understanding how the decision-making process works in theory and in practice.

The Rational Model

If you could know everything, you could make perfect decisions. How would an all-knowing person go about making a decision? This person would probably follow the rational model of decision making, illustrated in Figure 9.1.

Identify the Problem   According to this model, a decision maker first identifies the problem. Recall from Chapter 6 that it is important to distinguish the symptoms of a problem from the problem itself. Usually a supervisor notices the symptoms first, so that he or she has to look for the underlying problem.

For example, Dave Frantz finds that he has to work 60 hours a week to do his job as supervisor of a group of janitorial service workers. Dave works hard and spends little time socializing, so his effort is not the problem. He observes that he spends approximately half his time doing paperwork required by higher-level management. He decides that the major problem is that too much of his time is spent on paperwork. (Along the way, Dave also may find and resolve minor problems.)

FIGURE 9.1

The Rational Model of Decision Making

| Identify the problem. | Identify the alternative solutions. | Gather and organize facts. | Evaluate the alternatives. | Choose and implement the best alternative. | Get feedback and take corrective action. |

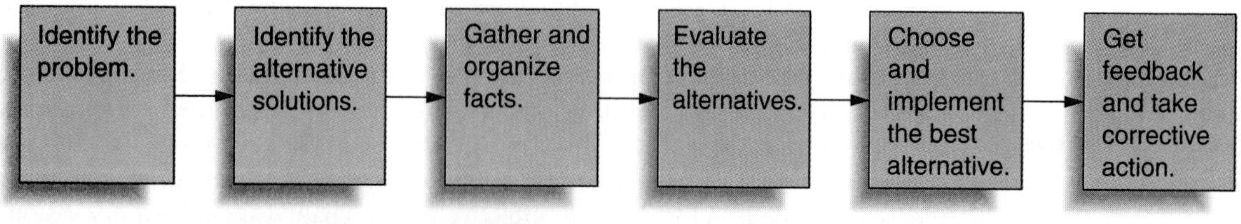

Identify Alternative Solutions   The next step is to identify the alternative solutions. In our example, Dave thinks of several possibilities. He might delegate the paperwork to other employees, hire a secretary, buy software that will automate some of the work, or persuade management to eliminate the required paperwork.

Gather and Organize Facts   Next, a decision maker gathers and organizes facts. Dave asks his manager if he really has to do all the paperwork; the manager says yes. From the human resources office, Dave gets information about the pay scale for secretaries. He evaluates which aspects of his work could be delegated, and he collects advertisements and magazine articles about various personal computers and software.

Evaluate Alternatives   A supervisor evaluates the alternatives from the information gathered. Dave determines that he cannot eliminate or delegate the paperwork. He knows that software will cost much less than a secretary, though a secretary would save more of his time. He predicts that his manager will be more open to buying the software than to hiring a secretary.

Choose and Implement the Best Alternative   A supervisor next chooses and implements the best alternative. In our example, Dave decides to buy the software and prepares a report showing the costs and benefits of doing so. He emphasizes how the company will benefit when he is more efficient and can devote more time to leading and controlling. He selects the program that he thinks will best meet his needs at a reasonable cost.

When evaluating and selecting alternatives, how can a supervisor decide which is best? Sometimes the choice is obvious, but at other times a supervisor needs formal criteria for making decisions, such as these:

- The alternative chosen should actually solve the problem. Ignoring the paperwork might enable Dave to leave work on time, but it would not solve the problem of how to get the job done.
- An acceptable alternative must be feasible. In other words, a supervisor should be able to implement it. For example, Dave learned that requesting less paperwork was not a feasible solution.
- The cost of the alternative should be reasonable in light of the benefits it will deliver. Dave's employer might consider a software program to be a reasonable expense, but the cost of a full-time secretary is high compared with the benefits of making Dave's job easier.

Get Feedback   The last step is to get feedback and take corrective action. In the example, Dave takes his proposal to his manager, who suggests some additions and changes, perhaps including helping others in the company to work with the new kind of reports Dave will be generating. Dave orders the software. When it arrives, he automates some of his work, using his experiences to improve on his original ideas.

When a decision will affect the course of someone's career or the expenditure of a lot of money, a supervisor will want to make the best decision possible. One way of doing so is to try to complete each of the steps in the rational model. In general, supervisors can benefit from using this model when they are making complex, formal decisions or when the consequences of a decision are great.

SUPERVISION AND DIVERSITY

Bringing Different Perspectives to Problem Solving

Mary Ellen Heyde is the Vehicle Line Director of Lifestyle Vehicles for Ford Motor Company, and she was responsible for the engineering and planning of the 1999 Windstar from concept (in 1995) all the way to production. Heyde is firmly convinced that "good ideas come when people with different perspectives work together on the same problem." For Heyde, that benefit is one of the biggest reasons that Ford's Dearborn, Michigan plant, where she is also the product manager for three other Ford models, always tries to hire people from backgrounds as diverse as possible.

"If you have a diverse workforce," says Heyde, "then you know that the customer's point of view will always be represented." Heyde cites the invaluable input of the many women on the Windstar minivan's design team and marketing committees, particularly helpful since most drivers of the Windstar are women. One of the women on the electrical team for the new minivan was the mother of young children, for instance, and she said the car's overhead light always woke her children up by turning on automatically when she opened the door at the end of a nighttime drive. What was intended as a safety feature was actually a problem for some of the vehicle's users. The problem was solved by introducing an option whereby only the floor lighting turns on when the door is opened, a feature the team called the "sleeping-baby mode."

But Ford's diverse employees are not the only ones who offer input that helps the company solve problems. Heyde mentions that families of employees are polled as well. Taking advantage of Take Our Daughters to Work Day, the design team asked children for their input on Ford products. And employees who lease their own cars through the firm are another source of inspiration—their spouses are routinely asked for their suggestions about the various cars they lease and drive.

"If we didn't get that kind of input," says Heyde, "then we'd miss out on good ideas."

Source: "Unit of 1," *Fast Company*, April 2000, p. 102.

Human Compromises

The example of the rational model of decision making may appear to be far removed from the daily experiences of most supervisors. Often supervisors have neither the time nor the desire to follow all these steps to a decision. Even when supervisors try to follow these steps, they often have trouble thinking of all the alternatives or gathering all the facts they need. Sometimes no alternative emerges as being clearly the best.

Given these human and organizational limitations, supervisors—like all decision makers—make compromises most of the time (see Figure 9.2). The resulting decision may be less than perfect, but it is typically one the decision maker is willing to live with. A supervisor who is aware of the kinds of compromises people make is more apt to be aware of when he or she is using them. In addition, a supervisor may find that although some kinds of compromises are useful in some situations, others are to be avoided as much as possible.

Simplicity   Although we often think we have approached a problem with a fresh perspective and have analyzed all the options, most people take a simpler approach. Usually what we are doing is simply mulling over our experiences and considering ways we have handled similar problems in the past. If we consider a few possibilities, we conclude that we have covered them all. People tend to select an alternative that they have tried before and that has delivered acceptable results. The downside of this kind of attempt at simplicity is that it tends to bypass innovative solutions, even though they sometimes deliver the best results. See "Supervision and Diversity" for some of the benefits of seeking innovation from new avenues.

■ FIGURE 9.2

Human Compromises in Decision Making

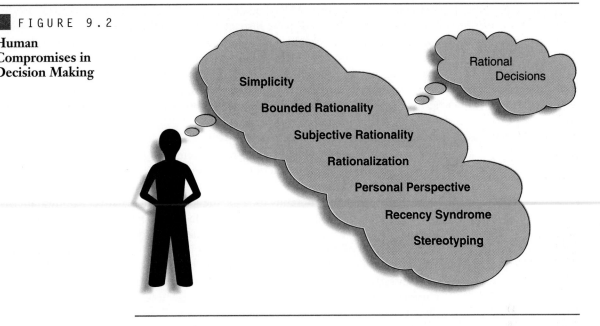

■ FIGURE 9.3

The Process of Bounded Rationality

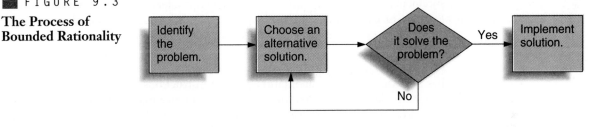

bounded rationality
Choosing an alternative that meets minimum standards of acceptability.

Bounded Rationality   When time, cost, or other limitations, such as the tendency to simplify, make finding the best alternative impossible or unreasonable, decision makers settle for an alternative they consider good enough. Choosing an alternative that meets minimum standards of acceptability is a form of **bounded rationality;** that is, a decision maker places limits, or *bounds*, on the *rational* model of decision making. (Figure 9.3 shows how bounded rationality works.) The decision maker considers alternatives only until one is found that meets his or her minimum criteria for acceptability.

For example, a supervisor who is fed up with tardiness might first be inclined to fire everyone who was late in a particular week. But she knows that will be demoralizing, will create a sudden and large need for hiring and training, and will probably not impress her manager. She rejects that alternative. Then she remembers that she gave "timeliness awards" last year, but that did not stop tardiness, so she rejects that alternative. Finally, she remembers reading an article that recommends spelling out the consequences of the undesirable behavior and then letting the employee experience those consequences. She decides to try that approach. There probably are other ways to solve the problem—maybe even better ways— but the supervisor does not spend any more time trying to think of them.

Subjective Rationality   When people analyze alternatives, they tend to rely on their intuition and gut instincts instead of on collecting impartial data. For example, a sales supervisor might estimate, "I think orders will be up next year, but just slightly, say, 2 percent." The sales supervisor did not arrive at that figure through marketing research or an analysis of industry data but relied on his experience with trends in demand for the product. Thus, even when the process for arriving at the decision is otherwise rational, the numbers used in the process may be subjective and thus not completely accurate.

Rationalization   People tend to favor solutions that they believe they can justify to others. For example, production supervisor Renata King knows that her manager focuses on containing costs. When Renata is considering alternative ways to approach a problem, she tends to favor the low-cost alternative. Another alternative might be more successful, but Renata feels that whatever the outcome, her manager is likely to appreciate her effort to keep costs down.

A version of this pattern of behavior was evident at AlliedSignal when Lawrence A. Bossidy became CEO. Bossidy met with customers and learned they were dissatisfied with the manufacturing firm's rate of filling orders as promised. Customers complained that this "order-fill rate" was just 60 percent, but Allied Signal employees argued it was really 98 percent. The employees' problem-solving efforts focused on justifying why Allied Signal's numbers were more correct. However, when employees realized that Bossidy was more interested in how to make customers happy than in arguing about statistics, they adopted the customers' measurements and began to tackle the underlying problems.[2] Like Bossidy, supervisors can benefit from rationalization by communicating what they consider important; employees will tend to make decisions that reflect those priorities.

Personal Perspective   In supervising computer programmers, Abraham Wassad has to review their documentation and the instructions they write for using their programs. Abraham pointed out to one programmer that some portions of his instructions needed clarification. "It's OK the way it is," insisted the programmer. "*I* understand it."

People often make this programmer's mistake: assuming everyone sees things the way they do. The programmer thinks the instructions must be clear to any (reasonable) person. Such assumptions can lead to incorrect decisions in many areas, including how much information to convey, what working conditions are most important to employees, or what product characteristics customers want. To avoid this problem, decision makers must find out what other people are thinking, then take those views into account.

Management trainer Rayona Sharpnack recounts a story about one of her clients, the marketing director of a software company, who was trying to solve the problem of the increasing cost of the printed documentation the firm sent out to all its customers. The marketing team brainstormed all kinds of options such as lower grades of paper, soy-based ink, small type, fewer graphics, and so on. Not until it dawned on team members that their customers might not all *want* the documentation did they hit upon the idea of sending them postcards to find out. The discovery that only 5 percent wanted the documentation saved the company $400,000 in one fiscal quarter.[3]

Recency Syndrome   People more readily remember events that have occurred recently than those that took place sometime in the past. This tendency is known as

recency syndrome
The tendency to more easily remember events that have occurred recently.

the **recency syndrome.** For example, a supervisor might remember that the last time she gave a negative performance appraisal the employee became hostile, but will not recall that a negative appraisal two years earlier led an employee to improve his performance. Clearly, in most situations, an event should not carry more weight simply because it is more recent. This is one reason that decision makers need to consider the alternatives as fully as is reasonable.

stereotypes
Rigid opinions about categories of people.

Stereotyping   Rigid opinions about categories of people are called **stereotypes.** Stereotyping interferes with rational decision making because it limits a decision maker's understanding of the people involved.[4] Stereotypes distort the truth that people offer a rich variety of individual strengths and viewpoints. For example, the stereotype that African-American people are athletic may seem flattering at face value but is insulting and misleading when applied to a particular African-American employee whose strengths are reliability and a gift for public speaking. No doubt, this employee would prefer to be recognized on the basis of his or her unique talents rather than on some stereotypical ones, and a supervisor who can do that will be best able to lead this employee.

The cure for stereotyping is *not* to assume that everyone is alike. Not only does this assumption oversimplify the situation, but it is, in effect, an insult to other people. It ignores the strengths and values people receive from their culture. Rather, a supervisor should make a conscious, ongoing effort to learn about the various groups of people represented in the workplace. The purpose is to acquire information that serves as a starting point for understanding others while recognizing that individuals within any group are unique.

In addition, a supervisor needs to be aware of his or her own stereotypes about people and situations. In making a decision, a supervisor should consider whether those stereotypes truly describe the situation at hand.

Guidelines for Decision Making

Should a supervisor always avoid human compromises in making decisions? Not necessarily. In some situations, seeking to match the rational model would be too costly and time-consuming. However, a supervisor has a variety of ways to make decisions more rationally. The following paragraphs provide further guidelines for making decisions in the workplace.

Consider the Consequences

A supervisor should be aware of the possible consequences of a decision. For example, hiring and firing decisions can have great consequences for the performance of the department. Purchases of inexpensive items are less critical than purchases of major equipment and computer systems. Some decisions affect the safety of workers, while others make only a slight difference in their comfort.

When the consequences of a decision are great, a supervisor should spend more time on the decision, following the rational model of decision making and seeking to include as many alternatives as possible. When the consequences of the decision are slight, a supervisor should limit the time and money spent in identifying and evaluating alternatives. A supervisor may choose to accept some of the human compromises described earlier.

Respond Quickly in a Crisis

When a nuclear reactor is overheating, the supervisor has no time to weigh each employee's qualifications and to select the best employee for each task in handling the crisis. When a store's customer is shouting about poor service, the supervisor has no time to list all the possible responses. Both cases require fast action.

In a crisis, a supervisor should quickly select the course of action that seems best. This is an application of bounded rationality. Instead of waiting to evaluate other alternatives, the supervisor should begin implementing the solution and interpreting feedback to see whether the solution is working. Based on the feedback, the supervisor may modify the choice of a solution.

David House of Bay Networks Inc. has spent a great deal of time teaching his staff how to improve their decision making. One of his "rules" offers supervisors another way to look at speed in critical decisions. Says House, "If you're not going to do anything differently tomorrow by making a decision today, then don't make it today. Situations change. . . . That's not an excuse to procrastinate. But the best decisions are just-in-time decisions. You should decide as late as possible—but before you need to take action."[5]

Inform the Manager

A supervisor's manager does not want to hear about every minor decision the supervisor makes each day. However, the manager does need to know what is happening in the department, so the supervisor should inform the manager about major decisions, including those that affect meeting departmental objectives, responses to a crisis, and any controversial decision.

When the manager needs to know about a decision, it is usually smart for a supervisor to discuss the problem before reaching and announcing the decision. The manager may see an aspect of the problem that has escaped the supervisor's attention or may have different priorities leading to a veto or modification of the supervisor's solution. For example, when a supervisor wanted to create a new position for a valued employee, her director gave approval on condition that the supervisor not increase her total budget. Knowing and adjusting for such information while weighing the alternatives is less embarrassing to the supervisor and avoids annoying the manager. Of course, in a crisis, the supervisor may not have time to consult with the manager and will have to settle for discussing the decision as soon as possible afterward.

Be Decisive Yet Flexible

Sometimes it is difficult to say which alternative solution is most likely to succeed or will bring the best results. Two alternatives may look equally good, or perhaps none of the choices look good enough. In such cases, a supervisor may find it hard to move beyond studying the alternatives to selecting and implementing one of them. However, avoiding a decision is merely another way of deciding to do nothing, and doing nothing is usually not the best choice. Furthermore, employees and peers find it frustrating to work with someone who never seems to make up his or her mind or get back to them with answers to their questions. Therefore, supervisors need to be decisive. (See "Tips from the Firing Line.")

Being decisive means reaching a decision within a reasonable amount of time. What is reasonable depends on the nature of the decision. For example, a supervi-

Making Better Decisions, Faster

If you've ever wished you could be a better decision maker, try a few of these ideas next time you face a decision or problem.

1. Make sure you have all the information you need. According to Donald Winkler, chairman and CEO of Ford Motor Credit Co., "Getting all of the facts is the key to good decision making."

2. Wait until the last minute to decide—but not a minute later. Know the difference between procrastinating and waiting for the last change in the marketplace or the final shift in the problem situation to occur. The best decisions are just-in-time decisions.

3. Don't be afraid of conflict. Tackle disagreement head-on and resolve it quickly. One way to reduce conflict is to agree, in writing, on exactly what the problem is.

4. If you're brainstorming a solution, remember the rules that underlie this technique: Have one conversation at a time (don't interrupt or allow interruptions), build on the ideas of others, don't prejudge a proposed solution, encourage wild ideas, and stay focused on the topic.

5. Make the right decision, not the best one. Waiting for the "best" solution to come along will leave you in the dust, with a backlog of other decisions waiting to be made. Pick a solution and go with it.

6. Disagree, but then commit to the solution. After you've been heard, get behind the decision and support it fully. Commitment is part of the job.

Sources: George Gendron, "FYI," *Inc.*, May 1998, p. 9; Michael Warshaw, "Have You Been House-Trained?" *Fast Company*, October 1998, pp. 46, 48; Keith Hammonds, "How Do We Break Out of the Box We're Stuck In?" *Fast Company*, November 2000, pp. 260–268.

---

sor should not spend hours deciding what assignments to give technicians each morning, but he or she would probably spend several days selecting a candidate to fill a job opening because this decision is more complex and its consequences are greater. The supervisor should pick the alternative that looks best (or at least acceptable) within the appropriate time frame for the decision, and then focus on implementing it.

Certain kinds of behavior are typical of a decisive supervisor. A decisive supervisor quickly clears his or her desk of routine matters, promptly referring them to the proper people, and keeps work moving. A decisive supervisor assumes complete responsibility for getting the facts needed when he or she must solve a problem. Finally, a decisive supervisor keeps his or her employees informed of what they are expected to do and how they are progressing relative to their objectives.

Being decisive does not mean a supervisor is blind to signs that he or she has made a mistake. When implementing a solution, a supervisor needs to seek feedback that indicates whether the solution is working. If the first attempt at solving a problem fails, a supervisor must be flexible and try another approach. Here David House recognizes that failure may coincide with conflict. His advice: "One way to make progress on a tough decision is to agree on what the question is. Agree on the wording and write it down. Debate often stems from having different ideas about what's being decided."[6] The wise supervisor will make sure all parties to the decision are clear about what's being determined.

Avoid Decision-Making Traps

Some supervisors seem to delight in emergency deadlines and crisis situations, and they act as though each decision is a life-or-death issue. But good planning can avert many crises; life-or-death issues are not the usual stuff of a supervisor's job.

"I Make Bad Decisions All the Time"

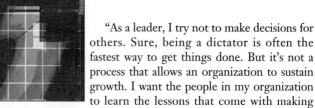

Pamela Lopker is chairperson and president of QAD, Inc., a multimillion-dollar California resource-planning software maker whose clients include Avon Products, PepsiCo, Ford, and Johnson & Johnson. Here's what Pamela says about decision making. How does it compare with your decision-making style as a supervisor?

"I make bad decisions all the time. But I've been successful because I've developed a process of identifying and changing those decisions quickly. I approach every decision with an eye to the long-term outcome. That's a hard method to adopt in a fast-paced business environment. But it's the only way to create sustainable value on either a professional or a personal level. The quick-fix method that I see so many companies rely on is just that—a quick fix. . . .

"As a leader, I try not to make decisions for others. Sure, being a dictator is often the fastest way to get things done. But it's not a process that allows an organization to sustain growth. I want the people in my organization to learn the lessons that come with making decisions: that everything is a compromise, that nothing is ever completely logical, but that you can deal with things through a logical decision-making process."

Source: *Fast Company* by Anna Muoio. Copyright © 1998 by Business Innovator Group Resources/Inc. Reproduced with permission of Business Innovator Group Resources/Inc. via Copyright Clearance Center.

Making a major issue out of each decision does not make the supervisor more important, but it does interfere with clear thinking. A supervisor must be able to put each issue into perspective so that he or she can calmly evaluate the alternatives and devote an appropriate amount of time to finding a solution.

Another trap for decision makers is responding inappropriately to failure. When a supervisor makes a wrong decision, the supervisor will look best if he or she acknowledges the mistake. Finding someone to blame only makes the supervisor seem irresponsible. At the same time, supervisors need not agonize over their mistakes. The constructive approach is to learn whatever lesson the mistake can teach and then to move on.

By trying to save time or work independently, some supervisors fail to draw on easily available information. One important source of information is precedent. Have some of the alternatives been tried before? If so, what was the outcome? Answering these questions can help a supervisor evaluate alternatives more realistically. For problems and decisions that are likely to recur, supervisors can set up a system for collecting information to use in future decisions. Ronald Mendell, a legal investigator in Austin, Texas, evaluates product failures by keeping records on a form that asks questions such as: How did the product fail? What activities and processes were going on when the product failed? Where else is this product used? Answers that show a pattern help Mendell diagnose the underlying problem.[7] Similarly, by consulting with other members of the organization or with outside experts, a supervisor often can find readily available data that will improve his or her decision.

Sometimes supervisors are tempted to promise too much. This mistake traps many supervisors because the promises keep people happy—at least until they are broken. For example, a supervisor may promise an angry employee a raise before being sure the budget can handle it. This promise may solve the immediate problem of the employee's anger, but it will backfire if the supervisor cannot deliver the raise. Similarly, a supervisor may tell her manager that she can continue meeting existing deadlines even while a new computer system is being installed. She is not sure of this, but making the promise is a way of avoiding a confrontation with her manager (until the department does miss a deadline). Ultimately, everyone will be more pleased if supervisors make realistic promises. Then it is possible to arrive at solutions that will work as expected. "Meeting the Challenge" suggests what one manager does when solutions don't work.

Another trap is to assume there is one "right" decision. David House suggests that supervisors instead should look for the *best* decision. "Every decision involves risk," he says. "And if there are 10 ways to do something, 8 of them will probably work. So pick 1 of the 8 and get going. Life's too short. You have 10 more decisions to make after this one.[8]

Tools for Decision Making

In preparing a budget for next year, LaTanya Jones, manager of a store's appliance department, needed to determine how many sales associates should work each day of the week. At a factory that produces air conditioners, production supervisor Pete Yakimoto had to determine why the rate of defects was rising and what to do to correct the problem. Pete's employees complained that they were making mistakes because they had to work too fast, and Pete wondered if hiring more workers could be justified economically.

Problems such as these are difficult to solve mentally. Usually a supervisor facing such complex decisions needs tools and techniques for analyzing the alternatives. Some widely used tools are probability theory, decision trees, and computer software.

Probability Theory

Sometimes a supervisor needs to choose which course of action will have the greatest benefit (or least cost), but a supervisor cannot completely control the outcome. Therefore, a supervisor cannot be 100 percent sure what the outcome will be. For example, a sales supervisor can tell salespeople whom to call on but cannot control the behavior of the customers. Pete Yakimoto in the previous example can recommend that new workers be hired, but he has only limited control over how the workers will perform. In statistical terms, situations with uncertain outcomes involve risk.

probability theory
A body of techniques for comparing the consequences of possible decisions in a risk situation.

To make decisions about risk situations, a supervisor can compare the consequences of several decisions by using **probability theory.** To use this theory, a supervisor needs to know or be able to estimate the value of each possible outcome and the likelihood (probability) that this outcome will occur. For example, a production supervisor is comparing two stamping presses. The supervisor wants to use a press to produce $1 million in parts per year. Press A costs $900,000, and Press B costs $800,000. Based on the suppliers' claims and track record, the supervisor believes there is a 90 percent chance that Press A will last 10 years (thus producing $10 million in parts) and only a 10 percent chance that it will fail after 5 years (thus producing $5 million in parts). The supervisor believes there is a 30 percent chance that Press B will fail after 5 years.

To use probability theory to make decisions about risk situations, the supervisor can begin by putting the possible outcomes into table format. Table 9.1 shows

TABLE 9.1		Five Years of Production	Ten Years of Production
Possible Outcomes for a Risk Situation	**Press A**	$5 million – $900,000 = $4.1 million	$10 million – $900,000 = $9.1 million
	Press B	$5 million – $800,000 = $4.2 million	$10 million – $800,000 = $9.2 million

Note: Outcomes are computed as value of production minus cost of press.

TABLE 9.2		Five Years of Production	Ten Years of Production
Expected Value of Possibilities	**Press A**	$4.1 million × .10 = $410,000	$9.1 million × .90 = $8.2 million
	Press B	$4.2 million × .30 = $1.3 million	$9.2 million × .70 = $6.4 million

Note: Values are computed as possible outcomes (from Table 9.1) times probability of outcome.

the possible outcomes for the stamping presses. In this case, the supervisor subtracted the cost of the press from the value of what the press could produce in 5 or 10 years. Notice that because Press B is cheaper, the possible outcomes for that press are greater. Remember, however, that Press B is also more likely to fail after 5 years. To find the *expected* value *(EV)* of each possible outcome, multiply the possible outcome *(O)* by the probability of that outcome *(P)*. Stated as a formula, $EV = O \times P$. Table 9.2 shows the results of this computation. The supervisor should select the press with the highest expected value, in this case, Press A.

Decision Trees

In the real world, most decisions involving probability are at least as complex as the example of purchasing machinery. Sorting out the relative value of the choices can be easier with the use of a graph. Thus, a supervisor may find it helpful to use a decision tree for making decisions in risk situations. A **decision tree** is a graph that helps in decision making by showing the expected values of decisions under varying circumstances.

As depicted in Figure 9.4, a decision tree shows the available alternatives, which stem from decision points. For each alternative, one of several chance events may occur. As before, the decision maker estimates the probability of each chance event occurring. To find the expected value of each outcome, the decision maker multiplies the probability by the value of the outcome $(EV = O \times P)$. The decision maker should select the alternative for which the expected value is greatest.

For example (see Figure 9.4), a sales supervisor is trying to decide whether to hire a new salesperson at a salary of $40,000. The supervisor estimates that with the new salesperson on board, there is a 60 percent chance that the department's sales will increase from $200,000 to $250,000. Without the new salesperson, the chance for the sales increase is only 50 percent. The supervisor assumes that, at worst, the department will hold steady in either case. The dollar value of each possible outcome is the amount of sales minus the cost of the choice (hiring or not hiring). To find the expected value of each choice, the supervisor multiplies the probability of each outcome by the value of that outcome. Assuming there is a

decision tree
A graph that helps decision makers use probability theory by showing the expected values of decisions under varying circumstances.

■ F I G U R E 9 . 4
A Simple Decision Tree

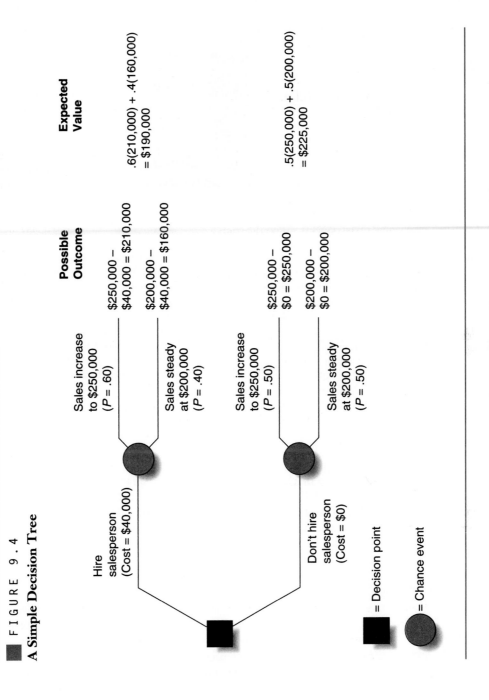

Expected
Value

.6(210,000) + .4(160,000)
= $190,000

.5(250,000) + .5(200,000)
= $225,000

Possible
Outcome

$250,000 –
$40,000 = $210,000

$200,000 –
$40,000 = $160,000

$250,000 –
$0 = $250,000

$200,000 –
$0 = $200,000

Sales increase
to $250,000
(P = .60)

Sales steady
at $200,000
(P = .40)

Sales increase
to $250,000
(P = .50)

Sales steady
at $200,000
(P = .50)

Hire
salesperson
(Cost = $40,000)

Don't hire
salesperson
(Cost = $0)

■ = Decision point

● = Chance event

SUPERVISION ACROSS INDUSTRIES

The Trucking Industry

Group Decision Making Helps Policy Become Reality

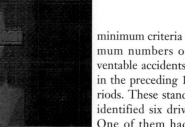

A family-owned trucking business was in a difficult situation. Facing external pressures like rising oil prices and insurance costs, as well as internal factors like high employee turnover and difficulty in recruiting new drivers, the firm was also trying to double in size during the 2000 calendar year. But its efforts to grow were hampered by ongoing disagreements within the company about how to enforce safety standards for existing drivers.

The safety department supervisor knew which drivers had poor safety records. But the operations department supervisor wanted to keep them on their jobs because they were productive and difficult to replace. So the safety policies that were already in place were never fully implemented, because to do so would have cost the company these drivers.

However, several highly publicized traffic accidents convinced the owner that the entire fleet was in danger of losing a great deal of its business. He convened a companywide meeting to develop a set of minimum criteria for drivers, including maximum numbers of moving violations, preventable accidents, and off-the-job violations in the preceding 12-, 24-, and 36-month periods. These standards, once enforced, easily identified six drivers who should be let go. One of them had been with the company since its founding and had a reputation for on-time delivery and excellent customer service.

It was a difficult decision, and the group debated for some time. But in the end, the supervisors decided that making exceptions to the rule was not in the fleet's best interest, and all six drivers with poor safety records were let go.

Without that decision, the new policies would have suffered the same fate as the old ones—being ignored when they were inconvenient. Supervisors in all fields may face similarly difficult decisions. In this case, willingness to turn policy into action led the way to improving both safety and the bottom line.

Source: Jim York, "Safety Scorecard," *Fleet Owner*, March 2001, pp. 34–35.

---

60 percent chance of sales increasing if the supervisor hires that salesperson (and a 40 percent chance of sales remaining steady), the expected value of hiring is .60($210,000) + .40($160,000), or $190,000. The expected value of not hiring is $225,000. Based on the greater expected value for not hiring, the supervisor would decide that it makes more economic sense not to hire a salesperson at this time.

Computer Software

decision-making software
A computer program that leads the user through the steps of the formal decision-making process.

Some computer programs have been developed to help people make decisions. This **decision-making software** leads the user through the steps of the formal decision-making process (see Figure 9.1). Besides having the user identify alternatives, the programs ask the user about his or her values and priorities.

For help in sorting out information, a supervisor might also use spreadsheet or database management software. Spreadsheet software, such as Lotus 1–2–3, Excel, and SuperCalc, helps the user organize numbers into rows and columns; it can automatically perform computations such as adding a column of numbers. A database management program, such as Access or ORACLE, systematically stores large amounts of data and makes it easy for the user to request and retrieve specific categories of data. A computerized index of periodicals at your library is an example of this kind of software. In addition, software companies are continually developing new ways to help users find and manipulate information. Among the best examples are OLAP (on-line analytical processing) tools such as Business Objects, Essbase, and Holos.

■ FIGURE 9.5

■ FIGURE 9.5

A Potential Drawback of Group Decision Making

DILBERT® by Scott Adams

These kinds of computer software do not make decisions for supervisors, but they can make it easier for supervisors to organize their thoughts and gather information. A supervisor still must creatively identify alternatives and use his or her judgment in selecting the best solution.

Group Decision Making

Some organizations allow or expect supervisors to work with a team or other group in arriving at a decision. For example, a supervisor might seek input from a team of employees in deciding how to meet production targets or encourage them to come up with a solution among themselves. The supervisor also might call on peers in other departments to share their expertise.

Advantages and Disadvantages

Group decision making has some advantages over going it alone. Group members can contribute more ideas for alternatives than an individual could think of alone. Since people tend to draw on their own experiences when generating and evaluating alternatives, a group will look at a problem from a broader perspective.

Also, people who are involved in coming up with a solution are more likely to support the implementation of that solution. They will better understand why the solution was selected and how it is supposed to work, and they will tend to think of it as *their* solution. (Chapter 3 elaborates on ways organizations are enjoying these benefits by establishing self-managing work teams and transforming the supervisor's role from commander to coach.)

Of course, group decision making also has disadvantages. First, an individual usually can settle on a decision faster than a group. Figure 9.5 illustrates this disadvantage humorously. Second, there is a cost to the organization when employees spend their time in meetings instead of producing or selling. A third drawback is that the group can reach an inferior decision by letting one person or a small sub-group dominate the process. Finally, groups sometimes fall victim to **groupthink,** or the failure to think independently and realistically that results when group members prefer to enjoy consensus and closeness.[9] Here are some symptoms of groupthink:

groupthink
The failure to think independently and realistically as a group because of the desire to enjoy consensus and closeness.

- An illusion of being invulnerable.
- Defending the group's position against any objections.
- A view that the group is clearly moral, "the good guys."
- Stereotyped views of opponents.
- Pressure against group members who disagree.
- Self-censorship, that is, not allowing oneself to disagree.
- An illusion that everyone agrees (because no one states an opposing view).
- Self-appointed "mindguards," or people who urge other group members to go along with the group.

During the making of the movie *The Bonfire of the Vanities,* many of the people involved had doubts about casting decisions and changes in the story line, but they did not tell the director, Brian DePalma. DePalma wondered about the wisdom of some of the decisions, but because no one objected, he convinced himself that his decisions were correct. Perhaps that is why the $50 million movie was a flop at the box office.[10]

When a supervisor notices that his or her group is showing the symptoms of groupthink, it is time to question whether the group is really looking for solutions. A supervisor who also is the group leader should draw forth a variety of viewpoints by inviting suggestions and encouraging group members to listen with an open mind. Another way to overcome groupthink is to appoint one group member to act as devil's advocate, challenging the position of the majority. When the group has reached a decision, the leader also can suggest that everyone sleep on it and settle on a final decision at a follow-up meeting.

Using Group Decision Making

Given the advantages and disadvantages of group decision making, a supervisor would be wise to involve employees in some but not all decisions. When a decision must be made quickly, as in an emergency, a supervisor should make it alone. Individual decisions also are appropriate when the potential benefit of a decision is so small that the cost of working as a group to make the decision is not justified. But when a supervisor needs to build support for a solution, such as measures to cut costs or improve productivity, the group process is useful. Group decision making also can be beneficial when the consequences of a poor decision are great; the benefits of a group's collective wisdom are worth the time and expense of gathering the input.

A supervisor can have a group actually make the decision, or a group may simply provide input, leaving more decision-making responsibility to the supervisor. For example, a supervisor might ask a group only to generate alternatives. If a group is to make the decision, a supervisor may let group members select any alternative, or a supervisor may give the group a few alternatives from which to choose. Whenever supervisors ask for input, they should be sure they intend to use the information. Employees are quickly wise to—and offended by—a supervisor who only pretends to be interested in their ideas.

Encouraging Participation   "Not everyone gets a change to decide, but everyone should have a chance to be heard. Without a doubt, the most vigorous debates

FIGURE 9.6

The Brainstorming Process

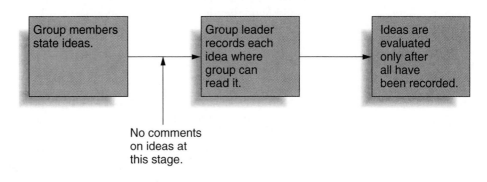

Group members state ideas.

Group leader records each idea where group can read it.

Ideas are evaluated only after all have been recorded.

No comments on ideas at this stage.

yield the best thinking." This advice from David House of Bay Networks emphasizes the benefits of involving all group members in a group decision.[11] Since a main benefit of making decisions as a group is the variety of opinions and expertise available, a supervisor leading a decision-making meeting should be sure that everyone is participating. One basic way of encouraging participation is for a supervisor to avoid monopolizing the discussion. The supervisor should focus on hearing participants' opinions. Also, some group members will find it easier than others to speak up. The supervisor should notice which participants are quiet and should ask their opinions about specific topics being discussed. Finally, a supervisor can encourage participation by reacting positively when people contribute ideas. A barrage of criticism or ridicule will quickly discourage group members from speaking.

Another barrier to participation is an "us-them" mentality that can pit team members against one another instead of letting them work together to solve a problem. Mark Turner, vice president of corporate risk at Ford Motor Credit Co., tells the following story:

> We were meeting with a group of managers from Ford Motor. On the first day, one of the Ford Motor guys piped up, "If you guys in credit would just do this." Don [Winkler, chairman and CEO of Ford Motor Credit] said, "Hang on. I'm an officer of Ford Motor Co. We're all part of Ford. If you're going to sit in this room and work on this team, you've got to drop this 'we' and 'they.' . . . I'm just trying to make the point that this is a collective effort."[12]

brainstorming
An idea-generating process in which group members state their ideas, a member of the group records them, and no one may comment on the ideas until the process is complete.

Brainstorming   Another way to generate ideas in a group is to use brainstorming. **Brainstorming** is an idea-generating process (see Figure 9.6) in which group members state their ideas, no matter how far-fetched these may seem. A member of the group records all the ideas, and no one may criticize or even comment on them until the end of the process.

Donald Winkler, chairman and CEO of Ford Motor Credit Co., has a unique method for keeping brainstorming on a positive track: He won't allow the word "but" to be spoken in his presence. Greg Smith, one of the company's vice presidents, reports that Winkler's feeling about this is so strong that at meetings in the office in Colorado Springs, "There is a jar sitting on a table. Every time someone says, 'but,' that person puts a dollar in the jar."[13]

Here are five rules for brainstorming suggested by Douglas Dayton, who with Steven Jobs developed the first commercial mouse and now runs the Boston office of IDEO, the product design and development firm.

1. Have one conversation at a time.
2. Build upon the ideas of others.
3. Defer judgment.
4. Encourage wild ideas.
5. Stay focused on the topic.[14]

Hearing other people's ideas often stimulates the thinking of group members. The supervisor can further open people's thought processes through such mind-expanding tactics as meeting in the work area rather than the usual conference room, asking people outside the group to identify problems, or asking employees to prepare for the meeting by individually listing problems to name at the meeting. Once all the ideas have been listed, the group can evaluate those that hold the most promise.

Creativity

Rebecca Liss, a branch operations manager with Kemper Securities, had to be creative when she hired Gail as a new employee. With Gail on board, Liss's group was larger than it ever had been, but there was no money in the budget for additional office space or a computer terminal for Gail. That meant two employees would somehow have to share a terminal. Working with her staff, Liss developed the idea to arrange the desks into an island formation with a computer terminal between the two employees who were to share it.

creativity
The ability to bring about something imaginative or new.

This example shows how creative thinking can lead to excellent solutions. **Creativity** is the ability to bring about something imaginative or new. With decision making, it means being able to generate innovative or different alternatives from those used in the past. When a problem seems unsolvable, the supervisor especially needs creativity to find a fresh approach.

A common notion is that some people are creative, whereas the rest of us are stuck with following routine and ordinary courses of action. Taking the Self-Quiz on page 235 will provide you with a measure of the state of your own creative skills. If you do not score as high as you would like, take heart—the evidence suggests that people can develop their ability to be creative.

Thinking More Creatively

A fundamental way to become more creative is to be open to your own ideas. When trying to solve a problem, think of as many alternatives as you can. Jot them all down without rejecting any; evaluate them only when you are done. This is like the group process of brainstorming. When you can, brainstorming with a group can help stimulate the creativity of the other participants as well as your own. Whether you are alone or in a group, practice should help your ideas flow more easily.

Years ago, advertising executive James Webb Young described a five-step technique for generating creative ideas[15]:

1. Gather the raw materials by learning about the problem and developing your general knowledge. Young says, "Constantly expanding your experience, both personally and vicariously, [matters] tremendously in an idea-producing job."[16]
2. Work over those materials in your mind. As you think of partial ideas, jot them down so you can refer to them later.

3. Incubate; let your unconscious mind do the work. Instead of thinking about the problem, do whatever stimulates your imagination and emotions, such as listening to music.
4. Identify an idea. It will probably pop into your head unexpectedly.
5. Shape and develop the idea to make it practical. Seek out constructive criticism.

Nearly three decades after Young developed this technique, it still remains practical.

Young points out that creative thinking is not always a conscious process. Sometimes creative ideas come from dreaming or daydreaming, or they will come to you while you are doing something else. If you are stuck on a problem, leave it for a while. Walk the dog, take a shower, work on a different task. Above all, do not neglect time for resting and daydreaming. If you are trying to solve the problem as a group, and the discussion is not going anywhere, adjourn or at least take a break, and then continue the discussion later. The veteran entrepreneur Norm Brodsky is a firm believer in the idea of taking a shower before finalizing a critical decision. He realized, however, that this wasn't always practical for a manager, so he automatically puts the decision off for 24 hours instead.[17] Supervisors will find many other ways to take a figurative "shower" to give their creativity a chance to kick in.

Here are just a few suggestions[18]:

1. See beyond the obvious. Things are not always what they seem, and rephrasing the question can sometimes lead you to a different, better, solution.
2. Don't take No for an answer. Be willing to take a risk.
3. Persist in spite of failure. Good ideas can come from anywhere, even from discarded "bad" ideas.
4. Make your own opportunities. Give luck, chance, and instinct their due.
5. Find new uses for people and things and new ways of doing things. Ask, "What haven't we done before?" instead of, "What's always worked in the past?"
6. Stretch your creative skills with puzzles, brain teasers, cryptograms, logic problems, and creative activities like poetry, painting, cooking, or carpentry. Remember to set aside quiet time to think.
7. Read biographies of creative people like artists, inventors, and innovators in all fields.
8. Start a file of "crazy" ideas. You never know when you might need one.
9. Have fun! Humor and play can break down barriers and help maintain the childlike sense of wonder on which creativity depends.

Establishing and Maintaining a Creative Work Climate

A supervisor can benefit from the entire work group's creativity by establishing a work climate that encourages creative thinking. The most important step a supervisor can take in this regard is to show that he or she values creativity. When employees offer suggestions, a supervisor should listen attentively and look for the positive aspects of the suggestions. A supervisor should attempt to implement employees' ideas and should give them credit.

When ideas fail, a supervisor should acknowledge that failure is a sign that people are trying. A supervisor should help employees see what can be learned from the failure. The aim is to avoid discouraging employees from making more suggestions in the future. As management trainer Rayona Sharpnack observes, "The only way to learn is through failure . . . the only way to grow is through experimentation, practice, and risk."[19]

Overcoming Barriers to Creativity

Often supervisors and employees have difficulty being creative because they are afraid their ideas will fail. A supervisor can overcome this barrier by accepting that failures by employees will occur. Overcoming your own fear of failure is more challenging; indeed, the organization may not always reward creativity. The best the supervisor can do is to keep in mind that a lack of creativity will probably prevent big successes as well as big failures.

If an idea does fail, a supervisor should acknowledge the problem and not try to pass the blame on to someone else. The emphasis should be on finding a solution, not on placing blame. Most managers admire supervisors who try ideas after careful thought and who focus on learning from mistakes rather than passing blame. A supervisor who prepares contingency plans (see Chapter 6) and is prepared to focus on solutions is likely to impress his or her superiors, even when the specific idea does not work out as hoped.

Another barrier to creativity is being overly busy. As described earlier, creative thinking requires time for quiet and rest. If a supervisor cannot get these at the workplace, he or she needs to allow time for thinking elsewhere—at home, while walking in the woods, while driving. For example, the supervisor can turn off the television for a while each evening. Besides reflection, another good substitute for TV watching is reading. The imagination required to read a book actually helps people develop their ability to think, but the average U.S. adult reads only minutes a day.

Isolation also interferes with creativity. Supervisors need to talk to co-workers in other departments of the organization. They need to talk and listen to their employees. Colleagues in other organizations can be a good source of ideas, as can friends and family members. However, the supervisor must be careful about spending a great deal of time with the same few people. They are less likely to be sources of fresh ideas than are new or less familiar acquaintances.

Summary

9.1   Identify the steps in the rational model of decision making.

According to the rational model, the decision maker first identifies the problem and then identifies the alternative solutions. Next, he or she gathers and organizes facts. The decision maker evaluates the alternatives and then chooses and implements the best alternative. Finally, he or she gets feedback and takes corrective action.

9.2   Discuss ways people make compromises in following the decision-making model.

People usually simplify the rational approach to decision making, selecting an alternative that they have tried before and that has delivered acceptable results. Choosing an alternative that meets minimum standards of acceptability is a form of bounded rationality. People tend to analyze alternatives subjectively, relying on intuition and in-

stinct, and they tend to favor solutions they can justify. People's analyses also tend to be clouded by adoption of a personal perspective, the tendency to remember recent events best, and the use of stereotypes.

9.3   Describe guidelines for making decisions.

Supervisors should be aware of the possible consequences of their decisions. In a crisis, a supervisor should respond quickly. With regard to crises and other situations that influence the department's performance, a supervisor should inform his or her manager about the decision, if possible, before making it. Supervisors should be decisive but flexible. They should avoid decision-making traps such as treating all problems as crises, responding inappropriately to failure, failing to draw on available information, and promising too much.

9.4 Explain how probability theory, decision trees, and computer software can help in making decisions.

Probability theory defines the expected value of an outcome in a risk situation as the value of the possible outcome times the probability of that outcome. The decision maker using this theory selects the outcome with the greatest expected value. A decision tree is a graph that shows the expected values of decisions under varying circumstances. Thus, it helps the decision maker use probability theory. Decision-making software leads the user through the rational decision-making process, and spreadsheet and database management software helps users organize their information. The software does not make the decision, but it helps the user think through the problem more logically.

9.5 Discuss advantages and disadvantages of making decisions in groups.

Group members can contribute more ideas for alternatives than an individual could alone. Also, people who are involved in coming up with a solution are more likely to support its implementation. Disadvantages are that groups make decisions more slowly than individuals, the process is more costly, and groups may fall victim to groupthink, actually suppressing different viewpoints.

9.6 Describe guidelines for group decision making.

A supervisor can benefit from group decision making when time permits and when the consequences of a poor decision justify the cost of group decision making. Group decision making is also useful when a supervisor needs to build support for the alternative selected. The group may actually make the decision, or it may provide input such as sug-

gested alternatives, letting the supervisor make the final decision. A supervisor leading a decision-making meeting should make sure that everyone is participating and should react positively when they do so. Brainstorming, in which members state their ideas no matter how far-fetched they may seem, often helps stimulate the thinking of group members.

9.7 Describe guidelines for thinking creatively.

A fundamental way to become more creative is to be open to your own ideas. When trying to solve a problem, think of as many alternatives as you can, without rejecting any. Some people use the five-step technique: gathering raw materials, thinking about the materials, incubating, identifying an idea, and shaping and developing the idea. Creative thinking is not always conscious; dreaming, daydreaming, and engaging in distracting activities actually can help generate ideas.

9.8 Discuss how supervisors can establish and maintain a creative work climate.

Supervisors should show that they value creativity. They should listen to and encourage suggestions. When ideas fail, supervisors should acknowledge that failure is a sign that people are trying. Instead of focusing on blaming, the supervisor should see what lessons can be learned from the failure.

9.9 Identify ways to overcome barriers to creativity.

Some barriers to creativity are fear of failure, excessive busyness, and isolation. To overcome these barriers, supervisors need to remember that failing inevitably accompanies trying, to set aside time for thinking and resting, and to communicate with co-workers and peers in other organizations.

Key Terms

decision, p. 211

bounded rationality, p. 215

recency syndrome, p. 217

stereotypes, p. 217

probability theory, p. 221

decision tree, p. 222

decision-making software, p. 224

groupthink, p. 226

brainstorming, p. 227

creativity, p. 228

Review and Discussion Questions

1. Andrea is in charge of scheduling the work for the service department of a car dealership. Lately, people in the sales department have been taking telephone calls from customers and promising that service work could be completed on a certain day or by a certain time. Consequently, everyone is unhappy— mechanics, salespeople, customers, and Andrea—because the work schedule is disrupted and the service department can't keep up with the promises made to customers. Using the rational model of decision making, what steps might Andrea take to correct the situation?

2. Define *bounded rationality*. Describe a situation in which you resorted to bounded rationality as a method of decision making. What were the results of your decision? Do you think this was the best way to make a decision under the circumstances? Why or why not?

3. Franklin Jones, a supervisor in the buying department for a department store, says, "I think these men's jackets are going to be hot this fall. Let's place a big order." What kind of compromises to rational decision making is he using in making his decision? Using the decision-making model, what would be a more rational approach?

4. In each of the following situations, what is interfering with the supervisor's ability to make the best decision? Suggest how the supervisors can improve their decision making.
    a. "I think this new answering machine model should be blue," said the design supervisor. "I like blue."
    b. "Let's conduct training at three o'clock on Fridays," said the customer service supervisor. "After all, it's been slow the last couple of Friday afternoons."
    c. "I'll bet we could boost sales by attracting more women," said the sales manager at an auto dealership. "To generate some traffic, we could hold a little fashion show or a makeup demonstration or something like that every week or so."

5. This chapter presents several guidelines for decision making: Consider the consequences, respond quickly in a crisis, inform the manager, be decisive but not inflexible, and avoid decision-making traps. How would such guidelines influence the way a nursing supervisor handles the following two situations?
    a. The supervisor is scheduling nurses for the next month.
    b. One of the nurses calls on Friday afternoon to say her father just died, so she will be out next week.

6. Philip is a supervisor who likes to work independently. Whenever he faces a new situation, he prefers to analyze it and make his decision without consulting other sources. How might this method of decision making impact the results of his decision? What might be a better way for Philip to proceed?

7. Rita McCormick is the supervisor of the state office that processes sales tax payments. She has noticed that workers are falling behind and wants to get authorization either to hire two more employees or to schedule overtime until the work gets caught up. Rita estimates that there is an 80 percent chance the workload will continue to be this high and a 20 percent chance that work will fall back to previous levels, which the current employees can handle during regular working hours. (She assumes there is no chance of less work in the future.) Because she will have to pay time and a half for overtime, she assumes that the annual cost of overtime will be $150,000, whereas a workforce with two more employees will cost only $140,000.
    a. Construct a decision tree for this problem.
    b. Which alternative should the supervisor choose?

8. What are some advantages of making decisions as a group? What are some disadvantages?

9. What are the symptoms of groupthink? What can a supervisor do to overcome groupthink in a team meeting?

10. Roberto Gonzalez wants to make his solutions more creative. When he has a problem to solve, he sits down at his desk and tries to generate as many alternative solutions as he can. Unfortunately, he usually gets frustrated before he comes up with an alternative that satisfies him, so he just picks an acceptable solution

and tries to implement it. How can Roberto modify his decision-making process to come up with more creative ideas?

11. How can supervisors foster creativity in their department or work group?

A SECOND LOOK

Does the creativity described at Hallmark Cards and Joe Designer mean letting employees do whatever they want? How can you apply some of the techniques described in the opening story?

SKILLS MODULE

CASE

Can the "Wrong" Decision Ever Be Right?

Chris Newell is the founder of the Lotus Institute (Cambridge, Massachusetts), whose mission is to explore how groupware technology overlaps cultural issues. His thoughts on decision making are instructive for supervisors:

"The crux of making good decisions isn't doing things right—it's making sure that you focus on the right things. As citizens of the Information Age, we're overwhelmed with data, reports, facts—much of it noise that we need to filter out before we can figure out what's relevant to a decision. So I've learned to hone my discrimination skills. But if you're exploring something that has no precedent—an idea, a product, a service—you can't rely solely on data to guide you. You have to rely on people too. I've developed a personal advisory council that I consult before tackling a big decision, a group of people who are anchored by similar values—though not necessarily by similar perspectives.

"Sometimes making the 'wrong' decision is the right thing to do. Last year, I decided to overrun my budget—to continue investing in Learn-ingSpace, a product that Lotus was unsure about investing in. I knew it was the right thing to do, even though I couldn't get the company to agree. When news of my decision surfaced on the radar of some key people, I got hammered. At times, I even doubted my own decision. A year later, LearningSpace has become one of Lotus's most important strategic products.

"I made one mistake: I didn't communicate all of the implications of going over budget. Otherwise, I wouldn't change a thing about what I did."

1. How many of this chapter's guidelines for decision making can you identify in Chris Newell's decision-making process?
2. How well have they worked for him? Do you think some are working better than others?
3. Are there any flaws in his process, or anything that you would advise him to do differently next time?

Source: Anna Muoio, ed., "Decisions, Decisions," *Fast Company*, October 1998, pp. 93–106.

■ SELF-QUIZ

How Creative Are You?

How many of the following apply to you? The more that apply to you, the more likely it is that you can think creatively.

1. I ask a lot of questions.
2. I enjoy word games and puzzles.
3. I write down all my ideas.
4. I know what time of day I am most likely to think of something new.
5. I read and listen to ideas that are contrary to my own beliefs.
6. I often wonder, "What if . . . ?"
7. I enjoy finding out how things work.
8. I make time every day to be alone in a quiet place.
9. I don't make assumptions about people or situations.
10. I read about my own field of work.
11. I read about areas outside my field of work.
12. I can think of more than one way to do most everyday activities.
13. I can laugh at my own mistakes.
14. I speak (or would enjoy learning) a second language.
15. I am willing to take risks.

Class Exercise

This exercise will test your ability to think creatively about a problem in order to help someone else come to a decision. Divide into teams of two and decide which of you is to represent the employee and which the supervisor. The employee wishes to persuade the supervisor, who is reluctant, to agree to a brief trial of telecommuting.

Take a few minutes for the "employee" to prepare. The "employee" should decide how to address the problem and then present a solution designed to overcome the "supervisor's" skepticism. The "supervisor" gets a few minutes to make his or her decision, then presents the steps in the process and the reasoning behind the answer. If both of you are satisfied with your performance, volunteer to role-play your problem-solving and decision-making scenario to the class.

Team-Building Exercise
Learning from Mistakes

Everyone who makes decisions makes some mistakes; the trick is to learn from them. Divide the class into teams and let each team member present one mistake he or she has made at work or in school, such as missing a deadline or appointment or misunderstanding some instructions. Discuss what the team can learn from each mistake, and choose the one mistake about which every member agrees he or she learned the most. Let each team present the winning mistake and list the lessons they drew from it.

PART FOUR

Skills of the Supervisor

10

I love e-mail. I think it is changing the world.
—Jeff Bezos, founder and CEO, Amazon.com

Communication

■ CHAPTER OUTLINE

How Communication Works
The Communication Process
Hearing versus Listening

Communicating Effectively
Communicate from the Receiver's Viewpoint
Learn from Feedback
Use Strategies for Effective Listening
Be Prepared for Cultural Differences

Barriers to Communication
Information Overload
Misunderstandings
Biases in Perception

Types of Messages
Nonverbal Messages
Verbal Messages
Technology and Message Types
Choosing the Most Effective Message Type

Communicating in Organizations
Direction of Communication
Formal and Informal Communication

■ LEARNING OBJECTIVES

After you have studied this chapter, you should be able to:

10.1 Describe the process of communication.

10.2 Distinguish between hearing and listening.

10.3 Describe techniques for communicating effectively.

10.4 Identify barriers to communication and suggest ways to avoid them.

10.5 Distinguish between verbal and nonverbal messages, and name types of verbal messages.

10.6 Identify the directions in which communication can flow in an organization.

10.7 Distinguish between formal and informal communication in an organization.

10.8 Discuss the role of the grapevine in organizations.

CAROL ROBERTS EMPHASIZES COMMUNICATION AT INTERNATIONAL PAPER

It's a difficult task to bear bad news. Soon after accepting the position of vice president of people development at International Paper, Carol Roberts realized there was a problem. While there were many ways for supervisors and employees to communicate at the firm, most of them weren't being used. The feedback loop for performance appraisal was open instead of closed and, as Carol said, "We weren't helping our people to progress, and we weren't progressing as a company."

However, Carol was well aware of her status as a brand-new employee and as a woman in a male-dominated industry. She was reluctant to communicate her concerns to her manager for fear that she would be seen as a complainer. Perhaps her message would be seen as an attempt to get ahead by criticizing others. Clearly this would be an important communication for Carol.

She realized she had three communication goals. First, she had to make supervisors and their managers aware that they weren't giving enough useful feedback to their employees on the front lines. Second, she needed to remind them that International Paper's future depended on developing its people, making the stakes for improving the delivery of feedback very high. Finally, Carol knew she had to communicate persuasively to overcome the perception that she was using the situation to promote herself.

With the help of an outside consultant, she set up a two-day meeting for the firm's 33 top managers. She opened by asking all of them for their help in solving the problem and letting them know she didn't have all the answers. Over the course of the meeting, her direct approach won them over, and she left the meeting with a plan for a solution. A year later, a new employee development program and a "watchdog" committee were in place. Carol's communication skills had carried her past dissent to a successful delivery of her message.

Source: Michael Warshaw, "Open Mouth. Close Career?" *Fast Company*, December 1998, pp. 241–251.

---

communication
The process by which people send and receive information.

Whether delivering good news or bad, supervisors must be able to communicate well to perform high-quality work. **Communication** is the process by which people send and receive information. The information may be about opinions, facts, or feelings. Even hard-nosed businesspeople need information about feelings; for example, a supervisor should know when his or her boss is angry or when employees are discouraged.

Communication is at the heart of the supervisor's job. To work with their manager, their employees, and supervisors in other departments, supervisors send and receive ideas, instructions, progress reports, and many other kinds of information. These and other communications can occupy three-quarters of a supervisor's workday. Thus, supervisors need to know how to communicate and how to do so effectively. This chapter describes basic communication skills and the types of communication that commonly occur in organizations.

How Communication Works

On March 13, 2001, Neil L. Patterson, chief executive of software developer Cerner Corp., sent an e-mail message to about 400 of his company's managers. In the memo Patterson demanded increased productivity and insisted that the managers put employees on time clocks, charge unapproved absences to vacations, reduce staff by 5 percent, and hold staff mettings at 7 A.M. and 6 P.M., and on Saturday mornings.

Two things made this communication unusual: It was extremely angry and rancorous, and it quickly found its way to other employees of the Kansas City firm and even onto a public Yahoo! message board where investors could see it.

The memo, which included phrases like "Hell will freeze over before this CEO implements another employee benefit in this culture" and "You have a problem and you will fix it or I will replace you," was never intended to be released to the public, and Patterson quickly apologized for it with a follow-up e-mail to employees and an interview with the *Kansas City Star*. Company spokesperson Stan Sword asserted that the original e-mail was "an overstatement" that arose from Patterson's passion for work—and that the employes understood that.

Still, the company's stock dropped 22 percent over the next three days, and *Fortune* magazine jokingly apologized for having recently chosen Cerner as one of the 100 best firms in the country to work for. While the stock price recovered within a few weeks, most observers say that Patterson's e-mail broke several rules of good communication, among them: don't communicate in anger, remain open to feedback, model effective leadership, and—rules particular to electronic communication—don't try to hold large-group discussions via e-mail and never forget that e-mail isn't private.[1]

At times all of us, like Neil Patterson, have found that simply talking or writing does not guarantee effective communication. Rather, our intended audience should be receiving and understanding the message.

The Communication Process

To describe and explain issues such as these, social scientists have attempted to diagram the communication process. As a result, we have a widely accepted model of how communication works. Figure 10.1 illustrates one version of this model.

Communication begins when the sender of a message encodes the message. This means the sender translates his or her thoughts and feelings into words, gestures, facial expressions, and so on. The sender then transmits the encoded message by writing, speaking, and other personal contact. If communication is working properly, the intended audience receives the message and is able to decode, or interpret, it correctly. Of course, mistakes do occur. Communication breakdowns may occur because of **noise;** that is, anything that can distort a message by interfering with the communication process. Examples of noise are distractions, ambiguous words, and incompatible electronic equipment used to transmit the message.

The sender of the message can recognize and resolve communication problems by paying attention to feedback. **Feedback,** in this sense, is the way the receiver responds—or fails to respond—to the message. Feedback may take the form of words or behavior. For example, an electronic Internet monitoring program detected four page views of Web pornography within 10 minutes at one Col-

noise
Anything that can distort a message by interfering with the communication process.

feedback
The way the receiver of a message responds or fails to respond to the message.

FIGURE 10.1

The Communication Process

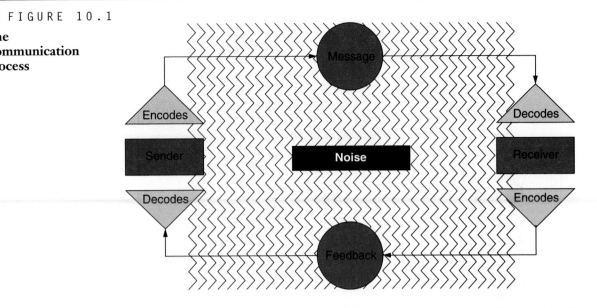

orado firm with only four employees, and at another larger firm in Denver, there were 3,000 online shopping transactions, 4,000 day-trading hits, and 500 pornography views within 5 days.[2] Whatever one may think about the merits of such surveillance, results like these tell supervisors that employees are not paying enough attention to their tasks. For Neil Patterson of Cerner, such results may be feedback indicating that he hasn't communicated clearly enough about how employees should use the Internet during work hours.

Hearing versus Listening

Notice in Figure 10.1 that the receiver must decode the message, meaning that the receiver as well as the sender has an active role to play in communication. If the receiver is not playing that role, communication is not occurring.

In many cases, this means the receiver of a message must *listen* to it rather than just *hear* it. Hearing means the brain is registering sounds. Most of us have at some point heard a parent nagging at us to clean our rooms or a co-worker complaining about working conditions, but we may not be listening. Listening means paying attention to what is being said and trying to understand the full message. This is the meaning of "decoding" a message. When parents nag or when co-workers complain, we often choose not to listen to them.

Thus, as the model of the communication process shows, when we want communication to work, we need to make sure that people are decoding messages as well as sending them. Because communication is an essential part of a supervisor's job, a supervisor must practice good listening skills as well as good writing and speaking skills. The next section discusses listening in greater detail.

Communicating Effectively

Supervisors need to understand the requests that cross their desks and the questions that employees raise. They need to know when the boss is angry or impressed. They need to ensure that employees understand their instructions. When

FIGURE 10.2

**Techniques
for Effective
Communication**

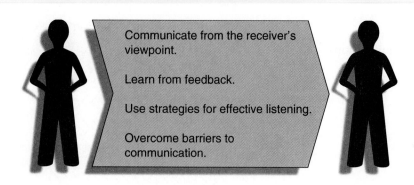

Communicate from the receiver's viewpoint.

Learn from feedback.

Use strategies for effective listening.

Overcome barriers to communication.

supervisors succeed in these responsibilities, they are communicating effectively. Figure 10.2 demonstrates that effective communication is most likely to occur when the parties communicate from the receiver's viewpoint, learn from feedback, use strategies for effective listening, and overcome barriers to communication.

Communicate from the Receiver's Viewpoint

Even though we know that other people do not share all our experiences, views, priorities, and interests, we find it is easy to forget this when we are communicating. But such differences make the intended audience more likely to ignore or misunderstand the messages we send. For example, a business owner may find it fascinating and noteworthy that the company has been in the family for four generations. Skilled sales personnel, on the other hand, know that customers would rather hear how the company's services will benefit them. The salespeople therefore communicate with the audience's viewpoint in mind; they focus on what the company can offer customers.

This sales principle applies to all kinds of communication. Simply put, if you want the receiver's attention, interest, and understanding, you must communicate from his or her viewpoint. Applying this principle includes tactics such as using understandable vocabulary, referring to shared experiences, and addressing the receiver's interests. Thus, in explaining to employees that the department will be reorganized, a supervisor should focus on topics such as job security and job design, not on how the changes will make the company more profitable or more like its nearest competitor. After all, employees naturally are most concerned about their own jobs.

Learn from Feedback

Feedback can help supervisors communicate effectively. When a supervisor sends a message, he or she generally expects a certain kind of response. Suppose a supervisor explains a policy requiring that all employees take their lunch breaks at some time between 11:00 A.M. and 1:00 P.M. One type of feedback would be the expressions on employees' faces—do they seem to understand or do they look confused? Employees also might respond verbally; one might ask whether employees are to take a two-hour lunch break. Another type of response comes from the employees' later behavior. If the employees understood the message, no one will be hav-

■ FIGURE 10.3

**Ten Rules for
Good Listening**

1. Remove distractions and give the speaker your full attention.
2. Look at the speaker most of the time.
3. When the speaker hesitates, give a sign of encouragement such as a smile or nod.
4. Try to hear the main point and supporting points.
5. Distinguish between opinions and facts.
6. Control your emotions.
7. Be patient; do not interrupt.
8. Take notes.
9. At appropriate times, ask questions to clarify your understanding.
10. Restate what you think the speaker's point is, and ask whether you heard correctly.

---

ing lunch after 1:00 P.M. By evaluating the words, facial expressions, and behavior of the people who received the message, the supervisor can determine whether they understood it.

When feedback indicates that a message was not received fully and correctly, the supervisor can try modifying it, so that it is better adapted to the receiver. The supervisor may have to eliminate sources of noise; for example, by talking in a location with fewer distractions or choosing clearer words.

Image National, a sign manufacturer based in Boise, Idaho, holds monthly meetings at which managers discuss the company's financial statements with employees. Feedback indicated that employees failed to understand the basics of the reports, so Ron Eardley, Image National's president, used a visual aid to clarify the message. He displayed a giant replica of a dollar bill to represent the company's total sales; as the chief financial officer read off the costs of sales, Eardley cut off portions of the dollar bill representing their proportion of total sales. Watching the dollar being "eaten away" brought home to employees that the company's sales dollars do not go straight to its owner's pockets.[3]

A supervisor also can use feedback when he or she is receiving a message. In particular, when a supervisor is uncertain about the meaning of a message, he or she can ask the sender to clarify it. Asking questions is usually a smarter tactic than guessing.

Use Strategies for Effective Listening

"Things just aren't done like they used to be," grumbled Tom Wiggins to Allen Pincham, his supervisor at the construction site. "Oh, boy," thought Allen, "here we go again with the complaining." Allen began studying some blueprints, ignoring Tom until he blew off some steam and returned to work. Later that week, the general contractor confronted Allen with a report he had received from Tom that some work was not being done according to code. Tom had complained that he had tried to inform Allen, but that his attempts were ignored.

Better listening could have saved the construction project much expense and could have saved Allen Pincham considerable embarrassment. Listening is a key part of communication, and most supervisors could be better listeners. (Test your own listening skills by taking the Self-Quiz on page 267.) Figure 10.3 lists 10 rules for being a good listener.

Effective listening begins with a commitment to listen carefully. A supervisor should not assume that a message will be boring or irrelevant and should instead decide to listen carefully and to try to identify important information. For example, when an employee complains frequently about seemingly petty matters, the complaints may hide a broader concern that the employee is not stating directly. If a supervisor does not have time to listen when someone wants to talk, he or she should schedule another time to continue the conversation.

A supervisor should also concentrate on the message and tune out distractions. A major type of distraction is planning one's own responses; another is assuming that the listener has nothing interesting to say. When tuning out distractions proves difficult, it may help to take brief notes of what the person is saying, focusing on the key points.

If the speaker uses words or phrases that evoke an emotional reaction, a supervisor must try to control those emotions so that they do not interfere with understanding. One way to respond is to consider whether the speaker is merely trying to vent emotions. In that case, the best response is to listen and acknowledge the emotions without agreeing or disagreeing. Wait until the employee is calm before trying to solve a problem. Then ask questions that seek out the facts underlying an emotional statement: "Stan, you say you are treated unfairly. Would you give me some examples?"

active listening
Hearing what the speaker is saying, seeking to understand the facts and feelings the speaker is trying to convey, and stating what you understand that message to be.

In many situations, a supervisor can benefit from using a technique called active listening, pioneered by psychologist Carl R. Rogers. **Active listening** is not only hearing what the speaker is saying but also seeking to understand the facts and feelings the speaker is trying to convey and then stating what you understand the message to be. The sample dialogues in Table 10.1 illustrate two types of listening. In Example 1, the supervisor is simply hearing the employee's words; in Example 2, the supervisor is using active listening. According to Rogers, active listening is a way that supervisors can help employees understand their situation, take responsibility, and cooperate. However, active listening is used effectively only when a supervisor demonstrates a genuine respect for employees and a belief in their ability to direct their own activities.[4]

Be Prepared for Cultural Differences

Supervisors today, more often than in the past, have employees or customers from cultures other than their own. Preparation for cultural differences can help supervisors communicate clearly with these people. To be prepared, supervisors can acquaint themselves with basic guidelines for cross-cultural communication[5]:

Stick to simple, basic words: "use," not "utilize," and "before," not "prior to." Every culture has its own slang and idioms, such as "over the hill" and "in the ballpark." People from other cultures, especially those who speak another language, may be unfamiliar with these terms. In addition, avoid using the jargon of your industry. If you have time to prepare the message in advance, as in the case of a letter or speech, ask a third person to read or listen to the message to make sure it is clear.

When speaking, talk slowly and pronounce words carefully. You do not need to speak loudly; a common error is to assume that a loud tone of voice is the only way to get the message across. Seek feedback by asking your listener what he or she has heard, but do not ask, "Do you understand?" Many people are too embarrassed to respond that they do not understand the message. The following clues also may indicate a lack of understanding:

■ TABLE 10.1

Hearing versus Active Listening

Example 1: Hearing	**Word-Processing Operator:** Hey, Wanda, is Finchburg kidding? He wants the whole report ready by the end of the day? That's impossible!
	Supervisor: But that's the job. You'll have to work as fast as you can. We're under tremendous pressure this week.
	Operator: Doesn't he realize we're behind schedule already because of the quarterly reports?
	Supervisor: Look, Don, I don't decide what the managers want. I just have to see that the work gets done, and that's what I'm trying to do.
	Operator: How can I tell my wife I'll be working late *again?*
	Supervisor: You'll have to handle that with her, not me.
Example 2: Active Listening	**Word-Processing Operator:** Hey, Wanda, is Finchburg kidding? He wants the whole report ready by the end of the day? That's impossible!
	Supervisor: Sounds like you're pretty upset about it, Phyllis.
	Operator: I sure am. I was just about caught up after doing all these quarterly reports. And now this!
	Supervisor: As if you didn't have enough work to do, huh?
	Operator: Yeah. I don't know how I'm gonna meet this deadline.
	Supervisor: Hate to work late again, is that it?
	Operator: That's for sure. I made other plans two weeks ago. Seems like everything we do around here is a big rush.
	Supervisor: I guess you feel like your work cuts into your personal time.
	Operator: Well, yeah. I know Finchburg needs this report to land a big customer. I guess that means that this job really *is* important. Maybe if Joel will help me by doing the tables, I can get out of here at a reasonable hour.

Source: Based on "Active Listening" by Carl R. Rogers and Richard E. Farson.

- Nods and smiles that are not directly connected to what you are saying.
- A complete lack of interruptions.
- Efforts to change the subject.
- A complete lack of questions.
- Inappropriate laughter.

Give your listener plenty of time to come up with questions. If you still are not sure that an employee has understood instructions, check on the progress of his or her work, allowing ample time to make any needed corrections or clarify what you meant.

Make sure you understand what the other person is saying. Ask for clarification when you need it. Help the speaker to relax, and invite him or her to speak more slowly. If you are having trouble understanding a word pronounced by a nonnative speaker of English, try asking the person to spell it. Most important, assume you can understand, and then try.

Learn about the communication styles used by people from different cultures, and try to match them when appropriate. For example, in some Far Eastern

Helping Workers Get the Work Done

At the Illinois factory of 3Com Corp, the 1,200 employees speak more than 20 different languages, including Tagalog, Gujarati, and Chinese. Although English is the common language, not everyone who is hired is immediately fluent. After failing to make himself understood in slow, repeated English words addressed to a janitor he thought was Polish, one supervisor found himself enlisting the help of a Serbian employee he thought could help. She couldn't. In fact, no one was sure what nationality the janitor was.

One place where 3Com can't afford to take such chances, however, is on the factory line where modems are produced around the clock. To ease the communication process between supervisors and employees, the firm has made it a practice to continually redesign the work to fit the workers. Laminated instruction sheets hang over most workstations; in addition to written directions, they include large color-coded drawings showing exactly what is to be done,

where, and with what components. Training, too, relies on plenty of illustrations and hands-on practice on the job.

Any line jobs that become too complex to teach to workers with language difficulties are quickly broken down into smaller parts. "The key," says director of manufacturing Mary Ellen Smith, "is that anyone can come in and do that job."

Supervisors have flexibility to group workers on the line in any way that helps meet their production goals. If it makes sense to put workers together who share a common language, they can do so. While employees still tend to lunch only with those who share their language, at least on the line they are finding ways to get the job done.

Source: Timothy Aeppel, "A 3Com Factory Hires a Lot of Immigrants, Gets Mix of Languages," *Wall Street Journal*, March 30, 1998, pp. A1, A12.

cultures, it is considered extremely rude to interrupt someone during a conversation, whereas people from Arabic cultures tend to tolerate interruptions as a sign of enthusiasm. Asians are likely to view loudness as rude, but a Middle Easterner is more often comfortable with it. In any case, a wise supervisor will avoid jumping to conclusions about an individual's character on the basis of cultural preferences.

Supervisors also can help their employees communicate by stressing the importance of keeping communication simple. Share what you learn about communication styles. Compliment employees as they make progress in cross-cultural communication. "Meeting the Challenge" demonstrates how one firm tries to overcome multiple-language barriers. In another example, Thomas Chen, founder of Crystal Window & Door Systems Ltd. in Flushing, New York, offers free English classes to his 200 employees, about three-quarters of whom are Chinese Americans. Bilingual staff members conduct the classes on evenings and weekends, and use multimedia and personal instruction to cover everything from conversational English to the technical vocabulary of the industry. On "English-only Fridays," everyone, including the company's growing population of Hispanic workers, gets to practice what has been learned in class. And since everyone is doing it, no feels uncomfortable.[6]

Barriers to Communication

The model of the communication process suggests where barriers to communication can arise. In general, the sender may fail to encode the message clearly, the message may be lost in transmission, or the receiver may misinterpret the message. In practice, these categories of problems often overlap. The resulting barriers may take the form of information overload, misunderstandings, and biases related to perception.

Information Overload

Today's world is often called the information age. People are bombarded with information daily. On the way to work, radio ads and billboards proclaim which brand of automobile or soft drink to buy. At the workplace, memos, magazines, and managers report on trends, policies, and responsibilities. During the course of a day, many employees get information from colleagues, computer screens, printed pages, and telephone calls. In the evening, family members and television announcers recount the day's news. People cope with this barrage of information by tuning out a lot of what they see and hear.

How can a supervisor respond to this barrier to communication? An important way is to give employees only information that will be useful to them. For example, when employees need instructions, a supervisor should think the instructions through carefully, so that new instructions don't have to be provided later. Also, a supervisor should be sure that employees are paying attention. The way to do this is to observe the people receiving the information and to look for feedback. A supervisor can say to an employee, "Do you understand what I want you to do? Try putting it in your own words." To his or her manager, a supervisor might say, "Do you think this idea supports your goals for the department?"

Misunderstandings

In decoding a message, the receiver of a message may make errors that lead to misunderstandings. This barrier can arise when a message is needlessly complicated. Imagine a supervisor's memo that reads, "The deterioration of maintenance practices will inevitably lead to conditions that will be injurious to our hitherto admirable safety record." The person who receives this memo is likely to misunderstand it because so much effort is required to figure out what the words mean. Instead, the supervisor could write, "Because the maintenance workers are no longer tuning up the machines each month, the machines are going to wear out and cause injuries."

When the supervisor is the receiver of a message, he or she needs to be careful to understand its true meaning. The supervisor should not hesitate to ask questions about unclear points. It is also helpful to check on the meaning with such responses as "So you'd like me to . . ." or "Are you saying that . . .?" A supervisor also needs to recognize when people are intentionally vague or misleading. On those occasions, the supervisor should interpret messages with particular care.

Likewise, supervisors should be aware that vulgar language is counterproductive at best and sometimes offensive. In a case currently pending grievance procedures, a customer service representative for Verizon Communications Inc. says she was fired for uttering a crude expletive during a disciplinary review. While the reaction may seem extreme, some companies like Verizon and General Motors do prohibit profanity. Experts disagree about whether supervisors can reasonably be expected to "listen to every word workers utter."[7]

Word Choices To avoid misunderstandings, a supervisor should be careful to make appropriate word choices when encoding the message. Besides choosing simple words, this means avoiding ambiguous words. If an employee asks, "Should I use the solvent in the bottle on the left?" the supervisor should not say, "Right."

■ TABLE 10.2

Two Ways to Address Comments to Others

	You Statements	I Statements
Examples	"You're so irresponsible!"	"I'm upset that you've missed the deadline for the third time. When someone in the department misses a deadline, the whole department looks bad. What can we do?"
	"At the next department meeting, you'd better be prepared and be on time, or you're going to be sorry when we review your salary."	"I was not pleased that you were late to the meeting and unprepared. I expect a higher standard of performance."
	"You're bugging the women with those dirty jokes, so just knock it off before we get in trouble."	"I have received complaints from two of the employees in the department that you are embarrassing them by telling dirty jokes. Our company policy and the law both forbid that type of behavior."
Likely response	Defensiveness, ignoring speaker.	Listening, collaborating on a solution.

Problems also can arise from using words that attribute characteristics to another person. Saying "You're so irresponsible!" leads an employee to tune out a message. Instead, a supervisor could describe specific behaviors and his or her own feelings: "That's the second time this week you've made that mistake. I get annoyed when I have to explain the same procedure more than once or twice." This approach is called using "I statements" instead of "you statements." Table 10.2 gives examples of the differences between the two types.

Choosing words carefully is especially important in addressing others. A careful supervisor uses the name of a co-worker or customer instead of "dear" or "honey" unless the supervisor is completely certain that the receiver in a business setting likes being called by such endearments.

Word choice is also an important element of clarity. Supervisors should avoid using language that obscures their meaning, such as this sentence from a prospectus sent to clients of Federated Investors: "Redemptions will be processed in a manner intended to maximize the amount of redemption which will not be subject to a contingent deferred sales charge."[8] One good way to check your written communication for clarity is to read it out loud before sending it.

Cross-cultural differences in meaning can lead to unintentional misunderstandings, as Anita Santiago, president and creative director of the Los Angeles advertising company that bears her name, well knows. In adapting the California Milk Processor Board's famous "Got Milk?" ad series for Spanish-speaking audiences, Santiago refocused the campaign on grandmothers serving milk to their grandchildren. One reason: When translated to Spanish, "Got milk?" means, "Are you lactating?"[9]

Cultural Differences   Another concern involves misunderstandings that result from cultural differences. For example, the mainstream culture in the United States places relatively great emphasis on expressing one's personal opinion. A supervisor from this culture thus could expect that employees would feel free to share ideas and express disagreements. In contrast, people from a culture that

■ TABLE 10.3

Cultural Differences in Communication

Aspect of Communication	Example
Language	Even within the United States, employees may speak many different languages.
Word choices	In the United States, a direct refusal is considered clear and honest; in Japan, it is considered rude and immature.
Gestures	In the United States, nodding means *yes* and shaking the head means *no;* the reverse is true in Bulgaria, parts of Greece, Turkey, and Iran.
Facial expressions	In mainstream American culture, people smile relatively often and view smiling as a way to convey goodwill. Someone from the Middle East might smile as a way to avoid conflict, and someone from Asia might smile to cover up anger or embarrassment.
Eye contact	Arabs often look intently into the other person's eyes as a way to know and work well with the other person; in England, blinking one's eyes is a sign that the other person was heard and understood.
Distance between speaker and listener	Middle Easterners may interpret standing a foot apart as an indication of involvement in a conversation; an American may interpret standing that close as a sign of aggression.
Context (situation in which message is sent and received)	Holding a business conversation during the evening meal is acceptable in the United States but rude in France.
Conversational rituals (phrases and behaviors that are customs, not meant to be interpreted literally)	In the United States, people often greet one another with "How are you?" not expecting an answer; in the Philippines, they ask, "Where are you going?" Men make more use of jokes and friendly put-downs; women more often use equalizers such as saying, "I'm sorry," and make requests indirectly.

Sources: Roger E. Axtell, *Gestures: The Do's and Taboos of Body Language around the World* (New York: Wiley, 1991); Philip R. Harris and Robert T. Moran, *Managing Cultural Differences*, 3d ed. (Houston: Gulf Publishing, 1991); Deborah Tannen, *Talking from 9 to 5* (New York: William Morrow, 1994); Sondra Thiederman, *Bridging Cultural Barriers for Corporate Success: How to Manage the Multicultural Work Force* (New York: Lexington Books, 1991); Chanthika Pornpitakpan, "Trade in Thailand: A Three-way Cultural Comparison" *Business Horizons*, March–April 2000, vol. 43, issue 2, pp. 61–70.

places a high value on harmony (e.g., Japan) might agree with the speaker out of politeness rather than a shared opinion. People from a culture that values demonstrating respect according to one's place in the hierarchy (e.g., Mexico or the Middle East) might be reluctant to express disagreement to a manager or other high-ranking person. A U.S. manager who was unfamiliar with such values might assume mistakenly that employees from these cultures were unable or unwilling to contribute their ideas.

To avoid misinterpreting the words and behavior of others, a supervisor must be familiar with the communication styles of the various cultures of people with whom he or she works. Table 10.3 identifies some aspects of communication affected by culture and provides examples of cultural differences. Information about the values and customs of different cultures, of course, does not apply to every member of any culture, but it can sensitize a supervisor to areas where extra care may be needed to promote understanding.

When interpreting communication styles, it can be useful to recognize women as a different cultural group from men in the United States. In other

Men Talk, Women Apologize

If you've ever suspected that men and women communicate differently at work, you are probably right. The next time you find yourself attending a meeting, whether of your peers, your subordinates, or your managers, you might find it helpful to be aware of some of the following behavior differences. Once aware, you can train yourself to overcome or avoid them.

- Men like meetings more than women do, but they fall asleep at them far more often.
- Men use put-downs to protect themselves from criticism, while women tend to apologize before they present information.
- Men are both self-effacing and self-promoting, whereas women are eager perfectionists.
- Men won't ask questions; women will.

- Men take up a lot of physical space, spreading their papers around the table, stretching, leaning back, getting up and walking around the room. Women usually sit still and find most office furniture too uncomfortable for lounging.
- Men speak out; women tend to raise their hands before speaking.
- Men talk more than women do so their ideas are more frequently adopted.
- Men will make up answers; women will admit they don't know something.

Source: Carol Hymowitz, "Men and Women Fall Back into Kids' Roles at Corporate Meetings," *Wall Street Journal*, December 15, 1998, p. B1.

words, although there are many sources of individual differences, men and women tend to communicate in gender-specific ways. For example, assertiveness in women is often viewed as being pushy or aggressive, so women tend to use a less assertive style of communication than men. Women also tend to value modesty and to describe their accomplishments as group rather than personal achievements. Supervisors who want to benefit fully from the talent of their women employees may have to take an active role in asking for their ideas and identifying their accomplishments.[10] For example, see "Supervision and Diversity" for some ways that men and women may communicate differently in meetings.

inference
A conclusion drawn from the facts available.

Inferences versus Facts Misunderstandings also can arise when the listener confuses inferences with facts. An **inference** is a conclusion drawn from the facts available. A supervisor may observe that an employee is not meeting performance standards. That would be a fact. If a supervisor says, "You're lazy!" he or she is making an inference based on the fact of the below-par performance. The inference may or may not be true.

Statements using the words *never* and *always* are inferences. A supervisor may claim, "You're always late"—knowing for certain that the employee has been late to work six days straight. However, the supervisor cannot know for certain what the employee *always* does.

One business writer tells the story of a manager who berated a supervisor and crew of maintenance workers as they stood by a piece of machine that was to be dismantled. The manager had concluded that the workers were "goofing off" and shouted at them to begin immediately. The supervisor explained that they were waiting for a required written work permit, which would outline the safety precautions they were to take. At this the manager apologized for jumping to a conclusion without knowing the facts.[11]

To overcome mistakes caused by treating inferences as facts, a supervisor should be aware of them. When sending a message, a supervisor should avoid

■ FIGURE 10.4

**A Drawing That
May Be Perceived in
More than One Way**

Source: Edwin G. Boring, "A New Ambiguous Figure," *American Journal of Psychology*, July 1930, p. 444. See also Robert Leeper, "A Study of a Neglected Portion of the Field of Learning—The Development of Sensory Organization," *Journal of Genetic Psychology*, March 1935, p. 62. Originally drawn by cartoonist W. E. Hill and published in *Puck*, November 8, 1915.

statements that phrase inferences as facts. When listening to a message, a supervisor should be explicit with his or her inferences. For example, a supervisor in a bakery could say, "When you tell me the test of the recipe was a failure, I assume you mean the quality of the bread is poor. Is that correct?"

Biases in Perception

**perceptions
The ways people see
and interpret reality.**

Based on their experiences and values, the sender and receiver of a message make assumptions about each other and about the message. The ways people see and interpret reality are known as **perceptions.** Look at the picture in Figure 10.4. What do you see? You may perceive either an old woman or a young woman.

When perceptions about others are false, messages might get distorted. Imagine that supervisor Al Trejo has decided his employees would like him to pay more attention to their day-to-day problems and successes. So Al stops by the desk of one of his employees, Kim Coleman, and asks, "What are you doing?" Based on her experiences, Kim believes that supervisors are quick to criticize, so she perceives that Al's question is intended to determine whether she is goofing off. Feeling defensive, Kim snaps, "My work, of course." Al then perceives that Kim does not want to discuss her work with him.

Prejudices   Broad generalizations about a category of people—stereotypes—can lead to negative conclusions about them. These negative conclusions are called **prejudices,** and they can distort perceptions. In our culture, it is common to attribute certain characteristics to women, African Americans, Asian Americans, blue-collar workers, and many other groups. Of course, these characteristics often do not apply to a particular person. Imagine that a male manager assumes women are irrational and highly emotional, and that a female supervisor who reports to him discusses her desire for a raise. Even if she outlines a series of logical points supporting her request, he may perceive her request as irrational and may respond by telling her to "take it easy, things will work out OK." If such poor communication continues, the supervisor might eventually quit in frustration.

prejudices
Negative conclusions about a category of people based on stereotypes.

The way to overcome communication barriers resulting from prejudices is to be aware of the assumptions we make. Are we responding to what a person is saying or to what he or she is wearing? Are we responding to the message or to the speaker's accent? To the words or to our beliefs about the person's race? Awareness enables the sender and the receiver of a message to focus on understanding rather than assuming.

Biases in Paying Attention   Perception begins when people pay attention to a message or other stimulus. However, biases occur even at this early stage of the perception process. People tend to pay more attention to a message that seems to serve their own self-interests. They also are more apt to hear messages that fit their existing viewpoints and to discount messages that contradict those viewpoints. Imagine that an employee suggests a new procedure, to which the supervisor responds, "Your idea will never work." The employee is more likely to think the supervisor is opposed to change than that the idea is unworkable.

The supervisor can combat biases in attention by phrasing messages carefully to appeal to the receiver. In the case of the new idea from an employee, the supervisor might say, "Thank you for your suggestion. I estimate that it will save us about $50 a month. Can you think of a way we can modify it so that implementing it will cost less than $1,500?" This response shows the supervisor was paying attention to the suggestion and recognized at least some of its merit.

Types of Messages

When Sandy walked into her cubicle at the insurance company where she worked, a note signed by her supervisor was on her desk: "See me," it read. "Uh-oh," thought Sandy nervously, "what did I do?"

Sandy walked into her supervisor's office and saw that he was smiling. "Congratulations," he said, "you got the raise we requested."

verbal message
A message that consists of words.

In this example, Sandy's supervisor communicated with her through a note, a facial expression, and spoken words. Two of the messages were **verbal messages;** that is, they consisted of words. The third—the smiling face—was a **nonverbal message;** that is, it was conveyed without words.

nonverbal message
A message conveyed without using words.

Nonverbal Messages

How can anyone get a point across without using words? While the idea of nonverbal messages might seem surprising or unimportant at first, we continuously send and receive messages through our facial expressions, posture, and other non-

■ FIGURE 10.5

The Etiquette of Proper Distance: Some Cross-Cultural Examples

- Americans, on average, stand 2 feet apart when conducting business.
- Middle Eastern males typically stand up to 18 inches apart.
- Asians and many African cultures leave a space of 3 feet or more.

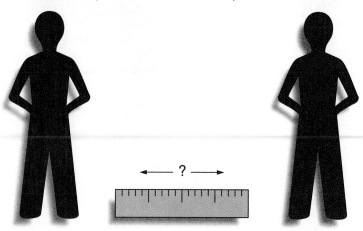

Source: Based on Sondra Thiederman, *Bridging Cultural Barriers for Corporate Success: How to Manage the Multicultural Work Force* (New York: Lexington Books, 1991), p. 132.

verbal cues. In the example of Sandy, the message conveyed by the supervisor's facial expression was as important as the verbal message, "See me." The smile, unlike the note, conveyed to Sandy that her supervisor had good news.

Major types of nonverbal messages are gestures, posture, tone of voice, facial expression, and even silence. We learn the meaning of many such messages simply by participating in our culture. From experience, we can recognize a friendly handshake, a cool silence in response to something we say, and the "proper" distance to stand from the person with whom we are talking, part of a concept known as personal space (see Figure 10.5). Imagine that a supervisor and an employee are discussing a problem concerning the employee's work. The employee drops her eyes, looking away from the supervisor. Based on the usual assumptions in American culture, a supervisor is apt to conclude that the employee is dishonest, uninterested, or guilty of something.

Because we learn the meaning of nonverbal messages from our culture, people from different cultures have different nonverbal vocabularies. In the previous example, if the employee is a Cambodian woman, she may be trying to communicate respect; according to Cambodian custom, looking her supervisor in the eye would be rude. The meanings of nonverbal cues may vary even among different groups of people born in the United States. Failure to recognize different interpretations of nonverbal signals can be misleading, as in the case of a European-American speaker who concludes, on the basis of eye contact, that an African-American listener is not interested in what he or she is saying.

A supervisor needs to send nonverbal signals communicating that he or she is businesslike and professional.[12] Some ways supervisors can send these signals are to sit or stand straight, use open hand gestures, and sit with their hands resting comfortably in their laps. Dressing conservatively signals that a supervisor commands respect and has self-control. Smiling when appropriate and shaking hands

Relative Contributions of Several Factors to Total Impact of a Message

When a message is both verbal and nonverbal, the nonverbal message may have more impact on the receiver than the words themselves. This pie chart shows the relative impact, expressed as a percent, of words, vocal tones (tone of voice), and facial expressions.

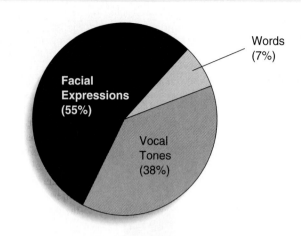

Source: Data from Albert Mehrabian, "Communication without Words," *Psychology Today*, September 1968, pp. 53–55.

readily indicate enthusiasm and interest. Finally, a pleasing, well-modulated tone of voice gets respect from others. A supervisor can develop such a voice by practicing with a mirror, video camera, or friend.

When a person is sending both verbal and nonverbal messages, the nonverbal message may have more influence on the receiver. This point was clearly understood by a group of protestors who opposed Citigroup's planned purchase of Associates First Capital, a firm that was under investigation at the time. The activists rallied before a courthouse in Durham, North Carolina, carrying red umbrellas, the symbol of Citigroup, with holes cut in them.[13] Figure 10.6 shows the weight that different components of a message may carry. If the relative importance of nonverbal communication seems surprising, imagine that someone is saying, "You're in trouble!" in an angry tone of voice. Now imagine the same person saying that while laughing. Are the messages identical?

Verbal Messages

Most nonverbal communication supplements verbal messages. People send verbal messages by speaking (oral communication) or writing (written communication). See "Tips from the Firing Line" for some ways to improve your voice mail communication.

Oral Communication   To communicate with employees, supervisors usually depend on oral communication. Every day they talk to employees to explain work duties, answer questions, assign tasks, check progress, and solve problems. This type of communication gives the supervisor an opportunity to send and receive many nonverbal cues along with the verbal ones. Thus, a supervisor can benefit from applying nonverbal communication skills when talking to employees. For example, the supervisor should use a well-modulated tone of voice and allow plenty of time for questions.

Most oral communication occurs face to face—in conversations, interviews, meetings, and formal presentations. (Meetings were discussed in Chapter 3.)

Ten Tips for Using Voice Mail

1. Speak slowly when leaving a message—and leave your phone number twice. The recipient shouldn't have to replay your message again and again.
2. Spell your name—so the recipient gets it right the first time.
3. Don't just leave your name and number—leave a message. You're much more likely to get a return call if the recipient knows what's up.
4. Make it quick. Take more than 60 seconds, and risk losing your audience.
5. Give your message a headline to help the recipient distinguish which calls are top priority.
6. Enunciate. The audio quality of voice mail varies dramatically. Speak up and state your business clearly.
7. Be specific about what you want. There's a good chance someone can leave the information you need on your voice mail, thus eliminating an unnecessary round of phone tag.
8. Avoid "thank-you" messages—they only add to voice mail overload and therefore are never welcome.
9. Keep your voice mail greeting short. If you must have a long greeting, tell the caller how to skip it in the future.
10. Don't leave repeat messages. Your second call is no more likely to be returned than your first. Try sending an e-mail instead.

The 10 Commandments of E-mail According to Intel

1. Don't use your inbox as a catchall folder for everything you need to work on. Read items once, and answer them immediately if necessary, delete them if possible, or move them to project-specific folders.
2. Set up a "Five Weeks Folder" that deletes its content automatically after five weeks. Use it as a repository for messages you're unsure about, such as that email you want to delete, but you're not sure if the guy's going to call you tomorrow and ask about it.
3. Assist colleagues' inbox-filtering efforts by agreeing on acronyms to use in subject lines that quickly identify action items and other important messages. Sample acronyms: <AR>, Action Required; <MSR>, Monthly Status Report.
4. Send group mail only when it is useful to *all* recipients. Use "reply-to-all" and "CC:" buttons sparingly.
5. Ask to be removed from distribution lists that you don't need to be on.
6. To cut down on pileup, use the "out-of-office" feature of your e-mail, in addition to your voice mail, to notify people when you are traveling.
7. When possible, send a message that is only a subject line, so recipients don't have to open the e-mail to read a single line. End the subject line with <EDM>, the acronym for End of Message.
8. Graphics and attachments are fun, but they slow down your ability to download messages when you're on the road. Use them sparingly.
9. If you're sending an attachment larger than 5 MB to a large group of recipients, consider putting it on the company's Web site or intranet instead.
10. Be specific. If you send a 20-page attachment, tell the recipient that the important information is on pages 2 and 17.

Sources: *Fast Company* by Quain and Alison Overholt. Copyright © 1998, 2001 by Business Innovator Group Resources/Inc. Reproduced with permission of Business Innovator Group Resources/Inc. via Copyright Clearance Center.

Technology offers an increasing selection of oral communication channels for people in different locations. We take telephone calls for granted; newer technologies include voice mail, teleconferencing, and videoconferencing.

Speaking before a group makes many supervisors nervous, but nervousness can be positive if it inspires supervisors to be well prepared.[14] Following these steps can help you to give a successful presentation:

1. Prepare a timeline of the steps you need to take, and mark the approximate date for each on your calendar to avoid procrastinating.

2. Find out something about your audience, as individuals if possible, or as a group. Assess what they already know and what they need to find out from you. What do they feel, and how can you motivate them?

3. Outline your presentation, including an effective opening. Begin with a brief story or an intriguing question. Try not to open with a joke.

4. Limit your main points—three is a reasonable number—and state them clearly as a preview of your presentation.

5. Use explicit transitions from each of your main points to the next, and sum up as you go along.

6. Move around the room (but don't pace), use natural gestures, and make eye contact with every part of the room. Vary your inflection and keep the audience involved. For instance, instead of saying, "The cashiers must wait for the stock workers to close," says, "Juan and Janet must wait for Cho and Mark before they close."

7. Use an effective closing that either refers back to your opening, summarizes your main points, or calls for action. Be considerate of your audience and end on time.

8. Still nervous? Remember that you can overcome most jitters by preparing, rehearsing (enlist a friend to practice on), checking and rechecking visual aids and audiovisual technology before you begin, and striking up a friendly conversation with someone who arrives early.

If you want more formal, in-depth help with speaking before a group, the organization may be willing to send you to one of the many training seminars available or to a speech class at a community college. Many people have benefited from participating in meetings of the Toastmasters organization. Practice not only can improve your public speaking skills but also diminish your anxiety.

The ability to speak confidently in any public setting is an important attribute for a supervisory or management career. William Converse relied on his communications skills to save his firm when the television show "Inside Edition" claimed that Alpine Industries' air purifiers actually polluted the air instead of cleaning it. With sales plummeting and a state investigation launched, Converse went on radio talk shows to counter the story.[15]

Written Communication   Many situations call for a record of what people tell one another. Therefore, much of the verbal communication that occurs in organizations is in writing. Common forms of written communication include memos, letters, reports, bulletin board notices, posters, and electronic messages.

Memos (short for *memoranda*) are an informal way to send a written message. At the top of the page, the sender types the date, receiver's name, sender's name, and subject matter. Because of their informality, memos lend themselves to communication within an organization.

People writing to someone outside the organization usually send a letter, which is more formal than a memo but has basically the same advantages and disadvantages. Both provide a written document for the receiver to review, and both take a relatively long time to prepare and deliver.

An analysis of how to meet a need or solve a problem takes the form of a report. A report describes the need or problem, then proposes a solution. Many reports contain charts and graphs to make the message easy to understand. Another helpful technique for a long report (more than two pages) is to start off with a paragraph that summarizes the contents. Busy managers can review what the report is about, even if they cannot read the full report right away.

Written messages also can be sent electronically by fax machine or e-mail. E-mail makes communication easier in many ways, but it has its complications, as we saw in the opening story about Neil Patterson of Cerner Corp. Another factor in the use of e-mail at work is privacy, or the lack of it. Many employers are aware that about 70 percent of all Internet surfing is done at work,[16] and the number of firms using electronic monitoring to check employees' e-mail, Internet, and phone use is growing. The American Management Association (AMA) recently reported that nearly 80 percent of major U.S. companies now do so, up from only 35 percent four years ago.[17]

E-mail and the use of the Internet are the most closely scrutinized activities, and about 25 percent of the firms in the AMA survey reported firing employees for misuse of electronic communications channels. One widely publicized incident occurred at Carlyle Group when a young new hire, transferred to the company's Seoul, South Korea, office, boasted by e-mail to a handful of former co-workers in New York about his lavish lifestyle and romantic exploits. The explicit message was forwarded to thousands of people on Wall Street and made its way to Carlyle's managers, whereupon the associate was forced to resign.[18]

To communicate a single message to many people, the organization may use posters and electronic or printed bulletin board notices. These are efficient but impersonal ways to send messages, so they usually supplement more personal types of communication. For example, if a factory's managers want to promote quality, they can use posters that say "Quality First." For the message to be effective, however, managers and supervisors also should praise individuals for doing quality work, discuss quality when evaluating performance, and set an example in the quality of their own work.

Wegman's Food Markets, Inc., is committed to diversity, and it uses an assortment of methods to get this message across to employees and customers alike. The firm's commitment statement is posted in all departments and break rooms and is displayed on the sales floor and printed on plastic shopping bags. A bulletin board about diversity is maintained in each store, and diversity was featured in a recent series of radio and television ads.[19]

Technology and Message Types

Developments in technology have provided an increasing number of ways to deliver messages. Among the more recent developments are e-mail, fax machines, teleconferencing, cellular phones, and videoconferencing.

These message types provide exciting options but make selecting a communications channel more difficult. Furthermore, the ability to send and receive information not only in the workplace but also in one's home, car, and airplane seat can contribute to the information overload described earlier in the chapter. Some employees may feel as if they are never able to fully leave their workplaces because they can be reached by fax or cellular phone wherever they are.

Choosing the Most Effective Message Type

With so many ways to send a message, which is the best for a supervisor to use? While face-to-face communication conveys the most information (words *plus* tone of voice *plus* body language *plus* immediate feedback), the most effective and efficient method for a message depends on the situation. Therefore, when deciding whether to call, meet with, or e-mail or fax a message to someone, the supervisor

SUPERVISION ACROSS INDUSTRIES

The Insurance Industry

Getting the Word Out at State Farm

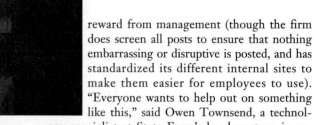

Diane Watkins probably didn't know that she was starting a communications revolution at State Farm Insurance, where she is a senior marketing specialist. Watkins, whose job is to help the company's sales agents improve their sales performance, simply decided to post her 10 most effective selling tips on the company's nationwide intranet. The results were startling.

Within just a few days, a dozen State Farm sales agents had read Watkins' "Best Practices" and posted tips of their own for others to see and use. In a couple of months, over 40 agents from around the country had joined an increasingly enthusiastic discussion on the message board Watkins had used, and hundreds more had read the comments.

A New York rep had suggested ways to get referrals in the Asian community. Other agents had discussed ways to persuade existing buyers of auto insurance to consider some of the company's other products. All this took place without any gimmick or reward from management (though the firm does screen all posts to ensure that nothing embarrassing or disruptive is posted, and has standardized its different internal sites to make them easier for employees to use). "Everyone wants to help out on something like this," said Owen Townsend, a technology specialist at State Farm's headquarters, in explaining the success of Watkins' initial post in sparking so many rich discussions. "People like seeing their names in print."

Like Watkins, supervisors in other areas can learn to get the most from communication technology. Among the reasons her simple idea worked to encourage useful communication via State Farm's intranet were: She posted information everyone could benefit from, her message was succinct and easy to absorb, there was a means for feedback, and everyone could participate.

Source: George Anders, "Best Practice: Inside Job," *Fast Company*, September 2001, pp. 177–185.

---

should consider time and cost limits, the complexity and sensitivity of the issue, the need for a record of the communication, the need for feedback, and the capabilities of the audience.

Time and Cost Limits   When the supervisor needs to reach someone in a hurry, a letter or memo may be too time-consuming. An employee might be easy to find at his or her desk or on the shop floor. Often, the fastest way to reach someone in the organization is to make a telephone call.

Modern technology shortens the time required to send messages. Fax, e-mail, and voice mail allow a supervisor to contact people who are away from the telephone much of the day or who are taking other calls. However, these technologies do not ensure that messages will be *received* quickly, because it is the receiver who decides when to pick up the fax or retrieve messages from voice mail or e-mail.

Like time, costs place some limits on the choice of communications media. When people who need to discuss an issue are located far apart, the costs of a videoconference may be less than the costs of bringing everyone together. For that reason, VeriFone, which provides credit card verification services, uses videoconferencing for initial interviews of job candidates (then flies in those who will receive follow-up interviews) and supplements visits to customers with quick updates through videoconferences.[20]

Complexity and Sensitivity of the Issue   A complex message is clearer if written. For example, the results of a survey or the analysis of a work group's performance are easier to understand in a written report. In a meeting, an oral report will be clearer if supplemented with written handouts, slides, posters, or overhead transparencies. When speed is critical in communicating complex information to someone outside the organization, it may be cost-effective to use a fax machine or a computer modem.

For emotionally charged issues or when the state of mind of employees is at issue, communicators need the information that comes from tone of voice, gestures, and facial expressions. Such information is also essential for assessing how well employees (especially new ones) are doing. Written communications such as e-mail are thus best-suited for objective messages. In contrast, sarcasm, humor, and emotion-laden messages are likely to be misinterpreted by receivers of e-mail. To avoid such problems, technology-savvy VeriFone bans the use of arguments and sarcasm on e-mail.[21]

The more sensitive a message or situation, the more opportunity there should be for nonverbal communication. Telephone calls, voice mail, and audio e-mail messages provide information through vocal tones. Most information, of course, comes from communicating face to face. Holding a one-on-one or group meeting allows the message sender to defuse anger and dispel misconceptions. It gives the receivers a chance to air their feelings and ask questions. For example, a supervisor who needs to discipline an employee must ensure that the employee understands the problem and has a chance to present his or her point of view. Similarly, an announcement of layoffs or restructuring should be made in person.

Need for a Record   As you will learn in Chapter 13, a disciplinary action calls for a written record as well as a face-to-face meeting. A supervisor needs to combine a written message with oral communication. Other actions that call for written records include placing an order and establishing goals for an employee or department.

Need for Feedback   The easiest way to get feedback is to send an oral message. The listeners at the meeting or on the telephone can respond immediately with comments and questions. If feedback is critical, face-to-face communication is more effective than a telephone conversation because the person delivering the message can watch facial expressions as well as hear reactions. Do people look confused, excited, angry, satisfied? If a supervisor explaining a new procedure says, "Do you understand?" and the employee responds with a doubtful "I guess so," a supervisor knows that an example or some other clarification is needed.

Capabilities of the Receiver   People will receive a message only if it comes through a channel they feel comfortable using. In many settings, for example, some employees lack reading skills. If a supervisor believes that an employee cannot read the message, he or she will need to find ways to deliver it through the spoken word, pictures, gestures, or some other means of communication. This situation arises when an employee cannot read at all or reads too poorly to understand a particular message. Some employees may read well in other languages but not in English; in such a case, the supervisor may want to make written messages available in other languages.

The issue of illiteracy is a sensitive one. Supervisors therefore must be tactful and look carefully for signs that employees have trouble reading. Employees with reading difficulties are typically embarrassed about this problem and try to hide it.

A potentially more widespread concern is the comfort and skill in using modern technology. Some people feel frustrated or angry when a voice mail system answers the telephone. Supervisors can help by recording an answering message that offers information such as when to expect a return call and how to reach an operator or secretary. Likewise, information offered online will seem convenient to some and inaccessible to others.

Communicating in Organizations

In business, government, and other organizations, communication tends to follow certain patterns. Understanding these patterns can help the supervisor make the best use of them.

Direction of Communication

downward communication
Organizational communication in which a message is sent to someone at a lower level.

Think back to the organization charts in Chapter 7. When someone sends a message to a person at a lower level, **downward communication** is occurring. A supervisor is receiving a downward communication when listening to instructions or an evaluation from his or her manager or when reading a memo from top management describing a new company policy. The supervisor is sending a downward communication when he or she discusses a problem with an employee or tells an employee how to perform a task. Employees expect to receive enough downward communication in order to understand how to do their jobs, and they typically like to know enough so that they understand what is going on.

upward communication
Organizational communication in which a message is sent to someone at a higher level.

When someone sends a message to a person at a higher level, **upward communication** is occurring. A supervisor is receiving an upward communication when an employee asks a question or reports a problem. A supervisor is sending an upward communication when he or she tells the manager how work is progressing or asks for a raise. Managers especially want to receive upward communications about controversial matters or matters affecting their own performance.

To be well informed and to benefit from employees' creativity, a supervisor should encourage upward communication. Writer and business consultant Denis Waitley advises sales managers to spend more time listening to their salespeople. Not only will sales managers get answers to their questions, but also they will help to create an organization that is continually learning and improving from the ideas of its people.[22]

A supervisor can enhance upward communication by applying the strategies for effective listening. A supervisor should respond to employees so they know their messages have been received. Another means of encouraging upward communication is to establish a formal way, such as a suggestion box, for employees to provide comments and suggestions. As part of an effort to institute total quality management, supervisors at the distribution branch of a major manufacturer of high-tech equipment began to meet once a month with each of their employees. These sessions are for sharing information, clarifying work priorities, and making supervisors aware of employee activities and abilities. A year into the program, the monthly meetings had helped to improve employee views of supervision and communications in the division.[23]

lateral communication
Organizational communication in which a message is sent to a person at the same level.

A message sent to a person at the same level is **lateral communication.** Supervisors send and receive lateral communications when they discuss their needs with co-workers in other departments, coordinate their group's work with that of other supervisors, and socialize with their peers at the company.

Why should a supervisor need to know about the directions of communication? One way a supervisor can use this information is to be sure that he or she is participating in communication in all directions: enough downward communication so that employees know what is expected of them and the supervisor understands what is happening in the organization; enough upward communication so that his or her manager is aware of the supervisor's accomplishments and employees feel encouraged to offer ideas; and enough lateral communication so that the work of the supervisor's department is well coordinated with the work of other departments.

Formal and Informal Communication

The communication that follows the lines of the organization chart is known as **formal communication,** which is directed toward accomplishing the goals of the organization. For example, when a supervisor discusses an employee's performance with that employee, the supervisor is helping the employee to perform high-quality work. When a supervisor gives the manager a report of the department's weekly activities, the supervisor is helping the manager perform his or her responsibilities for controlling.

However, much of the communication that occurs in an organization is directed toward meeting people's individual needs. For example, managers and employees alike may spend time discussing the performance of their favorite sports teams, the behavior of their children, and good places to eat lunch. This type of communication is called **informal communication.**

Gossip and Rumors

Much informal communication takes the form of gossip and rumors. Gossip is like small talk but centers around people. People use gossip to indicate what behavior is acceptable. Thus, employees gossiping about who got promoted or who is dating the new supervisor in the payroll department are typically airing and refining their views about promotion policies and love affairs between co-workers.

Rumors are explanations, sometimes unfounded, for what is going on around us. For example, if a factory gets a visit from the company's board of directors, employees at the factory may spread rumors that the factory is to be sold or the operations moved to South Korea. When people are afraid, they spread rumors to ease their fear while trying to get at the facts. Thus, rumors tend to circulate chiefly during crises and conflicts—and they are often false.

Although rumors and gossip are a fact of life in the workplace, it does not look good for a supervisor to participate in spreading either. As a member of management, a supervisor is expected to know and report the facts about company business. When a supervisor spreads gossip or rumors, word eventually will get around that he or she is responsible for the message. The following guidelines are useful to keep rumors and gossip under control[24]:

- Do not share any personal information about other employees, including your desire or intention to criticize or discipline an employee. Discuss the matters with others only when they truly need to know, such as discussing a personnel matter with your manager or someone in the human resources department.
- When you hear company information, such as plans for expansion or cutbacks, keep it to yourself until the organization makes an official announcement.

formal communication Organizational communication that is work-related and follows the lines of the organization chart.

informal communication Organizational communication that is directed toward individual needs and interests and does not necessarily follow formal lines of communication.

Otherwise, you could embarrass yourself and upset your manager or employees if the information is inaccurate or the plans fall through.

- If you hear a rumor, investigate it and find out the truth and the cause. The rumor may be a tip-off that employees are worried or angry about something, and it is the supervisor's job to address those concerns.

grapevine
The path along which informal communication travels.

The Grapevine   The path along which informal communication travels is known as the **grapevine.** The grapevine is important to supervisors because employees use it as a source of information. Thus, a supervisor must expect that employees sometimes have information before the supervisor has delivered it. Supervisors also must realize that employees may be getting incorrect information through the grapevine, especially in times of crisis or conflict.

When supervisors and employees work different hours, maintaining good communication can be particularly difficult. According to a recent survey by Coleman Consulting Group, which focuses on 24-hour business that employs shift workers, nearly 70 percent of such firms reported major communication breakdowns between management and shift workers. The poll surveyed more than 22,000 employees and found that their communication with management had declined to the status of grapevine information in nearly 90 percent of the cases. Just 11 percent reported receiving information directly from their supervisors, and 59 percent inferred that management did not really care about them.[25]

The grapevine springs up on its own, and managers are generally unable to control it. However, knowing about the grapevine can help the supervisor seek out and correct misinformation. The supervisor also can take some steps to see that at least some of the messages in the grapevine are positive and in line with the organization's objectives[26]:

- Regularly use the tools of formal communication to inform employees of the organization's version of events.
- Be open to discussion; be someone employees will turn to when they want a rumor confirmed or denied.
- Use performance appraisal interviews as a way to listen to employees as well as to give them information.
- Have a trusted employee act as a source of information about the messages traveling the grapevine.
- When it is necessary to clear the air, issue a formal response to a rumor.

Furthermore, if supervisors and other managers are exercising their leadership skills to create an environment in which employees can and want to make a positive contribution, both formal and informal communication are important. Supervisors will want to encourage communication among employees so that they can improve the ways they work together.

That was the goal of Lou Hoffman, who heads a San Jose, California, public relations firm. To spur more informal communication among the firm's 18 employees, Hoffman announced he would pay for the lunch of any two employees who ate together at the nearest restaurant. Furthermore, he divided the employees into two groups and offered a gift certificate to anyone who had lunch with each person in the other group. Everyone won a certificate, and Hoffman claims employees have begun solving more of their problems together, rather than expecting him to mediate every dispute.[27]

Summary

10.1 Describe the process of communication.
The communication process occurs when people send and receive information. It begins when someone encodes a message by putting it into words or nonverbal cues. The sender of the message transmits it by speaking or writing. Then the receiver of the message decodes, or interprets, it. Usually the receiver gives the sender feedback.

10.2 Distinguish between hearing and listening.
Hearing occurs when the brain registers sounds. Listening occurs when the person who hears sounds also pays attention and tries to understand the message.

10.3 Describe techniques for communicating effectively.
Effective communication is most likely to occur when the parties communicate from the receiver's viewpoint, learn from feedback, use strategies for effective listening, and overcome barriers to communication. To listen effectively, the listener should make a commitment to listen, set aside time for listening, and then concentrate on the message. The listener also should try to control his or her emotions, not letting an emotional reaction interfere with understanding. Active listening involves hearing what the speaker is saying, seeking to understand the facts and feelings the speaker is trying to convey, and stating what one understands the message to be.

Supervisors also should be prepared for cultural differences in order to communicate effectively. They should stick to simple words, avoid jargon, speak slowly, give the listener time to ask questions, ask for clarification, and learn about the communication styles of different cultures.

10.4 Identify barriers to communication and suggest ways to avoid them.
Barriers to communication include information overload, misunderstandings, perceptions and prejudices, and biases related to perception. Ways to avoid these barriers include giving employees only the information they need, encoding messages carefully and simply, observing feedback, avoiding name-calling, being aware of inferences and prejudices, and phrasing messages to appeal to the receiver.

10.5 Distinguish between verbal and nonverbal messages, and name types of verbal messages.
Verbal messages consist of words. Nonverbal messages are messages encoded without words, such as facial expressions, gestures, or tone of voice. Types of verbal messages include face-to-face discussions, telephone calls, memos, letters, reports, e-mail messages, faxes, and videoconferences.

10.6 Identify the directions in which communication can flow in an organization.
Organizational communication may flow upward, downward, or laterally. Upward communication travels to the sender's superior. Downward communication travels from manager to employees. Lateral communication flows between people at the same level.

10.7 Distinguish between formal and informal communication in an organization.
Formal communication travels along the lines of the organizational chart and is related to accomplishing the goals of the organization. Informal communication may travel in any direction between any members of the organization. It tends to be aimed at achieving personal, rather than organizational, objectives.

10.8 Describe the role of the grapevine in organizations.
The grapevine is the path of much of the organization's informal communications. Much of the information that travels through the grapevine is gossip and rumors. The supervisor generally cannot control this flow of information but should be aware that it exists and that he or she may have to correct misinformation. In addition, by encouraging communication with his or her employees, a supervisor may be able to ensure that some of the messages in the grapevine are positive.

Key Terms

communication, p. 239	prejudices, p. 252	lateral communication, p. 260
noise, p. 240	verbal message, p. 252	formal communication, p. 261
feedback, p. 240	nonverbal message, p. 252	informal communication, p. 261
active listening, p. 244	downward communication, p. 260	grapevine, p. 262
inference, p. 250	upward communication, p. 260	
perceptions, p. 251		

Review and Discussion Questions

1. Phyllis Priestley, a supervisor, wants to tell her boss what she plans to accomplish at a leadership seminar she will be attending next week. She decides to do so in the form of a memo. Briefly describe how this communication will follow the model shown in Figure 10.1.

2. Can a person be hearing but not listening well? Can a person be listening but not hearing well? Explain.

3. Every Monday morning, Ron Yamamoto, a supervisor, must attend a divisional meeting to discuss progress and make plans. Ron finds that most people at the meetings are long-winded and that the meetings as a whole are boring. However, he needs to know what is going on in the division. How can Ron listen effectively, even though he is bored?

4. Sheila James owns her own catering business employing four workers. She just got a contract to cater a wedding reception for a Chinese couple who speak very little English. What steps can Sheila take to make sure her communication with the couple is successful? As a supervisor, what steps might Sheila take with her employees to make sure they understand the couple's wishes as well?

5. In a staff meeting held to introduce new software that will provide office employees with information about the company's financial status, sales figures, and marketing plans, you notice that one of your employees is alternately staring out the window and doodling in his notebook. You are certain he is not paying attention. What barrier to communication might be occurring here? What steps might you take as a supervisor to overcome it?

6. The following examples describe some ways to send messages. Indicate whether each is verbal or nonverbal. For each verbal message, indicate whether it is oral or written.
   a. A long silence accompanied by an icy stare.
   b. A letter delivered by fax machine.
   c. Voice mail.
   d. Laughter.

7. As mail room supervisor, you need to report to your manager that a sack of mail has been misplaced (you are not sure how it happened). Would you want to send this message through written or oral communication? Would you want to deliver it face to face?
   Describe the form of communication you would choose and why you would choose it.

8. Nina Goldberg has been asked by her manager to give a presentation to employees about changes the company is going to make in health care benefits. Using the five steps described in this chapter, how should Nina go about preparing her presentation?

9. Face-to-face communication conveys the most information because the people communicating can learn from each other's body language and tone of voice as well as from the words themselves. However, why shouldn't a supervisor always choose face-to-face communication over other ways?

10. Lee Hamel is a busy supervisor. He rarely hears from his employees except when there is a production snag or scheduling problem. Lee figures that as long as things run smoothly, his employees are happy. Why might Lee's attitude be counterproductive in the long run?

What steps could he take to improve upward communication from his employees?

11. Which of the following organizational communications are formal? Informal?

    a. A memo providing information about the company picnic.

    b. A meeting at which employees discuss the department's goals for the month.

    c. A rumor about a new vacation policy.

    d. A discussion between a supervisor and an employee about who will win the World Series.

12. Should a supervisor participate in informal communication? If so, when? If not, why not?

A SECOND LOOK

In how many directions did Carol Roberts at International Paper need to communicate in order to make her point about performance feedback?

SKILLS MODULE

CASE

Communication: Right from the Start

Perhaps there is no more important time for a supervisor to communicate with an employee than on the employee's first day at the job. Many companies are beginning to recognize this, putting more and more emphasis on the formal communication known as orientation. Orientation involves mostly downward communication, showing the employee the "ropes" of the organization; but it also fosters upward communication.

At Great Plains Software in Fargo, North Dakota, new employees start out with an automatic three-month orientation period. They take eight classes in topics that range from e-mail to benefits to the company's overall vision. (Great Plains avoids the problem of information overload by dispensing with tedious hours of filling out forms and forcing new workers to read long policy manuals.) In addition, each new employee is teamed up with a more senior employee who acts as a designated "coach."

At the end of the program, the new hire's supervisor collects feedback from peers and the coach, then meets with the employee to discuss his or her future at Great Plains. Thus, the orientation program fosters formal and informal communication, as well as communication in all organizational directions. Lynn Dreyer, former vice president of human resources, claims that this program of communication fosters a "solid, long-term commitment to the company," unlike the one-day orientation that employees used to receive.

Other companies also have picked up on the importance of communication right from the start. Some, such as Southwest Airlines and Rosenbluth International, foster communication in even more unconventional ways than Great Plains. At Rosenbluth (a travel-services organization), new hires attend formal presentations at the Philadelphia headquarters; then they play communication games with each other; finally, they are served high tea by the CEO and other senior executives. "It lets [new employees] know that they really *do*

come first," explains Diane McFerrin Peters, a consultant for the company.

Southwest's orientation includes scavenger hunts and the organization's own version of "Wheel of Fortune." "People aren't just sitting around like giant sponges absorbing too much information," says Vice President Libby Sartain. Still, the needed information does travel to new hires. Underlying the party atmosphere is a highly structured program of formal communication: a history of the airline, a description of the company's vision, an outline of necessary customer care, and a listing of benefits.

After orientation, positive informal communication is encouraged through a buddy system. Each new hire is matched with an old hand in the Co-Hearts program. "It's somebody to have lunch with, to bounce ideas off of—a friend in the company," notes Sartain. Thus, good communication takes off right from the start.

1. Do you think these new approaches to communication through orientation will have a long-term effect on employees' performance at Great Plains, Rosenbluth, and Southwest? Why or why not?
2. The Co-Hearts program at Southwest encourages positive informal communication. How might it backfire?
3. What message do you think Rosenbluth's high tea service sends to employees? What steps must Rosenbluth's management take to make sure the gesture is effective?
4. "We try not to take ourselves too seriously," says Southwest Vice President Libby Sartain. What nonverbal signals might reveal the meaning of her message?

■ S E L F - Q U I Z

Are You an Effective Listener?

On the line before each statement, score yourself on a scale of 1 (seldom) to 10 (usually) to indicate how often that statement is true about you. Be as truthful as you can in light of your behavior in the last few meetings or gatherings you have attended.

_____   1. I listen to one conversation at a time.

_____   2. I like to hear people's impressions and feelings, as well as the facts of a situation.

_____   3. I really pay attention to people; I don't just pretend.

_____   4. I consider myself a good judge of nonverbal communications.

_____   5. I don't assume I know what another person is going to say before he or she says it.

_____   6. I look for what is important in a person's message, rather than assuming it is uninteresting and ending the conversation.

_____   7. I frequently nod, make eye contact, or whatever to let the speaker know I am listening.

_____   8. When someone has finished talking, I consider the meaning of his or her message before responding.

_____   9. I let the other person finish before reaching conclusions about the message.

_____   10. I wait to formulate a response until the other person has finished talking.

_____   11. I listen for content, regardless of the speaker's "delivery" style.

_____   12. I usually ask people to clarify what they have said, rather than guess at the meaning.

_____   13. I make a concerted effort to understand other people's points of view.

_____   14. I listen for what the person really is saying, not what I expect to hear.

_____   15. When I disagree with someone, the person feels that I have understood his or her point of view.

Total score: Add your total points. According to communication theory, if you scored 131–150 points, you strongly approve of your own listening habits, and you are on the right track to becoming an effective listener. If you scored 111–130, you have uncovered some doubts about your listening effectiveness, and your knowledge of how to listen has some gaps. If you scored 110 or less, you probably are not satisfied with the way you listen, and your friends and co-workers may not feel you are a good listener either. Work on improving your listening skills.

Source: From *Supervisory Management* by AMA. Copyright 1989 by American Management Association. Reproduced with permission of American Management Association via Copyright Clearance Center.

Class Exercise

You learned many principles in this chapter to help you improve your communication skills. This exercise reviews six of those principles and gives you a chance to see how you can use them to improve supervisory communications.

Instructions

1. Review the following list of communication principles:

   a. Use feedback to verify that your message has been received accurately.

   b. Practice active listening.

   c. Select appropriate method for sending your message.

   d. Be tuned in to nonverbal messages.

   e. Be well prepared when speaking before a group.

   f. Understand the important role of informal communication in the workplace, particularly rumors, gossip, and the grapevine.

2. Read the scenarios and determine which of the communication principles the supervisor violated. In each blank provided, write the letter of that principle from the list in step 1. The principle you choose should indicate the one that the supervisor could have used to achieve a more positive outcome. (*Hint:* Each principle will be used only once; there is one *most* correct answer for each.)

Scenario	Principle
On Tuesday afternoon, the plant manager gave each of the 12 supervisors throughout the plant a five-page document that spelled out some changes in the employee handbook that would be effective the following month. The plant manager instructed the supervisors to call departmental meetings sometime within the next three days to present the changes to their own staff. Jeff sent out a notice to his employees to be at a 45-minute meeting on Thursday afternoon. Several unexpected events occurred that demanded most of Jeff's time during the next two days. Jeff did manage to make it to the meeting; however, he had only a few minutes beforehand to skim the document. He ended up mostly reading aloud from the document at the meeting.	1. _____
Pete went to talk to his supervisor about a personal problem. He left the meeting feeling that he hadn't gotten through to his supervisor, who seemed preoccupied and distracted throughout their entire conversation.	2. _____
Sid was on his way out the door to meet a customer for a business lunch at a local restaurant. He stopped long enough to give about 90 seconds of hurried instructions on a task he needed one of his employees to do for a P.M. deadline that same day. Sid finished his instructions by glancing at his watch and saying, "I'm going to be late for my luncheon appointment. You got everything OK, didn't you?" The employee mumbled, "Yeah, I guess so," and Sid was out the door.	3. _____
Krista overheard one of the employees in her department telling someone on the phone that he had heard from a reliable source that the company was going to pink-slip 10 percent of the employees on Friday. Krista shook her	4. _____

head in disgust and thought to herself, "Another ridiculous rumor. With all the rumors floating around this place, I could spend all my time dispelling rumors. I'll let this one die a natural death on Friday; I don't have time to deal with it right now."

Shannon had a long "to do" list for the day and decided to dispense with as many items as she could first thing in the morning by using the e-mail system. She had gotten rid of six tasks by sending messages to the appropriate people. She sent a seventh message that contained confidential information about one of her employees. The next day Shannon's manager spoke with her about a negative situation that had arisen as a result of her seventh message being accessed by some people who should not have seen it. He told her to consider more carefully the messages she chose to send via e-mail.

5. _____

Michael had decided to delegate an important project to Susan, his most capable employee. He called Susan to go over some of the specifics of the project—one that he saw as a great opportunity for her to show higher management what she was capable of doing. Susan, however, did not share Michael's enthusiasm about her new work assignment. Michael ignored her expressionless face, and chose to respond to her verbal responses. For example, when he asked her whether she agreed this was an exciting project, she responded after a few seconds of silence with a mere yes.

6. _____

Source: This class exercise was prepared by Corinne Livesay, Belhaven College, Jackson, Mississippi.

Team-Building Exercise

Divide the class into groups of at least three people. In each group, decide on a scenario to consist of three sentences as follows:

1. The words, "I don't think that's right."
2. The sentence that came before it.
3. The sentence that came after it.

Also determine the physical setting and situation in which the sentences were spoken.

Let each group act out its scenario for the class. When all the scenarios have been presented, discuss the following:

• How did the context or situation change the meaning of "I don't think that's right?"

• How did the nonverbal behavior and setting differ in each scene?
• How could each group's "I don't think that's right" be paraphrased into a different sentence?
• Which component communicated the most information about the meaning of the scene—the words, the nonverbal behavior, or the situation?

Source: Adapted from Isa N. Engelberg and Dianna R. Wyann, *Working in Groups: Communication Strategies and Principles* (Boston: Houghton Mifflin, 1997).

11

In business, willingness is just as important as ability.
—**Paul G. Hoffman**

Motivating Employees

■ CHAPTER OUTLINE

■ LEARNING OBJECTIVES

After you have studied this chapter, you should be able to:

11.1 Identify the relationship between motivation and performance.

11.2 Describe content theories of motivation.

11.3 Describe process theories of motivation.

11.4 Explain when financial incentives are likely to motivate employees.

11.5 Describe pay plans using financial incentives.

11.6 Discuss the pros and cons of keeping pay information secret.

11.7 Identify ways supervisors can motivate their employees.

■ MILK AND COOKIES, ANYONE?

Every two weeks, when the consultants who work for Digital Pilot, a Dallas software firm, come to the office to meet with company president, Ronald Paige, and present their field reports, they are greeted by a tray of milk and cookies. The unusual snack is meant to disarm any reservations the team might have about speaking up during the meeting. Radical thinking is encouraged, and stories of failures as well as successes with such clients as IBM, Coopers & Lybrand, and USData Corporation are welcomed. "Around here, 'positive' doesn't mean 'perfect.' We want the good, the bad, and the ugly," says Paige, "as long as we can learn from it."

Each consultant gets a turn to tell stories of his or her most recent exploits in the field. The atmosphere is informal, but everyone knows the communications are important. Consultants who have distinguished themselves with the kind of bold thinking and risk taking the company encourages are rewarded with a Kudos candy bar tossed onto the table by the president. The motivational device may be unique but it seems to be working. Ronald says no one ever seems to eat the candy bars. They remain on employees' desks as a kind of trophy "because people are so damn proud of them."

Source: Cathy Olofson, "Milk & Cookies—and Kudos for Ideas," *Fast Company*, November 1998, p. 82.

motivation
Giving people incentives that cause them to act in desired ways.

Giving people incentives that cause them to act in desired ways is known as **motivation.** Among other things, supervisors must motivate their employees to do good work, to complete assignments on time, and to have good attendance. At Digital Pilot, the snacks and candy bars are a light-hearted but effective way to motivate the employees.

When employees are motivated and also have the ability—the necessary skills, equipment, supplies, and time—they are able to perform well (see Figure 11.1). Thus, the objective of motivating employees is to lead them to perform in ways that meet the goals of the department and the organization. Because supervisors are evaluated largely on the basis of how well their group as a whole performs, motivation is an important skill for supervisors to acquire.

How the supervisor can make good use of the link between employees' objectives and their performance is discussed in this chapter. Theories of what motivates employees and how the motivation process works are described, legal issues are identified, and the role of money as a motivator is discussed. Finally, practical ways that supervisors can motivate employees are suggested.

How Does Motivation Work?

"What's wrong with these people?" exclaimed Martha Wong about the sales clerks she supervises in the shoe department. "We pay them good wages, but when we hit a busy season like this, nobody's willing to put forth the extra effort

■ FIGURE 11.1

The Effect of Motivation on Performance

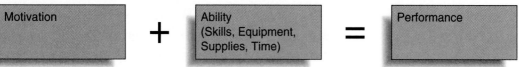

we need—giving up a break once in a while or even just moving a little faster." Martha needs to figure out what to do so that employees will *want* to keep customers happy during busy periods. Perhaps they expect more money, or perhaps they want something else, such as a feeling of being part of a team.

Imagine that supervisors like Martha could know exactly what motivates employees. For example, imagine that all salespeople are motivated solely by the money they earn and that social scientists have devised an accurate formula to determine how much money the company must pay to get a given amount of selling. Suppose that all secretaries are motivated by flexible work hours and all production workers are motivated by recognition from the plant manager. A company that knew this would be in a position to devise the kinds of rewards that employees want. The supervisor could hand out the rewards and would know that if employees had the necessary skills, they would do good work.

Of course, no such simple knowledge about motivation exists. Instead, supervisors have to rely on a variety of theories that social scientists have developed. None of the theories are perfect, proven explanations of how to get employees to behave in a certain way, but all give supervisors some guidance. Familiarity with the best-known theories can help supervisors think of ways to motivate their employees.

Content Theories

Some theories of motivation have focused on what things motivate workers. These are called content theories because they focus on the content of the motivators. Although money is the motivator that comes most readily to mind, some people respond more to other sources of satisfaction. To help you think about what motivates *you*, try the Self-Quiz at the end of this chapter (page 293).

Three researchers whose content theories of motivation are widely used are Abraham Maslow, David McClelland, and Frederick Herzberg.

Maslow's Hierarchy of Needs   Psychologist Abraham Maslow assumed that people are motivated by unmet needs. When a person's need for something is not met, the person feels driven, or motivated, to meet that need. To give a basic example, a person who needs food feels hungry and therefore eats something.

According to Maslow's theory, the needs that motivate people fall into five basic categories:

1. Physiological needs are needs required for survival: food, water, sex, and shelter.
2. Security needs keep you free from harm. In modern society, these might include insurance, medical checkups, and a home in a safe neighborhood.

■ FIGURE 11.2

Maslow's Hierarchy of Needs

3. Social needs include the desire for love, friendship, and companionship. People seek to satisfy these needs through the time they spend with family, friends, and co-workers.
4. Esteem needs are the needs for self-esteem and the respect of others. Acceptance and praise are two ways these needs are met.
5. Self-actualization needs describe the desire to live up to your full potential. People on the path to meeting these needs will not only be doing their best at work and at home but also will be developing mentally, spiritually, and physically.

Maslow argues that these needs are organized into a hierarchy (see Figure 11.2). The most basic needs are at the bottom of the hierarchy. People try to satisfy these needs first. At the top of the hierarchy are the needs people try to satisfy only when they have met most of their other needs. However, people may be seeking to meet more than one category of needs at a time.

Based on this view, people tend to rely on their jobs to meet most of their physiological and security needs through paychecks and benefits such as health insurance. Needs higher on the hierarchy can be satisfied in many places. For example, people satisfy some of their social needs through their relationships with family and friends outside of work, and they may seek to meet their self-actualization needs through volunteer work or membership in a religious organization. Nevertheless, people can also satisfy higher-level needs in the workplace. An employee who is applauded for solving a difficult problem or who takes pride in skillfully performing a craft such as carpentry is meeting some higher-level needs at work.

The rise of corporate social responsibility efforts combined with increasing need for volunteerism in many communities is allowing some firms to meet employees' higher-level needs with organized opportunities to do good. For instance, nonprofit groups in California's Orange County benefited from the efforts of more than 30,000 local employees who tackled more than 100 projects in the Volunteer Center's 2001 annual Volunteer Connection Day. Home Depot workers by the hundred repaired homes for the needy, and a group of hotel workers at Brea Embassy Suites collected diapers for needy mothers. Other employees of firms around the country work in soup kitchens, package and ship donated food, give time to counsel teens and seniors, raise funds for causes, and clean beaches and community parks. Said Monica Warthen, community relationships manager for Experian, an international computer services firm whose employees are active volunteers, "We believe that giving employees the opportunity to do things beyond their day-to-day work makes them more well-rounded, and therefore they feel better about their jobs and they're happier employees."[1]

Maslow's hierarchy is a widely cited view of motivation, but it has shortcomings. Critics (including Maslow himself) have noted that the theory is based on clinical work with neurotic patients and was not tested much for relevance to the work setting.[2] Are the needs identified by Maslow really all-inclusive? Do they describe people of many cultures, or just the majority of U.S. workers? The lack of studies investigating the hierarchy of needs makes it impossible to answer such questions with certainty. However, the popularity of Maslow's theory implies that it can be helpful in offering suggestions about what motivates people.

Applied to a work situation, Maslow's theory means that the supervisor must be aware of the current needs of particular employees. During a serious recession, a factory supervisor may find that many employees are highly motivated just to keep their jobs so they can pay their bills. In contrast, employees who are less worried about keeping a job may respond well to efforts to meet social needs.

At Nickelodeon, for instance, the offices themselves are designed to motivate employees by recognizing their creative contribution to the hot kids' television network. The décor is an explosion of bright, crayon colors and the walls are made of inviting surfaces like chalkboard, cord, and magnetic steel on which employees can display random thoughts, wild ideas, and jokes. Each show or department has its own brand, and its part of the office space has its own unique personality. "You don't think of it as a place where you come to work," says Nickelodeon's president Herb Scannell. "You think of it as a place where you come to play."[3]

In this era of increasing numbers of single parents and two-income families in the workforce, a practical concern of many employees is their need for flexibility in their work hours to balance the demands of home and work. Some organizations have responded with "family-friendly" policies, which typically include flexible work arrangements such as the following:

flextime
A policy that grants employees some leeway in choosing which 8 hours a day or which 40 hours a week to work.

job sharing
An arrangement in which two part-time employees share the duties of one full-time job.

- **Flextime**—This is a policy that grants employees some leeway in choosing which 8 hours a day or which 40 hours a week to work.
- *Part-time work*—For employees who can afford to work less than full time, this option frees them to spend more time meeting other needs. It is economically appealing to organizations because few offer a full range of benefits to part-time employees.
- **Job sharing**—To create part-time jobs, two employees share the duties of a single position.
- *Telecommuting*—Some employees can and want to work from home, keeping in touch by means of computer and telephone lines.

Harry Cedarbaum is a firm believer in job rotation, a new work time option offered by his employer, Booz, Allen & Hamilton, Inc., in New York. Caught between three children, a demanding job, and ailing parents who live in Europe, Harry needed to make time to help his parents close up their business. Booz Allen's new job rotation plan assigned him to a post as a recruiter at Columbia University, which allowed him to work fewer hours and help his parents out while still maintaining his employment with the firm. Although he received frequent job

SUPERVISION AND DIVERSITY

Accounting for Women

Before a 1996 research study, the intense environment at the accounting firm of Ernst & Young was creating unusually high turnover among the women it hired. Too many women employees were leaving every year, after struggling to reconcile the stress of the job with demands at home. Hiring and training replacements cost the firm $150,000 per person, and the replacements were often men. Supervisors recognized that such high turnover wasn't good for client relations, not to mention women who wanted to make accounting their career.

So Ernst & Young made some new ground rules for two of its California offices. Some of the changes included authorizing nontraditional ways for employees to entertain customers, such as family picnics and baseball outings, even an occasional manicure for a female client, instead of the traditionally male golf outings. Another new rule prohibits professionals from checking e-mail or voice mail over the weekend, a much more difficult challenge than it might seem for employees used to a high-pressure environment. Now, even if this rule means that a client has

to wait until Monday, the firm wants its people to have the weekends for themselves and their families.

A new casual dress policy is in effect, and supervisors are hiring more qualified administrative staff to lighten some of the workload of accountants. If an employee is still struggling to meet too many demands, projects are reassigned. When it evaluates each client's profitability to the firm, Ernst & Young is taking into account the stress on its employees and the potential rate of turnover each project might entail. The firm also has an in-house women's network that it may even expand to include former staffers. The hope is that the new definition of work will prevent women from leaving the firm in such high numbers, and that the firm's women and men will all have saner lives.

Source: Keith H. Hammonds and Gabrielle Saveri, "Accountants Have Lives, Too, You Know," *Business Week*, February 23, 1998, pp. 88, 90; Toddi Gunter, "Weaving an Old-Girls Network," *Business Week*, July 9, 2001, p. 115.

offers from other firms, Harry said, "I made a commitment to [Booz Allen], and they made a commitment to me. This loyalty is an incredible thing."[4]

The view among many human resources experts is that family-friendly policies are an important way to get and keep the best workers. "I think the concept is so simple," says Kathleen Sebelius, commissioner of the Kansas Insurance Department, referring to the department's policy that allows four-month-old Kallan Justice Gonzales to spend the day in his mother Julie's office. "It just allows a parent to be a caregiver. . . . Parents don't have to make choices about, 'Am I a parent or am I a worker?' "[5]

By a recent account, over 40 percent of employers offer flexible scheduling in some form.[6] See "Supervision and Diversity" for another way that firms are using family-friendly policies to motivate.

McClelland's Achievement-Power-Affiliation Theory   In the 1960s David McClelland developed a theory of motivation based on the assumption that through their life experiences, people develop various needs. His theory focuses on three such needs:

1. *The need for achievement*—the desire to do something better than it has been done before.
2. *The need for power*—the desire to control, influence, or be responsible for other people.
3. *The need for affiliation*—the desire to maintain close and friendly personal relationships.

According to McClelland, people have all these needs to some extent. However, the intensity of the needs varies from one individual to the next. The nature of a person's early life experiences may cause one of these needs to be particularly strong.

The relative strength of the needs influences what will motivate a person. A person with a strong need for achievement is more motivated by success than by money. This person tends to set challenging but achievable goals and to assess risk carefully. Someone with a strong need for power tries to influence others and seeks out advancement and responsibility. A person with a strong need for affiliation gives ambition a back seat in exchange for approval and acceptance.

This theory provides a possible explanation for some recent findings in a U.S. Department of Labor survey of women employees. According to that survey, a large proportion of low-income women reported that the best thing about going to work was being with their co-workers. As incomes rose, the importance of workplace relationships gave way to high ratings for being paid well.[7] We might guess that more of the women in low-paying positions had a high need for affiliation. Further, many of them may have developed this need through experiences that taught them they need to rely on the support of family and friends to help them in the struggle to meet work, safety, and family needs with limited resources.

McClelland's theory differs from Maslow's in that it assumes different people have different patterns of needs, whereas Maslow's theory assumes the same pattern of needs for all people. Thus, McClelland takes into account individual differences. Both theories, however, imply that supervisors must remember that employees are motivated by a variety of possibilities.

Herzberg's Two-Factor Theory   Frederick Herzberg's research led to the conclusion that employee satisfaction and dissatisfaction stem from different sources. According to this two-factor theory, dissatisfaction results from the absence of what Herzberg calls *hygiene factors*, which include salary and relationships with others. For example, someone whose pay is poor (e.g., a physical therapist earning $5,000 less than the average pay for the position) is going to be dissatisfied with the job. In contrast, satisfaction results from the presence of what Herzberg calls *motivating factors*, which include opportunities offered by the job. Thus, an employee who sees a chance for promotion is likely to be more satisfied with the current job than one who does not. Table 11.1 lists the items that make up hygiene and motivating factors.

■ T A B L E 1 1 . 1 **Two-Factor Theory:** **Hygiene Factors and** **Motivating Factors**	**Hygiene Factors**	**Motivating Factors**
	Company policy and administration	Opportunity for achievement
	Supervision	Opportunity for recognition
	Relationship with supervisor	Work itself
	Relationship with peers	Responsibility
	Working conditions	Advancement
	Salary and benefits	Personal growth
	Relationship with subordinates	

Herzberg found that employees are most productive when the organization provides a combination of desirable hygiene factors and motivating factors. Based on this theory, an organization cannot ensure that its employees will be satisfied and productive simply by giving them a big pay raise every year. Employees will also need motivating factors such as the ability to learn new skills and to assume responsibility. Like the other content theories, Herzberg's theory tells supervisors that they need to consider a variety of ways to motivate employees.

Process Theories

Another way to explain how motivation works is to look at the process of motivation instead of specific motivators. Theories that pertain to the motivation process are known as process theories. Two major process theories are Vroom's expectancy-valence theory and Skinner's reinforcement theory.

Vroom's Expectancy-Valence Theory   Assuming that people act as they do to satisfy their needs, Victor Vroom set out to explain what determines the intensity of motivation. He decided that the degree to which people are motivated to act in a certain way depends on two things:

1. *Valence*—the value a person places on the outcome of a particular behavior. For example, a person may highly value the prestige and the bonus that result from submitting a winning suggestion in a contest for improving quality.
2. *Expectancy*—the perceived probability that the behavior will lead to the outcome. A person in the example may believe that his or her idea has a 50–50 chance of winning the quality improvement contest.

Vroom's expectancy-valence theory says that the strength of motivation equals the perceived value of the outcome times the perceived probability of the behavior resulting in the outcome (see Figure 11.3). In other words, people are most motivated to seek results they value highly and think they can achieve.

This theory is based on employees' *perceptions* of rewards and whether they are able to achieve them. Employees may place different values on rewards than a supervisor, and they may have different opinions about their abilities. If a supervisor believes that a good system of rewards is in place but that employees are not motivated, the supervisor might investigate whether employees think they are expected to do the impossible. To learn this, supervisors must be able to communicate well (see Chapter 10).

Skinner's Reinforcement Theory   From the field of psychology comes reinforcement theory, pioneered by B. F. Skinner. Reinforcement theory maintains that

FIGURE 11.3

Vroom's Expectancy-Valence Theory

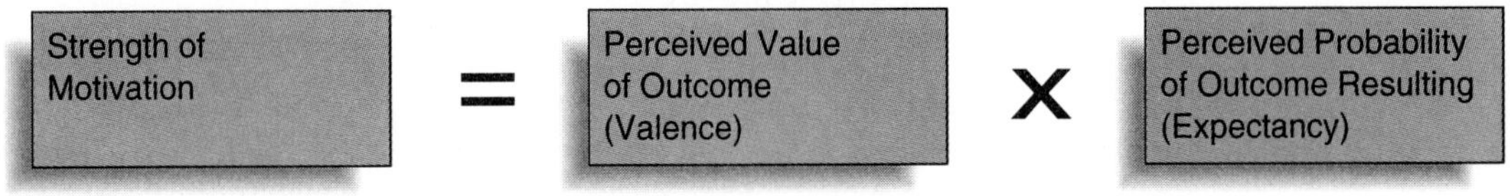

people's behavior is influenced largely by the consequences of their past behavior. Generally, people keep doing things that have led to consequences they like, and people avoid doing things that have had undesirable consequences. For example, praise feels good to receive, so people tend to do things that, in their experience, result in praise.

reinforcement
A desired consequence or the ending of a negative consequence, either of which is given in response to a desirable behavior.

Reinforcement theory implies that supervisors can encourage or discourage a particular kind of behavior by the way they respond to the behavior. They can administer **reinforcement,** which can involve either giving a desired consequence or ending a negative consequence in response to behavior the supervisor wants. Or the supervisor can administer **punishment,** which is an unpleasant consequence of the behavior the supervisor wants to end. As described in the story at the beginning of this chapter, when salespeople performed well, they earned bonuses or won contests—a form of reinforcement. The lowest-performing sales rep received the undesirable attention of winning a "prize" for rating at the bottom—a form of punishment. Using reinforcement theory to motivate people to behave in a certain way is known as **behavior modification.** In everyday language, we call it "using the carrot and the stick."

punishment
An unpleasant consequence given in response to undesirable behavior.

For long-term results, reinforcement is more effective than punishment. Psychologists have found that repeated punishment (or failure) can lead to an unhappy consequence called "learned helplessness." This means that if employees are punished repeatedly for failing in some aspect of their work, these employees will eventually believe that they are unable to succeed at the job. These employees begin to approach the job passively, believing that they will fail no matter what.

behavior modification
The use of reinforcement theory to motivate people to behave in a certain way.

Together, Vroom's and Skinner's process theories support the idea that supervisors motivate most effectively when they place less emphasis on punishing infractions and more on giving employees a desirable goal and the resources that enable them to achieve that goal. These theories are consistent with the new management style adopted by Andy Pearson, who ran PepsiCo. Inc. for nearly 15 years with a successful but abrasive style that earned him the reputation of being one of the 10 toughest bosses in the United States (according to *Fortune* magazine in 1980), partly for his track record of routinely firing the least productive 10 to 20 percent of the workforce. Now founding chairman of Tricon Global Restaurants Inc., the largest restaurant chain the world, Pearson has changed his style. Instead of asking employees, "So what?" he is asking himself, "If I could only unleash the power of everybody in the organization, instead of just a few people, what could we accomplish?"

Pearson recently told *Fast Company* magazine,

> A lot of people make the mistake of thinking that getting results is all there is to the job. They go after results without building a team or without building an organization that has the capacity to change. Your real job is to get results *and* to do it in a way that makes your organization a great place to work—a place where people enjoy coming to work, instead of just taking orders and hitting this month's numbers.[8]

Motivation Theories and the Law

Most of these motivation theories have one element in common: that supervisors must consider individual differences in designing rewards. What motivates one person may not motivate another, so supervisors need to offer a variety of rewards. At the same time, to avoid discrimination, employers must distribute benefits fairly.

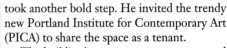

SUPERVISION ACROSS INDUSTRIES

Advertising

Creative Space Yields Creative Results

Dan Wieden is the founder and CEO of Wieden + Kennedy, a $780 million ad agency that has flourished in Portland, Oregon, for nearly 20 years. When the firm outgrew its original downtown headquarters, Wieden saw an opportunity not only to relocate to more spacious surroundings, but to accomplish another goal as well. "For us," he says, "this wasn't about the riddle of figuring out the cubicles or making the office space different than the next guy's. The job was figuring out how we can help people live creative lives. . . . If we're helping people lead surprising, audacious lives, that will infect everything else we do here."

Wieden knows well that motivating the creative staff of an ad agency is a large part of his role as CEO. To inspire a new way of thinking he selected a rapidly changing, mixed-use neighborhood in Portland's Pearl District, where a 90-year-old historical landmark building stood. After cutting out the central core of the building and creating a six-story atrium that doubles as a meeting area (it can accommodate the firm's entire 250-person staff), Wieden

took another bold step. He invited the trendy new Portland Institute for Contemporary Art (PICA) to share the space as a tenant.

The building's new roommates are a good match. Having an art organization in the building, with its creative staff and active exhibit space, has stimulated Wieden + Kennedy's staff to think in new ways and has also helped the firm contribute to the larger Portland community. Says Wieden, "If you can get people to stop thinking about making ads and to start thinking about making pieces of communication, then something fresh is apt to arrive."

Wieden made a surprising but successful choice in his building's new tenant. Supervisors can adapt his strategy and motivate their own staffs in any industry by encouraging the kind of creative thinking that leads to new and better ways of doing things. Fortunately, that doesn't require a landmark building, just the willingness to keep a mind as open as Wieden's new atrium.

Source: Ron Lieber, "Creative Space," *Fast Company*, January 2001, pp. 136–146.

Boston-based Work/Family Directions, which provides referral services, uses a formal procedure to balance these objectives with flexible scheduling. If employees want an alternative work arrangement such as flextime, telecommuting, or job sharing, they must fill out a form that details the hours and location they are requesting, the impact on the organization, and a proposal for overcoming any drawbacks of the arrangement. The company then decides whether to grant the request based on business-related concerns instead of the employee's reasons for requesting the arrangements.[9]

The types of rewards a supervisor may use are not entirely under his or her control. Not only does a supervisor have to follow the organization's policies, but a variety of laws require that employers provide certain types of benefits. For example, federal laws set requirements for overtime pay, rest breaks, health insurance for retirees, and many other areas. Most organizations have a human resources professional or department responsible for helping the organization comply with laws related to benefits. The details of these laws are beyond the scope of this book.

However, the requirements of the Family and Medical Leave Act of 1993 are worth noting because they affect the supervisor's role in scheduling work and staffing the department. Under this law, organizations with 50 or more employees within a 75-mile radius must give employees up to 12 weeks of unpaid leave to care for a newborn, adopted, or foster child within one year of the child's arrival. These employers also must offer this time off if employees need to care for a seriously ill child, parent, or spouse or if they themselves have medical conditions that prevent them from doing their jobs. During the time off, the employer must continue to pay the employee's health insurance premiums. The employer also must guarantee that the employee will be able to return to his or her job or an equivalent one. If the need for the leave is foreseeable, the employee must give the organization 30 days' notice.

Money as a Motivator

Some supervisors and other managers assume that the main thing employees want out of a job is money. Most people work to earn at least enough to get by. Though money is only one of many available ways to motivate employees, it is an important one.

Just how important was demonstrated at Ty Inc., the maker of Beanie Babies. Its employees worked hard all year in 1998 to keep small retailers stocked with the popular collectible toys, and at the end of the year all 300 of them received cash bonuses equal to their entire 1998 income. Many of them wept.[10]

When Money Motivates

The content theories of motivation imply that money motivates people when it meets their needs. Celia Talavera, a mother of four, takes a two-hour bus ride to reach her job as housekeeper at Lowes Santa Monica (California) Beach Hotel. She is in favor of a proposed new "living wage" ordinance that would raise her pay from $9.88 to $10.50, because it would provide a small amount for savings and benefits. "I am fighting for a living wage because I want to work there for a long time," she says.[11] The opportunity to earn more can also be very important to a college student, considering the high cost of college tuition and the potentially great impact of a college degree on the student's future lifestyle. A retired person or a married person whose spouse earns a comfortable income might work primarily for nonfinancial rewards such as a sense of accomplishment or the satisfaction derived from performing a needed service.

If money is to work as a motivator, employees must believe they are able to achieve the financial rewards the organization offers. Thus, if a theater company offers its staff a bonus for selling a given number of season-ticket subscriptions over the telephone, the bonus will motivate the employees only if they believe they can sell that many tickets. Or, if an organization pays a bonus for employee suggestions that improve quality, the bonus will motivate employees only if they believe they are capable of coming up with ideas.

Pay Plans Using Financial Incentives

financial incentives
Payments for meeting or exceeding objectives.

The way a pay plan is structured can influence the degree to which employees are motivated to perform well. Some pay plans offer bonuses, commissions, or other kinds of pay for meeting or exceeding objectives. For instance, a growing number of organizations tie raises and bonuses to success in retaining existing customers and meeting established quality goals. Others pay employees a higher rate for learning additional skills, including how to operate lift trucks and computer-controlled machinery and how to develop computer applications to do business globally. Such pay plans are said to use **financial incentives.**

Supervisors rarely have much say in the type of pay plan an organization uses. However, they can motivate better if they understand the kinds of pay plans that offer a financial incentive. Knowing whether the organization's pay system is designed to motivate gives a supervisor clues about the needs of employees for nonfinancial incentives. If the organization's pay plan includes financial incentives but the employees remain unmotivated, a supervisor might look for other kinds of motivators. On the other hand, if the organization's pay plan contains no financial incentives, a supervisor might seek permission to include money for bonuses in the department's budget.

piecework system
Payment according to the quantity produced.

Piecework System   The **piecework system** pays people according to how much they produce. This method is often used to pay independent contractors; that is, people who are self-employed and perform work for the organization. For example, a magazine might pay a writer a fixed rate for each word, or a clothing manufacturer might pay a seamster a set amount for each shirt sewed. Farmworkers may be paid according to how much they harvest. Unlike independent contractors, however, few employees are paid by this system.

Production Bonus System   Production department employees may receive a basic wage or salary plus a bonus that consists of a payment for each unit produced. Thus, an employee might earn $8.50 or more an hour plus $0.20 for each unit produced. This is called a production bonus system. If employees do not appear to be motivated by a production bonus system, the bonus may not be large enough to be worth the extra effort. Employees who work faster earn more money under such a system, but the pay system does not necessarily encourage high-quality work.

There are other types of bonus as well. When a boom in business coincided with a shortage of qualified workers, Alan Hirsch, owner of Dilworth Mattress Co. in Charlotte, North Carolina, had to scramble to find the 10 workers he needed to keep his operation running. He hit upon the idea of giving a $50 biweekly bonus to workers with perfect attendance for the past two weeks.[12]

Saga Software, an enterprise software developer based in Reston, Virginia, gives out nearly $300,000 in on-the-spot performance bonuses. Nearly half the firm's 800 employees earned between $500 and $5,000 in one recent year; if they chose to defer all or part of the bonus, the firm marked the award up by 50 percent.[13]

Increasingly popular for executive compensation packages are bonus plans with escalating payouts, in which the financial award is tied to such quantifiable measures as growth in sales, profits, cash flow, or the value of the firm.[14]

commissions
Payment linked to the amount of sales completed.

Commissions   In a sales department, employees may earn **commissions,** or payment linked to the amount of sales completed. For example, a real estate agent listed a house for her brokerage. Upon the sale of the house, the agent might receive a commission of 2 percent of the sale price. The selling agent and the brokerage also would get commissions.

Most organizations that pay commissions also pay a basic wage or salary. Otherwise, the financial uncertainty can worry employees to the point that it interferes with motivation. Some people, however, like the unlimited earnings potential of a commission-only job.

Other factors, too, can interfere with the successful use of commissions. In the case of Axxis, an audiovisual equipment rental company, CEO Stephen Smith found that guaranteeing sales reps' commissions almost proved the undoing of the company. For the first two months after Smith and his business partner mortgaged their homes to raise the capital they needed to attract a small but top-flight sales force, nobody sold anything. Business picked up after six months, but Smith, whose parents founded the firm, says, "In retrospect, it's the most insane thing I've ever done."[15]

Some firms have tried commission plans and abandoned them. Profsoft, a $27 million Virginia Beach firm that provides technical services and training, now pays its salespeople a salary and gives them a share of year-end profits. One problem with the old system, in which sales commissions were paid, was that the company's engineers, who helped with sales presentations but worked on lengthy bid proposals alone, felt it was unfair to reward just the sales reps with added pay. Not only is the new way seen as more fair, but "the technical people are involved all the time now," says cofounder Michael Adolphi, "and the salespeople help with the bids."[16]

Payments for Suggestions   To build employee participation and communication, many companies pay employees for making suggestions on how to cut costs or improve quality. Typically, the suggestion must be adopted or save some minimum amount of money before the employee receives payment. The size of the payment may be linked to the size of the benefit to the organization. In other words, an idea with a bigger impact results in a bigger payment.

Group Incentive Plans   Organizations today are focusing increasingly on ways to get employees and their supervisors to work together as teams. A financial incentive to get people to work this way is the **group incentive plan,** which pays a bonus when the group as a whole exceeds some objective. An organization measures the performance of a work unit against its objectives, then pays a bonus if the group exceeds the objectives. At Continental Airlines, every employee receives at least $65 in cash for each month that the airline ranks among the top three in on-time performance as rated by the U.S. Transportation Department or completes at least 80 percent of its flights on schedule. For every month that Continental ranks first, the bonus rises to $100 each.[17]

A frequently used type of group incentive is the **profit-sharing plan.** Under this kind of plan, the company sets aside a share of its profits earned during a given period, such as a year, and divides these profits among the employees. The assumption is that the better the work done, the more the company will earn and, therefore, the bigger the bonuses. In the past, profit sharing was limited chiefly to executives, but more companies today are sharing profits among all employees.

An increasing number of companies are adopting a **gainsharing** program, under which the company encourages employees to participate in making suggestions and decisions about improving the way the company or work group operates. As performance improves, employees receive a share of the greater earnings. Thus, gainsharing seeks to motivate not only by giving financial rewards but also by making employees feel they have an important role as part of a team.

Secrecy of Wage and Salary Information

In our society, money is considered a private matter, and most people do not like to talk about what they earn. Thus, in private (nongovernment) organizations, employees generally do not know one another's earnings, although supervisors know what their subordinates earn. In contrast, government employees' earnings are public information, often published in local papers, because taxpayers ultimately pay their wages and salaries.

---

group incentive plan
A financial incentive plan that rewards a team of workers for meeting or exceeding an objective.

profit-sharing plan
A group incentive plan under which the company sets aside a share of its profits and divides it among employees.

gainsharing
A group incentive plan in which the organization encourages employees to participate in making suggestions and decisions, then rewards the group with a share of improved earnings.

Does secrecy help or hurt the usefulness of money as a motivator? Certainly, it does not make sense to disclose information if it only embarrasses employees. Most employees overestimate what others earn. This overestimation can result in dissatisfaction because employees believe they are underpaid in comparison.

To motivate employees with the possibility of a raise and a belief that pay rates are fair, the organization must let them know what they can hope to earn. A typical compromise between maintaining privacy and sharing information is for the organization to publish pay ranges. These show the lowest and highest wage or salary the organization will pay an employee in a particular position. Employees do not know how much specific individuals earn, but the ranges show what they can expect to earn if they get a raise, promotion, or transfer to another position.

How Supervisors Can Motivate

The first part of this chapter addressed the theories of motivating. These theories suggested some practical ways supervisors can motivate. Several possibilities are summarized in Figure 11.4. In addition, "Tips from the Firing Line" suggests what recent research says about how supervisors can motivate others.

Making Work Interesting

When employees find their work interesting, they are more likely to give it their full attention and enthusiasm. In general, work is interesting when it has variety and allows employees some control over what they do. Work can be made more interesting through job rotation, job enlargement, job enrichment, and increased customer contact.

job rotation
Moving employees from job to job to give them more variety.

Job rotation involves moving employees from job to job to give them more variety. For example, the employees in a production department may take turns

---

■ FIGURE 11.4

Some Ways Supervisors Can Motivate Employees

- Making Work Interesting
  - Job rotation
  - Job enlargement
  - Job enrichment
  - Customer contact
- Having High Expectations
- Providing Valued Rewards
- Relating Rewards to Performance
- Treating Employees as Individuals
- Encouraging Participation
- Providing Feedback

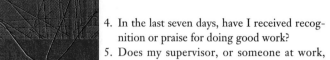

Can You Meet the Test of the "Q12"?

According to a recent Gallup Organization study, the single most important variable in employee productivity and loyalty is not pay or perks or benefits or even the workplace environment. Instead, it is the quality of the relationship between employees and their direct supervisors, which suggests that the greatest sources of satisfaction in the workplace are internal and even emotional in nature.

Their analysis of Gallup interviews with more than 1 million workers conducted over 25 years have led researchers Marcus Buckingham and Curt Coffman to conclude that 12 simple questions, which they call the "Q12," can strongly predict how well employees will perform in the workplace.

How well do your supervision skills stack up against the Q12? Here are the questions your employees might be asking themselves:

1. Do I know what is expected of me at work?
2. Do I have the materials and equipment I need to do my work right?
3. At work, do I have the opportunity to do what I do best every day?
4. In the last seven days, have I received recognition or praise for doing good work?
5. Does my supervisor, or someone at work, seem to care about me as a person?
6. Is there someone at work who encourages my development?
7. At work, do my opinions seem to count?
8. Does the mission/purpose of my company make me feel my job is important?
9. Are my co-workers committed to doing quality work?
10. Do I have a best friend at work?
11. In the last six months, has someone at work talked to me about my progress?
12. This last year, have I had opportunities at work to learn and grow?

Source: From Buckingham and Coffman, First Break All the Rules, Simon & Schuster, p. 28. Copyright © 1999 The Gallup Organization. All rights reserved. Reprinted with permission. Question items may not be reproduced or utilized outside of a Gallup Organization engagement.

---

cross-training
Training in the skills required to perform more than one job.

job enlargement
An effort to make a job more interesting by adding more duties to it.

job enrichment
The incorporation of motivating factors into a job—in particular, giving the employee more responsibility and recognition.

operating all the machines in the factory. Job rotation requires that employees have relatively broad skills. As a result, the supervisor or company must provide for **cross-training,** or training in the skills required to perform more than one job. The opportunity to learn new skills through cross-training can in itself motivate employees.

Job enlargement is an effort to make a job more interesting by adding more duties to it. Thus, a machine operator might be responsible not only for running a particular machine, but also for performing maintenance on the machine and inspecting the quality of the parts produced with the machine. As with job rotation, this approach assumes that variety in a job makes it more satisfying, with the result that employees are more motivated.

Job enrichment is the incorporation of motivating factors into a job. Herzberg called the factors that enrich a job "motivators." Generally, an enriched job gives employees more responsibility to make decisions and more recognition for good performance. Thus, enriched jobs are more challenging and, presumably, more rewarding. For example, instead of requiring salespeople in a department store to call a supervisor whenever a customer has a complaint, the store might authorize them to handle complaints as they see fit. They would have to call a supervisor only if solving the problem would cost the store more than some set amount, say, $500.

When modifying jobs to make them more interesting, the organization and supervisor must remember that not all employees are motivated by the same things at the same time. Thus, while some employees may eagerly accept the new variety in their jobs, others are likely to be less enthusiastic. Some workers may think jobs are being redesigned simply to get more work out of people for the same amount of money. A supervisor must be careful to emphasize the advantages of the new arrangement and to listen to employee reactions.

Work also can be made more meaningful by giving employees some contact with the people who receive and use their products (goods or services). Nurses and salespeople are routinely in contact with the people they serve, but production workers and accounting personnel have less customer contact. Sometimes a supervisor can arrange to have workers visit the users of the products. For example, a group of production workers might be sent to visit a customer who is having trouble operating a machine the company manufactures. The workers not only would be able to help the customer, but they might also get some ideas for making the machine better. Accounting personnel might meet the people in the company who use their reports to make sure they understand and are satisfied with the reports.

Having High Expectations

Effective motivation can lead to performance beyond employees' own expectations of themselves. When someone expects a lot of us, we often find that we can do a lot. When little is expected, we tend to provide little. In either case, the expectations are self-fulfilling.

The direct relationship between expectations and performance is known as the **Pygmalion effect.** The name comes from the Greek myth of Pygmalion, a king of Cyprus who carved a statue of a beautiful maiden and then fell in love with her. He so wished she were real that she became real.

According to the Pygmalion effect, a supervisor who says to an employee, "You're so dense, you never get the procedures right," will not motivate effectively. Instead, the employee will decide that understanding procedures is beyond his or her capacity. Therefore, a supervisor who wishes employees to set high standards for themselves must think and speak with the assumption that the employees are capable of meeting high standards. A supervisor might say, "These procedures are complicated, but I'm sure that if you study them regularly and ask questions, you can learn to follow them."

At SAS Institute Inc., a major software company based in Cary, North Carolina, benefits and perks include on-site day care, piano concerts at lunchtime, private offices for all, plenty of open space, paid maternity leaves, a lactation room, massages, a free medical clinic, a 55,000-square-foot athletic facility, tennis courts, walking trails, canoes and a lake to row them on, yoga classes, free car washes, an on-site farmer's market, a high school stocked with computers for employees' children, and a strictly enforced policy of a seven-hour workday. Overtime is distinctly frowned upon. Founder James Goodnight believes that if you treat people as if they will make a difference, they will. David Russo, the company's long-time head of human resources, elaborates on the role of expectations in translating all those benefits into top-flight performance at the $750-plus million company:

Says Russo, "If you're out sick for six months, you'll get cards and flowers, and people will come to cook dinner for you. If you're out sick on six Mondays in a row, you'll get fired. We expect adult behavior."[18]

Providing Rewards That Are Valued

The content theories of motivation indicate that a variety of rewards may motivate, but that not all employees will value the same rewards at the same time. The supervisor's challenge is to determine what rewards will work for particular

Pygmalion effect
The direct relationship between expectations and performance; high expectations lead to high performance.

MEETING THE CHALLENGE

Motivating without Cash

Here's a look at how supervisors at a handful of firms are using noncash incentives to motivate their employees.

Whole Foods Market (Austin, Texas) All 13,000 employees of this natural foods grocery chain are eligible to use "flexible credit dollars" to select the benefits they prefer. One might choose health insurance, while another might put all her money in the 401k plan. All employees also receive 20 percent discounts on all store purchases (which no other grocery firm offers), stock options after three years on the job, and bonuses for staff whose departments exceed their financial goals. Another benefit that's hard to beat is a six-week sabbatical, which any employee can earn after three years with the firm. Jody Hatch, human resources vice president, says, "We've found that the less restriction we place on people, the more they perform."

SAS Institute (Cary, North Carolina) Although this software firm does pay cash bonuses, its human resources vice president says, "We try to provide the best working environment we can. Cash is not how we motivate folks." Perks such as subsidized child care and a health center with medical staff are part of the picture; there are also basketball and racquetball courts, a soccer field, and a fitness center for employees.

Yahoo! (Santa Clara, California) Since its employees tend to work through lunch, managers of one of the Internet's most popular sites began a subsidized lunch program. The firm also runs seminars on personal finance for its employees, many of whom have become wealthy from their stock options in the firm. Free health care benefits for domestic partners are offered, along with a website full of resources for schools, day care, elder care, and even pet care. Trips to movie openings, restaurant parties, sports tournaments, and Ben & Jerry's ice cream complete the picture.

Boston Restaurant Associates, Inc. (Boston, Massachusetts) To improve performance in specific areas, the firm began offering stock options to employees. For instance, the "dough program" was begun to solve the problem of keeping pizza dough fresh during transport. The five dough makers who came up with an answer were awarded a total of 20,000 options. Exceeding profit goals and recruiting and retaining employees were the subject of other reward programs, and these earned employees a total of about 30,000 options. The options were given at the stock's current price, and employees could cash them in immediately if they chose.

Sources: Carol A. L. Dannhauser, "Beyond the Paycheck," *Working Woman*, October 1998, p. 40; Tamar Hausman, "The Dish-Out," *Wall Street Journal*, November 3, 1998, p. B20.

employees at particular times. This means appreciating the needs people are trying to meet and the variety of ways a supervisor can provide rewards.

Sometimes an outrageously attractive award serves not only to recognize a valued employee but also to motivate others who can't help but notice the result of outstanding performance. Gordon M. Bethune, chair of Continental Airlines, awarded a new Ford Explorer to Tampa, Florida reservations agent Wendy Pignataro for a period of perfect attendance. Pignataro and six other winners received their prizes before a crowd of hundreds of fellow employees at the company's Houston headquarters.[19]

Of course, there are some limits to a supervisor's discretion in giving rewards. Company policy or a union contract may dictate the size of raises employees get and the degree to which raises are linked to performance as opposed to seniority or some other measure. However, supervisors can use the theories of motivation, coupled with their own experience, to identify the kinds of rewards over which they have some control. For example, a supervisor has great freedom in administering rewards such as praise and recognition. Many supervisors have some discretion in job assignments. Employees who have a high need for achievement (McClelland's theory) or are trying to meet esteem or self-actualization needs (Maslow's theory) may appreciate opportunities for additional training. Employees who have a high need for affiliation or are seeking to meet social needs may appreciate being assigned to jobs where they work with other people. See "Meeting the Challenge" for some ideas for other noncash rewards.

Relating Rewards to Performance

The rewards that a supervisor uses should be linked to employee performance. Unfortunately, employees seldom see a clear link between good job performance and higher pay. If there is a connection, employees should be aware of it and understand it. Linking rewards to the achievement of realistic objectives is a way to help employees believe they can attain desired rewards. As Vroom's expectancy-valence theory described, rewards are most likely to motivate employees when the employees view them as achievable.

At Great Scott Broadcasting, an independent broadcasting company in Pottstown, Pennsylvania, sales reps for the company's eight radio stations in Maryland and Delaware must be knowledgeable about audience demographics, marketing protocol, and other key information about selling radio spots. With a game called Trivia Feud, general manager Cathy Deighan ensures that the reps have the information they need to answer clients' questions quickly and accurately. The competitive 15-minute game is played at every weekly sales meeting— "It can get pretty crazy," says Deighan—and each person on the winning team gets a prize, such as a gift certificate for dinner, a free car wash, or cash.[20]

The use of objectives is a basic way to link rewards to performance (see Chapter 6). For example, the management by objectives (MBO) system provides rewards when employees meet or exceed the objectives they have helped set for themselves. Thus, if a museum's cafeteria workers are supposed to leave their work areas spotless at the end of each shift, they know whether they have done what is necessary to receive their rewards, such as regular pay raises or extra time off.

Using clear objectives to help motivate employees is an important way to make sure that when employees try hard, they are trying to do the right things. The Von Maur department store chain has built an outstanding reputation by linking challenging goals to rewards. Employees are expected to deliver exceptional customer service "for every single customer, every single day." To reward such behavior, the stores hold weekly meetings at which thank-you notes from customers are read to employees. The subjects of those letters receive applause in addition to a prize such as movie tickets or cash.[21] (For a discussion of communicating goals and other information to employees, see Chapter 10.)

Treating Employees as Individuals

Most of the theories of motivation emphasize that different things motivate individuals to different degrees. A supervisor who wishes to succeed at motivating has to remember that employees will respond in varying ways. A supervisor cannot expect that everyone will be excited equally about cross-training or overtime pay. Some employees might prefer an easy job or short hours, so that they have time and energy for outside activities. *Business Week* editor Diane Brady, a working mother, was happy to find the privacy to pump breast milk for her infant son while on the job in her New York office.[22] "Pumping at work helps me feel close to my son while we're apart during the day," she says. Wolfgang Zwierner has waited tables at Brooklyn's famed Peter Luger Steak House for 38 years because, he says, "the job of a waiter is to like people. I make people comfortable. I spoil them if I can."[23] Figure 11.5 shows how U.S. workers rated job characteristics in a Gallup poll.

As much as possible, a supervisor should respond to individual differences. When a particular type of motivation does not seem to work with an employee, a supervisor should try some other motivator to see if it better matches the employee's needs.

■ FIGURE 11.5

Job Characteristics Rated Important by U.S. Workers

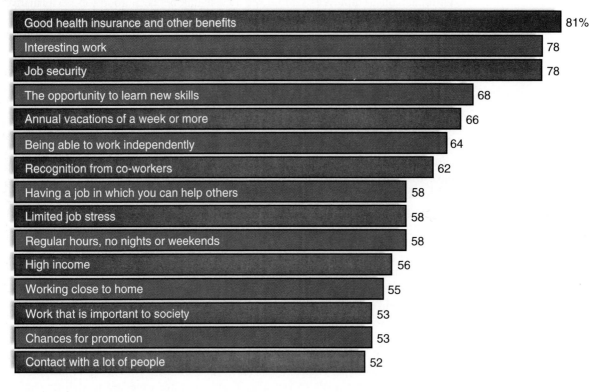

Job Characteristic	Percent
Good health insurance and other benefits	81%
Interesting work	78
Job security	78
The opportunity to learn new skills	68
Annual vacations of a week or more	66
Being able to work independently	64
Recognition from co-workers	62
Having a job in which you can help others	58
Limited job stress	58
Regular hours, no nights or weekends	58
High income	56
Working close to home	55
Work that is important to society	53
Chances for promotion	53
Contact with a lot of people	52

Source: Data from Gallup poll cited in Patricia Braus, "What Workers Want," *American Demographics*, August 1992, pp. 30–31 ff.

Encouraging Employee Participation

One way to learn about employees' needs and to benefit from their ideas is to encourage employees to participate in planning and decision making. As you read in Chapter 9, employees tend to feel more committed when they can contribute to decisions and solutions. They also are likely to cooperate better when they feel like part of a team.

Work/Family Directions established a task force of employees to develop its request form for flexible work arrangements, including which questions to use on the form. The company's founders maintain that this employee involvement contributed to a widely shared belief that the process of granting requests is fair.[24]

Another way to increase motivation through involvement is to ask for volunteers to do the jobs that no one wants. The idea is that assigning unpopular work usually results in a lower level of commitment. Asking subordinates for their advice about how tasks should be accomplished is another way to increase their involvement. Here, of course, listening to their input is critical to demonstrating sincerity.[25]

Providing Feedback

People want and need to know how well they are doing. Part of a supervisor's job is to give employees feedback about their performance. When the supervisor tells employees that they are meeting or exceeding objectives, the employees know that they are doing something right. When a supervisor tells employees that they are falling short of objectives, the employees know that they need to improve. Most people will try to improve when given a chance to do so.

Praise is an important kind of feedback. In monitoring employees, a supervisor should look for signs of excellent performance and let the employees know, in specific terms, that the good work is appreciated and that it benefits the organization.

There are many ways to deliver praise. For example, a nursing supervisor might write a memo to a nurse, in which the supervisor comments on the nurse's courteous manner with patients and how it gives patients a good impression of the hospital. Or, a police force supervisor might remark to an officer that the officer's paperwork is always complete and legible.

A supervisor does not have to use a dramatic approach to praising a behavior. Praise is so easy to give and its potential rewards are so great that the supervisor can and should use it routinely, as long as it is sincere.

Summary

11.1   Identify the relationship between motivation and performance.

To perform well, employees must be motivated. Motivation is giving people incentives to act in certain ways. For motivation to work, a supervisor needs to know what rewards employees value.

11.2   Describe content theories of motivation.

Content theories of motivation attempt to identify what motivates people. According to Maslow's theory, people are motivated by unmet needs. These needs fall into a hierarchy: physiological, security, social, esteem, and self-actualization. People attempt to satisfy lower-level needs before they focus on higher-level needs. According to McClelland, people have achievement, power, and affiliation needs. The intensity of each kind of need varies from person to person. Herzberg's two-factor theory says that employees are dissatisfied when hygiene factors are absent and satisfied when motivating factors are present.

11.3   Describe process theories of motivation.

Process theories explain how motivation works through its process. According to Vroom's expectancy-valence theory, the intensity of a person's motivation depends on the value the person places on the outcome of a behavior multiplied by the perceived probability that the behavior will actually lead to the outcome. People are most motivated to seek results they value highly and think they can achieve. Reinforcement theory, pioneered by B. F. Skinner, says that people behave as they do because of the kind of consequences they experience as a result of their behavior. The supervisor can therefore influence behavior by administering the consequences (in the form of reinforcement or punishment).

11.4   Explain when financial incentives are likely to motivate employees.

Money motivates people when it meets their needs. The employees must believe they are able to achieve the financial rewards the organization offers.

11.5   Describe pay plans using financial incentives.

Under a piecework system, employees are paid according to how much they produce. A production bonus system pays a basic wage or salary plus a bonus based on performance; for example, an amount per unit assembled. Commissions are payments tied to the amount of sales completed. Some organizations pay employees for making useful suggestions on cutting costs or improving quality. Group incentive plans pay a bonus when the group as a whole exceeds an objective. Profit-sharing and gainsharing plans are types of group incentives.

11.6 Discuss the pros and cons of keeping pay information secret.

Keeping pay secret respects employees' desire for privacy. However, to be motivated by the possibility of greater earnings and a sense that pay rates are fair, employees must know what they can hope to earn. Typically, an organization balances these needs by publishing pay ranges that show the least and most the organization will pay an employee in a particular job.

11.7 Identify ways supervisors can motivate their employees.

Supervisors can motivate employees by making work interesting through job rotation, job enlargement, job enrichment, and contact with users of the product or service. Other ways to motivate include having high expectations of employees, providing rewards that are valued, relating rewards to performance, treating employees as individuals, encouraging employee participation, and providing feedback, including praise.

Key Terms

motivation, p. 271	financial incentives, p. 280	job rotation, p. 283
flextime, p. 274	piecework system, p. 281	cross-training, p. 284
job sharing, p. 274	commissions, p. 281	job enlargement, p. 284
reinforcement, p. 278	group incentive plan, p. 282	job enrichment, p. 284
punishment, p. 278	profit-sharing plan, p. 282	Pygmalion effect, p. 285
behavior modification, p. 278	gainsharing, p. 282	

Review and Discussion Questions

1. Name and rank the five basic needs, from lowest to highest, that Maslow described in his hierarchy of needs. If a supervisor applies this hierarchy to his or her employees, what are some specific ways that employees' needs could be met?

2. What are some family-friendly policies that companies now have in place so that employees can balance home and work? What other family-friendly policies might help employees to meet the demands in their lives and thus motivate them at work?

3. What are the three categories of needs that McClelland identified in his theory? Which category of needs do you think is strongest for you?

4. What are the hygiene factors and motivating factors described by Herzberg? Consider your current job or one you held most recently. Which factors are (were) present at that job? How would you say they affect(ed) your level of satisfaction? Your level of motivation?

5. John Lightfoot believes he has a 75 percent chance of earning a bonus of $100. Mary Yu believes she has a 75 percent chance of qualifying for a raise of $1,000 a year. According to Vroom's expectancy-valence theory, is it correct to conclude that Mary will be more intensely motivated by her potential reward than John will be by his? Explain.

6. Andre Jones supervises computer programmers. He expects each programmer to turn in a progress report by quitting time each Friday.
    a. Name at least one way Andre can use reinforcement to motivate employees to turn in their reports on time.
    b. Name at least one way Andre can use punishment to motivate employees to turn in their reports on time.
    c. Which of these approaches do you think would be most successful? Why?

7. In which of the following situations do you think money will be an effective motivator? Explain.
    a. The economy is slow, and even though the salespeople think they are doing their best, sales are down. Sales supervisor Rita Blount tells the sales force that anyone

whose weekly sales are up by 10 percent next week will receive a $5,000 bonus.

b. A retailer such as Radio Shack announces that the top performer in the store will be a prime candidate for a management job in a store the company is opening in another state. Whoever takes the job will receive a raise of at least 9 percent.

c. A respiratory therapist who is the parent of two high school–age children can earn an extra $500 this month by accepting a schedule that involves working on weekends.

8. Which type or types of pay plan (piecework, production bonus, commission, payment for suggestions, group incentive) would work best in each of the following situations? Why?

a. A company wants to motivate employees in the manufacturing department to fulfill increased orders for wooden toys as the company tries to expand from a regional market to a national market.

b. A car dealership wants to emphasize teamwork in its service department.

9. Antonio Delgado supervises the police officers of the fourth precinct. Name some ways that he can make their work more interesting.

10. A supervisor at a mail-order catalog company reads a report stating that 15 percent of all orders subsequently are returned, but this figure is considered better than the industry average. How can she use the Pygmalion effect to motivate employees to reduce the number of returns even further?

11. What is wrong with each of the following attempts at motivation?

a. A sales supervisor for an insurance company believes that employees appreciate an opportunity to broaden their experiences, so she rewards the top performer each year with an all-expenses-paid leadership seminar. The seminar lasts a week and is conducted at a hotel in a city 200 miles away.

b. The supervisor of a hospital cafeteria awards one employee a $50 bonus each month. To give everyone an equal chance at receiving the bonus, the supervisor draws names written on slips of paper from a jar.

c. A maintenance supervisor in a pickle factory believes that qualified employees should be able to tell whether they are doing a good job. Therefore, the supervisor focuses motivation efforts on thinking up clever rewards to give out each year to the best performers.

A SECOND LOOK

How well do you think Digital Pilot is motivating its employees to share their experiences with each other and take the kind of risks Ronald Paige feels are necessary? Why?

SKILLS MODULE

CASE

Using Incentives to Build Sales

Abolishing salaries to jump-start sales may seem extreme, but Billy Ross credits just such a move with helping to turn around Super 1, his $14 million recreational vehicle (RV) dealership near Atlanta. When his salespeople were turning in below-par performances—closing a sale for only 1 out of every 200 customers who walked on the lot—Ross replaced their $250 weekly salary with a compensation plan that he hoped would promote more proactive selling. Salespeople now earn $10 cash for each customer whose information they capture (including, for example, name, address, and phone number), and $25 when a customer submits a written offer for an RV. Ross caps the total incentive package at $300 per week, but he also pays salespeople a hefty 20 percent commission on any RVs sold. All customer information goes into a database for follow-up calls and mailings.

Ross says most customers don't mind divulging their vital statistics, but if someone is reluctant, he encourages his salespeople to tell them about the $10 incentive. "Customers don't mind as much when they know they're helping the salesperson earn a weekly paycheck," he says. In the week after the initial contact, salespeople follow up with amiable "just-checking-to-see-if-you're-still-looking" calls, which Ross says are responsible for more than half the dealership's RV sales. He adds that the incentives have helped increase his closing percentage from 0.5 percent to 10.0 percent in one year. But most important, the incentives work. It's rare that someone doesn't nail the $300 cap, and sales staff turnover has been zero since October 1997.

1. Do Ross's results surprise you? Why or why not?
2. The new pay plan costs Ross more than the old (the cap is higher than the old salary and there are 20 percent bonuses on every sale). If it had not resulted in increased sales to cover the costs, what would you have advised Ross to do?
3. What other strategies can Ross add to the financial incentives he uses? Do you think they would be as effective? Why or why not?

Source: *Inc:.* The Magazine for Growing Companies by Shane McLaughlin. Copyright © 1998 by Business Innovator Group Resources/Inc. Reproduced by permission of Business Innovator Group Resources/Inc via Copyright Clearance Center.

SELF-QUIZ

What Motivates You?

What makes a job appealing to you? Rank the following job factors from 1 to 12. Assign 1 to the factor you consider most important and 12 to the factor you consider least important.

_____ 1. Work that is interesting and meaningful.

_____ 2. Good wages or salary.

_____ 3. Authority to make important decisions.

_____ 4. Comfortable work environment, such as a clean, modern laboratory, fancy store, or attractive office.

_____ 5. Likable co-workers.

_____ 6. Good relationship with supervisor.

_____ 7. Clear understanding of the department's and company's goals and performance requirements.

_____ 8. Appreciation and recognition for doing a good job.

_____ 9. Opportunities to learn new skills.

_____ 10. Prestigious title or occupation.

_____ 11. Chance for advancement.

_____ 12. Job security.

Class Exercise

If you have not already done so, answer the Self-Quiz questions. Then, by a show of hands, determine how many class members selected each response as most important and how many as least important. The instructor might tally the responses on the chalkboard or overhead projector or fill in the table below:

Discuss the following questions:

- Which response or responses did most class members choose as most important?
- Which response or responses did most class members choose as least important?
- Do you think these choices are typical of most employees today? Why or why not?
- How could a supervisor use this information to motivate employees?

NUMBER OF STUDENTS RATING THE ITEM

Self-Quiz Item	Most Important	Least Important
1.	_____	_____
2.	_____	_____
3.	_____	_____
4.	_____	_____
5.	_____	_____
6.	_____	_____
7.	_____	_____
8.	_____	_____

NUMBER OF STUDENTS RATING THE ITEM

Self-Quiz Item	Most Important	Least Important
9.	_____	_____
10.	_____	_____
11.	_____	_____
12.	_____	_____

Team-Building Exercise

Developing Motivational Methods

This chapter deals with one of the most challenging areas for supervisors: motivating employees. This exercise will help you develop a comprehensive list of motivating methods on which to draw when faced with employees whom you feel are not performing to their full potential.

Instructions

1. The table on page 295 shows five suggested categories of motivational methods and gives an example of each. Drawing on what you have learned about motivation in this class and elsewhere, list methods, techniques, and strategies that can serve as a source of ideas on how to motivate people.

2. For purposes of this exercise, do not be concerned about the economic impact of your ideas or a plan for carrying them out. For ex-

ample, if you suggest a bonus to reward your employees for good performance, there is no need to provide a formula for computing the bonus. At the same time, however, do not make ridiculous suggestions that would not make good business sense, such as suggesting that you reward all employees and their families with a two-week all-expenses-paid vacation to Bermuda.

3. Divide the class into groups. Then develop a group list that can be copied for each group member. There will undoubtedly be many days in your management career when you will be able to use this list to help you generate some ideas on how to motivate an unmotivated employee. Also, the list can be improved over time as you develop greater expertise as a motivational leader.

Things I can do to be a motivational leader	Characteristics of a motivating work environment	Ways to reward my employees for good performance	Strategies I can use to improve the way work is done	Organizational policies or benefits
Help employees set challenging yet achievable goals	Goods and services employees believe in	Publish achievements in company newsletter	Communicate clear performance standards	Flexible work schedule to accommodate personal and family needs

12

If you want to improve something, start measuring it. Then attach rewards to positive measurements, or penalties to negative ones, and you'll get results.
—Peter Lewis, CEO of Progressive Corporation

Improving Productivity

■ CHAPTER OUTLINE

The Productivity Challenge
Trends in Productivity in the United States
Constraints on Productivity

Measurement of Productivity

Improving Productivity by Controlling Quality

Improving Productivity by Controlling Costs
Determining Costs
Cost-Control Strategies

Employee Fears about Productivity Improvement

■ LEARNING OBJECTIVES

After you have studied this chapter, you should be able to:

12.1 Define *productivity*.

12.2 Identify constraints on productivity.

12.3 Describe how productivity and productivity improvements are measured.

12.4 Identify the two basic ways productivity may be improved.

12.5 Describe cost-control strategies available to supervisors.

12.6 Explain why employees have fears about productivity improvement, and tell how supervisors can address those fears.

PRODUCTIVITY AT KATZINGER, INC.

Diane and Steven Warren, owners of Katzinger Inc., called together their 37 employees. Food costs at the 100-seat restaurant and deli in Columbus, Ohio, were spiraling out of control and something had to be done. The Warrens had a plan.

As Diane recalls, the Warrens said, "You guys reduce food costs below 35 percent [of total sales], and we'll split the [savings] with you." Results were quick and dramatic. In the first month of the gainsharing plan, food costs fell 1.7 percent, and employees earned about $40 each. Since then there have been payouts nearly every month, some as high as $95. The managers of the restaurant, who knew where the waste was but didn't know how to put controls in place, each

met with their individual staffs to come up with ideas. Some, says Diane, were "amazingly simple, such as ordering fewer bagels so we wouldn't end up throwing so many away, and using the ends of tomatoes in soups and salads." Matching their orders for perishable foods more closely to what they expected to sell also helped reduce waste and drop costs.

The Warrens succeeded in raising the productivity of their restaurant by controlling costs, maintaining quality, and sticking to a simple plan that involved everyone in the organization.

Source: Abby Livingston, "Gain-sharing Encourages Productivity," *Nation's Business*, January 1998, pp. 21–22.

---

productivity
The amount of results (output) an organization gets for a given amount of inputs.

When the Warrens looked for ways to cut their costs without reducing sales or quality, they wanted to improve productivity. **Productivity** is the amount of results (output) an organization gets for a given amount of inputs (see Figure 12.1). Thus, productivity can refer to the amount of acceptable work employees do for each dollar they earn or the number of acceptable products manufactured with a given amount of resources.

This chapter takes a deeper look at the meaning of productivity and how it is measured. It describes the two basic ways to increase productivity: controlling quality and controlling costs. Ways that supervisors can participate in efforts to improve productivity are suggested.

The Productivity Challenge

Stiff competition from around the world is forcing U.S. businesses to pay attention to productivity. In addition, widespread opposition to paying higher taxes is forcing governments to make their operations more productive. To help improve productivity, supervisors must understand why it is important and what limits an organization's productivity.

■ FIGURE 12.1
**The Productivity
Formula**

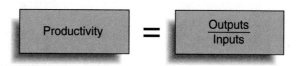

Trends in Productivity in the United States

When the productivity of organizations in a country is improving, people benefit. They can get goods and services at lower prices or with lower taxes than they otherwise could. Employers tend to pay higher wages and salaries to workers who are more productive. People also have access to more and better goods and services. Because of these benefits, statisticians keep track of productivity trends in various countries.

Overall, the performance of U.S. businesses has been mixed. The amount of goods and services produced by the average U.S. worker remains higher than that for any other industrialized nation. In 1995 the average output per hour in the manufacturing sector, measured against the index year 1992, was 113.8 percent for the United States and 111.0 for Japan, and in 2000 the figures were 144.7 percent for the United States and 132.6 for Japan.[1] The U.S. Department of Labor announced in the summer of 2001 that productivity was still rising despite a sharp economic slowdown, due to the fact that companies had used a combination of technology, layoffs, and reduced work hours to emerge from a nearly 20-year productivity slump. Results from the second quarter of 2001 showed that productivity rose again at a 2.5 annual rate for the quarter, as business produced about the same output but with less labor.[2]

Constraints on Productivity

When you read about ways to improve productivity, keep in mind that several constraints limit the impact of a supervisor or even of a higher-level manager. Supervisors and other managers should be aware of these constraints, so that they can either plan ways to overcome them or set realistic goals within them. Some of the most important constraints on productivity are management limitations, employee attitudes and skills, government regulations, and union rules.

Management Limitations   Operative employees will contribute to improving productivity only if they believe management is truly committed to this objective. All too often, however, employees believe management is more interested in the next quarter's profits than in producing high-quality goods or services as efficiently as possible. Employees become frustrated, especially when managers do not seem to listen to their ideas for improvements.

The most important way supervisors can overcome this constraint is to set a good example. Supervisors should demonstrate by their actions and words that they are interested in the department's productivity. This behavior includes seeing that the job is done right the first time, as well as using resources wisely, which, on a personal level, includes being well organized. To test your own level of personal productivity, take the Self-Quiz at the end of the chapter (page 316).

Supervisors also must communicate instructions clearly and plan carefully, so that employees are able to live up to managers' expectations. Furthermore, supervisors should listen to employees' concerns and ideas about improving productivity. If the organization has a formal program for submitting ideas, supervisors can offer to help employees write down or explain their suggestions. In organizations that allow or expect employee participation in planning and decision making, supervisors should encourage, not stifle, this participation.

Employee Attitudes and Skills   Improving productivity means making changes. People have a natural tendency to resist change because it is challenging and often frightening (see Chapter 15). Employees who have negative attitudes toward productivity improvements will not be motivated to make the changes work. Part of a supervisor's job is to identify employee attitudes and, when necessary, help employees take a more positive view. (The last section of this chapter addresses this issue in greater detail.)

The skills of employees also influence how effective productivity-building efforts will be. When an organization wants each member to contribute more to the goods or services it produces, each member must either work faster or do the job differently. Some employees are able to perform new tasks or do their jobs in a new way with little or no training. Other employees understand only one way of working. Supervisors can possibly overcome this constraint among employees who are willing to work simply by providing more training. When employees are either unwilling or unable to learn, this constraint is more difficult to overcome.

Attitudes and skills alike may require improvement when productivity suffers as a result of culture shock. Culture shock can be thought of as "the frustration and confusion that result from being constantly subjected to strange and unfamiliar cues about what to do and how to get it done."[3] Immigrant employees, supervisors of people from another culture, and employees whose cultures differ from that of most of their co-workers find that others do not respond to their behaviors in an expected manner. Furthermore, employees in a strange culture do not know how they are expected to behave and do not receive the credit they expect for their achievements, skills, and ideas. Common responses include depression, loneliness, aggression, short attention span, frustration, passivity, and quickness to fatigue.

How can a supervisor help prevent or correct the isolation, confusion, and aggression that can result from culture shock? The basic solution is more exposure to a variety of people. The more that people are exposed to diversity and the more they learn about it, the more comfortable they will be. Supervisors and their employees may benefit from formal training in this area. It is also helpful to be open and honest about the problem. Discussing feelings helps to diffuse culture shock and leads people to a better understanding of one another.

Government Regulations   Businesses and other organizations in the United States are regulated in many areas, including payment of overtime wages, disability compensation, environmental pollution, building codes, minimum safety standards, and child labor.

Following these regulations costs money, but the laws reflect the values of the majority in our society. For example, it might be cheaper to hire children to assemble electronic components, but few people want to return to the days of children laboring long hours within factory walls. Likewise, scrubbers on smokestacks cost money, but clean air to breathe is essential. Even when government regulations seem illogical or unreasonable, an organization can face serious penalties for ignoring or disobeying them. Thus, the proper role of supervisors and other managers is to know these regulations and seek ways of improving productivity without violating the law.

Union Rules   Union contracts typically specify rules for what tasks particular employees may do, what hours they may work, and how organizations may use employees. Sometimes an organization's managers see a way to improve productivity that violates one of these rules. For example, it might be more efficient to have two employees learn each other's jobs so they can get the work done even when one of them is away or busy. However, the union contract might contain a rule against this. Similarly, the International Brotherhood of Teamsters objected to certain aspects of UPS's restructuring. According to the Teamsters, hourly workers would be given authority over more senior employees, so the company had to negotiate these changes with the union. (UPS management maintains that the greater freedom and responsibility brought about by the changes are just what employees want.)[4]

When employers and unions collaborate on a solution, they can overcome such constraints, although the process usually takes time. If an organization explains how everyone will benefit from the changes, the union may agree to revise the contract, especially if the alternative is employee layoffs. Even though a supervisor can propose changes, it is not part of a supervisor's job to remove these constraints. Supervisors must do their best to get work done as efficiently as possible under the existing work rules.

Measurement of Productivity

The basic way to measure productivity is to divide outputs by inputs (see Figure 12.1). In other words, productivity is the amount of output produced with the inputs used. Table 12.1 provides examples of inputs and outputs for several types of organizations. The productivity equation can compare the output and input for an individual, a department, an organization, or even an entire country's paid workforce. The remaining discussion focuses on the direct concern of supervisors with the productivity of their department and their individual employees.

By applying basic arithmetic to the formula for productivity, the supervisor can see what has to change for productivity to increase. The right side of the equation is a fraction. Remember that when the top (numerator) of a fraction gets bigger, the number becomes greater. When the bottom (denominator) of a fraction gets bigger, the number becomes smaller. For example, 3/2 is greater than 1/2, and 1/5 is less than 1/3. To increase productivity, a supervisor needs to increase outputs, reduce inputs, or both.

Consider an employee who processes 96 driver's license applications in the course of an eight-hour day at the secretary of state's office. One way to measure this employee's productivity is 96/8, or 12 applications per hour (see Figure 12.2). A supervisor might note that a more experienced employee can process 20 applications per hour, so by this measure the first employee is less experienced than desirable and might require more training, motivation, or just more experience.

But the organization is also interested in the cost of the employee. So the supervisor might measure the input as the employee's cost per day (hourly wage times number of hours). If the employee earned $6 per hour, the productivity measure would be 96/($6 × 8), or 2 (see Figure 12.2). If the employee who

	Organization	Inputs	Outputs
TABLE 12.1 **Examples of Inputs and Outputs**	Bus line	Buses; gas, oil, and other supplies; terminals; drivers; ticket sellers; managers; tickets; schedules; funds; data	Transportation services to passengers
	Manufacturing firm	Trucks; plants; oil, rags, and other supplies; raw materials; purchased parts; production workers; supervisors; engineers; storekeepers; bills of material; inventory records; production schedules; time records; funds; data	Goods for use by customers
	Hospital	Ambulances; hospital rooms; beds, wheelchairs, X rays; receptionists; administrators; nurses; doctors; medicines; drugs; splints, bandages, food, and other supplies; medical charts; funds; data	Health care services to patients
	Police force	Cars and vans; offices; police officers; forms; handcuffs, radios, guns, office supplies, and other supplies; office furniture; equipment for forensic research; uniforms; funds; data	Protection of public safety

Source: Adapted from Samuel C. Certo, *Modern Management*, 6th ed., Allyn & Bacon, 1994.

FIGURE 12.2

Productivity Measurements

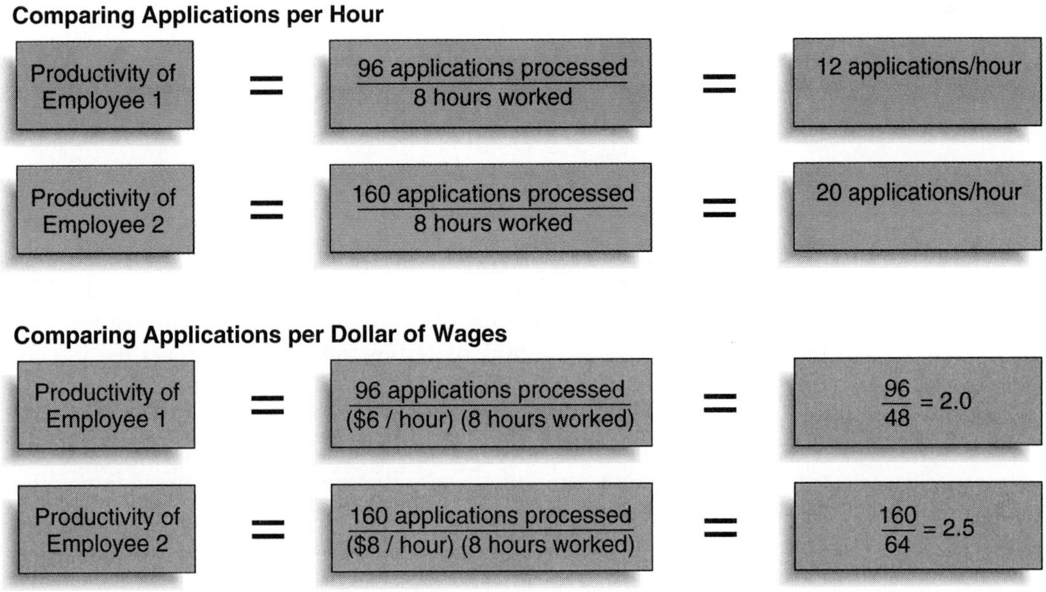

Comparing Applications per Hour

$$\text{Productivity of Employee 1} = \frac{96 \text{ applications processed}}{8 \text{ hours worked}} = 12 \text{ applications/hour}$$

$$\text{Productivity of Employee 2} = \frac{160 \text{ applications processed}}{8 \text{ hours worked}} = 20 \text{ applications/hour}$$

Comparing Applications per Dollar of Wages

$$\text{Productivity of Employee 1} = \frac{96 \text{ applications processed}}{(\$6 / \text{hour}) (8 \text{ hours worked})} = \frac{96}{48} = 2.0$$

$$\text{Productivity of Employee 2} = \frac{160 \text{ applications processed}}{(\$8 / \text{hour}) (8 \text{ hours worked})} = \frac{160}{64} = 2.5$$

■ FIGURE 12.3

Quantity without Quality Does Not Boost Productivity

"I don't get it! I turn out a record 370 units, and I don't even get a lousy 'thank you!'"

Source: From *Front Line Supervisor's Bulletin*, July 10, 1992. Reprinted with permission of Bureau of Business Practice, 125 Eugene O'Neill Drive, Suite 103, New London, CT 06320.

processes 20 applications per hour earns $8 per hour, that employee's productivity would be $160/(\$8 \times 8)$, or 2.5. Thus, the more experienced employee is more productive, even taking into account his or her higher wages.

Bear in mind that the "output" measured in the productivity formula is only goods and services of acceptable quality. A rude salesclerk and a production worker making defective components are not really productive. In these cases, the productivity formula would include only the number of correctly made components or the amount of sales made courteously and accurately. The production worker in the cartoon shown in Figure 12.3 has evidently missed this point.

Improving Productivity by Controlling Quality

Mistakes, errors, and rework are not just quality problems of the kind discussed in Chapter 2. They are also a drag on productivity. Poor quality can slow the output both of individuals and of the firm as a whole. That is why one of the supervisor's most important tasks is to think of and implement ways to get the job done right the first time.

Many of the quality-control strategies introduced in Chapter 2, such as Six Sigma, zero defects, and employee involvement, are applicable to productivity improvement. Though most of these initiatives are companywide programs that must be guided from the very top of the organization, supervisors play an important part. They can increase their own and their team or group's productivity by:

1. Understanding the goals of quality programs.
2. Accepting their own role in reaching those goals.

3. Helping subordinates contribute to quality goals.
4. Using their specific knowledge of the tasks and processes their teams perform to find unique ways to contribute to productivity.

Managers of the experimental SQA Division of office furniture maker Herman Miller understood the link between quality and productivity very well. This division, whose initials stood for "simple, quick, affordable," was so successful in reducing order-entry errors that the error rate dropped from 20 percent to almost zero. Now folded back into the main company so its achievements can be duplicated in other divisions, SQA cut faulty shipments enough to earn the highest customer-satisfaction rating in the industry.[5]

Improving Productivity by Controlling Costs

When supervisors and other managers look for ways to boost productivity, they often start by looking at their costs per unit of output, as was the case in this chapter's opening story. Productivity improves when the department or organization can do as much work at a lower cost. It also improves when output rises without a cost increase.

Determining Costs

Not surprisingly, before a supervisor can make intelligent decisions about how to trim costs, he or she has to know where the money is going. The most important source of such information is budget reports, described in Chapter 6. By reviewing budget reports regularly, a supervisor can see which categories of expenses are largest and identify where the department is spending more than it budgeted. Then a supervisor should spend time with workers, observing how they use the department's resources, including their time. The process of gathering information about costs and working with employees to identify needed improvements is part of a supervisor's control function.

Cost-Control Strategies

To lower costs, supervisors can use a number of strategies. (See the basic alternatives summarized in Figure 12.4.) These strategies are not mutually exclusive. Supervisors can get the greatest productivity by using as many of these strategies as will work. In deciding which strategies to use, supervisors should consider which will appeal to higher-level management, which will be acceptable to employees, and which involve areas within their control.

An important part of many of these strategies is encouraging and using employees' ideas for saving money. Operating the machines, preparing the reports, and serving clients or customers gives employees a close-up view of how things are done, enabling them to see the shortcomings of the organization's way of doing things.

Examples abound. Bic Corporation, the maker of pens, razors, and cigarette lighters, has a standing team of 15 production-line employees who meet once a week to review suggestions from the plant's suggestion boxes. Supervisors have 10 days to implement suggestions that the group approves, and Bic credits the program with increasing morale, productivity, and ultimately profits.[6] American Freightways of Harrison, Arkansas, opened a toll-free phone line for its employees

■ FIGURE 12.4

Cost-Control Strategies

Increase output.
Improve methods.
Reduce overhead.
Minimize waste.
Regulate or level work flow.
Install modern equipment.
Train and motivate employees.
Minimize tardiness, absenteeism, turnover.

to use in submitting ideas. Suggestions the company adopted include the addition of more forklifts and the installation of an automated billing system.[7] Dana Corporation, an auto parts maker headquartered in Toledo, Ohio, extended its suggestion program to four international companies it had recently acquired. It's likely the expanded program will prove worthwhile; the U.S. program is already a success. A recent suggestion from Kevin Bailey, a machine operator at Dana's Hopkinsville, Kentucky, plant, cost only $500 to implement but doubled production. Bailey's idea was simple. New automated equipment was being installed at a cost of $130,000 to speed production on a bracket press, and he recommended moving the press closer so he could reach it more easily, making his work more efficient. Although the Society for Human Resources Management notes that some managers ignore suggestions for months, defeating the purpose of soliciting them, Dana acted promptly. Bailey's suggestion "breezed right through," he said.[8]

Increase Output Remember that the numerator in the productivity equation (output/input) represents what the department or organization is producing. The greater the output at a given cost, the greater the productivity. Thus, a logical way to increase productivity is to increase output without boosting costs.

What does this mean in practical terms? Sometimes, by applying themselves, people can work faster or harder. Servers in a restaurant may find they can cover more tables, and factory production workers may find they can assemble more components. Of course, it is not always possible to increase output without sacrificing quality.

Needless to say, this method of improving productivity makes employees unhappy most frequently. A supervisor who wants to boost productivity by increasing output must first ensure that the new goals for output are reasonable. This could perhaps be learned by including employees in the decision-making process. A supervisor must also communicate the new goals carefully, emphasizing any positive aspects of the change. For example, a supervisor might mention that if employees are more productive, the organization has a chance to remain competitive without layoffs. In the end, improving productivity by increasing output works only when employees are motivated to do more (see Chapter 11).

Some companies are using technology to ensure productivity. Software programs that monitor e-mail and Internet usage have many uses, including protecting proprietary information and avoiding liability in hostile-environment discrimination suits. But companies also hope to cut down on the number of work hours employees report spending on shopping, visiting adult entertainment sites, planning trips, checking investments, and corresponding with friends and family. The American Civil Liberties Union and the American Management Association both report that about 76 percent of employers now use some form of electronic monitoring, though fewer inform employees of such surveillance.[9]

Improve Methods   There are only limited ways of doing the same thing better or faster. Reviewing and revamping the way things are done is the basic principle of reengineering, which led to productivity improvements at Liberty Mutual, an insurance and financial services company. At Liberty, the time from initial customer contact to the issuance of an insurance contract was 62 days, even though the actual preparation of a contract took only 3 days. The rest of the time was spent shuffling paperwork between departments, each of which had an independent computer system requiring that data be entered by hand. After studying this process, Liberty came up with a new method: Teams comprising members from each department would handle the entire process together. Not only has the new system cut the processing time by more than half, but it has enabled the company to offer quotes to more prospects and thus generate more sales.[10]

Mechanics at Boeing's Everett, Washington, plant now follow a new rule to cut down on the number of stray wrenches, bolts, and just plain debris left behind on finished planes. Each worker must check out his or her tools at the start of each shift and check them back in at the end. This simple procedure has gone a long way toward reducing the $4 billion a year the company was spending to repair planes damaged by left-behind items, such as a flashlight once found sealed inside a wing. Boeing even offers noncash prizes to employees for the most items retrieved from the planes, and the idea has been a big hit.[11]

A potentially powerful approach to improving methods is to apply the principles of job enlargement and job enrichment. Enlarging and enriching jobs makes them more interesting, which should motivate employees to deliver higher quality as well as work harder. UPS hopes to achieve that outcome by empowering its truck drivers to plan the routes they cover.[12]

Like managers at all levels, supervisors should be constantly on the lookout for ways to improve methods. Some ideas will come from supervisors themselves. (Chapter 9 provides suggestions for creative thinking.) Employees often have excellent ideas for doing the work better because they see the problems and pitfalls of their jobs. Supervisors should keep communication channels open and actively ask for ideas.

overhead
Expenses not related directly to producing goods and services; examples are rent, utilities, and staff support.

Reduce Overhead   Many departments spend more than is necessary for **overhead,** which includes rent, utilities, staff support, company cafeteria, janitorial services, and other expenses not related directly to producing goods and services. Typically, an organization allocates a share of the total overhead to each department based on the department's size. This means that a supervisor has limited control over a department's overhead expenses. However, a supervisor can periodically look for sources of needless expenses, such as lights left on in unoccupied

Where Productivity Means Never Having Anything in Stock

Speedy delivery is the biggest asset of giant online bookseller Amazon.com and the key to its success, along with its ability to offer customers 3.1 million titles to choose from. Yet the bookseller keeps very little in stock, which helps it control its overhead and thus its prices. Triggered by orders received online, books arrive daily from publishers and wholesalers and are quickly sorted by the warehouse staff, using a special numbering system for placement on the shelves. They are shelved based on how they are to be shipped, not by author or title, and they are tracked by inventory number.

The next step is for employees known as "pickers" to go through the shelves collecting books to fill specific orders. Supervisors expect that, depending on the size of the orders, pickers can fill between 25 and 100 orders a day. The books are delivered in carts to the sorting crew, which assigns them to bins for shipping. Some books take a quick detour for gift wrapping, and then the orders are packed, weighed, and set on pallets for those trucks waiting outside the door. In most cases, they leave the building the same day they arrived.

In this fast-paced 24-hour operation, "one department always looks out for the other department," says Cedric Ross, the distribution center's head of training. "Instead of being highly competitive, we try to see ourselves as one big team."

Sources: Paula L. Stepankowsky, "At Amazon.com Distribution Center, Virtual Wishes Turn into Real Books," *Wall Street Journal*, November 16, 1998, p. B7E; Robert D. Hof et al., "Amazon.com: The Wild World of E-commerce," *Business Week*, December 14, 1998, pp. 106–119.

---

areas or messy work areas that mean extra work for the janitorial staff. By reducing these costs to the company, a supervisor ultimately reduces the amount of overhead charged to his or her department.

Staff departments in particular can be guilty of contributing too much to the cost of overhead by generating unnecessary paperwork. Supervisors and their employees who produce or handle reports and forms should evaluate this paperwork, whether hard copy or electronic, to make sure it is needed. Another way to reduce the amount of paper is to make sure that when a procedure calls for a form with several parts, all the parts are actually used. "Meeting the Challenge" shows how one firm keeps productivity high with no stock in the warehouse.

Minimize Waste   Waste occurs in all kinds of operations. A medical office may order too many supplies and wind up throwing some away or taking up unnecessary storage space. A factory may handle materials in a way that produces a lot of scrap. A sales office may make unnecessary photocopies of needlessly long proposals, contributing more to landfills than to the company's profits.

idle time (downtime)
Time during which employees or machines are not producing goods or services.

A costly form of waste is **idle time,** or **downtime**—time during which employees or machines are not producing goods or services. This term is used most often in manufacturing operations, but it applies to other situations as well. In a factory, idle time occurs while a machine is shut down for repairs or while workers are waiting for parts. In an office, idle time occurs when employees are waiting for instructions, supplies, a computer printout, or a response to a question they asked the supervisor.

detour behavior
Tactics for postponing or avoiding work.

Another form of wasted time results from **detour behavior,** which is a tactic for postponing or avoiding work. Employees and their supervisors use a wide variety of detour behavior: A supervisor enjoys a cup of coffee and the newspaper before turning to the day's responsibilities or an employee stops by a colleague's desk to chat. Detour behavior may be especially tempting when a person's energy is low or when a person is facing a particularly challenging or unpleasant assignment. (The opposite of detour behavior is effective time management, discussed in Chapter 14.)

Sharon Katz Pearlman had been a lawyer with KPMG Peat Marwick, the accounting firm, for several years when she decided to try to reduce her typical 14-hour days. In her new four-day-a-week schedule, she found that by becoming more efficient, skipping lunch hours, and eliminating the chitchat that took place in the office, she was able to retain her high productivity. "I have to be very productive in whatever time I have," she said. Her firm recently recognized her achievement when her supervisor insisted on promoting her back to full-time status and making her a partner.[13]

Wasted time may be an even more important measure of lost productivity than wasted costs. Customer time counts, too, as United Airlines recognizes. Setting a new industry standard for productivity, United is adopting a plan that makes it a partner with American Airlines in allowing "interlining." Interlining makes electronic airline tickets for the two carriers. These tickets now account for about one-third of all air trips and are interchangeable with just a few keystrokes. The switch used to require converting the tickets to paper tickets first, which took time that passengers didn't always have. United also plans to extend the new method to its overseas partners such as Lufthansa.[14]

Supervisors should be on the alert for wasted time and other resources in their department. They can set a good example for effective time management and can make detecting waste part of the control process (see Chapter 6). Often, employees are good sources of information on how to minimize waste. The supervisor might consider holding a contest to find the best ideas.

Regulate or Level the Work Flow   An uneven flow of work can be costly (see Figure 12.5). When work levels are low, the result is idle time. When the department faces a surge in demand for its work, employees have to work extra hours to keep up. As a result, the department may have to pay workers overtime rates—one and a half or two times normal wages—during peak periods. In addition, people are rarely as efficient during overtime hours—they get tired—as they are during a normal workday. If a supervisor can arrange to have a more even work flow, the department can be staffed appropriately to get the job done during normal working hours, and fewer employees will be idle during slow periods.

A supervisor can take several steps to regulate departmental work flow:

1. A supervisor should first make sure that adequate planning has been done for the work required.
2. A supervisor may also find it helpful to work with his or her manager and peers or to form teams of employees to examine and solve work flow problems. Cooperation can help make the work flow more evenly or at least more predictably. For example, a manager who travels extensively may assign a great deal of work upon her return, not realizing that she is clustering deadlines instead of spreading them out for an even work flow. The sales department may be submitting orders in batches to the production department instead of submitting them as soon as they are received.
3. If the work flow must remain uneven, a supervisor may find that the best course is to use temporary employees during peak periods, an approach that can work if the temporary employees have the right skills.

■ FIGURE 12.5

The Costs of Uneven Work Flow

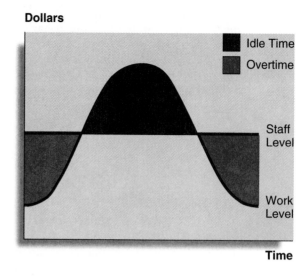

Dollars

Idle Time

Overtime

Staff Level

Work Level

Time

Install Modern Equipment Work may be slowed because employees are using worn or outdated equipment. If that is the case, a supervisor may find it worthwhile to obtain modern equipment. Although the value of installing modern equipment is obvious for manufacturing departments, many other workplaces can benefit from using modern equipment, including up-to-date computer technology.

In deciding to buy new equipment or in recommending its purchase, a supervisor needs to determine whether the expense will be worthwhile. One way to do this is to figure out how much money per year the new equipment will save, for example, in terms of lower repair costs, less downtime, and more goods produced. Then compute the number of years before the savings will offset the cost of buying the equipment, a time known as the **payback period.** A payback period is computed according to the first formula shown in Figure 12.6. Thus, if a computer system will cost $120,000 and is expected to save the office $40,000 per year, the payback period is three years ($120,000 ÷ $40,000 per year). Higher-level management or the finance department usually has an opinion on what payback period is acceptable for the organization.

Another way to evaluate whether an investment is worthwhile is to find the **average rate of return (ARR)** for that investment. ARR is a percentage that represents the organization's average annual earnings for each dollar of a given investment. An ARR of 15 percent means that each dollar invested yields income (or savings) of 15 cents a year. A basic formula for ARR is the second equation in Figure 12.6. For the computer system in the previous example, the ARR would be the $40,000 annual savings divided by the $120,000 cost, or .33—a 33 percent return. To determine whether this return is acceptable, a supervisor compares it with what the money spent could earn in another form of investment. Again, higher-level management or the finance department usually has established standards for this measure.

Payback period and ARR as described here are only two of the simplest ways to evaluate investments. Other, more complex, methods take into account factors such as the timing of payments and earnings. Software is available to compute

payback period
The length of time it will take for the benefits generated by an investment (such as cost savings from machinery) to offset the cost of the investment.

average rate of return (ARR)
A percentage that represents the average annual earnings for each dollar of a given investment.

FIGURE 12.6

Basic Formulas for Evaluating an Investment

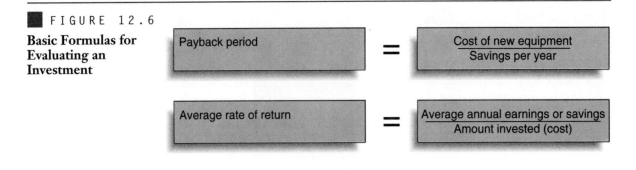

payback period, average rate of return, and other analyses of the financial worthiness of an investment.

Train and Motivate Employees To work efficiently, employees need a good understanding of how to do their jobs. Thus, a basic way to improve productivity is to train employees. "Supervision and Diversity" illustrates how supervisors can train and motivate telecommuters.

As you learned in Chapter 11, training alone does not lead to superior performance; employees also must be motivated to do good work. In other words, employees must want to do a good job. Motivation is a key tactic for improving productivity because employees are often in the best position to think of ways to achieve their objectives more efficiently. In China, the government hopes that a new policy mandating Saturdays off will improve productivity as workers try to get the same work done in five days instead of six. Josef Wilfling, general manager for Siemans AG in Shanghai, agrees: "People are visibly tired at the end of the day [with a six-day week]. This will help, I'm sure."[15]

See "Tips from the Firing line" for some ways that you can increase productivity by boosting morale.

Minimize Tardiness, Absenteeism, and Turnover Lack of motivation is often the problem underlying time lost to tardiness and absenteeism. When employees dislike their jobs or find them boring, they tend to use excuses to arrive late or not at all. Lost time is costly; in most cases, the organization is paying for someone who is not actually working. Furthermore, other employees may be unable to work efficiently without the support of the missing person. As a result, minimizing absenteeism and tardiness is an important part of the supervisor's job. (Chapter 13 provides some guidelines for this task.)

One way for supervisors to cut down on absenteeism may be to pay more attention to factors that cause undue stress for employees. CCH Inc. recently surveyed 800,000 workers in 401 companies around the United States and found that stress as a reason for work absences has increased dramatically in the last three years. Personal illness, in contrast, has declined by almost half. While some of the switch may be caused by employees reporting they feel stressed instead of calling in "sick," there seems little doubt that workers look on absenteeism somewhat differently now. Also on the increase are absences due to an "entitlement mentality," which translates as "I've worked hard; I deserve a day off."[16]

Absenteeism may be the first step to leaving the company. The employee misses more and more days, then finally quits altogether. The rate at which

SUPERVISION AND DIVERSITY

The Telecommuting Supervisor

How does a supervisor successfully manage telecommuters' productivity? Does the situation become more complicated when the supervisor is a telecommuter too?

To maintain productivity in a telecommuting environment, Ken Radziwanowski, who trains AT&T managers to supervise telecommuters, suggests choosing your telecommuting workers carefully. They need a high ability to work independently, the skill to create a productive home office free of distractions, excellent planning and organization skills, and computer expertise.

Once you've selected the right people, you can maintain productivity by relying on your supervisory skills. For instance, plan work flow and scheduling in advance, set clear goals and objectives, agree on what constitutes acceptable performance and how to measure it, establish reporting methods—such as written or oral reports, computer tracking, phone conferences, e-mail, or in-person meetings—and their frequency, and finally remember to give plenty of feedback on performance. Make sure you have off-site technical support for your people, and help them keep in touch with each other and with you by creating a way for them to share information electronically, such as shared online folders (something like an electronic office watercooler).

Tom Smithling is an AT&T telecommuting supervisor who works at home about four days each week. He maintains his own productivity by calling his boss regularly with status reports, using his in-office day to see his boss in person, and making sure he attends important meetings no matter what day they're scheduled. In working with his employees, he believes strongly in good communication techniques. Tom checks in with his people often, sometimes three or four times a day by phone. Because he may not always anticipate when they need coaching, he has learned to make his training very focused. He does this over the phone as well, and he finds it important to listen carefully (to make up for missing eye contact and body language in the conversation), and not to do anything else while on the phone, such as typing, reading e-mail, or doing other work.

Tom finds the connections he has forged are paying off. If a day or two goes by and he hasn't spoken to someone in his group, he finds they'll call him, if only to say hi. "It's almost as if they are lonesome," he says. "They want me to know they are working."

Sources: "When the Manager Telecommutes Too," *Getting Results*, January 1997, p. S2; "AT&T Trains Managers to Supervise Telecommuters," *Getting Results*, January 1997, p. S1.

---

turnover
The rate at which employees leave an organization.

employees leave an organization is known as **turnover.** High turnover is expensive, because the organization must spend a lot of money to recruit and train new employees. Therefore, an important part of controlling costs is to keep good employees by making the organization a place they want to stay.

Job sharing is an innovation that helps many workers, particularly women, stay in the workforce. Natalie Wolanin "desperately wanted to stay in my career" and jumped at the chance to share with Judy Schroeter-Deegan the job of manager of market research at the National School Board Association. "It does take support," says Natalie two years later, "it would be very tough otherwise." But the partners, their supervisor, and the human resources director are happy with the arrangement.[17] Such creative solutions can help supervisors maintain productivity by hiring and keeping valuable workers who are less motivated to leave.

Supervisors can minimize turnover by applying the principles of motivation. In general, supervisors should identify what employees want from their jobs and meet those needs when possible.

Using Morale Boosters to Improve Productivity

The link between productivity and morale has been demonstrated many times over, and few things sap morale more quickly than anger. As one writer notes, "It takes a great deal of managerial skill to maintain high morale and high productivity, but making people angry is a snap." Needless conflict is a time waster, too.

Here are some don'ts to help you avoid creating unnecessary dips in morale—and in turn, productivity.

1. Don't go over your boss's head. Skipping links in the chain of command is almost never a good idea.
2. Don't refuse a task just because "it's not in my job description." Negotiate if you must, but refusing to work doesn't raise productivity.
3. Don't pay selective attention to tasks. Doing only what you like to do will make more work for others, if not for you in the long run, and slows everyone down.
4. Don't nurse the feeling that you're being exploited. Suggesting that you are underpaid, overworked, or underappreciated won't get the job done or make you look good.
5. Don't pull rank by flaunting perks, leaving earlier than your subordinates, or misusing your authority. Respect subordinates' time as well.
6. Don't put others or their work down. People put forth their best effort when they know you know their worth.
7. Don't suggest that your subordinates can't be trusted or need you to monitor every detail. Trust builds morale.
8. Don't leave your people out of the loop. That lets them know they're not important and creates resentment, not results.
9. Don't carry out disciplinary actions in public. Have a high regard for employees' pride and self-esteem.
10. Don't back-stab your peers. Undermining them hurts you, too.
11. Don't invade others' territories, whether it is their area of responsibility or their desk or locker. The counterattack will be just as wasteful as your offensive.
12. Don't take credit you don't deserve. Even if you gain in the short term, it won't be worth it.

Source: Adapted from Terry L. Stawar, "A Dozen Ways to Make Enemies at Work without Even Trying," *Manage*, August 1, 1998, p. 23.

Employee Fears about Productivity Improvement

A highly productive organization is in an ideal position to thrive and grow. Thus, employees can benefit from productivity improvements. This is true especially when efforts to boost productivity focus on improving the quality of processes rather than simply cutting payroll costs. Even so, many employees react with fear when managers start talking about improving productivity.

During a recent speech to the National Association of Manufacturers, Dallas Federal Reserve Bank President Robert D. McTeer, Jr., told the following story:

> At the rate you're going with productivity improvements, the factory of the future may have only two employees: a man and a dog. The man's job will be to feed the dog. The dog's job will be to keep the man from touching the equipment.[18]

And, indeed, some observers expect that the Internet will eventually link not just pieces of factory equipment but also factories themselves, and perhaps even entire supply chains.[19]

Employees may have good reason to be fearful. Many have experienced or have heard of cost reductions leading to less overtime pay, more difficult work, and even layoffs. When layoffs occur, the people who are left behind often have to struggle to keep up with the work that still has to be done.

Supervisors must respond to these fears. Most importantly, they must be prepared with information. A supervisor who does not understand the types of changes to be made and the reasons for them should discuss the matter with his or her manager as soon as possible. After obtaining a clear view of the organization's plans and goals, a supervisor should present this information to the employees. In doing so, a supervisor should emphasize what the benefits will be and avoid dwelling on the negatives.

When a supervisor gives information about productivity improvement, employees should have an opportunity to ask questions. The supervisor who cannot answer some of the questions should promise to get answers—and then do so. Although information alone will not make employees enthusiastic about a productivity program, uninformed employees almost certainly will suffer from low morale.

In Chapter 15, we will take a closer look at how supervisors can help employees cope with the fears and related challenges that accompany productivity improvements and other types of change.

Summary

12.1 Define *productivity*.
Productivity is the amount of results (output) an organization gets for a given amount of inputs such as labor and machinery. Typically, it refers to the amount of acceptable work employees do for each dollar they earn or the number of acceptable products manufactured with a given amount of resources.

12.2 Identify constraints on productivity.
Management limits productivity when it does not seem truly committed to improving it. Employee attitudes and skills limit productivity when employees are unable or unwilling to meet standards for performance. Government regulations impose responsibilities on organizations that limit their productivity to achieve other objectives. A union contract may contain work rules that limit productivity.

12.3 Describe how productivity and productivity improvements are measured.
To measure productivity, divide the amount of outputs by the amount of inputs. Outputs are the amount of work done or goods and services produced, assuming that these are of acceptable quality. Inputs may be measured as dollars, hours, or both. Productivity increases when output increases, input decreases, or both.

12.4 Identify the two basic ways productivity may be improved.
Two ways to improve productivity are to control quality and to control costs. Controlling quality

involves minimizing defects or errors. Controlling costs involves producing the same amount of goods or services at a lower cost or producing more at the same cost.

12.5 Describe cost-control strategies available to supervisors.
A supervisor may increase output by having people or machines work faster or harder. A more effective approach may be to improve methods; that is, to get things done more efficiently. The supervisor may identify ways to reduce overhead and minimize waste, including idle time and wasted physical resources. Regulating or leveling the work flow can make staffing more efficient. Installing modern equipment reduces costs when the new equipment is more efficient. To cut costs related to personnel, a supervisor should see that workers receive adequate training and motivation, and he or she should take steps to minimize tardiness, absenteeism, and turnover.

12.6 Explain why employees have fears about productivity improvement, and tell how supervisors can address those fears.
Many employees are fearful of productivity improvements because many organizations make such changes through layoffs and extra work for the remaining employees. Supervisors can respond by keeping employees informed about the organization's plans, emphasizing the benefits, and listening to employees.

Key Terms

productivity, p. 297

overhead, p. 305

idle time (downtime), p. 306

detour behavior, p. 306

payback period, p. 308

average rate of return (ARR), p. 308

turnover, p. 310

Review and Discussion Questions

1. Frank Ouellette works at a government agency where neither managers nor employees seem to worry about how long it takes to complete an assignment. Should Frank's co-workers be concerned about productivity? Why or why not?

2. Anna Holt, a supervisor in a boot manufacturing plant, just received a memo from her manager informing her that productivity on her shift must increase by 10 percent during the next fiscal quarter. However, when she recently approached her manager about upgrading two of the machines, she was turned down. In addition, she knows that her employees' union will balk at an increase in the number of boots her group must produce in a given shift. What constraints on productivity does Anna face? How might she attempt to resolve them?

3. At the claims-processing office for All-Folks Insurance, 25 employees process 2,500 claims a day. The claims-processing office for Purple Cross Insurance uses a state-of-the-art computer system, and its 15 employees process 3,000 claims a day.
   a. Which office is more productive?
   b. At which office would you expect employees to be paid more? Why?

4. In question 3, suppose that half the claims processed by the employees at Purple Cross contain errors and all of the claims processed at All-Folks are done correctly. Which office would you say is more productive? Why?

5. Where can supervisors get information to help them determine costs?

6. How would you expect employees to respond to each of these efforts to cut costs?
   a. A plan to increase output by scheduling fewer rest breaks.
   b. A plan to increase output by hiring someone to bring supplies to laboratory workers, rather than having them get their own supplies.

7. Sam Marshall was just promoted to manager of a fast-food restaurant. The restaurant owner has asked Sam to look for ways to reduce overhead. What might be some sources of needless expense (that are under Sam's control), and what steps might Sam take to reduce these?

8. At a telemarketing office, 36 employees make telephone calls to people's homes, trying to sell services for the company's clients. When the employees arrive at work, the supervisor hands each of them a list of the homes to call. However, the supervisor is sometimes tied up in a meeting or on the telephone, so the employees have to wait to get their lists. They use the time to discuss their family or social lives and to surf the Internet.

   What productivity problem is occurring in this office? Suggest at least one way the supervisor can address this problem.

9. Rachel Roth supervises a shift of workers who manufacture ski clothing. Because of its seasonal nature, the work flow tends to be uneven, and Rachel feels that this hurts productivity. What steps might Rachel take to try to regulate the work flow in her department?

10. A maintenance supervisor learned that installing a type of high-efficiency light bulb in the building can save the organization $1,000 a year. Replacing the current system with the new one would cost about $2,500.
    a. What is the payback period for this system?
    b. What is the average rate of return?
    c. Do you think this is a worthwhile investment? Why or why not?

11. How does high turnover hurt productivity? What can a supervisor do to minimize turnover?
12. Why do employees sometimes resist productivity improvements? How can supervisors prepare for and respond to employee attitudes?

A SECOND LOOK

What accounts for the Warrens' success in the opening story? What other cost-cutting measures could they take? Would these measures affect quality?

SKILLS MODULE

CASE

Com-Corp Industries Keeps Productivity High

It's no coincidence that Com-Corp Industries, a metal-stamping shop that manufactures headlight parts, keeps productivity high with democratic management in which employees have a say in many aspects of their jobs. That's because president John Strazzanti started out at the bottom and has learned many lessons over the years in what keeps workers working, costs down, and quality high.

At his first job as a press operator in the stamping department at a plant that made bicycle parts, Strazzanti was eager to impress his boss. "The maximum number of parts ever produced from the machine I was assigned was 40,000 in a 10-hour shift," he recalls. "I went to work trying to learn how to make the machine run faster. By the end of the week I had produced 46,000 pieces." But Strazzanti's supervisor didn't give him the praise he expected; instead, the boss said, "I really think 50,000 is attainable. That's what I want you to shoot for." Instead of hitting 50,000 pieces, Strazzanti never reached more than 32,000 after that. It was a lesson he never forgot—one in how *not* to increase productivity.

Twenty-five years later, Strazzanti's Com-Corp employees earn above-market pay increases; they make decisions about compensation rates, get tenure, enjoy profit sharing, and they have access to all kinds of company information and training. All of this and more is written in the company's Policy and Procedure Manual. Thus, employees are motivated—and they produce.

To prevent management constraints on productivity, an internal corporate auditor reviews pertinent documents generated by supervisors, such as performance appraisals, purchasing records, and so forth. To control costs, the company charges managers with "maximizing the company's return on investment" in exchange for profit sharing.

Employee compensation costs also are controlled; the policy manual stipulates that employee decisions about compensation must be based on the economic rule of thumb that the marketplace determines the worth of employees' skills and services.

Com-Corp also tracks the costly rate of turnover and has identified two types. Positive turnover occurs when employees leave Com-Corp for jobs that are more challenging than the company can offer. Negative turnover occurs when workers leave for jobs that pay more, which signals that Com-Corp's pay rates are not always competitive in the marketplace. This occurrence is rare: In a recent year, Com-Corp experienced only a 2 percent negative turnover.

If productivity is measured in the amount of outputs an organization gets for its inputs, Com-Corp can mark its productivity high on the scale. The company has grown steadily since its incorporation more than 15 years ago, and it has never lost money.

1. If Strazzanti had to face union constraints on productivity, how do you think he might handle the situation?
2. Do you think Com-Corp's employees suffer from fears about productivity improvement? Why or why not?
3. Com-Corp has several ways of controlling costs. Do you think that its democratic management system also helps control quality? Why or why not?

■ SELF-QUIZ

Test Your Personal Productivity

Place a check mark next to each of the activities you do or habits you have formed. The more check marks, the more productive you can be.

_____ 1. I complete tasks right away, without procrastinating.

_____ 2. I take notes during meetings and conversations to avoid misunderstanding and omissions.

_____ 3. I plan tomorrow's work today by writing a few notes before quitting time.

_____ 4. I prioritize my tasks, tackling the most important or most difficult ones first every day.

_____ 5. I keep a follow-up file.

_____ 6. I plan realistic deadlines, allowing time for delays.

_____ 7. I keep my workspace or desk neat and uncluttered.

_____ 8. I delegate wherever possible and reasonable to my assistant and/or my subordinates.

_____ 9. I limit the number and length of phone calls and monitor my own use of the Internet.

_____ 10. I am not afraid to say no in order to protect the time I have available for the job.

Source: From Ted Pollock, "Increasing Personal Productivity," *Supervision*, March 2001. Reprinted by permission of © National Research Bureau, 320 Valley Street, Burlington, Iowa 52601.

Class Exercise

Imagine that you have been asked by the dean of students to act as host to a foreign-exchange student for a semester at your school. The student's major is identical to your own. The student speaks some English, but not as a primary language.

What steps would you take to maximize the student's productivity while at your school? What constraints might you face? How would you deal with potential culture shock? Write a plan outlining your ideas.

Team-Building Exercise
Measuring Teams' Productivity

This class exercise requires jigsaw puzzles, one for each five or six students in the class. Puzzles with no more than 500 pieces would probably work best.

Divide the class into teams for each puzzle. Each team works on its puzzle for 15 minutes. When time is up, the class discusses the following questions:

1. Compare the productivity of the teams. How should productivity be measured? When the whole class agrees on a proper measure, each team computes its own productivity.
2. Which team was most productive? Why? Did it use methods that could have helped the other groups?
3. How could you have improved the productivity of your team?

13

The only difference between a problem and a solution is that people understand the solution.

—Charles Kettering, engineer and inventor

Supervising "Problem" Employees

■ CHAPTER OUTLINE

■ LEARNING OBJECTIVES

After you have studied this chapter, you should be able to:

13.1 Identify common types of problem behavior among employees.

13.2 Explain why and when supervisors should counsel employees.

13.3 Describe counseling techniques.

13.4 Discuss effective ways of administering discipline.

13.5 Describe the principles of positive discipline and self-discipline.

13.6 Explain how supervisors can detect and confront troubled employees.

13.7 Specify how supervisors can direct troubled employees in getting help and then follow up on the recovery efforts.

13.8 Discuss the role of the supervisor's manager and the human resources department in helping the supervisor with problem employees.

■ TIME CARD ABUSE

Managers at a plant suspected that some employees were getting overtime pay for time not worked by them by having co-workers punch their time cards. Supervisors were told to check employees' time cards and verify that employees were on the job when their time cards indicated overtime. . . . One day, a supervisor pulled an employee's time card and saw that it indicated he was working overtime. When he couldn't find the employee, he concluded that the employee was not in the plant. The supervisor then instructed a security guard to watch the absent employee's time card and report if anyone else punched it. The security guard saw another employee punch the time card and notified the supervisor.

Based on the supervisor's report, the personnel manager conducted an investigation and verified that the employee punched the absent employee's card. Stating that the employee's action amounted to theft, the manager fired the employee under a company policy calling for immediate discharge for punching another employee's time card. At an arbitration hearing on the discharge, the employee denied the charge, asserting the security guard had made a mistake because she was relieving another worker at the time the card was punched and,

therefore, she could not have punched the card. She also claimed that other workers had been caught stealing from the company and had not been fired. She argued that her 10-year record of good work at the plant should be considered as a factor mitigating against discharge for a single offense.

The arbitrator upheld the discharge action. He said that even though the employee had long service at the plant, the serious nature of her infraction—an attempt to collect unmerited overtime pay by falsifying a co-worker's time card—could not be ignored. Although the employee denied punching the co-worker's card, the evidence suggested otherwise, according to the arbitrator. First, management already suspected that time cards were being punched incorrectly by other workers and was therefore able to alert the security guard to the problem. Second, the guard was employed by an outside contractor and had no reason to falsely implicate the employee. Concerning the employee's claim that she was relieving another worker when the time card was punched, the arbitrator noted that no witnesses were available to support the employee's contention.

Source: William E. Lissy, "Time Card Abuse: Labor Law for Supervisors," *Supervision*, May 1996, pp. 17 ff.

When a supervisor does a good job of leading, problem solving, communicating, and motivating, most employees will perform well. Even so, a supervisor occasionally faces the challenge of a "problem" employee, one who is persistently unwilling or unable to follow the rules or meet performance standards. In general, problem employees fall into two categories: (1) employees *causing* problems—for example, by starting fights or leaving early—and (2) employees *with* problems, such as an employee whose money worries are a distraction from work. By handling these troubled employees appropriately, a supervisor can help resolve the problem without hurting the morale or performance of other employees.

This chapter provides guidelines for supervising problem employees. It describes some common problems requiring special action on the part of a supervisor and explains two basic courses of action to take: counseling and discipline. The chapter also discusses how to help a troubled employee. Finally, the chapter describes the kinds of support a supervisor can expect from superiors, the human resources department, and other experts.

Problems Requiring Special Action

For the third straight Monday, Peter Dunbar had called in sick. The other employees were grumbling about having to do extra work to make up for his absences, and rumors were flying about the nature of Peter's problem. Peter's supervisor knew she would have to take action, beginning with some investigation into what the problem was.

When supervisors observe poor performance, they tend to blame the employee for lacking ability or effort. But when supervisors or employees need to explain their own poor performance, they may blame the organization or another person for not providing enough support. This inconsistency suggests that some digging is needed to uncover the true source of a performance problem. For example, the supervisor might consider the following questions:

- Has the employee performed better in the past?
- Has the employee received proper training?
- Does the employee know and understand the objectives he or she is to accomplish?
- Is the supervisor providing enough feedback and support?
- Has the supervisor encouraged and rewarded high performance?
- Are other employees with similar abilities performing well? Or are they experiencing similar difficulties?

Although persistent failure to perform up to standards results from many problems, the problems that supervisors most commonly encounter among employees are absenteeism and tardiness, insubordination and uncooperativeness, alcohol and drug abuse, and theft. Psychological problems also cause friction in the workplace; see "Supervision and Diversity."

Absenteeism and Tardiness

An employee who misses work, even part of a day, is expensive for an employer. The company frequently must pay for those unproductive hours—for example, by providing sick pay to an employee who calls in sick. In addition, the other employees may be less productive when they have to cover for someone who is absent or tardy.

Of course, employees who really are sick should take time off. The company provides sick days for good reasons: to allow employees to rest and recover and to prevent them from infecting the rest of the workforce. The problem arises with absences that are unexcused or recur with suspicious regularity. In addition, missing work is often a sign of a deeper problem, such as a family crisis, anger about something at work, or plans to leave the organization.

When Is a Disability Not a Disability?

In 1997, for the first time, the Equal Employment Opportunity Commission (EEOC) recorded more complaints of discrimination on the basis of emotional or psychiatric impairment than any other category, including HIV, substance abuse, and other health-related disabilities. The trend appeared set to continue into 1998 as well.

In one of the fastest-growing areas of employment law, the tide may be turning in employees' favor. Before new EEOC guidelines and a Supreme Court opinion were released in 1997 and 1998, respectively, companies won more than 90 percent of all court decisions under the Americans with Disabilities Act (ADA). In other words, when otherwise competent employees claimed they had been discriminated against because they were disabled by mental illnesses such as depression and schizophrenia, they lost because courts ruled they were not disabled.

Under the new guidelines, the EEOC has said that a mental disorder can be considered a disability

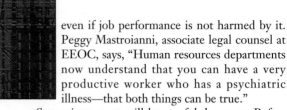

even if job performance is not harmed by it. Peggy Mastroianni, associate legal counsel at EEOC, says, "Human resources departments now understand that you can have a very productive worker who has a psychiatric illness—that both things can be true."

Supervisors must still be careful, however. Referring an employee to counseling or treatment may be charitable but it can be misconstrued. "The employee can turn around and claim that the employer perceives the employee as having a disability and is discriminating against the employee on that basis," says Harriet E. Cooperman, head of the labor and employment law group at Weinberg & Green in Baltimore. This advice is offered by James J. McDonald, Jr., of Fisher & Phillips, a California law firm: "Focus on the conduct, not on the condition. Don't try to play armchair psychiatrist."

Source: Geanne Rosenberg, "When the Mind Is the Matter," *New York Times*, November 7, 1998, pp. C1–C2.

A Xerox Corporation study recently found that work options such as flexible scheduling can reduce absenteeism by as much as 30 percent, suggesting that policies allowing workers to achieve a better balance of work and home life have much to offer.[1]

Insubordination and Uncooperativeness

When poor performance results from not understanding how to do a job, the solution is relatively simple. A supervisor must make sure that instructions are communicated clearly and that the employee is receiving the proper training. But sometimes an employee performs poorly or breaks rules because he or she chooses to do so. Such an employee may simply be uncooperative, or the employee may engage in **insubordination,** the deliberate refusal to do what a supervisor or other superior asks.

insubordination
Deliberate refusal to do what the supervisor or other superior asks.

Many kinds of negative behavior fall into these categories. An employee may have a generally poor attitude—criticizing, complaining, and showing a dislike for a supervisor and the organization. He or she might get into arguments over many kinds of issues. An employee may make an art form out of doing as little as possible. The employee might spend most of the day socializing, joking around, or just moving slowly. Another employee might regularly fail to follow rules—"forgetting" to wear safety equipment or sign out at lunchtime. Unfortunately, employee complaints of racism and retaliation have risen.[2]

The owner of a restaurant in Austin, Texas, relates the story of an extremely negative waitress: "She had nothing good to say about anything or anybody. Her

SUPERVISION ACROSS INDUSTRIES

Information Systems

When Laid-off Workers Take Revenge

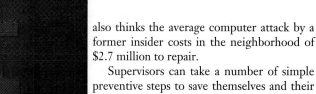

Laid-off information systems employees suddenly have high-tech weapons at hand if they are in the mood for revenge against their former employers. Those weapons are the very tools they worked with while employed. One systems administrator hacked his former employer's computers and published company secrets in a public chat room. Another encrypted all the patient files at the hospital from which she had been laid off and restored them only when promised a cash payout, severance pay, and immunity from prosecution. Another worker sent everyone at his old company a pornographic e-mail message, and one erased all the CEO's e-mail at his former firm. There was even a case in which a laid-off worker used a dead colleague's password to log back into the company's network because no one had yet deleted the dead man's profile.

In San Francisco, the FBI has seen the number of corporate computer break-ins by former employees jump from 3 to 15 in just a year. "This is just the tip of the iceberg," says James Hegarty, who supervises the agency's computer crime squad in Boston. "We think it's phenomenally underreported." The FBI also thinks the average computer attack by a former insider costs in the neighborhood of $2.7 million to repair.

Supervisors can take a number of simple preventive steps to save themselves and their firms from the loss and damage that an ex-employee-turned-saboteur can cause. Experts advise being aware of the six common traits of those who nurse grudges: a history of personal or social frustrations, heavy computer use, loose ethics, reduced loyalty, a sense of entitlement, and lack of empathy. Practical steps supervisors should take include shutting off employees' computer access just *before* they are terminated, letting workers know that divulging company secrets and invading computer computers are serious crimes, treating laid-off workers with respect so that grudges won't arise, and requiring all remaining employees to change their passwords. All this is, of course, in addition to the normal security precautions that supervisors should have in place, such as periodic sweeps of the computer systems to detect unauthorized access.

Source: Michelle Conlin and Alex Salkever, "Revenge of the Downsized Nerds," *Business Week*, July 30, 2001, p. 40.

constant complaints were affecting everyone—instead of her picking up others' upbeat attitudes, she was bringing everyone down." The last straw was her yelling at the owner on the restaurant floor during a busy period.[3]

Alcohol and Drug Abuse

The *Los Angeles Times* recently reported the following startling figures:

> On any given day, 5 percent to 17 percent of American workers arrive at their jobs under the influence of drugs or alcohol, according to Timothy Dimoff, a former narcotics detective. . . . About one in 10 employees uses illicit drugs or alcohol during work hours, according to the National Institute on Drug Abuse.
>
> Substance abusers miss an average of three weeks more per year than fellow employees and are three times more likely to be late. They're 16 times as likely to make use of health-care benefits, six times more likely to file workers' compensation claims and only two-thirds as productive as non-abusers, according to government agencies such as the departments of Labor and Health and Human Services. . . . Drug enforcement agencies estimate that as much as 25 percent of workplace drug abuse involves pharmaceuticals such as painkillers and tranquilizers.[4]

Steelcase, Inc., recently estimated the cost of treating each drug-abusing employee at $9,000 to $12,000 a year.[5]

The Americans with Disabilities Act (ADA), which prohibits discrimination on the basis of physical or mental disability, treats substance abuse arising from an addiction as a disability. Therefore, substance abuse may not be legal grounds for firing an employee. The supervisor should encourage the employee to get help, even if doing so requires adjusting the employee's work schedule or permitting the employee to take a disability leave to get treatment. In addition, actions taken with regard to the employee should focus on work performance, not on the substance abuse itself. For example, a supervisor might warn, "If I catch you picking fights with your co-workers again, I will have to suspend you." This warning addresses the employee's job-related behavior. (For more on the ADA and other laws against employment discrimination, see Chapter 16.)

Although a supervisor must treat each employee fairly and avoid discrimination, he or she also has responsibility for helping to ensure that the workplace is safe for employees and others. If an employee's suspected substance abuse is creating a hazard, a supervisor must act. Again, the key is to address job-related behavior. (See the section on troubled employees, page 334, which provides guidelines for handling employees who abuse drugs or alcohol.)

Workplace Violence

Security managers at the Fortune 1000 companies recently responded to a Pinkerton survey by saying that workplace violence is their number 1 security threat. It is estimated that there are about 2 million incidents of workplace violence per year, and according to the Bureau of Labor Statistics, since 1992 murder has been second only to highway accidents as the leading cause of death on the job. In 1999, 645 people were killed in the workplace.[6]

Kristin L. Bowl, spokesperson for the Society for Human Resource Management in Alexandria, Virginia, says that about 15 percent of incidents of workplace violence result from substance abuse, and the Department of Labor found that 96 percent of nearly a million women who suffer domestic abuse from former or current domestic partners are also victims of workplace violence. Bowl agrees, "Domestic violence is a contributing factor to workplace violence." Her agency suggests that nearly one in 10 violent incidents is perpetrated by a spouse or ex-spouse or by a boyfriend, girlfriend, or relative, and Bowl offers this advice: "Employers can help to obtain protective orders and provide escorts to cars for those who have to work late hours, along with many security measures they provide to employees in general."[7]

Domestic violence is estimated to cost U.S. companies $3 billion to $5 billion a year in sick leave and reduced productivity.[8] For this and other reasons, some companies, such as Philip Morris Co. and Liz Claiborne Inc., offer information and help for employees who are victimized at work or at home. Rona Solomon, deputy director of the Center for Elimination of Violence in the Family Inc. (Brooklyn, New York), advises that employee assistance programs can be important referrals for victims of violence, and that protecting the employee's privacy is a must.[9] "We don't know who goes in there [to counseling programs] and we don't keep records," says Philip Morris Management Corp.'s vice president of corporate affairs programs DeDe Thompson Bartlett.[10]

In the aftermath of workplace violence there are often psychological wounds among employees that must be allowed to heal. The wise supervisor refrains from adopting the role of counselor but rather remains alert to those who may need special help, such as a referral for professional assistance or even reassignment or time off. After a shooting at Navistar in Melrose Park, Illinois, in February 2001, in which a former employee killed four workers, about 20 percent of the workforce took the next day off, and many spent the following day in counseling sessions to deal with complex feelings of grief, stress, and even guilt.[11]

Theft

The largest cause of missing goods and money for retailers today is not shoplifting, which accounts for 33 percent of losses, but employee theft, which makes up 44 percent of losses. (Paperwork errors and vendor fraud make up the remaining 18 and 5 percent, respectively.)[12]

When the manager of a Beall's Outlet store in the Southeast began stealing small amounts of money from the cash register, she used various strategies to hide the thefts. Before long, she had taken $1,000, but even so her misdeed might have gone undetected save for new software the company had installed to monitor cash-register transactions. The computer program was able to monitor every sale, every voided sale, every "no sale," and every refund; and security personnel were able to set up survillance within three weeks of the first theft and collect enough evidence in the following week to confront the manager and file charges.[13] Such monitoring software is coming into more and more frequent use.

Not all thefts involve money or tangible goods. Employees can also "steal time" by giving the employer less work than they are paid for, taking extra sick leave, or altering their time cards. Lost time is also more and more often spent surfing the Internet. Various new kinds of software programs can block particular websites from employees' view and monitor Internet activity. Some of these "activity monitors" not only capture keystrokes and mouse movements (by recording how long certain windows stay active and open); they also create a complete record of the computer's use.[14] Privacy issues come into play when such tools are used, and some observers feel they imply a lack of trust on the employer's part that can be damaging to employee-employer relationships. Figure 13.1 summarizes average tangible losses per employee theft in various types of retail stores.

The theft of information is also a serious and growing problem, made even easier by new communications technology, as in the case of a supervisor at a magazine distributor on Long Island who was accused of leaking to brokers advance copies of *Business Week* magazine's "Inside Wall Street" column every week. The supervisor was accused of faxing the column to one of the brokers, who passed it along to several others, whose family and customers are believed to have made more than $200,000 in illegal profits.[15]

The widespread nature of employee theft indicates that supervisors must be on their guard against it. Besides following the broad guidelines in this chapter for handling employee problems, supervisors should take measures to prevent and react to theft. Each organization has its own procedures, varying according to type of industry. In addition, supervisors should carefully check the background of anyone they plan to hire (part of the selection process described in Chapter 16).

More careful checking would have saved some trouble for Cheryl Cwiklinski, who hired a bookkeeper who seemed like a dream, working long hours without taking breaks or days off. Unfortunately, this "model" employee was later found to be making out thousands of dollars in checks to herself and working the extra hours to cover her actions.[16]

Supervisors should make sure that employees follow all procedures for record keeping. They should take advantage of ways to build employee morale and

FIGURE 13.1

Losses per Employee Theft

Average, all stores
$1,023

Supermarket and grocery stores
$183

Department stores
$746

Men's, women's and children's apparel
$1,078

Discount stores
$1,123

Home centers, hardware, lumber and garden supply stores
$1,146

Source: From Jennifer S. Lee, "Tracking Sales at the Cashiers," *New York Times*, July 11, 2001. Copyright © 2001 The New York Times. Reprinted with permission.

involvement; employees who feel like a part of the organization are less likely to steal from it. Supervisors should make sure employees understand the costs and consequences of theft. Perhaps most important, supervisors should set a good example by following the principles of ethical behavior.

The Small Business Administration advises supervisors who suspect an employee is stealing not to investigate the crime themselves. Instead, they should report their suspicions to their manager and to the police or professional security consultants.

Counseling

If a supervisor responds to problem behavior immediately, he or she will sometimes be able to bring the problem to a quick end without complex proceedings. For example, a supervisor can respond to each complaint from an employee who constantly complains about the way things are done by calmly asking the employee to suggest some alternatives. Not only does this discourage complaining, but it may uncover some good, new ways of operating. In many cases, however, the supervisor must take further steps to demonstrate the seriousness of the problem behavior.

Often the most constructive way a supervisor can address problem behavior is through counseling. **Counseling** refers to the process of learning about an individual's personal problem and helping the employee resolve it. Employees themselves should be able to resolve a relatively simple problem, such as tardiness caused by staying up too late watching television, without the supervisor's help. For more complex problems, such as those stemming from financial difficulties or substance abuse, the solution will require getting help from an expert. Because counseling is a cooperative process between supervisor and employee, employees are likely to respond more positively to it than to a simple order that they "shape up or ship out."

counseling
The process of learning about an individual's personal problem and helping him or her resolve it.

Benefits of Counseling

Counseling benefits employees in several ways. It can ease their worries or help them solve their problems. Working cooperatively with a supervisor to resolve a problem gives employees a sense that the supervisor and organization are interested in their welfare. This belief in turn can improve job satisfaction and motivation. The resulting improvements in productivity benefit the employee through performance rewards.

The organization benefits, too. Employees who receive needed counseling are well motivated and more likely to meet performance standards. The changes in an employee's attitudes also carry over to the work of other employees. When personal problems affect one employee's work, the others suffer consequences such as working harder to make up for the problem employee's lapses. Also, being around someone with a negative attitude tends to drag down the spirits of others in the group. After counseling improves the problem employee's performance and attitude, the whole group tends to do better.

Appropriate Times to Counsel

A supervisor should counsel employees when they need help in determining how to resolve a problem that is affecting their work. Sometimes an employee will approach a supervisor with a problem, such as marriage worries or concern about doing a good job. At other times, a supervisor may observe that an employee seems to have a problem when, for example, the quality of the employee's work is declining.

It is essential for supervisors to remember that they lack training to help with many kinds of problems. They are not in a position to save a marriage, resolve an employee's financial difficulties, or handle an alcoholic family member. Only when qualified should a supervisor help an employee resolve the problem. In other cases, a supervisor should simply listen, express concern, and refer the employee to a trained professional. The human resources department may be able to suggest sources of help.

Counseling Techniques

Counseling involves one or more discussions between the supervisor and the employee. These sessions should take place in a location where there will be privacy and freedom from interruptions. The sessions may be directive or nondirective (see Figure 13.2).

directive counseling
An approach to counseling in which the supervisor asks the employee questions about the specific problem; when the supervisor understands the problem, he or she suggests ways to handle it.

Directive versus Nondirective Counseling The most focused approach to counseling is **directive counseling,** in which a supervisor asks an employee questions about a specific problem. The supervisor listens until he or she understands the source of the problem. Then the supervisor suggests ways to handle the problem.

For example, assume that Bill Wisniewski, a computer programmer, has been absent a number of times during the past month. The supervisor might ask, "Why have you been missing so many days?" Bill replies, "Because my wife has been sick, and someone needs to look after my kids." The supervisor would follow up with questions about the condition of Bill's wife (e.g., to learn whether the problem is likely to continue), the ages and needs of Bill's children, and so on. Then

FIGURE 13.2

Directive versus Nondirective Counseling

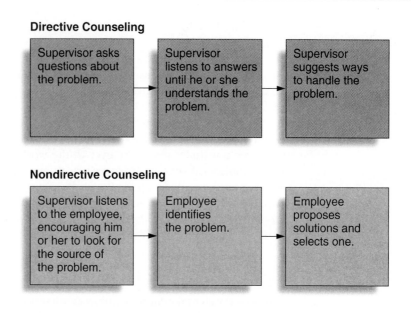

Directive Counseling

Supervisor asks questions about the problem. → Supervisor listens to answers until he or she understands the problem. → Supervisor suggests ways to handle the problem.

Nondirective Counseling

Supervisor listens to the employee, encouraging him or her to look for the source of the problem. → Employee identifies the problem. → Employee proposes solutions and selects one.

the supervisor might suggest finding alternative sources of care, perhaps referring Bill to a company program designed to help with such problems.

In most cases, a supervisor and employee will receive the greatest benefit when the supervisor helps the employee to develop and change instead of merely looking for a solution to a specific problem. To accomplish this, the supervisor can use **nondirective counseling.** With this approach, a supervisor should primarily listen, encouraging the employee to look for the source of the problem and to propose possible solutions. In the preceding example, a supervisor would ask open-ended questions such as "Would you tell me more about that?" Ideally, by working out his own solution, Bill would find that he has the ability to resolve many family problems without missing a lot of work.

nondirective counseling
An approach to counseling in which the supervisor primarily listens, encouraging the employee to look for the source of the problem and to propose possible solutions.

The Counseling Interview　The counseling interview starts with a discussion of what the problem is (see Figure 13.3). It then moves to consideration of possible solutions and selection of one solution to try. The interview ends with the supervisor scheduling a follow-up meeting.

The person who requested the counseling begins by describing the problem. If the employee requested help, the employee should begin. If the supervisor set up the interview because something seemed wrong, the supervisor should begin. The supervisor should focus on behavior and performance—what people do, not who they are—and encourage the employee to do the same. For example, if the employee says, "The other employees are prejudiced against me," the supervisor should ask the employee to describe what actions led to that conclusion. In addition, the supervisor should use the principles of active listening, described in Chapter 10.

Because counseling often takes place as a result of an employee's personal problems, the employee may be emotional during counseling sessions. The supervisor needs to be prepared for crying, angry outbursts, and other signs of emotion. He or she should be calm and reassure the employee that these signs of emotion

■ FIGURE 13.3

The Counseling Interview

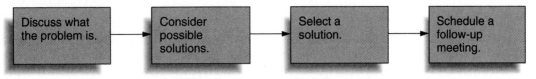

are neither good nor bad. Of course, there are appropriate and inappropriate ways to express emotions. Suppose that a salesperson in a hardware store has a 10-year-old son with behavior problems. It would not be appropriate for the salesperson to express his worry and frustration by snapping at customers.

Next, the supervisor and employee should consider ways to solve the problem. Instead of simply prescribing a solution, the supervisor usually can be more helpful by asking the employee questions that will help the employee come up with ideas. Employees are more likely to cooperate in a solution they helped to develop. Asking an employee to suggest solutions can be an especially effective way to end constant whining and complaining by that employee. When the supervisor and employee agree on a particular solution, the supervisor should restate it to make sure the employee understands. (Chapter 9 provides more detailed guidelines for mutual problem solving.)

Finally, the supervisor should schedule a follow-up meeting, which should take place just after the employee begins to see some results. At the follow-up meeting, employee and supervisor will review their plans and discuss whether the problem has been or is being resolved. For example, in the case of the salesperson in the hardware store, the supervisor might say, "I've noticed that we haven't received any more customer complaints about your service. In fact, one woman told me you went out of your way to help her." Notice that the supervisor is focusing on work performance, which the supervisor is qualified to discuss, rather than on the employee's family problems. If the employee replies, "Yes, I've been so much calmer ever since I started talking to that counselor about my son," the supervisor has a good indication that the employee is resolving the problem.

Discipline

"I can't stand Marcia's surly attitude any longer!" fumed Don Koh, Marcia's supervisor. "If she doesn't cut it out, she's going to be sorry." This supervisor is eager for the employee to experience the consequences of her behavior. However, despite the anger and frustration that can be generated by supervising a problem employee, a supervisor needs to apply discipline in constructive ways. **Discipline** is action taken by a supervisor to prevent employees from breaking rules. In many cases, effective discipline can quickly bring about a change in an employee's behavior.

discipline
Action taken by the supervisor to prevent employees from breaking rules.

Administering Discipline

In administering discipline, a supervisor should distinguish between discipline and punishment. (See the Self-Quiz on page 341 to help you determine the difference.) As described in Chapter 11, punishment is an unpleasant consequence given in response to undesirable behavior. Discipline, in contrast, is broader; it is a teaching process. The supervisor explains the significance and consequences of the employee's behavior, then, if necessary, lets the employee experience those consequences.

The specific ways in which a supervisor applies these steps may be dictated by company policies or the union contract, if any. Thus, a supervisor must be familiar with all applicable policies and rules. These should include respecting the rights of employees in the discipline process. Employees' rights include the following[17]:

- The right to know job expectations and the consequences of not fulfilling those expectations.
- The right to receive consistent and predictable management action in response to violations of the rules.
- The right to receive fair discipline based on facts.
- The right to question management's statement of the facts and to present a defense.
- The right to receive progressive discipline (described in the next section).
- The right to appeal a disciplinary action.

The Discipline Process   Before administering discipline in response to problem behavior, supervisors need to have a clear picture of the situation. They may observe the problem themselves or someone may tell them about the problem. In either case, supervisors need to collect the facts before taking further action.

As soon as possible, a supervisor should meet with the employees involved and ask for each employee's version of what happened. For example, a supervisor who believes that one of his or her employees is using the office telephone for excessive personal calls should not make hasty accusations or issue a general memo stating company policy about phone use. Rather, the supervisor should ask the employee directly and in private what his or her telephone conversations were about. In getting the employee's version of a problem, a supervisor should use good listening practices and resist the temptation to get angry.

When a supervisor observes and understands the facts behind problem behavior, disciplining an employee takes place in as many as four steps: warnings, suspension, demotion, and dismissal (see Figure 13.4). This pattern of discipline is "progressive" in the sense that the steps progress from the least to the most severe action a supervisor can take. A warning is unpleasant to hear but fulfills the important purpose of informing employees about the consequences of their behavior before more punitive measures are taken. Suspension, demotion, and discharge are more upsetting to an employee because they hurt the employee in the pocketbook.

■ FIGURE 13.4

Possible Steps in the Discipline Process

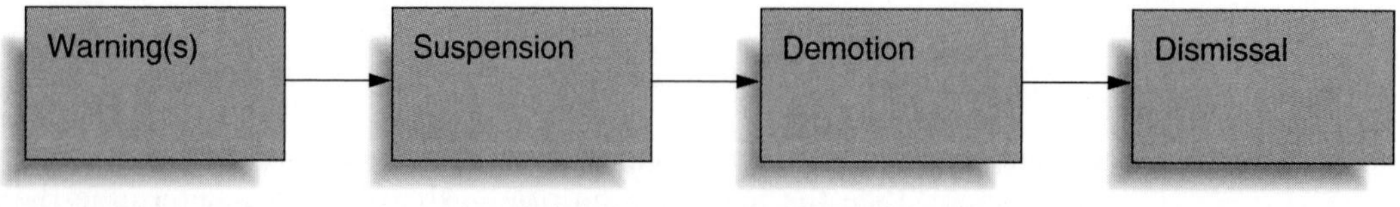

Warning   A warning may be either written or oral. Some organizations have a policy that calls for an oral warning followed by a written warning if performance does not improve. Both types of warning are designed to make sure that the employee understands the problem. A warning should contain the following information:

- What the problem behavior is.
- How the behavior affects the organization.
- How and when the employee's behavior is expected to change.
- What actions will be taken if the employee's behavior does not change.

Thus, a supervisor might say, "I have noticed that in the last two staff meetings, you have made hostile remarks. Not only have these disrupted the meetings, but they lead your co-workers to take you less seriously. I expect that you will refrain from such remarks in future meetings, or I will have to give you a suspension." As in this example, the warning should be brief and to the point.

In the case of a written warning, it is wise practice to ask the employee to sign the warning, which documents that the first step in the discipline process took place. If the employee refuses to sign the warning, even with minor changes, the supervisor should note the employee's refusal or should call in someone (such as the supervisor's manager) to witness the refusal.

suspension
Requirement that an employee not come to work for a set period of time; the employee is not paid for the time off.

Suspension   A **suspension** is the requirement that an employee not come to work for a set period of time, during which the employee is not paid. The length of the suspension might run from one day to one month, depending on the seriousness of the problem. Suspensions are useful when the employee has been accused of something serious, such as stealing, and the supervisor needs time to investigate.

demotion
Transfer of an employee to a job involving less responsibility and usually lower pay.

Demotion   A **demotion** is the transfer of an employee to a job having less responsibility and usually lower pay. Sometimes a demotion is actually a relief for an employee, especially if the employee has been goofing off or performing poorly because the job was more than he or she could handle. In such a case, the employee might welcome returning to a job where he or she is competent. More often, however, a demotion leads to negative feelings—a punishment that continues for as long as the employee holds the lower-level job.

dismissal
Relieving an employee of his or her job.

Dismissal   The permanent removal of an employee from a job is called **dismissal,** or termination or discharge. The organization cannot really regard dismissal as a success because it then has to recruit, hire, and train a new employee. Nevertheless, a supervisor sometimes must dismiss an employee who commits a serious offense or who will not respond to other forms of discipline. Occasionally an employee or supervisor may decide that correcting a problem is impossible, or at least too difficult or expensive. In addition to continued failure to correct problem behavior, dismissal may occur because an employee deliberately damages the organization's property, fights on the job, or engages in dangerous practices (e.g., a railroad engineer who drinks on the job).

Dismissing an employee is never easy; however, it is sometimes a necessary part of the job to ensure a positive work environment for the remaining employees. The owner in the previous example fired the difficult waitress at the Austin restaurant, and the next day the other staff members said their jobs were now much less stressful. Phil Roberts, president of the Premier Ventures restaurant group, comments: "As a manager, you are a leader. Employees depend on you to make decisions—even tough ones—that are for the good of the whole."[18] In addition, many organizations have policies requiring a supervisor to involve higher-level management before dismissing an employee. Supervisors should be familiar with any such policy and follow it.

In following the steps in the discipline process, a supervisor should keep in mind that the objective is to end the problem behavior. A supervisor takes only as many steps as are necessary to bring about a change in behavior: The ultimate goal is to solve the problem without dismissing the employee.

Guidelines for Effective Discipline When an employee is causing a problem—from tardiness to theft to lack of cooperation—the supervisor needs to act immediately. That is not always easy to do. Pointing out poor behavior and administering negative consequences are unpleasant tasks. However, by ignoring the situation, a supervisor is signaling that the problem is not serious. As a result, the problem gets worse. Seeing that the problem behavior leads to no consequences, an employee may increase it and other employees may follow this example.

In contrast, when Kathleen R. Tibbs was an in-flight supervisor with Eastern Airlines, she faced up to the unpleasant task of disciplining an employee with unacceptable attendance. Tibbs had the employee suspended for seven days. Her action inspired the employee to address the personal problems that led to her poor attendance. "Tips from the Firing Line" suggests how to handle poor performers appropriately.

When discussing the problem with an employee, a supervisor should focus on learning about and resolving the issue at hand. This meeting is no time for name-calling or for dredging up instances of past misbehavior. Nor is it generally useful for a supervisor to dwell on how patient or compassionate he or she has been. Instead, a supervisor should listen until he or she understands the problem, then begin discussing how to correct it in the future. Talking about behaviors instead of personalities helps the employee understand what is expected.

A supervisor should keep emotions in check. Although it is appropriate to convey sincere concern about the problem, a supervisor's other feelings are largely irrelevant and can even stand in the way of a constructive discussion. When an employee breaks the rules or seems unwilling to do a good job, it is only natural for a supervisor to feel angry. The supervisor should get control over this anger before confronting the employee in order to be objective rather than hostile. Being calm and relaxed when administering discipline tells an employee that the supervisor is confident of what he or she is doing.

Discipline should be a private matter. The supervisor should not humiliate an employee by reprimanding the employee in front of other employees. Humiliation only breeds resentment and may actually increase problem behavior in the future.

A supervisor also should be consistent in administering discipline. One way to do this is to follow the four steps of the discipline process outlined earlier. Also, a supervisor should respond to *all* instances of misbehavior rather than, for example, ignore a longstanding employee's misdeeds while punishing a newcomer. Consistency is a key part of preventing workplace violence; the most effective policy is widely thought to be one of zero tolerance. In other words, whenever *any* employee threatens or carries out *any* act of violence, the organization quickly responds with discipline in some form (whatever is most appropriate under the circumstances).[19] The guidelines for effective discipline are summarized in Figure 13.5.

Documentation of Disciplinary Action Employees who receive discipline sometimes respond by filing a grievance or suing the employer. To be able to justify his or

TIPS FROM THE FIRING LINE

Seven Pitfalls of Dealing with Poor Performers

With expectations high, competition stiff, and qualified employees more and more difficult to find, supervisors can find themselves in stressful situations when their subordinates "push the envelope" on the job.

Here are seven common pitfalls of dealing with poorly performing workers, and ways to overcome them.

1. *Using punishment instead of correction.* Some supervisors believe that being progressively more punitive will force the employee out and solve the problem. Besides the fact that this approach is counterproductive, another difficulty is that some employees treated this way will fight back. Instead, do whatever it takes to bring the poor performer up to the required level of skill or productivity.

2. *Assuming the problem will go away by itself.* Ignoring the problem, whether for fear of hurting the employee's feelings or from unwillingness to begin a difficult conversation, will not solve the difficulty. Help the employee to make his or her own decision about whether to correct the deficiency or move on to a job that is a better fit. Remember, the person not doing well is not neccessarily a bad employee. It could be a simple mismatch of job requirements and training or ability.

3. *Being overly concerned about legality.* Law and regulations are designed to ensure fair treatment, not to ensure that you keep unproductive people on board. Be sure you are not using laws and regulations as an excuse for not taking action, and remember that if you do the right thing by all employees and treat them as you would want to be treated, you will usually be within the law.

4. *Not hearing the employee out.* Giving the employee the chance to talk about his or her feelings is not the same thing as giving your subordinate the upper hand. A frank two-way conversation can often provide the information and means you need to begin taking steps to correct the employee's performance.

5. *Having low standards and low expectations.* Even those employees with the potential to surpass expectations will fail if their job descriptions are insufficient to reflect the expected level of performance. Make sure you yourself are clear about what the standards are and how they are measured, and communicate them to your employees.

6. *Conducting inadequate performance reviews.* An employee whose recent performance reviews lack any indication of problems may not even be aware that you are dissatisfied, and no human resources department would support your attempt to fire or even discipline the worker. Use regular performance reviews to point out areas of deficiency and suggest specific steps for improvement, and conduct interim reviews to note what improvements are taking place and when.

7. *Failing to document your concerns.* This is a simple step that is often overlooked. Write down performance deficiencies and date your notes, and don't forget to record positive information about performance improvements as well.

Source: From Michael P. Scott, "7 Pitfalls for Managers When Handling Poor Performers and How to Overcome Them," *Manage*, February 1, 2000. Reprinted with permission.

her actions, a supervisor must have a record of the disciplinary actions taken and the basis for the discipline. These records may be needed to show that the actions were not discriminatory or against company policy. As noted earlier, one type of disciplinary record is a signed copy of any written warning. In addition, other disciplinary actions should be recorded in the employee's personnel file, as directed by the human resources department.

Supervisors often use past performance appraisals as documentation of the need for disciplinary action. However, this often backfires because many supervisors are reluctant to give negative evaluations. A performance appraisal that has an employee's work recorded as average, adequate, or meeting only minimal standards does not support dismissal of that employee. This is why it is essential for the supervisor to give accurate performance appraisals (see Chapter 18).

FIGURE 13.5

Guidelines for Effective Discipline

> 1. Act immediately.
>
> 2. Focus on solving the problem at hand.
>
> 3. Keep emotions in check.
>
> 4. Administer discipline in private.
>
> 5. Be consistent.

Documentation is especially important when a supervisor must terminate an employee. Because the experience is so emotional, some former employees respond with a lawsuit. The employee's file should show the steps the supervisor took leading up to the termination and a record of the specific behaviors that led the supervisor to dismiss the employee.

Positive Discipline

positive discipline
Discipline designed to prevent problem behavior from beginning.

Ideally, discipline should not only end problem behavior, it should also prevent problems from occurring. Discipline designed to prevent problem behavior from beginning is known as **positive discipline,** or preventive discipline. An important part of positive discipline is making sure employees know and understand the rules they must follow. A supervisor also should explain the consequences of violating rules. For example, a production supervisor might explain that company policy calls for dismissal of any employee caught operating machinery while under the influence of drugs or alcohol.

A supervisor also can administer positive discipline by working to create the conditions under which employees are least likely to cause problems. Employees may engage in problem behavior when they feel frustrated. For example, if the organization sets a sales quota higher than salespeople think they can achieve, they may give up and goof off instead of trying their best. If computer operators complain that they need more frequent rest breaks to prevent health problems, and no changes are made, they may adopt a negative attitude toward the company's apparent lack of concern for their well-being. This reaction is related to another source of problem behavior: feeling as if one is not an important part of the organization. If employees conclude that they and management are at odds with one another, some may turn their energy toward seeing what they can get away with.

To combat such problems, a supervisor needs to be aware of and responsive to employees' needs and ideas. A supervisor should encourage upward communication, promote teamwork, and encourage employees to participate in decision making and problem solving. Effective use of motivation techniques also helps prevent the frustration and alienation that can lead to problem behavior. Finally, through good hiring and training practices, a supervisor can help to ensure that employee values, interests, and abilities are a good match with the job and the or-

MEETING THE CHALLENGE

Wainwright Industries Uses Quality and Teams to Create Positive Discipline and a Nonviolent Culture

When they set out to apply for the prestigious Malcolm Baldrige National Quality Award, owners of Missouri-based Wainwright Industries, a 275-employee shop that manufactures stamped and machined products, didn't think about violence—or the lack of it—in their workplace. But they soon discovered a correlation. After employees walked out on strike in the late 1970s, management decided they could no longer afford an adversarial relationship; certainly not if they were going to improve quality standards. "We decided it can't be we and they; it has to be us. We set about to try to develop that kind of environment," recalls David Robbins, vice president of Wainwright.

First, Wainwright gave employees more decision-making power; then employees decertified their union, whereupon Wainwright management declared all employees salaried workers. "Everybody in our company is paid whether they come to work or not," says Robbins, "and yet consistently, since 1984, we have had in excess of 99 percent attendance." However, discipline for tardiness and absenteeism does apply. "Obviously, when people are salaried, we expect them to come to work. If people show a propensity not to come to work, we take that pretty seriously," notes Robbins. Wainwright administers progressively severe penalties to employees who are consistently late or absent.

Then there's the introduction of teams—if a worker is too often late or absent, his or her teammates take it pretty seriously, too, because they have to make up the missing employee's work. In addition, "everybody is in a profit-sharing plan, so if somebody is on salary and not coming to work, that's eating into their profit sharing," Robbins continues.

Robbins believes that team motivation is a positive form of discipline. "I would much rather have the team be self-motivating, rather than for me to be involved in discipline. If the team tells Joe that he's letting them down, that's far more effective than anything I can do."

How do the positive discipline of the quality movement and teamwork promote a nonviolent work atmosphere? Robbins believes that Wainwright has created "an environment where people take more ownership in each other and the company. When you have that ownership, a lot of problems and frustrations are easier to deal with," and less apt to deteriorate into violence. The open communication that comes with quality and teamwork also means that managers are more aware of potential problems. In this type of atmosphere, "you're going to get threats reported more readily," explains manager Garry Mathiason. "You're going to get a clearer transmission of what the company values are."

Finally, the company offers an employee assistance program (EAP) in which counselors help employees deal with problems such as alcohol and drug abuse, financial difficulties, family matters, and the like. Wainwright management believes that if these problems are faced early on, they are less likely to undermine employees' performance at work. Wainwright makes certain that all employees know about the EAP so that "problems can be addressed proactively," according to Robbins.

Perhaps it's no surprise that Wainwright Industries won the Malcolm Baldrige National Quality Award.

Source: From "Creating a Violence-Free Company Culture," *Nation's Business*, February 1995. U.S. Chamber of Commerce.

---

decision-making leave
A day off during which a problem employee is supposed to decide whether to return to work and meet standards or to stay away for good.

ganization. See "Meeting the Challenge" to learn how one small company encourages positive discipline in these ways.

At some companies, positive discipline includes a day off with pay for employees who fail to respond to efforts to educate them about following the rules and meeting performance standards. During this suspension, known as a **decision-making leave,** the employees are supposed to decide whether to return to work and meet standards or to stay away for good. If the employees choose to come back, they work with a supervisor to develop objectives and action plans for improvement.

Finally, a supervisor should not only punish problem behavior but reward desirable kinds of behavior, such as contributing to the department's performance. For example, a supervisor should recognize those who make suggestions for improvements or who resolve sticky problems. (See Chapter 11 for specific ideas.)

Self-Discipline

An effective program of positive discipline results in self-discipline, in which employees voluntarily follow the rules and try to meet performance standards. Most people get satisfaction from doing a job well, so self-discipline should result when employees understand what is expected. Supervisors can help to encourage self-discipline by communicating not only the rules and performance standards, but the reasons for those rules and standards.

In addition, a supervisor who takes long lunch breaks or spends hours chatting with friends on the telephone or the Internet is in no position to insist that employees put in a full workday. If supervisors expect employees to follow the rules, they must set a good example by exercising self-discipline.

Troubled Employees

So far, this chapter has emphasized problems that can be solved by giving employees more information or helping them to change their behavior. However, some employees have problems that make them unable to respond to a simple process of discipline or counseling. These troubled employees include people who are substance abusers or have psychological problems.

Detection of the Troubled Employee

The first signs that a supervisor has a troubled employee tend to be the kinds of discipline problems described earlier in this chapter. A supervisor may notice that an employee is frequently late or that the quality of an employee's work has been slipping. If disciplinary action or counseling seems ineffective at resolving the problem, a supervisor may have a troubled employee.

In the case of substance abuse, the supervisor might notice signs that the employee has been using alcohol or drugs. The examples listed in Table 13.1 are among the most common behavioral signs. (Note that these are only hints that the employee might be using drugs or alcohol. There may be other explanations for these behaviors.) Perhaps a supervisor will even find the employee has possession of drugs or alcohol. When an employee is suspected of drug use, some organizations have a policy of confirming the suspicion through the use of drug testing.

Because there may be another explanation for symptoms that look like the effects of using alcohol or illicit drugs (e.g., taking prescription medications), a supervisor should avoid making accusations about what he or she believes is going on. For example, a supervisor should not say, "I see you've been drinking on the job." Instead, the supervisor should focus on job performance: "I see something is hurting the quality of your work this week. Let's talk about what the problem is and how to solve it."

Confrontation of the Troubled Employee

Ignoring a problem does not make it go away. Thus, hoping an alcoholic employee will seek help rarely works. It only helps the employee maintain the illusion that the substance abuse is not causing significant problems. After all, if the

■ TABLE 13.1 **Possible Signs of Alcohol or Drug Use**	Slurred speech. Clumsy movements and increased accidents. Personality changes. Decreased ability to work as part of a team. Smell of alcohol on the employee's breath. Growing carelessness about personal appearance and the details of the job. Increase in absenteeism or tardiness, along with unbelievable excuses. Daydreaming. Leaving the work area; making frequent visits to the rest room. Violence in the workplace.

boss does not complain, how bad can the work be? Therefore, when a supervisor suspects a problem, he or she needs to confront the employee.

The first step is to document the problem. A supervisor should keep notes of instances in which an employee's performance is not acceptable. When collecting this information, a supervisor should be sure to keep notes on all employees whose performance is slipping, not just the one person targeted.

When a supervisor has gathered enough supporting evidence, he or she should confront the employee. The supervisor should go over the employee's performance, describing the evidence of a problem. Then the supervisor should refer the employee to a source of counseling or other help by saying something like "I think something's troubling you, and I want you to see an employee assistance counselor." Finally, the supervisor should explain the consequences of not changing. In some cases, accepting help may be a requirement for keeping the job. Thus, the supervisor might say, "There's no shame in getting help, and we'll keep it private. But you are responsible for doing your job safely and up to standards. If you don't, I'll have to follow our disciplinary procedures for unacceptable performance."

Experts agree that this type of warning from a supervisor can be one of the most effective ways to motivate a substance-abusing employee to get help. "Job jeopardy is the standard that Employee Assistance Programs have always used to encourage employees to accept help," says Bill McGuire, Employee Assistance Program administrator for EG&G Florida, Inc., a contractor at the Kennedy Space Center. "This way, rather than being purely a carrot-or-stick approach, the interventions by a manager, then by the Employee Assistance Program, are integrated to address the intolerable situation and help the employee resolve the behavioral issue."[20]

During the confrontation, the employee may become angry or defensive. This reaction is common in such situations, so the supervisor should not take it personally or overreact. The employee also may come up with excuses that sound particularly sad and compelling. In any case, the supervisor must continue to focus on the employee's behavior on the job and the way the employee's behavior affects the organization. No matter how outraged the employee or how impressive or creative the excuse, the employee's behavior must improve.

Some caution is advisable, however. An employee violated a company policy against driving a company car after drinking and was given an ultimatum by her supervisor: Either attend an alcoholism treatment program or be fired. The employee, who was not an alcoholic, sued her employer under the Americans with Disabilities Act, claiming that the ultimatum and her eventual termination from the job were based on a perception of disability. It's unwise to assume everyone who abuses is an addict.[21]

Aid in and Evaluation of Recovery

Most organizations have developed procedures for providing help to troubled employees. When a supervisor believes that problems are occurring because an employee is troubled, the organization's procedures need to be investigated. In most cases, the place to start is with the human resources department.

The type of treatment program tends to depend on the size of the organization. Many small organizations refer troubled employees to a counseling service. Another policy is simply to tell the employee to get help or lose the job. A supervisor should be careful in pursuing the latter approach. If possible, the ultimate objective should be the employee's rehabilitation, not dismissal. Rehabilitation is not only more compassionate, it tends to be less costly than hiring and training a new employee, and it is less likely to violate laws prohibiting employment discrimination.

Other organizations, especially large ones, offer an **employee assistance program (EAP)**. An EAP is a company-based program for providing counseling and related help to employees whose personal problems affect their performance. It may be simply a referral service or it may be fully staffed with social workers, psychologists, nurses, career counselors, financial advisers, and other professionals. These programs are voluntary (employees do not have to participate unless they want to) and confidential (participation is a private matter).

As the diversity of the U.S. workforce has increased, employers have broadened their concept of the kinds of help troubled employees will need, and EAPs have expanded their services accordingly. Originally, EAPs focused on helping employees recover from substance abuse. Some of the relatively new services include financial or career counseling, referrals for child care and elder care, AIDS education and counseling, and "cultural adjustment counseling," which is directed toward helping employees work with others of a different cultural background. Without tolerating the employee's substance abuse, supervisors can still grant time off or flexibility in the work schedule to allow for attendance at recovery meetings.[22]

The reason for providing EAPs and other sources of counseling is to improve the employee's performance. It is up to the supervisor to see that the treatment plan is producing the desired results at the workplace. Any signs of improvement not related to performance (e.g., abstinence from alcohol) are irrelevant from the supervisor's point of view.

employee assistance program (EAP)
A company-based program for providing counseling and related help to employees whose personal problems are affecting their performance.

Sources of Support

Supervising problem employees is a delicate matter. Supervisors must be careful to motivate and correct rather than to generate hostility and resentment. At the same time, supervisors must be careful to follow organizational procedures, union requirements, and laws regarding fair employment practices. Fortunately, supervisors can get support from their superiors, the organization's human resources department, and outside experts.

When an employee fails to respond to initial attempts at counseling, a supervisor should try discussing the problem with his or her manager. The manager may be able to offer insights into how to handle the problem. In addition, some steps, such as suspension or dismissal, may require that the supervisor get authorization from a higher-level manager.

It is also wise to consult with the human resources department, which has information about company policies on discipline and how to document it. Human resources personnel can advise a supervisor on how to proceed without breaking laws, violating a contract with the union, or putting the organization at risk in case of a lawsuit. In addition, personnel specialists have expertise that can make them good sources of ideas on what to say or what corrective measures to propose. Sometimes just talking about a strategy helps a supervisor to think of new ways to approach the problem.

In small organizations with no human resources staff, a supervisor and his or her manager may agree that the problem requires the help of outside experts. They may contract with a consultant, a labor attorney, or a human relations specialist who provides services on a temporary basis. The fee paid to such an expert may seem high but can be far less than the cost of defending a wrongful-termination lawsuit. The local office of the Small Business Administration (SBA) also may be able to provide help. SBA assistance may include a referral to an executive in one of its programs for providing small businesses with free advice.

In sum, when an employee's problems or problem behavior threaten to disrupt the workplace, a supervisor should not despair. The effective use of counseling and discipline can solve many of these problems. When they do not, a variety of people inside and outside the organization stand ready to help.

Summary

13.1 Identify common types of problem behavior among employees.

The problems that supervisors most often encounter are absenteeism and tardiness, insubordination and uncooperativeness, alcohol and drug abuse, workplace violence, and employee theft.

13.2 Explain why and when supervisors should counsel employees.

Counseling helps employees solve their problems, which enables them to perform better at work. It therefore improves productivity as well as the attitudes and job satisfaction of employees. Supervisors should counsel employees when they need help in determining how to resolve a problem that is affecting their work. When an employee has a problem with which the supervisor is unqualified to help, the supervisor should refer the employee to a professional.

13.3 Describe counseling techniques.

Counseling consists of one or more discussions between the supervisor and the employee. These discussions may involve directive counseling, in which the supervisor asks the employee questions to identify the problem and then suggests solutions. Or the discussions may be nondirective, with the supervisor primarily listening and encouraging the employee to look for the source of the problem and identify possible solutions. At the beginning of the interview, the person who identified the problem describes it, focusing on behavior and performance. Next, the supervisor and employee consider ways to solve the problem. Finally, the supervisor schedules a follow-up meeting to review the planned solution and determine whether the problem is being resolved.

13.4 Discuss effective ways of administering discipline.

After collecting the facts of the situation, the supervisor should meet with the employee or employees involved and ask for their version of what has happened. The supervisor should use good listening techniques. Then the supervisor issues a warning. If necessary, the supervisor lets the employee experience the consequences of unsatisfactory behavior through suspension, demotion, and ultimately dismissal. The supervisor takes as many steps as are necessary to resolve the problem behavior. The supervisor should administer discipline promptly, privately, impartially, and unemotionally. The supervisor should document all disciplinary actions.

13.5   Describe the principles of positive discipline and self-discipline.

Positive discipline focuses on preventing problem behavior from ever beginning. It can include making sure employees know and understand the rules, creating conditions under which employees are least likely to cause problems, using decision-making leaves when problems occur, and rewarding desirable behavior. Effective positive discipline results in self-discipline among employees; that is, employees voluntarily follow the rules and try to meet performance standards. Supervisors who expect self-discipline from their employees must practice it themselves.

13.6   Explain how supervisors can detect and confront troubled employees.

The supervisor can look for discipline problems and investigate whether these are symptoms of personal problems. With substance abuse, the supervisor might notice signs that the employee is using alcohol or drugs. When the supervisor suspects that an employee is troubled, he or she should document the problem and then meet with the employee and describe the evidence of a problem, focusing on the employee's performance at work. The supervisor should refer the employee to a source of help and explain the consequences of not getting help. The supervisor should be careful not to overreact to an employee's emotional response or creative excuses.

13.7   Specify how supervisors can direct troubled employees in getting help and then follow up on the recovery efforts.

Supervisors should learn their organization's procedures for helping troubled employees and then follow those procedures. This may involve referring employees to help outside the organization or to the organization's employee assistance program. The supervisor is responsible for seeing that the employee's performance is improving, not for evaluating evidence of improvement unrelated to work.

13.8   Discuss the role of the supervisor's manager and the human resources department in helping the supervisor with problem employees.

The supervisor's manager and the human resources department can help the supervisor handle problem employees in ways that follow organizational guidelines, legal requirements, or union contracts. A supervisor should discuss the problem with his or her manager and the human resources department to get information about the organization's policies for handling problem employees and suggestions for handling the specific problem. The organization may offer an employee assistance program whose ultimate goal is the employee's rehabilitation.

Key Terms

insubordination, p. 320

counseling, p. 324

directive counseling, p. 325

nondirective counseling, p. 326

discipline, p. 327

suspension, p. 329

demotion, p. 329

dismissal, p. 329

positive discipline, p. 332

decision-making leave, p. 333

employee assistance program (EAP), p. 336

Review and Discussion Questions

1. Dennis McCutcheon supervises the employees who work in the building supplies department of a large discount hardware store. One of his employees, Kelly Sims, has been late to work every Tuesday and Thursday for the last three weeks. Sometimes she disappears for more than an hour at lunch. Although Kelly had a positive attitude when she started the job, recently Dennis has overheard her complaining to co-workers and being less than friendly to customers. Using the questions listed in the section "Problems Requiring Special Action" (page 319), how might Dennis go about uncovering the true source of Kelly's performance problem?

2. What is the difference between directive and nondirective counseling? Give an example of each in the form of a brief dialogue.

3. An employee explains to her supervisor that her performance has been slipping because she has been distracted and frightened by threats from her former husband.
   a. Should the supervisor counsel the employee about her job performance? Explain.
   b. Should the supervisor counsel the employee about the threats from her former husband? Explain.

4. While counseling an employee, a supervisor made the following statements. What is wrong with each statement? What would be a better alternative for each?
   a. "Your laziness is becoming a real problem."
   b. "Knock off the shouting! The way your performance has been lately, you have no right to be angry."
   c. "What you need to do is to take this job more seriously. Just focus on getting your work done, and then we won't have a problem."

5. What are the steps in the discipline process? In what kinds of situations would a supervisor take all these steps?

6. What additional type of information should be included in the following warning to an employee?

   "I noticed that you returned late from lunch yesterday and three days last week. This upsets the other employees because they get back promptly in order to give others a chance to take their breaks. Beginning tomorrow, I expect you to be back on time."

7. Describe four guidelines for disciplining employees effectively.

8. Jackie Weissman supervises a group of technicians in a laboratory that conducts medical tests. It is extremely important that the technicians follow lab procedures to obtain accurate test results. What steps can Jackie take to apply positive discipline with her group?

9. a. What are some signs that an employee has been abusing alcohol or drugs?
   b. Why should a supervisor avoid making a statement such as "You've been coming to work high lately"?

10. What steps should a supervisor take in confronting an apparently troubled employee?

11. Rick Mayhew's nine-year-old son was recently diagnosed with a chronic illness that is difficult and expensive to treat. In addition, Rick's elderly mother-in-law is going to be moving in to live with his family. Rick's supervisor has noticed that his performance has been suffering lately; he is often late to work, leaves early, and has trouble concentrating on his work. The supervisor does not want to lose Rick as an employee. Would an employee assistance program help Rick? Why or why not?

12. Tom Chandra has a problem with one of the production workers he supervises. The worker has been ignoring Tom's instructions about the new procedures for operating a lathe, preferring instead to follow the old procedures. What kind of help can Tom get from his manager and the human resources department in handling this problem?

A SECOND LOOK

What kind of problem behavior did the fired employee exhibit in the story in the chapter opening? If you were her supervisor, how would you have handled this situation?

SKILLS MODULE

General Electric: Is Insubordination Really a Disability?

Insubordination is the deliberate refusal to do what a supervisor asks. So how can it be called a disability? One former employee of General Electric tried to do just that, claiming that under the Americans with Disabilities Act (ADA), an employee with a disability must receive a reasonable accommodation from his or her employer.

Donald, the GE employee, claimed that he was unable to follow his supervisor's orders (this went on for more than 20 years). Further, he claimed that the source of his incapacity to follow orders was actually his supervisor, Gary. Gary continuously exacerbated Donald's "disability" to the point that Donald simply walked out of the plant one day. Instead of firing Donald, GE put him on decision-making leave; if he was insubordinate again, he *would* be fired.

Donald claimed that Gary did not treat him with respect, and when Gary made a request that Donald did not agree with, Donald argued. Gary threatened to fire him. Another manager encouraged Donald to obey the request, which he did. But when Gary later reminded Donald that he was still facing disciplinary action for previous insubordination, Donald lost his temper. Gary fired him.

Donald retaliated, taking his case to court under the ADA. He claimed that he had two disabilities. First, he stated that he suffered from "an emotional condition that is characterized by feelings of inferiority and unacceptability." This disability rendered him incapable of following orders. In a sideline, he claimed a related disability: tardiness. Thus, he claimed, GE must make a "reasonable accommodation" for his condition. Second, Donald stated that he was unable to get along with his supervisor (he considered this to be a handicap), and that GE should accommodate him on this as well. Then Donald made a final claim: that GE had intentionally inflicted emotional distress on him by firing him.

The judge didn't see things Donald's way. The court refused to view insubordination, tardiness, or an inability to get along with one's supervisor as legal disabilities. His termination was ruled legal as well. Donald was stuck looking for another job.

1. Do you think that Donald could be classified as a troubled employee? Why or why not?
2. What steps might Gary have taken in administering discipline to prevent Donald's eventual firing and the subsequent lawsuit? (Or do you think *anything* could have been done?)
3. Would counseling have helped Donald? Why or why not?

Source: From *Management Review* by Milton Bordwin. Copyright 1994 by American Management Association. Reproduced with permission of American Management Association via Copyright Clearance Center.

S E L F - Q U I Z

Can You Distinguish between Discipline and Punishment?

Write True or False on the line before each of the following statements.

_____ 1. If an employee failed to do something I requested, I would immediately dock his or her pay.

_____ 2. If I noticed that an employee was leaving work early on a regular basis, I would revoke his or her lunch privileges.

_____ 3. If I saw two employees arguing, I would ask each separately for his or her version of the story.

_____ 4. If I had to issue a warning to an employee, I would make certain that he or she understood exactly what behavior the warning referred to.

_____ 5. If an employee insults me personally, I will insult the employee in return, so that he or she understands how I feel.

_____ 6. No matter how angry I feel inside at an employee, I will not act hostilely.

_____ 7. If an employee is doing poorly, I will note that in the performance appraisal.

_____ 8. If an employee were late to work the day of the company picnic, I would force him or her to stay on the job rather than leave early with everyone else to attend the picnic.

_____ 9. If I smelled alcohol on the breath of an employee after lunch, I would immediately fire the person.

_____ 10. If I caught an employee violating a company policy, I would immediately discuss the behavior and its consequences with the person.

Scoring   True responses to statements 1, 2, 5, 8, and 9 illustrate punishment; True responses to statements 3, 4, 6, 7, and 10 illustrate discipline.

Class Exercise

The postal service has adopted a new disciplinary code that substitutes a letter of reprimand for the 7- to 14-day suspension without pay that repeated infractions once drew. As an extreme penalty, workers may be given one payless "day of reflection."

The post office feels the new policy treats "adults like adults." But the president of the National Rural Letter Carriers Association fears employees may see the new discipline as a mere "slap on the wrist."

Debate these two views.

Source: "World Week," *Wall Street Journal*, November 3, 1998, p. 1.

Team-Building Exercise

Handling Performance Problems

This is a role-playing exercise. One class member volunteers to take on the role of supervisor. Another classmate volunteers to be the problem employee. The scenario:

> Chris Johnson has been a teller in the main branch of a bank for five years. Lately, Chris has been making a lot of mistakes. Chris often counts out money wrong and has had to redo many receipts that contain errors. Customers have begun complaining about the mistakes Chris makes and the detached, distracted manner in which Chris provides service. But at Chris's most recent performance appraisal, just two months ago, Chris's overall rating was excellent, leading to a generous wage increase. Chris's supervisor, Pat Smith, must decide how to respond to the decline in Chris's performance.

Before the role play begins, the class discusses what the supervisor should do. Based on the information given, should Pat use counseling, discipline, both, or neither? Once the class agrees on a general strategy, the two volunteers act it out.

Then the class discusses what happened:

- Did the supervisor do a good job of applying the techniques selected? What did the supervisor do well? What could the supervisor have done better?
- Did the employee and supervisor arrive at a workable solution? Explain.
- How can the supervisor follow up to see whether the employee is improving?

14

The most important thing I've realized is that if you overcommit yourself to your work, you become valueless to your company.

—**Steven Wynne, President and CEO, Adidas America**

Managing Time and Stress

■ CHAPTER OUTLINE

Time Management
Understanding How You Use Time
Planning Your Use of Time
Controlling Time Wasters

Stress Management
Causes of Stress
Consequences of Stress
Personal Stress Management
Organizational Stress Management

A Word about Personality

■ LEARNING OBJECTIVES

After you have studied this chapter, you should be able to:

14.1 Discuss how supervisors can evaluate their use of time.

14.2 Describe ways to plan the use of time.

14.3 Identify some time wasters and how to control them.

14.4 List factors that contribute to stress among employees.

14.5 Summarize consequences of stress.

14.6 Explain how supervisors can manage their own stress.

14.7 Identify ways organizations, including supervisors, can help their employees manage stress.

■ DOES THE COMPUTER SAVE TIME, OR ADD STRESS?

The last 10 years have seen enormous changes in the magazine industry. Downsizing, restructuring, mergers, consolidations, and an influx of new technologies all have changed the landscape forever. Rhonda Duey, associate editor of *Hart's Oil and Gas World*, welcomes the industry's new reliance on computers. When her husband's job required the family to relocate, Rhonda was able to keep her job while giving up long commuting hours. She now does all her writing and editing online from her home.

Some supervisors, however, find the computer has increased their workload, not reduced it, and with that increase comes added stress. Elizabeth Crow, editor-in-chief of *Mademoiselle*, offers this assessment: "The efficiencies you realize in terms of time and control increase the amount of work you end up doing. You do more research, more writing and more rewriting, and you can do it longer."

Here's what Diane Potter, vice president and consumer marketing director of Times-Mirror magazines, has to say about computers. "Most of us are dealing with more work with fewer human resources. We are far more busy. There used to be an occasional lull seasonally. . . . That doesn't happen now. Peak time is all the time. . . . I don't believe people do their most creative thinking when they are under stress."

Finally, Sue Rice, senior vice president, human resources at Cahners Business Information, says, "Everyone feels stretched out and stressed out. That's sort of the nature of the workforce today. It's not only the work. It's the fact that you're accessible 24 hours a day by voice mail, the Internet, home faxes, car phones, and video conferencing."

Perhaps it's no wonder that many human resources managers believe that stress now accounts for nearly three times as many absences from work as it did only five years ago.

Sources: Barbara Love, "How Our Jobs Have Changed," *Folio*, April 1, 1998, pp. 46 ff; Leonard Wiener, "Ever Thought of Calling in Well?" *U.S. News & World Report*, November 9, 1998, p. 82.

A supervisor who has a bad day may feel as though everything is out of control. Instead of working on what he or she wants, the supervisor attempts to solve unexpected problems and to soothe upset employees and customers. While workdays like this affect employees and managers at all levels, they are a particular problem for supervisors because a supervisor's people-oriented job means solving many needs and conflicts. To minimize and cope with these difficulties, supervisors must manage time and stress.

This chapter describes basic techniques of time management and stress management. It identifies ways supervisors can control how they use time. Then it defines stress and describes its consequences. Finally, the chapter suggests ways supervisors themselves can cope with stress and also help employees to do so.

Time Management

Sean Mulligan's typical day is hectic. Just when he gets on the telephone, someone is at the door with a problem; he almost never finds the time to sit down and ponder the problem. By the end of the day, Sean is exhausted, but he would be hard-pressed to say what he accomplished. Lisa Ng's days are also busy, but when someone interrupts her, Lisa pulls out her calendar and makes an appointment for later. She starts out each day knowing what tasks are essential, and she always manages to complete them.

Which kind of supervisor would you rather have working for you? Which kind would you rather be? Time is the only resource we all have in equal shares: Everyone gets 24-hour days. To evaluate your own responses to time pressures, take the Self-Quiz on page 371.

Supervisors who are in control of their time find that their jobs are easier and that they can get more done. Needless to say, getting a lot done is a good way to impress higher-level management. The practice of controlling the way you use time is known as **time management.**

time management
The practice of controlling the way you use time.

Time management techniques can be as simple as putting things away as soon as you are done with them, using an appointment calendar to keep track of your schedule, and getting all the information you need *before* you start on a project. While this chapter provides broad guidelines for time management, each supervisor must work out the details. A look at the many different varieties of calendars, planners, and scheduling tools available in your nearest office-supply store, whether in paper form or as software, will convince you that no two people get organized in quite the same way.

Understanding How You Use Time

Before you can take control over the way you use time, you have to understand what you already are doing. A practical way to learn about your use of time is to keep a **time log.** This is a record of what activities you are doing hour by hour throughout the workday. Figure 14.1 provides an example. Each half-hour during the day, write down what you did during the previous half-hour. Do not wait until the end of the day; this level of detail is too difficult to remember.

time log
A record of what activities a person is doing hour by hour throughout the day.

After you have kept a time log for at least one typical week, review your log. Ask yourself the following questions:

- How much time did I spend on important activities?
- How much time did I spend on activities that did not need to get done?
- How much time did I spend on activities that someone else could have done (perhaps with some training)?
- What important jobs did I not get around to finishing?

From your review, you may see some patterns. Do you reserve a certain time of day for telephone calls or meetings? Do you frequently interrupt what you are doing to solve a problem or move on to something more interesting? Do you tackle the most important jobs first or the easiest ones? The answers to these and similar questions will help you see where you need to change. After you have tried applying the principles in this chapter for a while, you might want to try keeping a time log again to see how you have improved.

■ FIGURE 14.1

Format for a Time Log

Date _____

Time	Activity	Others Involved	Location
7:30–8:00			
8:00–8:30			
8:30–9:00			
9:00–9:30			
9:30–10:00			
10:00–10:30			
10:30–11:00			
11:00–11:30			
11:30–12:00			
12:00–12:30			
12:30–1:00			
1:00–1:30			
1:30–2:00			
2:00–2:30			
2:30–3:00			
3:00–3:30			
3:30–4:00			
4:00–4:30			
4:30–5:00			
5:00–5:30			

Keeping a time log is also helpful for people who feel out of control of their personal time. For example, if you are frustrated at how little time you spend with loved ones or if you cannot find the time for charitable work, keep a log of how you use your hours outside work. You may find that you are spending a lot of time on an unimportant activity that you can relinquish to free time for something else.

■ FIGURE 14.2

A Superhuman Level of Time Management

Source: Reprinted with permission of Nicole Hollander.

Planning Your Use of Time

Based on what you learned from keeping a time log, you can plan how to use your time better. Although few of us would want to achieve the level of time management portrayed in Figure 14.2, you need to make sure that the most important things get done each day before you move on to less important activities. You must set priorities. Thus, your planning consists of deciding what you need to do and which activities are most important.

Planning your use of time begins with the planning process described in Chapter 6. If you follow the guidelines in that chapter, you will routinely establish objectives for the year, specifying when each must be completed. With these yearly objectives in mind, you can figure out what you need to accomplish in shorter time periods—each quarter, month, and week. Review your objectives regularly, and use them to plan what you will need to accomplish each week and day.

Making a "To Do" List Many people find it helpful to spend a few minutes at the end of each week writing a list of things to do—what they must accomplish during the next week. When you have made your list, write an *A* next to all the activities that must be completed that week; these are your top priorities. Then write a *B* next to all the activities that are important but can be postponed if necessary. Label everything else *C*; these are your lowest priorities for the week. Schedule times for doing your A-level and B-level activities. If you have more time, work on your C-level activities. As you complete each activity on the "to do" list, check it off.

How do you know when is the best time to do the activities on your list? Here are some guidelines to follow for creating weekly and daily schedules:

- First, record all the activities that must take place at a set time. For example, you do not have any choice about when to schedule your regular Monday morning staff meeting or the appointment you made with your manager for three o'clock on Thursday.

FIGURE 14.3

Common Time Wasters

E-mail
Meetings
Phone calls
Paperwork
Unscheduled visitors

Procrastination
Perfectionism
Failure to delegate
Inability to say no

- Next, find times for your remaining A-level activities. Try to avoid scheduling them at the end of the day (on a daily plan) or week (on a weekly plan). If a crisis comes up, you will need another chance to finish these activities. Schedule your B-level activities next.
- Schedule the most challenging and most important activities for the times of day when you are at your best. If you are sleepy after lunch or get off to a slow start in the morning, schedule top-priority activities for times when you are more alert. Consultant Tom Peters reports that when writing a book, he worked from 4:00 A.M. to 7:30 A.M., napped for an hour, and then returned to work. He thus benefited from his most creative time, between 4:00 A.M. and 11:00 A.M.[1]
- Learn to use the calendar or scheduling tools built into your computer operating system. For instance, Microsoft's Microsoft Works Calendar not only allows you to record upcoming events, meetings, appointments, and holidays; it will also send you customized reminders of each (with audio signals, if you like). Other programs, such as Lotus Notes, will allow you to schedule a team meeting and post the day, time, and location on the calendars of all the team's members.
- Schedule time for thinking, not solely for doing. Remember that the creative process requires time for reflection (see Chapter 9).
- Do not fill up every hour of the day and week. Leave some time free to handle unexpected problems and questions from your employees and others. If problems do not occur, so much the better. You will have time for the C-level activities.

Controlling Time Wasters

Many supervisors find that certain activities and attitudes are what most often lead them to waste time. Figure 14.3 identifies the most common time wasters: e-mail, meetings, telephone calls, paperwork, unscheduled visitors, procrastination, perfectionism, failure to delegate, and inability to say no. Some of the activities are necessary, but a supervisor does not always manage the time spent on them wisely. "Tips from the Firing Line" summarizes some suggestions for managing time well.

Get More Time out of Every Day

Here are some tips from the editors of *Working Woman* magazine that can help you get organized and use your time effectively.

1. Make a "to do" list each night for the following day, and make one on Sunday for the following week. Include everything you want to accomplish, both business and personal, using two separate columns. Check things off as you accomplish them.

2. Figure out what time of day you're at your best and do your most mentally demanding work then. Save less stressful work for your ebb times, like after lunch or the evening.

3. Handle each piece of paper that crosses your desk just once. Answer it, forward it, file it, or throw it away.

4. Read your e-mail only once. Answer it, store it, print and file it, or delete it.

5. Keep your files in alphabetical order so you don't have to hunt for needed information.

6. Eliminate clutter everywhere in your life—at home and on your desk. This will make it easier for you to identify and focus on what's truly important.

7. Delegate routine tasks to others who can handle them efficiently at less cost to the company than you. Give clear instructions and set deadlines.

8. Instruct your subordinates about how to handle routine emergencies that they can control themselves.

9. Always extend the utmost courtesy to support personnel such as clerks and secretaries. Their goodwill can greatly expedite your work.

10. When you need to discuss something with a co-worker or subordinate, go to that person's office or work area. That way, when you've said what you need to say, you can leave promptly.

11. If your firm doesn't have them, create computer templates of the documents you use most frequently, such as letters, faxes, contracts, memos, and expense reports.

12. Always set and distribute your agenda for any meeting you convene, including the time the meeting will be over. Start promptly, don't wait for latecomers, and invite only those who need to contribute to the decision that must be made.

Source: June Rogoznica, "Beat the Clock," *Working Woman*, October 1998, pp. 58–59.

One business writer suggests there are fifteen different time wasters that plague supervisors. In addition to those in Figure 14.3, he cites working without a plan, working with fuzzy goals or too many goals, oversupervising, worrying, excessive socializing, pursuing perfectionism, putting off delivering bad news, correcting your own mistakes or those of others, waiting, attending meaningless meetings, dealing with those who don't put in a full day's work, and getting angry.[2]

Giving poor instructions is another source of waste. Instead of saving time, poorly expressed or incomplete instructions create errors or send employees back to you for clarification.[3]

Meetings   The main reason many supervisors hate meetings is that meetings often waste time. People slowly drift into the room, then devote time to chatting while waiting for latecomers. When the formal meeting finally gets under way, the discussion may drift off onto tangents, and the group may never complete the task that it gathered to carry out. Meetings like these are understandably a source of frustration.

When you attend a meeting chaired by someone else, it is hard to control wasted time. You can encourage careful use of time by being prompt. If meetings tend to start late, you might bring along some reading material or other work to do while you wait. If the discussion at the meeting seems irrelevant, you might try tactfully asking the speaker to explain how the current discussion will help in accomplishing the goal of the meeting.

When you call a meeting, you can use time wisely by starting promptly. If the discussion veers off course, politely remind participants about the subject at hand. It is also smart to set an ending time for the meeting. If you cannot solve the problem in the time allotted, schedule a follow-up meeting. (Chapter 3 provides more ideas for holding effective meetings.)

Telephone Calls and E-Mail   When other people call you, they usually have no way of knowing whether the time is convenient. Consequently, most of us get telephone calls when we are busy with something else. When they interrupt the work flow, telephone calls are time wasters.

One way to take control of your time is to remember that you are not a slave to the telephone. If you are fortunate enough to have a secretary to screen your calls, have that person answer your telephone when you are working on top-priority jobs. If you answer the telephone while you are in a meeting or doing something important, explain to the caller that you cannot give the call the attention it deserves at that time, and schedule a convenient time to call back. Of course, you have to use this approach carefully. If the person calling is your manager or a customer, the telephone call may be your top priority.

When you are placing calls yourself, think ahead. Schedule time for making calls each day, bearing in mind different time zones when calling long distance. Before you call someone, make sure you have the information you need close at hand; it does not make sense to place a client on hold while you fetch the file containing the answers he or she wanted. Not only does that waste time, it annoys the person who has to wait. If the person you are calling is not available, ask when you can reach him or her instead of simply leaving a message. That way, you have control over when the call will be made.

The telephone can be a time saver as well as a time waster. When you have a meeting or appointment on your calendar, call to confirm it. If you need to meet with someone away from the workplace, call to get directions rather than waste time by driving around and looking for the meeting place.

For all its apparent convenience, e-mail can absorb another major block of the supervisor's time. A recent study by Pitney Bowes estimated that the average office worker sends or receives an astounding 190 messages a day from all sources, including phones, pages, faxes, mail, and especially e-mail. About 82 million business workers now use e-mail, and electronic communication has "the potential for wreaking havoc on someone's workday," according to Mark Levitt, research manager at International Data Corporation. A senior scientist at RAND, a California think tank, adds, "There's a pressure to respond faster. Waiting a day is practically unheard of."[4]

To keep from being overwhelmed, supervisors should learn to prioritize their e-mail, delete junk mail unread, limit the number of messages sent and the number of recipients, and avoid forwarding or responding to chain letters or other kinds of nonbusiness correspondence. Business consultant and writer Jennifer White advises being ruthless about e-mail. One of her recommended strategies is to check your e-mail once and once only during each day, at a scheduled time. Checking it throughout the day destroys momentum and turns the task into a burden.[5]

Paperwork and Reading Material   Supervisors spend a lot of time reading and writing. They receive mail, reports, and magazines to read, and they must prepare reports, letters, and memos to send to others. Reading and writing are not necessarily a waste of time, but many supervisors do these activities inefficiently.

Most advice on how to manage paperwork is based on the principle of handling each item only once. Set aside specific time to read all the papers that cross your desk. At that time, decide whether each item is something you need to act on. If not, throw it away immediately. If you must act, then determine the most efficient response. An efficient way to respond to a memo is to write a brief response across the top and return the memo to the sender. If you have a secretary, you can keep a tape recorder by your side and dictate responses to letters as you read them. Or consider whether you can respond to a letter with a telephone call. If you learn that you must set time aside to do research or prepare a report, then schedule that time immediately.

Most supervisors have a multitude of magazines, newsletters, and newspapers to choose from. Each supervisor will find that some of these are very helpful, others somewhat helpful, and still others not relevant at all. To cut the time spent poring over the unhelpful publications, a supervisor should decide which ones are useful and cancel subscriptions to the rest. It is wise to look at the table of contents in the somewhat helpful publications for relevant information rather than to turn every page. A supervisor who finds that an internal company report he or she receives provides little useful information might ask to be taken off the distribution list.

Unscheduled Visitors   Supervisors are interrupted at times by unscheduled visitors: customers, peers, employees, salespeople, or anyone else who turns up without an appointment. Because seeing these people is an unplanned use of time, the interruptions can interfere with getting the job done. Figure 14.4 shows some broad guidelines for handling this potential problem.

When a supervisor regularly spends time with unscheduled visitors on unimportant matters, a lot of time gets wasted. The key is to know which interruptions

■ FIGURE 14.4

**Handling
Unscheduled
Visitors**

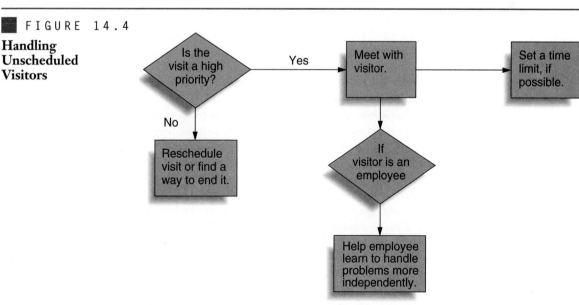

are important. For example, when an angry customer demands to see the manager and interrupts a supervisor in a store, an important part of the supervisor's job is to make that customer happy. When a supervisor's manager occasionally drops in to discuss an idea, the supervisor will probably have to work around the manager's schedule. But when a co-worker in another department stops in to report on his vacation or a salesperson shows up unannounced, the interruption does not carry a high priority.

With low-priority interruptions, the supervisor needs to take control over his or her time diplomatically. The supervisor might say to the co-worker back from vacation, "It's great to hear you had fun last week. Let's have lunch together so you can tell me about it." When salespeople call without an appointment, a supervisor can ask them simply to leave some literature. Another response to unscheduled visitors is to set a time limit. For example, the supervisor might say, "I've got five minutes. What's on your mind?" If the problem is urgent or seems to deserve more time, the supervisor can arrange to meet the visitor later for a specified amount of time.[6]

Standing is a useful signal. If you see an unwanted visitor heading toward your office, stand and meet the visitor at your door, then talk to the visitor there. This sends a message that you expect the conversation to be brief. Meeting with someone else at his or her desk or in a conference room allows you to get up and leave when you have completed your business. If you meet with someone in your office, standing up when you finish sends a signal that the meeting is over.

Interruptions from employees can be tricky to handle because part of a supervisor's job is to listen to employees and help them with work-related problems. At the same time, a constant stream of interruptions could mean that employees have too little training or authority to handle their work. If an employee interrupts with a problem, one approach is to listen and then ask, "What do you suggest we do about that?" This shows that the supervisor expects the employee to participate in finding solutions. With practice, the employee may learn to handle problems more independently.

If the problem is not urgent—for example, if it does not hold up an employee's work—a supervisor may want to schedule a later time when supervisor and employee can meet to work on the problem. At that later time, of course, the supervisor should give priority to the meeting with the employee and discourage interruptions from others. Thus, employees will learn that a supervisor will listen and work with them, though not necessarily on a moment's notice.

Procrastination   Sometimes it is hard to get around to starting an activity. Maybe you have to write a proposal to buy a new computer system. You are not quite sure how to write that kind of proposal, so you are grateful when the telephone rings. You talk for a while, and that conversation reminds you to follow up on an order with a supplier. So you make another telephone call. You get up to stretch your legs and decide it is a good time to check on how your employees are doing. Bit by bit, you manage to get through the entire day without doing any work on the proposal. This process of putting off what needs to be done is called **procrastination.**

procrastination
Putting off what needs to be done.

Procrastination is a time waster because it leads people to spend their time on low-priority activities while they avoid the higher priorities. The best cure for procrastination is to force yourself to jump in. To do that, focus on one step at a time. Decide what the first step is, then do that step. Then do the next step. You will find that you are building momentum and that the big job no longer seems so overwhelming.

If you need more incentive to get started, give yourself a reward for completing each step. For example, you might decide that as soon as you complete the first step, you will go for a walk in the sunshine, call a customer who loves your product, or take a break to open your mail. If the project seems thoroughly unpleasant, you can concentrate on the rewards. The ultimate reward of course is to finish the job.

Here are a few other tips for conquering procrastination[7]:

1. Pick one area at a time in which you tend to procrastinate and attack it. You might tend to put off starting new projects, for instance, or answering e-mail, or returning phone calls. Whatever the case, choose one task and start it.
2. Compartmentalize your work and force yourself to get through the task one step, one e-mail, or one phone call at a time. With each one you complete, begin the next one.
3. Try getting the biggest job done first, when you have the most energy. With that done, it's downhill the rest of the way.
4. Give yourself deadlines. Write them down where you can't miss them, and stick to them.
5. Don't pursue perfectionism; see the section below.

Perfectionism One reason people put off doing necessary work is that they are afraid what they do will not live up to their standards. Although high standards can inspire high performance, perfectionism can make people afraid to try at all. **Perfectionism** is the attempt to do things perfectly. It may sound like a noble goal, but human beings are imperfect. Expecting to be perfect therefore dooms a person to failure.

perfectionism
The attempt to do things perfectly.

Instead of being a slave to perfectionism, determine the highest standard you realistically can achieve. You may be able to meet a higher standard by drawing on the expertise of employees and peers. When you find yourself avoiding a difficult task, remind yourself that your goals are realistic, then give the job your best try.

Failure to Delegate Perfectionism often underlies the failure to delegate work. Even when someone else can do a job more efficiently in terms of that person's cost and availability, supervisors may resist delegating because they believe only they can really do the job right. This attitude stands in the way of appropriate delegating. In terms of time management, the result is that the supervisor has taken on too much work. Instead, the supervisor should learn to delegate effectively.

Inability to Say No To control your use of time, you must be able to say no when appropriate. However, it is easy to let other people and their demands control how we use our time, so we end up overextending ourselves by taking on more tasks than we can possibly do well. How do you react when someone asks you to chair a committee, manage a new project, or take an active role in a local charity? Most people are uncomfortable saying no when the opportunity is for a worthwhile project or they do not want to hurt somebody's feelings. But when we take on too many things, we cannot do our best at any of them.

If someone comes to you with an opportunity that will require a significant commitment of time, learn to tell the person politely that you will consider the offer and will reply later at some specific time. Then assess your present commitments and priorities. Decide whether you should take on this new task. You may decide that you have time for it, but in other instances you will have to decline, claiming that you do not have enough time to do justice to the task. If your life is already busy but the opportunity seems important, try asking yourself, "What activity am I willing to give up to make time for this new one?"

If your own supervisor asks you to take on an urgent new task, request help in deciding where the new task should fit into your current priorities, or ask what should be given up in order to accomplish the new project.[8]

For those times when you can't say no, try these tips:

1. Ask the person making the request how the two of you can plan better for the next time.
2. Remind the person that he or she now owes you one and, for example, could cover your shift next time you need time off.
3. Suggest your own timetable. For instance, say, "I can do that by the end of the week."
4. Put a time limit on your participation. For instance, explain that you can only give an hour and no more.[9]

Whatever you decide, a thoughtful approach does both yourself and the other person a favor. If you do not have the time to complete a task well and on schedule, it is better to give the other person a chance to find somebody else. None of us like to find out that the person we have been counting on is overcommitted and doesn't have enough time to do the job well.

Stress Management

stress

The body's response to coping with environmental demands.

Failure to manage time wisely is one reason supervisors find their jobs difficult. It is frustrating to leave the workplace knowing that you did not accomplish anything you really wanted to that day. Supervisors also have difficulty hearing a lot of complaints, working in a dangerous environment, and trying to live up to unrealistic expectations. To cope, supervisors can use the techniques of stress management.

Stress refers to the body's response to coping with environmental demands such as change, frustration, uncertainty, danger, or discomfort. Usually when we think of stress, we think of the response to problems—for example, arguments, cold, or long hours of work. Stress also results from the challenges that stimulate us and from the happy changes in our lives. Thus, buying a car is stressful, and so is getting married or promoted. People experiencing stress typically undergo physiological changes such as faster heartbeat, faster breathing, higher blood pressure, greater perspiration, greater muscle strength, and decreased gastric (stomach) functioning, among other changes.

Causes of Stress

The environmental demands that cause stress may arise in the workplace, in people's personal lives, and in the conflicts that may arise between the two.

Work-Related Causes Job factors linked to stress involve the organization's policies, structures, physical conditions, and processes (the way work gets done). Examples of each type are identified in Figure 14.5. Employees tend to experience the most stress if policies seem unfair and ambiguous, the structure makes jobs relatively unsatisfying, physical conditions are uncomfortable, and processes interfere with employee understanding of what is happening and how well they are doing.

FIGURE 14.5

Job Factors Linked to Stress

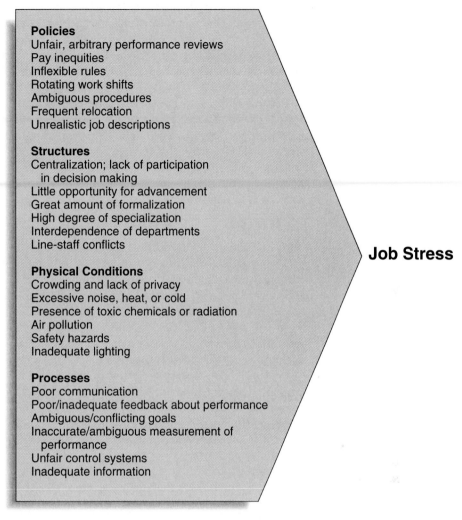

Policies
Unfair, arbitrary performance reviews
Pay inequities
Inflexible rules
Rotating work shifts
Ambiguous procedures
Frequent relocation
Unrealistic job descriptions

Structures
Centralization; lack of participation
   in decision making
Little opportunity for advancement
Great amount of formalization
High degree of specialization
Interdependence of departments
Line-staff conflicts

Physical Conditions
Crowding and lack of privacy
Excessive noise, heat, or cold
Presence of toxic chemicals or radiation
Air pollution
Safety hazards
Inadequate lighting

Processes
Poor communication
Poor/inadequate feedback about performance
Ambiguous/conflicting goals
Inaccurate/ambiguous measurement of
   performance
Unfair control systems
Inadequate information

Job Stress

Source: From *Modern Management: Diversity, Quality, Ethics & the Global Environment*, 6th edition, by Samuel C. Certo and Lee Graf. Copyright © 1994 Pearson Education, Inc.. Reprinted by permission of Pearson Education, Inc., Upper Saddle River, NJ.

David Stum, president of the Loyalty Institute at Aon Consulting, says that employees feel increasingly stressed by "the new corporate expectation . . . to do everything better, faster and cheaper." He notes that days lost from work because of stress increased 36 percent between 1995 and 1998, which Paul Rosch, president of the American Institute of Stress, tags with a cost to U.S. employers of $200 billion to $300 billion annually. That figure includes absenteeism, turnover, direct medical costs, workers' compensation and other legal costs, accidents, and diminished productivity.[10]

Recent studies of a representative sample of occupations done by the Bureau of Labor Statistics indicate that victims of occupational stress missed a median of 23 days of work in 1997, compared with only 5 days for all injuries and illnesses.

Workers in the financial, insurance, and real estate sectors account for 12 percent of all stress cases, while machine operators accounted for 15 percent and production supervisors 4 percent. Blue-collar workers accounted for most of the injuries and illnesses, while white-collar workers made up more than half the stress cases. Looking at the data by gender, the Bureau found that men accounted for two-thirds of the injuries and ailments, while women accounted for two-thirds of the stress cases.[11]

Recurring efforts at downsizing have contributed to a great deal of employee stress. Many employees see job cuts as a long-term trend that prevails without regard to whether they do their best or the organization earns a profit. A case in point is Pam Cromer, who worked for Westinghouse Electric Corporation in Pittsburgh. She worked up to 80 hours a week when the company was struggling during the early 1990s. One night part of her face went numb, which Cromer learned was caused from clenching her teeth too hard—the result of tension. Despite Cromer's willingness to sacrifice, she was laid off in cutbacks that occurred after she had been with Westinghouse 22 years. At a going-away party, her coworkers observed, "The winners get to leave, and the losers get to stay."[12]

A supervisor's own behavior also can be a source of stress for employees. A supervisor who communicates poorly, stirs up conflict, and metes out discipline arbitrarily is creating stressful working conditions. Other supervisory behaviors that can contribute to employee stress are demonstrating a lack of concern for employee well-being and checking up on every detail of an employee's work. If you've ever typed while someone peered over your shoulder, you know that you can almost feel your blood pressure rise.

Michael Gelman is the executive producer of *Live with Regis*, a freewheeling morning television show filmed in New York. Over the 13 years he has held the job, Gelman has found his own way of coping with the particular stress of working with Regis Philbin. "There are absolutely no second chances on live television," comments Gelman. "When things go awry and Regis grumbles and complains, I don't take it personally. It's all part of his shtick. We just move on . . . there is that 5 percent of the time when my feelings are indeed hurt and I want to blurt out, 'Wait a minute.' But that would be out of character."[13]

One writer suggests that before assuming employees can't manage their time, supervisors should check three stress-causing traps they may fall victim to: (1) giving ambiguous instructions, causing the employee to stop work and seek clarification; (2) interrupting subordinates with needless visits that interfere with concentration and momentum; and (3) keeping people waiting.[14]

Another source of stress is the sheer inability to leave the job behind when it's appropriate to do so. A recent *Inc.* magazine/Gallup survey listed several work activities and asked, "Did you do any of the following on vacation last year?" Here are the results[15]:

Activity	Percent Who Said Yes
Work.	17
Make phone calls to work.	35
Check e-mail.	19
Leave vacation for a meeting.	5
Cut vacation short because of work demands.	11

See "Supervision and Diversity" for some interesting comparisons of workweeks around the world.

It's Not Just the Job; It's the Hours on the Job

So you think you have a long workweek? Don't let the average worker from South Korea hear you complain, or people in Turkey or Argentina, for that matter.

On average, South Koreans put in 55.1 hours a week, which is more than workers from 31 other countries surveyed by Roper Starch Worldwide in New York. The survey, whose results were released last week, questioned 1,000 workers in each country.

Just behind the Koreans in hours worked were the Turks, at 54.1 a week, followed by the Argentines, at 53.5, and the Taiwanese, 53.4.

Workers in the United States, where economic growth has slowed, and in China put in the same amount of time on the job—42.4 hours, below the global average of 44.6.

Who works the least amount of hours each week? According to the study, it is the French, who average 40.3 hours and the Italians, at 40.5.

France cut its workweek to 35 hours from 39 hours about a year ago to tackle high unemployment levels and bolster the economy. In other industrialized countries, "we're beginning to see greater emphasis on balancing work and leisure," said Tom Miller, group senior vice president of Roper.

Type A personality A pattern of behavior that involves constantly trying to accomplish a lot in a hurry.

Type B personality A pattern of behavior that focuses on a relaxed but active approach to life

Personal Factors Even when faced with similar job factors and supervisory behavior, some employees will have a greater stress response than others. General feelings of negativism, helplessness, and low self-esteem can contribute to stress. In addition, some medical researchers have observed that the people who are more likely to have heart disease (presumably a sign of stress) tend to share a similar pattern of behavior, which the researchers named the Type A personality. A **Type A personality** refers to the behavior pattern of constantly trying to get a lot done in a hurry. It includes the behaviors listed in Table 14.1. Research suggests that some Type A people seem to thrive on their approach to life, whereas others—those prone to heart disease—have an excess amount of hostility along with the basic Type A characteristics. To help those at risk, physicians often recommend adopting contrasting behaviors, known collectively as a **Type B personality** (see Table 14.1).

Work-Family Conflict Stress also can be great for people who experience conflict between the demands of work and home. Women have traditionally borne the primary responsibility for homemaking and the family's well-being, so as a group they are particularly vulnerable to this source of stress. A survey of 311 female nurses aged 50 to 70 found that women who feel tension between demands from work and demands from home are at higher risk than other women of having serious heart disease. The risk was not associated with what the women achieved or how hard they worked, but with the degree to which they felt a conflict between career and family. At greatest risk were the women who believed that having a family interfered with advancement in their careers.[16]

Consequences of Stress

Stress is a fact of life. Indeed, life would be boring without some sources of stress, and most people seek out some degree of stress. Some people even are attracted to jobs billed as challenging or exciting—those likely to be most stressful. On the

TABLE 14.1 **Behavior Patterns Associated with Type A and Type B Personalities**	Type A	Type B
	Moving, walking, eating rapidly	Having varied interests
	Feeling impatient with people who move slower than you	Taking a relaxed but active approach to life
	Feeling impatient when others talk about something that is not of interest to you	
	Doing two or three things at the same time	
	Feeling unable to relax or to stop working	
	Trying to get more and more done in less and less time	

Source: Adapted from Meyer Friedman and Ray H. Rosenman, *Type A Behavior and Your Heart* (New York: Fawcett Crest, 1974), pp. 100–101, summarized in Jane Whitney Gibson, *The Supervisory Challenge: Principles and Practices* (Columbus, OH: Merrill Publishing, 1990), p. 309.

| FIGURE 14.6 **Stress Levels and Performance**

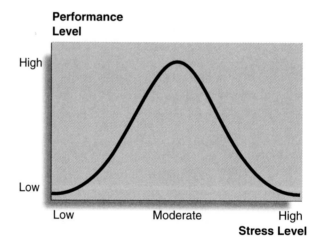

job, employees tend to perform best when they are experiencing a moderate degree of stress (see Figure 14.6).

However, too much stress brings problems, especially when the sources of stress are negative (e.g., a critical manager or unsafe working conditions). As Figure 14.6 indicates, performance falls when the amount of stress moves from moderate to high. In a highly stressful environment, people are more apt to come down with heart disease, high blood pressure, ulcers, and possibly other diseases. Because of illness and unhappiness, they take more time off from work. When employees are at work, the sources of stress may distract them from doing their best and may make them prone to having accidents.

TABLE 14.2 **Possible Signs of Excess Stress**	Decline in work performance.
	Increase in use of sick days.
	Increase in number of errors and accidents.
	Moodiness and irritability.
	Fatigue.
	Loss of enthusiasm.
	Aggressive behavior.
	Difficulty making decisions.
	Family problems.
	Apparent loss of concern for others and their feelings.*
	Feeling that it's impossible to help other people.*
	Feeling of inability to get your job done fully or well.*

*Possible signs of burnout.

Besides hurting the organization through poor performance and attendance, excess stress can hurt employees as individuals. People experiencing stress tend to feel anxious, aggressive, frustrated, tense, and moody. They may be overly sensitive to criticism, have trouble making decisions, and be more likely to have trouble maintaining mutually satisfying relationships with loved ones. They may be unable to get enough sleep. People under stress are also at risk for abusing drugs and alcohol.

Because of these potential negative consequences of stress, supervisors should notice when employees seem to be experiencing more stress than they can handle effectively. Table 14.2 lists some signs that indicate when employees may be experiencing excess stress. If some of these signs exist, a supervisor should try to reduce the stress employees are experiencing and recommend some coping techniques. (Approaches to stress management are described in the next section.)

Burnout   A person who cannot cope with stress over an extended period of time may experience burnout. **Burnout** is the inability to function effectively as a result of ongoing stress. Employees who are burned out feel drained and lose interest in doing their jobs. Typically, burnout occurs in three stages:

burnout
The inability to function effectively as a result of ongoing stress.

1. The employee feels emotionally exhausted.
2. The employee's perceptions of others become calloused.
3. The employee views his or her effectiveness negatively.

Burnout is worse than just needing a vacation. Therefore, it is important to cope with stress before it leads to burnout.

Some signs of excess stress that may indicate burnout are indicated in Table 14.2. Supervisors who observe these signs in employees not only should seek to reduce stress, but also should be sure that employees are being rewarded for their efforts. Burnout is especially likely to occur when people feel they are giving of themselves all the time, with little or no return. For that reason, burnout is reported widely among employees in the so-called helping professions, such as health care and teaching.

Personal Stress Management

Because stress arises from both personal and job factors, a full effort at stress management includes actions at both levels. Personal stress management is especially important for people who hold jobs that are by nature highly stressful, such as the supervisor of nurses in a hospital's intensive care unit or the supervisor of a crew of firefighters.

A variety of techniques are available for personal stress management: time management (discussed in the first part of this chapter), positive attitude, exercise, biofeedback, meditation, and well-rounded life activities. Supervisors can use these techniques to improve their own stress levels, and they also can encourage employees to use them.

Time Management Making conscious, reasoned decisions about your use of time helps prevent the stress that can result from wasted time or unrealistic goals. Thus, a good start for handling the stress related to balancing work and family responsibilities is to set priorities. For example, different people will have different views about whether a promotion is worth the price of moving or working weekends. Then set aside time for the things you consider important, scheduling time for friends and family members as well as work-related commitments. After all, as Rita Emmett says in her book, *The Procrastinator's Handbook: Mastering the Art of Doing It Now*, the real point of finding ways to accomplish necessary tasks in an efficient and timely way is to make time to enjoy the rest of what life has to offer.[17]

Don't forget to include time for resting and recharging. (See "Meeting the Challenge.") Bolstered by research reports showing a link to improved safety and job performance, some managers are even putting naps on their schedules. Claudio Stampi, a researcher on sleep strategies, explains:

> We've found that you get tremendous recovery of alertness—several hours' worth—out of a 15-minute nap. You can get temporary help through stimulation—coffee, exercise, brighter light, cooler temperatures—but you're actually fixing the problem by taking a nap.[18]

No wonder spending part of your lunch break with your head down on your desk has come to be called "power napping."

Time management principles are also useful for managing the stress of balancing work and home responsibilities. If family activities are on your "to do" list, you have a built-in response when another request conflicts with family time: "I have other commitments at that time." Also, being realistic about time is ultimately less frustrating than expecting yourself to handle everything. Instead of criticizing yourself for what you do not do, make an effort to give yourself a pat on the back for all the times you strike a balance between home and work commitments.

Positive Attitude As mentioned, people with a negative outlook tend to be more susceptible to stress. Thus, supervisors can reduce their stress response by cultivating a positive attitude. Ways to do this are to avoid making negative generalizations and to look for the positives in any situation. Saying to oneself, "This company doesn't care about us; all it cares about is profits" or "I'll never get the hang of this job," contributes to a negative attitude. A supervisor can consciously replace such thoughts with more positive ones: "The competition is tough these days, but we each can contribute to helping this company please its customers" and "This job is difficult, but I will plan a way to learn how to do it better."

Truck Drivers Battle Road Fatigue

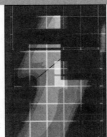

Many people who consistently work long hours—on overtime, double shifts, or to meet deadlines—know how fatigue can slow them down, impair decision-making ability, cause tempers to flare, and so forth. But what about workers whose fatigue endangers not only their own safety but also the safety of others?

Fatigue is a significant source—and consequence—of stress. Among truck drivers in recent years, it has led to an increase in fatalities on the road. According to the National Transportation Safety Board, 58 percent of 113 single-vehicle heavy truck accidents (in which the driver survived) in one year were linked to tired truck drivers, of whom 25 percent had violated rules pertaining to sleep. Most of the drivers involved in the accidents got only about five hours of sleep a night.

When interviewed anonymously, drivers admit to falsifying their log books, which document more sleep than they actually get. Some keep two sets of log books—one accurate, the other for inspectors. Although this practice is clearly unethical, the drivers claim they must stay on the road longer hours—and deliver for their companies or customers—or lose their jobs. Oliver Patton, editor of *Transport Topics* magazine, claims that government deregulation of the trucking industry "took trucking out of its protective envelope and plunged it into a market-based business." Thus, drivers work longer and often for less money.

There are some possible solutions to the sleep problem. One may come from the research being done for NASA by Dr. Claudio Stampi of the Institute for Circadian Studies, who is studying the positive effects of napping rather than long, uninterrupted hours of sleep. Nappers don't fall into deep sleep, he says, and thus awake more refreshed than people who sleep for many hours at a time. "The challenge is to train rescue workers or astronauts to adapt quickly to [a nap] schedule," says Stampi. Truck drivers could benefit, too.

Technology may also help. Satellites and cellular tracking could be used to track the progress of trucks, from their speed to the amount of time they spend on the road. In addition, inspectors may be able to use certain video games to measure alertness and agility among drivers on the road. In the meantime, most of us hope that truck drivers will have the good sense to pull over when they are tired, and grab a nap—or at least a cup of coffee.

Sources: Richard Saltus, "Study on Nap-Based Survival Could Be Workaholic's Dream," *Boston Globe*, September 4, 1995, pp. 17, 24; "Highway to Nod," *Economist*, April 8, 1995, p. 28.

In the positive examples, a supervisor is focusing on the areas over which he or she has control. This helps to defuse the sense of helplessness that can increase stress and contributes to a positive outlook.[19]

Maintaining a sense of humor also is important to a positive attitude. Consultant Diane C. Decker explains, "If we can laugh at ourselves and see the humor in situations, then we don't feel it's the end of the world."[20] Decker recommends developing a list of things that bring you joy, then cultivating those areas of your life. She arrived at this idea through her own experiences as manager with a manufacturer that was experiencing production problems. She worried about her own future and that of her employees; to beat the stress, she signed up for a class in being a clown. Spending time getting others to laugh helped Decker to relax and put her problems into perspective.

Exercise Experts on stress believe that the human body long ago developed a stress response to help people handle dangerous situations. Early peoples had to face storms or attacks by wild animals and human enemies. The basic responses are either to fight the danger or to run away. For this reason, the physical changes in response to stress are known as the "fight-or-flight syndrome."

Because the body's response to stress is to get ready for physical action, a logical way to respond to workplace stress is to look for an outlet through physical activity. Although it is never appropriate to punch your manager when he or she criticizes you or to run away when clients complain, other forms of exercise can provide a similar release without negative social consequences. Some people enjoy running, walking, or riding a bicycle before or after work—or as a way to get to work. Others prefer to work out at a health club, participate in sports, or dance. Besides letting off steam, exercising strengthens the body's organs so that they can better withstand stress.

Biofeedback   People who have devoted time to developing their awareness of such automatically controlled bodily functions as pulse rate, blood pressure, body temperature, and muscle tension have learned to control these functions. Developing an awareness of bodily functions in order to control them is known as **biofeedback.** People use biofeedback to will their bodies into a more relaxed state.

biofeedback
Developing an awareness of bodily functions in order to control them.

Meditation   While meditation has religious overtones for many people, in its general form it is simply a practice of focusing one's thoughts on something other than day-to-day concerns. The person meditating focuses on breathing, on a symbol, or on a word or phrase. People who practice regular meditation find that it relaxes them and that the benefits carry beyond the time spent meditating.

Well-Rounded Life Activities   For someone who gets all of his or her satisfaction and rewards from working, job-related stress is more likely to be overwhelming. No job is going to be rewarding all the time, so some of your satisfaction should come from other areas of life. For instance, if your manager is impatient and fails to praise you for completing an important project, you can offset those frustrations by enjoying the love of friends and family members or hearing the cheers of your softball teammates when you make a good play.

In other words, people who lead a well-rounded life are more likely to experience satisfaction in some area of life at any given time. This satisfaction can make stress a lot easier to cope with. Leading a well-rounded life means not only advancing your career but also devoting time to social, family, intellectual, spiritual, and physical pursuits. One person might choose to read biographies, join a volleyball team, and volunteer in a soup kitchen. Another person might take bicycle trips with the kids on weekends and be active in a religious congregation and a professional organization. These varied pursuits not only help people manage stress, they also make life more enjoyable.

Organizational Stress Management

Although employees can take many actions to cope with stress, a significant reduction in stress requires attacking it at its source. Many sources of stress may arise from the policies and practices of the organization and its management. Therefore, any serious effort at stress management must include organizational interventions.

Organizational stress management can operate on several levels. Supervisors can adjust their behavior so that they do not contribute unnecessarily to employee stress. Also, many organizations have helped employees manage stress through means such as job redesign, environmental changes, and wellness programs. Al-

■ TABLE 14.3 How Supervisors Can Minimize Organizational Stressors	Prepare employees to cope with change.	• Communicate thoroughly. • Provide adequate training to handle any new work demands. • Skip unnecessary changes during times of transition.
	Foster a supportive organizational climate.	• Make policies and procedures flexible. • Establish fair policies and administer them fairly. • Investigate whether work can be done in more efficient ways that reduce work overload. • Make sure employees understand what is expected of them. • Praise individual and group successes.
	Make work interesting.	• Give employees some control over decisions and work processes. • Match the challenge level to employees' abilities. • Assign a variety of tasks.
	Encourage career development.	• Communicate with employees about their career prospects in the organization. • Encourage employees to take advantage of any career counseling programs available through the organization. • Make time to discuss career goals with employees.

Sources: Based on information in Samuel C. Certo, *Modern Management*, 6th ed. (Boston: Allyn and Bacon, 1994), pp. 308–310; Fred Luthans, *Organizational Behavior* (New York: McGraw-Hill, 1985), pp. 146–148.

though a supervisor rarely can carry out all these measures single-handedly, he or she may be in a position to recommend them to higher-level managers. Also, a supervisor who knows about any stress management measures offered by the organization is in a better position to take advantage of them and to recommend them to employees.

Behavior of the Supervisor Understanding sources of stress can help supervisors behave in a manner that minimizes unnecessary stress and enhances employee confidence. Supervisors should avoid behavior that contributes to raising employee stress levels. For instance, knowing that feelings of helplessness and uncertainty contribute to stress, supervisors can minimize such feelings through clear communication and regular feedback. Where possible, supervisors also can empower employees to make decisions and solve problems, thereby giving them more control. Table 14.3 summarizes some basic approaches to reducing stress in the workplace.

As noted earlier, employees with low self-esteem tend to be more susceptible to stress than those with high self-esteem. Therefore, supervisors should avoid behavior that can damage self-esteem; for example, put-downs and criticism with no clue about how to improve. Better still, supervisors should behave in esteem-enhancing ways, including the generous use of praise (when it can be offered sincerely) and feedback to employees about how their efforts add value to the work group or the organization as a whole.

Changes in the Job Recall from Figure 14.5 that many characteristics of a job can be sources of stress. Just a few of the job factors linked to stress are unfair policies, ambiguous procedures, lack of opportunities for advancement, and poor communication. A supervisor has at least some control over many of these matters. For example, supervisors can improve their ability to be fair and to communicate instructions clearly and precisely.

In general, an important part of stress management involves identifying job factors linked to stress and then modifying those factors when possible. Sometimes a supervisor cannot act alone to make a change; for example, he or she may not be powerful enough to resolve conflicts with another department. In such cases, a supervisor should be sure that higher-level management knows about the stress-related job factors and how they are affecting employees.

When the sources of stress include boring or overly difficult jobs, the organization may be able to change the job requirements to make them less stressful. As described in Chapter 11, a routine job can be made more interesting through job enlargement or job enrichment. An overly difficult job can be made less so by giving employees further training or by reassigning some responsibilities so that the work is divided more realistically.

Environmental Changes   As shown in Figure 14.5, some characteristics of the job environment can add to employee stress. For example, it is a strain on employees to cope with noise, poor lighting, uncomfortable chairs, and extremes of heat and cold. When possible, an organization should reduce stress by fixing some of these problems. A supervisor is frequently in an excellent position to identify needed environmental changes and to report them to the managers who can make the changes. That is likely to be the case when employees complain about uncomfortable chairs or dark work areas.

Wellness Programs   Most organizations provide their employees with health insurance, and many also take an active role in helping employees stay well. The usual way to do this is to provide a **wellness program,** or organizational activities designed to help employees adopt healthful practices. These activities might include exercise classes, stop-smoking clinics, nutrition counseling, and health screening such as cholesterol and blood-pressure tests. Some organizations even have constructed exercise facilities for employees. Aetna, the life insurance company, has five modern health clubs. Steelcase, the maker of office furniture, has six wellness workers on its staff, including an exercise physiologist and three health educators.[21]

Text 100 is an $18 million international public relations agency at which employees get two "duvet days" in addition to their regular vacation and sick time. If they don't feel like getting up, employees can call in, take a "duvet day," and get back under the covers, no questions asked.[22]

At Union Pacific, the wellness program identifies employees at high risk for health problems, then teaches them how to gradually shed unhealthy habits. The program, run by Kersh Wellness Management, measures cholesterol and blood pressure. Employees at high risk are counseled individually in how to reduce fat and add exercise. For instance, counselor Patsy Parker has helped one employee make one change a month, such as substituting mustard for mayonnaise on sandwiches and extending his nightly walk by 15 minutes.[23]

Reebok International Ltd. in Stoughton, Massachusetts, has a fitness center that offers massage therapy, yoga, mind strengthening, and traditional fitness activities. The programs have grown since the center opened, and classes are usually nearly full, with about half the plant's 1,600 employees signed up.[24]

Big companies aren't the only ones with wellness programs. Highsmith, a supplier of library products, invites each of its 240 employees and their spouses to

wellness program
Organizational activities designed to help employees adopt healthy practices.

participate in annual screenings measuring cholesterol, blood pressure, percentage of body fat, and general fitness. Based on how well the employee scores, he or she receives a 50, 25, or 12.5 percent reduction in health insurance premiums. (Doctors may sign waivers for employees with conditions beyond their control.) To help employees improve their scores, the company provides on-site instruction in exercise, weight control, nutrition, and smoking cessation.[25]

Highsmith, Union Pacific, and the other companies with wellness programs aren't just bringing down stress levels. They are also slashing costs related to unhealthy employees. Highsmith's president reports that savings in health insurance and related costs completely cover the expenses of its wellness program. According to Union Pacific, the $1.2 million a year it spends on promoting healthy behavior saves the company three times that amount in reduced medical costs alone. Aetna reports that employees who exercise cost the company $282 a year less to insure than its other employees. Steelcase estimates its wellness program has saved $20 million over a decade.[26]

The Adolph Coors Company opened its wellness center in 1982. The center is free for all 6,000 full- or part-time employees and their families. Coors' most recent cost-benefit analysis of the wellness program found annual incremental costs of poor employee health running from over $1,300 to more than $6,300 per employee, with total costs in the millions of dollars. The firm is now working with the University of Michigan to build a health cost database for those who participate in the center.[27]

Given the benefits of wellness programs, it makes sense for supervisors to participate in and support them. When possible, supervisors can avoid scheduling activities that conflict with participation in the programs. They can encourage employees to participate and they can set good examples by their own participation. However, supervisors should focus on encouraging all employees to participate in the program instead of singling out employees and encouraging them to make specific changes such as losing weight or cutting out cigarettes. After all, having a specialist conduct the wellness program frees the supervisor to concentrate on work-related behaviors—and avoid charges that the supervisor has discriminated against an employee with a disability such as obesity or addiction to nicotine.

A Word about Personality

The guidelines given in this chapter for managing time and stress have worked for many people. However, the degree to which a person will succeed at using any particular technique depends in part on that person's personality. This text does not explore psychological theory, but a brief look at one approach to understanding personality types may be helpful. The Myers-Briggs Type Indicator is a test that classifies people into 16 personality types based on the work of psychiatrist Carl Jung.[28] These 16 personality types describe the traits a person has along four dimensions (see Figure 14.7). For example, one individual might be an extrovert, an intuitive, a feeler, and a perceiver. Another person will have a different combination of four traits. These traits are not considered good or bad; each has its own strengths and weaknesses.

Knowing your personality type suggests suitable techniques for managing your own time and stress. Thus, an introvert may find that meditation is a pleasant way to relieve stress, whereas an extrovert may find meditation impossible but dancing with friends refreshing. Judgers have an easy time applying such time

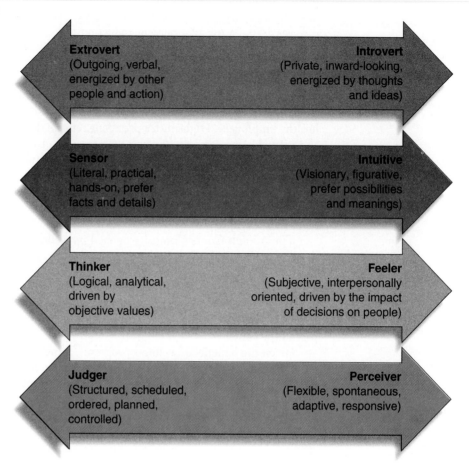

■ FIGURE 14.7

A Basis for Categorizing Personality Types

According to the Myers-Briggs Type Indicator, a person's personality traits fall somewhere along each of these four dimensions.

Source: Adapted from Otto Kroeger and Janet M. Thuesen, "It Takes All Types," *Newsweek*, Management Digest advertising section, September 7, 1992.

management aids as "to do" lists. Perceivers also make those lists, but they lose them and cannot seem to make time to find them. To manage their time, these personality types need heroic amounts of self-discipline—or maybe a job that requires flexibility more than structure.

When you discern that a particular way of behavior does not fit your personality type, you have a choice. You can make the effort to develop the contrasting trait. For instance, a feeler might list logical criteria for making a decision that must be objective. Or you can avoid situations that require you to behave in ways unsuited to your personality. If the feeler in the previous example really hates making decisions objectively, this person might seek out a job or organization where highly subjective decisions are valued.

In addition, recognizing different personality types can help you understand the behavior of other people. For example, if you think your manager's head is always in the clouds, perhaps he or she is an intuitive and you are a sensor. Such insights alone can ease a great deal of stress.

Summary

14.1 Discuss how supervisors can evaluate their use of time.

A practical way to evaluate time use is to keep a time log. A supervisor enters his or her activities for half-hour periods throughout the workday. After a week or two of keeping the time log, a supervisor reviews the information to see whether the time is being used efficiently.

14.2 Describe ways to plan the use of time.

A supervisor can plan the use of time by making a list of things to do for the day or week, then rate each item on the list as A (things that must be done), B (things that are important but can be postponed if necessary), or C (everything else). A supervisor then schedules specific times for completing the A- and B-level activities. When time permits, a supervisor works on the C-level activities. A supervisor should not fill up every hour of the day, so that free time is available to handle unexpected problems. A supervisor can plan his or her time with the help of a variety of computer software programs designed specifically for time management. A supervisor also can use programs called desktop organizers.

14.3 Identify some time wasters and how to control them.

Many meetings waste time. The supervisor who calls a meeting can start the meeting on time, keep the discussion on track, and end it on time. A supervisor can control telephone calls by having someone screen them, by returning calls at the same time every day, by preparing for calls to be made, and by scheduling calls instead of leaving messages. To handle paperwork and reading material, a supervisor should handle each item only once, decide which items are essential, dictate responses or make telephone calls when possible, and designate a time for reading. With unscheduled visitors, a supervisor can schedule a later meeting, stand to signal that a meeting is ending or will be short, or specify a time limit for the discussion.

The best way to handle procrastination is to tackle the project one step at a time, giving oneself rewards along the way. To combat perfectionism, a supervisor should set high but reasonable standards. Perfectionism is a cause of failure to dele-

gate, so a supervisor must strive to delegate work effectively. Finally, supervisors sometimes find themselves taking on too many projects. The solution is to say no to projects they do not have time to complete properly.

14.4 List factors that contribute to stress among employees.

Certain job factors linked to stress involve the organization's policies, structures, physical conditions, and processes. Notably, when employees feel out of control and if the workplace is unsafe or unpredictable, employees will suffer more from the effects of stress. Personal factors also can make a person more vulnerable to stress. Such factors include general feelings of negativism, helplessness, low self-esteem, and a Type A personality—constantly trying to get a lot done in a hurry. Conflicts between work and personal life may be a further source of stress.

14.5 Summarize consequences of stress.

Stress is the body's response to coping with environmental demands. These demands can come from change, frustration, uncertainty, danger, and discomfort. Stress can be stimulating, but an excessive amount of it leads to illness and lowered performance. People under stress feel anxious, aggressive, frustrated, tense, and moody, and they may overreact to criticism. They are also at risk for abusing drugs and alcohol. When a person cannot cope with stress over an extended period of time, the person may experience burnout.

14.6 Explain how supervisors can manage their own stress.

Supervisors and others can manage stress by using time management, having a positive attitude, getting exercise, using biofeedback, meditating, and leading a well-rounded life. These actions do not reduce the amount of stress the person is under, but they do make a person better able to handle it.

14.7 Identify ways organizations, including supervisors, can help employees manage stress.

Supervisors and other managers can seek to eliminate or minimize the job factors linked to stress. They should communicate clearly, give regular feedback to employees, and empower workers to make decisions and solve problems. Supervisors also should behave in ways that enhance employees' self-esteem. In addition, they can make jobs more interesting through job enlargement or job enrichment, and can make certain that the work environment is safe and comfortable. Organizations also can offer wellness programs that provide services such as health clinics, instruction in exercise and weight control, and nonsmoking programs.

Key Terms

time management, p. 345	stress, p. 354	burnout, p. 359
time log, p. 345	Type A personality, p. 357	biofeedback, p. 362
procrastination, p. 352	Type B personality, p. 357	wellness program, p. 364
perfectionism, p. 353		

Review and Discussion Questions

1. For one week keep a time log of your activities at work or at school. Follow the format of Figure 14.1. What does it tell you about your own time management habits?

2. Refer to the cartoon in Figure 14.2. Describe an experience in which you succeeded in turning a delay (or other frustrating setback, such as a person not showing up for an appointment with you) into a positive use of your time.

3. Demetrius Jones prepared the following list of things to do:

Performance appraisal for Angela	A
Clean out files	C
Finish report due Wednesday	A
Prepare a plan for training employees	B
Find out why Kevin has been making more errors lately	B
Read professional journals	C

   a. Which activities does Demetrius consider most important? Least important?
   b. Which activities should Demetrius schedule for times when he is at his best?
   c. If Demetrius fits all these activities onto his weekly schedule and finds he has time left over, what should he do about the "free" time?

4. Assume you are the supervisor of social workers at a hospital. One of your co-workers, a nursing supervisor, asks you to meet with him in his office to discuss a mutual problem. When you arrive at the agreed-upon time, he says, "I'll be right back as soon as I deliver these instructions to one of the nurses and grab a cup of coffee." After you get started 10 minutes later, the supervisor takes several telephone calls, interrupting the meeting for 5 minutes at a time. "Sorry," he says after each call, "but that call was important." An hour into the meeting, you have not made much progress toward solving your problem.
   a. How would you feel in a situation like this? How does your co-worker's behavior affect your performance? How does it affect his performance?
   b. How could you react in this situation to improve your use of time?

5. Imagine that you came to work an hour early so that you could get started on a large proposal that you have due in a week. Fifteen minutes into the project, a co-worker stops by to tell you about her recent vacation. After she leaves, your manager pokes his head into your office and asks if you can spare a minute. Finally, you settle into your proposal. Five minutes after the official start of the workday, one of your employees comes into your office and informs you that she is going to resign. What is the best way to handle each of these unscheduled visitors?

6. You know that you have an important assignment to complete by the end of the week, but you put off starting it on Monday because you want to get everything else out of the way first. In addition, you want a clean slate so that you can concentrate and do a perfect job. Sud-

denly on Thursday, you realize you can't possibly finish the assignment by the next day. You've procrastinated all week. What steps could you have taken to avoid procrastinating and thus complete the assignment on schedule?

7. Which of the following are sources of stress? Explain.
   a. A supervisor who gives you vague and confusing instructions and then criticizes your results.
   b. Buying a house.
   c. Working at a boring job.
   d. Getting a promotion to a supervisory position you have wanted for a year.

8. Sales supervisor Anita Feinstein does not understand all the fuss about stress. She feels stimulated by a job that is exciting and contains many challenges. Does her attitude show that stress is not harmful? Explain.

9. Describe the signs of burnout. Describe the three stages of burnout. What should a supervisor do when he or she observes burnout in an employee?

10. Name five job factors linked to stress over which a supervisor could have some control.

11. How do the following responses help a person cope with stress?
    a. Exercising.
    b. Using biofeedback.
    c. Meditating.
    d. Participating in a wellness program.

A SECOND LOOK

Over which changes brought about by the computer do you think the employees in the opening story can exercise control? How would greater control reduce the stress they experience?

SKILLS MODULE

CASE

Is It OK Not to Be Perfect?

Debra Chatman Finely worked hard for 15 years to become vice president of marketing at Prudential Reinsurance Company/Everest Reinsurance Company in New Jersey. But instead of boosting her self-esteem, her success nearly cost Debra her health.

Concerned that being the highest-ranking African American in a mostly white company put extra performance pressure on her, Debra determined to outperform her co-workers and vowed she would never make a mistake on the job. When she hit the inevitable bumps in the road, she first became depressed, then forced herself to work even harder. She put in regular late nights and weekends in the office and studied hard for meetings. "My work was a large part of my identity. How well I performed determined how good I felt about myself," she says now.

Finally, however, Debra realized that the stress of trying to achieve the impossible—perfection—was becoming a serious problem. She quit her job, found professional counseling, and began working on a master's degree in psychology. Now she's changed her outlook on perfection. "I'm not afraid to make mistakes if I know I've done my best. Sometimes I can even find pleasure or humor in my shortcomings—it's such a relief."

1. What warning signs might have suggested to Debra that her goals for her own performance were unrealistically high?
2. How do you handle your mistakes? Do you think your strategy adds stress to your life and, if so, how can you improve it?
3. What role do you think humor plays in relieving stress? Thinking of a job or jobs you have held, how might such humor be acceptable at work?
4. How can you check your expectations of yourself against others' expectations of you?

Source: Kellye M. Garrett, "Give Perfectionism the Boot," *Black Enterprise*, November 1998, p. 181.

SELF-QUIZ

How Well Do You Use Technology to Manage Time?

How well do you use technology to save and manage time? Complete this simple quiz to find out. Each of the following statements represents a simple, yet tried-and-true method of timesaving technology. Rate yourself on each: If you practice the method regularly, give yourself a "3." Practice it sometimes; give yourself a "2." Practice it rarely; you get a "1." And if you never practice it, you receive a "0." Now, take a moment to complete the quiz.

1. I skim professional journals via the Web.	3	2	1	0
2. I send agendas, meeting minutes, assignment summaries, and other notices to co-workers and employees using e-mail.	3	2	1	0
3. I maintain working files in a single, readily accessible directory, enabling me to work on current projects whenever I have spare moments.	3	2	1	0
4. Using planning or spreadsheet software, I list and monitor objectives, strategies, and tasks necessary for the completion of my goals.	3	2	1	0
5. I group tasks related to each software package together, and complete each group of related tasks at the same time.	3	2	1	0
6. I organize documents with an intuitive file structure.	3	2	1	0
7. I maintain a perpetual "to-do" list on a computerized task manager or in a special file, checking off items as they are completed.	3	2	1	0
8. Using numerical rankings in a spreadsheet, I analyze and identify priorities.	3	2	1	0
9. I maintain my calendar and other key information using portable digital technology.	3	2	1	0
10. 1 have software that maintains my key organizational resources, such as contacts, tasks, events, and crucial records.	3	2	1	0
11. I maintain "idea files" into which I post thoughts, jottings, and potential tasks.	3	2	1	0
12. I use e-mail to forward documents to co-workers.	3	2	1	0
13. I associate related files to each other with html links.	3	2	1	0
14. I consolidate Web searches into a specific time of the day or week.	3	2	1	0
15. I conduct "off-line" Web searches to save time.	3	2	1	0

16. Through e-mail, discussion lists and team software, I participate in virtual meetings.   3   2   1   0

17. Using shared directories, I post public files containing policies, forms, and other information regularly used by the people around me.   3   2   1   0

18. I transfer files from my office computer to my home or laptop, and vice-versa.   3   2   1   0

19. I have begun using voice input to save keyboarding or personal dictating time.   3   2   1   0

20. I append the names of files with dates for easy retrieval.   3   2   1   0

21. I use my computer to send broadcast faxes and e-mails when appropriate.   3   2   1   0

22. I maintain a directory and bookmarks of commonly used reference materials.   3   2   1   0

23. I use shortcuts, such as templates and macros, to speed up my work.   3   2   1   0

24. I handle business transactions online.   3   2   1   0

25. I maintain financial data in a simple accounting program or, if appropriate, using spreadsheet or database software.   3   2   1   0

26. I maintain files for every person I work with, detailing meeting summaries, assignments and other notes.   3   2   1   0

27. I automatically create multiple drafts of a document, noting relevant changes with each successive draft.   3   2   1   0

28. I automate correspondence and mailing functions using mail merge features.   3   2   1   0

29. I use spreadsheet software to prepare budgets, expense reports, statistical analyses and other numerical data.   3   2   1   0

Now, total your score and figure out where you stand. If you rated between 75 and 90, congratulations! You're developing some outstanding timesaving technology skills. A rating between 50 and 74 means that you've learned a number of practical skills, and you're probably aware of the many ways technology can help you master time. Maintain your commitment to learn more. A rating below 50 means that you may have some catch-up to do. If you find yourself in this category (and even if you don't) review the principles noted in this time quiz. Read up on the latest technology. Take a course or seminar to learn how you can better use these remarkable tools in your daily life.

Source: From Richard G. Ensman, "Technology and Time Management: How Do You Rate?" *Manage*, November 1, 2001. Reprinted with permission.

Class Exercise

Each student, in turn, tells the class how he or she wastes time. The instructor lists the ways on the chalkboard or overhead projector. Then the class discusses the list.

- Which time wasters are most common?

- Are they really just time wasters, or are they also stress reducers?

Source: The idea for this exercise was provided by Sylvia Ong, Scottsdale Community College, Scottsdale, Arizona.

Team-Building Exercise

What Kind of Team Member Are You?

Divide the class into teams of four or five students. Assign each team an imaginary project with a completion date (or have the teams come up with one on their own). Suggested projects are cleaning up one of the common areas used by students at the school, recruiting classmates to participate in a fund-raising activity, or developing publicity for an upcoming arts event. Then have the teams (1) make a "to do" list outlining how they plan to set priorities for the project and use their time; (2) note how they plan to control time wasters; and (3) describe how they plan to manage any stress associated with trying to complete the project properly and on schedule.

At the end of the exercise, have students identify themselves as Type A or Type B personalities and discuss how this contributes to the way they approach getting things done as team members.

15

The Net was forcing us to learn fast, change fast, even fail fast. The only thing wrong with making mistakes would be not learning from them.
—**Scott Cook, cofounder, Intuit**

Managing Conflict and Change

■ CHAPTER OUTLINE

Conflict
Positive and Negative Aspects of Conflict
Types of Conflict

Managing Interpersonal Conflict
Strategies
Initiating Conflict Resolution
Responding to a Conflict
Mediating Conflict Resolution

Change in the Workplace
Sources of Change
Resistance to Change
Implementing Change
Proposing Change

Organization Politics and Power
Sources of Power
Types of Power
Political Strategies
Building a Power Base
Establishing a Competitive Edge
Socializing

■ LEARNING OBJECTIVES

After you have studied this chapter, you should be able to:

15.1 List positive and negative aspects of conflict.

15.2 Define types of conflict.

15.3 Describe strategies for managing conflict.

15.4 Explain how supervisors can initiate conflict resolution, respond to a conflict, and mediate conflict resolution.

15.5 Identify sources of change, and explain why employees and supervisors resist it.

15.6 Discuss how supervisors can overcome resistance and implement change.

15.7 Describe the types of power supervisors can have.

15.8 Identify common strategies for organization politics.

■ CHANGING THE RIGHT THINGS

For nearly 40 years Motel 6 built its multimillion-dollar business and its reputation on offering a few consistent services to business travelers—clean but plain rooms, simple friendly service, and low, low prices. Its advertising slogan expressed its homey atmosphere: "We'll leave the light on for you" was as resistant to change over the years as the motel chain itself.

Recently, however, recovering from a downturn in the hotel industry and in its own fortunes in particular, the chain began making some changes on its front lines. Management spent $600 million to overhaul and redesign every one of the 85,000 rooms in its nearly 800 motels. Some were upgraded, although the addition of landscaping and central heating and air conditioning won't make them luxurious. The chain is also considering attracting a new type of business traveler, the extended-stay guest, who seeks low-priced rooms with separate areas for working and cooking. And, in a break from its long history of company ownership, the chain is selling franchises to open new motels, especially in smaller communities where it has not competed before.

What all these changes mean for the long-term future of Motel 6 is still unclear, but the first results are in and they are promising. The chain was one of the highest scorers in a 2000 survey of 10,000 leisure and business hotel guests, conducted by J. D. Power and Associates, the California-based market research firm. And in a reader survey by the *Los Angeles Times*, a recent guest had this to say about the chain: "The rooms are freshly painted, with new carpets and new bedspreads. It's a budget hotel, but the rooms are clean and nice." And from another guest: "I love that Motel 6."

The chain's front-line supervisors were the ones who implemented and oversaw many of the changes, which meant disruptions in the work of nearly all their staff while painters, decorators, and contractors went to work. None of these crews could be allowed to interfere with the smooth operations of the rest of the hotel, which meant that many short-term changes in procedures and schedules had to be made to accommodate the renovations. For Motel 6's supervisors, change was all in a day's work.

Source: Edwin McDowell, "Not Just Leaving the Light On," *New York Times*, October 28, 1998, pp. C1–C2; "Survey Picks Top Hotels in 5 Price Ranges," *Atlanta Journal-Constitution*, September 3, 2000, p. K4; "Destination: California & Nevada: Readers Poll," *Los Angeles Times*, August 13, 2000, p. L1.

In any organization, conflicts and changes are bound to occur. Whether these are constructive or destructive depends significantly on the supervisor's ability to manage them.

This chapter addresses conflict management by examining the nature of conflict and ways to respond to conflict constructively. The chapter also discusses the role of change in the workplace and how supervisors can implement it. Finally, the chapter discusses an aspect of organizational behavior that often affects the management of both conflict and change—organization politics—describing how supervisors can use politics ethically and effectively.

Conflict

conflict
The struggle that results from incompatible or opposing needs, feelings, thoughts, or demands within a person or between two or more people.

In the context of this book, **conflict** refers to the struggle that results from incompatible or opposing needs, feelings, thoughts, or demands within a person or between two or more people. If supervisor Janet Speers sees that an employee she likes is taking home office supplies, her feelings for the employee come into conflict with her belief that stealing is wrong. If her feelings and belief are both strong, she will have difficulty resolving the issue. Likewise, if two employees disagree over how to fill out time sheets for sick days, there is a conflict between the employees. In this case, the organization should have a clear procedure to make the conflict easy to resolve.

Positive and Negative Aspects of Conflict

Sometimes conflict is a positive force that can bring about necessary changes. Imagine that a business that develops computerized information systems has hired a new systems analyst, Jordan Walsh, the first African American in the company. Jordan gets all the boring and routine jobs—filing, running errands, proofreading the documentation. If he acts cheerful, the other employees will assume there is no conflict (although he may feel one internally). Of course, this situation is not good for Jordan; he feels insulted, is bored every day, and misses out on the experience he needs to develop his career. This arrangement is also bad for the employer, who is paying for a systems analyst but not benefiting from his talents. Furthermore, Jordan may quit, and the company will have to bear the expense of repeating the hiring process. However, if Jordan complains to his supervisor about his limited role, the conflict will surface, and the resolution may leave everyone, including Jordan, better off. Thus, when conflict serves as a signal that a problem exists, it can stimulate a creative response.

Ongoing conflict also has negative consequences. People who are engaged in disputes are under stress, which takes a physical toll. In addition, people who are busy arguing and trying to persuade others to take their sides are not involved in more productive activities. Finally, depending on the source of the conflict, the people involved may be angry at management or the organization, so they may vent their anger in ways that are destructive to the organization, such as taking extra time off or sabotaging equipment.

The consequences of conflict may depend partly on the way that it is resolved. If people treat a conflict as an opportunity for constructive problem solving and change, the outcomes may well be positive. If people routinely see conflict as a need for someone to win at someone else's expense, or for a manager to impose control, the conflict is more likely to have negative consequences.

frustration
Defeat in the effort to achieve desired goals.

Most notably, when conflict is viewed as a win-lose proposition, the loser will experience **frustration;** that is, defeat in the effort to achieve desired goals. An employee who has her request for a flextime arrangement turned down experiences frustration. So does an employee who can't convince a prospective customer to return his phone calls. Most of us can handle a little frustration philosophically,

■ FIGURE 15.1

Types of Conflict

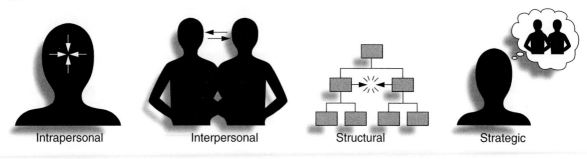

with words such as "Oh, well, I can't always have my own way" or "No one can have it all." However, repeated frustration tends to generate anger. A frustrated employee may engage in destructive behavior such as sabotage, aggression, insubordination, and absenteeism. (Chapter 13 covers the supervision of employees who engage in such behaviors.) To head off problems arising from frustration, this chapter will emphasize those forms of conflict resolution aimed at finding a solution satisfactory to all parties.

Types of Conflict

Before a supervisor can respond effectively to a conflict, he or she needs to understand the real nature of that conflict. Who is involved? What is the source of the conflict? A supervisor is likely to respond differently to a conflict that results from a clash of opinions than to one stemming from frustration over limited resources.

As defined, conflict may arise within an individual (intrapersonal) or between individuals or groups. The basic types of conflict involving more than one person are called interpersonal, structural, and strategic (see Figure 15.1).

Intrapersonal Conflict   An intrapersonal conflict arises when a person has trouble selecting from among goals. Choosing one of two possible goals is easy if one is good and the other bad. For example, would you rather earn $1 a year as a drug dealer or $1 million a year as the microbiologist who discovered a cure for cancer? Of course, we rarely are faced with such unrealistically easy choices. Most choices fall into three categories:

1. A choice between two good possibilities (e.g., having a child or taking an exciting job that requires travel year-round).
2. A choice between two mixed possibilities (e.g., accepting a promotion that involves moving away from your family or keeping your current, but monotonous, job to be near your family).
3. A choice between two bad possibilities (e.g., reorganizing your department in a way that requires either laying off two employees or eliminating your own position).

Because these choices are not obvious, they result in conflict.

Supervisors should consider whether they or their organization are contributing unnecessarily to intrapersonal conflicts. For example, do they reward unethical behavior or pressure employees to behave unethically? If so, they are setting up conflicts between employees' values and their desire to be rewarded.

Similarly, Felice Schwartz, founder and retired president of Catalyst, a research and advisory firm, maintains that measuring employees' worth in terms of how many hours they work creates conflicts between commitment to family and commitment to work. In the years immediately following World War II, many people accepted the expectation that women would resolve this conflict by always putting family first, and men by always putting work first. Today, however, fewer employees will settle for these extreme choices. Schwartz recommends that managers be more realistic and measure employee contributions in terms of productivity, not hours spent at the workplace.[1]

In many cases, a supervisor lacks the expertise to resolve an intrapersonal conflict. When supervisors notice that an employee is struggling with an intrapersonal conflict, they should consider who might be able to help. People with skills in handling various types of intrapersonal conflicts include psychologists, religious advisers, and career counselors.

Interpersonal Conflict Conflict between individuals is called interpersonal conflict. Supervisors may be involved in interpersonal conflicts with their manager, an employee, a peer, or even a customer. In addition, they may have to manage conflicts between two or more of their employees. Interpersonal conflicts may arise from differing opinions, misunderstandings of a situation, or differences in values or beliefs. Sometimes two people just rub each other the wrong way. (Chapter 8 provides an in-depth discussion of leading employees, and a section later in this chapter describes some approaches to managing interpersonal conflict.)

One concept gaining in popularity is "emotional intelligence," or the ability to manage emotions and interpersonal relationships. Sometimes divided into the four components of self-awareness, self-management, social awareness, and social skills, emotional intelligence is being introduced in training programs at organizations as diverse as giant American Express, the U.S. Air Force, and Cooperative Printing, a 45-employee Minneapolis firm.[2] The hope is that by giving supervisors and managers a way to deal with their and others' emotions, such training will reduce conflict and improve performance.

Structural Conflict Conflict that results from the way the organization is structured is called structural conflict. Conflict often arises between line and staff personnel, and production and marketing departments are often at odds. In the latter example, marketing wants to give customers whatever they ask for, and production wants to make what it can easily and well.

Structural conflict often arises when various groups in the organization share resources, such as the services of a word-processing or maintenance department. Each group wants its jobs handled first, but the support department obviously cannot help everyone first.

When structural conflict arises between two groups of employees reporting to a supervisor or between a supervisor's group and another group, the supervisor may be able to help minimize or resolve it by providing opportunities for the two groups to communicate and get to know each others' viewpoints, having them collaborate on achieving a mutually desirable goal, and giving each group training or experience in what the other group does.

To help his office employees appreciate the efforts of his blue-collar workers, Oil Changers CEO Larry Read requires each white-collar employee (including each manager) to work on the shop floor one day each month, greeting customers and performing nontechnical tasks as a part of a shop team. According to Read, this improves communication between the two groups of employees and helps the office staff see the practical impact of their decisions.[3]

If some employees involved in a structural conflict report to another supervisor, managing the conflict requires the cooperation of the two supervisors. Engaging that cooperation may require appropriate use of political tactics, discussed in the last section of this chapter.

Because supervisors do not establish an organization's structure, they have limited impact on the sources of structural conflict. However, they do need to be able to recognize it. Knowing that a conflict is structural frees a supervisor from taking the issue personally and alerts him or her to situations that require extra diplomacy. A supervisor also may be able to understand the other party's point of view and communicate it to his or her employees.

Strategic Conflict Most of the conflicts described so far arise unintentionally when people and groups try to work together. However, sometimes management or an individual intentionally will bring about a conflict to achieve an objective. This is referred to as a strategic conflict. For instance, a sales department might hold a contest for the highest sales volume and the most impressive example of delighting a customer. Or a manager might tell two employees that they are both in the running for a retiring supervisor's job. In both examples, the intent is to use competition to motivate employees to do exceptional work.

Managing Interpersonal Conflict

Restaurant manager Phyllis Jensen schedules the hours each server will work during the upcoming week. She has noticed that one of the servers, Rich Yakima, scowls when he gets his assignments and does so for hours afterward. Phyllis asked Rich about it, and he replied, "You know just what the problem is. You know I've been wanting an evening off every weekend so I can go out with my girlfriend, but every week you have me working Friday and Saturday nights. And I've noticed that Rita and Pat always get the hours they want." Responding to problems such as this is known as **conflict management.**

conflict management
Responding to problems stemming from conflict.

Strategies How can Phyllis manage the conflict involving Rich? She can begin by recognizing the various strategies available for conflict management: compromise, avoidance, smoothing, forcing a solution, and confrontation or problem solving (see Figure 15.2). Based on her understanding of these strategies, Phyllis can choose the most appropriate one for the circumstances. To see which conflict management strategy you tend to select most frequently, take the Self-Quiz on page 401.

compromise
Settling on a solution that gives each person part of what he or she wants; no one gets everything, and no one loses completely.

Compromise One conflict management strategy is to reach a **compromise,** which means that the parties to the conflict settle on a solution that gives both of them part of what they wanted. No party gets exactly what it wanted, but neither loses entirely either. Both parties presumably experience a degree of frustration—but at a level they are willing to live with.

FIGURE 15.2

Strategies for Conflict Management

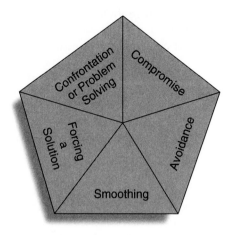

People who choose to compromise are assuming they cannot reach a solution completely acceptable to everyone, but they would rather not force someone to accept a completely disagreeable choice. In that sense, compromise does not really solve the underlying problem; it works best when the problem is relatively minor and time is limited.

Avoidance and Smoothing Conflict is unpleasant, so people sometimes try to manage conflict by avoiding it. For example, if sales supervisor Jeanette Delacroix finds the people in the human resources department stuffy and inflexible, she can avoid dealing with that department. When contact with human resources is absolutely necessary, Jeanette can delegate the responsibility to a member of the sales force. A related strategy is **smoothing,** or pretending that no conflict exists.

These strategies make sense if you assume that all conflict is bad. If you successfully avoid or smooth over all conflicts, life looks serene on the surface. However, people do disagree, and sometimes people with opposing viewpoints have important ideas to share. Avoiding those conflicts does not make them go away, nor does it make opposing points of view any less valid or significant. Therefore, it is important to be selective in avoiding or smoothing over conflicts. These strategies are most useful for conflicts that are not serious and for which a solution would be more difficult than the problem justifies.

This point is especially important with regard to today's diverse workforce. A person's point of view often seems puzzling, irritating, or downright incorrect to someone of another race, age, or sex. It takes extra work to understand people who are different from us. However, a supervisor must give equal attention to the views of all employees, not only those the supervisor understands best. Pretending that everyone is looking at a situation the same way does not make it so. It can even foster a belief among some employees that the supervisor is discriminating against them.

At the same time, people in many non-Western cultures believe it is best to avoid conflicts, placing a higher value on harmony than on "telling it like it is."[4] People with these values are less likely than employees from Western cultures to complain to their supervisor or to deliver bad news. Thus, a supervisor may not

smoothing
Managing a conflict by pretending it does not exist.

realize there is a problem, such as a dispute between employees or a possibility that a task will be completed late. A supervisor must tactfully ensure that employees know that the supervisor wants to be aware of any problems in order to help resolve them.

Forcing a Solution   Because ignoring or avoiding a problem does not make it go away, a supervisor may want to try a more direct approach to ending a conflict. One possibility is to force a solution. This means that a person or group with power decides what the outcome will be. For example, if machinist Pete Desai complains to his supervisor that he never gets overtime assignments, the supervisor can respond, "I make the assignments, and your job is to do what you're told. This weekend it's going to be Sue and Chuck, so make the best of it." Or if two supervisors present conflicting proposals for allocating space among their departments, a committee of higher-level managers could select one proposal, allowing no room for discussion.

In an organization with self-managed work teams, another twist on forcing a solution is more likely. The team may decide that instead of reaching a consensus on some issue, the team will simply vote on what to do. The majority makes the decision.

Forcing a solution is a relatively fast way to manage a conflict, and it may be the best approach in an emergency. Reaching consensus, for example, tends to be difficult and time-consuming, whereas a team can vote on an issue quickly. However, forcing a solution can cause frustration. In organizations seeking teamwork and employee empowerment, forcing a solution works against those objectives by shutting off input from employees with a minority viewpoint.[5] The bad feelings that accompany frustration and exclusion from decision making may lead to future conflict.

conflict resolution
Managing a conflict by confronting the problem and solving it.

Confrontation or Problem Solving   The most direct—and sometimes the most difficult—way to manage conflict is to confront the problem and solve it. This is the conflict management strategy called **conflict resolution.** Confronting the problem requires listening to both sides and attempting to understand rather than to place blame. Next, the parties should identify the areas on which they agree and the ways they can both benefit from possible solutions. Both parties should examine their own feelings and take their time at reaching a solution. (Chapter 9 provides further guidelines for problem solving.)

Confronting and solving a problem makes a different assumption about the conflict than other strategies for conflict management, which tend to assume that the parties have a *win-lose conflict.* In other words, the outcome of the conflict will be that one person wins (i.e., achieves the desired outcome), and the other person must lose. In contrast, conflict resolution assumes that many conflicts are *win-win conflicts,* in which the resolution can leave both parties better off. Frustration is avoided and both sides feel like winners.

Initiating Conflict Resolution

When a supervisor has a conflict with another person, he or she needs to resolve that conflict constructively. Otherwise, the conflict is unlikely to go away on its own. When initiating conflict resolution, a supervisor should act as soon as he or she is aware of the problem. As the problem continues, a supervisor is likely to get increasingly emotional about it, which only makes resolution more difficult.

According to Don Weiss, president of Self-Management Communications, Inc., emotions can't be avoided in conflict situations but they can be controlled. "The whole person comes to work, and emotions play a legitimate role in a person's life. Therefore, feelings—the other person's and your own—must be respected, but when emotions and feelings interfere with the ordinary conduct of business or with a person's ability to function well, you're obligated to address them in a rational manner. It's to the other person's benefit as well as to the benefit of the organization."[6]

Prepare for conflict resolution by understanding what the conflict is. Focus on behavior (which people can change), not on personalities (which they cannot change). What is the action that is causing the problem, and how does that action affect you and others? For example, you might tell a supervisor in another department, "I haven't been getting the weekly sales figures until late Friday afternoon. That means I have to give up precious family time to review them over the weekend, or else I embarrass myself by being unprepared at the Monday morning staff meetings."

When used politely, this type of approach even works with one's manager. You might say, "I haven't heard from you concerning the suggestions I made last week and three weeks ago. That worries me, because I think maybe I'm giving you too many ideas or not the right kind."

After you have stated the problem, listen to how the other person responds. If the other person does not acknowledge there is a problem, restate your concern until the other person understands or until it is clear that you cannot make any progress on your own. Often a conflict exists simply because the other person has not understood your point of view or your situation. When you have begun communicating about the problem, the two of you can work together at finding a solution. Restate your solution to be sure that both of you agree on what you are going to do (see Figure 15.3).

FIGURE 15.3

Initiating Conflict Resolution

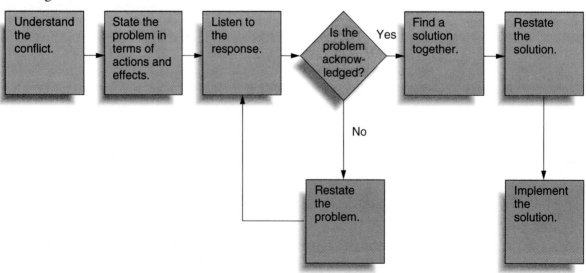

Responding to a Conflict

Sometimes a supervisor is party to a conflict that is bothering someone else. When the other person makes the supervisor aware of the conflict, it is up to the supervisor to respond in a way that makes a solution possible. If an employee says, "You always give me the dirty assignments," it is not helpful to get angry or defensive.

Understand the Problem   The constructive way to respond to a conflict is first to listen to the other person and try to understand what the problem is really about. If the other person is emotional, let that person vent those feelings, then get down to discussing the problem. Try to interpret the problem in the terms you would use to express the problem yourself. Avoid statements of blame, and find out what specific actions the other person is referring to. For example, when an employee says, "You always give me the dirty assignments," you can ask the employee to give specific examples and then describe how he or she feels about the behavior.

Understanding the problem can be complicated if one of the people involved has a "hidden agenda"—a central concern that is left unstated. Typically, a person with a hidden agenda is angry or upset about something but directs those feelings toward some other issue. For example, a colleague in another department explodes, "What's wrong with you? The numbers in your report are off by a mile!" Your colleague is not really angry because you made a mistake. He is nervous because he has to make a presentation to the board of directors, and he wonders if the incorrect numbers are your way to mislead him, so that he looks uninformed and you get the promotion he wants. Or maybe your colleague simply has had a frustrating day, and your mistake is the last straw.

If another person's feelings seem to be out of proportion to the problem he or she is describing, look for a hidden agenda. Finding one can save you from trying to resolve the wrong conflict. In addition, when you are upset about something yourself, it is usually more constructive to describe the problem directly than to leave others guessing at your hidden agenda.

Work on a Solution   When you understand the problem, build an environment of working together on a solution. To do this, agree with some aspect of what the other person has said. In the example, you might say, "You've really disliked your last three assignments." Then you and the other person should be ready to begin identifying possible solutions. The final step is to agree on what the solution will be and how you will carry it out. Figure 15.4 summarizes this approach.

FIGURE 15.4

Responding to a Conflict

| Listen to the complaint. | Interpret the problem in terms of actions and effects. | Agree with something the other person said. | Find a solution together. | Agree on how to carry out the solution. | Implement the solution. |

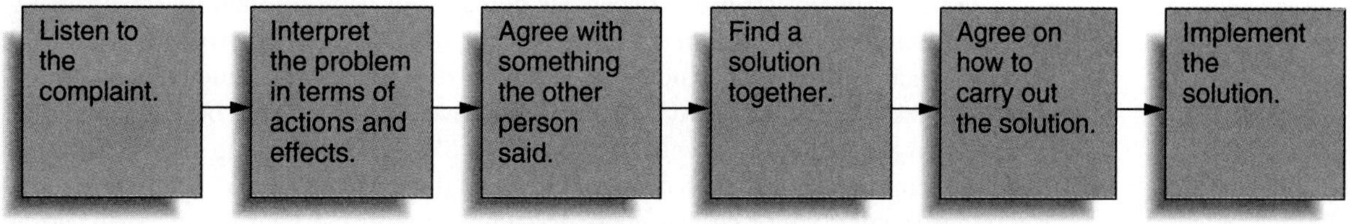

Mediating Conflict Resolution

Sometimes a supervisor is not personally involved in a conflict, but the parties ask the supervisor to help resolve it. If the parties to the conflict are peers of the supervisor, getting involved can be risky, and the supervisor might be wiser to tactfully refer the peers to a higher-level manager. If the parties to the conflict are the supervisor's employees, then mediating the conflict is part of the supervisor's job and an important way to keep the department functioning as it should.

To mediate a conflict, a supervisor should follow these steps:

1. Begin by establishing a constructive environment. If the employees are calling each other names, have them focus on the issue instead of such destructive behavior.
2. Ask each person to explain what the problem is. Get each person to be specific and to respond to the others' charges.
3. When all parties understand what the problem is, have them state individually what they want to accomplish or what will satisfy them.
4. Restate in your own words what each person's position is. Ask the employees if you have understood them correctly.
5. Have all participants suggest as many solutions as they can. Begin to focus on the future.
6. Encourage the employees to select a solution that benefits all of them. They may want to combine or modify some of the ideas suggested.
7. Summarize what has been discussed and agreed on. Make sure all participants know what they are supposed to do in carrying out the solution, and ask for their cooperation.

Throughout this process, continue your efforts to maintain a constructive environment. Keep the emphasis off personalities and blame; keep it on your mutual desire to find a solution.

Other useful strategies include meeting with the parties separately first, to give each a chance to air his or her views. Then meet with everyone and explain your ground rule: "You're on safe ground so don't hold back, but everything you say must be in the best interest of the other person." Stop the discussion if anyone can't adhere to the rules, and finish by explaining that you expect them to continue having more open conversations with one another as a result of the meeting.[7]

Change in the Workplace

Conflict is both a cause and a consequence of change. When people experience a conflict, they manage it by making changes to the situation or to their attitudes. When change occurs—in the workplace and elsewhere—conflict accompanies the need to let go of familiar behaviors and attitudes.

When the conflicts are between the demands of work and family, the growing desire of employees to balance the two rather than choose one over the other has forced organizations to consider the adoption of policies and values that are more family-friendly.[8] So far, many organizations have concluded that because the labor pool is large, they simply will hire those people who are willing to work the 50 hours or more a week often required for a high-powered career. However, some employees will leave or choose a less prestigious career path within an organization if their work responsibilities heavily conflict with family demands. Perhaps organizations should consider whether they would benefit if people who insist on making time for their families held a greater number of key decision-making positions.

The greater desire to balance work and home life is only one of many sources of change in the workplace today. A survey of U.S. companies found that 84 percent were undergoing at least one major business change, such as adopting innovative information technology or reengineering business processes.[9] External sources of change include higher expectations for quality and stiffer foreign competition.

Because of these and many other changes, the success of organizations (i.e., profitability, in the case of businesses) depends on how well they adapt to changes in their environment. For example, an organization must respond when a new competitor enters the marketplace or a new law limits how it may operate.

Change is a fact of organizational life, so supervisors do not decide *whether* organizations should change but *how* to make the changes work. They can do this better if they recognize the various factors that can affect the success of a change:

- *The change agent*—The person trying to bring about the change should have skills in implementing change and solving the related problems, as well as expertise in the area affected.
- *Determination of what to change*—Any changes should make the organization more effective in delivering high quality.
- *The kind of change to be made*—The change can involve process and equipment; policies, procedures, and job structure; and people-related variables such as attitudes and communication skills.
- *Individuals affected*—Some people are more open to change than others. Also, people will see some changes as beneficial to them but other changes as harmful.
- *Evaluation of change*—An evaluation can indicate whether it is necessary to modify the change process or make further changes.

Supervisors are the organization's primary link to operative employees, so they must understand how employees are likely to respond to changes, be able to communicate information about the changes to employees, and help employees respond positively. See "Tips from the Firing Line" for some ways to stay resilient in the face of change.

Sources of Change

Changes can originate with management, employees, or external forces (see Figure 15.5). Organizations change when management sees an opportunity or a need to do things better. A need may arise because performance is inadequate. Examples of an opportunity are a new computer system that is more efficient or a new procedure that can lead to higher-quality service.

Sometimes even if the improvement is incremental, management will see a need for change. This was the case when Pitney Bowes Credit Corporation in Shelton, Connecticut, transformed itself from a big but bland division of Pitney Bowes Inc. to what Matthew Kissner, president and CEO, calls his "idea factory." The colorful new office space is full of unusual details that mark it as "a fun space that would embody our culture," he says. "This place wasn't broken. But we knew we could make it better."[10]

Even an organization's employees may bring about changes. Forming a union could lead to changes in the way management reaches agreements with employees and the conditions under which employees work. Many organizations actively respond to employee suggestions on how to improve quality and cut costs.

TIPS FROM THE FIRING LINE

Resilience Rules

Andrew Shatté and his colleagues at Adaptiv Learning Systems, a consulting firm based in King of Prussia, Pennsylvania, teach people at such companies as Ford and Nortel Networks how to stay resilient in the face of adversity. It's an important skill for leaders to have at any time, but in a period of challenge and change, it is especially crucial. Here are some of the principles that they teach.

1. *Explain yourself.* Dealing effectively with a problem or a setback starts with how you explain it—to yourself and to those around you. "Too many people learn negative or helpless ways of thinking," Shatté says. "But they can unlearn them and adopt more resilient ways of thinking. Once you're aware of your explanatory style, listen for a pattern. Ask yourself why this happened, and listen to what you say." Some people tend to explain setbacks as temporary, while others view them as permanent. Do you tend to cast blame on others, or do you explain everything as your fault? Each style needs to be offset with logic and perspective.
2. *Don't overreact.* "In most rough situations, people tend to describe what went wrong in terms of 'always' and 'everything,' Shatté says. For instance, when a boss criticizes part of a presentation or report, many people say to themselves, "My reports are always bad," or "I bet I'm one step away from getting canned." Shatté and his colleagues teach people to counter those standard overreactions with a more accurate evaluation. Most of the time, things aren't as bleak as we make them out to be.
3. *Act fast, but don't rush to judgment.* It's important to be honest when you run into a setback—but it's also important to be sure you understand what's really going on. Adaptiv worked with a European company that was selling whiskey in a country that preferred vodka. The country also had an active black market. Whiskey sales had hit the skids. The company's executives blamed the sales team. Everyone knew there was a problem, and everyone rushed to judgment about the cause. The real problem, it turns out, involved the sales force's lack of training. Armed with the proper analysis, both sides worked the problem.
4. *Keep it in perspective.* Ask yourself: What's the worst thing that can happen? What's the best outcome that we can hope for? And then keep pressing yourself about the accuracy of those scenarios. "People most need to work on being accurate and candid about what has happened," Shatté says. "Then they can take strides to remedy the situation."

Source: *Fast Company* by Rekha Balu. Copyright © 2001, 2001 by Business Innovator Group Resources/Inc. Reproduced with permission of Business Innovator Group Resources/Inc. via Copyright Clearance Center.

FIGURE 15.5

Sources of Change

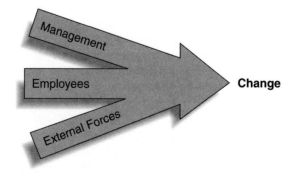

As the U.S. workforce becomes increasingly diverse in terms of age, race, and sex, the forces for change from employees are likely to strengthen. People of diverse backgrounds can offer a greater variety of creative solutions. In addition, the challenge of working harmoniously with different kinds of people can itself lead to a push for changes, such as provisions for different religious holidays or guidelines on how to treat people fairly.

Other changes are imposed from outside. New laws and regulations often lead to changes within organizations. A local government organization might have to make changes in response to voters' refusal to approve a tax increase. A series of lawsuits might cause an organization to reexamine how it makes a product. The size and composition of the workforce may affect whom the organization hires and how much training it provides.

Economic trends also are important. For example, businesses usually are able to seek growth more aggressively when the economy is expanding. But during downturns change is also common and can be especially difficult. Many large firms have recently experienced cutbacks. At the end of 2000, for instance, Gillette Co. announced the elimination of 8 percent of its workforce, or 2,700 jobs, and the closing of eight factories, a follow-up to a management shakeup on the heels of more than two years of disappointing financial performance.[11]

In 1998 the London Futures Exchange announced a sweeping reorganization to cut its costs in half within the next year, letting several hundred employees go in response to growing competition.[12] The same year, the fashion industry felt the pinch of changing tastes, a slowdown of consumer confidence, and a long series of mergers and consolidations in the retailing industry. While some big design houses faced negative changes as a result of these economic factors, many smaller, independent design companies were thriving, rethinking their business practices to survive in leaner times.[13]

Resistance to Change

Any change, such as the adoption of a new procedure in the workplace or the completion of a major training program, requires work. People are fearful because change carries the risk of making them worse off, as happened to the staffers laid off by the politician in Figure 15.6. At a financial services company, the announcement of a reengineering effort quickly was followed by widespread rumors predicting massive layoffs, bankruptcy, and a dramatic increase in employee workloads.[14]

People's resistance to change is greatest when they are not sure what to expect or why the change is necessary. Change stirs up fear of the unknown, another normal human response. Furthermore, when people do not understand the reasons for change, the effort to change does not seem worthwhile. (See "Meeting the Challenge" to learn how one company dealt with change—and managers who resisted it.)

Sometimes even when change is positive, it meets resistance. At Xerox Corporation, employees complained that it took too long for them to receive reimbursements for expenses incurred in the course of business. Xerox undertook a benchmarking study of 26 other firms to try to find a solution to its problem and came up with a new system that entailed the use of more than one corporate credit card, new forms to fill out, and no cash advances. The advantage was, employees no longer had to worry about being reimbursed. But, said Warren D. Jeffries, manager of customer services benchmarking for Xerox, "everyone resisted the changes, even those that were unhappy with the old way."[15]

■ FIGURE 15.6

A Change That Leaves Employees Worse Off

Source: Courtesy of Tribune Media Services.

Implementing Change

To implement change, a supervisor must overcome resistance to it, ensure that the change is made, and create the conditions in which the change is likely to last. Noted behavioral scientist Kurt Lewin has set forth a model for this process (see Figure 15.7).[16] Lewin's model indicates that a successful change has three phases:

1. *Unfreezing*—People recognize a need for change.
2. *Changing*—People begin trying to behave differently.
3. *Refreezing*—The new behavior becomes part of employees' regular processes.

This model makes two assumptions about the change process. First, before a change can occur, employees must see the status quo as less than ideal. Second, when employees begin changing, the organization must provide a way for the new behavior to become established practice.

Unfreezing   In the unfreezing phase, the supervisor or other person responsible for implementing the change must spell out clearly why a change is needed. AlliedSignal's CEO, Lawrence Bossidy, describes this step colorfully, as the "burning platform theory of change":

> When the roustabouts are standing on the offshore oil rig and the foreman yells, "Jump into the water," not only won't they jump but they also won't feel too kindly toward the foreman. There may be sharks in the water. They'll jump only when they themselves see the flames shooting up from the platform. . . . The leader's job is to help everyone see that the platform is burning, whether the flames are apparent or not.[17]

In essence, then, unfreezing means overcoming resistance to change.

Many changes require not only performing new tasks but also adopting new attitudes, such as a willingness to assume decision-making responsibility and a strong commitment to customer value. Employees may have difficulty changing their attitudes, especially if they are unsure about management's sincerity.[18] Also, management needs to address employee resistance arising from fears about the

Engelhard Engineers Change through Teams

Faced with the hard business realities of the 1980s, Engelhard, a large, New Jersey–based chemical and engineered materials company, decided that reengineering was the answer. To reduce costs and increase production speed, the organization forced its own solution by laying off 500 salaried employees from corporate staff to operations management. And Engelhard found itself no better off. L. Donald LaTorre, president and chief operating officer, now admits, "We learned that we really didn't change the work, we just eliminated people. This made us realize that we had to change the work as well."

LaTorre still wanted to cut costs and boost production. The petroleum catalyst division of the company found a way to do it, but this required a multimillion-dollar plant expansion. LaTorre OK'd the proposal, but said that the expansion had to pay for itself. The plant needed new customers. Thus, the cross-functional sales teams charged with change were born.

Teams included members from sales, distribution, and manufacturing, so that the teams would benefit from different viewpoints. For instance, someone in distribution might learn from someone in sales how customers wanted products packaged and delivered. The teams were so effective that the increased capacity in the new plant was sold out within six months.

The teams did not always operate smoothly, however. Conflict was a natural part of the process, and not everyone in the division bought in to the new ideas and changes brought about by team decisions. The greatest resistance actually came from middle managers, who felt threatened by changes. "We've had to move some of our resisters out," notes LaTorre, "but we got such good early results that there's been a lot of peer pressure to go along with the change."

Ultimately, the petroleum catalyst division of Engelhard increased its global market share by 35 percent. That's a success story, but it is important to recognize that change—even successful change—is difficult for everyone involved. At Engelhard, those who could not accept change were forced to look for other jobs, but this also points to the important role of all employees, both managers and hourly workers: For an organization to change, people must be willing to change it.

Source: Michael Hammer and Steven A. Stanton, "Beating the Risks of Reengineering," from *The Reengineering Revolution*, excerpted in *Fortune*, May 15, 1995, pp. 108–109, 114. Courtesy of HarperCollins Publishers.

FIGURE 15.7

Lewin's Model of Change

---

change. The organization relies heavily on supervisors—as management's link to operative employees—to carry out this responsibility, for which they need good communication skills (see Chapter 10). The following guidelines may help as well[19]:

• Tell employees about a change as soon as you learn about it.
• Make sure employees understand what the change is, then explain how the change is likely to affect them.
• Be as positive about the change as possible, citing any benefits to the employees. These might include more interesting jobs or bigger bonuses. At the same time, don't get caught up in parroting the company's point of view.

- Describe how the organization will help employees cope. Will there be training in how to follow new procedures? Will the organization provide counseling or other assistance to employees being laid off? What will happen to employee benefits?
- Do not try to hide bad news, including the possibility that some employees will lose their jobs. But be professional and don't needlessly communicate your own worries.
- Give employees plenty of opportunity to express concerns and ask questions. It is better for a supervisor to hear concerns and questions than to let them circulate in the rumor mill, where information may be misleading or incorrect.
- Answer as many questions as you can and get the answers to the rest as soon as possible. If you can't provide complete information, say, "Let me tell you what I know.
- Keep alert to your company's status in the marketplace and let your employees know about it. Are new orders coming in? Are new products or services ready to roll out? Any team will be more productive if members feel they understand what is happening in the company as a whole, and if their supervisor is a dependable source of accurate and positive information.
- When employees are upset, listen to expressions of sadness and anger without argument. It is unfair and unwise to tell employees they are overreacting. People experience change subjectively, and one subjective experience is as valid as another.

In listening to and answering questions, bear in mind that some employees will not think of questions until some time has passed. Therefore, provide opportunities for employees to ask questions on an ongoing basis, not just at the time a change is announced.

Changing   When employees appreciate the need for a change and have received any necessary training, they are ready to begin altering their behavior. The key to implementing change is to build on successes. A supervisor should determine those aspects of the change over which he or she has control, then seek to carry them out successfully. A supervisor should point out each success the group achieves along the way. As employees see the change achieving desirable results, they are more likely to go along with it and even embrace it.

Price Pritchett, who heads a Dallas-based firm specializing in organizational change, offers supervisors the following advice, using the example of a change to reduce bureaucracy:

> Set a dramatic example. One of the surest ways to get your team members' attention is to strike a high-profile and irreversible blow against bureaucracy yourself. You might, for example, take the shelf-full of regulation manuals and policies that govern your department's procedures and dump them all in the trash. The point here is to make a statement that will get your staff to sit up and take notice—and realize just how serious you are about making significant changes.[20]

On a practical level, building on successes generally entails starting with basic changes in behavior, rather than beginning with an effort to change values. Values, by their nature, are more resistant to change. To induce changes in behavior, the change effort should include tangible or intangible rewards for the desired behavior. As employees experience positive outcomes, their attitudes become more positive, and their values may shift as well.

This was the process AT&T followed when it wanted its research staff to be more oriented toward customer needs. The company charged the first-level manager of each research group with fulfilling the company's technology needs in a particular business area instead of focusing strictly on excellence in terms of a particular scientific discipline. Success would be measured in terms of how well the group satisfied customers by helping to meet their needs. The scientists at first viewed the new approach as a lowering of standards, but gradually they saw that useful advances in technology were at least as significant as achievements that won the admiration of their scientific colleagues.[21]

A supervisor who has control over scheduling a change should establish reasonable deadlines. As employees meet each deadline, the supervisor can point out their on-time achievements. For example, imagine that an accounting department is installing a new computer system. Instead of focusing simply on whether everyone is using the system properly, a supervisor can establish dates for setting up various pieces of equipment and learning to operate different parts of the system. Then the supervisor can note that the terminals arrived on time, that everyone learned how to log on and enter their password in a single training session, and so on.

A supervisor also might have control over which people are directly involved in the change or the order in which people get involved. The supervisor of the accounting department might recognize that some employees are already enthusiastic about the new system or are flexible and open to change. These people should learn the system first; then they can spread their enthusiasm around and help other employees when it is their turn to learn.

Similarly, if a group of employees work well together and enjoy each other's company, a sensible approach is to keep these employees together. For example, the change of adding another shift might proceed more smoothly if informal groups are not split into different shifts. In contrast, when a change involves bringing together two groups of employees from different organizations, locations, or shifts, a supervisor might build cooperation by teaming up employees from each group.

Refreezing   The change process is complete only when employees make the new behavior part of their routine. However, because new procedures are less comfortable than the old and familiar ones, employees may revert to their old practices when the initial pressure for change eases. In organizations that do not manage change effectively, managers may assume a change effort has succeeded simply because employees modified their behavior according to instructions. But if employees merely fulfill the basic requirements of a change without adjusting their attitudes, and if the organization has not arranged to reinforce and reward the change, backsliding is likely.

Backsliding is a natural response among employees, but it can become a problem unless a supervisor acts to get everyone back on track. A supervisor should remind employees about what they have achieved so far and what is expected of them in the future (see the principles of motivation described in Chapter 11). An important part of refreezing is for employees to be rewarded for behavior that shows they have made the desired change.

Proposing Change

In many situations, a supervisor wants to make a change but needs to ask higher-level management for authority to implement it. A supervisor also is wise to ask his or her manager about changes that are controversial, difficult to implement, or of major importance. These situations require a supervisor to make a proposal to higher-level management.

To propose a change effectively, the supervisor should begin by analyzing it. How will it help the organization better achieve its goals? Will it improve quality or productivity? What steps are required to carry it out? How much will it cost? Who will carry it out? What training will be required? Only when the answers to these questions confirm that the change is beneficial and feasible is the supervisor in a valid position to continue with the proposal.

Recall that the change process begins with convincing others of the need for a change (unfreezing, in Lewin's model). Some organizations actively cultivate suggestions for improvement, making it relatively easy for a supervisor to sell a change. In other organizations, management may view change more cautiously. Thus, it is often important for a supervisor to begin by helping management see the situation giving rise to the need for a change. A supervisor may have to do this before he or she even mentions changing something.

Once a supervisor's groundwork has prepared management for the proposal, a supervisor should have one ready to submit. Except for simple changes, a supervisor should make proposals in writing. The beginning of a proposal should contain a brief summary of what the change is and why it is desirable. Then the supervisor can provide details about the procedure for change and the costs and benefits involved. (For more suggestions about upward communication and reports, see Chapter 10; for guidelines on maintaining good relations with your manager, see Chapter 8.)

Organization Politics and Power

organizational politics
Intentional acts of influence to enhance or protect the self-interest of individuals or groups.

power
The ability to influence people to behave in a certain way.

Implementing change and resolving conflicts are easier for a person who has a relatively strong position in the organization. Thus, supervisors can most effectively manage conflict and change if they are able to improve their positions with an organization. Together, the activities through which people do this are called **organizational politics.** Improving one's position is not in itself good or bad; therefore, politics also is not innately good or bad. Political skills *are* important, however. They help a supervisor obtain the cooperation and support of others in the organization. More about organizational politics is available in the Appendix which follows this chapter.

The usual way that people use politics to improve their positions is by gaining power. **Power** is the ability to influence people to behave in a certain way. For instance, one supervisor says, "I wish everyone would be at work on time," yet employees continue to come in late. Another supervisor gets employees so excited about their contribution to the company that they consistently arrive at work on time and perform above what is required of them. The second supervisor has more power than the first.

Sources of Power

Editorial supervisor Stan Bakker has a decade-long track record of turning manuscripts into best-sellers. When he tells one of the editors on his staff how to handle a particular author or manuscript, the editor invariably follows Stan's directions. Why? Partly because Stan is the boss, and partly because the editors respect his expertise. Thus, Stan's power comes both from his position in the company and from his personal characteristics.

position power
Power that comes from a person's formal role in an organization.

Power that comes from a person's formal role in an organization is known as **position power.** Every supervisor has some position power with the employees he or she supervises. Higher-level managers, in turn, have a greater degree of position power.

personal power
Power that arises from an individual's personal characteristics.

In contrast, **personal power** is power that arises from an individual's personal characteristics. Because a person does not need to be a manager in an organization to have personal power there, employees sometimes view a co-worker as an informal leader of their group. If a supervisor announces a reorganization, one employee may successfully urge everyone to rally around the new plan—or may undermine morale by making fun of the changes. The informal leader in a group could be someone that other employees see as having expertise or being fun to work with.

Supervisors cannot eliminate personal power in subordinates, but they should be aware of it so they can use it to their advantage. A supervisor can watch for problems that might arise when the supervisor and an informal leader have conflicting goals. Perhaps more important, a supervisor can seek ways to get an informal leader on his or her side; for example, a supervisor might announce a decision to the informal leader first or discuss plans with that person.

Types of Power

Because power comes from their personal characteristics as well as their position in the organization, supervisors can have a variety of types of power. A supervisor who has less position power than he or she would like might consider the following types of power to see whether some can be developed. These types are summarized in Table 15.1.

Legitimate power comes from the position a person holds. Thus, a supervisor has legitimate power to delegate tasks to employees. To exercise legitimate power effectively, a supervisor needs to be sure employees understand what they are directed to do and are able to do it.

Referent power comes from the emotions a person inspires. Some supervisors seem to light up the room when they enter; they have a winning personality that includes enthusiasm, energy, and genuine enjoyment of the job. People like working for such a supervisor and often perform beyond the call of duty because they want the supervisor to like them. A person with referent power is often called "charismatic."

■ TABLE 15.1
Types of Power

Power Type	Arises From
Legitimate	The position a person holds
Referent	The emotions a person inspires
Expert	A person's knowledge or skills
Coercive	Fear related to the use of force
Reward	Giving people something they want
Connection	A person's relationship to someone powerful
Information	Possession of valuable information

Expert power arises from a person's knowledge or skills. Employees respect a supervisor who knows the employees' jobs better than they do. Their respect leads them to follow the supervisor's instructions. For example, the head of a company's research and development team might be a scientist who is well regarded in the field. Researchers could be expected to ask for and rely on this supervisor's advice.

Coercive power arises from fear related to the use of force. A supervisor who says, "Be on time tomorrow, or you're fired!" is using coercive power. This type of power may get results in the short run, but in the long run employees come to resent and may try to get around this supervisor. A supervisor who often relies on coercive power should consider whether he or she is doing so at the expense of developing other, more appropriate types of power.

Reward power arises from giving people something they want. The reward given by a supervisor might be a raise, recognition, or assignment to a desired shift. A supervisor who plans to rely on reward power to lead employees had better be sure that he or she is able to give out rewards consistently. Often supervisors are limited in this regard. Company policy may put a ceiling on the size of raises to be granted or there may be only a few assignments that really thrill employees.

Connection power is power that stems from a person's relationship to someone powerful. Imagine that two supervisors are golfing buddies. One of them gets promoted to the job of manager of purchasing. The other supervisor has connection power stemming from his relationship to the new manager. Similarly, if one of the organization's employees is the daughter of a vice president, she has connection power as a result of that family relationship. Connection power can be a problem for the organization and its managers when the people who have it place the interests of their relationship ahead of the interests of the organization. Nevertheless, it is a fact of organizational life.

Information power is power that arises from possessing valuable information. Someone who knows which employees are targeted in the next round of layoffs or when the department manager will be out of town has information power. The secretaries of top managers have information power as well as connection power.

Political Strategies

A person's political strategies are the methods the person uses to acquire and keep power within the organization. Depending on the particular strategies a person chooses and how he or she uses those strategies, they may be ethical or unethical. The following strategies commonly are used in organizations[22]:

- *Doing favors*—People remember favors and generally are willing to help out or say a good word in return. However, doing favors solely to create an obligation is unethical.
- *Making good impressions*—Those who are skilled at organization politics know that it is important to create a positive image of themselves. Not only do they look their best, but they make sure their accomplishments are visible.
- *Cultivating the grapevine*—The saying "knowledge is power" applies to one's position in the organization. Therefore, power is greater for those who are connected to the grapevines that carry information in the organization (see Chapter 10). Ways to get connected include serving on committees and developing friendships and informal contacts.
- *Supporting the manager*—The supervisor's manager can be a powerful ally. Therefore, it is important to help the manager look good.

SUPERVISION AND DIVERSITY

Women and Men and Power

Do men and women use power differently? Here are some thoughtful answers from women.

I believe that "gathering" is at the crux of how women view and use power differently from men. . . . It's not easy to find the freedom to operate with a "gathering" style—even though there is plenty of research documenting that collaborative approaches offer the best chance of producing high-quality results.—*Sharon Patrick, President and COO, Martha Stewart Living (New York)*

In my 30 years in the labor movement, "pushy broad" is one of the nicer names that I've been called. . . . I'm tenacious. Sometimes I'm ornery. But I always find ways to get things done. . . . Women who want to be leaders have to be up-front and honest about it—not only with themselves but also with the men they work with and the men they share their lives with.—*Linda Chavez-Thompson, Executive Vice President, AFL-CIO (Washington D.C.)*

For years, I've seen women trying to act like men. More recently, I've seen men trying to act like women. It won't work. The only way to be powerfully successful, whether you're a man or a woman, is to be who you are.—*Janice Gjertsen, Business Development, Digital City New York (New York)*

There are a few points about power that apply to both sexes—but are especially relevant to women. First, you need a good relationship with those in power in order to be able to learn from them. Second, people who have power don't always have something to teach you. Third, the best way to learn is to ask questions—even if doing so makes you feel uncomfortable. Fourth, real power comes from within, not from your official position. And finally, the power to contribute—to make a difference in a fast-changing world—should never be confused with power over others.—*Wendy Luhabe, Managing Partner, Bridging the Gap (South Africa)*

Source: *Fast Company* by Anna Muoio. Copyright © 1998 by Business Innovator Group Resources/Inc. Reproduced with permission of Business Innovator Group Resources/Inc. via Copyright Clearance Center.

- *Avoiding negativism*—People have more respect for those who propose solutions than for those who merely criticize.
- *Giving praise*—People like to be praised, and written compliments are especially valuable. As long as the praise is sincere, the supervisor can offer it to anyone, even his or her manager.

"Supervision and Diversity" demonstrates how women may strategize their use of power differently from men.

Building a Power Base

At the heart of organization politics is building a base of power. The particular approach used varies with the kinds of power an employee or manager might acquire. Figure 15.8 summarizes some possible approaches. Some people take on more responsibility in an effort to become needed in the organization. Others seek control over resources; the supervisor with more employees or a bigger budget is considered to be more powerful.

An important way supervisors can build their power bases is to please their managers. Peers and subordinates who recognize that a supervisor has a close relationship with the manager tend to treat the supervisor carefully to avoid antagonizing the manager.

To do favors so that others will be in one's debt is yet another approach. Bribery of course is unethical, but there are many ethical ways to do favors for others. A supervisor might offer to stay late to help a co-worker finish a project or

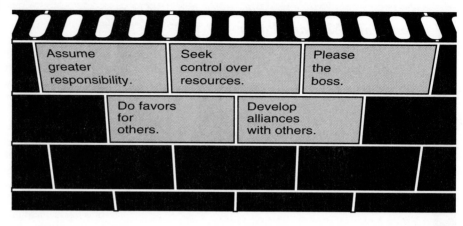

Assume greater responsibility.

Seek control over resources.

Please the boss.

Do favors for others.

Develop alliances with others.

jump-start the co-worker's car on a cold day. When the supervisor needs help or a favorable word from someone, the co-worker probably will be happy to return the favor.

Doing favors can help a supervisor with one of the other techniques for building a power base: developing alliances with others in the organization. A supervisor who has many people on his or her side is able to get more done and to build a good reputation. This does not mean supervisors have to hang around with greedy, pushy, or unethical co-workers. Instead, they should identify people they admire as potential allies. Alliances can be built with these people by earning their trust, keeping them informed, and developing comfortable relationships through common interests.

Establishing a Competitive Edge

On the assumption that there are limits to the number of promotions and other goodies available, organization members seek to gain a competitive edge. They try to stand out so that when raises, promotions, and choice assignments are handed out, they will be the recipients. Ethical efforts to establish a competitive edge generally are based on trying to do an exceptional job.

Some unethical approaches to establishing a competitive edge are spreading lies and rumors about peers and taking credit for the ideas and work of subordinates. Trying to look good at the expense of someone else may be effective at first, but when the truth comes out the person who uses this tactic winds up the biggest loser. Other people learn to distrust such a person. In the long run, the most successful way to look exceptional is to produce exceptional results.

Socializing

At many organizations, part of the game of getting ahead includes socializing with co-workers. Perhaps the people who get promoted the fastest are those who on occasion play golf with the boss or go out for a drink after work. Depending on a supervisor's behavior in these situations, socializing can be helpful or it can put an end to an employee's career growth.

Common sense can help the supervisor handle socializing appropriately. For example, a supervisor who gets drunk at a party is likely to behave foolishly. Likewise, dating a subordinate is an invitation to trouble. If the relationship lasts, other employees are likely to be jealous of the subordinate and to doubt the supervisor's ability to be fair. If the relationship does not work out, the supervisor could be set up—justly or unjustly—for charges of sexual harassment by an angry subordinate. (For an explanation of sexual harassment, see Chapter 19.)

In general, the wisest course is to be sensible but natural. For example, a supervisor should not push to become a buddy of the manager or of subordinates. Nor should a supervisor use social occasions as an opportunity to make a big impression; showing off is hardly an effective way to build relationships.

Summary

15.1 List positive and negative aspects of conflict.

When it leads to necessary changes, conflict is a positive force because it signals that a problem exists. However, ongoing conflict puts people under stress and takes up time that could be spent more productively. When conflict involves anger at management or the organization, it may lead to destructive behavior.

15.2 Define types of conflict.

Conflict may be intrapersonal, taking place within one person. Conflict between individuals is called interpersonal. Structural conflict results from the way the organization is structured. Strategic conflict is brought about intentionally to achieve some goal, such as motivating employees.

15.3 Describe strategies for managing conflict.

One strategy is to compromise, or agree to a solution that meets only part of each party's demands. Another approach is to avoid the conflict or to pretend it does not exist (smoothing). Forcing a solution occurs when a person with power selects and imposes the outcome. None of these strategies tries to solve the underlying problem, and all assume that the situation is win-lose for those involved. Confronting and solving the problem, called conflict resolution, assumes that a conflict can be a win-win situation.

15.4 Explain how supervisors can initiate conflict resolution, respond to a conflict, and mediate conflict resolution.

To initiate conflict resolution, a supervisor must begin by understanding what the conflict is. The supervisor then states the problem and listens to the response; when the parties are communicating, they can find a solution and agree upon what each person will do.

To respond to a conflict, a supervisor should listen to the other person and try to understand the problem. Then the supervisor can build cooperation by agreeing with part of the statement and working with the other person to reach a solution.

To mediate conflict resolution, a supervisor begins by establishing a constructive environment, then asks each person to explain what the problem is and state what he or she wants. Next the supervisor restates each position, asks for suggested solutions, and encourages the parties to select a mutually beneficial solution. Finally, the supervisor summarizes what course of action has been agreed upon.

15.5 Identify sources of change, and explain why employees and supervisors resist it.

Change can come from management in response to an opportunity or need to do things better. It can come from employees in the form of unionizing or making suggestions. Change can be imposed by external forces such as the government. Employees and supervisors resist change because it typically requires extra effort and sometimes leaves people worse off. Other reasons for resisting change are fear of the unknown and worry that one is incapable of making the change.

15.6 Discuss how supervisors can overcome resistance and implement change.

To overcome resistance to change, supervisors can recognize and respond to employees' feelings. They also can keep employees informed about the change, being realistic but emphasizing any benefits. The supervisor should give employees opportunities to ask questions about the change. To implement change, the supervisor should build on successes. This includes communicating successes as they occur, setting reasonable deadlines for the steps that must be taken, and involving first the people who are most likely to be enthusiastic about the change.

15.7 Describe the types of power supervisors can have.

Supervisors can have legitimate power, which comes from their position in the organization; referent power, which comes from the emotions they inspire in others; expert power, which comes from their knowledge or skills; coercive power, which comes from fear related to their use of force; reward power, which comes from giving people something they want; connection power, which comes from their relationships to people in power; and information power, which comes from the possession of valuable information.

15.8 Identify common strategies for organization politics.

Political strategies commonly used in organizations include doing favors, making good impressions, cultivating the grapevine, supporting the manager, avoiding negativism, and giving praise.

Key Terms

conflict, p. 376

frustration, p. 376

conflict management, p. 379

compromise, p. 379

smoothing, p. 380

conflict resolution, p. 381

organization politics, p. 392

power, p. 392

position power, p. 393

personal power, p. 393

Review and Discussion Questions

1. On her first day on the job, Jenna's supervisor introduces her incorrectly to her co-workers, mispronouncing her name. For several weeks after that, Jenna's co-workers, intending to be friendly, pronounce her name incorrectly. Jenna goes along with it, not wanting to jeopardize her new relationships. Finally, feeling uncomfortable about the situation, Jenna approaches her supervisor about the mistake. Is this a positive or negative conflict? Why?

2. Imagine that you are a production supervisor at a hand-tool manufacturer such as Snap-On Tools. Your manager says, "I know you were looking forward to your trip to Hawaii next month, but we will be stepping up production, and three new employees will be joining your group. I wish you would consider staying to make sure everything goes smoothly."
   a. What is the nature of the conflict in this situation? In other words, what two goals is it impossible for you to achieve at the same time?
   b. List as many possible solutions as you can think of to resolve this conflict.
   c. Which solution do you prefer? How could you present it to your manager?

3. Identify each of the following conflicts as interpersonal, structural, or strategic.
   a. The production department's goal is to make parts faster, and the quality-control department wants slower production to reduce the rate of defects.
   b. A salesperson does not take telephone messages for her co-workers because she believes she has a better chance of being the department's top performer when her co-workers do not return their calls.
   c. One cashier at a supermarket is much older than the others, and he does not spend much time talking to them. The other cashiers criticize him for not being a team player.

4. Why does compromise generally leave both parties feeling frustrated?

5. Rachel Gonzalez supervises servers at a restaurant. She knows that many of them are upset about the hours she has scheduled for them, but she believes that people should not argue.

So she avoids discussing the subject, and she posts the following week's schedule just before leaving for the day. What is wrong with Rachel's approach to conflict management? What would be a better way to manage this conflict?

6. Ron Herbst is a supervisor in a clinical laboratory. He has noticed that one employee regularly comes to work in a surly mood. The employee is getting his work done on time, but his attitude seems to be affecting other employees.

    a. How can Ron initiate conflict resolution with this employee? How should he describe the problem?

    b. If the employee responds to Ron's statement of the problem by saying, "I'm fine. Don't worry about me," what should the supervisor do and say?

7. The managers of a soft-drink bottling company decide that production workers will each learn several jobs and rotate among those jobs. They have read that this technique improves productivity, and they believe that workers will be happier because their jobs will be more interesting. However, many of the employees and their supervisors are reluctant to make the change. What could explain their resistance?

8. What are the factors that can affect the success of a change?

9. How can a supervisor overcome resistance to change?

10. What is the primary reason that efforts for change within an organization fail? What can a supervisor do to avoid this failure and to ensure that change will be successful?

11. What are the two basic sources of power available to a supervisor? Which do you think is more important to the supervisor's effectiveness? Why?

12. Which type or types of power is the supervisor exerting in each of the following situations?

    a. A sales supervisor promises a $50 bonus to the first salesperson to close a sale this week.

    b. One day a month, a supervisor orders in pizza and joins her employees for lunch. The employees look forward to these gatherings because the supervisor joins them in recounting funny stories, and she usually is able to fill them in on some management plans.

    c. A supervisor in the bookkeeping department got his job thanks to a referral from his father, who regularly plays racquetball with the company's president. Since the supervisor was hired, the president has visited the bookkeeping department a couple of times to see how he is doing. The manager of the department is very diplomatic in his criticism of the supervisor.

    d. When the employees in a word-processing department make many errors per page or a particularly glaring error, their supervisor posts the offending pages on the department bulletin board to shame the employees into performing better.

13. A sales supervisor believes she could be more effective if she had more cooperation from the company's credit department. If the credit of potential customers could be approved faster, her salespeople could close more sales. What political tactics would you recommend that the sales supervisor consider to get more cooperation from the credit department?

A SECOND LOOK

How can Motel 6's supervisors help employees work with changes like new ownership and a new type of clientele?

SKILLS MODULE

CASE

Conflict and Change: Breyers Ice Cream Melts in Philadelphia

Ice cream used to be one of those unchanging symbols of American life, like baseball or the Sears catalog. But baseball went on strike, and the original Sears catalog folded. And in Philadelphia, the traditional scoop of vanilla fell off the cone when 130-year-old Breyers (now owned by Kraft) announced that it was closing its 71-year-old plant, leaving 240 workers without jobs.

"This has always seemed like the perfect job for me," laments Frank Avent, a 53-year-old Breyers employee facing the layoff. "[Breyers ice cream] has always been my favorite dessert. Until now." Avent worked at the plant for 25 years.

The situation at Breyers is the same one many American companies have had to face in recent years. Operating in a city with high business taxes, an aging infrastructure, and high crime rates, Breyers management concluded it must leave the city where the company was founded. In addition, modernizing the existing plant would have cost $15 million. Trying to get the public and employees to see the benefits of the change, John Gould, Jr., spokesman for Good Humor–Breyers (now based in Wisconsin) claims, "We believe the Philadelphia operation is one that we can close without adversely affecting production."

But the closing does affect jobs, often ones held by people for many years or from one generation to the next. "It's a shame they're leaving Philly. It really is," comments Rich Hunter, a mechanic who has been with Breyers for 12 years. "My father used to work here, too. We've got pictures of this place from [the time] when horse-and-buggies used to deliver the ice cream."

If some workers seem nostalgic, others are angry and mistrustful of the organization. "They knew what they were getting when they bought this place," observes Roney Brabham, a production worker for 18 years, "but they never even tried to fix it up. Where does that leave us?"

Union representatives agree. "Big business once again shows its concern for the bottom line and its lack of concern for working men and women," notes Edward Henderson, head of the Teamsters Local 463, which represents 184 workers at the plant.

If these workers and their union reps resist change, it is understandable: People are losing jobs. Implementing change will not be easy for supervisors, who must deal with the reality of layoffs—and may face layoffs themselves. In this case, the freeze-unfreeze-refreeze model of change may be more difficult to carry out than usual: It's nearly impossible to get the ice cream back into the cone.

1. What three points of view are expressed in this case?
2. Is there any way to initiate some type of conflict resolution in the Breyers case? If so, how?
3. Do the workers have any potential power? If so, what type or types might they have? How could they use it?
4. What steps might supervisors take to implement the change as painlessly as possible?

Source: From "Closing of Breyers Is a Bitter Chapter for Employees, City," *Boston Globe*, September 5, 1995. Reprinted with permission of The Associated Press.

SELF-QUIZ

What Is Your Conflict-Handling Style?

Everyone has a basic style for handling conflicts. To identify the strategies you rely upon most, indicate how often each of the following statements applies to you. Next to each statement, write *5* if the statement applies often, *3* if the statement applies sometimes, and *1* if the statement applies never.

When I differ with someone . . .

_____   1. I explore our differences, not backing down, but not imposing my view either.

_____   2. I disagree openly, then invite more discussion about our differences.

_____   3. I look for a mutually satisfactory solution.

_____   4. Rather than let the other person make a decision without my input, I make sure I am heard and also that I hear the other person out.

_____   5. I agree to a middle ground rather than look for a completely satisfying solution.

_____   6. I admit I am half wrong rather than explore our differences.

_____   7. I have a reputation for meeting a person halfway.

_____   8. I expect to say about half of what I really want to say.

_____   9. I give in totally rather than try to change another's opinion.

_____ 10. I put aside any controversial aspects of an issue.

_____ 11. I agree early on, rather than argue about a point.

_____ 12. I give in as soon as the other party gets emotional about an issue.

_____ 13. I try to win the other person over.

_____ 14. I try to come out victorious, no matter what.

_____ 15. I never back away from a good argument.

_____ 16. I would rather win than end up compromising.

To score your responses, add your total score for each of the following sets of statements:

Set A: statements 1–4   Set C: statements 9–12

Set B: statements 5–8   Set D: statements 13–16

A score of 17 or more on any set is considered high. Scores of 12 to 16 are moderately high. Scores of 8 to 11 are moderately low. Scores of 7 or less are considered low.

Each set represents a different strategy for conflict management:

- Set A = Collaboration (I win, you win)
- Set B = Compromise (Both win some, both lose some)
- Set C = Accommodation (I lose, you win)
- Set D = Forcing/domination (I win, you lose)

Source: From *Supervision: Managerial Skills for a New Era*, by Von der Embse. Copyright © 1987 Pearson Education, Inc. Reprinted by permission of Pearson Education Inc., Upper Saddle River, NJ.

Class Exercise

This exercise is based on role playing. One class member takes the role of a supervisor, and two class members act as the employees. The supervisor leaves the room for five minutes as the employees act out the following scenario:

> Pat and Chris work in a word-processing department, preparing reports and letters on computer terminals. Pat trips on the cord to Chris's computer, shutting it off and erasing the project Chris was working on. Chris is upset. If Chris does not finish the job by the end of the day, the failure to meet a deadline will show up on Chris's performance records and hurt Chris's chances for getting a raise. In addition, the manager who requested the work will be upset, because this is an important project.

This is a basic scenario; the employees should be creative in adding details. For example, they can address the following questions:

- Did Pat erase the files on purpose?
- Has Pat ever done something like this before?
- Do these employees otherwise get along?

- Are communications in general and this conflict in particular complicated by some difference between the employees (age, sex, race, etc.)?

After the two class members have acted out the scene, the supervisor returns to the room, and the role playing continues as the employees bring their conflict to the supervisor. The supervisor should try to manage the conflict.

When the supervisor is satisfied with how the conflict has been handled (or when 10 minutes have elapsed), the class discusses the following questions:

1. Did the supervisor understand the real problem? If not, what was the real problem?
2. Did the supervisor and employees solve the problem? Was the solution a good one?
3. In what ways was the supervisor effective in resolving the conflict? How could the supervisor improve his or her approach?
4. What other possible solutions might the supervisor and employees have considered?

Team-Building Exercise

Role-Playing Types of Power

Divide the class into teams of five or more students. Each student receives a card marked with the type of power he or she possesses: legitimate, referent, expert, coercive, reward, connection, or information. (If the group is small, some students may have two types of power.) Students should not show other team members which card they have. Each team has a goal: to convince the rest of the

class that changing something (e.g., holding class in the evening instead of the afternoon) is a good idea.

Using the different kinds of power, each team presents its idea to the class. Afterward, the class should discuss how effective each team was, how effective individual team members were, and what type of power was most effective in getting people to respond positively to the idea of change.

Appendix: Organizational Politics*

Most students of supervision find that study of organizational politics intriguing. Perhaps this topic owes its appeal to the antics of Hollywood's corporate villains who get their way by stepping on anyone and everyone. As we will see, however, organizational politics includes, but is not limited to, dirty dealing. Organizational politics is an ever-present and sometimes annoying feature of modern work life. "According to 150 executives from large US companies, office politics wastes an average of 20% of their time; that's 10 weeks a year."[1] On the other hand, organizational politics is often a positive force in modern work organizations. Skillful and well-timed politics can help you get your point across, neutralize resistance to a key project, or get a choice job assignment.

Roberta Bhasin, a district manager for US West, put organizational politics into perspective by observing the following:

> Most of us would like to believe that organizations are rationally structured, based on reasonable divisions of labor, a clear hierarchical communication flow, and well-defined lines of authority aimed at meeting universally understood goals and objectives.
>
> But organizations are made up of *people* with personal agendas designed to win power and influence. The agenda—the game—is called corporate politics. It is played by avoiding the rational structure, manipulating the communications hierarchy, and ignoring established lines of authority. The rules are never written down and seldom discussed.
>
> For some, corporate politics are second nature. They instinctively know the unspoken rules of the game. Others must learn. Managers who don't understand the politics of their organizations are at a disadvantage, not only in winning raises and promotions, but even in getting things *done*.[2]

We explore this important and interesting area by (1) defining the term *organizational politics*, (2) identifying three levels of political action, (3) discussing eight specific political tactics, (4) considering a related area called *impression management*, and (5) discussing how to manage organizational politics.

Definition and Domain of Organizational Politics

"*Organizational politics* involves intentional acts of influence to enhance or protect the self-interest of individuals or groups."[3] An emphasis on *self-interest* distinguishes this form of social influence.

Supervisors are endlessly challenged to achieve a workable balance between employees' self-interests and organizational interests. When a proper balance exists, the pursuit of self-interest may serve the organization's interests. Political behavior becomes a negative force when self-interests erode or defeat organizational interests. For example, researchers have documented the political tactic of filtering and distorting information flowing up to the boss. This self-serving practice put the reporting employees in the best possible light.[4]

Uncertainty Triggers Political Behavior

Political maneuvering is triggered primarily by *uncertainty*. Five common sources of uncertainty within organizations are

1. Unclear objectives.
2. Vague performance measures.
3. Ill-defined decision processes.
4. Strong individual or group competition.[5]
5. Any type of change.

Regarding this last source of uncertainty, organization development specialist Anthony Raia noted, "Whatever we attempt to change, the political subsystem becomes active. Vested interests are almost always at stake and the distribution of power is challenged."[6]

Thus, we would expect a field sales representative, striving to achieve an assigned quota, to be less political than a supervisor working on a variety of projects. While some supervisors stake their career success on hard work, competence, and a bit of luck, many do not. These people attempt to gain a competitive edge through some combination of the political tactics discussed below. Meanwhile, the salesperson's performance is measured in actual sales, not in terms of being friends with the boss or taking credit for others' work. Thus, the supervisor would tend to be more political than the field salesperson because of greater uncertainty about management's expectations.

Because employees generally experience greater uncertainty during the earlier stages of their careers, are junior employees more political than more senior ones? The answer is yes, according to a survey of 243 employed adults in upstate New York. In fact, one senior employee nearing retirement told the researcher: "I used to play political games when I was younger. Now I just do my job."[7]

Three Levels of Political Action

Although much political maneuvering occurs at the individual level, it also can involve group or collective action. Figure A illustrates three different levels of political action: the individual level, the coalition level, and the network level.[8] Each level has its distinguishing characteristics. At the individual level, personal self-interests are pursued by the individual. The political aspects of coalitions and networks are not so obvious, however.

FIGURE A

Levels of Political Action in Organizations

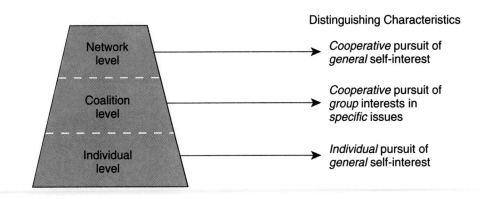

People with a common interest can become a political coalition by fitting the following definition. In an organizational context, a *coalition* is an informal group bound together by the *active* pursuit of a *single* issue. Coalitions may or may not coincide with formal group membership. When the target issue is resolved (a sexually harassing supervisor is fired, for example), the coalition disbands. Experts note that political coalitions have "fuzzy boundaries," meaning they are fluid in membership, flexible in structure, and temporary in duration.[9]

Coalitions are a potent political force in organizations. Consider the situation Charles J Bradshaw faced in a finance committee meeting at Transworld Corporation; Bradshaw, president of the company, opposed the chairman's plan to acquire a $93 million nursing home company:

> [The senior vice president for finance] kicked off the meeting with a battery of facts and figures in support of the deal. "Within two or three minutes, I knew I had lost," Bradshaw concedes. "No one was talking directly to me, but all statements addressed my opposition. I could tell there was a general agreement around the board table." . . .
>
> Then the vote was taken. Five hands went up. Only Bradshaw voted "no."[10]

After the meeting, Bradshaw resigned his $530,000-a-year position, without as much as a handshake or good-bye from the chairman. In Bradshaw's case, the finance committee was a formal group that temporarily became a political coalition aimed at sealing his fate at Transworld. Coalitions on the corporate boards of American Express, IBM, and General Motors also ousted the heads of those giant companies.

A third level of political action involves networks.[11] Unlike coalitions, which pivot on specific issues, networks are loose associations of individuals seeking social support for their general self-interests. Politically, networks are people oriented, while coalitions are issue oriented. Networks have broader and longer term agendas than do coalitions. For instance, Avon's Hispanic employees have built a network to enhance the members' career opportunities.

Political Tactics

Anyone who has worked in an organization has firsthand knowledge of blatant politicking. Blaming someone else for your mistake is an obvious political ploy. But other political tactics are more subtle. Researchers have identified a range of political behavior.

■ TABLE A

Eight Common Political Tactics in Organizations

Political Tactic	Percentage of Managers Mentioning Tactic	Brief Description of Tactic
1. Attacking or blaming others	54%	Used to avoid or minimize association with failure. Reactive when scapegoating is involved. Proactive when goal is to reduce competition for limited resources.
2. Using information as a political tool	54	Involves the purposeful withholding of distortion of information. Obscuring an unfavorable situation by overwhelming superiors with information.
3. Creating a favorable image (impression management)	53	Dressing/grooming for success. Adhering to organizational norms and drawing attention to one's successes and influence. Taking credit for others' accomplishments.
4. Developing a base of support	37	Getting prior support for a decision. Building others' commitment to a decision through participation.
5. Praising others (ingratiation)	25	Making influential people feel good ("apple polishing").
6. Forming power coalitions with strong allies	25	Teaming up with powerful people who can get results.
7. Associating with influential people	24	Building a support network both inside and outside the organization.
8. Creating obligations (reciprocity)	13	Creating social debts ("I did you a favor, so you owe me a favor")

Source: Adapted from R. W. Allen, D. L. Madison, I. W. Porter, P. A. Renwick, and B. T. Mayes. "Organizational Politics: Tactics and Characteristics of Its Actors," *California Management Review*, Fall 1979, pp. 77–83.

One landmark study, involving in-depth interviews with 87 managers from 30 electronics companies in southern California, identified eight political tactics. Top-, middle-, and supervisors were represented about equally in the sample. According to the researchers: "Respondents were asked to describe organizational political tactics and personal characteristics of effective political actors based upon their accumulated experience in *all* organizations in which they had worked."[12] Listed in descending order of occurrence, the eight political tactics that emerged were

1. Attacking or blaming others.
2. Using information as a political tool.
3. Creating a favorable image. (Also known as *impression management*.)[13]
4. Developing a base of support.
5. Praising others (ingratiation).
6. Forming power coalitions with strong allies.
7. Associating with influential people.
8. Creating obligations (reciprocity).

Table A describes these political tactics and indicates how often each reportedly was used by the interviewed managers.

■ TABLE B

Are You Politically Naive, Politically Sensible, or a Political Shark?

Characteristics	Naive	Sensible	Sharks
Underlying attitude	Politics is unpleasant.	Politics is necessary.	Politics is an opportunity.
Intent	Avoid at all costs.	Further departmental goals.	Self-serving and predatory.
Techniques	Tell it like it is.	Network; expand connections: use system to give and receive favors.	Manipulate; use fraud and deceit when necessary.
Favorite tactics	None—the truth will win out.	Negotiate, bargain.	Bully; misuse information: cultivate and use "friends and other contacts."

Source: From J. K. Pinto and O. P. Kharbanda, "Lessons for an Accidental Profession." Reprinted with permission from *Business Horizons*, March–April 1995. Copyright © 1995 by The Trustees at Indiana University, Kelley School of Business.

The researchers distinguished between reactive and proactive political tactics. Some of the tactics, such as scapegoating, were *reactive* because the intent was to *defend* one's self-interest. Other tactics, such as developing a base of support, were *proactive* because they sought to *promote* the individual's self-interest.

What is your attitude toward organizational politics? How often do you rely on the various tactics in Table A? You can get a general indication of your political tendencies by comparing your behavior with the characteristics in Table B. Would you characterize yourself as politically *naive*, politically *sensible*, or a political *shark?* How do you think others view your political actions? What are the career, friendship, and ethical implications of your political tendencies?[14]

Impression Management

Impression management is defined as "the process by which people attempt to control or manipulate the reactions of others to images of themselves or their ideas."[15] This encompasses how one talks, behaves, and looks. Most impression management attempts are directed at making a *good* impression on relevant others. But, as we will see, some employees strive to make a *bad* impression. For purposes of conceptual clarity, we will focus on *upward* impression management trying to impress one's immediate supervisor. Still, it is good to remember that *anyone* can be the intended target of impression management. Parents, teachers, peers, employees, and customers are all fair game when it comes to managing the impressions of others.

A Conceptual Crossroads

Impression management is an interesting conceptual crossroads involving self-monitoring and organizational politics.[16] Perhaps this explains why impression management has gotten active research attention in recent years. High self-monitoring employees ("chameleons" who adjust to their surroundings) are likely to be more inclined to engage in impression management than would low self-monitors. Impression management also involves the systematic manipulation of attributions. For example, a supervisor will look good if upper management is encouraged to attribute organizational successes to her efforts and attribute problems and failures to factors beyond her control. Impression management definitely fits into the realm of organizational politics because of an overriding focus on furthering one's *self-interests*.

Making a Good Impression

If you "dress for success," project an upbeat attitude at all times, and avoid offending others, you are engaging in favorable impression management—particularly so if your motive is to improve your chances of getting what you want in life.[17] There are questionable ways to create a good impression, as well. For instance, Stewart Friedman, director of the University of Pennsylvania's Leadership Program, recently offered this gem:

> Last year, I was doing some work with a large bank. The people there told me a story that astounded me: After 7 PM, people would open the door to their office, drape a spare jacket on the back of their chair, lay a set of glasses down on some reading material on their desk—and then go home for the night. The point of this elaborate gesture was to create the illusion that they were just out grabbing dinner and would be returning to burn the midnight oil.[18]

Impression management often strays into unethical territory.

An analysis of the influence attempts reported by a sample of 84 bank employees (including 74 women) identified three categories of favorable upward impression management tactics.[19] Favorable upward impression management tactics can be *job-focused* (manipulating information about one's job performance), *supervisor-focused* (praising and doing favors for one's supervisor), and *self-focused* (presenting oneself as a polite and nice person). Take a short break from your studying to complete the questionnaire in Table C. How did you do? A moderate amount of upward impression management is a necessity for the average supervisor today. Too little, and busy managers are liable to overlook some of your valuable contributions when they make job assignment, pay, and promotion decisions. Too much, and you run the risk of being branded a "schmoozer," a "phony," and other unflattering things by your co-workers.[20] Excessive flattery and ingratiation can backfire by embarassing the target person and damaging one's credibility. Also, the risk of unintended insult is very high when impression management tactics cross gender, racial, ethnic, and cultural lines.[21] International experts warn:

> The impression management tactic is only as effective as its correlation to accepted norms about behavioral presentation. In other words, slapping a Japanese subordinate on the back with a rousing "Good work, Hiro!" will not create the desired impression in Hiro's mind that the expatriate intended. In fact, the behavior will likely create the opposite impression.[22]

Making a Poor Impression

At first glance, the idea of consciously trying to make a bad impression in the workplace seems absurd. But an interesting new line of impression management research has uncovered both motives and tactics for making oneself look *bad*. In a survey of the work experiences of business students at a large northwestern

U.S. university, more than half "reported witnessing a case of someone intentionally looking bad at work"[23] Why? Four motives came out of the study:

(1) *Avoidance:* Employee seeks to avoid additional work, stress, burnout, or an unwanted transfer or promotion. (2) *Obtain concrete rewards:* Employee seeks to obtain a pay raise or a desired transfer, promotion, or demotion. (3) *Exit:* Employee seeks to get laid off, fired or suspended, and perhaps also to collect unemployment or worker's compensation. (4) *Power:* Employee seeks to control, manipulate, or intimidate others, get revenge, or make someone else look bad.[24]

Within the context of these motives, *unfavorable* upward impression management makes sense.

Five unfavorable upward impression management tactics identified by the researchers are as follows:

- *Decreasing performance*—restricting productivity, making more mistakes than usual, lowering quality, neglecting tasks.
- *Not working to potential*—pretending ignorance, having unused capabilities.
- *Withdrawing*—being tardy, taking excessive breaks, faking illness.

■ TABLE C

How Much Do You Rely on Upward Impression Management Tactics?

Instructions
Rate yourself on each item according to how you behave on your current (or most recent) job. Add your circled responses to calculate a total score. Compare your score with our arbitrary norms.

Job-Focused Tactics   Rarely Very Often
1. I play up the value of my positive work results and make my supervisor aware of them.   1—2—3—4—5

2. I try to make my work appear better than it is.   1—2—3—4—5

3. I try to take responsibility for positive results, even when I'm not solely responsible for achieving them.   1—2—3—4—5

4. I try to make my negative results not as severe as they initially appear to my supervisor. 1—2—3—4—5

5. I arrive at work early and/or work late to show my supervisor I am hard worker.   1—2—3—4—5

Supervisor-Focused Tactics
6. I show an interest in my supervisor's personal life.   1—2—3—4—5

7. I praise my supervisor on his/her accomplishments.   1—2—3—4—5

8. I do personal favors for my supervisor that I'm not required to do.   1—2—3—4—5

9. I compliment my supervisor on her or his dress or appearance.   1—2—3—4—5

10. I agree with my supervisor's major suggestions and ideas.   1—2—3—4—5

Self-Focused Tactics
11. I am very friendly and polite around my supervisor.   1—2—3—4—5

12. I try to act as a model employee around my supervisor.   1—2—3—4—5

13. I work harder when I know my supervisor will see the results.   1—2—3—4—5

Total score = ____

Arbitrary Norms
13–26   Free agent
27–51   Better safe than sorry
52–65   Hello, Hollywood

Source: Adapted from S. J. Wayne and G. R. Ferris, "Influence Tactics, Affect, and Exchange Quality in Supervisor-Subordinate Interactions: A Laboratory Experiment and Field Study," *Journal of Applied Psychology*, October 1990, pp 487–499.

- *Displaying a bad attitude*—complaining, getting upset and angry, acting strangely, not getting along with co-workers.
- *Broadcasting limitations*—letting co-workers know about one's physical problems and mistakes (both verbally and nonverbally).[25]

Recommended ways to manage employees who try to make a bad impression can include affording them more challenging work, greater autonomy, better feedback, supportive leadership, clear and reasonable goals, and a less stressful work setting.[26]

Managing Organizational Politics

Organizational politics cannot be eliminated. A supervisor would be naive to expect such an outcome. But political maneuvering can and should be managed to keep it constructive and within reasonable bounds. Harvard's Abraham Zaleznik put the issue this way: "People can focus their attention on only so many things. The more it lands on politics, the less energy—emotional and intellectual—is available to attend to the problems that fall under the heading of real work.[27]

An individual's degree of politicalness is a matter of personal values, ethics, and temperament. People who are either strictly nonpolitical or highly political generally pay a price for their behavior. The former may experience slow promotions and feel left out, while the latter may run the risk of being called self-serving and lose their credibility. People at both ends of the political spectrum may be considered poor team players. A moderate amount of prudent political behavior generally is considered a survival tool in complex organizations. Experts remind us that

---

■ TABLE D

Some Practical Advice on Managing Organizational Politics

To Reduce System Uncertainty
Make clear what are the bases and processes for evaluation.

Differentiate rewards among high and low performers.

Make sure the rewards are as immediately and directly related to performance as possible.

To Reduce Competition
Try to minimize resource competition among managers.

Replace resource competition with externally oriented goals and objectives.

To Break Existing Political Fieldoms
Where highly cohesive political empires exist, break them apart by removing or splitting the most dysfunctional subgroups.

If you are an executive, be keenly sensitive to managers whose mode of operation is the personalization of political patronage. First, approach these persons with a directive to "stop the political maneuvering." If it continues, remove them from the positions and preferably, the company.

To Prevent Future Fieldoms
Make one of the most important criteria for promotion an apolitical attitude that puts organizational ends ahead of personal power ends.

Source: D. R. Beeman and T. W. Sharkey, "The Use and Abuse of Corporate Politics." Reprinted with permission of *Business Horizons*, March–April 1987, p 30. Copyright © 1987 by the Board of Trustees at Indiana University, Kelley School of Business.

. . . political behavior has earned a bad name only because of its association with politicians. On its own, the use of power and other resources to obtain your objectives is not inherently unethical. It all depends on what the preferred objectives are.[28]

With this perspective in mind, the practical steps in Table D are recommended. Notice the importance of reducing uncertainty through standardized performance evaluations and clear performance-reward linkages.[29] Measurable objectives are the supervisor's first line of defense against negative expressions of organizational politics.[30]

PART FIVE

Supervision and Human Resources

16

You can't compromise on the people you use. We need people who are confident and believe in what they do and can stand and face the wind when it blows hard.
—Joakim Jonason, creative director, Care Anholt Jonason

Selecting Employees

■ CHAPTER OUTLINE

Roles in the Selection Process

Selection Criteria

Recruitment
Looking Inside the Organization
Looking Outside the Organization

The Selection Process
Screening from Employment Applications and Résumés
Interviewing Candidates
Administering Employment Tests
Conducting Background and Reference Checks
Making the Selection Decision
Requesting a Physical Examination

Legal Issues
Antidiscrimination Laws
Workplace Accessibility
Immigration Reform and Control Act

■ LEARNING OBJECTIVES

After you have studied this chapter, you should be able to:

16.1 Discuss common roles for supervisors in the selection process.

16.2 Distinguish between job descriptions and job specifications, and explain how they help in selecting employees.

16.3 List possible sources of employees.

16.4 Identify the steps in the selection process.

16.5 Discuss how a supervisor should go about interviewing candidates for a job.

16.6 Define types of employment tests.

16.7 Summarize the requirements of antidiscrimination laws.

16.8 Explain how hiring decisions are affected by the Americans with Disabilities Act (ADA).

16.9 Describe the requirements of the Immigration Reform and Control Act (IRCA) of 1986.

■ THE HIRING BOARD GAME

The Equal Employment Opportunity Commission recently announced that it will actively focus on uncovering discrimination in hiring situations, making training for managers and supervisors more important than ever before. In one recent survey, 100 frontline supervisors were asked to identify illegal employment interview questions, and no supervisor did so correctly.

To make sure it stays within the law, Tower Records is taking employment law training seriously, with a game. Instead of assigning books and giving lectures, employment law trainers in its human resources department dress up as game pieces and gather on a giant game board laid out on the floor of a conference room at Tower's Sacramento, California, headquarters. Groups of Tower store managers and supervisors team up to answer questions about hiring and disciplinary situations.

The object of the "game," of course, is to answer as many questions correctly as possible. For each correct answer, you advance your "game piece" one space on the board. Incorrect answers are flagged for discussion. Tower's human resources manager for employee relations, Renee Gromacki, says the game is "a little crazy," but it works.

Source: Susan J. Wells, "The Hunt for Bias in Hiring," *New York Times*, March 8, 1998, Business section, p. 12.

For legal reasons and because it makes good business sense, hiring should be done with care. Thus, it is in the supervisor's best interests to do a good job in helping to select employees. Enthusiastic, well-qualified people are more likely to deliver high quality than indifferent, unqualified people. This is especially true in today's leaner organizations; when fewer employees are getting the work done, each employee has a greater impact on the organization's overall performance. In fact, as *Inc.* magazine reported, finding qualified employees had become the greatest challenge facing small business owners in 1996,[1] and large firms are finding it just as difficult to find and retain good people.

This chapter addresses the supervisor's role in selecting employees, which often entails working with the organization's human resources (or personnel) department. The chapter explains how supervisors define needed qualities of jobs and employees by preparing job descriptions and job specifications. It describes how organizations can recruit candidates and decide whom to hire. Finally, it addresses some legal issues that supervisors and others in the organization must be aware of when hiring.

Roles in the Selection Process

A supervisor's role in the selection process can vary greatly from one organization to another. In small organizations, a supervisor may have great latitude in selecting employees to fill vacant positions. Other organizations have formal procedures that require the human resources department to do most of the work, with the supervisor simply approving the candidates recommended. In most cases, as at Tower Records, a supervisor works to some extent with a human resources department. In this way, a supervisor benefits from that department's skills in screening and interviewing candidates, and from its familiarity with laws regarding hiring practices.

As described in Chapter 3, a growing number of organizations expect employees to work on teams. At the least, the use of teamwork requires the selection of employees who will be effective team members. A supervisor might therefore try to identify candidates who are cooperative and skilled in problem solving or who have helped a team achieve good results in the past. In other cases, the use of teamwork dramatically changes a supervisor's role in the selection process. When teamwork takes the form of self-managing work teams, a team generally interviews candidates and recommends or selects new team members. A supervisor, as team leader, needs to understand the principles of selection so that he or she can coach employees in carrying out the process. The organization's human resources staff supports the team, rather than the individual supervisor.

Selection Criteria

job description
A listing of the characteristics of a job, including the job title, duties involved, and working conditions.

job specification
A listing of the characteristics desirable in the person performing a given job, including educational and work background, physical characteristics, and personal strengths.

To select the right employees, the supervisor, team (if applicable), and human resources department have to be clear about what jobs need to be filled and what kind of people can best fill those jobs. A supervisor or self-managed team provides this information by preparing job descriptions and job specifications, consulting with the human resources department as needed. Table 16.1 details basic kinds of information to include in job descriptions and job specifications.

A **job description** is a listing of the characteristics of the job—that is, the observable activities required to carry out the job. A written job description typically includes the title of the job, a general description, and details of the duties involved. As you will see later in this chapter, it is important for the job description to spell out the essential duties of the job. When appropriate, a job description may also describe working conditions. Figure 16.1 shows a sample job description for a maintenance technician.

A **job specification** is a listing of the characteristics desirable in the person performing the job. These include four types of characteristics[2]:

1. *Knowledge*—Information required to perform tasks in the job description.
2. *Skills*—Proficiency in carrying out tasks in the job description.
3. *Abilities*—General enduring capabilities required for carrying out tasks in the job description.
4. *Other characteristics*—Any additional characteristics related to successful performance of the essential tasks (e.g., personality characteristics).

A job specification for the maintenance technician's position therefore would include characteristics such as knowledge about the company's vehicles and shop equipment, skills in repairing these things, broad mechanical abilities, and a commitment to high-quality work.

A supervisor (or team with the supervisor's coaching) should provide the information that applies to the particular job. If a job description and job specification already exist for a position, a supervisor should review them to make sure they reflect current needs. Preparing and using these materials helps a supervisor

■ TABLE 16.1
Contents of the Job Description and Job Specification

Job Description	Job Specification
Job title	Education
Location	Experience
Job summary	Availability to work overtime
Duties, including backup functions during peak periods	Skills—technical, physical, communication, and interpersonal
Productivity and quality standards	Training
Machines, tools, and equipment	Judgment and initiative
Materials and forms used	Emotional characteristics
Relationships—supervision and teams, if any	Physical effort
Working conditions	Unusual sensory demands (sight, smell, hearing, etc.)

Source: From *Modern Management*, 8th edition, by Samuel C. Certo. Copyright © 2000 Pearson Education, Inc. Reprinted by permission of Pearson Education, Inc., Upper Saddle River, NJ.

■ FIGURE 16.1
Sample Job Description: Maintenance Mechanic

General Description of Job General maintenance and repair of all equipment used in the operations of a particular district. Includes the servicing of company vehicles, shop equipment, and machinery used on job sites.

1. *Essential Duty (40%): Maintenance of Equipment*
   Tasks: Keep a log of all maintenance performed on equipment. Replace parts and fluids according to maintenance schedule. Regularly check gauges and loads for deviances that may indicate problems with equipment. Perform nonroutine maintenance as required. May involve limited supervision and training of operators performing maintenance.

2. *Essential Duty (40%): Repair of Equipment*
   Tasks: Requires inspection of equipment and a recommendation that a piece be scrapped or repaired. If equipment is to be repaired mechanic will take whatever steps are necessary to return the piece to working order. This may include a partial or total rebuilding of the piece using various hand tools and equipment. Will primarily involve the overhaul and troubleshooting of diesel engines and hydraulic equipment.

3. *Essential Duty (10%): Testing and Approval*
   Tasks: Ensure that all required maintenance and repair has been performed and that it was performed according to manufacturer specifications. Approve or reject equipment for readiness to use on a job.

4. *Essential Duty (10%): Maintain Stock*
   Tasks: Maintain inventory of parts needed for the maintenance and repair of equipment. Responsible for ordering satisfactory parts and supplies at the lowest possible cost.

Nonessential Functions
   Other duties as assigned.

Source: From Raymond Noe, John R. Hollenbeck, Barry Gerhart, and Patrick M. Wright, *Human Resource Management: Gaining a Competitive Advantage*, 1994. Copyright © 1994 by The McGraw-Hill Companies. Reproduced with permission of The McGraw-Hill Companies.

base hiring decisions on objective criteria—how well each candidate matches the requirements of the job. Without them, a supervisor risks hiring people solely because he or she likes them better than others.

Recruitment

recruitment
A process of identifying people interested in holding a particular job or working for the organization.

To select employees, the supervisor and human resources department need candidates for the job. Identifying people interested in holding a particular job or working for the organization is known as **recruitment,** which involves looking for candidates from both inside and outside the organization.

Looking Inside the Organization

Many employees are eager to accept a promotion. Less commonly, employees welcome the variety of working in a new department or at a different task even when the transfer does not involve more money or prestige. These changes can be a source of motivation for employees.

Increased motivation is only one way the organization benefits from promotions and transfers. In addition, the promoted or transferred employees start the new job already familiar with the organization's policies and practices. It may be easier to train new people for entry-level jobs than to hire outsiders to fill more complex positions.

To find employees who are interested in and qualified for a vacant position, a supervisor or human resources department recruits within the organization. Internal recruitment is conducted in two basic ways: through job postings and employee referrals. A job posting is a list of the positions that are vacant in the organization. Typically, a job posting gives the title of the job, the department, and the salary range. In addition, a supervisor's employees may be able to recommend someone for the job—friends or relatives who do not currently work for the organization or qualified candidates they have met through trade or professional groups. Some organizations pay employees a bonus for referrals if the candidate is hired.

Looking Outside the Organization

A growing organization will especially need to look outside the organization for at least some of its employees. New hires are less familiar with the organization, but they bring fresh ideas and skills that the organization currently lacks. The basic ways to identify qualified candidates outside the organization are through advertising, employment agencies, and schools.

Help wanted advertisements are a popular way to recruit candidates for a job. Most people at some time or another read the want ads in their local newspapers to see what jobs are available. Organizations also can advertise in journals and magazines directed toward a specialized audience. For example, a research laboratory looking for a writer might advertise in *Technical Communications* and a manufacturer looking for an engineer to develop new products might advertise in *Design News.* Advertising in these kinds of specialized publications limits the recruiting to candidates with a background (or at least an interest) in the relevant field.

Employment agencies seek to match people looking for a job with organizations looking for employees. These agencies may be government run, in which

The Food Service Industry

Combating High Turnover by Hiring Right the First Time

Would you put off opening your restaurant for the lunchtime crowd because you couldn't find "the right people" to serve it? Richard Melman did. Melman heads Lettuce Entertain You Enterprises in Chicago, and he looks at the hiring decision this way: "If your average server waits on 30 people a night and that person works six nights a week, he or she will be dealing with 180 customers each week. If you don't have the right people in place, you're making a big mistake."

High turnover is a given in some industries, and the food industry is no exception. A recent survey by Food Industry News revealed that 71 percent of foodservice operators who responded said they had a hard time attracting and retaining people in whom they could have confidence. Consultant Wayne Outlaw says managers and supervisors need to ask themselves, "Where can I get employees?" in the same way they ask, "Where can I get customers?"

Outlaw believes the best source of valued employees is employee referral programs. "If the [referral] program is not working," he says, "it's either not being implemented properly, or you have to ask yourself, 'How happy are my employees?'"

Supervisors in firms of all kinds can take a hint from Paulette Brewer, owner of the landmark Green Barn Restaurant in Red Bluff, California. Brewer looks at résumés of prospective employees carefully, and she never hires without asking for a business reference and a personal reference to substantiate a candidate's integrity and dependability. Another suggestion comes from Outlaw, who says that asking employees to pitch in to fill a vacant slot while you look for a replacement creates the kind of extra burden that leads people to quit. "Managers need to be recruiting at all times," he advises, "even when fully staffed—and get enough notice to bring in the new employee."

Source: Polly M. LaHue, "Bad Attitude," *Restaurant Hospitality*, February 2001, pp. 30–36.

case they do not charge for their services, or private. Many private agencies charge the employer for locating an employee while some charge the person searching for a job. In either case, the agency collects a fee only when someone is hired. Using an agency makes sense when the organization lacks the time or expertise to carry out an effective recruiting effort. (In addition, organizations are increasingly relying on agencies to recruit all types of temporary employees.) Agencies also help screen candidates, a step in the selection process described in the next section.

Online recruiting is becoming more popular as a way to match candidates to jobs. Many firms find the ease of updating their help wanted ads to be a big advantage of the Internet, as well as the chance to reach job seekers all over the country at very little expense. Cisco Systems, IBM, Sprint, and Progressive Insurance are just a few of the large companies that include recruitment pages on their web sites.[3] There are also sites like Monster.com devoted exclusively to job listing. A recent survey by Inc. magazine revealed that about 60 percent of the computer-related companies in the Inc. 500 find Internet recruiting to be helpful, while among firms in industries such as consumer goods, telecommunications, and health care only 3 to 4 percent found it useful.[4]

Depending on the requirements of the job, a supervisor might want employees who recently have graduated from high school, a community college, a trade school, a prestigious university, or some other type of school. In such cases, the organization might seek job candidates through schools of the desired type. Large organizations that expect to hire many recent graduates sometimes send recruiters to talk to students at the targeted schools. Many schools also arrange various kinds of listings of employers who are interested in hiring. Recruiting through schools is a way to limit candidates to those with the desired educational background.

Humphrey Chen needed to hire employees for ConneXus, a service through which radio listeners can identify the titles and artists of songs using their cell phones. Chen took a novel route to recruiting through MIT, his alma mater. He e-mailed the head administrative assistant in the computer science department and asked her to mention some of ConneXus' current job openings in the next mass e-mail she sent to students alerting them to class and exam schedules. A week later, Chen had hired four MIT students, three as interns and one full-time.[5]

The Selection Process

In recent years, organizations typically have had many more candidates than they have needed to fill their vacant positions. Thus, once an organization has identified candidates for a job, it begins the major work: the selection process. Through this process, the supervisor and human resources department seek the person who is best qualified to fill a particular job. Figure 16.2 shows how the various steps in the selection process narrow the field of candidates. Usually the human resources department does the initial screening, and the supervisor makes the final decision.

■ FIGURE 16.2

The Selection Process

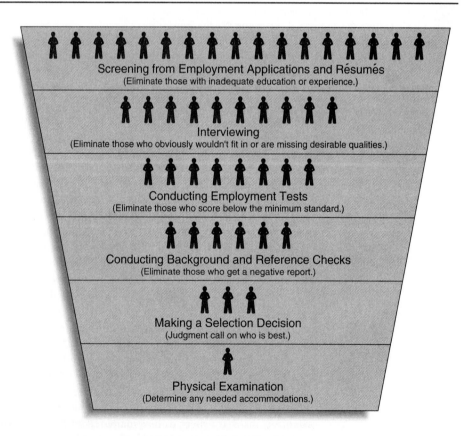

Screening from Employment Applications and Résumés
(Eliminate those with inadequate education or experience.)

Interviewing
(Eliminate those who obviously wouldn't fit in or are missing desirable qualities.)

Conducting Employment Tests
(Eliminate those who score below the minimum standard.)

Conducting Background and Reference Checks
(Eliminate those who get a negative report.)

Making a Selection Decision
(Judgment call on who is best.)

Physical Examination
(Determine any needed accommodations.)

Screening from Employment Applications and Résumés

Candidates for a job respond to recruitment by filling out an employment application or sending in a résumé. Figure 16.3 shows a sample employment application. The first stage of the selection process is to review the applications or résumés to screen out candidates who are unqualified or less qualified than others. The objective of screening is to narrow the pool of applicants to the number that the supervisor or human resources department wants to interview for the job.

Usually someone in the human resources department takes care of the screening process, comparing the applications or résumés with the job description prepared by the supervisor and eliminating the candidates who obviously fail to meet the qualifications called for in the job description.

Supervisors seldom participate actively in this process, but sometimes they know of a candidate that they would like to consider. In such cases, the name of this person is sent to the human resources department with the request that the person be included in the selection process. Rarely does the human resources department screen out a person that a supervisor wants included.

Interviewing Candidates

When the human resources department has narrowed the list of candidates to a few people, the next step is to interview them. Objectives of interviewing include narrowing the search for an employee by assessing each candidate's interpersonal and communication skills, seeing whether the supervisor and employee are comfortable with one another, and learning details about the information the candidate has provided on the application or résumé. In addition, each candidate has an opportunity to learn about the organization, which helps in the decision about accepting a job offer.

Learning and carrying out effective interviewing practices sometimes may seem like a lot of trouble to a supervisor. When tempted to look for shortcuts, a supervisor should bear in mind the significance of selection interviews. For any new employee, the organization will spend tens, maybe hundreds, of thousands of dollars on salary, benefits, and training. Thus, collecting the information needed for making the right hiring decision is at least as important as doing the research for making other investments of comparable size. Viewed in this light, carefully preparing for and conducting a selection interview is well worth the time and effort.

Patsy Moore-Talbott, a consultant for InterChange, a consulting and outplacement firm, offered this advice on interviewing. She suggests that interviewers and candidates both need to be prepared. "The interview needs to be more of a conversation and less of an interrogation. We need to find out who these people really are, instead of who they think we want them to be. So encourage them to tell you their stories. . . . But give them warning about the direction of the interview. Tell them to be prepared to discuss the times they were really excited. And ideally the process of preparing for the interview will help candidates get in touch with those things that excite them in work."[6]

Who Should Interview?   The initial interview with a job candidate frequently is conducted by someone in the human resources department. Depending on an organization's policies and practices, a supervisor may participate in later interviews. For this reason, a supervisor can benefit from understanding how to interview effectively.

FIGURE 16.3

Sample Employment Application

APPLICATION FOR EMPLOYMENT

(PRE-EMPLOYMENT QUESTIONNAIRE) (AN EQUAL OPPORTUNITY EMPLOYER)

PERSONAL INFORMATION

DATE

NAME (LAST / FIRST / MIDDLE) SOCIAL SECURITY NUMBER

PRESENT ADDRESS (STREET / CITY / STATE / ZIP)

PERMANENT ADDRESS (STREET / CITY / STATE / ZIP)

PHONE NO. ARE YOU 18 YEARS OR OLDER? Yes ☐ No ☐

ARE YOU EITHER A U.S. CITIZEN OR AN ALIEN AUTHORIZED TO WORK IN THE UNITED STATES? Yes ☐ No ☐

EMPLOYMENT DESIRED

POSITION DATE YOU CAN START SALARY DESIRED

ARE YOU EMPLOYED NOW? IF SO MAY WE INQUIRE OF YOUR PRESENT EMPLOYER?

EVER APPLIED TO THIS COMPANY BEFORE? WHERE? WHEN?

REFERRED BY

EDUCATION	NAME AND LOCATION OF SCHOOL	*NO OF YEARS ATTENDED	*DID YOU GRADUATE?	SUBJECTS STUDIED
GRAMMAR SCHOOL				
HIGH SCHOOL				
COLLEGE				
TRADE, BUSINESS OR CORRESPONDENCE SCHOOL				

LAST / FIRST / MIDDLE

GENERAL

SUBJECTS OF SPECIAL STUDY OR RESEARCH WORK

SPECIAL SKILLS

ACTIVITIES: (CIVIC, ATHLETIC, ETC.)

EXCLUDE ORGANIZATIONS, THE NAME OF WHICH INDICATES THE RACE, CREED, SEX, AGE, MARITAL STATUS, COLOR OR NATION OF ORIGIN OF ITS MEMBERS.

U.S. MILITARY OR NAVAL SERVICE RANK PRESENT MEMBERSHIP IN NATIONAL GUARD OR RESERVES

*The Age Discrimination in Employment Act of 1967 prohibits discrimination on the basis of age with respect to individuals who are at least 40 years of age.

TOPS FORM [illegible] (CONTINUED ON OTHER SIDE) LITHO IN U.S.A.

FORMER EMPLOYERS (LIST BELOW LAST THREE EMPLOYERS, STARTING WITH LAST ONE FIRST).

DATE MONTH AND YEAR	NAME AND ADDRESS OF EMPLOYER	SALARY	POSITION	REASON FOR LEAVING
FROM				
TO				
FROM				
TO				
FROM				
TO				
FROM				
TO				

WHICH OF THESE JOBS DID YOU LIKE BEST?

WHAT DID YOU LIKE MOST ABOUT THIS JOB?

REFERENCES: GIVE THE NAMES OF THREE PERSONS NOT RELATED TO YOU, WHOM YOU HAVE KNOWN AT LEAST ONE YEAR.

	NAME	ADDRESS	BUSINESS	YEARS ACQUAINTED
1				
2				
3				

THE FOLLOWING STATEMENT APPLIES IN: MARYLAND & MASSACHUSETTS. (Fill in name of state)
IT IS UNLAWFUL IN THE STATE OF ____________ TO REQUIRE OR ADMINISTER A LIE DETECTOR TEST AS A CONDITION OF EMPLOYMENT OR CONTINUED EMPLOYMENT. AN EMPLOYER WHO VIOLATES THIS LAW SHALL BE SUBJECT TO CRIMINAL PENALTIES AND CIVIL LIABILITY.

Signature of Applicant

IN CASE OF EMERGENCY NOTIFY (NAME / ADDRESS / PHONE NO.)

"I CERTIFY THAT THE FACTS CONTAINED IN THIS APPLICATION ARE TRUE AND COMPLETE TO THE BEST OF MY KNOWLEDGE AND UNDERSTAND THAT, IF EMPLOYED, FALSIFIED STATEMENTS ON THIS APPLICATION SHALL BE GROUNDS FOR DISMISSAL.

I AUTHORIZE INVESTIGATION OF ALL STATEMENTS CONTAINED HEREIN AND THE REFERENCES LISTED ABOVE TO GIVE YOU ANY AND ALL INFORMATION CONCERNING MY PREVIOUS EMPLOYMENT AND ANY PERTINENT INFORMATION THEY MAY HAVE, AND RELEASE ALL PARTIES FROM ALL LIABILITY FOR ANY DAMAGE THAT MAY RESULT FROM FURNISHING SAME TO YOU.

I UNDERSTAND AND AGREE THAT, IF HIRED, MY EMPLOYMENT IS FOR NO DEFINITE PERIOD AND MAY, REGARDLESS OF THE DATE OF PAYMENT OF MY WAGES AND SALARY, BE TERMINATED AT ANY TIME WITHOUT PRIOR NOTICE AND WITHOUT CAUSE."

DATE SIGNATURE

DO NOT WRITE BELOW THIS LINE

INTERVIEWED BY DATE

REMARKS:

NEATNESS ABILITY

HIRED: ☐ Yes ☐ No POSITION DEPT.

SALARY/WAGE DATE REPORTING TO WORK

APPROVED: 1. EMPLOYMENT MANAGER 2. DEPT. HEAD 3. GENERAL MANAGER

This form has been designed to strictly comply with State and Federal fair employment practice laws prohibiting employment discrimination. This Application for Employment Form is sold for general use throughout the United States. TOPS assumes no responsibility for the inclusion in said form of any questions which, when asked by the Employer of the Job Applicant, may violate State and/or Federal Law.

An organization may support the use of teamwork by having teams (or several team members) interview job candidates. According to James H. Shonk, president of the Team Center in Ridgefield, Connecticut, team input into the selection process can contribute to lower turnover among team members.[7] Team interviews also provide evidence of how a candidate interacts with a team. At Gates Rubber's plant in Siloam Springs, Arkansas, a job candidate meets first with the personnel department, then with a group of three people from different parts of the plant. Plant manager Burt Hoefs explains, "We're evaluating communications skills, work attitudes, and general confidence levels. Since all the work of the plant is done in teams, we're also focusing on an applicant's ability to respond well in a group setting."[8] When interviews are conducted by teams, a supervisor needs to combine skills in interviewing with skills in facilitating group processes (see Chapters 3 and 9).

Preparation for the Interview   To prepare for an interview, an interviewer should review the job description and develop a realistic way to describe the job to candidates. An interviewer also should review an applicant's résumé or job application, and consider whether the information given there suggests some specific questions to ask. Suppose the interviewer wants to know why a candidate chose a particular major in school or switched fields—say, leaving a job as a salesperson to become a mechanic. The interviewer also will want to inquire about any time gaps between jobs. Finally, the interviewer should arrange for an interview location that meets the conditions described in the next section.

Interview Conditions   Most job candidates feel at least a little nervous. This can make it hard for an interviewer to tell what a person would be like on the job. Therefore, it is important for an interviewer to conduct the interview under conditions that put a candidate at ease. Good interview conditions include privacy and freedom from interruptions. Seating should be comfortable. Some interviewers sit next to the candidate at a small table, rather than behind a desk, to create a less formal, more equal setting. Candidates also can be put at ease by offering them a cup of coffee and taking a minute or two for comments on a general, noncontroversial topic such as the weather.

Privacy is sometimes difficult for a supervisor to arrange. Many supervisors do not have an office with a door to close. If possible, a supervisor should arrange to use a conference room or someone else's office. At the very least, a supervisor interviewing in a cubicle should hang a Do Not Disturb sign outside.

Content of the Interview   After making the candidate comfortable, an interviewer should begin by asking general questions about the candidate's background and qualifications. An interviewer should also ask a candidate about his or her goals and expectations concerning the job. The following questions are among those most commonly asked[9]:

- Why do you want to work for our company?
- What kind of career do you have planned?
- What have you learned in school to prepare for a career?
- What are some of the things you are looking for in a company?
- How has your previous job experience prepared you for a career?
- What are your strengths? Weaknesses?
- Why did you attend this school?

■ FIGURE 16.4

The Interviewing Process

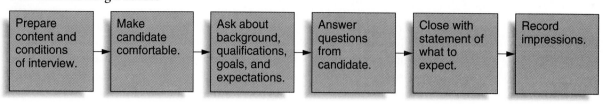

- What do you consider to be one of your most worthwhile achievements?
- Are you a leader? Explain.
- How do you plan to continue developing yourself?
- Why did you select your major?
- What can I tell you about my company?

When the interviewer has asked enough questions to gauge the candidate's suitability for the position, he or she should give the candidate a chance to ask questions. This not only can help the candidate learn more, but it can give the interviewer insight into the candidate's understanding and areas of concern.

The interviewer should close the session by telling the candidate what to expect regarding the organization's decision about the job, such as a telephone call in a week or a letter by the end of the month. As soon as the candidate has left, the interviewer should jot down notes of impressions about the candidate. Memories fade fast, especially when the interviewer meets many candidates. Figure 16.4 summarizes the steps in the interviewing process.

The questions an interviewer asks must be relevant to performance of the job. This means that an interviewer may not ask questions about the candidate's age, sex, race, marital status, children, religion, and arrest (as opposed to conviction) record. For example, an interviewer may not ask, "So, are you planning to have any children?" or "What nationality is that name?" Such questions violate antidiscrimination laws, described later in this chapter. Table 16.2 (on pages 425–426) identifies many permissible and impermissible questions. A supervisor who is in doubt about whether a particular question is allowable should check with the human resources department before asking it.

structured interview
An interview based on questions the interview has prepared in advance.

unstructured interview
An interview in which the interviewer has no list of questions prepared in advance but asks questions based on the applicant's responses.

Interviewing Techniques   The person who conducts the interview may choose to make it structured, unstructured, or a combination of the two. A **structured interview** is one based on questions an interviewer has prepared in advance. By referring to the list of questions, the interviewer covers the same material with each candidate. In an **unstructured interview,** an interviewer has no list of questions prepared in advance but thinks of questions based on an applicant's responses. An unstructured interview gives an interviewer more flexibility but makes it harder to be sure that each interview covers the same material.

A practical way to combine these two approaches is to prepare a list of questions that must be covered with each candidate. Then, an interviewer who wants the candidate to clarify a response to a particular question asks a follow-up question such as "Please tell me about your reasons for handling the problem that

■ TABLE 16.2

Permissible and Impermissible Questions for Selection Interviews

Category	Interviewer May Ask	Interviewer May Not Ask
Name	Current legal name; whether candidate has ever worked under another name	Maiden name; whether candidate has ever changed his or her name; preferred courtesy title (e.g., Ms., Miss, Mrs.)
Address	Current residence; length of residence	Whether candidate owns or rents home, unless it is a bona fide occupational qualification (BFOQ) for the job; name and relationship of person with whom applicant resides
Age	Whether the candidate meets a minimum age requirement set by law (e.g., being 21 to serve alcoholic beverages)	Candidate's age; to see a birth certificate; how much longer candidate plans to work before retiring; dates of attending elementary or high school; how applicant feels about working for a younger (or older) boss
Sex	Candidate's sex if it is a BFOQ (e.g., a model or restroom attendant)	Candidate's sex if it is not a BFOQ
Marital and family status	Whether the candidate can comply with the work schedule (must be asked of both sexes if at all)	Candidate's marital status; whether the candidate has or plans to have children; other family matters; information about child care arrangements; questions about who handles household responsibilities; whether candidate is seeking work just to supplement the household income
National origin, citizenship, race, color	Whether the candidate is legally eligible to work in the United States; whether the candidate can prove this, if hired	Candidate's national origin, citizenship, race, or color (or that of relatives); how candidate feels about working with or for people of other races
Language	List of languages the candidate speaks or writes fluently; whether the candidate speaks or writes a specific language if it is a BFOQ	Language the candidate speaks off the job; how the candidate learned a language
Arrests and convictions	Whether the candidate has been convicted of a felony; other information if the felony is job related	Whether the candidate has ever been arrested; information about a conviction that is not job related
Height and weight	No questions	Candidate's height or weight
Health history and disabilities	Whether the candidate is able to perform the essential functions of the job; how (with or without accommodation) the candidate can perform essential job functions	Whether the candidate is disabled or handicapped; how candidate became disabled; health history; whether the candidate smokes; whether the candidate has AIDS or is HIV positive
Religion	Whether the candidate is a member of a specific religious group when it is a BFOQ; whether the candidate can comply with the work schedules	Religious preference, affiliations, or denomination; name of applicant's priest, pastor, rabbi, or other religious leader

(continued)

█ TABLE 16.2
(*concluded*)

Category	Interviewer May Ask	Interviewer May Not Ask
Religion	Whether the candidate is a member of a specific religious group when it is a BFOQ; whether the candidate can comply with the work schedules	Religious preference, affiliations, or denomination; name of applicant's priest, pastor, rabbi, or other religious leader
Personal finances	Credit rating if it is a BFOQ	Candidate's credit rating; other information about personal finances, including assets, charge accounts; whether candidate owns a car
Education and work experience	Job-related education and experience	Education and experience that are not job related
References	Names of people willing to provide references; names of people who suggested that the candidate apply for the job	Reference from a religious leader
Military service	Information about job-related education and experience; whether candidate was dishonorably discharged	Dates and conditions of discharge; eligibility for military service; experience in foreign armed services
Organizations	List of memberships in job-related organizations such as unions or professional or trade associations	Memberships in any organizations that are not job related and would indicate race, religion, or other protected group; candidate's political affiliation

Sources: Richard D. Irwin, Inc., "Management Guidelines," Appendix 2, December 1, 1991; Robert N. Lussier, *Supervision: A Skill-Building Approach* (Homewood, IL: Irwin, 1989), pp. 254–55; and Janine S. Pouliot, "Topics to Avoid with Applicants," *Nation's Business*, July 1992, pp. 57–58; Gary Dessler, *Human Resource Management* (Upper Saddle River, NJ: Prentice Hall, 2000), p. 234.

way." An interviewer need not ask the questions in the order written so long as all of them are covered eventually. Based on a candidate's comments, an interviewer may want to move to a question further down on the list. Even though the format varies somewhat from candidate to candidate, this approach ensures that an interviewer does not omit important topics from some interviews.

open-ended question
A question that gives the person responding broad control over the response.

closed-ended question
A question that requires a simple answer, such as yes or no.

Within either a structured or an unstructured interview, an interviewer may ask questions that are open-ended or closed-ended. An **open-ended question** is one that gives the person responding broad control over the response. A **closed-ended question** is one that requires a simple answer, such as yes or no. An example of an open-ended question is "What experiences in your past job will help you carry out this one?" Examples of closed-ended questions are "Did you use a Macintosh computer on your last job?" and "Which shift do you prefer to work?"

Open-ended questions tend to be more useful in interviewing, because they lead a candidate to provide more information. For example, to learn how thoroughly a candidate has researched the job—an indication of how serious he or she is about the position—an interviewer might ask, "What would you look for if you were hiring a person for this position?" Loretta M. Flanagan, who directs Westside Future, an organization dedicated to reducing infant mortality, uses open-ended questions to learn about the human relations and problem-solving skills of job candidates. For example, she might pose this question to a candidate for a case worker position:

> A high, drug-using pregnant woman comes into the office, wanting immediate help. She has missed two previously scheduled appointments. The case manager is busy with another client and has a second client arriving in 20 minutes. How do you handle such competing demands?

Of course, there is no single correct answer. Flanagan looks for candidates who show an ability to set priorities and to justify the course of action selected.

Because the candidate decides how to answer an open-ended question, the answer sometimes is not clear enough or specific enough. Then, the interviewer will want to probe for more details, possibly saying, "Can you give me an example of that?" or "What do you mean when you say your last job was 'too stressful'?"

Problems to Avoid   When conducting an interview, a supervisor needs to avoid some common errors in judgment. One of these is making decisions based on personal biases. For example, a supervisor may dislike earrings on men or certain modish hairstyles worn by women. However, these characteristics are unlikely to indicate how well a candidate would carry out a job. Likewise, being a friend or relative of a supervisor is not a good predictor of job performance. Making a hiring decision based on these and other biases can lead an interviewer to exclude the person who is best qualified.

halo effect
The practice of forming an overall opinion on the basis of one outstanding characteristic.

Another source of errors is the **halo effect,** which means forming an overall opinion on the basis of one outstanding characteristic. For example, many people will evaluate someone's personality on the basis of the person's handshake. "She has a firm grasp," an interviewer might think with regard to a candidate. "I can tell that she's energetic, decisive, and gets along well with people," when the candidate might not have any of those desirable traits. An interviewer needs to look for evidence of each trait, not just lump them all together.

See "Tips from the Firing Line" for some suggestions for avoiding another common error, forming erroneous first impressions.

A supervisor also needs to avoid giving candidates a misleading picture of the organization. If a candidate seems desirable, it can be tempting to describe the organization in glowing terms so that the candidate will want to work there. But if the reality is not so wonderful, the new employee is bound to be disappointed and angry. He or she may even quit. On the other hand, within the bounds of realism, a supervisor should give a good impression of the organization and its people. Even a candidate who is not the best person for the job may someday be a customer or be in a position to influence other people's views about the organization.

Administering Employment Tests

From a résumé or employment application, it is relatively easy to see where a candidate worked and went to school, but how can you tell whether a candidate really has the skills to do the job? Just because Pete Wong works for the marketing division at a candy company does not mean he knows how to sell candy (maybe that is why he wants to leave). Just because Ruth Petersen got a college degree in engineering does not mean she can apply her knowledge to working with a team to prepare the layout of an actual plant.

Strategies for Countering First Impressions

Pierre Mornell is a psychiatrist, writer, and consultant in the field of executive selection. He believes that most of us form strong first impressions, often during the first 30 seconds of an interview, and that our personal biases affect these and later judgments that we make about job candidates. To try to ensure that our first impressions are as free of bias as possible, Mornell offers the following advice.

1. *Listen very carefully to the person's story.* Mornell suggests talking only 20 percent of the time during interviews and listening the other 80 percent. "To avoid the biggest mistake I see made in most interviews—that is, talking too much—I suggest that you ask *all* your questions up front," he suggests. Let the candidate do most of the talking.

2. *Make your questions count.* One question Mornell likes to ask job candidates is, "Do you have any questions for me?" That lets him know whether the person has done any research about the firm and can demonstrate a real interest in and knowledge of the job. He

also tells candidates, "The company will be checking your background. Will there be any surprises?" Keep questions simple and clear, Mornell advises, and of course, be aware of what is and isn't legal to ask.

3. *Think contrarily.* By this Mornell means considering opposites. For instance, if a candidate is focused on the past, he asks about the person about the present. If an applicant talks in generalities, he asks about specifics.

4. *Always check the candidate's past record.* Mornell advises *never* skimping on the background check, since the applicant's track record is a more important consideration in the hiring decision than personal biases or first impressions.

Source: *Inc.: The Magazine for Growing Companies* by Pierre Mornell. Copyright © 2000 by Business Innovator Group Resources/Inc. Reproduced with permission of Business Innovator Group Resources/Inc. via Copyright Clearance Center.

One way to see whether employees have the necessary skills is to administer an employment test. A variety of employment tests are available:

aptitude test
A test that measures a person's ability to learn skills related to the job.

proficiency test
A test that measures whether the person has the skills needed to perform a job.

psychomotor test
A test that measures a person's strength, dexterity, and coordination.

- A test that measures an applicant's ability to learn skills related to the job is known as an **aptitude test.**
- An applicant may take a **proficiency test** to see whether he or she has the skills needed to perform a job. An example is a word-processing test for a secretarial position.
- For jobs that require physical skills, such as assembling, an applicant may take a **psychomotor test,** which measures a person's strength, dexterity, and coordination.
- Sometimes organizations also use personality tests, which identify various personality traits. Psychologist Martin Seligman maintains that optimism is associated with successful performance of sales jobs. He tested his theory at MetLife by conducting an experiment in which the hiring of one group of salespeople was based on traditional measures, while that of another group was based on their high scores on a test measuring optimism. According to Seligman, the optimists outperformed not only the control group but also MetLife's entire sales force.[10]
- Finally, some organizations test for drug use, especially where the use of drugs by employees poses a serious safety risk, as in the case of machine operators or pilots. Such tests are controversial, but they are legal in most states.[11]

Usually the human resources department handles the testing of applicants.

The Wall Street Journal reports that some employers now are screening job applicants for their attitudes toward drug use, workplace violence, and sexual harassment. According to one industrial psychologist, traditional background checks can show only whether a prospective employee has a past history of abuses, while attitude testing is believed by some to indicate future tendencies. BTi Employee Screening Services, Inc., in Dallas, uses an attitude survey in its own hiring. John Pate, vice president of operations, told *The Wall Street Journal*, "You like to know what people are thinking. You don't want to hire your problems."[12]

Some tests contain language or other biases that make them easier for employees of one ethnic group than another. Using these tests could violate antidiscrimination laws, described later in this chapter. If a supervisor wants to use employment tests, the tests should be reviewed by the human resources department or an outside expert to ensure that they are not discriminatory.

Despite these restrictions, employers can be creative in devising employment tests. At Flash Creative Management, an information technology company, owner David Blumenthal instructs each job candidate to "check the company's references" by calling a list of customers and asking them what type of company Flash is. He then asks the companies to indicate their impression of the candidate—whether the person asked intelligent questions, whether the customer would like working with the candidate, and so on. Blumenthal believes this source of information is critical because each of Flash's employees has direct contact with clients. In addition, the process tests a candidate's willingness and ability to follow through with the assignment. An added benefit is that the practice communicates to a candidate the strength of Flash's commitment to customer service; a candidate who isn't interested in working for such a company can opt out during the selection process.[13]

Conducting Background and Reference Checks

It is a simple fact that many résumés and job applications contain false information. In a recent survey by the Society of Human Resource Management of its members, 90 percent of the respondents said they had discovered falsified information while checking a reference. At the top of the list of things job applicants lie about are their former employers, the length of time they worked there, their past salaries and titles, and their criminal records. According to one expert, "People put their best foot forward on their résumé, but on an application and in interviews, they often forget the image they constructed for themselves."[14]

A basic way to verify that the information on a job application or résumé is correct is to check references. Not only can checking an employee's background save the organization from hiring an unqualified person, but it can protect the organization from lawsuits. The courts have held employers responsible for crimes committed by an employee whose background at the time of hire was not investigated reasonably, with the result that the organization hired someone with a history of misdeeds for a position where he or she could do harm.[15]

A supervisor or a member of the human resources department may call or write to schools and former employers, or the organization may pay an employee screening company to do a background check. The relatively small fee to use one of these companies can be money well spent by an organization that is too small for a human resources staff.

Applicants may give several kinds of references:

- *Personal references*—people who will vouch for the applicant's character.
- *Academic references*—teachers or professors who can describe the applicant's performance in school.

Auditioning for a Job

Support Technologies Inc. is a firm that provides help desk services for corporations. In need of employees who can "hit the ground running," the firm decided to audition its prospective hires in typical situations with experienced employees and supervisors. It's a system that takes some time up front but saves supervisors time in the long run by ensuring that good workers are hired.

Here's what founder Cliff Oxford says about the audition process:

> Once we get serious about a candidate, we invite that person to spend a day with the whole company—working with us as we do our jobs. The two main things we're looking for: Is [the candidate] willing to speak out, to challenge the status quo? Will [he or she] fit in?
>
> A typical situation runs like this: For most of the morning, a candidate might work with our help desk professionals—our front line—as they field calls.

This is not the most glamorous work, but it's who we are. The last thing we want is to hire someone who's indifferent to service.

Later this person might work with a marketing or sales executive—maybe going over marketing strategy or brainstorming about some marketing collateral. Most of all, we're looking for opinions, criticism, and concrete solutions to problems. Finally, the person might sit in on a senior-management meeting. There can be a lot of passion in those meetings. We encourage conflict. We ask, Does this candidate jump into the fray?

At the end of the audition, we do an informal survey about reactions to the candidate. We come to a consensus fast. We've hired some great people who have made a big difference, and we've managed to avoid some potential disasters.

Source: Cathy Olofson, "Hire Fast, but Audition First," *Inc.*, December 1998, p. 52.

- *Employment references*—former employers who can verify the applicant's work history.

Most people can think of a friend or teacher who can say something nice about them, so the main use of personal and academic references is to screen out the few cases of people who cannot do so.

Previous employers are in the best position to discuss how an applicant performed in the past. However, to avoid lawsuits from former employees, many organizations have a policy of giving out very little information about past employees. Often a background check will yield only that the applicant did in fact hold the stated position during the dates indicated. Some employers may be willing to discuss the applicant's performance, salary, promotions, and demotions. Because previous employers are cautious about what they disclose, a telephone call to a former supervisor may be more fruitful than a written request for information. People are sometimes willing to make off-the-record statements over the telephone that they will not commit to writing.

Making the Selection Decision

The final decision of whom to hire is usually up to the supervisor. Typically, more than one person will survive all the preceding steps of the screening process. As a result, the final decision is usually a judgment call. One firm "auditions" promising candidates; see "Meeting the Challenge."

A supervisor can handle the dilemma of several well-qualified people being considered for a position by looking for additional relevant selection criteria. In practice, skillful hiring decisions often reflect a variety of issues, from how the decision will be perceived by higher-level managers to how comfortable a supervisor feels with the candidate.[16] Supervisors sometimes choose an employee like themselves, so they will feel comfortable; they also might select a person whose strengths differ from and thus balance their own strengths. A supervisor can improve his or her selections by applying the principles of effective decision making covered in Chapter 9.

When a supervisor has selected the candidate to hire, the human resources department or supervisor offers the job to the candidate. The person who offers the job is responsible for negotiating pay and fringe benefits and for settling on a starting date. If none of the candidates a supervisor has identified seem satisfactory, no candidate has to be picked and the recruiting process can be repeated. Perhaps the organization can look in new places or try to attract better candidates by offering more money.

Requesting a Physical Examination

In the past, many organizations have required that job candidates pass a physical examination. However, since Congress passed the Americans with Disabilities Act (described later in this chapter), experts have advised that employers request a physical exam only after a job offer is made.[17] A physical examination after the job offer helps the organization determine whether the person is physically able to fulfill job requirements, yet the timing of the exam reduces the risk that someone will sue the company for refusing to hire him or her because of a disability. Another use of the physical exam is to determine whether the person is eligible for any life, health, and disability insurance that the company offers as benefits.

An illness, disability, or pregnancy may not be used as the basis for denying a person a job unless it makes the person unable to perform the essential functions of the job. If a physical examination suggests a condition that may interfere with the person's ability to perform these essential functions, the company—very likely someone in the human resources department—should ask the candidate how it can adapt the equipment or job to accommodate that person. Because of these limitations on the use of information from physical examinations, most organizations will want the human resources department to handle the exams and the issue of how to accommodate employees with disabilities. A supervisor can then focus on a candidate's experience and talents.

Legal Issues

Congress has passed laws that restrict employment decisions. Most of these laws are designed to give people fair and equal access to jobs based on their skills, not on their personal traits such as race or physical disabilities. Whatever a supervisor's role in selecting employees, he or she must be aware of the laws affecting hiring in order to help ensure that the organization's actions are legal.

Antidiscrimination Laws

Certain federal laws prohibit various types of employment discrimination.

- Under Title VII of the Civil Rights Act of 1964 (commonly known as Title VII), employers may not discriminate on the basis of race, color, religion, sex, or

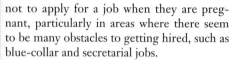

Expectant Job Seekers

The woman who interviewed Marie Pusateri for a supervisory job at an Internet communications company probably remembers her clearly. Marie was six months pregnant at the time and, fearful that she might be discriminated against, she carried her coat in front of her all the time. As last, however, she admitted she was pregnant, and the interviewer replied, "No problem. I'm pregnant, too."

Pregnant women do not always find such a straightforward welcome in hiring situations. Although federal law prohibits discrimination against expectant mothers, the Equal Employment Opportunity Commission receives between 3,000 and 4,000 complaints about such behavior a year. Some women feel that they risk not getting a job offer if they try to evade or challenge illegal questions about whether they are pregnant. And some women simply decide not to apply for a job when they are pregnant, particularly in areas where there seem to be many obstacles to getting hired, such as blue-collar and secretarial jobs.

Martha Baker, whose nonprofit group for women, Non-Traditional Employment for Women, trains and places women in industries like plumbing and heavy equipment, says she does not counsel pregnant women not to interview, but that most women in the program come to that decision on their own. Perhaps that is one reason why working women who become pregnant often decide to remain in their current jobs.

Source: Ingrid Eisenstadter, "Yes, I'll Take a Seat, and the Job Offer, Too" *New York Times*, March 18, 1998, Business section, p. 12.

Equal Employment Opportunity Commission (EEOC) The federal government agency charged with enforcing Title VII of the Civil Rights Act.

national origin in recruiting, hiring, paying, firing, or laying off employees, or in any other employment practices. The government agency charged with enforcing this law is the **Equal Employment Opportunity Commission (EEOC).** The EEOC investigates charges of discrimination and may pursue a remedy in court or arrange for mediation (which means an impartial third party hears both sides and decides how to resolve the dispute).

- The Age Discrimination in Employment Act of 1967, as amended in 1978 and 1986, prohibits employers from discriminating on the basis of age against people over 40 years old.

- The Rehabilitation Act of 1973 makes it illegal to refuse a job to a disabled person because of the disability, if the disability does not interfere with the person's ability to do the job.

- The Pregnancy Discrimination Act of 1978 makes it unlawful to discriminate on the basis of pregnancy, childbirth, or related medical conditions. A job applicant recently won a ruling against Wal-Mart for its failure to hire her because she was pregnant.[18] Supervisors should be aware that while such cases are quite rare, they can occur. See "Supervision and Diversity" for more information.

- Disabled veterans and veterans of the Vietnam War receive protection under the Vietnam Era Veterans Readjustment Act of 1974, which requires federal contractors to make special efforts to recruit these people. (This is a type of affirmative action, described shortly.) In deciding whether a veteran is qualified, an employer may consider the military record only to the extent it is directly related to the specific qualifications of the job.

Figure 16.5 illustrates the categories of workers protected by the antidiscrimination laws.

Although some people criticize these laws as a burden on employers, bear in mind that organizations should benefit from making employment decisions on the

FIGURE 16.5

Categories of Workers Protected by Antidiscrimination Law

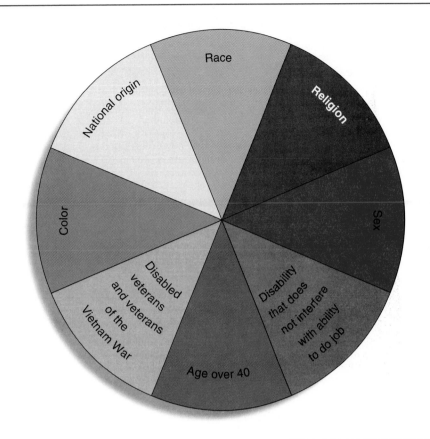

basis of people's knowledge, skills, and abilities instead of incidental personal traits such as race, age, or sex.

As the managers of many organizations have observed the growing diversity of the workforce and their customers, they have decided that simply avoiding discrimination is too limited a policy. They have adopted policies called "managing diversity." A report by the Society of Human Resource Managers and Commerce Clearing House defined managing diversity as "the management of an organization's culture and systems to ensure that all people are given the opportunity to contribute to the business goals of the company."[19] At an organization that effectively manages diversity, managers and employees create a climate in which all employees feel respected and able to participate.

Managing diversity implies that the organization is hiring and promoting a variety of people. For this and other purposes, many organizations have established affirmative action programs. **Affirmative action** refers to plans designed to increase opportunities for groups that traditionally have been discriminated against. In effect, these plans are an active attempt to promote diversity in the organization, not just to treat everyone the same way. See "Supervision and Diversity" in Chapter 1 for some perspective on the issue of affirmative action and recent challenges to the concept.

Some people mistakenly think that affirmative action means setting up artificial quotas that favor some groups at the expense of others. However, organizations can increase opportunities in other ways. Besides using training to create a

affirmative action
Plans designed to increase opportunities for groups that traditionally have been discriminated against.

TABLE 16.3 **Disability Status under the Americans with Disabilities Act**	**"Disability" Includes**	**"Disability" Does Not Include**
	Substantial limitation preventing a person from conducting a major life activity	Cultural and economic disadvantages
	Physical and mental impairments	Common personality traits, such as impatience
	History of using drugs as the result of an addiction	Pregnancy
	Severe obesity (weight in excess of 100 percent of the norm or that arises from a medical disorder)	Normal deviations in weight, height, or strength
		Temporary or short-term problems
		Illegal drug users disciplined for current abuse
		Illegal drug use that is casual (not related to addiction)

Note: People with disabilities are protected from employment discrimination only to the extent that their disability does not prevent them from performing the essential functions of the job.

Source: From "What Constitutes a Disability?" *Nation's Business,* June 1995, U.S. Chamber of Commerce.

pool of qualified applicants, some companies make a point of doing some of their recruiting at schools where many students are members of racial minorities.

Recent ballot initiatives in California and Washington aim to curtail affirmative action programs in hiring by state and local governments. People who favor affirmative action policies argue that because several candidates often have the qualifications to fill any given job, intentionally giving some jobs to people from disadvantaged groups is not only ethical but supports the achievement of the benefits related to diversity. Whatever your opinion of affirmative action, it is important to note that—except for employers that have federal contracts or subcontracts—organizations are not required by law to set up these programs. Rather, affirmative action programs are one possible response to laws against discrimination.

Workplace Accessibility

In 1990 Congress passed the Americans with Disabilities Act (ADA), which prohibits employers with more than 15 employees from discriminating on the basis of mental or physical disability in hiring and promotion. A person who can perform the essential functions of a job may not be prevented from doing so simply because the person has a mental or physical disability. Table 16.3 summarizes criteria for disability status under the ADA. Organizations also must avoid discrimination in public accommodations, transportation, government services, and telecommunications.

One benefit to organizations that comply with the ADA is that it encourages employers to take advantage of a large pool of potential workers whose talents are often ignored. The National Organization on Disability estimates that 70 percent of the nation's 49 million disabled people are unemployed.[20] But more and more companies, including Charles Schwab, Ford Motor, Honeywell, Johnson & Johnson, and Wells Fargo, are finding out why a 30-year study by DuPont showed that the job performance of disabled workers was equal to or better than that of their fully functioning peers. When quadriplegic Chris Harmon applied for a job at Crestar Bank, the recruiter who hired him had to put a pen in his mouth for him so he could sign the job application. But now that he has been hired as a telephone customer service representative, Harmon uses voice-activated technology to operate his computer and bring the information he needs to the screen. No one calling the bank ever realizes that he is disabled.[21]

Accommodations for Employees with Disabilities   To comply with the ADA, employers must make accommodations for employees with disabilities if the necessary accommodations are "readily achievable"that is, easy to carry out and possible to accomplish without much difficulty or expense. Businesses may receive a tax credit of up to $15,000 to help offset the cost of making their establishments accessible.

This law extends beyond wheelchair accessibility to require accommodations for any eligible disabled employee, including those with impaired sight and hearing, arthritis, high blood pressure, hearing impairment, and heart disease. Thus, accommodations might include door handles that are easy to manipulate and TDD telephones for hearing-impaired employees. For employees with mental disabilities, appropriate accommodations may include the following measures[22]:

- Modifications to work areas to permit maximum concentration and minimum distraction.
- Flexible schedules to counteract fatigue (e.g., longer and more frequent rest breaks).
- Time off to receive treatment for the disability.

In addition, organizations can head off many problems related to mental disabilities by making extra coaching and counseling available to employees as needed.

A number of ways to accommodate disabled workers draw on communication technology. Chris Sullivan runs the first investment service for deaf and hard-of-hearing investors at Merril Lynch's Plainsboro, New Jersey, offices. Deaf since infancy, he devised a way to use a TTY, or telephone teletypewriter, to enable specially trained operators to act as go-betweens in phone calls between deaf and hearing people. Brian Dickinson writes his newspaper column in Rhode Island with the help of the Eyegaze computer, which uses a special camera and computer keyboard to allow him to write using only his eyes. Amyotrophic lateral sclerosis (Lou Gehrig's disease) has left him unable to use any other part of his body.[23]

What Supervisors Can Do   Supervisors can take several steps to comply with the ADA. One is to review and revise job descriptions.[24] Because an organization cannot discriminate against those who can perform the essential functions of the job, each job description should indicate what is essential. It should focus on the results the employee must achieve instead of the process for achieving those results. For example, a job description for a telephone lineworker might say "Repair telephone lines located at the top of a pole" but not "Climb telephone poles." In addition, supervisors should make sure that production standards are reasonable; current employees should meet those standards.

When interviewing candidates, a supervisor should be careful not to ask whether they have a physical or mental condition that would prevent them from performing the job. Rather, after making a job offer, the organization will seek to accommodate any impairments the person may have. Similarly, the supervisor should not ask for candidates' health history, including any on-the-job injuries that candidates have suffered.

Immigration Reform and Control Act

By passing the Immigration Reform and Control Act (IRCA) of 1986, Congress gave employers responsibility for helping to discourage illegal immigration. IRCA forbids employers to hire illegal immigrants and requires them to screen candidates to make sure that they are authorized to work in the United States. At the same time, however, employers may not use these requirements as a rationale for discriminating against candidates because they look or sound "foreign."

This means that the employer must verify the identity and work authorization of *every* new employee. To do this, the employer can ask each new employee to show such documentation as a valid U.S. passport, unexpired Immigration Authorization Service document, unexpired work permit, birth certificate, driver's license, or social security card.[25] In large organizations, this law primarily affects the human resources department, giving it an extra task in the hiring process. In small organizations, however, a supervisor may be responsible for verifying that all his or her new employees are authorized to work in the United States.

Summary

16.1   Discuss common roles for supervisors in the selection process.

In most cases, a supervisor works with a human resources department in the selection process. If the organization depends on teams, a supervisor might try to identify candidates who are cooperative and skilled in problem solving or who have helped a team achieve good results in the past. If a team is making the selection, the supervisor as team leader needs to understand the principles of selection so that he or she can coach employees in carrying out the selection process. A supervisor also prepares job descriptions and job specifications, consulting with the human resources department as needed.

16.2   Distinguish between job descriptions and job specifications, and explain how they help in selecting employees.

A job description is a listing of the characteristics of the job—observable activities required to carry out the job. A job specification is a listing of characteristics desirable in the person performing the job. The two forms help show how well each candidate matches the job requirements.

16.3   List possible sources of employees.

An organization may recruit inside and outside the organization. Current employees may be promoted or transferred to fill job openings, or they may recommend people for jobs at the organization. Outside the organization, employees can be recruited through help wanted advertisements, employment agencies, and schools.

16.4   Identify the steps in the selection process.

Based on employment applications or résumés, the staff of the human resources department screens out unqualified candidates. Next, the human resources department or the supervisor interviews candidates. An organization may administer employment tests. Background and reference checks are conducted on candidates in whom the organization is still interested. A supervisor makes a selection decision, after which a candidate may be asked to take a physical examination.

16.5   Discuss how a supervisor should go about interviewing candidates for a job.

First, a supervisor should prepare for the interview by reviewing the job description and each applicant's résumé or job application, planning questions, and arranging for a place to conduct the interview that offers privacy and freedom from interruptions. When a candidate arrives, a supervisor should make him or her comfortable and then ask about the candidate's goals and expectations for the job. Questions must be relevant to performance of the job and should include both open-ended and closed-ended questions. The interviewer should avoid making common errors in judgment, such as personal biases, or offering misleading information about the organization. Then a candidate should have a chance to ask questions. A supervisor should close the interview by telling a candidate what to expect. As soon as the candidate leaves, the supervisor should make notes of his or her impressions.

16.6 Define types of employment tests.
Aptitude tests measure a person's ability to learn job-related skills. Proficiency tests measure whether a person has the skills needed to perform a job. Psychomotor tests measure strength, dexterity, and coordination. Personality tests identify personality traits. Some organizations also test for drug use. Physical examinations may be required after a job offer is made.

16.7 Summarize the requirements of antidiscrimination laws.
The organization, including the supervisor, must avoid actions that discriminate on the basis of race, color, religion, sex, national origin, age over 40 years, or physical or mental disability, including pregnancy-related disabilities. These laws apply to recruiting, hiring, paying, firing, and laying off employees and to any other employment practice. In addition, federal contractors and subcontractors must use affirmative action to encourage the employment of minorities and veterans of the Vietnam War. When evaluating veterans' qualifications, an employer may use only the portions of the military record that are related to job requirements.

16.8 Explain how hiring decisions are affected by the Americans with Disabilities Act (ADA).
The ADA prohibits discrimination on the basis of mental or physical disability against people who can perform the essential functions of a job. Instead, employers must make accommodations for employees with disabilities if the necessary accommodations are readily achievable. To comply with the law, supervisors should review and revise job descriptions to make sure they indicate what functions of the job are essential. When interviewing candidates, a supervisor should avoid asking about disabilities and a candidate's health history.

16.9 Describe the requirements of the Immigration Reform and Control Act (IRCA) of 1986.
Under IRCA, employers are responsible for helping to discourage illegal immigration. They may not hire people who are not authorized to work in the United States, yet they may not discriminate against people who simply appear to be foreigners. Thus, employers must verify the identity and work authorization of every new employee.

Key Terms

job description, p. 416

job specification, p. 416

recruitment, p. 418

structured interview, p. 424

unstructured interview, p. 424

open-ended question, p. 426

closed-ended question, p. 426

halo effect, p. 427

aptitude test, p. 428

proficiency test, p. 428

psychomotor test, p. 428

Equal Employment Opportunity Commission (EEOC), p. 432

affirmative action, p. 433

Review and Discussion Questions

1. Think of your current job or a job you recently held. Write a job description and a job specification for the job. How well do (or did) you match the requirements of the job?

2. A business executive said that people tend to make the mistake of hiring in their own image. What does this mean? How does this tendency make it more difficult for an organization to build a diverse workforce?

3. In recruiting for each of the following positions, what source or sources of candidates would you recommend using? Explain your choices.
   a. A receptionist for a city government office.
   b. A printing press operator.

    c. A graphic artist for an advertising agency.

    d. A nurse for an adult day care facility.

4. Describe what happens during the screening process. What does the human resources department look for when reading employment applications and résumés?

5. Supervisor Lisa Kitzinger is interviewing candidates for a computer operator job. Lisa works in a cubicle, and she has a secretary who could help during the interview process. What can Lisa do to put candidates at ease?

6. Which of the following questions is (are) appropriate for a job interview for the position of office manager for an automobile dealership?

    a. Do you attend church regularly?

    b. Do you know how to use our computer and telecommunications systems?

    c. Are you familiar with our line of cars?

    d. Are you married?

    e. Aren't you close to retirement age?

    f. What skills did you develop at your previous job that you feel would be helpful in this job?

7. How can an interviewer combine the techniques of the structured and unstructured interview?

8. Donald Menck, the supervisor on a boatbuilding line, interviews a male job candidate who comes to the interview dressed in a jacket and tie. Menck is surprised by the candidate's clothing, which is more formal than what is needed on the job; he is also impressed. He assumes that the candidate is intelligent and motivated. What common error in judgment is Menck making? What steps should he take during the interview to overcome it?

9. An airline has a policy that all its employees must receive a physical examination before they start working for the company. At what point in the selection process should the company request the examination? How may the airline use this information?

10. Which of the following actions would be considered discriminatory under federal laws? Explain your answers.

    a. A company creates a policy that all employees must retire by age 65.

    b. A supervisor gives the biggest raises to men, because they have families to support.

    c. A company that recruits at colleges and universities makes at least 20 percent of its visits to schools that are historically black.

    d. In a department where employees must do a lot of overtime work on Saturdays, a supervisor avoids hiring Jews because Saturday is their day of rest and worship.

11. Joel Trueheart supervises customer service representatives for a toy company. The employees handle complaints and questions from customers calling the company's toll-free telephone number. To fill a vacancy in the department, Joel has reviewed many résumés and is in the process of interviewing a few candidates. One of the most impressive résumés is that of Sophia Ahmad, but when Joel meets her, he is startled to observe that she is blind. What should Joel do to make sure he is complying with the Americans with Disabilities Act?

12. What steps must employers take to ensure that they are complying with the Immigration Reform and Control Act?

A SECOND LOOK

What kinds of hiring questions do you think Tower Records' human resource trainers are concerned about? Construct your own list of permissible interview questions for a Tower supervisor.

SKILLS MODULE

CASE

Peer Interviews

Peer interviewing has become a standard practice when hiring nurses at Children's Hospital Medical Center (CHMC) in Cincinnati, Ohio. Before beginning, a pilot project was initiated to try out peer interviewing. All interviewers were required to participate in a half-day workshop. The workshop included an overview of the selection process, legal aspects of interviewing, the Americans with Disabilities Act preemployment inquiry requirements, and techniques for interviewing and selecting candidates. Workshop participants reviewed sample applications, résumés, and videotaped vignettes of mock interviews.

An interview process record delineated the sequence of events in the interview process, and tracked the interviewer-applicant pairs and dates of interviews. A Clinical Nurse Interview Summary Tool provided a succinct format to evaluate each candidate's abilities in four areas: general, clinical practice, communication skills, and professional practice. The manager and peer interviewer completed the summary tool, which is used to compare applicants. Sample questions covered the four areas evaluated on the summary tool and provided a starting place for interview comment. Emphasis is placed on individualizing these sample questions within each department.

Qualifications for peer interviewers, determined by peer selection committee members, include:

- Current employment as a clinical nurse.
- A minimum of one year's experience in the department.
- Performance that reflected advanced clinical skills and a commitment to family-centered care.
- Well-developed communication skills, including the ability to promote positive interpersonal relationships.
- A positive representative of clinical nursing and the department's shared governance philosophy.
- An expressed interest in the project.

Six months into the project, 10 new employees were surveyed. Newly hired nurses stated the advantages of peer interviewing: getting a staff perspective of the unit, getting to know the staff, feeling more confident and comfortable with the unit, receiving a better understanding of nursing on the unit, and feeling welcome and important.

Peer interviewers felt that being part of the selection process fostered cohesiveness and team building. They were able to review the application several hours or days before the interview, interview the applicant, and discuss the candidate with the manager after the interview. The peer interviewers identified two difficulties: preparing for an interview in the middle of a patient care day and having one open position and several qualified candidates.

Twenty nurses were tracked for a year following their date of hire; only one of the newly hired nurses has terminated her employment. All departments at CHMC now have clinical nurses prepared as peer interviewers. The project committee continues to meet and refine the peer interviewing process.

1. What accounts for the successful retention rate of newly hired nurses in the peer interviewing program at CHMC?
2. Are there any ways the process might be improved? How can nursing supervisors help overcome the two problems cited by the peer interviewers?
3. How would you apply the positive features of the hospital's peer interview program to another industry in which you have some experience?

Source: From Susan R. Allen et al., "Peer Interviewing: Sharing the Selection Process," *Nursing Management*, March 1998, p. 46. Reprinted with permission of Lippincott Williams & Wilkins.

■ SELF-QUIZ

Would You Hire You?

One of the criteria supervisors look for in a job candidate is a good fit with the company culture. Use this quiz to determine what you value in your own work environment, and you'll have a better idea what kind of firm might want to hire you.

The 54 items below cover the full range of personal and institutional values you'd be likely to encounter at any company. Divide the list of items into the 27 choices that would be evident in your ideal workplace, and the 27 that would be least evident. Keep dividing the groups in half until you can rank-order them, and then fill in the numbers of your top and bottom 10 choices in the space provided. Test your fit in a hiring situation by seeing whether the company's values match your top and bottom 10.

Your top 10 choices:

_____ _____ _____ _____ _____ _____ _____ _____ _____ _____

Your bottom 10 choices:

_____ _____ _____ _____ _____ _____ _____ _____ _____ _____

The Choice Menu
You are:

1. Flexible
2. Adaptable
3. Innovative
4. Able to seize opportunities
5. Willing to experiment
6. Risk taker
7. Careful
8. Autonomy seeker
9. Comfortable with rules
10. Analytical
11. Attentive to detail
12. Precise
13. Team oriented
14. Ready to share information
15. People oriented
16. Easygoing
17. Calm
18. Supportive
19. Aggressive
20. Decisive
21. Action oriented
22. Eager to take initiative
23. Reflective
24. Achievement oriented
25. Demanding
26. Comfortable with individual responsibility
27. Comfortable with conflict
28. Competitive
29. Highly organized
30. Results oriented
31. Interested in making friends at work
32. Collaborative
33. Eager to fit in with colleagues
34. Enthusiastic about job

Your company offers:

35. Stability
36. Predictability
37. High expectations of performance
38. Opportunities for professional growth
39. High pay for good performance
40. Job security
41. Praise for good performance

42. A clear guiding philosophy
43. A low level of conflict
44. An emphasis on quality
45. A good reputation
46. Respect for the individual's rights
47. Tolerance
48. Informality
49. Fairness

50. A unitary culture throughout the organization
51. A sense of social responsibility
52. Long hours
53. Relative freedom from rules
54. The opportunity to be distinctive, or different from others

Source: From Matt Siegel, "The Perils of Culture Conflict," *Fortune*, November 9, 1998. Copyright © 1998 Time, Inc. All rights reserved.

Class Exercise

This chapter has covered the steps involved in making sound employee selection decisions. Finding employees who have the necessary skills to meet today's workplace challenges is not an easy task. Most organizations are facing similar challenges: adapting to technological changes, improving quality, dealing with workforce diversity, reorganizing work around teams, and empowering employees at all levels to improve customer service. This exercise focuses on the skills employers are looking for in today's job candidates, and it provides practice in developing interview questions that will help you in your evaluation of prospective employees.

Instructions:
1. Study Table 1.
2. Match the letter of each specific skill from Table 1 with the appropriate descriptor in Table 2. (Each answer will be used only once. The first two answers have been done for you in the left-hand column.)
3. In the space after each descriptor in Table 2, write an interview question to ask job candidates that will give you insight into their abilities in each area; assume you are interviewing job candidates to fill a job as bank teller. (The first two are already filled in, to give you an idea of some sample questions.)

■ TABLE 1 Sixteen Job Skills Crucial to Success		
Category of Skill	**Specific Skills in Each Category**	
Foundation Competence	*a*	Knowing how to learn
	b	Reading
	c	Writing
	d	Computation
Communication	*e*	Listening
	f	Oral communication
Adaptability	*g*	Creative thinking
	h	Problem solving
Personal management	*i*	Self-esteem
	j	Goal setting and motivation
	k	Personal/career development
Group effectiveness	*l*	Interpersonal skills
	m	Negotiation
	n	Teamwork
Influence	*o*	Organizational effectiveness
	p	Leadership

Source: Adapted from Anthony P. Carnevale, *America and the New Economy*, 1991, Jossey-Bass.

■ TABLE 2

Descriptors of Specific Skills

Answer	Descriptor and Interview Question
i	1. Employers want employees who have pride in themselves and their potential to be successful. *Question: Can you describe a task or project you completed in your last job that you were particularly proud of?*
h	2. Employers want employees who can think on their feet when faced with a dilemma. *Question: If you had a customer return to your teller window and claim, in a rather loud and irritated voice, that you had made a mistake, how would you handle the situation?*
	3. Employers want employees who can assume responsibility and motivate co-workers when necessary. *Question:*

Answer	Descriptor and Interview Question
	4. Employers want employees who will hear the key points that make up a customer's concerns. *Question:*
	5. Employers want employees who can learn the particular skills of an available job. *Question:*
	6. Employers want employees who can resolve conflicts to the satisfaction of those involved. *Question:*
	7. Employers want employees who have some sense of the skills needed to perform well in their current jobs and who are working to develop skills to qualify themselves for other jobs. *Question:*
	8. Employers want employees with good mathematics skills. *Question:*
	9. Employers want employees who can work with others to achieve a goal. *Question:*
	10. Employers want employees who can convey an adequate response when responding to a customer's concerns. *Question:*
	11. Employers want employees who have some sense of where the organization is headed and what they must do to make a contribution. *Question:*

(*continued*)

TABLE 2
(concluded)

Answer	Descriptor and Interview Question
	12. Employers want employees who can come up with innovative solutions when needed. *Question:*
	13. Employers want employees who can clearly and succinctly articulate ideas in writing. *Question:*
	14. Employers want employees who know how to get things done and have the desire to complete tasks. *Question:*
	15. Employers want employees who can get along with customers, suppliers, and co-workers. *Question:*
	16. Employers want employees to be analytical, to summarize information, and to monitor their own comprehension of the reading task. *Question:*

Source: The class exercise was prepared by Corinne Livesay, Belhaven College, Jackson, Mississippi.

Team-Building Exercise

Role Playing the Selection Process

This exercise simulates an abbreviated version of the selection process. Imagine that the manager of a family-style restaurant such as Denny's needs to hire a server. Working together, the class develops a job description and job specification. The instructor records them on the chalkboard or overhead projector. When in doubt about the details, class members should use their imaginations. The objective is for the class to agree that these two lists are reasonable and complete.

When the job description and job specification are complete, the class develops a list of interview questions that would indicate whether a candidate is appropriate for this job. Besides creating questions to ask, the class also might consider other ways to determine this information during an interview (e.g., observing some aspects of the candidates' behavior).

Next, four class members take on the following parts for a role play:

1. Restaurant manager.
2. Candidate 1: a college student with eagerness but no restaurant experience.
3. Candidate 2: a woman who appears to be about 60 years old and who had eight years' experience as a server during the 1960s.
4. Candidate 3: a man with four years' experience as a server in five different restaurants.

The class members taking these roles should feel free to add details to these descriptions of "themselves." The person acting as the restaurant manager interviews each candidate for no more than five minutes each. (A real interview would probably last much longer.)

The role-playing interviews could be videotaped and then played back during the discussion.

Finally, the class discusses one or both of these topics:

1. *Selecting a candidate:* By a show of hands, the class votes for which candidate they would recommend hiring. What are your reasons for choosing that particular candidate?

2. *Interviewing techniques:*
   - Did the restaurant manager interview objectively, based on the criteria determined at the beginning of the exercise?
   - Did the interview cover all the important points?
   - Did the manager use open-ended or closed-ended questions?
   - How did the manager's style of questioning help or hurt the information-gathering process?
   - Did the candidates have a chance to ask questions?
   - Did the manager obey the antidiscrimination laws?
   - How did the interviewing experience feel to the candidates? To the manager?

17

If you believe in training and developing people, you don't necessarily need a huge training budget. . . . You start with your own behavior.

—Jeffrey Pfeffer, professor, Stanford University Graduate School of Business

Providing Orientation and Training

■ CHAPTER OUTLINE

Orientation of New Employees
Benefits of Orientation
The Supervisor's Role
Orientation Topics
Orientation Methods

Training
The Training Cycle
Assessment of Training Needs
Types of Training

Coaching to Support Training

Evaluation of Training

■ LEARNING OBJECTIVES

After you have studied this chapter, you should be able to:

17.1 Summarize reasons for conducting an orientation for new employees.

17.2 Discuss how a supervisor and the human resources department can work together to conduct an orientation.

17.3 Identify methods for conducting an orientation.

17.4 Describe the training cycle.

17.5 Explain how supervisors can decide when employees need training.

17.6 Define major types of training.

17.7 Describe how a supervisor can use coaching and mentoring to support training.

17.8 Discuss how a supervisor can evaluate the effectiveness of training.

■ TRAINING PEOPLE TO MOVE HEAVEN AND EARTH

Why is the Ritz-Carlton the only hotel company to have received the prestigious Malcolm Baldrige National Quality Award? One reason might be the rigorous customer service training every one of its 16,000 employees receives. The chain's senior vice president of human relations, Leonardo Inghilleri, says, "We tell our employees to move heaven and earth to satisfy a customer. We have to equip them to do that—every day."

How is the ongoing training conducted? One of the firm's steadfast policies is a daily 10-minute briefing at the beginning of every shift. Workers and supervisors gather for training, operations news, and a reminder of the company philosophy. A weekly calendar

of topics for the meetings is e-mailed from the president's office to each hotel. For one energizing moment each day during these sessions, everyone in the company's 34 hotels around the world focuses on the same issue.

Here is a sample agenda. "First, we introduce the topic of the week. Second, we revisit one of our 'customer service basics.' Finally, we run through operational issues that are specific to each department: anything from the specials on the menu to an upcoming meeting with an investor. Ten minutes after the meeting begins, everyone is back at work."

Source: Cathy Olofson, "The Ritz Puts On Stand-Up Meetings," *Fast Company*, September 1998, p. 62.

Supervisors are responsible for making sure their employees know what to do and how to do it. Good selection practices ensure that employees are capable of learning their jobs and perhaps already know how to carry out many of the tasks they were hired to perform. However, especially in view of the intense changes faced by most organizations, even the best employees need some degree of training. In this context, **training** refers to increasing the skills that will enable employees to better meet the organization's goals.

training
Increasing the skills that will enable employees to better meet the organization's goals.

Businesses in the United States spend $54 billion annually on formal training, nearly $500 per employee according to *Training* magazine's year 2000 industry report.[1] Yet some firms are seeing change ahead, in a recent finding by the Center for Workforce Development, which states that up to 70 percent of what employees know about their jobs they learn informally from the people with whom they work.[2] That means that formal training may account for only about 30 percent of what employees learn. The implication for supervisors is that they will play an ever-greater role in training the employees with whom they work, relying less on formal training programs in the future.

At TalentFusion, Inc., training in team building, for instance, is about as informal as it can get. A recruitment agency that operates both on and off the Internet, TalentFusion holds weekly soccer games are part of employee training. "The game isn't about proficiency in soccer," explains CEO David Pollard. "It's about proficiency in team building and being goal-oriented, two things that translate perfectly to our work off the field."[3]

■ FIGURE 17.1

Specific Types of Training Provided by U.S. Companies

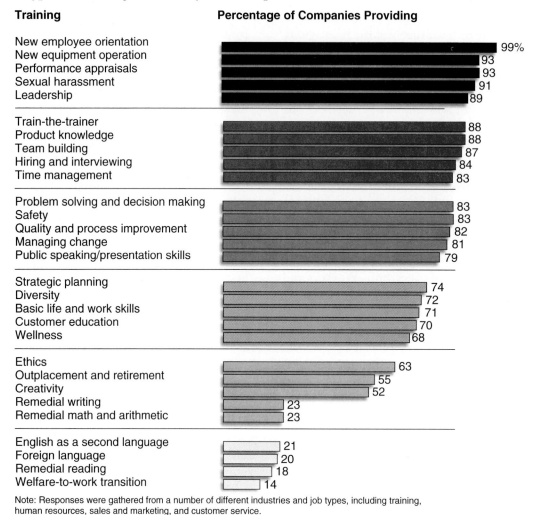

Training	Percentage of Companies Providing
New employee orientation	99%
New equipment operation	93
Performance appraisals	93
Sexual harassment	91
Leadership	89
Train-the-trainer	88
Product knowledge	88
Team building	87
Hiring and interviewing	84
Time management	83
Problem solving and decision making	83
Safety	83
Quality and process improvement	82
Managing change	81
Public speaking/presentation skills	79
Strategic planning	74
Diversity	72
Basic life and work skills	71
Customer education	70
Wellness	68
Ethics	63
Outplacement and retirement	55
Creativity	52
Remedial writing	23
Remedial math and arithmetic	23
English as a second language	21
Foreign language	20
Remedial reading	18
Welfare-to-work transition	14

Note: Responses were gathered from a number of different industries and job types, including training, human resources, sales and marketing, and customer service.

Source: Data from *Training* magazine, Industry Report 2000, http://www.trainingsupersite.com/publications/archive/training/2000/010/010correction.htm accessed on August 26, 2001.

Employee training, however it is conducted, meets important needs. New employees need a chance to learn the specific ways things are done in the organization. In addition, employees are best equipped to contribute in a changing workplace when they have an opportunity to learn new skills and improve existing ones through a variety of training programs. Well-trained employees can deliver higher quality than poorly trained people. Training can improve productivity by holding down a variety of costs: overtime pay for employees unfamiliar with their jobs, workers' compensation and lost time of employees injured when they fail to follow safe practices, lawsuits arising from misconduct such as sexual harassment (discussed in Chapter 19), and much more. Finally, well-trained employees are likely to be more satisfied because they know what they are doing and how it contributes to achieving the organization's goals. Figure 17.1 shows areas in which U.S. companies were conducting training, according to a recent survey.

This chapter describes types of training for employees and how supervisors can participate. It begins by laying out the supervisor's role in orientation, the employee's first learning experience. Next, the chapter discusses types of training available once employees are on board and explains how supervisors can assess when training is needed. The chapter also addresses the growing expectation that supervisors supplement formal training with coaching or mentoring. Finally, the chapter describes why and how to evaluate training efforts.

Orientation of New Employees

orientation
The process of giving new employees the information they need to do their work comfortably, effectively, and efficiently.

Do you remember your first day at your current or most recent job? When you arrived, you might not have known where you would be working or where the rest rooms were. You probably did not know your co-workers or how they spent their lunch hour. You might not have known the details of how to carry out your job, including where and how to get the supplies or materials you would need.

The uncertainty you felt is common to new employees in all kinds of organizations. For that reason, supervisors should assume that all employees need some form of orientation. In this context, **orientation** refers to the process of giving new employees the information they need to do their work comfortably, effectively, and efficiently. As you can see from Figure 17.1, *Training* magazine's recent survey found that 99 percent of companies sampled offered employees a formal orientation program. Even in organizations where someone else is responsible for carrying out a formal orientation program, supervisors themselves must ensure that their employees begin their jobs with all the information they need.

Benefits of Orientation

An employee who spends the day hunting for the photocopier, trying to figure out how to operate a cash register, or looking for someone to explain how to fill out a purchase order is not working efficiently. The primary reason organizations have orientation programs is that the sooner employees know basic information related to doing their jobs, the sooner they can become productive. They can work faster and with fewer errors, and their co-workers and supervisor can spend less time helping them.

Not only does orientation give new employees the knowledge they need to carry out their work, it also reduces their nervousness and uncertainty. This frees new employees to focus on their jobs rather than their worries, which not only boosts employee efficiency but also reduces the likelihood they will quit.

Another reason for conducting orientation is to encourage employees to develop a positive attitude. The time spent on an orientation session shows that the organization values the new employees. This will almost certainly add to employees' feelings of satisfaction and desire to cooperate as part of the organization. It can make new employees feel more confident that joining the organization was a good idea. In addition, work is more satisfying when we know how to do it well. The organization benefits because employees with positive attitudes tend to be more highly motivated, so they are more likely to do good work.

The benefits to employees' attitudes are among the reasons that Great Plains Software in Fargo, North Dakota, went from a one-day to a three-month orientation program. When employees join Great Plains, they take eight formal classes on topics ranging from e-mail to employee benefits to the company's vision. Each employee is assigned to a mentor, who provides personal coaching. (Mentoring is discussed later in this chapter.) Great Plains found that after it started the more intense orientation program, new employees had a better opinion of the company.[4]

At Motorola Semiconductor Products Sector in Phoenix, Arizona, training in Six Sigma methods (discussed in Chapter 2) is now included in every new employee's orientation. The company's quality engineering manager Craig Erwin says that Six Sigma, considered a "stretch goal," continues to yield improvements in product reliability and quality, "in spite of increasing product complexity and higher customer expectations." Including the training in employee orientation not only alerts every work to Six Sigma's importance in the firm; it also gives each new hire a head start in achieving the goal of continuous improvement.[5]

The Supervisor's Role

In a small organization, supervisors often are responsible for conducting the orientation of their employees. If you are one of those supervisors, look for ways to adapt the principles in this chapter to your group's particular needs.

Large organizations more often have a formal orientation program conducted by the human resources department. Even so, supervisors have a role in orientation. While the formal orientation program focuses on information pertaining to the organization as a whole, supervisors still must convey information about the specifics of holding a particular job in a particular department. If you are a supervisor under these circumstances, learn which of the topics and methods your human resources department already covers, then consider ways you and your employees can handle any remaining ones. See "Tips from the Firing Line" for ways to manage the "honeymoon" period.

Orientation Topics

When the human resources department and supervisor share responsibility for conducting an orientation, the human resources department typically covers topics related to the organization's policies and procedures, including hours of work and breaks; location of company facilities such as the lunchroom and exercise facilities; procedures for filling out time sheets; and policies regarding performance appraisals, pay increases, and time off. The human resources department also handles the task of having new employees fill out the necessary paperwork such as enrollment forms for insurance policies and withholding forms for tax purposes. The person conducting the orientation should explain each of these forms to new employees.

A supervisor is responsible for orientation topics related to performing a particular job in a particular department. A supervisor explains what the department does and how these activities contribute to the goals of the organization. A supervisor who covered this information in the selection interview should repeat it during the orientation process. As described later, the supervisor's orientation should point out the locations of facilities the employee will need to use and explain any of the department's own policies and procedures.

A supervisor's orientation also should provide instructions on how to perform the job. A supervisor may be able to explain a simple job at one time, but most jobs are more complex and will require a supervisor to first give an overview of the job's responsibilities and then, over the course of days or weeks, show the em-

Helping New Employees Make the Transition

Here are seven ways supervisors can help employees make a successful transition from new hire to valued subordinate.

1. *Clarify your expectations up front.* New employees in particular may feel shy about asking questions about tasks and procedures they don't understand. Don't assume they know all they need to; take the initiative instead, and go over your expectations point by point to make sure the new person is comfortable with and understands them.
2. *Don't assume qualification equal success.* Even those with strong credentials and related experience may have weaknesses in areas that are critical to job success. Begin coaching right away to help solve problems.
3. *Spell out important points about business goals and company culture.* Cover topics like overall company strategy, market share, and projections for the firm's future. Even those who transfer in from another area of the same firm may need to be given this information, and knowledge and culture can differ from one department to another.
4. *Help nurture the network.* Don't allow your new hire to work in a vacuum. Identify direct reports, subordinates, major clients, colleagues, counterparts in other areas, and so on. Offer specific suggestions for building solid relationships with key people in the new person's sphere.
5. *Be honest about potential pitfalls and past mistakes.* Learning from mistakes is one of the most valuable learning experiences we can have. Talk with your new employee about former workers who quit or were fired and explain what went wrong and why. (If you can't do so because you don't conduct exit interviews with departing employees, start holding them now.)
6. *Have regular assimilation reviews.* The "honeymoon period" in any new job lasts about six months, during which time you should meet with your new hire about once a month to discuss the job, review performance, and ask for feedback.
7. *Make coaching resources available before a crisis occurs.* Don't wait until an employee is in trouble or thinking of quitting before you take action. Coach your new hires through their transition periods and provide the motivation needed to succeed.

Source: " 'Honeymoon' Hint for Managers," *Supervision*, May 1, 2001. Reprinted by permission of © National Research Bureau, 320 Valley Street, Burlington, IA.

ployee how to perform different aspects of the job. To build morale while training, a supervisor also can explain why the employee's job is important—that is, how it contributes to meeting department and organizational objectives.

A supervisor should prepare and follow a checklist of the topics to cover during orientation of new employees. Figure 17.2 is adapted from a checklist distributed to supervisors at Swift and Company; it is printed on a two- by three-inch card so supervisors can easily refer to it. In preparing a checklist, a supervisor should include items that fit his or her particular situation.

Orientation Methods

The methods a supervisor uses will depend on the organization's policies and resources. For example, a large organization with a human resources department may provide a handbook of information for new employees and spell out orientation procedures to follow. A small organization may expect individual supervisors to develop their own orientation methods. Some common methods include using an employee handbook, conducting a tour of the facilities, and encouraging the involvement of co-workers.

Employee Handbook If the organization publishes an employee handbook, a new employee should be introduced to this document during the orientation. An

■ FIGURE 17.2

Sample Checklist for Orientation

SUPERVISORS' CHECKLIST
The Right Start for New Hourly Paid Employees

A. Explain (before employee starts the job):
1. Rate of pay, including overtime.
2. Pay day.
3. Initial job or assignment.
4. Hours—call out—holiday pay—no tardiness.
5. Starting and quitting time.
6. Lunch period—relief periods.
7. Whom to call if unable to come to work (give name and phone number on card).
8. Work clothes arrangement— laundry.
9. No smoking areas.
10. Safety rules—no running—mesh gloves— reporting all accidents, etc.
11. Sanitation—this is a food factory.
12. Name benefits (will explain later).
13. Possible job difficulties—sore muscles or hands, dizziness, nausea, etc. (encourage to stick it out).
14. Buying of company products.
15. Nothing from plant without order.
16. Importance of quality product.

B. Show:
1. Locker—rest rooms.
2. Lunch room.
3. Where employee will work—introduce to supervisor and immediate co-workers.
4. Explain the job—use JIT.
C. Talk to new employee (to encourage):
1. Twice first day.
2. Once each day the next four days.
D. After one week, explain:
1. Vacation.
2. S & A.
3. Hospitalization.
4. EBA—Group.
5. Pension.
6. Suggestion plan.
7. Union contract, if organized plant (probationary period).

Source: Adapted from a Swift and Company document.

employee handbook
A document that describes an organization's conditions of employment, policies regarding employees, administrative procedures, and related matters.

employee handbook describes an organization's conditions of employment (e.g., attendance, behavior on the job, performance of duties), policies regarding employees (e.g., time off, hours of work, benefits), administrative procedures (e.g., filling out time sheets and travel expense reports), and related matters. A supervisor should show a new employee what topics are covered in the handbook and explain how to use it to find answers to questions. For example, an employee might use the handbook to learn how long he or she must work to qualify for three weeks' vacation.

Tour of Facilities   Another important orientation method is to give the employee a tour. The tour might start with the employee's own work area, which should already be prepared with the supplies, tools, or equipment the employee will need. The supervisor then shows the employee the locations of physical facilities he or she will need to know about, including rest rooms, water fountain, coffee station, fax, and photocopier, and where to get supplies, parts, or other materials needed to do the job.

During the tour, the supervisor should introduce the new employee to the people he or she will be working with. Friendly, positive words during introductions can help make the new employee part of the team. In introducing a new nurse to her colleagues in the hospital, a supervisor might say, "This is Janet Strahn. She's one of the top graduates from Northern, and I know we're all going to appreciate her help." In introducing a new maintenance mechanic to a machine operator in the department, a supervisor might say, "Pedro is the guy you'll need if your machine goes down." In both examples, the supervisor is emphasizing the importance of the new employee to the department.

Involvement of Co-Workers   A new employee's co-workers have an important role to play in orientation. Their behavior goes a long way toward making the new employee feel either welcome or like an outsider. Therefore, a supervisor should ask all employees to help welcome newcomers. If the organization tries to build team spirit through activities such as clubs and sports teams, a supervisor should see that these are well publicized so that new employees can participate easily. A supervisor may encourage co-workers to invite a new employee to join them on breaks and at lunch. On the employee's first day, a supervisor can help a new employee feel welcome by inviting him or her to lunch.

Follow-Up   Besides the initial information giving, orientation should involve follow-up. A supervisor should check with new employees at the end of the first day and the first week to make sure they understand what they are supposed to be doing and know where to get what they need. At all times, a supervisor should encourage employees to ask questions.

Of course, a supervisor should not stop following up after one week. Regularly checking on the performance and progress of employees is part of a supervisor's control responsibilities, particularly in technical professions.[6]

Training

As mentioned earlier, employees need continued training even after they have worked for the organization for years. Training shows employees how to do the basics of their jobs and then helps them improve their skills. It also helps employees adapt to changes in the workplace. Because change occurs in every organization, the need for training continues (see Chapter 15).

The Training Cycle

The process of providing training takes place in a cycle of steps (see Figure 17.3). The first step is to assess needs for training. As described in the next section, assessment of training needs is part of a supervisor's job. In addition, higher-level management or the human resources department may identify a need for various kinds of training. The next three steps involve planning the training. Then someone conducts the training as planned. Finally, the training should be evaluated.

Planning Steps   A supervisor or other person proposing the training begins the planning stage by setting objectives for it. These objectives are based on a comparison of the current level and the desired level of performance and skills. In other words, they specify progress from the current level to the desired level. The training objectives should meet the criteria for effective objectives (see Chapter 6). Thus, they should be written, measurable, clear, specific, and challenging but achievable. Training objectives also should support the organization's goals by helping to develop the kind of employees who can make the organization more competitive. At Welch's Inc., a sizable portion of training funds is devoted to

FIGURE 17.3

The Training Cycle

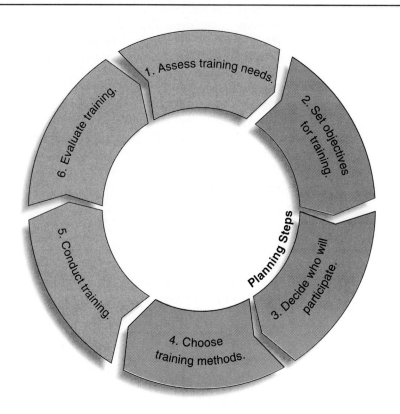

developing interpersonal skills such as decision making, teamwork, and conflict resolution. These skills support the organization's need to have employees who are flexible and responsive to change.[7]

A supervisor also decides who will participate in the training program. For example, training how to prevent and avoid sexual harassment applies to all employees, so everyone in the department would participate. But training how to operate a new piece of equipment would include only those who would use that equipment. This decision may take into account the interests and motivation levels of employees, as well as their skills. For example, an employee who is eager to advance in the organization will want to participate in many training activities to develop a variety of skills. An employee who is interested primarily in job security will probably want just enough training to keep up to date on how to perform the job.

The last step in planning training is to choose the training methods. Some training methods are described later in this chapter. If selecting a training method is part of a supervisor's role, he or she may wish to consult with the human resources department or a training expert to learn which techniques will best meet the objectives of the training.

Implementation   Once the training has been planned, someone conducts it in a timely manner. In some cases, the trainer may be a supervisor. A department's employees may be qualified to conduct some kinds of training, such as demonstrating how to use a computer system. In other cases, a professional trainer is more appropriate. The choice depends on the expertise of a supervisor or employee, the content and type of training, and the time and money available for training. A supervisor with a big budget and little expertise in a particular area of training is most likely to use an in-house or outside expert. Training topics most often tackled by a supervisor are those about the specific job or department instead of company policies and values, interpreting the company's performance, or working effectively as a team.

When a supervisor is conducting the training, he or she can benefit from applying principles of learning.[8] One of these principles is that adults generally get the most out of training if they are taught a little at a time over a long period, especially if the training is seeking to change behavior rather than merely add to the learner's store of knowledge. Thus, shutting down for a day of training would be less effective than scheduling a half hour every week or so. According to educators, another learning principle is that people retain only the following percentages of what is taught[9]:

- 10 percent of what they read.
- 20 percent of what they hear.
- 30 percent of what they see.
- 50 percent of what they see and hear.
- 70 percent of what they see and describe.
- 90 percent of what they describe while doing.

The implication, of course, is that supervisors and other trainers need to supplement or replace reading assignments and lectures with more effective means of teaching, particularly those that get the learner actively involved. That is most likely to occur when classes are small—no more than about 25 people. Finally, motivation is as important to successful learning as it is to other employee activities. Training will therefore be most effective when it reflects the principles of motivation discussed in Chapter 11.

Evaluation   After the training is over, the supervisor evaluates the results. Did it meet the objectives? The last section of this chapter discusses the evaluation of training in greater detail. Evaluation completes the training cycle by helping the supervisor identify needs for additional training.

Assessment of Training Needs

Whether or not supervisors conduct much of their employees' formal training, they are still responsible for recognizing needs for training. With input from the employees, supervisors should determine the areas of training that employees will need and schedule the times for them to receive it.

Needs assessment should be an ongoing, not an occasional, concern of supervisors. Change is such a dominant force today that organizations depend on a workforce that continually learns and develops to give them a competitive edge.

A supervisor has several ways to identify training needs. First, a supervisor can observe problems in the department that suggest a need for training. For example, if a restaurant's customers are complaining about the quality of service, the manager might conclude that some or all of the staff needs training in how to satisfy customers. Or if forms sent from one department to another frequently contain a similar type of error, the department's supervisor should investigate why the people filling out the forms are making this type of mistake. Although frequent questions from employees are not necessarily a "problem," they do indicate that employees may need training in some area.

Certain areas of change also signal a need for training, and a supervisor should pay attention to them and consider what new knowledge and skills employees will need to keep abreast. If an organization encourages employee empowerment and teamwork, employees will need to know how to make decisions, evaluate team efforts, and listen to team members. When new technology (from a competitor, supplier, or elsewhere) affects an organization or the individuals in it, employees will need to learn about that technology and gain skill in applying it. If a department or its base of customers is becoming more diverse, employees will need to learn how to respect, communicate with, and achieve objectives with different cultures.

Another way to obtain information about training needs is to ask employees. Employees frequently have opinions about what they must learn to do a better job. At a minimum, supervisors and employees should discuss training needs during performance appraisals (see Chapter 18). In addition, a supervisor should encourage employees to communicate their needs as they arise.

Finally, a supervisor can identify training needs when carrying out the planning function. Executing plans often requires that employees receive training in new skills or procedures. For example, if the organization will be introducing a new product, salespeople will have to be able to communicate its benefits to customers, and customer service staff will have to be able to answer questions about it.

Besides recognizing these signals, a supervisor also should evaluate them. Do they indicate a need for training or for something else? Sometimes poor performance is not a training problem, but a motivation problem. Errors or defects may be a symptom that employees lack resources or cooperation from elsewhere in the organization. Frequent questions may signal a need for better communication instead of (or in addition to) training. Before spending money on training, a supervisor should consider whether it is the best response to these signals. A good place to begin may be to ask the relevant employees to help find the underlying issue (see Chapter 19).

Mandatory Training   A supervisor is not the only one to decide when training is required. Government regulations, union work rules, or company policy may dictate training in certain circumstances. If the state mandates a number of continuing education classes for teachers, if the union requires an apprenticeship of so many months for pipe fitters, or if the company's top managers decide that everyone should take a class in total quality management, the supervisor's job is to make sure that his or her employees get the required training. The supervisor does so primarily through decisions related to scheduling and motivation.

Learning Environment   Along with planning for formal training sessions, supervisors can help organizations meet the need for training by fostering a climate that values learning. This kind of climate has been called a "learning environment." Jack Welch, former chairman of General Electric, says he has learned a great deal from the managers who report to him and encourages them to challenge his ideas. "G.E. has what I like to call a culture of learning," he says, "and that means learning from anyone."[10]

Another way to foster a learning environment is to set a good example. Supervisors should develop their own knowledge and skills through a variety of means, from reading to attending seminars. Also, supervisors should share information generously

What Would You Like to Learn?

Where can supervisors learn about drawing, Japanese bookbinding, harmonica, chess, and introduction to golf?—at InspireU, the training program offered to and by the employees of Agency.com, an interactive consulting company.

All the training courses in the popular in-house "university" are free and are offered after work or during lunch. About one-third of the company's employees take them, and that number is expected to grow every term. A potentially powerful force for both developing and retaining employees, the light-hearted program offerings also focus on work-related issues at least half the time.

Serious course titles that apply to supervisory employees include Management 101, Database Management, Running Brilliant Meetings and Discussions,

Copywriting, Accounting Management, and Computer Programming. There is a great deal of crossover among departments. In addition to learning new skills, the employees, who are mostly young with liberal arts backgrounds, also learn about other departments and the operation of the company as a whole.

Amy Brennan, assistant office manager, feels the courses have not only improved her business skills but also helped her devise a career track within the firm. "It helped me to figure out where I want to move . . . to learn about every part of this company and the industry."

Source: Amy Joyce, "Oddball Courses among Consulting Firm's Valued Perks," *Washington Post*, November 29, 1998, p. H4.

with employees. They can enable employees to learn from one another by encouraging them to exchange what they have learned through their education, training activities, and experience. When employees request time and other resources for training, a supervisor should view the training as an investment to be evaluated, not merely a distraction from the "real work" of the organization. See "Supervision and Diversity" for the variety of courses some firms can make available.

Types of Training

A variety of types of training are available for employees (see Figure 17.4). Most organizations use a variety of training methods. When BMW planned a new factory in Spartanburg, South Carolina, it also planned a combination of classroom and on-the-job training. In the classroom setting, employees learn the skills required for working on a team: communications, participation in a diverse workforce, and facilitating group processes.[11]

In selecting or recommending a type of training, a supervisor should consider the expense relative to the benefits, the resources available, and trainees' needs for practice and individualized attention. No matter what type of training is used, a supervisor should be sure that the trainer understands the objectives of the training and how to carry them out. A supervisor also should counsel employees who seem discouraged and praise them when they show progress.

On-the-Job Training   In many cases, the easiest way to learn how to perform a job is to try it. Teaching a job while trainer and trainee do the job at the work site is called **on-the-job training.** The trainer—typically a co-worker or supervisor—shows the employee how to do the job, and then the employee tries it.

on-the-job training
Teaching a job while trainer and trainee perform the job at the work site.

An employee who learns in this way benefits from being able to try out the skills and techniques being taught. The results tell immediately whether the employee understands what the trainer is trying to teach. However, on-the-job

Types of Training

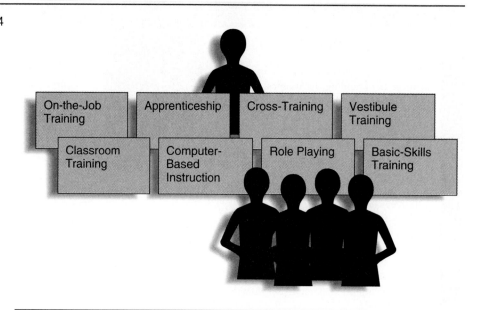

training carries the risk that an inexperienced employee will make costly and even dangerous mistakes. Thus, this type of training is most suitable when the tasks to be learned are relatively simple or the costs of an error are low. For more complex or risky tasks, it may be wiser to use other forms of training before or instead of on-the-job training.

apprenticeship
Training that involves working alongside an experienced person, who shows the apprentice how to do the various tasks involved in a job or trade.

Apprenticeship   Many tradespeople learn their trades through an **apprenticeship.** This involves working alongside an experienced person, who shows the apprentice how to do the various tasks involved in the trade. Thus, apprenticeship is a long-term form of on-the-job training. (Many apprenticeship programs also require that apprentices complete classroom training.) Most apprenticeships are in the building trades, such as carpentry and pipe fitting.

For example, the National Electrical Contractors Association and International Brotherhood of Electrical Workers (NECA-IBEW) has recently begun offering 3- to 5-year apprenticeships that promise on-the-job training, college credits, competitive pay, and health and pension benefits. The organization hopes to train more than 100,000 electricians and information technology system installers through the program.[12]

An apprenticeship program is more complicated to set up than simple on-the-job training for individual tasks. However, it is one way to help a supervisor meet training needs that require months or years of learning.

Cross-Training   As you learned in Chapter 11, an increasing number of organizations are using job rotation, meaning that employees take turns performing various jobs. Job rotation requires that employees learn to perform more than one job. Teaching employees another job so that they can fill in as needed is known as cross-training. Employees who have completed cross-training can enjoy more variety in their work, and their supervisor has more flexibility in making assignments. The resulting flexibility also makes cross-training necessary for many forms of teamwork. See "Meeting the Challenge" for more advantages of cross-training.

Cross-Training for Flexibility

Supervisors might think they have enough to do just to train the people who work for them. Many consultants today, however, advise them to do even more—to train everyone in the department to do every job. This "cross-training" helps the team produce more and better work by building flexibility into getting the job done, and it can also help meet supervisors' goals of developing the skills of the people for whom they are responsible. That in turn improves morale in the group, another benefit for the supervisor.

Here are three big advantages of cross-training, as seen by companies that have adopted the practice. Do they apply to your subordinates as well?

- *Every employee can help a customer.* Even the receptionist for The Chip, a computer technical-support and repair company, is trained in computer repair. That way, says president Chip Meyer, the whole company acts as a help desk for its clients.

- *Every employee knows how to sell.* Nick Nicholson runs the Ecology Group, a recycling and waste-

management firm. He's proud that one of his accounting staff was able to increase business with a client who called about a big accounting problem. "I don't think he could have done that if he hadn't had sales training," says Nick.

- *No employee is indispensable.* At Greenpages, a computer reseller, each new employee gets two months of intensive training in every job function in the company, including sales, purchasing, credit services, and customer support. Two highly cross-trained individuals are able to fill almost any position in the company for any length of time, invaluable for covering sick leave, vacations, maternity leaves, and so on. While they're generalists in all the firm's functions, CEO Kurt Bleicken says the skills they offer are "better than starting over from square one."

Source: Christopher Caggiano, "Sign of the Cross-Training Times," *Inc.*, December 1998, pp. 122–123.

In planning cross-training, a supervisor should make sure that employees spend enough time practicing each job to learn it well. Some jobs are more complex than others and will require more training time. Also, some employees will learn a given job faster than others.

Linda Reimer's boss, Dennis Brozak, noticed her when she was a 40-something part-timer working at the copy machine and began training her because he thought she had promise. Over a two-year period Brozak, the founder of a $4 million firm called Design Basics, showed Reimer how to do everything from managing human resources to producing a catalog, managing operations, and handling new-product development. "I wanted to find out a lot about her," he said. "Can she manage and motivate people? Can she delegate accurately and appropriately? And she had to be able to fire people when necessary. She has a big heart, but she passed that test, too." Eventually, Brozak had cross-trained Reimer well enough for her to take over as president of the firm.[13]

vestibule training
Training that takes place on equipment set up in a special area off the job site.

Vestibule Training While on-the-job training is effective, it is not appropriate as initial training for jobs that have no room for errors, such as piloting or nursing. In those cases, people learn principles or techniques before doing the actual job. A type of training that allows employees to practice using equipment off the job is called **vestibule training.** The employees undergoing vestibule training use procedures and equipment set up in a special vestibule school. For example, a large retail store might set up a training room containing cash registers, or an airline might use a simulated cabin for training flight attendants.

Vestibule training is appropriate when the organization hires people who do not already know how to use its equipment. Employees learn to operate the equipment without the pressure of accidents occurring, customers getting impatient, or other employees depending on a minimum amount of output. The expense of vestibule training or other off-the-job training is higher because employees are not producing goods or services for the organization while they undergo the training. However, if the organization hired only people who already had all the necessary skills, it would probably have to pay more and might have difficulty finding enough qualified candidates.

At Espresso Connection, a small chain of drive-through coffee bars in Washington State, Christian Kar slashed his marketing budget to pay for additional employee training, realizing that impressing customers with good service was the real key to increasing sales. When it came to knowing how to use the firm's equipment and prepare drinks, new employees used to learn by doing. But Kar hired several part-time trainers and developed a special hands-on facility where new employees spend a week using the machines and learning how to make various coffee drinks. Only when they've mastered the basics do recruits go on to another 40 hours of on-the-job training at one of the stores. Under the new program, training also includes the specifics of high-quality customer service. Peak-hour sales have doubled since training began. "The training has definitely helped," says Kar.[14]

Classroom Training   Other than vestibule training, about 73 percent of off-the-job training involves some form of classroom instruction.[15] This training takes place in a class or seminar where one or more speakers lecture on a specific topic. Seminars are available from a variety of sources on many topics, so a supervisor who is considering attending or sending employees to a seminar should first make sure that the topic will be relevant to job performance. Classroom training also can occur at the workplace, even if the organization lacks the time or facilities for formal classes.

The main advantage of classroom training is that the person conducting it can deliver a large quantity of information to more than one person in a relatively short span of time. Depending on the format and trainer, it can be a relatively inexpensive way to convey information. A disadvantage is that most of the communication travels in one direction—from the lecturer to the audience. One-way communication is less engaging and memorable. In addition, classroom training rarely allows the learners to practice what they are learning.

Classroom training therefore benefits from the trainer's ability to maintain a high level of interest. Training manager Karen Delahunty runs a one-day financial education course for The Body Shop USA and starts off by leading her class through the creation of a fictitious home-based beauty company. "There's product being whipped up on stage," she says. "Facials and all. We'll break eggs, sometimes go so far as to put facials on my face. I try to keep them laughing, because people don't learn unless they're having fun."[16]

Classroom training can also be more effective when it includes computer-based instruction and role playing.

Computer-Based Instruction   At a growing number of organizations, computer software is taking the place of classroom-based trainers. In fact, according to *Training* magazine, about 13 percent of training courses are delivered via computer-based training with no live instructor involved.[17] Computer-based instruction typically uses a computer to present information, generate and score test questions, keep track of the trainee's performance, and tell the trainee what activities to do next. This type of training is a common way of learning to use a new

TABLE 17.1

**E-Learning Offers
10 Major
Advantages**

1. Real-time learning and application of critical knowledge. E-learning is immediate and up-to-date.

2. Learner-centric training. E-learning changes the focus of training from instructor to learner. It is tailored to the learner's responsibilities and capabilities, creating relevant applications.

3. Ability to attract, train, and retain employees. The number one reason for loss of key employees is that they feel their company has not invested sufficient resources for their professional development.

4. Personalized training. An effective e-learning system learns about its users and tailors its offerings to their learning style, job requirements, career goals, current knowledge, and preferences.

5. Ownership of learning. E-learning empowers people to manage their own learning and development plans. Ownership of learning is crucial for individual growth and retention of employees.

6. Simulation. We learn by doing. E-learning is an innovative way of simulating each learning experience with content provided by top professionals.

7. Collaboration. This is done through either joint problem-solving or the sharing of ideas and experience among study groups and chat rooms. Collaboration is the path to effective learning and innovative processes.

8. Ability to train anytime and anywhere. Training in a virtual information classroom is now possible anytime, anywhere.

9. Cost effectiveness. Costs can be applied to each learner, and results measured against costs. And, e-learning is less intrusive to daily work duties, saving time and money through less interruption of employees regularly scheduled duties.

10. Quantifiable results. E-learning can be effectively measured in terms of knowledge gain and retention. With e-learning, corporations can track progress, report results, and specify additional subject matter. This is where ROI will be recognized by the employer and employee.

Source: From "e-learning Offers 10 Major Advantages," by Bray J. Brockbank, *Executive Excellence*, July 2001. Reprinted with permission.

computer program; the software comes with a series of lessons that give the user a chance to try using it. Computer-based training that employs the Internet is commonly referred to as e-learning. Table 17.1 lists ten major advantages that e-learning offers organizations.

Some firms have already put themselves on the leading edge of integrating technology into workforce training, such as AT&T, Ford, Intel, Aetna Life & Casualty, and even the U.S. government.[18] In its broadest sense, computer-aided instruction is termed "distance learning" by the U.S. Distance Learning Association, which offers the following definition: Distance learning is "the delivery of education or training through electronically mediated instruction including satellite, video, audio, audiographic computer, multimedia technology and learning at a distance." A possible scenario might run like this:

> On a service call, an appliance repair technician is asked to fix a broken refrigerator but discovers that he hasn't worked on this particular model before. No problem—he pulls out his laptop computer, accesses a phone line and within moments downloads

schematics and technical data on the appliance. The technician can also reach immediate, interactive technical assistance that literally talks him through repair procedures.

interactive multimedia
Computer software that brings together sound, video, graphics, animation, and text and adjusts content based on user responses.

Computer-based instruction is becoming more engaging and widespread because of the growing affordability of **interactive multimedia.** This is software that brings together sound, video, graphics, animation, and text. The best interactive multimedia programs adjust the course content based on the student's responses to questions. Interactive multimedia typically is delivered on CD-ROM, a storage medium that many personal computers can use. By a recent count, 80 percent of Fortune 500 companies were using interactive multimedia training.[19] Accenture uses interactive multimedia to create simulations in which trainees practice answering questions and otherwise interacting with digitized images of clients. Retailer JCPenney uses interactive multimedia to train customer service representatives in its credit card division. The computer simulates phone calls from customers, so the reps can actually practice handling irate (and reasonable) customers.

Some computer-based training uses simulations. The computer displays conditions that an employee might have to face. For example, a flight simulator would show pilot trainees the cockpit and the view from the window. Another simulation might be of dials and other readouts monitoring the performance of machinery. A trainee uses the computer's keyboard or some other device to respond to the situation displayed by a computer, and the simulator responds by showing the consequences of the trainee's actions. This enables the trainee to practice responding to conditions without suffering the real consequences of a mistake, such as a plane crashing or a boiler exploding.

Computer-based instruction has a significant cost advantage over other methods when there are many trainees. An organization may not have to pay a trainer. In addition, trainees can work at their own pace, eliminating the frustration that arises from a class moving too fast for them to understand material or too slow to maintain their interest. A good training program can help trainees learn faster or better than they might through another training technique. At JCPenney, customer service representatives trained with interactive multimedia reach peak proficiency in one-third less time than employees who had more traditional training. Accenture credits interactive multimedia for employees having "deeper competencies, more skill and knowledge."[20]

Even small companies can benefit from computer-based training. Sherman Assembly Systems of San Antonio, Texas is a contract manufacturer of electronic cable assemblies. Many of its employees are former welfare recipients who have received job training from Goodwill Industries but who still lack high school diplomas. To help them achieve their general equivalency diplomas (GEDs), CEO Michael Sherman enlisted the help of a local college to supply a Web-based GED program that runs on a couple of dedicated computers in the company's conference room.[21]

Some people, however, are nervous about using a computer. A supervisor or other trainer must serve as a source of encouragement and help for these people. Also, some forms of computer-based instruction do not allow employees to work as a team, ask questions, or exchange ideas. When these features of training are important, a supervisor should choose software that offers these capabilities, supplement the computer-based training, or select other training methods.

Experts offer the following advice for successfully implementing a computer-assisted training program[22]:

SUPERVISION ACROSS INDUSTRIES

Union Workers

Learning the Ropes

Training for union workers is on the increase, according to experts, and the reasons are varied. Foremost is the increasingly technical nature of work—computerized equipment and sophisticated technology not available a few short years ago require specialized training to use and operate. Another factor is the new emphasis on getting workers at all levels to increase their productivity and creativity, and to "think like management." Changing federal laws regarding safety and waste-handling standards create the need for training as well.

Still another reason is provided by Marshall Goldberg, executive director of the Association for Joint Labor and Management Education Programs. "Unions are becoming more and more involved in the personal development of their members," says Goldberg. "Unions are developing relationships with management to take on joint responsibility for the education and training of hourly workers throughout their careers."

Some training programs consist of apprenticeships, others of classroom or workshop exercises like those run by consultant Ellen Cooperperson of East Northport, New York. Cooperperson's training program focuses on building communication skills and incorporates cartoon characters and nursery rhymes to make her points. The value of training for increasing frictionless cooperation among workers is obvious, she feels. "For floor supervisors, this means they have to be able to lead others they might never have worked with before and might not meet again. So they can't rely on personal connections or prior knowledge about the person. They have to be able to read body language, pick up on changes of vocal tone and call on other communication skills."

Michael Bender, chief executive of the Bana Electric Corporation and a board member of the Joint Apprenticeship and Training Committee of the International Brotherhood of Electrical Workers, takes a similar view of the benefits of training, and not just for supervisors. "Everyone gets a lot smarter," he says. "And you really can't be too smart, after all."

Source: Warren Strugatch, "Investing in More Training for Hourly Workers," *New York Times*, September 2, 2001, p. LI-6.

1. Tell learners what they will be able to do after the training.
2. Include rewards, such as money, time off, better working conditions, new tools and equipment, or career opportunities.
3. Minimize noise and interruptions in the learning environment and maximize access, speed, and ease of use.
4. "Chunk" instruction into segments of 20 minutes or less.
5. Vary the media, including a variety of audio, video, and print materials as well as simulations and interactive tools.
6. Give legitimate feedback.
7. Remember to incorporate the human touch via chat rooms, e-mail, electronic office hours, audio streaming, or online mentoring.
8. Reinforce learning with questionnaires or "alumni" chat sessions.

role playing
A training method in which roles are assigned to participants, who then act out the way they would handle a specific situation.

Role Playing To teach skills in working with other people, an organization may use **role playing.** This method involves assigning roles to participants, who then act out the way they would handle a specific situation. Some of the exercises in this book use role playing. A technique that enhances the usefulness of role playing is to videotape the session and play it back so participants can see how they looked and sounded.

Role playing gives people a chance to practice the way they react to others, making it especially useful for training in human relations skills such as communicating, resolving conflicts, and working with people of other races or cultures. People who have acted out a particular role—for example, the role of supervisor—

generally have more sympathy for that person's point of view. The major potential drawback of role playing is that, to be most useful, it requires a trainer with expertise in conducting it.

At New York–based Internet media company MaMaMedia.com, which produces Web-based "playful learning" products for children under 12, employees learn by doing, but as children do. "We try to approximate the way children learn through exploration, fun, surprise, and imagination," says Rebecca Randall, executive vice president of marketing and brand development. "One of the best ways to provoke thought is by engaging people in games, play, activities, theater, and role playing."[23]

Basic-Skills Training An often-heard complaint among employers today is that it is increasingly difficult to find enough employees with the basic skills necessary to perform modern jobs. An increasing number of employers are responding to this problem by conducting their own training in basic skills. Organizations that offer such programs not only improve the skills of their workers but also attract and keep employees who are highly motivated. However, basic-skills education offers some challenges to the employer. One is that employees may resist attending because they are embarrassed or afraid the organization will punish them if it finds out they do not have basic skills. To address this challenge, an organization should name the program carefully, calling it something like "workplace education" or "skills enhancement." Supervisors and other managers should reassure employees that participating in the program does not place their jobs in danger. In addition, experts recommend rewarding employees for participating in a basic-skills program.

Coaching to Support Training

coaching
Guidance and instruction in how to do a job so that it satisfies performance goals.

After employees have received training, a supervisor should take on the role of coach to help them maintain and use the skills they have acquired. **Coaching** is guidance and instruction in how to do a job so that it satisfies performance goals. The concept comes from sports, where a coach constantly observes team members in action, identifies each player's strengths and weaknesses, and works with each person to help him or her capitalize on strengths and improve on weaknesses. The most respected coaches generally encourage their team members and take a personal interest in them.

In a business context, coaching involves similar activities. As coach, a supervisor engages in regular observation, teaching, and encouragement to help employees develop so that they in turn can help the team succeed. Much of this coaching is done informally to back up the more formal training process.

In this role, a supervisor observes employees' performances daily and provides feedback. To encourage employees, a supervisor should praise them when they meet or exceed expectations. A supervisor should consider whether good performance is evidence that the employees can be given key responsibilities or have strengths that should be further developed. When an employee makes a mistake, the supervisor should work with the employee, focusing on the problem itself, rather than any perceived deficiencies in the employee's character. Together, the supervisor and employee should decide how to correct the problem—perhaps through more training, a revised assignment, or more reliable access to resources. A supervisor and employee should work on only one problem at a time, with the supervisor continually looking for signs of employee progress. Figure 17.5 summarizes the process of coaching.

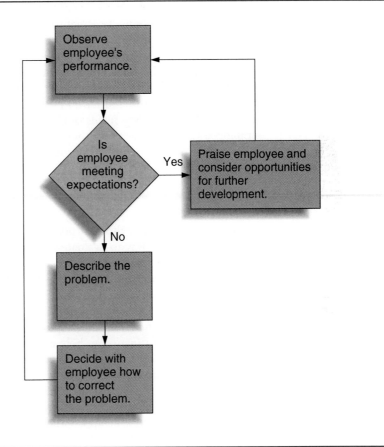

■ FIGURE 17.5

The Coaching Process

The process of coaching is different from simply telling employees what to do. It emphasizes learning about employees, then drawing on and developing their talents. (The Self-Quiz on page 472 can help you evaluate your coaching potential.) Acting as a coach is especially appropriate for supervisors in organizations that encourage employees to participate in decision making and teamwork.

Mentoring In some cases, a supervisor may focus coaching efforts on one employee. This practice is called **mentoring,** or providing guidance, advice, and encouragement through an ongoing one-on-one work relationship. A supervisor should not use a mentoring relationship as an excuse for failure to encourage all employees in the work group. However, mentoring may be an appropriate way to support the training of an employee who has especially great potential, needs extra attention to contribute fully, or has been assigned to the supervisor for that purpose. Some organizations use mentoring of minority and female employees to help them learn to navigate in a setting where communications styles, values, expectations, and so on differ from what they are used to.

At public relations firm FitzGerald Communications, in Cambridge, Massachusetts, new employees work with "buddies" from the client account teams for their first 90 days on the job. They then pick their own mentors, with whom they will meet several times over the course of the next year. The company takes

mentoring
Providing guidance, advice, and encouragement through an ongoing one-on-one work relationship.

mentoring so seriously that it has produced an 18-page mentoring handbook. The mentoring partners sign a contract to commit to the program, and both give their input in annual employee reviews.[24]

Some of the activities that mentors undertake include listening or acting as a sounding board, sharing knowledge and experience, guiding employees to discover the results of their own behavior, sharing what they know about opportunities in the organization and its future direction, looking beyond the needs of the company to focus on the needs of the person, and getting directly involved in the employee's career. One thing they don't do is give advice. The employee is best qualified to solve his or her own problems.[25]

Evaluation of Training

A supervisor is often in the best position to determine whether training is working. The most basic way to evaluate training is to measure whether the training is resolving the problem. Are new employees learning their jobs? Is the defect rate falling? Do employees use the new computer system properly? Are customers now praising the service instead of complaining about it? Looking for answers to such questions is central to the control process, described in Chapter 6.

Other people, including the employees who have participated in the training, also can provide information to help evaluate training. They might fill out a questionnaire (see Figure 17.6) or the organization might set up a team of people to evaluate the organization's training methods and content.

If the evaluation suggests that training is not meeting its objectives—as was the case with KG&E—the training may have to be modified or expanded. The type of training may not be appropriate for the training needs. For example, new employees who are having difficulty learning job skills may not have enough opportunity to practice what they are being taught. To identify what kinds of changes to make, the supervisor can ask questions such as the following:

- Was the trainer well prepared?
- Did the trainer communicate the information clearly and in an interesting way?
- Did the training include visual demonstrations in addition to verbal descriptions of how to do the task?
- Were the employees well enough prepared for the training program?
- Did the employees understand how they would benefit from the training?
- Did employees have a chance to ask questions?
- Did the employees receive plenty of praise for their progress?

To retain experienced managers at a manufacturing plant purchased from General Electric, Gates Energy Products human resource manager Robin Kane conducted a needs assessment to identify necessary skills and critical issues. She then designed a "new manager development program" consisting of courses that met for two days a month for nine months to cover such issues as team leadership skills, goal setting, motivating, delegating and time management, problem solving, decision making, negotiating, and managing conflict and change. Though the plant was later sold again, Kane was able to evaluate the program based on her goal of retaining managers: Turnover remained very low.[26]

Whatever the outcome, training represents a cost to the organization. Consequently, it is worth conducting only when it leads to improved performance, as

■ FIGURE 17.6

Questionnaire for Evaluating Training

Title of Program _____

Date _____ **Job Title** _____

Directions: Please indicate your response to each question and return this questionnaire to the program leader. Your responses are confidential. DO NOT SIGN YOUR NAME ON THIS EVALUATION INSTRUMENT.

1. In my opinion, this program was: (check one)
   ____ Excellent ____ Very good ____ Good ____ Fair ____ Poor
2. Did the program meet the objectives stated in the outline given to you? (check one)
   ____ Yes ____ No
3. Did the program meet your expectations? (Check one)
   ____ Yes ____ No If you checked no, please explain _____
   _____
4. Were the training facilities adequate? (Check one)
   ____ Yes ____ No If you checked no, please explain _____
   _____
5. In my opinion, the instructor was: (check one)
   ____ Excellent ____ Very good ____ Good ____ Fair ____ Poor
6. How important was each of these training elements? (check one for each element)
   Videotapes   ____ Very important ____ Worthwhile ____ Not important
   Role playing   ____ Very important ____ Worthwhile ____ Not important
   Lecture   ____ Very important ____ Worthwhile ____ Not important
   Handouts   ____ Very important ____ Worthwhile ____ Not important
   Group discussion ____ Very important ____ Worthwhile ____ Not important
7. To what extent did you participate in the program? (check one)
   ____ A lot ____ Just enough ____ Somewhat ____ Not at all
8. How much will the content of this program help you to perform your job responsibilities? (check one)
   ____ A lot ____ Just enough ____ Somewhat ____ Not at all
9. What other types of training programs are of interest to you? Indicate your preferences. _____
   _____
10. How can this program be improved? Indicate your suggestions. _____
   _____
11. Other comments and suggestions. Please indicate any other comments/suggestions that you feel will be useful in planning future training programs.
   _____
   _____
   _____
   _____
   _____

Source: Donald S. Miller and Stephen E. Catt, *Human Relations: A Contemporary Approach* (Homewood, IL: Richard D. Irwin, 1989), p. 330. Used by permission.

measured by increased quantity, quality, or both. Training that does not produce results should be changed or discontinued. In organizations where supervisors and others are selective and use only training that meets evaluation criteria, training programs are not just an expense, but a valuable investment in the organization's human resources.

Summary

17.1   Summarize reasons for conducting an orientation for new employees.

The primary reason to conduct an orientation is that the sooner new employees know basic information related to their job, the sooner they can become productive. Orientation also reduces the nervousness and uncertainty of new employees, and it helps them to develop a positive attitude by boosting job satisfaction.

17.2   Discuss how a supervisor and the human resources department can work together to conduct an orientation.

In a small organization, a supervisor may conduct most or all of the orientation. In a large organization, the human resources department may handle most of the task. In either case, it is up to the supervisor to convey information about the specifics of holding a particular job in a particular department. This includes explaining what the department does and what the new employee's job entails. Typically, the human resources department covers topics related to the organization's policies and procedures.

17.3   Identify methods for conducting an orientation.

During the orientation, a new employee should be introduced to the organization's employee handbook. A supervisor (or someone else) should give the employee a tour of the workplace, pointing out facilities the employee will need to use. During the tour, the employee should be introduced to the people with whom he or she will be working. A supervisor should instruct other employees in their role of welcoming a new employee. At the end of the first day and the first week, the supervisor should follow up to make sure the new employee understands the new job.

17.4   Describe the training cycle.

First, a supervisor (or someone else) assesses training needs. The next three steps cover planning the training: setting objectives, deciding who will participate, and choosing the training method. Then someone (a supervisor, an employee, or a professional trainer) conducts the training. The last step is to evaluate the success of the training. Evalua-

tion sometimes suggests needs for additional training.

17.5   Explain how supervisors can decide when employees need training.

A supervisor may observe problems in the department that indicate a need for training. Areas of change may signal training needs. A supervisor may ask employees about the kinds of training they need or may identify training needs when carrying out the planning function. Finally, some training may be mandated by government regulations, union work rules, or company policy.

17.6   Define major types of training.

The organization may use on-the-job training, which involves learning while performing a job. Related training methods are apprenticeship and cross-training (i.e., training employees in more than one job). The training also may take place off-site through vestibule training or in a classroom. Classroom training can be more effective when it includes computer-aided instruction (particularly interactive multimedia) and role playing. Some computer-aided instruction involves simulations. Finally, in an organization where employees lack basic skills such as the ability to read directions or work with numbers, the organization may offer basic-skills training.

17.7   Describe how a supervisor can use coaching and mentoring to support training.

To help employees maintain and use the skills they have acquired, a supervisor takes on the role of coach, guiding and instructing employees in how to do a job so that it satisfies performance goals. The supervisor observes employee performance and provides feedback on it. Supervisor and employee work together to devise a solution to any problem. Then the supervisor reviews the employee's performance to make sure the employee understood what to do and is doing it. A supervisor may act as a mentor to an employee, providing guidance, advice, and encouragement through an ongoing one-on-one work relationship. Some organizations use mentoring of minority and female employees as a way to help them learn to navigate unfamiliar work situations.

17.8 Discuss how a supervisor can evaluate the effectiveness of training.

To evaluate training, a supervisor measures whether the problem addressed by the training is being solved. In addition, participants in the training may fill out a questionnaire in which they evaluate their experience. When training is not producing the desired results, a supervisor should attempt to find out why and then correct the problem.

Key Terms

training, p. 447

orientation, p. 449

employee handbook, p. 452

on-the-job training, p. 457

apprenticeship, p. 458

vestibule training, p. 459

interactive multimedia, p. 462

role playing, p. 463

coaching, p. 464

mentoring, p. 465

Review and Discussion Questions

1. Describe a job or activity for which you received training. What was the purpose of this training?

2. Describe a situation in which you received an orientation. What did the orientation consist of? How was the orientation different from training?

3. When Al DeAngelis started his new job as a computer programmer, he arrived in his department at 9:30 A.M., after having spent time in the human resources department filling out forms. Marcia Eizenstadt, Al's supervisor, shook his hand and said, "Al, I'm so glad you're starting with us today. We need your talents tremendously." Then, explaining that she would be tied up all day in important planning meetings, Marcia showed Al to his desk and gave him an employee handbook to look at. "Read this carefully," said Marcia. "It'll tell you everything you need to know about working here. By tomorrow or the next day, I hope we'll be able to sit down and go over your first assignment." Al spent the rest of the day reading the manual, wishing for a cup of coffee, and trying to smile pleasantly in response to the quizzical looks he was getting from other employees passing by and glancing into his cubicle.

    a. What aspects of Al's orientation were helpful?

    b. How could it have been improved?

4. What are the steps in the training cycle?

5. Who determines when training is needed? What are some indications of a need for training?

6. Phil Petrakis supervises the housekeepers at a hotel in a big city. Phil has found that the easiest and fastest way to train his staff is to give them a memo describing whatever new policy or procedure he wants to teach. When the employees have read the memo, the training is complete—it is as simple as that. What is wrong with this approach?

7. Which type or types of training would you recommend in each of the following situations? Explain your choices.

    a. Teaching air-traffic controllers how to help pilots land planes safely.

    b. Improving the decision-making skills of production workers so they can better participate in the company's employee involvement program.

    c. Teaching a plumber how to replace sewer lines.

    d. Teaching a receptionist how to operate the company's new telephone system.

8. At a department meeting, production supervisor Lenore Gibbs announced, "Starting next month the company will be offering a class for any of you who can't read. It will take place after work in the cafeteria." How do you think employees with reading difficulties would react to Lenore's announcement? How can she phrase the announcement so that employees will be more likely to attend the class?

9. What is coaching? Why is it especially appropriate in organizations that encourage employee involvement and teamwork?

10. What is a mentor? What steps might a mentor take to help a Japanese employee who has been transferred from the Tokyo office to company headquarters in the United States? How might these actions help the employee and the organization?

11. Think back to the training you described in question 1. Evaluate its effectiveness. In what ways might it have been improved?

A SECOND LOOK

In the ongoing training at Ritz-Carlton, there appears to be no formal evaluation stage (Part 6 of the training cycle). How do you think evaluation is conducted?

SKILLS MODULE

CASE

Orientation at Web Industries

Web Industries is a small company known as a converter. It cuts materials into smaller sizes for use by manufacturers. Until recently, Web's new employees got the same training as new employees at many small companies: next to nothing. A supervisor would show a new employee how to operate machines and someone would describe the company's benefits package. It was up to the employee to sink or swim.

That changed as the company's managers began to recognize that although they thought they were too busy to train employees, they were spending just as much time fixing problems caused by the lack of training. Charles Edmunson, Web's vice president of manufacturing, gathered a cross-section of employees to brainstorm about the company's training needs. He then devised an orientation plan that calls for 20 hour-long sessions, which take place daily for four weeks.

The trainers are Web employees, including general managers, plant managers, customer service representatives, machine operators, maintenance workers, and office workers. Each trainer of a new employee covers an aspect of the orientation with which he or she is familiar. Trainers follow an outline prepared by Edmunson. They may add examples but not skip any section of the outline. Involving employees in the training builds a sense of commitment to the company and responsibility for the success of new employees. This approach is consistent with the company's overall emphasis on teamwork and employee involvement.

The orientation program covers the topics shown in Table A. According to Edmunson, some of the most important material is the information about the company, its goals, and employees' future with Web. Edmunson believes that this kind of information is easy to forget if it is not part of a formal orientation program. To make sure that all existing employees are familiar with the information, some Web plants started having all employees participate in the training.

Other topics covered in the orientation show employees how to help the company meet its goals. For example, making employees aware of the value of parts enables them to treat the parts with the care necessary to keep costs under control. Explains Edmunson, "We've got spacers for the machines that are an eighth of an inch wide and precision-ground, and they might be worth 25 or 30 bucks. They just look like little washer tubes. A new guy, if he's not aware that this is an expensive piece, may end up tossing it in the trash dumpster." Similarly, by explaining that the company competes for business by providing customized service, the trainers let new employees know the importance of catering to customers' demands.

When employees have completed the four weeks of orientation, they evaluate the program, indicating areas that need improvement. As a result, the orientation program has been updated once so far, and additional improvements are being considered.

1. Based on the information in Table A, does Web's orientation program appear to cover all the relevant topics? If not, what is missing?
2. What aspects of orientation should Web's supervisors handle? Consider that supervisors can both supplement and repeat what is covered during the formal orientation.
3. If you were a production supervisor at Web, how would you feel about having one of your machine operators take an hour or two each month to conduct training for new employees? Explain.

Source: *Inc.: The Magazine for Growing Companies*, by Leslie Brokaw. Copyright © 1991 by Business Innovator Group Resources/Inc. Reproduced with permission of Business Innovator Group Resources/Inc. via Copyright Clearance Center.

TABLE A **Topics Covered in Web Industries Orientation**	Week	Topics
	1	Welcome; Your Job; The Work Orders; Record Keeping; Your Benefits
	2	Our Business; Teamwork; Math for Converting; Packaging Standards; Maintenance Awareness
	3	Growing Our Company; Safety; Work Order Review; Record Keeping Review; How We Compete for Customers
	4	Your Future at Web; Constant Improvement; Math Review; Packaging Review; The ESOP (employee stock ownership plan)

Source: Adapted from Leslie Brokaw, "The Enlightened Employees Handbook," *Inc.*, October 1991.

SELF-QUIZ

Could You Coach Someone?

This quiz is designed to evaluate your potential for acting as a coach in support of training. Write True or False before each of the following statements.

_____ 1. The best way to get something done is to do it yourself.

_____ 2. If I give someone clear instructions, I know that person will get the job done without my checking on him or her.

_____ 3. I don't mind if someone asks me questions about how to do a job.

_____ 4. If I give someone instructions on how to perform a task, it's that individual's responsibility to complete it.

_____ 5. I like to let people know when they've done something right.

_____ 6. If someone makes a mistake, we focus on solving the problem together.

_____ 7. If someone makes a mistake, I correct the problem myself.

_____ 8. If someone doesn't follow company procedures, I assume he or she hasn't read the company handbook.

_____ 9. I think that interactive multimedia software is the best form of training for everyone.

_____ 10. Training a new employee shouldn't last more than a week.

Scoring: True responses to statements 2, 5, and 6 show good potential for coaching. True responses to the other statements show that you need to become aware of the needs of individuals, then work on drawing on and emphasizing their talents.

Class Exercise

One or more students volunteer to teach the class a skill. If possible, the volunteers should have time to prepare their "training session" before the class meets. Some "trainers" might like to work as a team. Suggestions for skills to teach follow; use your creativity to add to the list:

- Folding paper hats.
- Doing a card trick.
- Communicating a message in sign language.
- Making punch for a party.
- Setting the clock on a VCR.

After the training session or sessions, the class discusses the following questions:

1. How can you evaluate whether this training was successful? If possible, try conducting an evaluation of what the class learned. What do the results of this evaluation indicate?
2. What training techniques were used? Would additional or alternative techniques have made the skill easier to learn? What changes would have helped?

Team-Building Exercise

Orienting a New Team Member

Divide the class into teams of four or five. Select (or ask for a volunteer) one member of each team to play the role of a newcomer to the school (the newcomer might pose as a transfer student, a student from another country, or the like). The rest of the team will do its best to orient the newcomer to the school. Team members might want to take responsibility for different areas of knowledge; for example, one might draw a map of campus and town for the newcomer, pointing out bus routes and important or useful locations; another might volunteer information on study groups or social activities. At the end of the session, the newcomer should evaluate and discuss how effective the orientation was.

18

The imperial rater of nine grades seldom rates men according to their merits but always according to his likes and dislikes.
    —**Chinese writer of the Wei dynasty (fourth century A.D.)**

Appraising Performance

■ THE NEW WAVE IN EVALUATION

Steve Nadeau, vice president of human resources for Gwinnett Health System, a hospital with 3,300 employees in Lawrenceville, Georgia, had a problem. "The old-fashioned, paper-and-pencil performance review didn't work well for us," he said. "Evaluations were late, employees said it was too subjective, and managers didn't like the system." The problems snowballed and could even have affected the hospital system's accreditation by the Joint Commission on Accreditation of Healthcare Organizations, which evaluates more than 19,500 health care organizations in the United States.

Then Nadeau purchased a software program designed to support employee evaluations in the health care industry, and after a long period of testing and customizing the system with criteria specifically developed for the hospital, the program was implemented. Employees and managers were trained to use the program over a period of about two months, and the results were well worthwhile. "Employees have liked it from the start," says Nadeau.

The new system ties pay to performance, uses five employee ratings based on standards set by the hospital's managers, and reduces subjective input with modules that managers can customize but do not need to write from scratch. Although the system supports the hospital's traditional formal, manager-to-employee annual review, it also allows for input from co-workers, called 360-degree reviews, and it can incorporate the handwritten content of evaluation checklists designed for the two-thirds of Gwinnett's employees who don't have regular access to a computer. Since software-based performance appraisals like this one focus on results rather than on personality traits, the new system is likely to be seen as more objective and fair than the old one.

Source: Gail Dutton, "Making Reviews More Efficient and Fair," *Workforce*, April 2001, pp. 76–81.

---

performance appraisal
Formal feedback on how well an employee is performing his or her job.

Formal feedback on how well an employee is performing on the job is known as a **performance appraisal** (or a performance review or performance evaluation). Most organizations require that supervisors conduct a performance appraisal on each of their employees regularly, typically once a year. Therefore, supervisors need to know how to appraise performance fairly.

This chapter discusses reasons for conducting performance appraisals and describes a process for appraising performances systematically. It describes various types of appraisals used by organizations today. It tells how to avoid biases and how to conduct an appraisal interview.

Purposes of Performance Appraisal

Performance appraisals provide the information needed by employees to improve the quality of their work. To improve, employees need to hear how they are doing. As described in Chapters 7 and 10, a supervisor should provide frequent feedback. Performance appraisals supplement this informal information with a more thought-out, formal evaluation. (Employees who get enough informal feedback probably will not be surprised by the results of the appraisal.) A formal performance appraisal ensures that feedback to an employee covers all important aspects of the employee's performance.

Based on this information, the employee and supervisor can plan how to improve weak areas. In this way, performance appraisals support the practice of coaching, described in Chapter 17. For instance, at Van Kampen Investments in Oakbrook Terrace, Illinois, managers and supervisors use the review process to ask employees about their goals. "If an employee wants to go from customer service to finance, for example," says Jeanne Cliff, senior vice president of human resources, "what's the next step? Managers outline that for them, and give employees written goals and performance development plans."[1]

An appraisal also can help motivate employees. Most people appreciate the time their supervisor spends discussing their work, as well as praise for good performance; just hearing the supervisor's viewpoint can be motivating. Employees also tend to put forth the greatest effort in the areas that get appraised. Therefore, by rating employees on the kinds of behavior it considers important, an organization encourages them to try hard in those areas and keeps skilled workers in the firm. In a 1998 survey of information technology workers, more than 80 percent of those who responded said that receiving feedback and having individual development plans were among the top factors that would make them less likely to leave their firms.[2] And consider the case of Ransom, a union employee who had been with the same aerospace company for 18 years and had received exactly one face-to-face performance review with a supervisor in all that time. "No matter what I did," he says, "nobody reviewed my work and I never got noticed. After a while, I stopped being so concerned about performance."[3]

Above all, supervisors should remember that performance appraisals are part of the ongoing control process. Ron Adler, CEO of Laurdan Associates of Potomac, Maryland, says that the purpose of a performance appraisal should not be to mete out punishment or avoid lawsuits. "It's a method of getting action," he stresses, "either asking employees to keep doing what they're doing, or to change."[4] At Imagio, a public relations and advertising company, that question is asked quickly: New hires have 30 days to prove themselves before their first performance review. If they haven't shown that they are self-starters with team spirit, they are likely to be let go, with three weeks' severance pay. Ralph Fascitelli, the company's CEO, says that the rest of his growing firm is in accord with the policy, which acts as a control on productivity. "When someone is let go," he explains, "everyone understands that that person wasn't carrying their weight."[5]

Finally, performance appraisals provide important records for the organization. They are a useful source of information when deciding on raises, promotions, and discipline, and they provide evidence that these were administered fairly. A performance appraisal also provides documentation on employees whose behavior or performance is a problem. (For more on supervising problem employees, see Chapter 13.)

A Systematic Approach to Appraising Performance

To deliver their potential benefits, appraisals must be completely fair and accurate. Supervisors therefore should be systematic in appraising performance. They should follow a thorough process, use objective measures when possible, and avoid discrimination.

FIGURE 18.1

The Process of Performance Appraisal

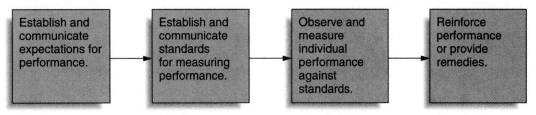

The Appraisal Process

The appraisal process takes place in four steps (see Figure 18.1). A supervisor establishes and communicates expectations for performance and standards for measuring performance. A supervisor also observes individual performance and measures it against the standards. Based on this information, a supervisor reinforces performance or provides remedies.

Establish and Communicate Expectations for Performance   During the planning process, a supervisor determines what the department or work group should accomplish (see Chapter 6). Through action plans, a supervisor spells out who is to do what to accomplish those objectives. From this information, it is relatively easy to specify what each employee must do to help the department or work group meet its objectives. One approach is to list the three to five major responsibilities of each position; the appraisal then focuses on these responsibilities.

For example, suppose Francine Bloch supervises the delivery personnel for a chain of appliance stores in Dallas. Each driver is expected to operate the vehicle safely, deliver every appliance without damaging anything, and be polite to customers.

A supervisor must make sure employees know and understand what is expected of them. To do this, a supervisor should make sure that objectives for the employees are clear, and he or she should communicate them effectively (see Chapter 10). Employees are most likely to understand and be committed to objectives when they have a say in developing them. More and more firms now require that supervisors and employees together set mutually acceptable performance goals.

Establish and Communicate Standards for Measuring Performance   Because expectations for performance are objectives, each expectation should be measurable (see Chapter 6). In appraising performance, a supervisor's task includes deciding how to measure employees' performance and then making sure employees know what will be measured. For instance, if an employee's job requires him or her to "deal with ambiguity," some criteria that could be set to measure this behavior could include:

- Shifting gears quickly.
- Seeing the big picture quickly.
- Making decisions without having "perfect" information.
- Valuing diverse ways of handling problems.[6]

With Francine's employees, the standards would include delivering all appliances without damage, having zero accidents or traffic tickets, and receiving no complaints from customers about service.

Observe and Measure Individual Performance against Standards   Through the control process, a supervisor should continuously gather information about each employee's performance. This is an ongoing activity, not something the supervisor saves to do when filling out appraisal forms. As consultant Carol Booz says, if managers and supervisors can "find a system to keep track of all of the things their employees have done during the review period, they won't view the process as much of a chore."[7] When preparing a performance appraisal, a supervisor compares this information with the standards for the employee being appraised. In the example, Francine would keep records of uncompleted deliveries, damage, accidents, traffic tickets, and customer complaints (and compliments). When appraising a particular employee's performance, she can see how often those problems arose with the employee.

Reinforce Performance or Provide Remedies   To keep employees motivated and informed, a supervisor needs to tell them when they are doing something right, not just when they are making a mistake. Thus, the final step of the appraisal process includes reinforcement for good performance. This can be as simple as pointing out to employees where they have performed well. For example, Francine might compliment one of the drivers on a letter of praise from a customer. A supervisor might want to comment that this information will be placed in the employee's permanent record with the organization.

Where performance falls short of the standards, an employee needs to know how to improve. A supervisor may state a remedy, but asking the employee to help solve the problem is often more effective. In the case of a driver who has received two traffic tickets for illegal left turns, Francine might point out this situation and ask the driver for an explanation. The driver might reply that he was confused because he was lost. With that information, Francine and the driver can work together to get the driver better acquainted with finding his way around Dallas.

Francine and the driver are treating the underlying problem (the driver's difficulty in finding his way around), rather than the symptom (the traffic tickets). Therefore, the driver's performance in this area can improve in the future. In general, to move beyond discussing symptoms to uncover the underlying problems, a supervisor and employee can ask which of the following kinds of causes led to the poor performance:

- *Inadequate skills*—If the problem is the employee's lack of certain skills, a supervisor should see that the employee gets the necessary training, as described in the previous chapter.
- *Lack of effort*—If the problem is a lack of effort on the employee's part, a supervisor may need to apply the principles of motivation discussed in Chapter 11.
- *Shortcomings of the process*—If organizational or job-related policies and procedures reward inefficient or less than high-quality behavior, the supervisor and employee may be able to change the way work is done.
- *External conditions*—If the problem is something beyond the control of supervisor and employee (e.g., a poor economy, lack of cooperation from another department, or a strike by suppliers), the appraisal standards and ratings should be adjusted so that they are fair to the employee.

- *Personal problems*—If performance is suffering because the employee has personal problems, a supervisor should handle the situation with counseling and discipline (see Chapter 13).

In investigating the underlying problem, a supervisor may gain important insights by asking what can be done to help the employee reach goals. Before the appraisal is over, an employee should have a clear plan for making necessary changes.

What to Measure in an Appraisal

Waitress Kelly O'Hara was furious as she walked out of her performance appraisal interview. "Irresponsible!" she muttered to herself, "Lazy! Who does he think he is, calling me those things? He doesn't know what he's talking about." Kelly's reaction shows that labeling people with certain characteristics is not a constructive approach to conducting an appraisal. Labels tend to put people on the defensive, and they are difficult, if not impossible, to prove.

Instead, a performance appraisal should focus on *behavior* and *results*. Focusing on behavior means that the appraisal should describe specific actions or patterns of actions. Focusing on results means describing the extent to which an employee has satisfied the objectives for which he or she is responsible. If Kelly's supervisor had noted that he had received several complaints about slow service, he and Kelly could have worked on a plan to minimize these complaints. Perhaps the problem was not even Kelly's behavior, but recurrent backlogs in the kitchen. The focus on meeting objectives would be more constructive than simply evaluating Kelly as "lazy," because it tells an employee exactly what is expected. This focus is also more fair, especially if the employee helped to set the objectives.

In many cases, a supervisor uses an appraisal form that requires drawing conclusions about the employee's personal characteristics. For example, a supervisor might need to rate an employee's dependability or attitude. Although such ratings are necessarily subjective, a supervisor can try to base them on observations about behavior and results. One approach is to record at least one specific example for each category rated. A rating on a personal characteristic seems more reasonable when a supervisor has evidence supporting his or her conclusion.

EEOC Guidelines

As described in Chapter 16, the Equal Employment Opportunity Commission (EEOC) is the government agency charged with enforcing federal laws against discrimination. The EEOC published the Uniform Guidelines on Employee Selection Procedures, which include guidelines for designing and implementing performance appraisals. In general, the behaviors or characteristics measured by a performance appraisal should be related to the job and to succeeding on the job. For example, if the appraisal measures "grooming," then good grooming should be important for success in the job. Because of this requirement, a supervisor and others responsible for the content of performance appraisals should make sure that what they measure is still relevant to a particular job.

Just as hiring should be based on a candidate's ability to perform the essential tasks of a particular job, so appraisals should be based on the employee's success in carrying out those tasks. The ratings in a performance appraisal should not be discriminatory; that is, they should not be based on an employee's race, sex, or other protected category but on an employee's ability to meet standards of performance.

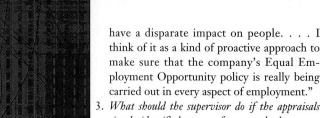

SUPERVISION AND DIVERSITY

Appraising Employees Fairly

Recent lawsuits based on performance appraisals have claimed unfairness to women, minorities, and older workers. These suits suggest to Carole O'Blenes, a partner in the law office of Proskauer Rose (New York), that there is a high potential for mistakes and misunderstandings to enter the evaluation process. Here are her suggestions for avoiding problems.

1. *What should a supervisor do about rating employees' subjective traits like enthusiasm or aggressiveness that could be considered to work against a certain gender or race or age group?* "It's preferable from a legal perspective that performance appraisals focus on behaviors rather than attitudes. So instead of rating someone on enthusiasm, you could phrase it in terms of behavior, like `takes on extra responsibility.' Ask what enthusiasm really means, why it's important."

2. *What should the supervisor do if, after a round of appraisals, a large number of women or minorities have received poor reviews?* "Examine those appraisals very carefully to see if there are criteria being applied that have a disparate impact on people. . . . I think of it as a kind of proactive approach to make sure that the company's Equal Employment Opportunity policy is really being carried out in every aspect of employment."

3. *What should the supervisor do if the appraisals simply identified poor performers who happen to be women or minorities?* "That can happen as easily as having three males who are lousy performers. . . . But you don't have to wait until you're hit with a lawsuit—or those women are being fired—before saying, "Gee, did we do something wrong here?" You know in advance. You've looked at it so that if there's a mistake, you can correct it, and if there isn't, you're in a position to defend it. You know where you stand."

Source: From *Workforce* by Gillian Flynn. Copyright 2001 by ACC Communications, Inc. Reproduced with permission of ACC Communications, Inc. via Copyright Clearance Center.

Furthermore, an employee should know in advance what those standards are, and the organization should have a system in place for employees to ask questions about their ratings. See "Supervision and Diversity."

Performance Appraisals and Pay Reviews

Many organizations review an employee's wage or salary level at the time of the performance appraisal. This reinforces the link the company makes between performance and pay increases. An employee with an excellent rating would be eligible to receive the largest allowable increase, whereas someone rated as a poor worker might not get any raise or only a cost-of-living increase.

However, reviewing pay and performance at the same time presents a potentially serious drawback.[8] Employees tend to focus on the issue of money, so a supervisor has more difficulty using the performance evaluation as an opportunity for motivating and coaching. Thus, many experts recommend conducting the two types of reviews at separate times. A supervisor of course has little choice in this matter. A supervisor who must review pay rates at the same time as performance should make an extra effort to emphasize performance, and it is especially important to provide coaching and feedback about performance throughout the year.

Types of Appraisals

Many techniques have been developed for appraising performance. The human resources department or higher-level management usually dictate which type the supervisor will use. An organization that has all supervisors use the same approach establishes a way to keep records showing performance over time, especially when an employee reports to more than one supervisor during his or her employment. Although a supervisor has to use the appraisal format selected for the whole organization, he or she may be able to supplement it with other helpful information. A supervisor can use the "Comments" section of a preprinted form or attach additional information to it.

Graphic Rating Scales

graphic rating scale
A performance appraisal that rates the degree to which an employee has achieved various characteristics.

The most commonly used type of appraisal is the **graphic rating scale,** which rates the degree to which an employee has achieved various characteristics, such as job knowledge or punctuality. The rating is often scored from 1 to 5, for example, with 5 representing excellent performance and 1 representing poor performance. Some appraisal forms include space for comments, so that a supervisor can provide support for his or her ratings. Figure 18.2 is a sample appraisal form using a graphic rating scale.

The main advantage of a graphic rating scale is that it is relatively easy to use. In addition, the scores provide a basis for deciding whether an employee has improved in various areas. However, the ratings themselves are subjective; what one supervisor considers "excellent" may be only "average" to another. Also, many supervisors tend to rate everyone at least a little above average. Some appraisal forms attempt to overcome these problems by containing descriptions of excellent or poor behavior in each area. Other rating scales pose a different problem by labeling performance in terms of how well an employee "meets requirements." Presumably, the supervisor wants *all* employees to meet the requirements of the job. However, scoring everyone high on this scale may be seen as a rating bias (on the assumption that not everyone can be a "top performer"), rather than successful management of human resources.[9]

Paired-Comparison Approach

paired-comparison approach
A performance appraisal that measures the relative performance of employees in a group.

The **paired-comparison approach** measures the relative performance of employees in a group. A supervisor lists the employees in the group and then ranks them. One method is to compare the performance of the first two employees on the list. A supervisor places a check mark next to the name of the employee whose performance is better, then repeats the process, comparing the first employee's performance with that of the other employees. Next, the supervisor compares the second employee on the list with all the others, and so on until each pair of employees has been compared. The employee with the most check marks is considered the most valuable.

A supervisor also can compare employees in terms of several criteria, such as work quantity and quality. For each criterion, a supervisor ranks the employees from best to worst, assigning a 1 to the lowest-ranked employee and the highest score to the best employee in that category. Then all the scores for each employee are totaled to see who has the highest total score.

The paired-comparison approach is appropriate when a supervisor needs to find one outstanding employee in a group. It can be used to identify the best candidate for a promotion or special assignment. However, paired comparison makes some employees look good at the expense of others, which makes this technique less useful as a means of providing feedback to individual employees. It is especially inappropriate as a routine form of appraisal in situations calling for cooperation and teamwork.[10]

■ FIGURE 18.2

Sample Graphic Rating Scale

Name _____ Dept. _____ Date _____

		Outstanding	Good	Satisfactory	Fair	Unsatisfactory
Quantity of work	Volume of acceptable work under normal conditions Comments:	☐	☐	☐	☐	☐
Quality of work	Thoroughness, neatness, and accuracy of work Comments:	☐	☐	☐	☐	☐
Knowledge of job	Clear understanding of the facts or factors pertinent to the job Comments:	☐	☐	☐	☐	☐
Personal qualities	Personality, appearance, sociability, leadership, integrity Comments:	☐	☐	☐	☐	☐
Cooperation	Ability and willingness to work with associates, supervisors, and subordinates toward common goals Comments:	☐	☐	☐	☐	☐
Dependability	Conscientious, thorough, accurate, reliable with respect to attendance, lunch periods, reliefs, etc. Comments:	☐	☐	☐	☐	☐
Initiative	Earnestness in seeking increased responsibilities. Self-starting, unafraid to proceed alone Comments:	☐	☐	☐	☐	☐

Source: John M. Ivancevich, *Human Resource Management: Foundations of Personnel*, 7th ed. (New York: Irwin/McGraw-Hill, 1998), p. 272. Copyright © 1998 by The McGraw-Hill Companies. Reproduced with permission of The McGraw-Hill Companies.

This approach is not without its problems, however. In the last couple of years blacks and women at Microsoft, U.S. citizens at Conoco, and older workers at Ford Motor Company have filed class-action suits claiming that these firms discriminated in assigning grades. Microsoft defends the system, which is also used by other major companies like Cisco Systems, Intel, Enron, and General Electric. "We want to give the highest compensation to the very top performers," says Microsoft's senior vice president for human resources, Deborah Willingham. The company says it has checks and balances in the system to ensure fairness and that employees are largely responsible for the rating criteria and can appeal their ratings. Conoco and Ford have also denied any discriminatory intent. Some critics, like David Thomas of Harvard Business School, contend that "companies are playing their version of 'Survivor,'" however, and Cisco planned to use its grading system as one way to identify the 5,000 workers it recently said it would lay off.[11]

■ FIGURE 18.3

Sample Forced-Choice Appraisal

Instructions	Rank from 1 to 4 the following sets of statements according to how they describe the manner in which _____ performs
	(name of employee)

the job. A rank of 1 should be used for the most descriptive statement, and a rank of 4 should be given or the least descriptive. No ties are allowed.

1. _____ Does not anticipate difficulties

   _____ Grasps explanations quickly

   _____ Rarely wastes time

   _____ Easy to talk to

2. _____ A leader in group activities

   _____ Wastes time on unimportant things

   _____ Cool and calm at all times

   _____ Hard worker

Source: John M. Ivancevich, *Human Resource Management: Foundations of Personnel*, 7th ed. (New York: Irwin/McGraw-Hill, 1998), p. 274. Copyright © 1998 by The McGraw-Hill Companies. Reproduced with permission of The McGraw-Hill Companies.

Forced-Choice Approach

forced-choice approach
A performance appraisal that presents an appraiser with sets of statements describing employee behavior; the appraiser must choose which statement is most characteristic of the employee and which is least characteristic.

In the **forced-choice approach,** the appraisal form gives a supervisor sets of statements describing employee behavior. For each set of statements, a supervisor must choose one that is most characteristic and one that is least characteristic of the employee. Figure 18.3 illustrates part of an appraisal form using the forced-choice approach.

These questionnaires tend to be set up in a way that prevents a supervisor from saying only positive things about employees. Thus, the forced-choice approach is used when an organization determines that supervisors have been rating an unbelievably high proportion of employees as above average.

Essay Appraisal

Sometimes a supervisor must write a description of the employee's performance, answering questions such as "What are the major strengths of this employee?" or "In what areas does this employee need improvement?" Essay appraisals often are used along with other types of appraisals, notably graphic rating scales. They provide an opportunity for a supervisor to describe aspects of performance that are not thoroughly covered by an appraisal questionnaire. The main drawback of essay appraisals is that their quality depends on a supervisor's writing skills.

Behaviorally Anchored Rating Scales (BARS)

behaviorally anchored rating scales (BARS)
A performance appraisal in which an employee is rated on scales containing statements describing performance in several areas.

Some organizations pay behavioral scientists or organizational psychologists to create **behaviorally anchored rating scales (BARS).** These scales rate employee performance in several areas, such as work quantity and quality, using a series of statements that describe effective and ineffective performance in each area. In

Sample Behaviorally Anchored Rating Scale (BARS)

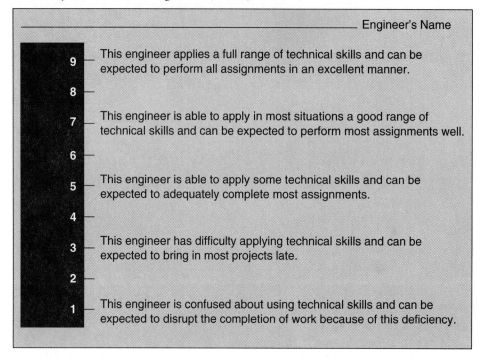

Source: John M. Ivancevich, *Human Resource Management: Foundations of Personnel*, 7th ed. (New York: Irwin/McGraw-Hill, 1998), p. 277. Copyright © 1998 by The McGraw-Hill Companies. Reproduced with permission of The McGraw-Hill Companies.

each area, a supervisor selects the statement that best describes how an employee performs. The statements in the rating scales are different for each job title in the organization. Figure 18.4 shows a behaviorally anchored rating scale measuring the performance area of engineering competence.

The major advantage of using BARS is that they can be tailored to the organization's objectives for employees. In addition, the BARS approach is less subjective than some other approaches because it uses statements describing behavior. However, developing the scales is time-consuming and therefore relatively expensive.

Checklist Appraisal

A checklist appraisal contains a series of questions about an employee's performance. Figure 18.5 shows the format for this kind of appraisal. A supervisor answers yes or no to the questions. Thus, a checklist is merely a record of performance, not an evaluation by a supervisor. The human resources department has a key for scoring the items on the checklist; the score results in a rating of an employee's performance.

While the checklist appraisal is easy to complete, it has several disadvantages. The checklist can be difficult to prepare, and each job category will probably require a different set of questions. Also, a supervisor has no way to adjust the answers for any special circumstances that affect performance.

FIGURE 18.5

Sample Checklist Appraisal

	Yes	No
1. Does the employee willingly cooperate with others in completing work assignments?	____	____
2. Does the employee have adequate job knowledge to perform duties in a satisfactory manner?	____	____
3. In terms of quality, is the employee's work acceptable?	____	____
4. Does the employee meet deadlines for the completion of work assignments?	____	____
5. Does the employee's record indicate unexcused absences?	____	____
6. Does the employee follow safety rules and regulations?	____	____

Source: Stephen E. Catt and Donald S. Miller, *Supervision: Working with People*, 2d ed. (Homewood, IL: Richard D. Irwin, 1991), p. 374.

Critical-Incident Appraisal

critical-incident appraisal
A performance appraisal in which a supervisor keeps a written record of incidents that show positive and negative ways an employee has acted; the supervisor uses this record to assess the employee's performance.

To conduct a **critical-incident appraisal,** a supervisor keeps a written record of incidents that show positive and negative ways an employee has acted. The record should include dates, people involved, actions taken, and any other relevant details. At the time of the appraisal, a supervisor reviews the record to reach an overall evaluation of an employee's behavior. During the appraisal interview, a supervisor should give an employee a chance to offer his or her views of each incident recorded.

This technique has the advantage of focusing on actual behaviors. However, keeping records of critical incidents can be time-consuming and, even if a supervisor is diligent, important incidents could be overlooked. Also, supervisors tend to record negative events more than positive ones, resulting in an overly harsh appraisal.

Work-Standards Approach

work-standards approach
A performance appraisal in which an appraiser compares an employee's performance with objective measures of what the employee should do.

To use the **work-standards approach,** a supervisor tries to establish objective measures of performance. A typical work standard would be the quantity produced by an assembly-line worker. This amount should reflect what a person normally could produce. A supervisor then compares an employee's actual performance with the standards.

Although the work-standards approach has been applied largely to production workers, the principle of objectively measuring outcomes make sense for a variety of jobs. A recent review of performance appraisals recommends describing each job in terms of 6 to 16 results that the organization wants accomplished.[12] The job results associated with customer service positions, for instance, might include "Serves customers by providing service requested." Then quality standards are established for achieving each result. The quality standard for the previous example might be "Customers are treated with courtesy at all times. Questions and requests are responded to promptly."[13] Under this system, performance appraisals would focus on two issues: Did the employee meet the quality standards? If not, what changes are required to the work process, access to resources, training, motivation, and so on?

SUPERVISION ACROSS INDUSTRIES

Education

Grading the Teacher

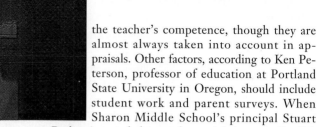

Educators might agree that the ultimate measure of teacher success is student performance. Traditionally, however, teachers have been compensated based on seniority, not results. Some school districts would like to see that change, though merit pay for teachers will be a tough sell. In the meantime, how is classroom performance to be evaluated?

It turns out there are nearly as many different ways to appraise teachers and offer feedback as there are classrooms. Some school districts rely on the traditional method of classroom observations. Even when the observer takes notes on a laptop computer instead of a scratch pad, the method is still basically the same.

But because a problem teacher with professional status and tenure can be difficult to remove from the classroom, in a process as agonizing as it is lengthy, many administrators prefer to work with person-to-person coaching and feedback to try to resolve difficulties and get teachers back on track. And some teachers themselves are responding with innovative approaches to the appraisal process.

Hard data about student performance from standardized test scores gives an incomplete picture of the teacher's competence, though they are almost always taken into account in appraisals. Other factors, according to Ken Peterson, professor of education at Portland State University in Oregon, should include student work and parent surveys. When Sharon Middle School's principal Stuart Berkowitz needed to evaluate eighth-grade English teacher Julie Belcher, Belcher was ready. She met Berkowitz with a in-depth discussion of her classroom projects, including a student book review website and an experiment intended to stimulate student participation. Belcher's goal was to focus less on superficial factors like classroom management and more on teaching goals and student understanding.

Supervisors in education as well as in other fields can readily appreciate that weather appraisal is based on performance, results, or both, there is little to lose from being prepared to present yourself and your achievements in the best light.

Sources: Ronald Brownstein, "National Perspectives: Make the Buck Stop with Teachers by Linking Raises to Student Results," *Los Angeles Times*, February 5, 2001, p. A5; Laura Pappano, "What Makes an A+ Educator? Reforms Provoke Reassessment of Teacher Evaluations," *Boston Globe*, February 11, 2001, p. C5.

Management by Objectives (MBO)

Chapter 7 introduced management by objectives (MBO) as a planning tool. In an organization that uses MBO, a supervisor will also use this approach for appraising performance. A supervisor compares each employee's accomplishments with the objectives for that employee. If the employee has met or exceeded his or her objectives, the appraisal will be favorable. The main advantages of this system are that an employee knows what is expected and a supervisor focuses on results rather than more subjective criteria.

The Police Department of Madison, Wisconsin, recently replaced its traditional appraisals with a system of individual goal setting, leadership training, and employee involvement. A survey of 12 metropolitan police departments conducted by the U.S. Department of Justice later found that Madison's 500-member force had the highest satisfaction level among citizens, and each year it receives more than 1,000 applications for about two dozen job openings.[14]

Assessments by Someone Other than the Supervisor

Supervisors cannot know how an employee behaves at all times or in all situations. Nor can supervisors always appreciate the full impact of an employee's behavior on people inside and outside the organization. To supplement what supervisors do know, other people might offer insights into an employee's behavior. For this reason, supervisors may combine their appraisals with self-assessments by the employee or with appraisals by peers and customers. Appraisals of supervisors and other managers also may come from their subordinates. Combining several sources of appraisals is called **360-degree feedback.**[15]

360-degree feedback
Performance appraisal that combines assessments from several sources.

At Photo Disc, supervisors and employees agree on the names of 6 to 10 peers, internal customers, team members, supervisors, and subordinates, all of whom complete a three-page review form that analyzes core aspects of the employee's performance such as teamwork and follow-through. A consultant compiles the results and acts as a safeguard against "stacked" ratings. Then the employee and the supervisor discuss the results, and the employee proposes a development plan based on any training needs that have been revealed.[16] And at Trinity Communications, Inc., a small marketing firm based in Boston, each employee is reviewed by both colleagues and clients. "It can be scary," founding partner Nancy Michalowski says of the process. "The challenge is to be constructive so that you all can continue to work together."[17]

To use self-assessments, a supervisor can ask each employee to complete an assessment before the appraisal interview. Then the supervisor and employee compare the employee's evaluation of his or her own behavior with the supervisor's evaluation. This can stimulate discussion and insights in areas where the two are in disagreement.

peer reviews
Performance appraisals conducted by an employee's co-workers.

Appraisals by peers—often called **peer reviews**—are less common, but their use is growing. Com-Corp Industries uses peer reviews to balance an appraisal that is affected by a supervisor's feelings about an employee. If the peer reviews conflict with a supervisor's appraisal, the company's human resources director investigates the source of the discrepancy.[18] Employees who work in teams usually appraise the performance of their team members. The teams do this in meetings, where they discuss each team member's strengths and areas needing improvement. Presumably, employees will react more positively to peer reviews in which all employees participate in the appraising on an equal basis than to peer reviews used occasionally for selected employees. See "Meeting the Challenge" to learn how one firm appraises its work teams.

The drive to please customers in a highly competitive market, coupled with a desire for practical information on performance, has encouraged some companies to institute programs in which customers appraise employees' performance. Major companies using customer appraisals include IBM, Sears, Ameritech, and Motorola. National Fuel Gas Distribution Corporation, headquartered in Buffalo, New York, asks its major customers to assess salespeople's performance in several areas, including product knowledge and problem-solving ability.[19] Even outside competitors can be a good source of general feedback.[20] They can tell you how others see you, including customers, and sometimes they will share information about how they have faced problems similar to yours. Be prepared to offer some nonclassified information in return.

At an increasing number of major corporations, subordinates rate how well their bosses manage. Typically, ratings are anonymous, to protect the workers. The purpose of these subordinate appraisals is to give managers information they can use to supervise more effectively and to make their organization more competitive. The appraisals also support the trend toward giving operative employees a greater voice in how an organization is run.

Hyde Manufacturing Company is one company that's working hard to incorporate a new feedback system.[21] This 120-year-old company is responding to tougher competition by shifting to a team-based operation that calls for employees

Reviewing Teams

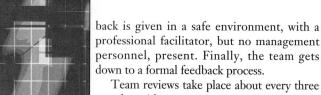

If supervisors find it hard to review employees one on one, how do they review teams?

Con-Way Transportation Services, a subsidiary of CNF, has an answer. Teams evaluate themselves, in a process called the team improvement review. Instead of focusing on judging, the team members ask themselves questions such as, "What are we doing that's working? What are we doing that's not working? How can we change that? Was there something I should have noticed? Could I have helped?"

The basis for successful appraisals was laid when the 100-member team was formed. The first step was to create an agreement about how to do things; that agreement includes a definition of excellent performance against which to measure team results. Then there's the appraisal process itself, which has three distinctive features. First, it separates feedback sessions from salary reviews, to take the pressure off employees reluctant to affect co-workers' salaries. Second, feedback is given in a safe environment, with a professional facilitator, but no management personnel, present. Finally, the team gets down to a formal feedback process.

Team reviews take place about every three months, with preparation starting a week before when members rate the team's performance on 31 criteria, using a scale of 1 to 5. During the review, team performance is discussed and individual performance is covered in the context of the team. Each person writes down his or her own strengths and "things to work on," which are passed around the room so everyone can comment on everyone else's list. Interestingly enough, the "things to work on" that each person comes up with are usually the same ones the team wishes they'd work on too.

Source: Gina Imperato, "How Con-Way Reviews Teams," *Fast Company*, September 1998, p. 152.

to review their team leaders with confidential, anonymous questionnaires. A pilot program begun in late 1994 grew into a system in which shop-floor workers review their team leaders and team leaders review their business-unit leaders, who in turn assess the director of manufacturing operations. Says Hyde's human resources director Dick Ayers, "None of us scored as well as we thought we would. . . . How people feel about this exercise is only going to be as good as the action we take to improve on weaknesses." Future refinements to the new system will probably include reports back to employees about how supervisors plan to act on the results of their reviews.

Benefits of 360-Degree Feedback Combining several sources of performance appraisal can correct some of the appraisal biases described in the next section. It also can provide information that is more useful for problem solving and employee development than the typical results of a traditional top-down appraisal. After New York–based Teleport Communications Group had customers rate the performance of its salespeople, sales rep Maryann Cirenza learned of shortcomings that helped her refocus on activities the customers found more valuable.[22] Similarly, Joe Malik, who manages a team of engineers at AT&T, was surprised to learn from a subordinate review that his employees were not focused merely on day-to-day challenges, but expected him to communicate a vision and a mission for his group.[23] Coming from one person, such challenges can be easy to ignore. When combined voices force a person to listen, the resulting improvements can enhance the person's long-term career prospects.

Guidelines for 360-Degree Feedback New software programs make 360-degree feedback easier by streamlining the assessment process, cutting administrative costs, and reducing the possibility of error.[24] A few questions to ask about such software before investing in it might include:[25]

- Do you want to gather cross-functional information to compare performance throughout your organization?
- Do you want to use the system for purposes beyond employee development, such as organizational climate and customer satisfaction surveys?
- How important is total respondent confidentiality?
- If you value accountability, what impact will that have on your concerns for confidentiality? For example, do you want to track survey completion by the respondents, examine potential collusion among raters, or help them improve the quality of their feedback?

For 360-feedback to be effective, the person managing the review process should ensure that the responses are anonymous. Subordinates especially may be afraid to respond honestly if they think that the person being reviewed will retaliate for negative comments. Anonymity is greater if the responses are pooled into a single report rather than presented one by one. Collecting appraisals from more than three or four people also increases the likelihood of protecting respondents' privacy.[26]

Sources of Bias

harshness bias
Rating employees more severely than their performances merit.

leniency bias
Rating employees more favorably than their performances merit.

central tendency
The tendency to select employee ratings in the middle of a scale.

proximity bias
The tendency to assign similar scores to items that are near each other on a questionnaire.

Ideally, supervisors should be completely objective in their appraisals of employees. Each appraisal should directly reflect an employee's performance, not any biases of a supervisor. Of course, this is impossible to do perfectly. We all make compromises in our decision-making strategies and have biases in evaluating what other people do. Supervisors need to be aware of these biases, so that their effect on the appraisals can be limited or eliminated. Figure 18.6 shows some sources of bias that commonly influence performance appraisals.

Some supervisors are prone to a **harshness bias,** that is, rating employees more severely than their performance merits. New supervisors are especially susceptible to this error, because they may feel a need to be taken seriously. Unfortunately, the harshness bias also tends to frustrate and discourage workers, who resent the unfair assessments of their performance.

At the other extreme is the **leniency bias.** Supervisors with this bias rate their employees more favorably than their performance merits. A supervisor who does this may want credit for developing a department full of "excellent" workers. Or the supervisor may simply be uncomfortable confronting employees with their shortcomings. The leniency bias may feel like an advantage to the employees who receive the favorable ratings, but it cheats the employees and department of the benefits of truly developing and coaching employees.

A bias that characterizes the responses to many types of questionnaires is **central tendency,** which is the tendency to select ratings in the middle of the scale. People seem more comfortable on middle ground than taking a strong stand at either extreme. This bias causes a supervisor to miss important opportunities to praise or correct employees.

Proximity means nearness. The **proximity bias** refers to the tendency to assign similar scores to items that are near each other on a questionnaire. If a supervisor assigns a score of 8 to one appraisal item, this bias might encourage the supervisor to score the next item as 6 or 7, even though a score of 3 is more accurate. Obviously, this can result in misleading appraisals.

Sources of Bias in Performance Appraisals

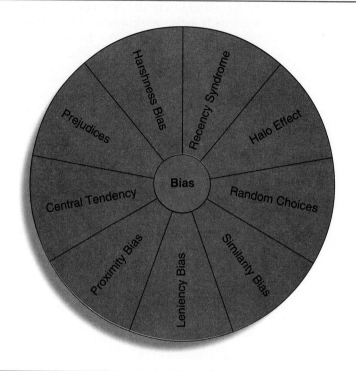

When using a type of appraisal that requires answers to specific questions, a supervisor might succumb to making *random choices*. A supervisor might do this when uncertain how to answer or when the overall scoring on the test looks undesirable. For example, if a supervisor thinks an appraisal is scoring an employee too low, he or she might give favorable ratings in some areas where the supervisor has no strong feelings. Supervisors who catch themselves making random choices should slow down and try to apply objective criteria.

The **similarity bias** refers to the tendency to judge others more positively when they are like ourselves. Thus, we tend to look more favorably on people who share our interests, tastes, background, or other characteristics. For example, in appraising performance, a supervisor risks viewing a person's performance in a favorable light because the employee shares his or her flair for dressing in the latest fashions. Or a supervisor might interpret negatively the performance of an employee who is much shyer than the supervisor.

As described in Chapter 9, the *recency syndrome* refers to the human tendency to place the most weight on events that have occurred most recently. In a performance appraisal, a supervisor might give particular weight to a problem the employee caused last week or an award the employee just won whereas he or she should be careful to consider events and behaviors that occurred throughout the entire period covered by the review. The most accurate way to do this is to keep records throughout the year, as described earlier with conducting a critical-incident appraisal.

The *halo effect*, introduced in Chapter 16, refers to the tendency to generalize one positive or negative aspect of a person to the person's entire performance. Thus, if supervisor Ben Olson thinks that a pleasant telephone manner is what

similarity bias
The tendency to judge others more positively when they are like yourself.

makes a good customer service representative, he is apt to give high marks to a representative with a pleasant voice, no matter what the employee actually says to the customers or how reliable the performance.

Finally, the supervisor's *prejudices* about various types of people can unfairly influence a performance appraisal. A supervisor needs to remember that each employee is an individual, not merely a representative of a group. A supervisor who believes that African Americans generally have poor skills in using standard English needs to recognize that this is a prejudice about a group, not a fact to apply to actual employees. Thus, before recommending that a black salesperson needs to improve her speaking skills, a supervisor must consider whether the salesperson really needs improvement in that area or whether the supervisor's prejudices are interfering with an accurate assessment. This is especially important in light of the EEOC guidelines discussed earlier in the chapter.

The Performance Appraisal Interview

The last stage of the appraisal process—the stage at which a supervisor reinforces performance or provides remedies—occurs in an interview between supervisor and employee. At this time, a supervisor describes what he or she has observed and discusses this appraisal with the employee. Together they agree on areas for improvement and development. If you have never been a supervisor, apply the questions to the way your current or most recent supervisor has appraised your performance.

Supervisors often dread conducting appraisal interviews. Pointing out another person's shortcomings can be an unpleasant experience. To overcome these feelings, it helps to focus on the benefits of appraising employees. Supervisors can cultivate a positive attitude by viewing the appraisal interview as an opportunity to coach and develop employees.

Purpose of the Interview

Quite simply, the purpose of holding an appraisal interview is to communicate information about an employee's performance. Once a supervisor has evaluated an employee's performance, the supervisor needs to convey his or her thoughts to the employee. An interview is an appropriate setting for doing so because it sets aside time to focus on and discuss the appraisal in private. The interview is also an opportunity for upward communication from the employee. By contributing his or her viewpoints and ideas, an employee can work with the supervisor on devising ways to improve performance.

Preparing for the Interview

Before the appraisal interview, a supervisor should allow plenty of time for completing the appraisal form. The form should be completed carefully and thoughtfully, not in a rush during the hour before the interview. Besides filling out the form, a supervisor should think about the employee's likely reactions to the appraisal and should plan how to handle them. A supervisor also should be ready with some ideas for correcting problems noted in the appraisal.

A supervisor should notify the employee about the appraisal interview ahead of time. Giving a few days' or a week's notice allows the employee to think about his or her performance. Then the employee can contribute ideas during the interview.

In addition, a supervisor should prepare an appropriate meeting place. The interview should take place in an office or other room where supervisor and employee will have privacy. The supervisor should arrange to prevent interruptions such as telephone calls.

Conducting the Interview

At the beginning of the interview, a supervisor should try to put an employee at ease. Employees are often uncomfortable at the prospect of discussing their performance. An offer of coffee and a little small talk may help to break the ice.

The supervisor can begin by reviewing the employee's self-appraisal, if one was completed, with the employee, asking him or her to give reasons for the various ratings. Then a supervisor describes his or her rating of the employee and how he or she arrived at it. A supervisor can start by describing overall impressions and then explain the contents of the appraisal form. A supervisor should explain the basis for the ratings, using specific examples of the employee's behavior and results. Most employees are waiting for the "bad news," so it is probably most effective to describe areas for improvement first, followed by the employee's strengths. People need to know what they are doing well so that they will continue on that course, realizing that their efforts are appreciated. See "Tips from the Firing Line" for some suggestions on communicating during the interview.

After describing the evaluation of the employee's performance, a supervisor should give the employee time to offer feedback. The employee should be able to agree or disagree with the supervisor's conclusions, as well as to ask questions. This is an important time for the supervisor to keep an open mind and apply the listening skills discussed in Chapter 10. Hearing the employee's reactions is the first step toward resolving any problems described in the appraisal.

Problem Solving and Coaching   When the supervisor and employee understand each other's point of view, they should reach a decision on how to solve problems described in the appraisal. Together they can come up with a number of alternatives and select the solutions that seem most promising. Sometimes the best solution is for the employee to make behavioral changes; at other times, the supervisor may need to make changes, such as keeping the employee better informed or improving work processes.

Proponents of quality management—notably W. Edwards Deming—have criticized performance appraisals for connecting rewards mainly to individual performance.[27] The problem, they say, is that how well employees perform depends mainly on the organization's systems. Quality work can't be performed by an employee who lacks needed information, authority, or materials. With this in mind, supervisors should be open to ways in which improving performance is a mutual effort. (Chapter 9 provides further guidelines for decision making and problem solving.)

Besides problem solving, appraisal interviews often include time for discussion related to coaching the employee and helping the employee to develop a career with the organization. Strengths and shortcomings identified in the performance appraisal often provide indications of areas in which the supervisor and employee could work together to develop desirable skills through further training or experience. Discussing employees' potential for growth and improvement is essential. As AlliedSignal's Lawrence A. Bossidy once told a manager, "You have to keep growing just to stay where you are," much less to advance in the organiza-

TIPS FROM THE FIRING LINE

Doing a Better Job with Job Reviews

The guidelines below can provide a framework for improving employee evaluations in any work setting.

- Review evaluations written by other experienced supervisors to see what works and what doesn't.
- Keep notes throughout the evaluation period. Don't rely on recall at the end of the time.
- Seek input from other observers when appropriate.
- Base written evaluations on multiple, firsthand observations.
- Know what you're looking for. Evaluate the right things. Concentrate exclusively on factors directly related to job performance.
- Don't include rumors, allegations, or guesswork as part of your written evaluations.
- Be complete. Include the good, the bad, and the ugly. Don't be afraid to criticize. Don't forget to praise.
- Focus on improvement. Use the evaluation to set goals for better performance.
- Never use an evaluation as a threat or as punishment.
- Supplement periodic written evaluations with frequent verbal feedback. Negative written evaluation should never come as a surprise.
- Don't put anything in writing which you wouldn't say to the employee in person.

- Don't beat around the bush or sugarcoat needed criticism. Say what has to be said and move on.
- If checklists are part of the evaluation, be sure written comments are consistent with the items checked.
- Be as specific as possible. Use examples. Glittering generalities don't help much in targeting action or improvement plans.
- Relate evaluations to previous reviews. Are things better? Worse? The same?
- Allow plenty of time to prepare evaluations properly. Don't work under pressure.
- Never complete an evaluation when you are angry or frustrated.
- Choose words carefully. The goal is clarity.
- Let the evaluation "cool" overnight before distributing it.
- Be willing to change an evaluation if new information becomes available.

Source: From Robert D. Ramsey, "How to Write Better Employee Evaluations," *Supervision*, June 1998, pp. 5 ff. Reprinted by permission of © National Research Bureau, P.O. Box 1, Burlington, Iowa, 52601-0001.

---

tion.[28] However, employees tend to have difficulty shifting their focus away from pay and past performance especially when performance appraisals are directly or indirectly tied to pay levels.[29] A supervisor therefore should not use performance appraisal interviews as a substitute for coaching on a continuing basis.

Signatures At the end of the interview, the supervisor and employee usually are required to sign the appraisal form. By doing so, they acknowledge that the interview has been conducted and that the employee has read and understood the form. If the employee refuses to sign, the supervisor can explain that this is all the employee's signature means. If that explanation does not persuade the employee to sign, the supervisor can note on the appraisal form that the employee refused to sign and can check with the human resources department regarding what procedures to follow next. The employee should receive a copy of the appraisal form.

The supervisor should close the interview on a positive note, with a comment such as, "You've been doing a great job," or, "I think that with the plans we've made, your work will soon be up to standards." Figure 18.7 summarizes the interviewing process.

Follow-Up Even after the interview is over, a supervisor continues appraising performance. He or she needs to follow up on any actions planned during the

■ FIGURE 18.7

The Process of Conducting a Performance Appraisal Interview

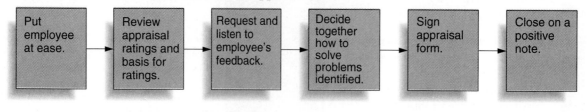

interview. Is the employee making the promised changes? Is the supervisor providing the resources, such as training, that are necessary for improvements to occur? This follow-up should be an ongoing process, not an activity left for the next year's performance appraisal.

Summary

18.1 Summarize benefits of conducting performance appraisals.

Performance appraisals provide information necessary for employees to improve the quality of their work. Appraisals can motivate employees by demonstrating the interest of the supervisor and the organization in them, keeping them informed, and indicating the important areas of performance. Performance appraisals also provide important records for the company, which managers use to make decisions on raises, promotions, and discipline.

18.2 Identify the steps in appraising performance systematically.

First, a supervisor establishes and communicates expectations for performance; then he or she establishes and communicates standards for measuring performance. A supervisor observes each employee's performance, measuring it against the standards. Finally, a supervisor provides reinforcement for acceptable or excellent performance and works with the employee to develop remedies for inadequate performance.

18.3 Discuss guidelines for avoiding discrimination in performance appraisals.

As much as possible, an appraisal should focus on objective measures of behavior and results—specifically, how well an employee carries out the essential tasks of the job. The behaviors and employee characteristics measured should be related to the job and to succeeding on the job.

18.4 Compare types of appraisals.

Graphic rating scales rate the degree to which an employee has achieved various characteristics, such as job knowledge and punctuality. The paired-comparison approach measures the relative performance of employees in a group. The forced-choice approach presents a supervisor with sets of statements describing employee behavior, and the supervisor chooses the statements which are most characteristic of the employee and which are least. An essay appraisal includes one or more paragraphs describing an employee's performance. Behaviorally anchored rating scales (BARS) rate employee performance in several areas by using a series of statements that describe effective and ineffective performance in each area. A checklist appraisal consists of a series of yes-or-no questions about an employee's performance. A critical-incident appraisal is based on an ongoing record of incidents in which an employee has behaved positively or negatively. The work-standards approach is based on establishing objective measures of performance, against which an employee's performance is compared. Management by objectives is a system of developing goals with employees and comparing their performance to those goals. In addition, a supervisor may combine several sources of appraisal in 360-degree feedback, having employees prepare self-assessments, obtaining peer assessments and customer assessments, or asking for appraisals (usually anonymous) of the supervisor.

18.5 Describe sources of bias in appraising performance.

Supervisors who want to prove they are tough may succumb to the harshness bias, rating employees too severely. Supervisors who hate to deliver bad news may succumb to the leniency bias, rating employees too favorably. The central tendency leads some supervisors to give their employees rankings in the middle of the scale. The proximity bias refers to the tendency to assign similar scores to items that are near each other on a questionnaire. Random choices sometimes are made when an appraiser is uncertain about answers or uncomfortable with an overall rating. The similarity bias is the tendency of people to judge others more positively when they are like themselves. The recency syndrome may lead a supervisor to give too much weight to events that have occurred recently. The halo effect leads an appraiser to use one positive or negative trait to describe a person's entire performance. Finally, people are influenced by their prejudices about groups.

18.6 Explain the purpose of conducting performance appraisal interviews.

The purpose of conducting an interview is to communicate the supervisor's impressions of an employee's performance to that employee. In addition, it is an opportunity for an employee to present his or her viewpoint and ideas so that supervisor and employee can work together on improving performance.

18.7 Tell how supervisors should prepare for a performance appraisal interview.

A supervisor should take as much time as necessary to complete an appraisal form thoughtfully. A supervisor also should think about how the employee is likely to react and should plan how to handle his or her reactions. A supervisor should be ready with ideas for resolving problems noted in the appraisal. A supervisor should notify the employee about the interview ahead of time and should prepare an appropriate place to meet without interruptions.

18.8 Describe guidelines for conducting the interview.

First, a supervisor should attempt to put the employee at ease. Then the supervisor and employee should go over the self-appraisal, if any, and the supervisor's appraisal of the employee. The supervisor should focus first on areas for improvement and next on areas of strength. The employee should have time to give feedback; then the supervisor and employee should work together to develop solutions to any problems identified. The supervisor and employee sign the appraisal form, and then the supervisor closes with a positive comment. After the interview, the supervisor needs to follow up to make sure that planned actions are taken.

Key Terms

performance appraisal, p. 475

graphic rating scale, p. 481

paired-comparison approach, p. 481

forced-choice approach, p. 483

behaviorally anchored rating scales (BARS), p. 483

critical-incident appraisal, p. 485

work-standards approach, p. 485

360-degree feedback, p. 487

peer reviews, p. 487

harshness bias, p. 489

leniency bias, p. 489

central tendency, p. 489

proximity bias, p. 489

similarity bias, p. 490

Review and Discussion Questions

1. What is a performance appraisal? How do organizations benefit from using performance appraisals?
2. June Pearson was just promoted to supervisor of the bookkeeping department at an insurance company. Based on the company's schedule for appraising performance, she needs to conduct an appraisal of Ron Yamamoto, one of the employees, only a month after she started the job. June cannot find any records

of goals established for Ron, so she asks his peers and others with whom he has contact to describe Ron's performance. Based on this information, June completes an appraisal form and conducts an interview.

a. Which steps of the systematic approach to appraising performance has June omitted?

b. How do you think Ron will react to this interview?

c. Can you think of anything else June could have done to improve this particular appraisal? Explain.

3. Name and describe briefly the five kinds of causes of poor performance.

4. Which of the following are appropriate ways to measure an employee's performance?

a. Day after day, more than three customers are lined up at Janet's cash register, so her supervisor concludes that she is a slow worker.

b. Jonathan smiles a lot, so his supervisor assumes he is happy.

c. Wesley is late to work every Wednesday morning, so his supervisor plans to find out the cause.

d. Nick habitually takes longer to deliver pizzas than his company promises its customers, so his supervisor notes that he is inefficient.

e. Production in the group that Caitlin oversees has fallen off somewhat in the last two months, so her supervisor discusses with her the possible reasons.

5. How can a supervisor avoid illegal discrimination in performance appraisals?

6. At a manufacturing company in south suburban Chicago, one policy stated that each manager and employee must be appraised at one-year intervals. At the same time, the company conducts a review of the person's wages or salary, usually giving at least a small raise. In recent years, like many manufacturers, this company has become concerned about reducing costs. The policy about conducting performance appraisals has been modified: managers' appraisals now must be conducted *at least* a year after the manager's salary was last reviewed. One supervisor was reviewed in December of one year, then in February (14 months later), and then in May of the third year.

a. What reasons do you think the supervisor's manager had for delaying the performance appraisals so that they were more than a year apart?

b. What effects do you think the delays had on the supervisor?

7. What type of performance appraisal is used most frequently? What are advantages and disadvantages of this approach?

8. What type of performance appraisal was (or is) used at your most recent job? How effective do you think it is? Why?

9. At a company that sells X-ray equipment, an important new sales territory is opening up. Patrick O'Day, the supervisor of the company's sales force, wants to assign the territory to the best-qualified salesperson. How can Patrick compare the performance of the members of the sales force to select the best candidate for the job?

10. Give an advantage and a disadvantage of using each of the following types of appraisals:

a. Essay appraisal.

b. Behaviorally anchored rating scale (BARS).

c. Checklist.

d. Critical-incident appraisal.

11. Which type of bias does each of the following situations illustrate?

a. Anne Compton is a new supervisor. To make sure that her employees and her manager take her judgments seriously, she gives each of her employees a lower rating than the previous supervisor did.

b. Ron is late in completing Noreen's written performance appraisal. To finish it as quickly as possible, he looks it over and adds some negative ratings to an overall positive review so that it looks balanced.

c. Renee really likes her new employee, Joan. Recently, Joan and her family moved to the same town in which Renee lives; their children attend the same school; Renee and Joan even enjoy lunchtime shopping together. When it comes time for Joan's performance review, Renee rates Joan high in every category.

12. Reginald DeBeers hates conducting appraisal interviews, so he has the process down to a science. Fifteen minutes before the end of the workday, he meets with the employee who is

to be appraised. He gets right down to business, explaining what the employee's ratings are and how he arrived at each number. Then the employee and supervisor sign the form. By then, it is quitting time, and Reginald rises to shake hands with the employee, saying either "Keep up the good work" or "I'm sure you'll do better next time."

What parts of the interviewing process does Reginald omit? What are the consequences of leaving out these steps?

A SECOND LOOK

Which steps in a systematic performance appraisal are evident in the Gwinnett Health System story at the beginning of this chapter?

SKILLS MODULE

CASE

Appraising Employees in a Dental Office

Jill Strode supervises the office staff in a dental office. One of Strode's accomplishments was to develop a system for appraising the performance of the employees she supervises.

For each employee, Strode spells out the specific areas of responsibility that will be evaluated. The areas she evaluates match the responsibilities stated in the employee's job description. Thus, for the checkout receptionist, Jill indicates that she will evaluate how that person handles five areas of responsibility, including checkout procedures and telephone communications. In evaluating how an employee handles each area, Strode looks for specific traits, such as knowledge, initiative, innovation, and courtesy. The following excerpts from an appraisal of the checkout receptionist illustrate the format of the appraisals:

JOB RESPONSIBILITY: Checkout Procedures and Folder Routing . . .

Accuracy: Very good overall. Attention to details is superb in all areas. Seldom forgets any part of the "checkout" procedure.

Example: Ability to pick up on errors made in charting, double-checking folders for missed steps (insurance, scheduling, etc.), thoroughness.

Innovation: Below average. This area has remained unchanged since we installed the system. Procedural changes have been suggested by the supervisor and implemented by the checkout receptionist. Needs improvement.

Example: Complaints with folder errors and patient flow have been verbalized; however, no suggestions for changes or improvement in procedures have been offered. Space limitations in checkout area still a concern . . . suggestions for improvements?

To review the performance appraisal with the employee, Strode sets up a formal appraisal meeting. She has developed the following agenda list of topics to cover during the meeting:

1. Review specific areas of responsibility that will be evaluated. Make any changes or additions if needed.
2. Appraisal for each specific area.
   a. Set goals for improvement and change (at least two improvements/changes for each).
   b. Set training dates, if needed.
   c. Get feedback from staff on appraisal from supervisor.
3. Overall appraisal of traits as exemplified in daily activities and actions.
4. Review goals and training dates.
5. Questions and answers from list.
6. Open forum for discussion: employee to supervisor.

Strode then follows up to make sure that the employee and supervisor carry through on the goals and plans they established during this interview.

1. Based on the information given, what type of performance appraisal has Strode developed?
2. Would you consider this a useful type of appraisal for clerical employees in a dental practice? Can you suggest any additions or improvements?
3. Based on the agenda Strode uses for appraisal interviews, what principles of effective appraisals does she follow?

Source: Jill Strode.

SELF-QUIZ

How Well Do You Accept Evaluations?

It can be difficult for any of us to accept judgment or criticism, and sometimes we may become emotional and fail to listen. This little quiz should help you find out how well you are prepared to receive feedback, which is just as important for a supervisor as giving it. Ask yourself the following questions.

1. Do I prepare for my performance review by gathering examples of work I've done well and compliments I've received from colleagues?
2. Have I been accomplishing what my job description calls for? Have I accepted and fulfilled my responsibilities on major assignments?
3. Have I improved on the job, learned additional skills, and/or taken on greater responsibilities?
4. Have I created a list of things about my performance that I can improve? Have I prioritized weaknesses and selected three to work on immediately?
5. Do I tell myself during the review, "I need to listen to this. It will help me grow personally and professionally"?
6. Do I stay tuned in to what I am hearing?
7. Can I remain objective and unemotional as far as possible?
8. Do I hold back from interrupting?
9. Do I summarize and restate what I hear to be sure I have heard it correctly?
10. Do I ask for specific and action-oriented feedback?
11. Have I created an action plan for attaining my goals?
12. Do I follow up to assess my own progress?

Source: Susan Vaughn, "Rethinking Employee Evaluations," *Los Angeles Times*, April 8, 2001, p. W1; "Give Yourself a Job Review," *American Salesman*, May 2001, pp. 26–27.

Class Exercise

Figure 18.1 provides an overview of how supervisors conduct performance appraisals. This exercise elaborates on that model by showing you how you can use *ManagePro* (trademark of Avantos Performance Systems)—the first product of its kind in a new category of business productivity software: goal and people management (GPM)—to improve your performance management skills.*

Instructions   You are one of 17 supervisors at Tybro, a major toy manufacturer in the Midwest. Place yourself in the following scenario:

Scenario   During a meeting with your boss, he shows you an article from *The Wall Street Journal*, "PC Program Lets Machines Help Bosses Manage People," and says to you, "I want to find out more

---

*Permission granted by Avantos Performance Systems, Inc., to include the *ManagePro* information contained in this exercise. For further information on *ManagePro*, contact Avantos Performance Systems, 5900 Hollis Street, Suite C, Emeryville, CA 94608, or call 1-800-AVANTOS.

■ TABLE A **Needs Focused on by *ManagePro***	**Employees' Performance Needs**	**Management Process**
	"Tell me what we're trying to achieve, and let's agree on what is expected of me."	*Set clear, measurable goals* that support the key business objectives with specific checkpoints and due dates.
	"Let's discuss how I'm doing."	*Monitor progress on each goal* at a frequency determined by the capability of the people involved.
	"Help me to improve."	*Provide adequate feedback and coaching* to keep people informed and help them improve performance. Surveys consistently show that employees have very little sense of what their boss thinks of their performance. Giving regular feedback to your people and helping them through coaching are critical parts of managing.
	"Reward me for my contribution."	*Evaluate, recognize, and reward people's contributions.* If people feel that performance pays off, they will work harder to achieve success.

about whether *ManagePro*, the software program reviewed in this article, could help our Tybro supervisors and managers, and I'd like you to be the one to answer that question for me. Probably the best way for you to find out is to register to attend the one-day *ManagePro* seminar, and then you can make your recommendation when you return, based on your hands-on experience."

You attend the seminar and learn a great deal about the performance management process. Following are some of the highlights of what you learned about *ManagePro*.

***Overview of* ManagePro**   The seminar trainer explained that *ManagePro* is based on fundamental, proven management processes that meet the basic performance needs that your employees have (see table A).

Throughout the day you learned how these processes are reinforced throughout *ManagePro* in (1) the way the program is structured, (2) the tools it provides, and (3) the advice available in the Management Advisor.

Program Structure   As you try out the program, you find that information is simple to enter using fill-in-the-blank forms, outlines, and spreadsheet-like tables. Information is also easy to view and

manipulate at multiple levels of detail. You find yourself quickly manipulating the program, using your mouse and pointing and clicking at the icons of what you need. Everything is very intuitive and easy to follow. Changes made through any part of the program at any level are reflected automatically throughout the program. For example, if you reorganize your goals in the Goal Planner/ Outliner, the changes automatically are reflected in the People Status Board.

Some of the key features of *ManagePro* include the following:

- The Goal Planner/Outliner allows you to organize your goals. Goals can be divided into layers of subgoals, given start and due dates, and delegated to a person or team. Click-and-drag movements makes it easy to organize and reorganize goals. (See Figure A.)
- The Goal Status Board gives a view of pending goals and their progress. Color-light indicators alert you to items that require action. For example, yellow means at least one subgoal is behind schedule. (See Figure B.)
- The People/Team Planner allows you to organize people, track goals associated with people, and manage information on feedback, coaching, and performance reviews.

FIGURE A

Stay Organized

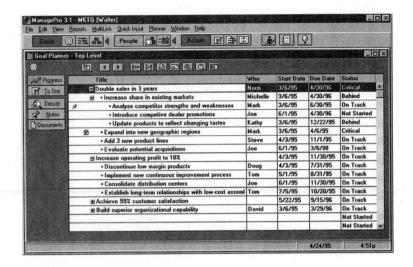

FIGURE B

Stay on Top of Your Goals

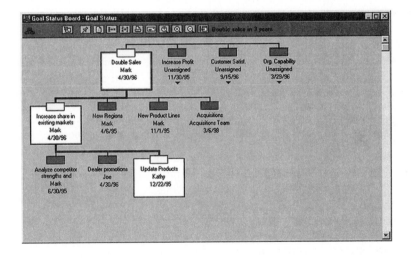

• The People Status Board prompts you periodically to consider getting updates on goal progress and to consider giving feedback, coaching, and recognition at a frequency determined by you for each individual or team. For example, you can have *ManagePro* remind you to give a certain employee feedback every three months. This will help you build up your people management discipline so that important activities and processes do not fall between the cracks. (See Figure C.)

Tools Some of *ManagePro's* support tools include the following:

• The Calendar displays year-, month-, week-, and day-at-a-glance graphic views of events and deadlines.

■ FIGURE C

**Effectively Manage
Your People**

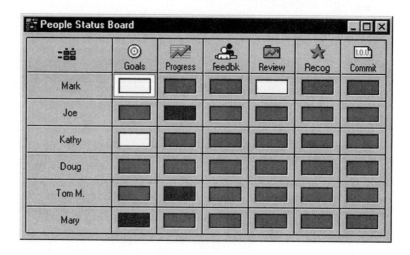

- The Action List provides a customizable view of action items and status relating to all goals and actions in *ManagePro*, including people management actions such as progress reviews.
- The Reports allow you to generate a variety of standard reports on goals, planning, calendars, action lists, and people management information.

Management Advisor One other major component of the program is accessed by selecting the Management Advisor button, which allows you to receive context-sensitive management tips and techniques compiled by experts. The Management Advisor helps new supervisors learn and apply management processes on the job; it also provides a refresher and specific diagnostic support for the experienced supervisor.

Team-Building Exercise

Designing an Appraisal

Divide the class into teams of four or five students. Each team will design a performance appraisal intended to evaluate the performance of either the president of the university or the president of the United States (or some other prominent person chosen by the class or the instructor). First, each

Conclusion

You return to your office the following day and sit down at your desk to prepare your recommendation to your boss on *ManagePro*. You definitely are sold on the idea that Tybro supervisors (and for that matter, all levels of management at Tybro) would benefit greatly by using this GPM software. In support of your recommendation, you will answer the following questions:

1. What management processes does *ManagePro* support?
2. What three features of *ManagePro* most impressed you as beneficial to improving your performance management and that of your company as a whole? Why?

team should choose which type of appraisal is best suited to evaluate the person's performance. Next, team members decide the content of the appraisal (what questions should be asked). Finally, the class as a whole should discuss which types of appraisals were selected and why, and why certain questions were chosen.

19

I would like to see where the labor movement is once again the driving force for the future direction of the nation.

—Anthony Mazzocchi, an official of the Oil, Chemical, and Atomic Workers Union

The Impact of the Law

■ LEARNING OBJECTIVES

After you have studied this chapter, you should be able to:

19.1 Summarize the basic purpose of the OSHAct and describe the supervisor's responsibilities under the act.

19.2 Identify basic categories of health and safety hazards in the workplace.

19.3 Discuss common safety and health concerns and how employers are addressing them.

19.4 Describe workplace safety and health programs, including their benefits and the supervisor's role in them.

19.5 Explain a supervisor's role during a union organization drive and collective bargaining.

19.6 Provide guidelines for working with a union steward and handling grievances.

19.7 Explain a supervisor's role in preventing strikes and operating during a strike.

19.8 Discuss how a supervisor should respond to charges of sexual harassment and prevent it from occurring.

■ WHERE THERE'S SMOKE . . .

It's becoming commonplace—the sight of huddled workers outside their office buildings, drawing the last bit of smoke into their lungs before they return to work from their furtive cigarette break. According to the National Cancer Institute, U.S. workplaces are rapidly becoming smoke free, with 65 percent of respondents to a recent survey saying they worked in places where smoking is not allowed. In 1993 that number was only 47 percent.

White-collar workplaces are more likely to be smoke free than service-oriented or blue-collar workplaces. And there are more smoking bans in the North than in the South. What does it all mean for employees?

Some people feel that the workplace has become a much healthier environment since the bans started taking effect. Even some smokers apparently don't want to be surrounded by smoke all day. Smokers bound by nonsmoking rules at work may consider quitting, which would increase the benefits to themselves and to others. But there may be a persistent backlash from those who cherish the right to smoke. According to the National Smokers Alliance, "Smokers have been unfairly characterized as second-class citizens who don't have the same rights as nonsmokers." The practice of smoking outside the workplace, some feel, forces workers into extreme cold and heat, which is seen as unfair and counterproductive.

Nevertheless, the evidence continues to mount that, in terms of employee health, where there's smoke, there's danger.

Source: Amy Joyce, "Smoke-Free Workplaces Spreading Like Wildfire," *Washington Post*, November 15, 1998, p. H4.

Most supervisors today are well aware that maintaining the safety and health of employees is a major task. This responsibility is just one of many imposed by the federal government on organizations operating in the United States. Other chapters have addressed some additional responsibilities. Chapter 3 discussed labor laws that limit the ways in which organizations can use teamwork. Chapter 11 introduced the impact of the law on the scope of benefits organizations must offer employees. Chapters 16 and 18 explored laws intended to ensure fair employment practices.

This chapter covers three areas in which federal laws govern the actions of organizations. First, it describes the role of the federal government in regulating safety and health in the workplace. It then describes safety and health hazards, organizational programs for promoting safety and health, and the role of the supervisor in this area. Next, the chapter discusses unions—their impact and the laws governing the interaction of organizations with unions and unionizing efforts. Finally, the chapter examines sexual harassment. It suggests ways to prevent sexual harassment and appropriate responses when an employee claims sexual harassment has occurred.

Government Regulation of Safety and Health

According to the Bureau of Labor Statistics, in 1999 more than 6.3 million occupational injuries and illnesses occurred among the almost 108 million workers in the private sector.[1] Furthermore, these problems are not limited to factory settings. For example, the industries with the highest incidence rates of occupational injuries in 1999 were scheduled air transportation and the nursing and personal care industries.[2] Not only is the challenge of preventing these problems widespread, but many injuries and illnesses reported today are newly recognized—complaints such as injuries related to repetitive motion and the less-than-optimal design of workstations.

Many organizations recognize that safeguarding the well-being of employees in the workplace is not only ethical but also essential to attracting and keeping qualified personnel. Unfortunately, this view has not always prevailed. As a result, the government has stepped in to regulate the safety and health of the workplace.

Terrible accidents occurred when the Industrial Revolution brought together inexperienced workers with new and unfamiliar machinery. Beginning primarily in the early 1900s, state governments passed inspection laws and set up workers' compensation programs to provide benefits for employees injured on the job. In 1913 Congress created the Department of Labor, whose duties include the improvement of working conditions. In spite of such actions, however, public sentiment in favor of further protection continued to grow.

Occupational Safety and Health Act (OSHAct) of 1970

Occupational Safety and Health Act (OSHAct) of 1970
The federal law that sets up government agencies to conduct research on occupational health and safety, set health and safety standards, inspect workplaces, and penalize employers that do not meet standards.

The most far-reaching of the laws regulating workplace safety and health is the **Occupational Safety and Health Act (OSHAct) of 1970.** The law is intended "to assure so far as possible every working man and woman in the nation safe and healthful working conditions and to preserve our human resources." The OSHAct sets up government agencies to conduct research regarding occupational health and safety, set health and safety standards, inspect workplaces, and penalize employers that do not meet standards. Penalties can be severe, including fines of $7,000 per day for failure to correct a violation and jail terms of six months for falsifying records to deceive inspectors.

OSHA and NIOSH

Occupational Safety and Health Administration (OSHA)
The agency of the federal government charged with setting and enforcing standards for workplace health and safety.

The OSHAct established two federal agencies to see that employers carry out its provisions. The **Occupational Safety and Health Administration (OSHA),** a part of the U.S. Department of Labor, is the agency charged with setting and enforcing standards for workplace health and safety. People often think of OSHA standards as pertaining mainly to factory-related issues such as personal protective equipment (e.g., gloves, safety shoes) and guards on machinery. However, many OSHA standards pertain to health and safety issues that arise in offices, including recently proposed standards for air quality and prevention of repetitive-motion injuries. (These topics are discussed later in the chapter.)

To see that organizations are meeting its standards, OSHA's inspectors may visit companies but must show a search warrant before conducting an inspection. "Between state and federal [inspections], we do about 85,000 inspections a year total, out of about 6 million workplaces," says former OSHA assistant secretary

Charles Jeffress. The agency also hosts a website with special areas for small businesses and links to online advisers. It has placed compliance-assistance specialists in its regional offices and also hosts forums and training sessions around the country.[3] OSHA also operates a program of free on-site consultations through which independent consultants evaluate an organization's work practices, environmental hazards, and health and safety program. If an organization follows the consultant's recommendations, it bears no penalties for the shortcomings identified.

OSHA's regulations have sometimes been criticized as excessively far-reaching and costly to implement. In the closing days of the Clinton administration, new rules went into effect that would have required employers to tell workers about common ergonomic injuries, which affect between 1 million and 1.8 million U.S. workers a year, and to take certain steps to remedy reported problems while providing full pay and benefits to injured workers with temporary work restrictions. OSHA and business leaders disagreed strongly about the cost of implementing the new rules, and President George W. Bush immediately repealed them.[4]

The **National Institute for Occupational Safety and Health (NIOSH)** is the government agency responsible for conducting research related to workplace safety and health. It is a part of the Department of Health and Human Services. NIOSH provides OSHA with information necessary for setting standards.

National Institute for Occupational Safety and Health (NIOSH)
The agency of the federal government responsible for conducting research related to workplace safety and health.

The Supervisor's Responsibility under the OSHAct

Given the extent of OSHA regulations and the thousands of pages interpreting those regulations, supervisors cannot be familiar with every regulation. However, supervisors do need to understand what kinds of practices are required to preserve health and safety in their departments. In addition, the OSHAct imposes some specific responsibilities that apply to supervisors.

The OSHAct requires that supervisors keep records of occupational injuries and illnesses. They must record these on OSHA forms within six working days after learning of the injury or illness. Figure 19.1 details which types of accidents and illnesses must be recorded.

A supervisor also may have to accompany OSHA officials when they conduct an inspection. These inspections occur in response to a request by an employer, a union, or an employee, or when OSHA's own schedule calls for them. (An employer may not penalize an employee for requesting an investigation or reporting a possible violation.) During the inspection, it is important to be polite and cooperative. This is not always as easy as it sounds because the inspection may come at an inconvenient time, and a supervisor may view it as unwanted interference. However, being uncooperative is no way to foster good relations with the agency and could even lead the inspectors to be tougher than they otherwise might be.

Because chemical hazards are widespread in the modern workplace, OSHA has issued a right-to-know rule requiring that employees be informed about the chemicals used where they work. Each organization must have available information about what chemical hazards exist in the workplace and how employees can protect themselves against those hazards. The information must include labels on containers of chemicals and hazardous materials, as well as Material Safety Data Sheets (MSDSs), both of which identify the chemicals, describe how to handle them, and identify the risks involved. A supervisor should make certain that this information is available for all chemicals that are brought into, used in, or produced at the workplace he or she supervises. If a supervisor finds that some infor-

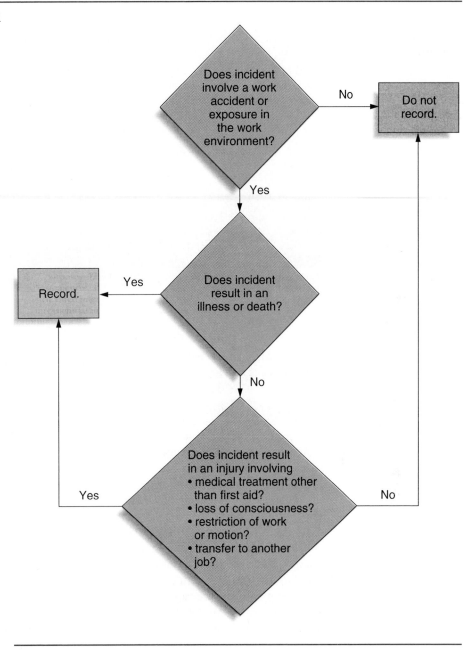

■ FIGURE 19.1

**Accidents and
Illnesses That Must
Be Recorded under
OSHAct**

mation still is needed, the suppliers of the chemicals and other hazardous substances should be able to provide it.

Types of Safety and Health Problems

Because supervisors have an important role to play in maintaining a safe and
healthy workplace, they need to be aware of problems that commonly arise, including health hazards and safety hazards. People tend to associate both classes of

FIGURE 19.2

Types of Health Hazards

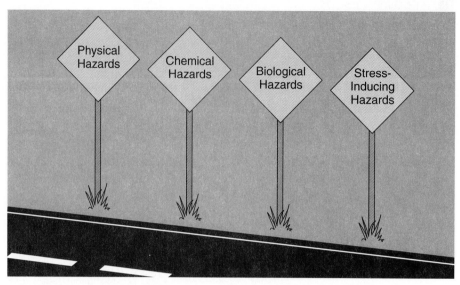

hazards with factory settings, but hazards can arise in any work setting, from offices to police cars.

Health Hazards

As a result of stressful working conditions, an air-traffic controller developed a stomach ulcer. A clerical employee believes that sharing a poorly ventilated room with a photocopier has caused her dizzy spells. These are examples of conditions in the work environment that may gradually hurt the health of the people there. Such conditions are **health hazards.** In general, health hazards may be physical, chemical, biological, or stress-inducing (see Figure 19.2).

Physical health hazards include noise, vibration, radiation, temperature extremes, and furniture and equipment that are not designed properly for the user's comfort. For instance, operating noisy equipment can impair an employee's hearing. Exposure to radiation can make a person more vulnerable to cancer. Improperly designed furniture can contribute to muscle aches and repetitive-motion disorders (described later in this chapter).

Chemical hazards may be present in dusts, fumes, and gases. They include chemicals that are carcinogenic (causes of cancer). Examples of chemical hazards are asbestos, coal dust, lead, and benzene. People in office buildings may be exposed to chemicals from synthetic carpeting, tobacco smoke, and other sources. OSHA has proposed regulations for indoor air quality. The research into the sources of such pollution is incomplete and there is strong resistance from smokers and the tobacco industry, so the proposed standards emphasize providing adequate ventilation, separate smoking rooms, or going outdoors to smoke.[5]

Even airplane travel can pose unexpected health hazards when the air quality on the plane is poor. A recent flight from Los Angeles to the East Coast made an unscheduled landing in Chicago where paramedics met the crew and passengers, who suffered loss of motor skills and mental alertness, inability to judge the pas-

health hazards
Conditions in the work environment that may gradually hurt the health of the people there.

■ FIGURE 19.3

Common Job-Related Injuries and Illnesses and Corresponding Days of Work Generally Missed

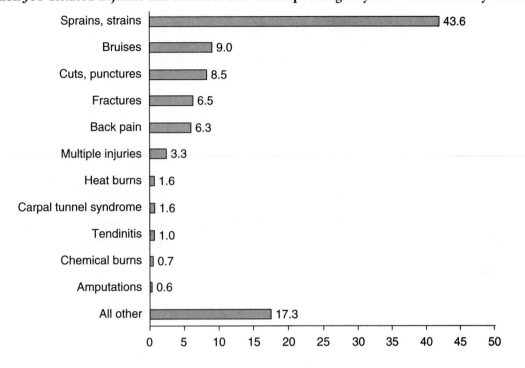

Source: NIOSH *Worker Health Chartbook 2000.* DHHS (NIOSH) Publication No. 2000-127. http://www.cdc.gov/niosh/pdfs/2000-127d.pdf

sage of time, apathy, and even loss of consciousness. The problems were found to be due to bad air. Recycled air saves the airplanes $60,000 per plane per year, but some believe that these savings come at too high a price. The Centers for Disease Control and Prevention and NIOSH are looking into continued complaints about carbon dioxide levels, and overly dry air on planes, and other health hazards.[6]

Biological hazards include bacteria, fungi, and insects associated with risks to people's health. Modern office buildings, which tend to be sealed tight against the elements, can be fertile ground for such health hazards. Likewise, overwatering plants can encourage the growth of molds in the standing water, and those molds can circulate on air currents, making employees ill.

Stressful working conditions also may harm the health of employees. For example, employees may be more apt to suffer from stress-related illnesses if their work requires them to take risks, please an unpredictable supervisor, or witness a lot of suffering. (Chapter 14 describes the consequences of stress and ways to manage it.)

Safety Hazards

safety hazards
Conditions in the workplace that may lead to an injury-causing accident.

A **safety hazard** is a condition in the workplace that may lead to an injury-causing accident. Common types of injuries include cuts, broken bones, burns, and electric shocks. Figure 19.3 shows several common job-related injuries and illnesses, along with corresponding days of work lost. At their most serious, injuries can lead to death. NIOSH reports that each day an average of 9,000 U.S. workers sustain disabling injuries on the job, 16 die from an injury sustained at work, and 137 die from work-related diseases. A NIOSH-funded study of the costs of such injuries and illnesses revealed that the cost to businesses is about $171 billion annually, compared to costs of about $33 billion for AIDS and $108 billion for cancer.[7] In general, safety hazards arise from personal behavior (i.e., unsafe acts) or conditions of the physical environment. As Figure 19.3 shows, unsafe acts cause the majority of accidents.

Types of Safety Hazards   Personal behavior as a safety hazard refers to practices by managers and employees that create an environment in which accidents may occur. This behavior may be as basic as carelessness or as obvious as drinking on the job. Sometimes employees cause a safety hazard by refusing to follow proper procedures or use safety equipment such as goggles or gloves. Supervisors and other managers can contribute by failing to enforce safety measures or requiring employees to work such long hours that they do not get enough rest to think clearly. NIOSH's *Worker Health Chartbook 2000* reported that in 1997 motor-vehicle-related incidents were the leading cause of fatal workplace injury.[8] Therefore, supervisors should be especially concerned about encouraging safe behavior among employees who spend work time in vehicles—delivery personnel, salespeople, employees who take business trips, and so on.

Some employees are said to be accident-prone—that is, more likely to have accidents than other people. These employees tend to act on impulse, without careful thought, and do not concentrate on their work. Many employees who are vulnerable to accidents have negative attitudes about their jobs, co-workers, or supervisors. Perhaps they find the work boring. Sometimes people who are otherwise careful are vulnerable to accidents. When people are struggling with personal problems or do not get enough sleep, they may become accident-prone. Therefore, a supervisor needs to pay attention to the behavior of all employees in order to recognize which of them are especially at risk for causing an accident on any given day. A supervisor may need to restrict the activities of an employee who is temporarily accident-prone or even to send that person home. If the problem continues, a supervisor may have to use the counseling and discipline procedures described in Chapter 13.

Hazardous working conditions that can lead to accidents are as varied as a messy work environment, electrical cords lying where people might trip over them, poor lighting, and a lack of protective devices on machinery. A study by Liberty Mutual that used BLS and workers' compensation data found that falls and slips were the second and third most costly types of work-site injuries in the United States in 1998.[9] And even language barriers can contribute to work hazards, as in the case of a young Hispanic worker who slipped from a wet roof and was paralyzed. His supervisor, who did not speak Spanish, said that the worker did not speak English and that made it difficult to communicate to him that the roof was dangerously slick.[10]

Responses   A supervisor who observes unsafe conditions should take one of the following actions, listed in order of priority:

1. Eliminate the hazard.
2. If the hazard cannot be eliminated, use protective devices such as guards on machinery.
3. If the hazard cannot be guarded, provide warnings, such as labels on the hot parts inside photocopiers.

Curing Ergonomic Problems

Ergonomics, or the practice of designing equipment and furniture to support the human body at work, has drawn much attention in the last few years as a way to prevent repetitive stress injuries like carpal tunnel syndrome, eyestrain, backache, and neck and shoulder pain. If your workstation is uncomfortable, you may not be able to ask for a whole new office purely on ergonomic grounds. But there are a few things you can do to alleviate any strain on your body. Here are some ideas.

1. *Your computer monitor.* If you can see your clothing reflected on your screen when your computer is turned off, or you see the active screen more clearly when shading your eyes with a piece of paper, there is too much glare reaching your eyes. Wearing darker clothing is a quick fix. Some others include adjusting your screen so the background is light and the characters dark, reducing the overhead lighting, and shielding the top of the monitor with a manila folder to reduce the light bouncing off it. The best solution, while more expensive, is a glare screen or filter specially designed for computer monitors.

2. *Your keyboard.* Try working with your forearms and hands at the same level, so the angle between them is flat. This should help prevent discomfort and even injury. Unfortunately, there is little agreement as to whether ergonomically designed keyboards are useful, although adjustable platforms or supports are generally recommended. The healthiest position is for the front of the keyboard to be slightly higher than the back, so the keyboard slopes away from you at an angle of about 10 or 12 degrees.

3. *Your chair.* Poor circulation, back pain, and fatigue are just a few of the results of poor seating. The quickest solution to an inadequate chair is a rolled-up towel or small inflatable pillow placed behind the small of the back. The best solution, of course, is a correctly designed chair with as many adjustable features as possible, including seat height, armrest height, seat tilt, and backrest tilt.

4. *Your mouse.* To keep your mouse responsive to your slightest touch and avoid the need for repeated clicking, take it apart and clean it every few weeks. Get a mouse that fits the shape of your hand and position it as close to your side as possible.

Source: Lisa Lee Freeman, ed., "Ergo Woes," *Working Woman,* December–January 1999, pp. 69–70.

4. If you cannot remove or guard the hazard on your own, notify the proper authority. Recommend a solution, then follow up to make sure that the condition has been corrected.

For Frank Clemente, Cargo Service Center's facility supervisor at Chicago's O'Hare International Airport, one of the busiest airports in the world, safety is especially important. Because forklifts often banged and damaged the dock doors at the warehouse, creating a situation in which the doors no longer closed securely, moisture would form on the floor and around the threshold, making the warehouse floor slippery and hazardous. So the company has now installed "knockout" dock doors, which consist of panels that fit into tracks mounted on the wall. If the doors are dislodged, they can easily be remounted, eliminating the dangerous conditions.[11]

Back and neck injuries account for many workplace injuries, so a supervisor should especially seek measures to prevent and correct safety hazards causing such injuries. Ways to prevent back injuries include designing the job to minimize injuries, training employees to use lifting techniques that minimize strain on the back, reducing the size or weight of objects to be lifted, using mechanical aids, and making sure that workers assigned to do a job are strong enough to do it safely. The position that puts the most stress on the back is sitting. Supervisors of office employees therefore should be sure that employees have comfortable chairs and enough opportunities to stand up and move around. See "Tips from the Firing Line" for some ergonomic suggestions for your work area.

Common Concerns

Several common concerns about safety and health in the workplace are especially significant because they are widely occurring, or at least widely discussed. These include smoking, alcoholism and drug abuse, problems related to the use of computers, repetitive-motion disorders, and AIDS.

Smoking   An estimated 57 million individuals in the United States currently smoke cigarettes, risking serious health consequences such as cancer, heart disease, and high blood pressure. With more than 430,000 deaths in the United States each year being attributable to tobacco use, smoking is the leading preventable cause of death and disease in the country.[12] Environmental ("second-hand") tobacco smoke is thought to cause between 3,000 and 6,000 lung cancer deaths of nonsmokers each year.[13] It is also implicated in coronary heart disease, sudden infant death syndrome, asthma, bronchitis, emphysema, and pneumonia.[14] Besides being a health hazard, cigarette smoking is a safety hazard; lit cigarettes can cause burns, fires, or explosions when handled carelessly or near flammable substances.

Because the consequences of cigarette smoking are potentially serious, many organizations have restricted the amount of smoking allowed in the workplace, as seen in the opening story. In many locations, the restrictions also are required by state or local law. A 1999 survey of 17 states and the District of Columbia conducted by the American Medical Association found that official workplace policies that limited smoking in public, common, or work areas were in effect at 87 to 97 percent of firms. As of the end of 1999, laws that restrict smoking in government work sites were in effect in the District of Columbia and 43 states, 11 of which prohibit smoking entirely.[15] Supervisors can help to minimize the effects of smoking in the workplace by enforcing the organization's restrictions and by providing encouragement and recognition to employees who are trying to quit smoking.

Alcoholism and Drug Abuse   Alcoholism and drug abuse are serious problems in the workplace and can be costly to the organization. One reason is that people who are under the influence of these substances are more likely to be involved in accidents. Many organizational policies therefore call for strong action when an employee is found to be under the influence.

Part of the supervisor's role in promoting safety is counseling and disciplining employees with these problems. (For more information on how supervisors should respond, refer to Chapter 13.)

video display terminal (VDT)

The screen on which a computer displays information.

Problems Related to Computer Use   Nearly half of U.S. workers now use computers on the job. As computers have become increasingly common in all kinds of work environments, people have attributed some health problems to computer use. Many of the concerns involve the use of **video display terminals (VDTs),** the screens on which computers display information. Users of VDTs have complained that working with or near these screens causes a variety of health problems. Working for extended periods in front of a VDT also can lead to sore muscles in the back, arms, legs, and neck. Some reports have suggested that VDT use also is linked to pregnancy problems, notably miscarriages, through the radiation emitted by the VDTs. At this time, research results neither support nor refute a link between VDT use and pregnancy risks.

Fortunately, the problems associated with VDT use can be reduced or eliminated. A workstation that includes VDTs should be well designed for comfort, including features such as an adjustable and detachable keyboard, display screens that tilt up and down, brightness and contrast controls, and a flexible copy holder that reduces the distance between the screen and the source material.[16] In addition, lighting that minimizes glare and an adjustable chair and worktable should be provided. Employees who use VDTs should take rest breaks. NIOSH recommends a 15-minute break after two continuous hours of VDT use, or after one hour if the use involves intense concentration. One way to provide breaks is to rotate assignments so that employees spend only part of the day working with a VDT. To minimize the possible risks of radiation, VDTs should be at least four feet from one another, and employees should sit at least two feet from the sides and back of any screen.[17] Those who are concerned about radiation also may wish to install radiation shields on their computers or to use only low-emission VDTs.

Instead of staring at a standard VDT, a growing number of computer users are pulling on headsets to take advantage of a new technology called virtual reality. **Virtual reality** is a three-dimensional computer-generated environment that gives the user a sensation of being part of that environment.[18] Employees already are using it to test products and receive training. Although learning to fly a new jet aircraft with virtual reality avoids some of the obvious safety hazards of actually piloting the jet, it does involve some health hazards. The use of virtual reality, especially for extended periods, has been associated with nausea and headaches. A few users even experience flashbacks hours or days later. The design of virtual reality systems may eventually reduce some of this "cybersickness," and supervisors can help by providing frequent breaks for employees using these systems.

People who type into computers for long stretches of time may also be susceptible to repetitive-motion disorders, discussed next.

Repetitive-Motion Disorders   Advances in machinery and electronic equipment have enabled workers to perform repetitive functions at an increasingly rapid pace. Unfortunately, the repeated application of force to the same muscles or joints can result in injuries known as **repetitive-motion disorders.** According to OSHA, musculoskeletal disorders, or MSDs (injuries and disorders of soft tissues include muscles, tendons, ligaments, joints, and cartilage and the nervous system), account for 34 percent of all lost-workday injuries and illnesses and $1 of every $3 spent on workers' compensation.[19]

An example of these disorders is carpal tunnel syndrome, which involves pain in the wrist and fingers. This is a common complaint among those who type at a keyboard all day or perform other tasks involving the wrist, such as making the same cut in chickens all day long at a poultry processor. Some people in the newspaper business have speculated that stiff competition for jobs in that field has forced many reporters and columnists to try to cope with the pain rather than complain about it.

Back problems are another major cost to employees and employers, accounting for an estimated $50 billion per year in workers' compensation alone. An additional $50 billion is spent each year on indirect costs such as finding and training substitute workers and running physical conditioning and reduced-work programs to help ease employees back into their jobs. And of course, reduced workplace productivity is a cause for concern. "If you look at lost work time," says Professor Alan Hedge of Cornell University's Department of Design and Environmental Analysis, "it's the tip of the iceberg. When you're hurting at work you're not as effective."[20]

To prevent repetitive-motion disorders, an organization can take several measures, including designing jobs and workstations to allow for rests, using

virtual reality
A three-dimensional computer-generated environment that gives the user a sensation of being part of that environment.

repetitive-motion disorders
Injuries that result from repeatedly applying force to the same muscles or joints.

ergonomics
The science concerned with the human characteristics that must be considered in designing tasks and equipment so that people will work most effectively and safely.

adjustable furniture, and avoiding awkward movements and bad posture. This type of response to the problem is an application of **ergonomics,** the science concerned with the human characteristics that need to be considered in designing tasks and equipment so that people will work most effectively and safely. While supervisors need not be experts in ergonomics, they can cultivate an awareness of these issues. Another measure is to encourage employees who are in pain to seek medical attention right away. Supervisors should never tell their employees to work through pain, as this may aggravate an existing injury.

AIDS (acquired immunodeficiency syndrome)
The incurable and fatal illness that is caused by the HIV virus.

AIDS   Although other illnesses are more widespread, probably the most feared is **AIDS,** caused by HIV, the human immunodeficiency virus. The biggest reason for the fear is that AIDS remains incurable and fatal. Fortunately, people cannot catch it from touching a person with AIDS or sharing a drinking fountain or rest room; the HIV virus is transmitted through the exchange of bodily fluids, which can occur through sexual activity, blood transfusions, and the sharing of contaminated hypodermic needles, as well as between an infected mother and a fetus.

Most of the activities involving the transmission of HIV would not occur in the workplace. The major exception is health care institutions where hypodermic needles are used. These institutions should have procedures for the proper handling and disposal of the needles to prevent the spread of AIDS and other serious diseases such as hepatitis.

In most work settings, the major concern about AIDS is how to treat employees who are HIV-positive or who have AIDS. Both fairness and federal antidiscrimination laws dictate treating these employees in the same way as anyone else with a disability. As long as the employees can perform their jobs, they should be allowed to remain. At some point, an organization may have to make reasonable accommodations to allow them to continue working, such as allowing an ill employee to complete job assignments at home.

When an employee has AIDS, a supervisor must confront the fears that other employees are likely to have about working with that employee. With help from the human resources department, a supervisor may need to educate other employees about AIDS and how it is transmitted. Despite these efforts, some employees may shun a co-worker with AIDS. Therefore, the supervisor and others in the organization must do their best to protect the confidentiality of a person with AIDS. If an employee with AIDS or the employee's co-workers are having trouble coping, the supervisor may wish to refer them to the organization's employee-assistance program, if one exists. (These programs are described in Chapter 13.)

Workplace Programs to Promote Safety and Health

Many employers have instituted formal programs to promote the safety and health of employees. The program may include training, safety meetings, posters, awards for safe performance, and safety and health committees. A typical committee includes operative employees and managers, perhaps with a membership that rotates among the employees. In a recent study of occupational safety and health committees in the public sector in New Jersey, it was found that committees with more worker involvement were associated with fewer reported illnesses and injuries.[21] The duties of a health and safety committee can include regularly inspecting work areas, reviewing employees' suggestions for improving health and safety, and promoting awareness about safety. The committee also might sponsor the organization's contests or awards for safe practices.

Many organizations have extended their safety and health programs to cover off-duty conduct by employees that contributes to health problems. These efforts may be part of a *wellness program* (see Chapter 14). For example, some wellness programs seek to discourage employees from smoking altogether (not just restricting smoking at work), and others seek to teach healthy eating and exercise habits.

In 1998, about 93 percent of employers had wellness programs, up from 76 percent in 1992. Responding to data showing that 97 million in the United States are overweight, for instance, and that obesity costs upwards of $90 billion in health care costs and lost productivity, companies such as Bank One Corporation have begun nutrition and exercise programs. Carla Crnkovic, a computer programmer for Bank One, has attended such a program for several years. "I lost 110 pounds," she said, "my blood pressure came down to normal and my cholesterol level dropped 40 points. It's wonderful."[22]

Benefits

By reducing the number and severity of work-related injuries and illnesses, safety and health programs can cut the costs to organizations in a number of areas. (See "Meeting the Challenge.") These include health and workers' compensation insurance, defense of lawsuits, repair or replacement of equipment damaged in accidents, and wages paid for lost time. The savings can be significant. In addition, safety and health programs can motivate employees, reduce turnover, and help prevent pain and suffering among employees and their families. Finally, an organization that is a safe and healthy place to work is more likely to enjoy good relations with the government and community and should have an easier time recruiting desirable employees.

Characteristics of an Effective Program

A safety and health program is effective when it succeeds in minimizing the likelihood that people will be injured or become ill as a result of conditions in the workplace, when all levels of management demonstrate a strong commitment to the program, and when employees believe that the program is worthwhile. In addition, all employees need to be trained in the importance of safety and ways to promote health and safety in the workplace. This training should give employees an ongoing awareness of the need to behave in safe ways. Finally, an organization should have a system for identifying and correcting hazards before they do damage. In addition to those mentioned elsewhere in this chapter, workplace hazards can include pesticides, loose carpeting, cleaning products, toner, markers, correction fluid, artificial lighting, dark stairways, needles or syringes, lead-based paint (in older buildings), noise, carbon dioxide, radon, x-rays, perfume, radioactive materials and waste, biological waste, poisonous substances, and tools and equipment that don't "fit" the employee.[23]

Role of the Supervisor

Top management's support of safety measures is important; the organization may even have a safety director or other manager responsible for safety programs. Nevertheless, it is up to supervisors to see that employees follow safety precautions. After all, it is the supervisors who observe and are responsible for the day-to-day performance of employees. Unfortunately, some supervisors must witness a

MEETING THE CHALLENGE

The Lower Cost of Good Health and Safety Practices

It's no revelation that workplace accidents cause companies money. Insuring against those accidents may cost even more. (Nationally, workers' compensation premiums cost businesses about $65 billion per year.) For small companies, trying to find an affordable workers' compensation insurance plan (which covers employees injured or rendered ill on the job) can be a nightmare. (Larger companies can foot the bill for their own self-insurance plans; smaller companies can't.) Ethically—and in some states, legally—companies must take care of their employees through some type of disability or workers' compensation insurance, no matter how difficult the task may be.

Recently, more small businesses have turned to self-insured groups, or SIGs. Some even have launched these groups themselves. For instance, a group of 70 small jewelry manufacturers and related businesses pooled their resources in a nonprofit trust to pay their own workers' comp bills. The Jewelry Industry Risk Management Association now has 144 members. Most of the growth in self-insurance has come from groups like this.

These groups don't just pay bills; they encourage their members to develop safe workplaces so that the bills diminish. Here's the financial incentive for this practice: Because each SIG holds its own funds in reserve, any surplus received from premiums and not spent on medical bills is returned as a "dividend" to the members.

SIGs hire administrators to manage their operations, develop safety training for workers, manage cases and claims, and oversee the finances. Mike Follick, president of Abacus Management Group Inc., in Rhode Island, describes the philosophy of a successful SIG: "I look at this not just as a way of helping with workers' comp costs but also helping small business develop certain problem-solving and management skills, which can then be applied to other areas." Abacus as well as other SIG administrators teach injury prevention and other methods for reducing the need for workers' comp claims. Once a case is taken on, Abacus follows the worker's recuperation closely.

At the encouragement of Abacus, SIG member Greylawn Foods, a distributor of refrigerated foods that employs 45 people, gives new hires a B200 back exam, which measures how much weight a person can lift safely. Because most jobs at Greylawn require a lot of lifting, the company needs to establish a baseline for workers' capacity to lift. That way, if an employee gets hurt lifting on the job, there is a record of how much weight he or she reasonably could have been expected to handle. "The B200 is expensive, but it is worth every penny," comments Greylawn president Sidney Goldman.

SIG members and their administrators know that keeping their employees healthy and safe translates to greater productivity—something on which most workers and employers agree. "You *must* care about the employees," declares Jack Curley of Steve Connolly Seafood in Boston. "You want them to get better from any type of injury. You want to preserve their paycheck for them, to the extent possible, to bring them back for 'light duty' at the earliest moment." (Light duty is less demanding work at full pay while a worker is recovering to full health.) For workers and their employers, even light duty is better than no duty at all.

Source: Roberta Reynes, "Do-It-Yourself Workers' Comp," *Nation's Business*, April 1995, pp. 26–28, and U.S. Chamber of Commerce.

serious injury before they appreciate why they must enforce safety rules and procedures. Supervisors who avoid enforcing these rules because they are afraid employees will react negatively are missing the point of why the rules exist. They also are failing to recognize that they have an important role in maintaining a safe and healthy workplace.

Training and Hazard Prevention   A supervisor needs to see that employees understand and follow all procedures designed to maintain safety and health. New employees must be well trained in how to do their job safely; more experienced employees need training when they take on new responsibilities or when the organization introduces new procedures, materials, or machinery. In addition, employees need reminders about safe practices. Besides comments from the supervisor, the reminders can include posters, items in the company or department newsletter, and presentations by one employee to the others. Statistics about the department's performance, such as number of accidents during this year compared with last year, can be posted on bulletin boards or reported in the newsletter. In addition, OSHA requires that companies with more than 10 employees display the safety and health poster shown in Figure 19.4, which provides information about employees' rights under the OSHAct.

Some special concerns arise with regard to educating workers who are or may become pregnant. A Supreme Court ruling prohibits employers from forbidding pregnant workers from holding hazardous jobs, a policy that, if permitted, could force women to choose between holding a job and having a baby. Nevertheless, women who remain in these jobs may sue an employer for damages if a child is born with injuries caused by hazardous working conditions. The acceptable way to protect women employees of childbearing age is to emphasize information. They should be informed of any pregnancy-related risks of work assignments. A supervisor also may encourage employees to ask for a reassignment to a less hazardous job if they become pregnant. (The organization may not reduce the employee's pay, benefits, or seniority rights.) If the employee cannot be reassigned, the organization can give the employee leave during her pregnancy, including full pay and a guarantee of getting the job back after the baby is born.

Another situation calling for special attention is the supervision of shift workers, who also need additional guidance in safe practices. Employees will be more alert and better able to concentrate if they adapt their overall lifestyle to working night shifts or rotating shifts. They must make an extra effort to get enough quality sleep during the day, seeking out a quiet, dark, cool place for doing so. People who are naturally alert late at night will probably sleep best if they do so right after working at night, whereas others will do better if they sleep just before going in to work at night. People who work a night shift also will be more comfortable if they eat relatively light foods during their shift, avoiding heavy, greasy items.

A supervisor should encourage all employees to participate in the promotion of safe and healthy conditions. One way to do this is to emphasize that employees share in the responsibility for creating a safe work setting. In addition, a supervisor should be responsive to employee complaints related to safety, seeing that the health and safety committee or the appropriate individual investigates these complaints. Any hazardous conditions should be corrected immediately.

Prompt Responses   A supervisor who observes a violation of health and safety guidelines should respond immediately and consistently. Failure to react is a signal to employees that the guidelines are not really important. First, a supervisor should determine why the violation occurred. Does the employee understand what the proper procedures are? If the employee understands the procedures but still resists following them, the supervisor should try to find out why. For example, if an employee complains that some safety equipment is uncomfortable to use, investigating the complaint may turn up a more effective alternative, such as a greater selection of safety glasses or a way to set up a job so that less safety equipment is required. Despite complaints, however, a supervisor must insist that employees follow safety procedures, even when they seem inconvenient. If the safety rules are violated, a supervisor may have to take disciplinary action. (See Chapter 13 for a discussion of discipline.)

FIGURE 19.4

OSHA Safety and Health Poster

You Have a Right to a Safe and Healthful Workplace.
IT'S THE LAW!

- You have the right to notify your employer or OSHA about workplace hazards. You may ask OSHA to keep your name confidential.

- You have the right to request an OSHA inspection if you believe that there are unsafe and unhealthful conditions in your workplace. You or your representative may participate in the inspection.

- You can file a complaint with OSHA within 30 days of discrimination by your employer for making safety and health complaints or for exercising your rights under the *OSH Act*.

- You have a right to see OSHA citations issued to your employer. Your employer must post the citations at or near the place of the alleged violation.

- Your employer must correct workplace hazards by the date indicated on the citation and must certify that these hazards have been reduced or eliminated.

- You have the right to copies of your medical records or records of your exposure to toxic and harmful substances or conditions.

- Your employer must post this notice in your workplace.

The *Occupational Safety and Health Act of 1970 (OSH Act)*, P.L. 91-596, assures safe and healthful working conditions for working men and women throughout the Nation. The Occupational Safety and Health Administration, in the U.S. Department of Labor, has the primary responsibility for administering the *OSH Act*. The rights listed here may vary depending on the particular circumstances. To file a complaint, report an emergency, or seek OSHA advice, assistance, or products, call 1-800-321-OSHA or your nearest OSHA office: • Atlanta (404) 562-2300 • Boston (617) 565-9860 • Chicago (312) 353-2220 • Dallas (214) 767-4731 • Denver (303) 844-1600 • Kansas City (816) 426-5861 • New York (212) 337-2378 • Philadelphia (215) 861-4900 • San Francisco (415) 975-4310 • Seattle (206) 553-5930. Teletypewriter (TTY) number is 1-877-889-5627. To file a complaint online or obtain more information on OSHA federal and state programs, visit OSHA's website at **www.osha.gov**. If your workplace is in a state operating under an OSHA-approved plan, your employer must post the required state equivalent of this poster.

1-800-321-OSHA
www.osha.gov

U.S. Department of Labor • **Occupational Safety and Health Administration** • **OSHA 3165**

Quality of Work Life   By combating fatigue, boredom, and dissatisfaction, which can make an employee accident-prone, a supervisor can promote safety and health. These efforts may include improving the quality of work life by making jobs more interesting and satisfying. Although no one has proved that there is a link between quality of work life and employee safety and health, it seems reasonable to assume that interested, satisfied employees will tend to be healthier and more careful. (Chapter 11 offers some guidelines for expanding and enriching jobs.)

In the case of shift workers, a supervisor can help minimize fatigue by encouraging the organization to place employees on a single shift or to rotate shifts so that employees go to work later and later, rather than earlier and earlier or in no steady pattern. Making sure there is bright lighting also will help employees stay alert at night.

Setting an Example   As with any other area where the supervisor wants employees to behave in a certain way, the supervisor must set a good example and follow safe practices. For example, a supervisor who uses tools improperly, creates a tower of soft-drink cans on a filing cabinet, or tries to troubleshoot a photocopier without first turning off the power is voiding the effect of even the most eloquent lecture on safety in the workplace.

Below are some other ways in which supervisors can set an example about safety. Most of these carry little or no financial cost.[24]

1. Be a fanatic about health and safety. Make it a top priority in your factory, shop, or office.
2. Establish a Safety Committee with responsibility for conducting periodic safety audits.
3. Heighten worker awareness through safety training programs, regularly scheduled safety campaigns, and celebration of National Safety Week.
4. Reward suggestions for improved health and safety measures.
5. Make cleanliness more than a virtue. Make it a requirement.
6. Distribute a safety and emergency procedures and instructions manual.
7. Post emergency phone numbers in prominent locations throughout the workplace.
8. Conduct safety evacuation drills where appropriate.
9. Insist that all hazardous substances and materials be tightly sealed and properly stored.
10. When you say that hard hats are required on the work site, mean it!
11. Install appropriate smoke detectors, alarms, and fire extinguishers.
12. Strictly enforce company no-smoking rules and introduce a no-perfume policy when necessary.
13. Clearly mark all hazardous items and zones.
14. Never condone or encourage safety short-cuts.

Labor Relations: The Supervisor's Role

Concerns related to health and safety are among those that spurred the formation of unions as we know them in the United States during the late 1800s. Employees, who then worked as long as 12 hours each day, banded together to persuade employers to shorten work hours, pay higher wages, and improve safety. Today unions continue to negotiate with organizations over similar issues.

■ FIGURE 19.5

Union Membership as a Percentage of the Employed U.S. Workforce

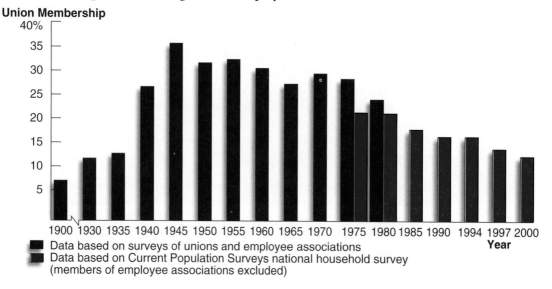

Sources: C. Chang and C. Sorrentino, "Union Membership in 12 Countries," *Monthly Labor Review* 114, no. 12 (1991), pp. 46–53; L. Troy and N. Sheflin, *Union Sourcebook* (West Orange, NJ: Industrial Relations Data and Information Services, 1985); Bureau of Labor Statistics, *Handbook of Labor Statistics* (Washington, DC, 1992); *Statistical Abstract of the United States: 1995* (Washington, DC, 1995), p. 444; Bureau of Labor Statistics, 1998 data (http://stats.bls.gov/news.release/union2.nws.htm); Bureau of Labor Statistics Union Members Summary, http://stats.bls.gov/news.release/union2.nr0.htm.

Wagner Act
Federal law intended to define and protect the rights of workers and employers, encourage collective bargaining, and eliminate unfair labor practices.

In 1935 the federal government passed the **Wagner Act** (also called the National Labor Relations Act). This law aims to define and protect the rights of workers and employers, encourage collective bargaining, and eliminate unfair practices (e.g., violence and threatening to fire employees who join a union). Following passage of the Wagner Act, union membership tripled (see Figure 19.5). As a percentage of the total workforce, union membership peaked in the 1940s.

Union membership has since fallen to below 14 percent of the workforce in 2000.[25] This drop accompanies a decline in the industrial sector of the economy, where membership was traditionally strongest. The power of unions has also declined along with the numbers. During the 1980s, many unions made major concessions in negotiations with employers.

labor relations
Management's role in working constructively with unions that represent the organization's employees.

The processes by which supervisors and other managers work constructively with unions constitute the management discipline of **labor relations**. Effective labor relations cannot eliminate all conflicts between labor and management, but it does provide a relatively low-cost means of resolving conflict through discussion rather than confrontation. Labor relations take place through activities such as organization drives and collective bargaining.

The Organization Drive

An organization drive is the union's method of getting its members elected to represent the workers in an organization. Management typically resists these drives because it believes that a union will interfere with managers' ability to make deci-

SUPERVISION ACROSS INDUSTRIES

Manufacturing

Making Safety Count

Emerald Packaging Inc. is a family-run bag-manufacturing firm in Union City, California. During the 1990s, while its insurance premiums rose steadily, the company also experienced high reported injuries among its 100-member factory work force. Most incidents were minor, but three required costly medical treatment and the expense of disability pay while workers took weeks to recover. Finally, by 1999, Emerald's annual insurance costs had risen 30 percent.

Kevin Kelly, an officer in the firm, decided to reduce the number of accidents from 24 a year to a maximum of 12, and to ensure that none cost the company lost time on the job. He set out to discover the causes of the minor injuries and found that workers, especially the most experienced ones, were simply neglecting basic safety measures, such as wearing protective glasses. One such worker had suffered three similar injuries from flying bits of plastic and was still not taking required precautions.

In a move that could well be a model for other supervisors facing similar problems, Kelly instituted a

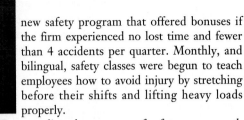

new safety program that offered bonuses if the firm experienced no lost time and fewer than 4 accidents per quarter. Monthly, and bilingual, safety classes were begun to teach employees how to avoid injury by stretching before their shifts and lifting heavy loads properly.

"By pounding the message of safety . . . month after month," says Kelly, "we slowly but surely changed the culture of our factory." Kelly also credits peer pressure with helping to improve the company's safety record. By early 2001, the factory had gone 850 days without anyone's missing work because of an injury, and the average annual rate of worker injuries was down to 8, well below the goal.

Unfortunately, deregulated insurance premiums prevented Emerald's rate from dropping, but Kelly is sure it would be higher still if it were not for the success of the new safety program.

Source: Kevin Kelly, "It Doesn't Hurt as Much," *Business Week*, April 2, 2001, p. 19.

---

sions in the best interests of the company. Managers also fear that the union will convert employees' loyalty to the company into loyalty to the union. The union tries to persuade employees that management has never had their interests at heart and that they will be better off if they let the union bargain collectively with management.

The process of organizing begins when a few employees decide they want to be represented by a union or when union leaders target an organization as a likely candidate. Union representatives then go to the company to organize. If at least 30 percent of the employees sign an authorization card stating they want the union to represent them, the union may request an election. The employees vote by secret ballot. If a majority of the voting employees favor the union, the union becomes the representative of *all* employees in the bargaining unit.

Although managers generally want to keep unions out, federal law says supervisors and other managers may not restrain employees from forming or joining a union. Supervisors are allowed to state their views about unions, but they may not threaten employees with punishment for forming or joining a union, and they may not promise rewards for working against the union. A supervisor who is unsure about what kinds of comments are permitted should consult with the organization's human resources department. A union in turn may not try to pressure employees into joining. Supervisors who think the union is violating this law should inform the human resources department.

Collective Bargaining

collective bargaining
The process of seeking to reach a contract spelling out the rights and duties of unionized workers and their employer.

Typically, workers and managers have differing views on a variety of issues; after all, the fundamental reason for unions is to give workers a stronger voice when differences arise. The basic process for resolving such differences is **collective bargaining**—the process of seeking to reach a contract spelling out the rights and duties of unionized workers and their employer. Typically, bargaining begins when the union and management set forth their demands. Because the two parties usually differ on what is acceptable, they discuss how to resolve the major areas of conflict. If they need help in resolving a conflict, they may call in a **mediator,** or **conciliator,** a neutral person who helps the two sides reach agreement.

mediator or conciliator
A neutral person who helps opposing parties in an organization reach agreement.

A supervisor seldom has a direct role in collective bargaining. However, management may ask a supervisor to provide information that will help during the bargaining process. This is another reason why the supervisor should keep careful records concerning employees.

The Labor Contract

A typical labor contract contains provisions such as guidelines for union membership; procedures for handling grievances; policies about regular and overtime pay, benefits (including vacations and holidays), and work hours; and agreements concerning safety and health. A supervisor must abide by the terms of this contract, so he or she must be familiar with it. A supervisor who is unfamiliar with the labor contract may unintentionally cause a problem by, for example, asking an employee to do something forbidden by the contract or using a procedure for discipline that is prohibited. Ignoring a provision in the contract, such as the length of rest periods, may be interpreted as an agreement to change the contract. A supervisor also should treat all employees fairly and consistently. Not only is this good practice whether or not there is a union, but federal law prohibits supervisors and other managers from discriminating against union members.

union steward
An employee who is the union's representative in a particular work unit.

Working with the Union Steward   Part of a supervisor's job under a labor contract is to maintain a good relationship with the union steward. A **union steward** is an employee who serves as the union's representative in a particular work unit. Employees go to the union steward with their contract-related questions and complaints.

To minimize conflict and to resolve problems that arise, a supervisor needs to cooperate with the union steward. The supervisor should treat a union steward with respect and tell him or her about problems and upcoming changes. If the supervisor and union steward have a cooperative relationship, they often can resolve problems themselves rather than subject the organization and its employees to the cost and stress of an ongoing dispute.

grievance
A formal complaint that the terms of a labor contract have been violated.

Grievances   Employees who believe they have been treated unfairly under the terms of the labor contract may bring a formal complaint, or **grievance.** Typically, when an employee brings a grievance, he or she first meets with the supervisor and union steward to look for a solution. Most of the time, the three of them can resolve the problem. If not, higher-level managers and union representatives meet to seek a solution. If they cannot reach an agreement, both parties might agree to bring in an outside **arbitrator,** a neutral person who reaches a decision on how to resolve a conflict. Both parties must adhere to the terms set by the arbitrator.

arbitrator
A neutral person who reaches a decision on the resolution of a conflict; both parties must adhere to the decision.

To avoid this costly and time-consuming process, supervisors should make sure that employees have a chance to be heard. In many cases, a supervisor can resolve conflicts before an employee even files a grievance. When a grievance is filed, a supervisor should take it seriously. This means gathering complete information and trying to resolve the problem as quickly as possible. Conflicts that are allowed to continue are likely to seem more significant to both parties.

Strikes

strike
Refusal by employees to work until there is a contract.

Occasionally, the parties are unable to reach an agreement during collective bargaining, so the employees vote to go on strike. During a **strike,** employees leave their jobs and refuse to come back until there is a contract. The use of strikes has been declining in recent decades. According to the U.S. Department of Labor's Bureau of Labor Statistics, there were 381 major strikes in 1970, 187 in 1980, 44 in 1990, and only 39 in 2000.[26] In general, striking during the term of a contract—a **wildcat strike**—is illegal.

wildcat strike
Refusal by employees to work during the term of a labor contract.

The Supervisor's Role in Preventing Strikes   Although a supervisor has little control over any agreement reached during collective bargaining by union and management representatives, he or she does have a role in minimizing the likelihood of a strike. Treating employees fairly and reasonably fosters good relations between employees and management. In this kind of climate, employees are less likely to desire a strike. Good communication practices also enable employees to understand management's point of view and give them a chance to vent their frustrations while staying on the job.

The Supervisor's Role during a Strike   Once the employees have voted to strike, there is little a supervisor can do to resolve the conflict. If the circumstances of the strike do not involve unfair labor practices by an employer, the employer may hire replacement workers. Then the supervisor must tackle the challenge of training and getting to know a new workforce. The supervisor will have to adjust goals and expectations to allow for the new employees' inexperience.

When a wildcat strike takes place, a supervisor should follow the practices listed in Table 19.1, notably, to observe carefully what is occurring and to encourage

■ TABLE 19.1
Guidelines for Supervising during a Wildcat Strike

Stay on the job.
Notify higher management by telephone or messenger.
Carefully record the events as they happen.
Pay strict attention to who the leaders are, and record their behavior.
Record any lack of action by union officials.
Report all information as fully and as soon as possible to higher management.
Encourage employees to go back to work.
Ask union officials to instruct employees to go back to work.
Do not discuss the cause of the strike.
Do not make any agreements or say anything that might imply permission to leave work.
Make it clear that management will discuss the issue when all employees are back at work.

Source: From Leslie W. Rue and Lloyd L. Byars, *Supervision: Key Link to Productivity*, 6th ed. (New York: Irwin/McGraw-Hill, 1999), p. 263. Copyright © 1999 by The McGraw-Hill Companies. Reproduced with permission of The McGraw-Hill Companies.

employees to abide by the contract and return to work. At no time should the supervisor make agreements or even discuss the problem that led to the wildcat strike.

Sexual Harassment

sexual harassment
Unwelcome sexual advances, requests for sexual favors, and other sexual conduct that interferes with work performance or creates a hostile work environment.

TWA, Dial Corporation, Wal-Mart, Mitsubishi, and several metropolitan police departments are among the employers who have faced sexual harassment suits in recent years.[27] Such suits dramatically highlight the issue of sexual harassment, a category of behavior prohibited by laws against sex discrimination. As defined by the Equal Employment Opportunity Commission (EEOC), **sexual harassment** is "unwelcome sexual advances, requests for sexual favors, and other verbal and physical conduct of a sexual nature" that "has the purpose or effect of unreasonably interfering with an individual's work performance or creating an intimidating, hostile, or offensive work environment." It may include any of the behaviors listed in Table 19.2. The perpetrator and victim may be either male or female. (About 13 percent of all complaints filed with the EEOC are filed by men.[28]) The victim does not need to prove that sexual harassment caused psychological harm, only that it was unwelcome. (The Self-Quiz on page 531 can help you determine how well you understand sexual harassment and what to do about it.)

The number of sexual harassment charges filed with the EEOC has increased dramatically. For example, the number of claims of sexual harassment filed in 2000 was 15,836, about 50 percent more than in 1992.[29] These numbers suggest that the problem is persistent and extensive.

Responding to Charges of Sexual Harassment

A charge of sexual harassment is a serious one. Court decisions have held employers liable for the misdeeds of their employees unless an organization actively tries to prevent the misbehavior and responds effectively when it does occur. Therefore, when an employee charges a member of an organization with sexual harassment, a supervisor must take the problem seriously. There are no exceptions to this rule—not the attractiveness of the victim nor the supervisor's opinion of a man who is offended by centerfold pictures.

■ TABLE 19.2
Behaviors That May Constitute Sexual Harassment

Suggestive remarks.
Teasing or taunting of a sexual nature.
Unwelcome physical conduct or sexual advances.
Continual use of offensive language.
Sexual bantering.
Bragging about sexual prowess.
Office or locker-room pinups.
"Compliments" with sexual overtones.
A demand for sex in return for retaining a job or being promoted.

Source: Based on Michael A. Verespej, "New-Age Sexual Harassment," *Industry Week*, May 15, 1995, p. 66.

SUPERVISION AND DIVERSITY

When the Joke Isn't Funny

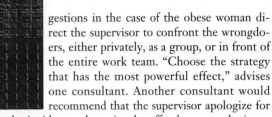

An obese worker experienced severe emotional distress when employees in her office circulated an unflattering cartoon that made reference to her weight. Although her supervisor prevented the incident from going any further, several employees were upset by the event and morale was damaged.

There are no federal antidiscrimination laws concerning weight or body shape, but most legal experts agree that firms that permit co-workers to harass one another on such grounds are asking for trouble. In some local jurisdictions, it is indeed illegal to discriminate on the basis of personal appearance, and someone whose obesity is due to a medical problem may be protected by the Americans with Disabilities Act, which prohibits bias against the disabled. At least one such case has in fact been brought.

Supervisors need to be prepared to handle situations in which harassment occurs. Some experts' suggestions in the case of the obese woman direct the supervisor to confront the wrongdoers, either privately, as a group, or in front of the entire work team. "Choose the strategy that has the most powerful effect," advises one consultant. Another consultant would recommend that the supervisor apologize for the incident and require the offenders to apologize as well. Any further actions should be disciplined, and while management should be careful not to draw any unnecessary attention to the victim, all supervisors should be instructed that no one will be permitted to treat fellow workers cruelly.

Source: Kirstin Downey Grimsley, "When Employees Don't Get the Picture on Cruel Office Jokes," *Washington Post*, November 15, 1998, p. H4.

A supervisor must see that the complaint is investigated properly. Generally, the investigation involves a third party, such as a personnel official, interviewing everyone involved. This official, the supervisor, and the parties involved should keep the investigation confidential. The supervisor must avoid also expressing an opinion or imposing his or her interpretation on the situation.

Whether harassment occurs depends on how the behavior affects the recipient, not on the intent of the person performing the behavior. Thus, if lewd jokes and pornographic pictures create a climate that feels hostile and intimidating to an employee, it does not matter that the person who told the jokes and hung up the pictures thought only that they were funny. Not surprisingly, perceptions vary from one person to another.

If the investigation indicates that sexual harassment did occur, the problem must be corrected. One approach that does *not* work is ignoring the offensive behavior in the hope that it will go away. The victim telling the offender to stop is effective more than half the time. Because of differences in perceptions, it may be helpful to describe not only the offending behavior but the kind of behavior that would be acceptable. In addition, a supervisor needs to work with the human resources department to identify a prompt and firm response to charges that are proven. The response might be to move the employee to another department or shift, or even to fire him or her. In any case, discipline should be appropriate and swift, occurring the same day if possible or at least within a week.

Preventing Sexual Harassment

An employee who sexually harasses another employee hurts the organization in several ways. First, the person who is being harassed is upset and unable to work as effectively as possible. If that person complains, disciplining the harasser may involve transferring or dismissing him or her, resulting in the loss of an otherwise qualified employee. And if the harassed person sues, the company faces the embarrassment and expense of defending itself in court. It is clearly in the organization's best interests to prevent harassment.

Some people have complained that concern about sexual harassment has poisoned the workplace—that they no longer feel safe paying friendly compliments. However, respecting the viewpoints and emotional comfort of all employees simply makes sense. See "Supervision and Diversity" for an example. The same is true of ensuring employees' safety and health, and of practicing good labor relations. In each case, a supervisor is recognizing that good employee relations is at the heart of cultivating the organization's most important resources: its employees.

Summary

19.1 Summarize the basic purpose of the OSHAct, and describe the supervisor's responsibilities under the act.

OSHAct set up two government agencies (OSHA and NIOSH) to conduct research regarding occupational health and safety, set health and safety standards, inspect workplaces, and penalize employers that do not meet standards. According to OSHAct, a supervisor must keep records of occupational injuries and illnesses, accompany OSHA officials on inspections of the workplace, and disseminate information about chemicals used in the workplace.

19.2 Identify basic categories of health and safety hazards in the workplace.

Health hazards may be physical, chemical, biological, or stress inducing. Safety hazards include personal behavior (i.e., unsafe acts) and unsafe conditions of the physical environment.

19.3 Discuss common safety and health concerns and how employers are addressing them.

Cigarette smoke can cause a variety of illnesses in smokers and the people who breathe secondhand smoke. As a result, many organizations have banned or limited smoking in the workplace. The abuse of alcohol and other drugs can be costly, so organizations have policies for responding to employees with these problems. Extended use of video display terminals can result in eyestrain and muscle aches, and they possibly contribute to miscarriages among pregnant employees. Organizations can address these problems with rest breaks, ergonomically designed workstations, and seating that places employees a safe distance from the screen.

Repetitive-motion disorders can result when employees repeatedly apply force to the same muscles or joints. Applying ergonomics to the design of jobs and workstations can minimize such problems. Many employees are afraid of working near someone with AIDS; however, the means of transmitting this disease are limited. A supervisor may need to provide an employee who has AIDS with reasonable accommodations and educate the employee's co-workers about this disease.

19.4 Describe workplace safety and health programs, including their benefits and the supervisor's role in them.

Workplace safety and health programs may include training, safety meetings, posters, awards for safe performance, and safety and health committees. These programs can cut costs by reducing work-related injuries and illnesses. In addition, safety and health programs can motivate employees, reduce turnover, and help prevent pain and suffering for employees and their families. A supervisor needs to make sure that employees understand and follow safety measures, and should encourage all employees to participate in the promotion of these measures. A supervisor must respond immediately to a violation of health and safety guidelines. A supervisor also should set a good example for employees.

19.5 Explain a supervisor's role during a union organization drive and collective bargaining.

During an organization drive, a supervisor may state his or her views about the union. However, a supervisor may not threaten employees about forming or joining a union and may not promise rewards for working against the union. If the union tries to coerce employees into supporting the union, the supervisor should report those activities. During collective bargaining, a supervisor provides management with information that will help it bargain.

19.6 Provide guidelines for working with a union steward and handling grievances.

A supervisor should cooperate with the union steward and treat that person with respect. He or she should tell the steward about problems and upcoming changes and should try to resolve problems with the steward rather than let them escalate. A supervisor should try to avoid grievances by giving employees a chance to be heard and trying to resolve conflicts. When a grievance is filed, a supervisor should take it seriously, gathering information and trying to resolve the problem as quickly as possible.

19.7 Explain a supervisor's role in preventing strikes and operating during a strike.

A supervisor should foster good relations with employees by treating them fairly and communicating effectively. This minimizes the chance that employees will want to strike. During a strike, a supervisor may have to train and oversee replacement workers. During a wildcat strike, a supervisor should observe carefully what is occurring and encourage employees to go back to work. A supervisor should not make agreements or even discuss the problem that led to the wildcat strike.

19.8 Discuss how a supervisor should respond to charges of sexual harassment and prevent it from occurring.

When an employee charges a member of the organization with sexual harassment, a supervisor must take the problem seriously, without exception. He or she must see that the complaint is investigated properly and avoid expressing an opinion or imposing an interpretation on the situation. A supervisor should work with the human resources department to identify a prompt and firm response to charges that are proven true. In many cases, sexual harassment can be prevented through training and greater awareness of different points of view between men and women.

Key Terms

Occupational Safety and Health Act (OSHAct) of 1970, p. 505

Occupational Safety and Health Administration (OSHA), p. 505

National Institute for Occupational Safety and Health (NIOSH), p. 506

health hazards, p. 508

safety hazards, p. 509

video display terminal (VDT), p. 512

virtual reality, p. 513

repetitive-motion disorders, p. 513

ergonomics, p. 514

AIDS (acquired immunodeficiency syndrome), p. 514

Wagner Act, p. 520

labor relations, p. 520

collective bargaining, p. 522

mediator or conciliator, p. 522

union steward, p. 522

grievance, p. 522

arbitrator, p. 522

strike, p. 523

wildcat strike, p. 523

sexual harassment, p. 524

Review and Discussion Questions

1. Describe the two government agencies established by the Occupational Safety and Health Act of 1970. What is their role in promoting safety and health in the workplace?

2. Keith Navarro is a new supervisor at a supermarket. He is worried that OSHA has so many regulations that it is impossible to keep track of them all. What general guidelines can you give Keith about his responsibilities under the OSHAct?

3. Give an example of the following types of health and safety hazards:
   a. Physical
   b. Chemical
   c. Biological
   d. Stressful working conditions
   e. Personal behavior

4. Betsy Lee is the supervisor of the central files department of a large professional association. She is concerned about the number of minor injuries caused by employees tripping, dropping stacks of files, and colliding. Two employees have complained that lighting is often poor because lightbulbs are not immediately replaced when they burn out. What actions should Betsy take to minimize the safety hazards in her department?

5. What can supervisors do to minimize the effects of each of the following hazards?
   a. Cigarette smoking in the workplace.
   b. Extended use of video display terminals.

6. What are the benefits of workplace health and safety programs?

7. A clothing manufacturer wants to set up a safety and health program. What characteristics should this program have to be effective?

8. Julie Lindholm supervises a shift of workers who sew together teddy bears for a toy manufacturer. What steps should she be taking to implement her company's health and safety measures?

9. A foreman notices that an employee is not wearing the safety goggles required for operating a piece of grinding equipment. How should the foreman respond? What actions should he take?

10. Supervisor Sandy Berkmann recently learned that several of his employees approached a union to conduct an organization drive. Sandy feels somewhat hurt by their action, believing that it is a reflection on his supervisory skills. He also thinks the union will be a disruptive force among his workers. By law, what may Sandy do or not do during the organization drive? What do you think would be the best way for Sandy to behave, so that the process is beneficial to everyone?

11. During the term of a labor contract, a group of employees becomes angry about a new policy they believe is unfair, and they leave their work areas to walk off the job. In an effort to keep them working, their supervisor calls out, "Hey, not so fast! Why don't you tell me what the problem is, and we'll work out a solution." Is this an acceptable way for the supervisor to handle the situation? Explain.

12. One of Jim Seifert's women employees tells him that a male supervisor—a good friend of Jim's—has repeatedly made sexually explicit comments to her that embarrass and offend her. What should Jim do about the situation?

A SECOND LOOK

The chapter-opening story contrasts the feelings of smokers and nonsmokers. What would you do as a supervisor to balance the rights and concerns of these two groups?

SKILLS MODULE

CASE

Building Safety from the Ground Up

When Kenny Davis began working as a welder at Canam Steel Corporation's headquarters in Point of Rocks, Maryland, the job was going to be temporary. He wanted to earn some money until he found a position as a teacher and a marching band director.

At that time Canam had no formal safety of job task training. Although they fabricated steel joists, girders, and trusses, the facility's 360 employees were not required to wear protective equipment such as hard hats, gloves, or safety spectacles. Housekeeping was lax and employees had no faith in the safety department.

Having had previous experience as a patient care technician at a hospital, Davis was given the responsibility of treating injured employees and determining whether outside medical assistance was necessary. Davis's interest in safety started to build when he realized many of the injuries he treated were preventable and had occurred because of a lack of training or a blatant disregard for safety on the part of both management and employees. Safety became a personal issue when a fire occurred in a 50-gallon drum on the shop floor.

"An employee grabbed a fire extinguisher. It was empty. He grabbed another one . . . empty. We grabbed four empty fire extinguishers before we found one that worked. I took those fire extinguishers and threw them into the office of the safety director. I was that angry. My safety was threatened," remembered Davis. Subsequently, he began to speak up whenever he saw what he thought was a safety violation. When the safety director left, Davis was offered his position. . . .

When Davis took over the safety program, it consisted of a 27-page safety manual which was virtually ignored by management and employees. Realizing he would not learn much from the existing safety program and materials, Davis met with Maryland OSHA compliance officers, health officials from local hospitals, members of the local fire department, representatives from the Maryland Department of the Environment, the company's attorney, and risk management and loss control professionals from Canam's insurers.

He attended safety management classes and seminars, watched safety videos, and read everything he could get his hands on. He went into the facility and talked to employees "because they do the job every day and they know where to find hazards," said Davis. . . .

One of the first things Davis did was require employees and supervisors to report every incident. "Our incidence rate went up at first, but we got a better idea of where near misses and accidents were occurring and what we could do to prevent them." Once he had solid numbers, Davis found it easier to sell proactive safety measures to management. For example, when Davis proposed that employees be issued hard hats, company officials resisted. Then he informed them that three head injuries had occurred in one 48-hour period.

"Up until then, management was reactive to safety. They waited until someone got injured before they made changes. Just one of those head injuries could cost us more in workers' compensation than hard hats for employees," said Davis.

As part of the incident review process, Davis met with supervisors and discussed employees who were seemingly "accident prone." He taught supervisors how to recognize unsafe behavior and showed them ways to incorporate safety awareness into their daily work schedules. "By tracking incidents, I could tell supervisors where to find hazards," said Davis. "Then they could take 5 or 10 minutes at the start of their shifts, look in those areas, and eliminate hazards if they saw them."

He scheduled meetings with employees who had repeated accidents and included their supervisors and union representatives. The causes of the accidents were discussed and, if necessary, the employees were retrained. The purpose of the meetings was to prevent future accidents and injuries, not place blame.

Through these and other efforts, workers' compensation costs are now one-fifth what they were when Davis started, and employees take an active role in their own safety and the safety of their co-workers.

1. What was wrong with Canam Steel's safety program when Davis took it over?
2. Davis recommends that supervisors work proactively with agencies like OSHA and the Environmental Protection Agency. What advantages do you see in his strategy?

3. What role did supervisors play in getting Davis's safety program established and accepted at Canam?

Source: S. L. Smith, "Stand-Up Safety," *Occupational Hazards*, November 1998. Copyright © 1998 by Penton Media, Inc. Reprinted with permission.

■ SELF-QUIZ

How Well Do You Understand Sexual Harassment?

Mark each of the following statements True or False.

_____ 1. Sexual harassment applies only to comments or actions made by men toward women.

_____ 2. There are no laws defining sexual harassment.

_____ 3. If I intend my remarks to be friendly, they cannot be interpreted as sexual harassment.

_____ 4. A court may find a company legally responsible for sexual harassment by one of its employees.

_____ 5. Sometimes the best way to deal with sexual harassment is to ignore it.

_____ 6. To keep things from escalating, a supervisor should personally investigate an employee's charge of sexual harassment.

_____ 7. A supervisor's opinion of both the victim and the person charged can provide valuable information in a sexual harassment investigation.

_____ 8. Discipline for sexual harassment should take place as soon as possible.

_____ 9. Showing someone pornographic pictures at the workplace does not constitute sexual harassment.

_____ 10. Because men and women often interpret behavior differently, education about sexual harassment could help prevent it.

Scoring: The correct response to statements 4, 8, and 10 is True; to all other statements, False.

Class Exercise

Suppose students could be represented by a union. How might they benefit? How would this change their relationship with their instructors and the university? Appoint someone in the class to play the role of union representative and someone to play the role of "supervisor." Hold an organization drive meeting, in which students as well as the union rep and supervisor participate. At the end of the meeting, allow students to vote on whether they want the union to represent them. (Note: Course grades or other benefits can be considered "pay" if issues of compensation are discussed.)

Team-Building Exercise

Conducting a Safety Inspection

Divide the class into teams of two to four members each. At the end of the class session or between sessions, the teams will look for and list health and safety hazards on campus or in some other prescribed area. Team members may choose the area of campus to visit and investigate, or the instructor may assign the teams to specific areas (e.g., parking lots, recreation areas, bookstore, classrooms). Before the teams begin, it may be helpful for the class as a whole to discuss what kinds of hazards they ex-

pect to find—wet floors, dangerous intersections, unmarked fire extinguishers, uncomfortable chairs at VDTs, sources of stress, and so on.

At the next class session, each team reports its findings to the class. The instructor may invite the campus security director to sit in on this discussion.

Source: This exercise is based on ideas submitted by Debbie Jansky, Milwaukee Area Tech Institute, Milwaukee, Wisconsin; James Mulvihill, Mankato Technical Institute, Mankato, Minnesota; and Sylvia Ong, Scottsdale Community College, Scottsdale, Arizona.

Notes

Chapter 1

1. Rolf Mlumentritt and Neil Hardie, "The Role of Middle Management in the Knowledge-Focused Service Organization," *Journal of Business Strategies*, Spring 2000, pp. 37–48.

2. W. H. Weiss, "Management Challenges as a Result of Information and Technological Changes," *Supervision*, February 2001, pp. 9–12.

3. Bureau of Labor Statistics, 1998 data, available at http://stats.bls.gov/news.release/ecopro.table1.htm.

4. "The Diversity Myth," *American Demographics*, June 1, 1998, pp. 39 ff; Susan Sachs, "Hispanic New York Shifted in 1990s," *New York Times*, May 22, 2001.

5. "Women Are Going to the Dogs (and Cats and Birds)," *New York Times*, April 18, 2001, p. G1.

6. David Raths, "Bridging the Generation Gap," *Infoworld*, November 8, 1999, p. 84.

7. William P. Anthony, "Managing Diversity, Then and Now," *Wall Street Journal*, July 3, 1992, p. A6.

8. "Visible Signs of Relief," *Inc.*, May 2001, p. 67.

9. Timothy P. Henderson, "Retailers Use E-Supervision Technology to Manage and Maintain Security at Multiple Sites," *Stores*, February 2001, pp. 64–66.

10. "The Salaryman Rides Again," *Economist*, February 4, 1995, p. 64.

11. Gene Koretz, "Big Payoffs from Big Layoffs," *Business Week*, February 24, 1997, p. 30; John Simons, "Despite Low Unemployment, Layoffs Soar," *Wall Street Journal*, November 18, 1998, p. A2.

12. Noel M. Tichy and Ram Charan, "The CEO as Coach: An Interview with AlliedSignal's Lawrence A. Bossidy," *Harvard Business Review*, March–April 1995, pp. 69–78.

13. Frank Quisenberry, "World-of-Work Changes Signal New Roles for Service Supervisors," *Service Edge*, November 1994, p. 7.

14. Lin Grensing-Pophal, "Training Supervisors to Manage Workers," *HR Magazine*, January 1999.

15. Gene Ference, "Coaching Plan Helps Managers Increase Employee Commitment," *Hotel & Motel Management*, April 2, 2001, p. 16.

16. Amy Joyce, "Fear of Flying Higher: Out of Your Comfort Zone and into the Uncertainties of Management," *Washington Post*, November 23, 1998, p. F9.

Chapter 2

1. David Rocks, "Reinventing Herman Miller," *Business Week*, May 3, 2000, accessed at www.businessweek.com/2000/00 14/b3675047.htm?scriptFramed.

2. Jane Erwin and P. C. Douglas, "It's Not Difficult to Change Company Culture," *Supervision*, November 1, 2000, p. 6.

3. Keith Bradsher, "Ford Has Hartsher Words for Lates Recalled Tires," *New York Times*, June 15, 2001, p. C4.

4. Mary Connelly, "Ford Works with Suppliers to Ensure Quality Standards," *Automotive News*, April 30, 2001, p. 36.

5. "QC Software Cuts Inspection Time 80%," *Manufacturing Engineering*, April 2001, pp. 116–120.

6. Larry Adams, "Boeing: Quality Starts with a Hole," *Quality*, September 1, 2000, pp. 44–52.

7. Veronica T. Hychalk, "How Do We Quantify Quality?" *Nursing Management*, March 1, 2001, p. 16.

8. Michael Glowacki, "Site Visit: Elkay Manufacturing Company, A Tale of Two Sites," *Journal for Quality & Participation*, March 1, 2000, pp. 59–61.

9. Roy Duff, "Why TQM Fails—and What Companies Can Do about It," *Quality Digest*, February 1995, pp. 50–52.

10. Roberto Ceniceros, "Insurance Department Takes Team Approach to Quality," *Business Insurance*, April 30, 2001, p. 92.

11. "TQM 101: The Basics of Total Quality Management," *Commitment Plus* (Quality and Productivity Management Association), November 1991, pp. 1–4.

12. Marcia Stepanek, "What Does No. 1 Do for an Encore?" *Business Week*, November 2, 1998, pp. 112–113.

13. John P. Walsh, "The Quest for Quality," *Hotel & Motel Management*, May 7, 2001, pp. 36–38.

14. www.thequalityportal.com/q_6sigma.htm, accessed June 17, 2001.

15. Erwin and Douglas, "It's Not Difficult to Change Company Culture."

16. Gregory T. Lucier and Sridhar Seshadri, "GE Takes Six Sigma Beyond the Bottom Line," *Strategic Finance*, May 2001, pp. 40–46.

17. Erwin and Douglas, "It's Not Difficult to Change Company Culture."

18. Ibid.

19. Andrea Gabor, "Quality Revival, Part 2: Ford Embraces Six Sigma," *New York Times*, June 13, 2001, p. C5.

20. Lucier and Seshadri, "GE Takes Six Sigma Beyond the Bottom Line."

21. www.nist.gov/public_affairs/factsheet/baldfaqs.htm, accessed June 17, 2001.

22. Walsh, "The Quest for Quality."

23. "Quality's Future: What Should Happen Isn't Necessarily What Will Happen," *QI*, TQM Archives, May 1, 2001.

24. www.nist.gov/public_affairs/factsheet/baldfaqs.htm, accessed June 17, 2001, and press release dated April 6, 2001.

25. www.iso.ch/.

26. Nancy Chase, "Beyond Compliance," *Quality*, December 1, 1998, p. 62.

27. Julie Gallagher, "Firms Work to Establish FS 9000 Standards," *Insurance & Technology*, June 2001, p. 18.

28. John Guaspari, "A Cure for 'Initiative Burnout,'" *Management Review*, April 1995, pp. 45–49.

29. Oren Harari, "Why Don't Things Change?" *Management Review*, February 1995, pp. 30–32.

30. "Changes in Satisfaction Demands and Technology After the How's, What's, Why's of Measurement," *Service Edge*, January 1995, pp.1–3, 5.

31. "Tips from a Pro: Getting People to Care about Quality," *Practical Supervision*, sample issue, p. 6.

Chapter 3

1. "Keeping the Idea Pipeline Flowing," *Business Week*, September 18, 2000, p. EB104.

2. R. B. Lacoursiere, *The Life Cycle of Groups. Group Development Stage Theory* (New York: Human Service Press, 1980).

3. W. H. Weiss, "Teams and Teamwork," *Supervision*, July 1998, p. 9.

4. "The Trouble with Teams," *Economist*, January 14, 1995, p. 61.

5. Edward Wong, "Nike Trying New Strategies for Women," *New York Times*, June 19, 2001, p. C1.

6. John Holusha, "TV Station Moves from Old Hotel to New Studio," *New York Times*, December 23, 1998, p B6.

7. Charles Fishman, "Engines of Democracy," *Fast Company*, October 1999, pp. 174–202.

8. Barbara B. Buchholz and Margaret Crane, "Nurturing the Team Spirit at Growing Green," *Your Company*, Spring 1995, pp. 10–11, 14–16.

9. See, for example, "The Trouble with Teams."

10. Norihiko Shirouzu, "Job One: Ford Has Big Problem beyond the Tire Mess," *Wall Street Journal*, May 25, 2001, p. A1.

11. "Guidelines for Implementing Self-Directed Work Teams," *Supervisory Management*, March 1995, p. 10.

12. Ibid.

13. "What Mentors Shouldn't Do," *Supervisory Management*, March 1995, p. 5.

14. Edward Glassman, "Self-Directed Team Building without a Consultant," *Supervisory Management*, March 1992, p. 6.

15. Rebecca J. Johnson, "Deep Sinkers," *Journal of Business Strategy*, May–June 1995, pp. 62–63.

16. Chuck Salter, "Life in the Fast Lane," *Fast Company*, October 1998, pp. 172–178.

17. "The Trouble with Teams."

18. "The Dream Team," *Supervisory Management*, May 1995, p. 10.

19. Donald J. McNerney, "Team Compensation," *Management Review*, February 1995, p. 16.

20. Stephen D. Solomon, "Hard Questions," *Inc.* 500, 1998, pp. 146–164.

21. Aaron Bernstein, "Putting a Damper on That Old Team Spirit," *Business Week*, May 4, 1992, p. 60.

22. Glenn Burkins, "Anitunion Group Tries to Use NAFTA to Push for Teams at Nonunion Firms," *Wall Street Journal*, April 14, 1999, p. A2.

23. Michael P. Cronin, "Team Penalty," *Inc.*, May 1993, p. 29.

24. David F. Girard-diCarlo, Michael J. Hanlon, and Caren E. I. Naidoff, "Legal Traps in Employee Committees," *Management Review*, November 1992, pp. 27–29.

25. Cronin, "Team Penalty."

26. "Avoid Labor Law Violations in Employee Involvement Programs," *NIBA News Bulletin* (Northern Illinois Business Association), March 1992, p. 11; Bernstein, "Putting a Damper on That Old Team Spirit."

27. Isa N. Engleberg and Dianna R. Wynn, *Working in Groups: Communication Principles and Strategies* (Boston: Houghton-Mifflin, 1997), p. 199.

28. Polly LaBarre, "Work Fast, Learn Even Faster," *Fast Company*, October 1998, p. 52.

29. Erika Germer, "Huddle Up!" *Fast Company*, December 2000, p. 86.

30. Salter, "Life in the Fast Lane."

Chapter 4

1. Samuel Greengard, "50% of Your Employees Are Lying, Cheating & Stealing," *Workforce Online*, October 1, 1997. http://www.workforceonline.com/members/research/corporate_culture/3057.html.

2. Ibid.

3. Chan Sup Chang et al., "Offering Gifts or Bribes? Code of Ethics in South Korea," *Journal of Third World Studies*, Spring 2001, pp. 125–139.

4. Quoted in "The Holiday Spirit," *Total Quality Newsletter*, December 1992, p. 8.

5. Matt Murray, "Wounded Phar-Mor Found a Healer in Antonio Alvarez," *Wall Street Journal*, May 26, 1995, pp. B1, B6.

6. Stephen Barr, "Clintons' Plight a Handy Reminder of the Perils of Accepting Inappropriate Gifts," *Washington Post*, December 11, 2001, p. C2.

7. James Cox, "Inmates Teach MBA Students Ethics from Behind Bars: University of Maryland Class Clarifies Moral Consequences," *USA Today*, May 24, 2001, p. B01.

8. "Good Grief," *Economist*, April 8, 1995, p. 57.

9. "Fast Fact," *Fast Company*, September 2000, p. 96.

10. "Hard Graft in Asia," *Economist*, May 27, 1995, p. 61.

11. Ibid.

12. Becky Ebenkamp, "The Gift That Keeps Offending," *Brandweek*, December 11, 2000, p. 22.

13. Libby Estell, "Think Globally, Give Graciously," *Incentive*, November 2000, pp. 47–50.

14. Carol Hymowitz, "CEOs Set the Tone for How to Handle Questions of Ethics," *Wall Street Journal*, December 22, 1998, p. B1.

15. Geanne Rosenberg, "Truth and Consequences," *Working Woman*, July–August 1998, p. 79.

16. Pat Widder, "More Corporations Learning that Ethics Are Bottom-Line Issues," *Chicago Tribune*, June 7, 1992, p. 6.

17. John O'Brien, "Whistle-Blowers Face Risks, Rewards," *Syracuse Herald American*, June 10, 2001, p. B1ff.

18. Tim Smart, "This Man Sounded the Silicone Alarm—in 1976," *Business Week*, January 27, 1992, p. 34.

19. "Erin Brockovich to Give Keynote Address and Upcoming 15th Annual World Gaming Congress and Expo," *PR Newswire*, June 20, 2001.

Chapter 5

1. Samuel C. Certo, *Modern Management*, 8th ed. (Upper Saddle River, NJ: Prentice Hall, 2000), p. 528.

2. Robert McNatt, ed., "Gender Neutral Benefits," *Business Week*, May 15, 2000, p. 14.

3. Tamar Lewin, "Oregon's Gay Workers Given Benefits for Domestic Partners," *New York Times*, December 10, 1998, p. A20.

4. Richard W. Judy and Carol D'Amico, *Workforce 2020: Work and Workers in the 21st Century* (Indianapolis, IN: Hudson Institute, 1997) http://www.hudson.org.

5. http://stats.bls.gov/news.release/ecopro.t05.htm, accessed June 28, 2001.

6. Bruce Felton, "Technologies That Enable the Disabled," *New York Times*, September 14, 1997, p. C1; Gene Koretz, "How to Enable the Disabled," *Business Week*, November 6, 2000, p. 36.

7. Debra Nussbaum, "When a Company Splits Its Identity," *New York Times*, April 19, 1998, p. BU12.

8. Mia Trinephi, "Boulevard de Triomphe," *Business Week*, May 4, 1998, pp. 26D, F.

9. Rudolph F. Verderber, *Communicate!* 8th ed. (Belmont, CA: Wadsworth, 1996), p. 45.

10. Keith Bradsher, "From Factory to the Top of Saturn," *New York Times*, December 20, 1998, sec. 3, p. 2.

11. Carey Goldberg, "Single Dads Wage Revolution One Bed-time Story at a Time," *New York Times*, June 17, 2001, pp. A1, A16.

12. "Workforce 2020: A Vision of the Future," *Worklife Report* 10, no. 4 (1997), p. 11.

13. "Not Everybody Prefers to Be Out Fishing," *Business Week*, October 12, 1998, p. 8.

14. "The Job-Huntin' Blues," *Business Week*, December 14, 1998, p. 8.

15. David Raths, "Bridging the Generation Gap," *Info World*, November 8, 1999, p. 84.

16. "Older and Wiser," *Business Week*, May 22, 2000, p. F6.

17. Quoted in Jason Chervokas and Tom Watson, "Senior Surfers: A Quiet but Potent Net Market," *Digital Nation*, October 3, 1997.

18. Shirley B. Waldrum and H. Gerald Niemira, "Age Diversity in the Workplace," *Employment Relations Today*, Winter 1997, pp. 67ff.

19. These ideas are based on Raymond V. Lesikar, John D. Pettit, Jr., and Marie E. Flatley, *Lesikar's Basic Business Communication*, 7th ed. (Homewood, IL: Irwin, 1996), p. 552.

20. Except where noted, these examples are taken from Kitty O. Locker, *Business and Administrative Communication*, 4th ed. (New York: Irwin/McGraw-Hill, 1997), pp. 313–14.

21. Lesikar et al., *Lesikar's Basic Business Communication*, p. 553.

22. Ibid., p. 563.

23. Ibid.

24. John Cloud, "Why Coors Went Soft," *Time*, November 2, 1998, p. 70.

25. Gary Dessler, *Human Resources Management*, 7th ed. (Upper Saddle River, NJ: Prentice Hall, 1997), p. 267.

26. "New Ripples in the Tide Against Job Discrimination," *New York Times*, March 22, 2000, p. G1.

Chapter 6

1. Melissa Larson, "Manage Your Project before It Manages You," *Quality Online* 36, no. 9, p. 64.

2. Keith H. Hammonds, "Leaders for the Long Haul," *Fast Company*, July 2001, pp. 56–58.

3. Christina Duff and Bob Ortega, "How Wal-Mart Outdid a Once-Touted Kmart in Discount-Store Race," *Wall Street Journal*, March 24, 1995, pp. A1, A4.

4. Peter Galuszka et al., "P&G's Hottest New Product: P&G," *Business Week*, October 5, 1998, pp. 92, 96.

5. Heath Row, "Road Rules," *Fast Company*, November 1998, p. 72.

6. William Keenan, Jr., "Numbers Racket," *Sales & Marketing Management*, May 1995, pp. 46–66ff.

7. Marshall Loeb, "Jack Welch Lets Fly on Budgets, Bonuses, and Buddy Boards," *Fortune*, May 29, 1995, pp. 1345–1347.

8. Scott Heimes, "Changes in Satisfaction Demands and Technology Alter the How's, What's, Why's of Measurement," *Service Edge*, January 1995, pp. 1–3, 5.

9. "The Big Picture: Keeping Tabs on Employees Online," *Business Week*, February 19, 2001, p. 16.

10. Matthew L. Wald, "Safety Panel Cites Poor Oversight of Buses Used in Public Transit," *New York Times*, November 18, 1998, p. B9.

11. "Is Maintenance Really Doing Its Job?" *Maintenance Management*, June 10, 1995, pp. 1–3, 7.

12. Leah Curtin and Roy L. Simpson, "Quality of Care and the 'Low Hanging Fruit,'" *Health Management Technology*, September 1, 2000, p. 48.

13. Duff and Ortega, "How Wal-Mart Outdid a Once-Touted Kmart," p. A4.

14. Lin Grensing-Pophal, "Training Supervisors to Manage Workers," *HR Magazine*, January 1999. Vol. 44, issue 1, pp. 67–72.

Chapter 7

1. "Sales Systems Help Digital Move to Account Based Selling," advertisement in *Sales & Marketing Management*, January 1992, p. 32.

2. "After Re-engineering, What's Next?" *Supervisory Management*, May 1995, pp. 1, 6.

3. "Another New Model . . . ," *Economist*, January 7, 1995, pp. 52–53.

4. See, for example, Peter F. Drucker, "The Network Society," *Wall Street Journal*, March 29, 1995, p. A14.

5. Barbara Bobo, "Building a Business Using Contractors," *Nation's Business*, June 1995, p. 6.

6. Joel Kotkin and David Friedman, "Why Every Business Will Be Like Show Business," *Inc.*, March 1995, pp. 64–66.

7. Anne Marie Borrego, "Inside Play," *Inc.*, September 2001, pp. 74–80.

8. Steve Liesman, "Texaco Plans Restructuring, Job Cuts as Depressed Oil Prices Hurt Industry," *Wall Street Journal*, November 13, 1998, p. A4.

9. Sarah Gracie, "Delegate Don't Abdicate," *Management Today* (London), May 1999, pp. 92–94.

10. "Shhh . . . the Best Kept Secret at The Ritz-Carlton Is . . . ," *Re-designing Customer Service*, May 1995, pp. 1–2.

11. Brad Lee Thompson, *The New Manager's Handbook* (Burr Ridge, IL: Irwin, 1995) p. 42.

12. "Shhh . . . the Best Kept Secret at The Ritz-Carlton."

13. The factors described in this paragraph are based on Harold Koontz, "Making Theory Operational. The Span of Management," *Journal of Management Studies*, October 1966, pp. 229–243; and Raymond L. Hilgert and Theo Haimann, *Supervision: Concepts and Practices of Management*, 5th ed. (Cincinnati, OH: South-Western Publishing, 1991), pp. 189–190.

14. "Too Much Work, Too Little Time," *Business Week*, July 16, 2001, p. 12.

15. Jill Hecht Maxwell, "One Man, One Computer, 1,431 Lawn Mowers," *Inc. Tech 2001*, No. 2, pp. 46–50.

16. W. H. Weiss, "The Art and Skill of Delegating," *Supervision*, Sept. 2000, pp. 3–5.

17. Daniel Gross, "Take It from the Top," *Working Woman*, July–August 1998, pp. 40–43.

18. Kirk Johnson, "Rescuers' Mission Remains Steadfast," *New York Times*, July 4, 2001, pp. B1, B7.

19. Gross, "Take It from the Top."

20. Mark Henricks, "Who's the Boss?" *Entrepreneur*, January 1995, pp. 54–55.

21. "Getting Things Done through People," *Front Line Supervisor's Bulletin* (Bureau of Business Practice), July 10, 1992, pp. 1–2.

22. Geoffrey Brewer, "The New Managers," *Sales & Marketing Management—Performance*, March 1995, pp. 31–35.

23. Alex Markels, "A Power Producer Is Intent on Giving Power to Its People," *Wall Street Journal*, July 3, 1995, pp. A1, A12.

Chapter 8

1. Patrick Sweeney, "What's the Difference Between Leaders and Managers?" *Franchising World*, May–June 2001, pp. 64–65.

2. Kevin Kelly, "You Can't Make Leaders," *Business Week Enterprise*, December 7, 1998, p. ENT 28.

3. Peter L. Thigpen, "Creating the Covenant" *Quality Digest*, August 1992, pp. 63–64.

4. Douglas McGregor, *The Human Side of Enterprise* (New York: McGraw-Hill, 1960).

5. Geoffrey Brewer, "The New Managers," *Sales & Marketing Management—Performance*, March 1995, pp. 31–35.

6. R. S. Dreyer, "Getting Along," *Supervision*, May 2001, p. 20.

7. Thomas Petzinger, Jr., "Competent Workers and a Complex Leader Keep Big Oil in Check," *Wall Street Journal*, December 4, 1998, p. B1.

8. Cheryl Dahle, "Natural Leader," *Fast Company*, December 2000, pp. 268–280.

9. Jeff Weinstein, "Service Lessons from Most-Admired Companies," *Restaurants and Institutions*, December 15, 1994, pp. 34, 38.

10. Wolf J. Rinke, "Leading for Results," *Executive Excellence*, March 2001, p. 12.

11. Joseph Lipsey, personal correspondence.

12. John A. Byrne, "Jack, a Special Report," *Business Week*, June 8, 1998, pp. 91–112.

13. Tom Peters, "Rule #3, Leadership Is Confusing as Hell," *Fast Company*, March 2001, pp. 124–140.

Chapter 9

1. Quoted by Tom Peters in "Rule #3: Leadership Is Confusing as Hell," *Fast Company*, March 2001, p. 124.

2. Noel M. Tichy and Ram Charan, "The CEO as Coach: An Interview with AlliedSignal's Lawrence A. Bossidy," *Harvard Business Review*, March–April 1995, pp. 69–78.

3. Cheryl Dahle, "Natural Leader," *Fast Company*, December 2000, pp. 268–280.

4. For a valuable discussion on eliminating stereotypes in organizations, see Bryan Gingrich "Individual and Organizational Accountabilities Reducing Stereotypes and Prejudice within the Workplace" *Diversity Factor*, Winter 2000, vol. 8, issue 2, pp. 14–19.

5. Michael Warshaw, "Have You Been House Trained?" *Fast Company*, October 1998, pp. 46–48.

6. Ibid.

7. "Parts Problems—Detecting Product Defects," *Maintenance Management*, June 10, 1995, p. 6.

8. Warshaw, "Have You Been House Trained?"

9. See Irving L. Janis, *Groupthink: Psychological Studies of Policy Decisions and Fiascoes*, 2d ed. (Boston: Houghton Mifflin, 1982).

10. Aimee L. Stern, "Why Good Managers Approve Bad Ideas," *Working Woman*, May 1992, pp. 75, 104.

11. Warshaw, "Have You Been House Trained?"

12. Keith H. Hammonds, "How Do We Break Out of the Box We're Stuck In?" *Fast Company*, November 2000, pp. 260–268.

13. Ibid.

14. George Gendron, "FYI," *Inc.*, May 1998, p. 9.

15. James Webb Young, *A Technique for Producing Ideas* (Chicago: Crain Communications, 1975).

16. Ibid., pp. 59–60.

17. Norm Brodsky, "Hurry Up and Wait," *Inc.*, November 1998, pp. 27–28.

18. These suggestions are adapted from Charles Butler, "Seriously Silly," *Business Week Frontier*, September 18, 1999, p. F14; Keith Hammonds, "How Do We Break Out of the Box We're Stuck In?"; and Robert D. Ramsey, "The Creative Side of Supervision," *Supervision*, May 1, 2001, p. 8.

19. Dahle, "Natural Leader." *Fast Company*, December 2000, pp. 268–280.

Chapter 10

1. Mary Helen Gillespie, "CEO's Weaknesses Displayed," *Boston Globe*, April 8, 2001, p. J15; "Electronic Invective Backfires," *Workforce*, June 2001, p. 20; Edward Wong, "A Stinging Office Memo Boomerangs," *New York Times*, April 5, 2001, p. B1.

2. Jennifer Beauprez, "Many Companies Monitor Workers' Web-Surfing Habits," *Denver Post*, March 13, 2000, p. C1.

3. Michael P. Cronin, "You Gotta Get a Gimmick," *Inc.*, November 1994, p. 134.

4. Carl R. Rogers and Richard E. Farson, "Active Listening," reprinted in William V. Haney, *Communication and Interpersonal Relations: Text and Cases*, 6th ed. (Homewood, IL; Irwin, 1992), pp. 158–159.

5. This section is based on Rose Knotts and Sandra J. Hartman, "Communication Skills in Cross-Cultural Situations," *Supervisory Management*, March 1991, p. 12; and Sondra Thiederman, *Bridging Cultural Barriers for Corporate Success: How to Manage the Multicultural Work Force* (New York: Lexington Books, 1991); Sandy Cameron "Understanding Cultural Differences: Tips for Working with International Staff and Campers," *Camping Magazine*, July–August 2000, vol. 73, issue 4, pp. 24–25.

6. Leigh Buchanan, "The English Impatient," *Inc.*, May 2001, p. 68.

7. Eve Tahmincioglu, "The 4-Letter-Word Patrol Is in Pursuit," *New York Times*, June 27, 2001, p. G1.

8. "Clean It Up Or Else," *Business Week*, October 26, 1998, p. 8.

9. Anita Santiago with Julie Dunn, "A Hard Lesson, Learned Door to Door," *New York Times*, July 16, 2000, p. B2.

10. Deborah Tannen, *Talking from 9 to 5* (New York: William Morrow, 1994).

11. Ken Fracaro, "Two Ears and One Mouth," *Supervision*, February 1, 2001, p. 3.

12. The ideas in this paragraph are based on Catherine R. Benson and Arlene M. Sperhac, "Image Building: Putting Your Best Foot Forward," *Healthcare Trends & Transition*, January 1992, pp. 26–29ff.

13. Richard A. Oppel, Jr., and Patrick McGeehan, "Along with a Lender, Is Citigroup Buying Trouble?" *New York Times*, October 22, 2000, section 3, pp. 1, 15 (photo).

14. The ideas in this list are drawn from Harriet Rubin, "Like the King, King David Knew How to Strum a Person Like an Instrument," *Fast Company*, November 2000, pp. 410–413; Belinda E. Puetz et al., "Helpline," *RN*, April 2001, p. 23; Mary Munter, *Guide to Managerial Communication*, 5th ed. (Upper Saddle River, NJ: Prentice Hall, 2000); and Edward Bailey, *Writing & Speaking at Work* (Upper Saddle River, NJ: Prentice Hall, 1999).

15. "Indecent Exposure," *Inc.*, 500, 1998, p. 86.

16. Ann Therese Palmer, "Up-Front: I-Way Patrol," *Business Week*, June 11, 2001, p. 14.

17. Gene Koretz, "Economic Trends: Big Bro Is Eyeing Your E-Mail," *Business Week*, June 4, 2001, p. 30.

18. Andrew Ross Sorkin, "An E-Mail Boast to Friends Puts Executive Out of Work," *New York Times*, May 22, 2001.

19. "Diversity at Wegman's Food Markets, Inc.," *Network Newsletter* (The Workplace Diversity Network) 3, no. 1 (February 1997).

20. William R. Pape, "Beyond E-mail," *Inc. Technology*, Summer 1995, pp. 27–28.

21. Ibid., p. 27.

22. William Keenan, Jr., "The Man in the Mirror," *Sales & Marketing Management*, May 1995, pp. 95–97.

23. Carrie A. Miles and Jean M. McCloskey, "People: The Key to Productivity," *HR Magazine*, February 1993, pp. 40–45.

24. Based on *The Front Line Supervisor's Standard Manual* (Waterford, CT: Bureau of Business Practice, 1989), pp. 42–43.

25. Elaine McShulskis, "24-Hour HR," *HR Magazine*, November 1997, p. 22.

26. Based on Mortimer R. Feinberg, "How to Get the Grapevine on Your Side," *Working Woman*, May 1990, p. 23; Ray Alastair, "Profiting from the E-mail Grapevine" *Marketing*, October 11, 2001, p. 27.

27. Donna Fenn, "Out to Lunch," *Inc.*, June 1995, p. 89.

Chapter 11

1. Scott Martelle, "Businesses Develop New Take on Giving: More Companies Find that Urging Workers to Volunteer in the Community Boosts Their Image, Staff Morale and Skills," *Los Angeles Times*, April 27, 2001, pp. B1.ff.

2. See, for example, Abraham Maslow, *Eupsychian Management* (Homewood, IL: Irwin, 1965); C. P. Alderfer, "An Empirical Test of a New Theory of Human Needs," *Organization Behavior and Human Performance* 4 (1969), pp. 142–175.

3. Michael Warshaw, "Nick Tunes into Kids," *Fast Company*, February–March 1998, pp. 120–129.

4. Aaron Bernstein, "We Want You to Stay, Really," *Business Week*, June 22, 1998, pp. 67–72.

5. Pam Belluck, "A Bit of Burping Is Allowed, If It Keeps Parents on the Job," *New York Times*, December 4, 2000, pp. A1, A22.

6. Alessandra Bianchi, "The Strictly Business Flextime Request Form," *Inc.*, May 1995, pp. 79–81.

7. Carol Kleiman, "Survey Says Personal Friends Can Be Perk for Women Personnel," *Chicago Tribune*, March 30, 1995, sec. 3, p. 3.

8. David Dorsey, "Andy Pearson Finds Love," *Fast Company*, August 2001, pp. 78–86.

9. Bianchi, "The Strictly Business Flextime Request Form."

10. Thomas Petzinger, Jr., "Looking Beyond Profit to Long-Term Value," *Wall Street Journal*, January 8, 1999, p. B1.

11. Barbara Whitaker, "'Living Wage' Ordinance Both Delights and Divides," *New York Times*, May 29, 2001, p. A13.

12. Dean Foust et al., "Wooing the Worker," *Business Week Online*, May 22, 2000, http://www.businessweek.com:/2000/00_21/b3682139.htm?scriptFramed accessed on August 13, 2001.

13. Mike Hofman, "Hot Tip: Performance Bonuses with an Extra Kick," Inc.Com, http://www.inc.com/articles/details/0,3532,ART20579,00.html accessed on August 13, 2001.

14. "Custom Packaging for Paychecks," Inc.Com, http://www.inc.com/articles/details/0,3532,ART19340,00.html accessed on August 13, 2001.

15. "Daddy, I Crashed the Company," *Inc.*, October 15, 1998, http://www2.inc.com/search/14230.html, accessed on August 13, 2001.

16. "No-Quota Noncoms," Inc.Com, http://www.inc.com/articles/details/0,3532,ART11397,00.html accessed on August 13, 2001.

17. Laurence Zuckerman, "Happy Skies of Continental," *New York Times*, February 27, 2001, pp. C1, C15.

18. Michelle Conlin and Kathy Moore, "Dr. Goodnight's Company Town," *Business Week*, June 19, 2000, pp. 192–200; Charles Fishman, "Sanity Inc.," *Fast Company*, January 1999, pp. 85–96.

19. Zuckerman, "Happy Skies of Continental."

20. Erika Germer, "Tell Them What They've Won!" *Inc.*, April 2001, p. 70.

21. Mary Peterson Kauffold, "Taking Care of Business," *Chicago Tribune*, February 26, 1995, sec. 18, pp. 1–2.

22. Diane Brady, "Give Nursing Moms a Break at the Office," *Business Week*, August 6, 2001, p. 70.

23. Alan Feuer, "Leading a Porterhouse Ballet," *New York Times*, June 11, 2001, pp. B1, B4.

24. Bianchi, "The Strictly Business Flextime Request Form," p. 79.

25. David K. Lindo, "Supervisors Must Speak Up," *Supervision*, January 2000, p. 14.

Chapter 12

1. http://stats.bls.gov/news.release/prod4.t01.htm, accessed on October 9, 2001.

2. David Leonhardt, "Productivity Still Gaining Despite Slump," *New York Times*, August 8, 2001, pp. C1, C2.

3. John M. Ivanvevich, *Human Resource Management*, 7th ed., (New York: Irwin/McGraw-Hill, 1998), p. 123.

4. Robert Frank, "Efficient UPS Tries to Increase Efficiency," *Wall Street Journal*, May 24, 1995, pp. B1, B4.

5. David Rocks, "Reinventing Herman Miller," *Business Week Online*, April 3, 2000, www.businessweek.com:/2000/00_14/b3675047.htm?scriptFramed, accessed on June 16, 2001.

6. Julie Flaherty, "Suggestions Rise from the Floors of U.S. Factories," *New York Times*, Arpil 18, 2001, P. C1, C7.

7. "Work Week," *Wall Street Journal*, February 9, 1999, p. A1.

8. Ibid.

9. Mary-Kathryn Zachary, "Technology and Employment Law," *Supervision*, March 2000, p. 19–26.

10. Michael Hammer and Steven A. Stanton, "Beating the Risks of Reengineering," *Fortune*, May 15, 1995, pp. 105–106 ff.

11. Lorraine Woellert, "O.K., Think—Where Is That Wrench?" *Business Week*, November 16, 1998, p. 8.

12. Frank, "Efficient UPS Tries to Increase Efficiency."

13. Reed Abelson, "Part-Time Work for Some Adds Up to Full-Time Job," *New York Times*, November 2, 1998, p. A1.

14. David Leonhardt, "Flying United with Paperless Tickets," *Business Week*, January 11, 1999, p. 6.

15. Joseph Kahn, "China's New Slogan: Workers of the World Take the Day Off!" *Wall Street Journal*, May 4, 1995, p. A9.

16. "Why Workers Don't Show Up," *Business Week*, November 16, 1998, p. 8.

17. "Job Sharing: A Case Study," *HR Magazine*, January 1966.

18. Darnell Little and Adam Aston, "Even the Supervisor Is Expendable," *Business Week*, July 23, 2001, P. 78.

19. Ibid.

Chapter 13

1. Rudy M. Yandrick, "Help Employees Reach for the Stars," *HR Magazine*, January 1997, p. 96.

2. Aaron Bernstein, "Racism in the Workplace," *Business Week*, July 30, 2001, pp. 64–67.

3. Beth Lorenzini and Brad A. Johnson, "Restaurant Wars," *Restaurant and Institutions*, May 1, 1995, pp. 148 ff.

4. Susan Vaughn, "Career Challenge: Firms Looking Closer at Costs of Addiction," *Los Angeles Times*, June 3, 2001, p. W1.

5. Jane Easter Bahls, "Drugs in the Workplace," *HR Magazine*, February 1998, cover story.

6. "Top Threat: Workplace Violence Remains No. 1 Nemesis," *Security*, June 2001, pp. 9–12; Mike France with Michael Arndt, "Office Violence: After the Shooting Stops," *Business Week*, March 12, 2001, pp. 98–100.

7. "Top Threat: Workplace Violence Remains No. 1 Nemesis."

8. Matthew Flamm, "Domestic Violence Victims Gaining Help in Workplace," *Crain's New York Business*, March 12, 2001, pp. 33, 38; Mike Hofman, "The Shadow of Domestic Violence," *Inc.*, March 2001, p. 85.

9. Matthew Flamm, "Domestic Violence Victims Gaining Help in Workplace."

10. Ibid.

11. France with Arndt, "Office Violence: After the Shooting Stops."

12. Jennifer S. Lee, "Tracking Sales and the Cashiers," *New York Times*, July 11, 2001, pp. C1, C6.

13. Ibid.

14. P. J. Connolly, "Activity Monitors Raise Ethical and Legal Questions Regarding Employee Privacy," *InfoWorld*, February 12, 2001, p. 57E.

15. Ann Davis and Aaron Lucchetti, "Magazine Vendor in Insider-Trading Case," *Wall Street Journal*, January 28, 1999, pp. C1, C24.

16. Wilma Randle, "When Employees Lie, Cheat or Steal," *Working Woman*, January 1995, p. 55.

17. List of rights provided by Corinne R. Livesay, Liberty University, Lynchburg, VA.

18. Lorenzini and Johnson, "Restaurant Wars," p. 158.

19. Michael Barrier, "The Enemy Within," *Nation's Business*, February 1995, pp. 18–24.

20. Yandrick, "Help Employees Reach for the Stars."

21. Jane Easter Bahls, "Dealing with Drugs: Keep It Legal," *HR Magazine*, March 1998, pp. 104 ff.

22. Ibid.

Chapter 14

1. Tom Peters, "You, Too, Can Manage without a Time Manager," *Chicago Tribune*, August 3, 1992, sec. 4, p. 5.

2. Robert D. Ramsey, "15 Time Wasters for Supervisors," *Supervision*, June 2000, p. 10.

3. Ted Pollock, "Mind Your Own Business," *Supervision*, March 2001, pp. 17–19.

4. Tammy Reiss, "You've Got Mail, and Mail, and Mail . . . ," *Business Week*, July 20, 1998, p. 6.

5. quoted in "Quitting Time!" *Incentive*, October 2000, p. 142.

6. http://www.getmoredone.com accessed on August 19, 2001.

7. Ted Pollock, "Mind Your Own Business," *Supervision*, May 2001, p. 17.

8. http://www.getmoredone.com accessed on August 19, 2001.

9. Ibid.

10. Gail Dutton, "Cutting Edge Stressbusters," *HR Focus*, September 1, 1998, p. 11.

11. Alisa Tang, "Sick or Stressed Out: Workplace Absence, by Job and Gender," *New York Times*, December 1, 1999, p. G1.

12. Frank Grazian, "Are You Coping with Stress?" *Communication Briefings* 14, no. 1, p. 3.

13. Michael Gelman with Jobert E. Abueva, "The Boss: No 2nd Chances on Live TV," *New York Times*, February 14, 2001, p. C8.

14. Ted Pollock, "Make Your Criticism Pay Off," *Supervision*, October 1998, p. 24.

15. Jeffrey Seglin, "1998 Inc./Gallup Survey: Americans at Work," *Inc.*, June 1998, p. 91.

16. Matt Murray, "Amid Record Profits, Companies Continue to Lay Off Employees," *Wall Street Journal*, May 4, 1995, pp. A1, A4.

17. Emily Burg, review of *The Procrastinator's Handbook*, www.workingwoman.com/wwn/article.jsp?contentId=5745&ChannelID=212 accessed on June 14, 2001.

18. Alex Markels, "Shhh! Napping Is Trying to Tiptoe into the Workplace," *Wall Street Journal*, June 26, 1995, pp. A1, A6.

19. Grazian, "Are You Coping with Stress?"

20. Carol Kleiman, "Turning Stress Control into a Laughing Matter," *Chicago Tribune*, August 6, 1995, sec. 8, p. 1.

21. Shawn Tully, "America's Healthiest Companies," *Fortune*, June 12, 1995, pp. 98–100ff.

22. Stephanie Gruner, "Looking to Reduce Employee Stress," *Inc.*, November 1998, p. 106.

23. Tully, "America's Healthiest Companies," p. 104.

24. Dutton, "Cutting Edge Stressbusters."

25. Donna Fenn, "Healthy Workers Cost Less," *Inc.*, May 1995, p. 137.

26. Tully, "America's Healthiest Companies."

27. Dutton, "Cutting Edge Stressbusters."

28. Seth A. Berr; Allan H. Church; Janine Waclawski "The Right Relationship is Everything: Linking Personality Preferences to Managerial Behaviors" Human Resource Development Quarterly, Summer 2000, Volume 11, Issue 2, pp. 133–157.

Chapter 15

1. Sue Shellenbarger, "Felice Schwartz: From the Mommy Track to the Zigzag Track," *Wall Street Journal*, May 3, 1995, p. B1.

2. Joshua Kendall, "Can't We All Just Get Along?" *Business Week*, October 9, 2000, p. F18; Tony Schwartz, "How Do You Feel?" *Fast Company*, June 2000, pp. 296–313.

3. Michael P. Cronin, "No More 'Us versus Them,'" *Inc.*, May 1994, p. 150.

4. For an interesting related study, see: Catherine H. Tinsley and Jeanne M. Brett, "Managing Workplace Conflict in the United States and Hong Kong," *Organizational Behavior and Human Decision Processes*, vol. 85, issue 2, 2001, pp. 360–381.

5. Jerry Wisinski, "What to Do about Conflicts?" *Supervisory Management*, March 1995, p. 11.

6. Don Weiss, "Saying the Right Thing at the Right Time," *Getting Results*, February 1997, p. 4.

7. Belinda E. Puetz et al., "Helpline," *RN*, April 2001, p. 23.

8. See, for example, Sharman Stein, "Making a Life or a Living?" *Chicago Tribune*, May 18, 1995, sec. 1, pp. 1, 12.

9. Catherine Romano, "Managing Change, Diversity and Emotions," *Management Review*, July 1995, pp. 6–7.

10. Scott Kirsner, "Designed for Innovation," *Fast Company*, November 1998, p. 54.

11. David Armstrong, "Gillette Will Cut 8% of Work Force, Close Plants under Restructuring Plan," *Wall Street Journal*, December 19, 2000, p. 1.

12. Alan Cowell, "London Futures Exchange to Reorganize," *New York Times*, November 3, 1998, p. C4.

13. Sharon R. King, "Staying in Vogue," *New York Times*, November 4, 1998, pp. C1, C4.

14. Michael Hammer and Steven A. Stanton, "Beating the Risks of Reengineering," *Fortune*, May 15, 1995, pp. 105–106 ff.

15. Claudia H. Deutsch, "Competitors Can Teach You a Lot, but the Lessons Can Hurt," *New York Times*, July 18, 1999, p. BU 4.

16. Kurt Lewin, "Frontiers in Group Dynamics: Concept, Method, and Reality of Social Sciences—Social Equilibrium and Social Change," *Human Relations*, June 1947, pp. 5–14.

17. Noel M. Tichy and Ram Charan, "The CEO as Coach: An Interview with AlliedSignal's Lawrence A. Bossidy," *Harvard Business Review*, March–April 1995, pp. 69–78.

18. Hammer and Stanton, "Beating the Risks of Reengineering," p. 106.

19. Some of the suggestions in this list are adapted from William W. Hull, "Coping with Threatening Change," *Supervision*, May 1, 2001, p. 3; others are from David W. Mann, "Why Supervisors Resist Change and What You Can Do About It," *Journal for Quality & Participation*, May 1, 2001, pp. 20–22.

20. Minda Zetlin, "Coping with Red Tape Lovers," *Getting Results*, February 1997, p. 6.

21. Arno Penzias, "New Paths to Success," *Fortune*, June 12, 1995, pp. 90–92, 94.

22. Jim Barlow, "The Ins and Outs of Office Politics," *Houston Chronicle*, May 17, 2001, p. C1; Donald S. Miller and Stephen E. Catt, *Human Relations: A Contemporary Approach* (Homewood, IL: Irwin, 1989), pp. 200–202.

Appendix to Chapter 15

1. C. Pasternak, "Corporate Politics May Not Be a Waste of Time," *HRMagazine*, September 1994, p. 18.

2. R. Bhasin, "On Playing Corporate Politics," *Pulp & Paper*, October 1985, p. 175. Also see N. Gupta and G. D. Jenkins, Jr., "The Politics of Pay," *Compensation & Benefits Review*, March–April 1996, pp. 23–30.

3. R. W. Allen, D. L. Madison, L. W. Porter, P. A. Renwick, and B. T. Mayes, "Organizational Politics: Tactics and Characteristics of Its Actors," *California Management Review*, Fall 1979, p. 77. Also see K. M. Kacmar and G. R. Ferris, "Politics at Work: Sharpening the Focus of Political Behavior in Organizations," *Business Horizons*, July–August 1993, pp. 70–74. A comprehensive update can be found in K. M. Kacmar and R. A. Baron, "Organizational Politics: The State of the Field, Links to Related Processes, and an Agenda for Future Research," in *Research in Personnel and Human Resources Management*, vol 17, ed G. R. Ferris (Stamford, CT: JAI Press, 1999), p. 1–39.

4. See P. M. Fandt and G. R. Ferris, "The Management of Information and Impressions: When Employees Behave Opportunistically," *Organizational Behavior and Human Decision Processes*, February 1990, pp. 140–158.

5. First four based on discussion in D. R. Beeman and T. W. Sharkey, "The Use and Abuse of Corporate Politics," *Business Horizons*, March–April 1987, pp. 26–30.

6. A. Raia, "Power, Politics, and the Human Resource Professional," *Human Resource Planning*, no. 4, 1985, p. 203.

7. A. J. DuBrin, "Career Maturity, Organizational Rank, and Political Behavioral Tendencies: A Correlational Analysis of Organizational Politics and Career Experience," *Psychological Reports*, October 1988, p. 535.

8. This three-level distinction comes from A. T. Cobb, "Political Diagnosis: Applications in Orgaizational Development," *Academmy of Management Review*, July 1986, pp. 482–496.

9. An excellent historical and theoretical perspective of coalitions can be found in W. B. Stevenson, J. L. Pearce, and L. W. Porter, "The Concept of 'Coalition' in Organization Theory and Research," *Academy of Management Review*, April 1985, pp. 256–268.

10. L. Baum, "The Day Charlie Bradshaw Kissed Off Transworld," *Business Week*, September 29, 1986, p. 68.

11. See K. G. Provan and J. G. Sebastian, "Networks within Networks: Service Link Overlap, Organizational Cliques, and Network Effectiveness," *Academy of Management Journal*, August 1998, pp. 453–463.

12. Allen, Madison, Porter, Renwick, and Mayes, "Organizational Politics: Tactics and Characteristics of Its Actors," p. 77.

13. See W. L. Gardner III, "Lessons in Organizational Dramaturgy: The Art of Impression Management," *Organizational Dynamics*, Summer 1992, pp. 33–46.

14. For more on political behavior, see A. Nierenberg, "Masterful Networking," *Training & Development*, February 1999, pp. 51–53.

15. A. Rao, S. M. Schmidt, and L. H. Murray, "Upward Impression Management: Goals, Influence Strategies, and Consequences," *Human Relations*, February 1995, p. 147.

16. See P. M. Fandt and G. R. Ferris, "The Management of Information and Impressions: When Employees Behave Opportunistically," *Organizational Behavior and Human Decision Processes*, February 1990, pp. 140–158; W. L. Gardner and B. J. Avolio, "The Charismatic Relationship: A Dramaturgical Perspective," *Academy of Management Review*, January 1998, pp. 32–58; L. Wah, "Managing—Manipulating?—Your Reputation," *Management Review*, October 1998, pp. 46–50; and M. C. Bolino, "Citizenship and Impression Management: Good Soldiers or Good Actors?" *Academy of Management Review*, January 1999, pp. 82–98.

17. For related research, see M. G. Pratt and A. Rafaeli, "Organizational Dress as a Symbol of Multilayered Social Identities," *Academy of Management Journal*, August 1997, pp. 862–898.

18. S. Friedman, "What Do You Really Care About? What Are You Most Interested In?" *Fast Company*, March 1999, p. 90. Also see B. M. DePaulo and D. A. Kashy, "Everyday Lies in Close and Casual Relationships," *Journal of Personality and Social Psychology*, January 1998, pp. 63–79.

19. See S. J. Wayne and G. R. Ferris, "Influence Tactics, Affect, and Exchange Quality in Supervisor-Subordinate Interactions: A Laboratory Experiment and Field Study," *Journal of Applied Psychology*, October 1990, pp. 487–499. For another version, see Table 1 (p. 246) in S. J. Wayne and R. C. Liden, "Effects of Impression Management on Performance Ratings: A Longitudinal Study," *Academy of Management Journal*, February 1995, pp. 232–260.

20. See R. Vonk, "The Slime Effect: Suspicion and Dislike of Likeable Behavior toward Superiors," *Journal of Personality and Social Psychology*, April 1998, pp. 849–864; and M. Wells, "How to Schmooze Like the Best of Them," *USA Today*, May 18, 1999, p. 14E.

21. See P. Rosenfeld, R. A. Giacalone, and C. A. Riordan, "Impression Management Theory and Diversity: Lessons for Organizational Behavior," *American Behavioral Scientist*, March 1994, pp. 601–604; R. A. Giacalone and J. W. Beard, "Impression Management, Diversity, and International Management," *American Behavioral Scientist*, March 1994, pp. 621–636; and A. Montagliani and R. A. Giacalone, "Impression Management and Cross-Cultural Adaptation," *The Journal of Social Psychology*, October 1998, pp. 598–608.

22. M. E. Mendenhall and C. Wiley, "Strangers in a Strange Land: The Relationship between Expatriate Adjustment and Impression Management," *American Behavioral Scientist*, March 1994, pp. 605–620.

23. T. E. Becker and S. L. Martin, "Trying to Look Bad at Work: Methods and Motives for Managing Poor Impressions in Organizations," *Academy of Management Journal*, February 1995, p. 191.

24. Ibid., p. 181.

25. Adapted from Ibid., pp. 180–181.

26. Based on discussion in Ibid., pp. 192–193.

27. Data from G. R. Ferris, D. D. Frink, D. P. S. Bhawuk, J. Zhou, and D. C. Gilmore, "Reactions of Diverse Groups to Politics in the Workplace," *Journal of Management*, no. 1, 1996, pp. 23–44. For other findings from the same database, see G. R. Ferris, D. D. Frink, M. C. Galang, J. Zhou, K. M. Kacmar, and J. L. Howard, "Perceptions of Organizational Politics: Prediction, Stress-Related Implications, and Outcomes," *Human Relations*, February 1996, pp. 233–266. Also see M. L. Randall, R. Cropanzano, C. A. Bormann, and A. Birjulin, "Organizational Politics and Organizational Support as Predictors of Work Attitudes, Job Performance, and Organizational Citizenship Behavior," *Journal of Organizational Behavior*, March 1999, pp. 159–174.

28. A. Drory and D. Beaty, "Gender Differences in the Perception of Organizational Influence Tactics," *Journal of Organizational Behavior*, May 1991, pp. 256–257. Also see L. A. Rudman, "Self-Promotion as a Risk Factor for Women: The Costs and Benefits of Counterstereotypical Impression Management," *Journal of Personality and Social Psychology*, March 1998, pp. 629–645; and J. Tata, "The Influence of Gender on the Use and Effectiveness of Managerial Accounts," *Group & Organization Management*, September 1998, pp. 267–288.

29. See S. J. Wayne and R. C. Liden, "Effects of Impression Management on Performance Ratings: A Longitudinal Study," *Academy of Management Journal*, February 1995, pp. 232–260.

30. Rao, Schmidt, and Murray, "Upward Impression Management: Goals, Influence Strategies, and Consequences," p. 165.

31. Also see A. Tziner, G. P. Latham, B. S. Prince, and R. Haccoun, "Development and Validation of a Questionnaire for Measuring Perceived Political Considerations in Performance Appraisal," *Journal of Organizational Behavior*, March 1996, pp. 179–190.

32. S. A. Akimoto and D. M. Sanbonmatsu, "Differences in Self-Effacing Behavior between European and Japanesee Americans." *Journal of Cross-Cultural Psychology*, March 1999, pp. 172–173.

33. A. Zaleznik, "Real Work," *Harvard Business Review*, January–February 1989, p. 60.

34. C. M. Koen, Jr, and S. M. Crow, "Human Relations and Political Skills," *HR Focus*, December 1995, p. 11.

35. For more on workplace, see "Smart Workplace Politics," *Supervisory Management*, September 1994, pp. 11–12; J. A. Byrne, "How to Succeed: Same Game, Different Decade," *Business Week*, April 17, 1995, p. 48; and M. Moats Kennedy, "Political Mistakes of the Newly Promoted," *Across the Board*, October 1995, pp. 53–54.

36. See L. A. Witt, "Enhancing Organizational Goal Congruence: A Solution to Organizational Politics," *Journal of Applied Psychology*, August 1998, pp. 666–674.

Chapter 16

1. Elyse M. Friedman, "The New Economy Almanac," *Inc.'s The State of Small Business 1997*, p. 108.

2. Raymond A. Noe, John R. Hollenbeck, Barry Gerhart, and Patrick M. Wright, *Human Resource Management: Gaining a Competitive Advantage* (Burr Ridge, IL: Austen Press, 1994), p. 207.

3. Samantha Drake, "Recruitment Agenda," *HR Magazine*, December 1996; Alice Starcke, "Internet Recruiting Shows Rapid Growth," *HR Magazine*, August 1996.

4. Christopher Caggiano, "The Truth about Internet Recruiting," *Inc.*, December 1999, p. 156.

5. Donna Fenn, "Scour Power: Smart Recruiters Are Turning the Internet Inside Out in Search of Employees," *Inc. Tech 2000*, no. 4, p. 111–188 (sidebar, p. 113).

6. Martha I. Finney, "Playing a Different Tune: Using the Hidden Assets of Employees," *HR Magazine*, December 1996.

7. "Experts Discuss Pitfalls, Advantages of Team-Based Systems," *Employee Relations Weekly*, April 18, 1994, pp. 415–416.

8. "Best Practices: Hiring," *Inc.*, March 1994, p. 10.

9. John M. Ivancevich, *Human Resource Management*, 7th ed. (New York: Irwin/McGraw-Hill, 1998), p. 701.

10. John Anderson, "Don't Leave Home without It," *Selling*, March 1995, pp. 68–71.

11. "Drug Testing: The Things People Will Do," *American Salesman*, March 2001, pp. 20–24.

12. "Work Week," *Wall Street Journal*, December 22, 1998, p. A1.

13. Donna Fenn, "Check My References—Please!" *Inc.*, April 1995, p. 111.

14. Kari Haskell, "Liar, Liar, You're Not Hired; Even White Lies Hurt Job Hunters," *New York Times*, May 30, 2001, p. G1.

15. Gary Dessler, *Human Resource Management*, 8th ed. (Upper Saddle River, NJ: Prentice Hall, 2000), p. 173.

16. Susan Kostal, "Picking the Best Person for a Key Job," *Working Woman*, December 1994, pp. 54, 56, 58.

17. Dessler, *Human Resource Management*, pp. 49–52. http://www.nchrtm.okstate.edu/files/EMPLOYER.TXT accessed on August 21, 2001.

18. Sue Shellenbarger, "Work and Family," *Wall Street Journal*, January 27, 1999, p. B1.

19. Sharon Nelton, "Nurturing Diversity," *Nation's Business*, June 1995, pp. 25–27.

20. Bruce Felton, "Technologies That Enable the Disabled," *New York Times*, September 14, 1997, p. B1.

21. Michelle Conlin, "The New Workforce," *Business Week*, March 20, 2000, pp. 64–68.

22. "Accommodations for Employees with Mental Disability," *Supervisory Management*, April 1995, p. 5.

23. Felton, "Technologies That Enable the Disabled."

24. These guidelines draw upon http://www.nchrtm.okstate.edu/files/EMPLOYER.TXT accessed on August 24, 2001.

25. Dawn D. Bennett-Alexander and Laura B. Pincus, *Employment Law for Business*, 2d ed. (New York: Irwin/McGraw-Hill, 1998), p. 558.

Chapter 17

1. www.trainingsupersite.com/publications/archive/training/2000/010/010high.htm accessed on August 26, 2001.

2. Jack Stack, "The Training Myth," *Inc.*, August 1998, p. 41.

3. Erika Germer, "Not Just for Kicks," *Fast Company*, March 2001, p. 70.

4. Reported in Nancy K. Austin, "Giving New Employees a Better Beginning," *Working Woman*, July 1995, pp. 20–21, 74.

5. Jane Erwin and P.C. Douglas, "It's Not Difficult to Change Company Culture," *Supervision*, November 1, 2000, p. 6.

6. Diane Walter, "A View from the Floor," *Training*, July 2001, p. 76.

7. Eileen Davis, "What's on American Managers' Minds?" *Management Review*, April 1995, pp. 14–20.

8. A number of these points are mentioned in Edward Shaw, "The Training-Waste Conspiracy," *Training*, April 1995.

9. David L. Goetsch, *Industrial Supervision in the Age of High Technology* (New York: Merrill, 1992), p. 407.

10. Claudia Deutsch, "Five Questions for John F. Welch, Jr.," *New York Times*, March 18, 2001, p. BU 7.

11. "Experts Discuss Pitfalls, Advantages of Team-Based Systems," *Employee Relations Weekly*, April 18, 1994, pp. 415–416.

12. "High School Grads Find Apprenticeships Hot Ticket to Cool Careers and Big Bucks," *PR Newswire*, June 11, 2001.

13. Mike Hofman, "The Leader Within," *Inc.*, September 1998, p. 127.

14. Emily Barker, "High-Test Education," *Inc.*, July 2001, pp. 81–82.

15. www.trainingsupersite.com/publications/magazines/training/010delivery.htm accessed on August 26, 2001.

16. John Case and Karen Carney, "Open-Book Management: Fun Ways to Learn about P&L," *HR Magazine*, February 1996.

17. www.trainingsupersite.com/publications/magazines/training/010delivery.htm accessed on August 26, 2001.

18. Bill Leonard, "Work and Training Overlap," *HR Magazine*, April 1996.

19. Wendy Marx, "The New High-Tech Training," *Management Review*, February 1995, pp. 57–60.

20. Ibid.

21. Leigh Buchanan, "City Lights: In the Bank," *Inc.*, May 2001, p. 68.

22. Jim Moshinskie, "Tips for Ensuring Effective E-Learning," *HR Focus*, August 2001, pp. 6–7.

23. Cathy Olofson, "Play Hard, Think Big," *Fast Company*, January 2001, pp. 64.

24. Anne Marie Borrego, "Using Mentors to Build Loyalty," *Inc.*, February 2000, pp. 121.

25. "What Mentors Do to Help Others Attain Potential," *Getting Results*, April 1997, p. C1.

26. Leon Rubis, "Mission Possible: Manager Training Helped Company Digest Big Bite," *HR Magazine*, December 1, 2000, pp. 60–62.

Chapter 18

1. Carla Johnson, "Employee, Sculpt Thyself . . . with a Little Help," *HR Magazine*, May 2001, pp. 60–64 (sidebar).

2. Ibid.

3. Carla Johnson, "Making Sure Employees Measure Up," *HR Magazine*, March 2001, pp. 36–41.

4. Ibid.

5. D. M. Osborne, "Good Morning, You're Fired," *Inc. 500*, 2000, p. 192.

6. Jonathan A. Segal, "86 Your Appraisal Process?" *HR Magazine*, October 2000, pp. 199–206.

7. Lin Grensing-Pophal, "Motivate Managers to Review Performance," *HR Magazine*, March 2001, pp. 44–48.

8. See, for example, Edward E. Lawler III, "Performance Management: The Next Generation," *Quality Digest*, February 1995, pp. 29–31.

9. Greg Boudreaux, "What TQM Says about Performance Appraisal," *Quality Digest*, February 1995, pp. 32–35.

10. Lawler, "Performance Management"; Boudreaux, "What TQM Says about Performance Appraisal."

11. Carol Hymowitz, "In the Lead: Ranking Systems Gain Popularity but Have Many Staffers Riled," *Wall Street Journal*, May 15, 2001, p. B1; Reed Abelson, "Companies Turn to Grades, and Employees Go to Court," *New York Times*, March 19, 2001, p. A1; Matthew Boyle, "Performance Reviews: Perilous Curves Ahead," *Fortune*, May 28, 2001, pp. 187–188.

12. Boudreaux, "What TQM Says about Performance Appraisal."

13. Ibid., p. 34.

14. Dayton Fandray, "The New Thinking in Performance Appraisals," *Workforce*, May 2001, pp. 36–40.

15. Brian O'Reilly, "360° Feedback Can Change Your Life," *Fortune*, October 17, 1994, pp. 93–94ff,; Marcie Schorr Hirsch, "360 Degrees of Evaluation," *Working Woman*, August 1994, pp. 20–21.

16. Stephanie Gruner, "Feedback from Everybody," *Inc.*, February 1997, p. 102.

17. Alison Stein Wellner, "Everyone's a Critic," *Business Week Small Biz*, April 2001, p. 18.

18. Teri Lammers Prior, "If I Were President . . . ," *Inc.*, April 1995, pp. 56–61.

19. Lisa Holton, "Look Who's in on Your Performance Review," *Selling*, January–February 1995, pp. 47–48ff.

20. Marilyn Moats Kennedy, "So How'm I Doing?" *Across the Board*, June 1997, p. 53.

21. Stephanie Gruner, "Turning the Tables," *Inc.*, May 1996, p. 87.

22. Holton, "Look Who's in on Your Performance Review."

23. O'Reilly, "360° Feedback Can Change Your Life," pp. 94, 96.

24. *Business Wire*, December 9, 1998.

25. "360-Degree Software Vendor Shootout," *HR Magazine*, December 1998.

26. Hirsch, "360 Degrees of Evaluation."

27. Boudreaux, "What TQM Says about Performance Appraisal"; Lawler, "Performance Management."

28. Noel M. Tichy and Ram Charan, "The CEO as Coach: An Interview with AlliedSignal's Lawrence A. Bossidy," *Harvard Business Review*, March–April 1995, pp. 69–78.

29. Lawler, "Performance Management," p. 29.

Chapter 19

1. http://stats.bls.gov/special.requests/ocwc/oshwc/osh/os/osnr0011.txt, Table 1, accessed on September 20, 2001.

2. Ibid., Table 4.

3. Christina LeBeau, "Breakway (A Special Report): Second Thoughts—Not Tough Enough? At Smaller Firms, Less OSHA Oversight and More Deaths and Injuries," *Wall Street Journal*, March 19, 2001, pp. 14ff.

4. Julie N. Lynem, "Body Politic: Battle Over Ergonomics Laws," *San Francisco Chronicle*, August 5, 2001, p. W1.

5. http://www.aerias.org/c_doc_149.htm, accessed on September 20, 2001.

6. Gayle Hanson, "In-Flight Air Recycling Fouls Friendly Skies," *Insight on the News*. February 17, 1997, p. 18; Julie Flaherty "Flight Attendants Demand Cleaner In-Flight Air," *Reuters*, January 4, 2001, pp. C1, C7.

7. http://www.cdc.gov/niosh/about.html, accessed on September 20, 2001.

8. "Worker Health Chartbook," *Professional Safety*, December 2000, p. 1.

9. "Watch Your Step: Workplace Injuries Cost a Bundle," *U.S. News & World Report*, March 26, 2001, p. 10.

10. Steven Greenhouse, "Hispanic Workers Die at a Higher Rate," *New York Times*, July 16, 2001, p. A11.

11. "Safety on the Docks," *Warehousing Management*, July 2001, pp. 33–37.

12. U.S. Department of Health and Human Services Fact Sheet, January 8, 2001, www.hhs.gov/news/press/2001pres/01fstbco.html, accessed on September 20, 2001.

13. National Cancer Institute Monographs, http://dccps.nic.nih.gov/TCRB/NCI_MONOGRAPHS/INDEX.htm, accessed on September 20, 2001.

14. "State-Specific Prevalence of Current Cigarette Smoking among Adults and the Proportion of Adults Who Work in a Smoke-Free Environment, United States, 1999," *Journal of the American Medical Association*, December 13, 2000, pp. 2865–2866.

15. Ibid. and CDC Fact Sheet, www.cdc.gov/tobacco/research_data/adults_prev/mm4943al_factsheet.htm, accessed on September 20, 2001.

16. "Ergonomics: The Study of Work, 2000 (Revised)," www.osha-sic.gov/Publications/Osha3125.pdf, p. 9, accessed on September 20, 2001.

17. Paula M. Noaker, "The Search for Agile Manufacturing," *Manufacturing Engineering*, November 1994, pp. 40–43.

18. Jon Van, "Actual Side Effects from Virtual Reality," *Chicago Tribune*, August 14, 1995, sec. 4, pp. 1, 3.

19. "Ergonomics: The Study of Work, 2000 (Revised)," www.osha-sic.gov/Publications/Psha3125.pdf, p. 6, accessed on September 20, 2001.

20. Robert J. Grossman, "Back with a Vengeance," *HR Magazine*, August 2001, pp. 36–46.

21. Adrienne E. Eaton and Thomas Nocerino, "The Effectiveness of Health and Safety Committees: Results of a Survey of Public-Sector Workplaces," *Industrial Relations*, April 2000, pp. 265ff.

22. Milt Freudenheim, "Employers Focus on Weight as Workplace Health Issue," *New York Times*, September 6, 1999, p. A15.

23. Robert D. Ramsey, "Handling Hazards in the Workplace," *Supervision*, May 2000, pp. 6–8.

24. These suggestions are excerpted from Ramsey, "Handling Hazards in the Workplace."

25. Bureau of Labor Statistics Union Members Summary, http://stats.bls.gov/news.release/union2.nr0.htm, accessed on September 20, 2001.

26. Bureau of Labor Statistics press release, February 9, 2001, ftp://146.142.4.23/pub/news.release/wkstp.txt, accessed on September 20, 2001.

27. "Dial Suit Becomes Class Action," *New York Times*, August 17, 2001, p. C10; Katherine E. Finkelstein, "T.W.A. to Pay $2.6 Million to Settle Harassment Suit," *New York Times*, May 25, 2001, p. B6; Michelle Conlin and Wendy Zellner, "Is Wal-Mart Hostile to Women?" *Business Week*, July 16, 2001, pp. 58–59.

28. "Sexual Harassment Charges: EEOC & FEPAs Combined: FY 1992–2000," http://www.eeoc.gov/stats/harass.html, accessed on September 20, 2001.

29. Ibid.

Glossary

accountability The practice of imposing penalties for failing to adequately carry out responsibilities and of providing rewards for meeting responsibilities. 14

action plan The plan for how to achieve an objective. 132

active listening Hearing what the speaker is saying, seeking to understand the facts and feelings the speaker is trying to convey, and stating what you understand that message to be. 244

affirmative action Plans designed to increase opportunities for groups that traditionally have been discriminated against. 433

ageism Discrimination based on age. 114

agenda A list of the topics to be covered at a meeting. 74

AIDS (acquired immunodeficiency syndrome) The incurable and fatal illness that is caused by the HIV virus. 514

apprenticeship Training that involves working alongside an experienced person, who shows the apprentice how to do the various tasks involved in a job or trade. 458

aptitude test A test that measures a person's ability to learn skills related to the job. 428

arbitrator A neutral person who reaches a decision on the resolution of a conflict; both parties must adhere to the decision. 522

authoritarian leadership A leadership style in which the leader retains a great deal of authority. 187

authority The right to perform a task or give orders to someone else. 165

average rate of return (ARR) A percentage that represents the average annual earnings for each dollar of a given investment. 308

behavior modification The use of reinforcement theory to motivate people to behave in a certain way. 278

behaviorally anchored rating scales (BARS) A performance appraisal in which an employee is rated on scales containing statements describing performance in several areas. 483

benchmarking Identifying the top performer of a process, then learning and carrying out the top performer's practices. 45

biofeedback Developing an awareness of bodily functions in order to control them. 362

bona fide occupational qualification (BFOQ) Acting roles that call for persons of very young or very advanced age. 115

bounded rationality Choosing an alternative that meets minimum standards of acceptability. 215

brainstorming An idea-generating process in which group members state their ideas, a member of the group records them, and no one may comment on the ideas until the process is complete. 227

budget A plan for spending money. 136

burnout The inability to function effectively as a result of ongoing stress. 359

central tendency The tendency to select employee ratings in the middle of a scale. 489

chain of command The flow of authority in an organization from one level of management to the next. 171

closed-ended question A question that requires a simple answer, such as yes or no. 426

coaching Guidance and instruction in how to do a job so that it satisfies performance goals. 464

code of ethics An organization's written statement of its values and its rules for ethical behavior. 89

cohesiveness The degree to which group members stick together. 64

collective bargaining The process of seeking to reach a contract spelling out the rights and duties of unionized workers and their employer. 522

commissions Payment linked to the amount of sales completed. 281

communication The process by which people send and receive information. 239

compromise Settling on a solution that gives each person part of what he or she wants; no one gets everything, and no one loses completely. 379

conceptual skills The ability to see the relation of the parts to the whole and to one another. 5

concurrent control Control that occurs while the work takes place. 146

conflict The struggle that results from incompatible or opposing needs, feelings, thoughts, or demands within a person or between two or more people. 376

conflict management Responding to problems stemming from conflict. 379

conflict resolution Managing a conflict by confronting the problem and solving it. 381

contingency planning Planning what to do if the original plans don't work out. 133

controlling The management function of ensuring that work goes according to plan. 10, 140

corporate culture Beliefs and norms that govern organizational behavior in a firm. 109

counseling The process of learning about an individual's personal problem and helping him or her resolve it. 324

creativity The ability to bring about something imaginative or new. 228

critical-incident appraisal A performance appraisal in which a supervisor keeps a written record of incidents that show positive and negative ways an employee has acted; the supervisor uses this record to assess the employee's performance. 485

cross-training Training in the skills required to perform more than one job. 284

decision A choice from among available alternatives. 211

decision tree A graph that helps decision makers use probability theory by showing the expected values of decisions under varying circumstances. 222

decision-making leave A day off during which a problem employee is supposed to decide whether to return to work and meet standards or to stay away for good. 333

decision-making skills The ability to analyze information and reach good decisions. 5

decision-making software A computer program that leads the user through the steps of the formal decision-making process. 224

delegating Giving another person the authority and responsibility to carry out a task. 172

democratic leadership A leadership style in which the leader allows subordinates to participate in decision making and problem solving. 187

demotion Transfer of an employee to a job involving less responsibility and usually lower pay. 329

department A unique group of resources that management has assigned to carry out a particular task. 611

departmentalization Setting up departments in an organization. 162

detour behavior Tactics for postponing or avoiding work. 306

directive counseling An approach to counseling in which the supervisor asks the employee questions about the specific problem; when the supervisor understands the problem, he or she suggests ways to handle it. 325

discipline Action taken by the supervisor to prevent employees from breaking rules. 327

discrimination Unfair or inequitable treatment based on prejudice. 110

dismissal Relieving an employee of his or her job. 329

diversity Characteristics of individuals that shape their identities and the experiences they have in society. 108

downtime Time during which employees or machines are not producing goods or services. 000

downward communication Organizational communication in which a message is sent to someone at a lower level. 260

employee assistance program (EAP) A company-based program for providing counseling and related help to employees whose personal problems are affecting their performance. 336

employee handbook A document that describes an organization's conditions of employment, policies regarding employees, administrative procedures, and related matters. 452

employee involvement teams Teams of employees who plan ways to improve quality in their areas of the organization. 36

empowerment Delegation of broad decision-making authority and responsibility. 173

Equal Employment Opportunity Commission (EEOC) The federal government agency charged with enforcing Title VII of the Civil Rights Act. 432

ergonomics The science concerned with the human characteristics that must be considered in designing tasks and equipment so that people will work most effectively and safely. 514

ethics The principles by which people distinguish what is morally right. 89

exception principle The control principle stating that a supervisor should take action only when a variance is meaningful. 144

feedback The way the receiver of a message responds or fails to respond to the message. 240

feedback control Control that focuses on past performance. 146

financial incentives Payments for meeting or exceeding objectives. 280

flextime A policy that grants employees some leeway in choosing which 8 hours a day or which 40 hours a week to work. 274

forced-choice approach A performance appraisal that presents the appraiser with sets of statements describing employee behavior; the appraiser must choose which statement is most characteristic of the employee and which is least characteristic. 483

formal communication Organizational communication that is work-related and follows the lines of the organization chart. 261

formal groups Groups set up by management to meet organizational objectives. 59

frustration Defeat in the effort to achieve desired goals. 376

functional authority The right given by higher management to specific staff personnel to give orders concerning an area in which the staff have expertise. 166

functional groups Groups that fulfill ongoing needs in the organization by carrying out a particular function. 59

gainsharing A group incentive plan in which the organization encourages employees to participate in making suggestions and decisions, then rewards the group with a share of improved earnings. 282

Gantt chart Scheduling tool that lists the activities to be completed and uses horizontal bars to graph how long each activity will take, including its starting and ending dates. 137

goals Objectives, often those with a broad focus. 128

grapevine The path along which informal communication travels. 262

graphic rating scale A performance appraisal that rates the degree to which an employee has achieved various characteristics. 481

grievance A formal complaint that the terms of a labor contract have been violated. 522

group Two or more people who interact with one another, are aware of one another, and think of themselves as a group. 57

group incentive plan A financial incentive plan that rewards a team of workers for meeting or exceeding an objective. 282

groupthink The failure to think independently and realistically as a group because of the desire to enjoy consensus and closeness. 226

halo effect The practice of forming an overall opinion on the basis of one outstanding characteristic. 427

harshness bias Rating employees more severely than their performances merit. 489

health hazards Conditions in the work environment that may gradually hurt the health of the people there. 508

homogeneity The degree to which the members of a group are the same. 65

human relations skills The ability to work effectively with other people. 5

idle time Time during which employees or machines are not producing goods or services. 306

inference A conclusion drawn from the facts available. 250

informal communication Organizational communication that is directed toward individual needs and interests and does not necessarily follow formal lines of communication. 261

informal groups Groups that form when individuals in the organization develop relationships to meet personal needs. 59

insubordination Deliberate refusal to do what the supervisor or other superior asks. 320

interactive multimedia Computer software that brings together sound, video, graphics, animation, and text and adjusts content based on user responses. 462

internal locus of control The belief that you are the primary cause of what happens to yourself. 186

ISO 9000 A series of standards adopted by the International Organization of Standardization to spell out acceptable criteria for quality systems. 45

job description A listing of the characteristics of a job, including the job title, duties involved, and working conditions. 416

job enlargement An effort to make a job more interesting by adding more duties to it. 284

job enrichment The incorporation of motivating factors into a job—in particular, giving the employee more responsibility and recognition. 284

job rotation Moving employees from job to job to give them more variety. 283

job sharing An arrangement in which two part-time employees share the duties of one full-time job. 274

job specification A listing of the characteristics desirable in the person performing a given job, including educational and work background, physical characteristics, and personal strengths. 416

knowledge skill The ability to utilize e-mail, voice mail, fax, intranet, and the internet to manage and distribute continuous streams of data. 5

labor relations Management's role in working constructively with unions that represent the organization's employees. 520

laissez-faire leadership A leadership style in which the leader is uninvolved and lets subordinates direct themselves. 187

lateral communication Organizational communication in which a message is sent to a person at the same level. 260

leading Influencing people to act or not act in a certain way. 10, 184

leniency bias Rating employees more favorably than their performances merit. 489

line authority The right to carry out tasks and give orders related to the organization's primary purpose. 166

Malcolm Baldrige National Quality Award An annual award administered by the U.S. Department of Commerce and given to the company that shows the highest-quality performance in seven categories. 44

management by objectives (MBO) A formal system for planning in which managers and employees at all levels set objectives for what they are to accomplish; their performance is then measured against those objectives. 133

mediator or **conciliator** A neutral person who helps opposing parties in an organization reach agreement. 522

mentoring Providing guidance, advice, and encouragement through an ongoing one-on-one work relationship. 465

motivation Giving people incentives that cause them to act in desired ways. 271

National Institute for Occupational Safety and Health (NIOSH) The agency of the federal government responsible for conducting research related to workplace safety and health. 506

nepotism The hiring of one's relatives. 95

network organizations Organizations that maintain flexibility by staying small and contracting with other individuals as needed to complete projects. 165

noise Anything that can distort a message by interfering with the communication process. 240

nondirective counseling An approach to counseling in which the supervisor primarily listens, encouraging the employee to look for the source of the problem and to propose possible solutions. 326

nonverbal message A message conveyed without using words. 252

norms Group standards for appropriate or acceptable behavior. 63

objectives The desired accomplishments of the organization as a whole or of part of the organization. 128

Occupational Safety and Health Act (OSHAct) of 1970 The federal law that sets up government agencies to conduct research on occupational health and safety, set health and safety standards, inspect workplaces, and penalize employers that do not meet standards. 505

Occupational Safety and Health Administration (OSHA) The agency of the federal government charged with setting and enforcing standards for workplace health and safety. 505

on-the-job training Teaching a job while trainer and trainee perform the job at the work site. 457

open-ended question A question that gives the person responding broad control over the response. 426

operational planning The development of objectives that specify how divisions, departments, and work groups will support organizational goals. 129

organic structure Organizational structure in which the boundaries between jobs continually shift and people pitch in wherever their contributions are needed. 164

organizational politics Intentional acts of influence to enhance or protect the self-interest of individuals or groups. 392

organizing Setting up the group, allocating resources, and assigning work to achieve goals. 9, 159

orientation The process of giving new employees the information they need to do their work comfortably, effectively, and efficiently. 449

overhead Expenses not related directly to producing goods and services; examples are rent, utilities, and staff support. 305

paired-comparison approach A performance appraisal that measures the relative performance of employees in a group. 481

parity principle The principle that personnel who are given responsibility must also be given enough authority to carry out that responsibility. 169

payback period The length of time it will take for the benefits generated by an investment (such as cost savings from machinery) to offset the cost of the investment. 308

peer reviews Performance appraisals conducted by an employee's co-workers. 487

perceptions The ways people see and interpret reality. 251

perfectionism The attempt to do things perfectly. 353

performance appraisal Formal feedback on how well an employee is performing his or her job. 475

performance report A summary of performance and comparison with performance standards. 147

personal power Power that arises from an individual's personal characteristics. 393

piecework system Payment according to the quantity produced. 281

planning Setting goals and determining how to meet them. 9, 128

policies Broad guidelines for how to act. 132

position power Power that comes from a person's formal role in an organization. 393

positive discipline Discipline designed to prevent problem behavior from beginning. 332

power The ability to influence people to behave in a certain way. 167, 392

precontrol Efforts aimed at preventing behavior that may lead to undesirable results. 146

prejudice Preconceived judgments or negative conclusions about an individual or a category of people based on stereotypes. 110, 252

probability theory A body of techniques for comparing the consequences of possible decisions in a risk situation. 221

problem A factor in the organization that is a barrier to improvement. 145

procedures The steps that must be completed to achieve a specific purpose. 132

process control Quality control that emphasizes how to do things in a way that leads to better quality. 33

procrastination Putting off what needs to be done. 354

product quality control Quality control that focuses on ways to improve the product itself. 33

productivity The amount of results (output) an organization gets for a given amount of inputs. 297

proficiency test A test that measures whether the person has the skills needed to perform a job. 428

profit-sharing plan A group incentive plan under which the company sets aside a share of its profits and divides it among employees. 282

program evaluation and review technique (PERT) Scheduling tool that identifies the relationships among tasks as well as the amount of time each task will take. 138

proximity bias The tendency to assign similar scores to items that are near each other on a questionnaire. 489

psychomotor test A test that measures a person's strength, dexterity, and coordination. 428

punishment An unpleasant consequence given in response to undesirable behavior. 278

Pygmalion effect The direct relationship between expectations and performance; high expectations lead to high performance. 285

quality control An organization's efforts to prevent or correct defects in its goods or services or to improve them in some way. 33

recency syndrome The tendency to more easily remember events that have occurred recently. 217

recruitment A process of identifying people interested in holding a particular job or working for the organization. 418

reinforcement A desired consequence or the ending of a negative consequence, either of which is given in response to a desirable behavior. 144, 278

repetitive-motion disorders Injuries that result from repeatedly applying force to the same muscles or joints. 513

responsibility The obligation to perform assigned activities. 167

role conflicts Situations in which a person has two different roles that call for conflicting types of behavior. 63

role playing A training method in which roles are assigned to participants, who then act out the way they would handle a specific situation. 463

roles Patterns of behavior related to employees' positions in a group. 62

rules Specific statements of what to do or not to do in a given situation. 132

safety hazards Conditions in the workplace that may lead to an injury-causing accident. 509

scheduling Setting a precise timetable for the work to be completed. 137

self-concept A person's self-image. 198

self-managing work teams Groups of 5 to 15 members who work together to produce an entire product. 67

sexism Discrimination based on gender stereotypes. 112

sexual harassment Unwelcome sexual advances, requests for sexual favors, and other sexual conduct that interferes with work performance or creates a hostile work environment. 113, 524

similarity bias The tendency to judge others more positively when they are like yourself. 490

Six Sigma A process-oriented quality-control method designed to improve the product or service output to 99.97 percent perfect. 42

smoothing Managing a conflict by pretending it does not exist. 380

span of control The number of people a manager supervises. 171

staff authority The right to advise or assist those with line authority. 166

staffing Identifying, hiring, and developing the necessary number and quality of employees. 9

standards Measures of what is expected. 141

statistical process control (SPC) A statistical quality-control technique using statistics to monitor production quality on an ongoing basis and making corrections whenever the results show the process is out of control. 35

statistical quality control Looking for defects in parts or finished products selected through a sampling technique. 34

status A group member's position in relation to others in the group. 64

stereotypes Generalized, rigid opinions about categories of people. 111, 217

strategic planning The creation of long-term goals for the organization as a whole. 129

stress The body's response to coping with environmental demands. 354

strike Refusal by employees to work until there is a contract. 523

structured interview An interview based on questions the interviewer has prepared in advance. 424

supervisor A manager at the first level of management. 3

suspension Requirement that an employee not come to work for a set period of time; the employee is not paid for the time off. 329

symptom An indication of an underlying problem. 145

task groups Groups that are set up to carry out a specific activity and then disband when the activity is completed. 59

team A group of people who must collaborate to some degree to achieve common goals. 67

team building Developing the ability of team members to work together to achieve common objectives. 71

technical skills The specialized knowledge and expertise used to carry out particular techniques or procedures. 5

Theory X A set of management attitudes based on the view that people dislike work and must be coerced to perform. 189

Theory Y A set of management attitudes based on the view that work is a natural activity and that people will work hard and creatively to achieve objectives they are committed to. 189

Theory Z A set of management attitudes that emphasizes employee participation in all aspects of decision making. 190

360-degree feedback Performance appraisal that combines assessments from several sources. 487

time log A record of what activities a person is doing hour by hour throughout the day. 345

time management The practice of controlling the way you use time. 345

total quality management (TQM) An organizationwide focus on satisfying customers by continuously improving every business process for delivering goods or services. 39

training Increasing the skills that will enable employees to better meet the organization's goals. 447

turnover The rate at which employees leave an organization. 310

Type A personality A pattern of behavior that involves constantly trying to accomplish a lot in a hurry. 357

Type B personality A pattern of behavior that focuses on a relaxed but active approach to life. 357

union steward An employee who is the union's representative in a particular work unit. 522

unity of command The principle that each employee should have only one supervisor. 170

unstructured interview An interview in which the interviewer has no list of questions prepared in advance but asks questions based on the applicant's responses. 424

upward communication Organizational communication in which a message is sent to someone at a higher level. 260

value The worth a customer places on a total package of goods and services relative to its cost. 46

variance The size of the difference between actual performance and a performance standard. 143

verbal message A message that consists of words. 252

vestibule training Training that takes place on equipment set up in a special area off the job site. 459

video display terminal (VDT) The screen on which a computer displays information. 512

virtual reality A three-dimensional computer-generated environment that gives the user a sensation of being part of that environment. 513

Wagner Act Federal law intended to define and protect the rights of workers and employers, encourage collective bargaining, and eliminate unfair labor practices. 520

wellness program Organizational activities designed to help employees adopt healthy practices. 364

whistleblower Someone who exposes a violation of ethics or law. 98

wildcat strike Refusal by employees to work during the term of a labor contract. 523

work-standards approach A performance appraisal in which the appraiser compares an employee's performance with objective measures of what the employee should do. 485

zero-defects approach A quality-control technique based on the view that everyone in the organization should work toward the goal of delivering such high quality that all aspects of the organization's goods and services are free of problems. 36

Index